Nietzsche and Critical Social Theory

Studies in Critical Social Sciences Book Series

Haymarket Books is proud to be working with Brill Academic Publishers (www.brill.nl) to republish the *Studies in Critical Social Sciences* book series in paperback editions. This peer-reviewed book series offers insights into our current reality by exploring the content and consequences of power relationships under capitalism, and by considering the spaces of opposition and resistance to these changes that have been defining our new age. Our full catalog of *SCSS* volumes can be viewed at https://www.haymarketbooks.org/series_collections/4-studies-in-critical-social-sciences.

Nietzsche and Critical Social Theory

Affirmation, Animosity, and Ambiguity

Edited by

Christine A. Payne

Michael J. Roberts

Haymarket Books

Chicago, IL

First published in 2019 by Brill Academic Publishers, The Netherlands

Published in paperback in 2020 by
Haymarket Books
P.O. Box 180165
Chicago, IL 60618
773-583-7884
www.haymarketbooks.org

ISBN: 978-1-64259-363-1

Distributed to the trade in the US through Consortium Book Sales and Distribution (www.cbsd.com) and internationally through Ingram Publisher Services International (www.ingramcontent.com).

This book was published with the generous support of Lannan Foundation and Wallace Action Fund.

Cover design by Jamie Kerry and Ragina Johnson.

Printed in the United States.

10 9 8 7 6 5 4 3 2 1

Library of Congress Cataloging-in-Publication data is available.

Contents

Acknowledgements

The chapters collected here in this volume are drawn from papers presented at the *Nietzsche and Critical Social Theory: Affirmation, Animosity, Ambiguity* conference held at San Diego State University in January 2017 (https://nietzsche.sdsu.edu/). We would like to thank Dean Norma Bouchard of the College of Arts and Letters at SDSU for the generous support provided for our conference. In addition, we would like to thank Professor Mark Wheeler, Chair of the Philosophy Department at SDSU, Professor William Nericcio, Director of the MALAS program at SDSU, Professor Sandra Wawrytko, Director of the Center of Asian and Pacific Studies at SDSU, Professor Minjeong Kim, Chair of the Sociology Department at SDSU, Professor Enrico Marcelli from the Sociology Department, Ginger Shoulders, Communications and Web Services Coordinator in the College of Arts and Letters at San Diego State, and Professor David Fasenfest, editor of the journal *Critical Sociology* for providing the support necessary to make the conference a success. Special thanks also to Professor Fasenfest for his support for our special guest-edited issue on *Nietzsche and Critical Sociology* in the March 2019 issue of *Critical Sociology*. We hope the readers of this volume will also consult that issue. Most importantly we thank each of the authors in this volume who graciously accepted our invitation to contribute to this collection.

Notes on Contributors

Peter Atterton
is Professor of Philosophy at San Diego State University. He has published many articles on Levinas, as well as on other figures in Continental philosophy, and has translated various interviews and essays by Levinas. He is co-author of *On Levinas* (Wadsworth, 2004); and co-editor of *The Continental Ethics Reader* (Routledge, 2003), *Levinas and Buber: Dialogue and Difference* (Duquesne University Press, 2004), *Animal Philosophy: Essential Readings in Continental Thought* (Continuum, 2004), *Radicalizing Levinas* (SUNY Press, 2010), and *Face to Face with Animals: Levinas and the Animals Question* (SUNY Press, 2019). He is currently working on a book-length study of Levinas and naturalism.

Babette Babich
is an author and philosopher who teaches at Fordham University in Manhattan and, on occasion, at the Humboldt University in Berlin. She has written eight books, including *The Hallelujah Effect: Music, Performance Practice and Technology* (London 2016), *Un politique brisée* (Paris 2016) and *Nietzsches Wissenschaftsphilosophie* (Oxford 2011) and edited 14 collective volumes, including, most recently, *Reading David Hume's »Of the Standard of Taste«* (Berlin 2019) and *Hermeneutic Philosophies of Social Science* (Berlin 2017).

T.J. Berard
is an Associate Professor of Sociology at Kent State University (Ohio, USA). His research addresses relations between identities and inequalities in law, crime, deviance, social problems, social control and subcultures. He is a recipient of the Shils-Coleman prize in sociological theory from the Theory Section of the American Sociological Association, and a past Chair of the Crime and Juvenile Delinquency division of the Society for the Study of Social Problems.

Jung Min Choi
received his B.A. at UC Berkeley and finished his Ph.D. at York University in Toronto, Canada. He is an associate professor in the department of sociology at San Diego State University. He has published, all guided by anti-essentialist philosophies and community-based approaches, on critical pedagogy, race and racism, globalization and the bankruptcy of neolibersalism. He is the recipient of more than 30 Excellence in Teaching Awards and is currently President of The Dignified Learning Project, a non-profit education-based organization in San Diego.

Dawn Herrera
works at the juncture of critical and normative theory to transform the terms through which we frame and evaluate political life. A Mellon Fellow, she holds a Ph.D. from the University of Chicago's Committee on Social Thought. She lives in Chicago, where she lectures at the University of Chicago and the School of the Art Institute.

Douglas Kellner
is George Kneller Chair in the Philosophy of Education at UCLA and is author of many books on social theory, politics, history, and culture. His most recent books are *American Nightmare: Donald Trump, Media Spectacle, and Authoritarian Populism* (2016); and *The American Horror Show: Election 2016 and the Ascendency of Donald J. Trump* (2017). Kellner's website is at http://www.gseis.ucla.edu/faculty/kellner/kellner.html which contains several of his books and many articles.

Eve Kornfeld
is Senate Distinguished Professor and Professor of History at San Diego State University She earned her B.A. at Princeton University and her M.A. and Ph.D. in History at Harvard University. Her books were published in the Bedford Series in History and Culture of St. Martin's Press, and her articles appeared in the *William and Mary Quarterly, Journal of the Early Republic, Journal of American Studies, Canadian Review of American Studies, New England Journal of History, Pennsylvania History, History Teacher,* and the *Journal of American Culture.* She has served on the governing board of the American Culture Association. She received SDSU's Excellence in Teaching Award in the Humanities and Social Sciences in 2017, and the Senate Excellence in Teaching Award in 2018.

Ishay Landa
is Associate Professor of Modern History at the Israeli Open University, in Ra'anana. His research interests include political theory – especially fascism, Marxism, and liberalism – and popular culture. He has written four books: *The Overman in the Marketplace: Nietzschean Heroism in Popular Culture* (Lexington, 2007), *The Apprentice's Sorcerer: Liberal Tradition and Fascism* (Brill, 2010), *The Roots of European Fascism: 1789–1945* (in Hebrew, the Open University Press, 2015), and *Fascism and the Masses: The Revolt Against the Last Humans, 1848–1945* (Routledge, 2018). His essays and lectures deal with diverse topics such as fascism, consumerism, religion and atheism, and take on different writers and thinkers, for example, Friedrich Nietzsche, Martin Heidegger, Georges Bataille, or J.R.R. Tolkien. He has won several scholarships, among

them a Post-doc fellowship with distinction: "Gerhard Martin Julius Schmidt Minerva Fellowship," for a research conducted at TU Braunschweig, Germany (2006–2008), and more recently, the Alon Fellowship for Outstanding Young Researchers, awarded by the Council of Higher Education, Israel (2009–2012).

Kristin Lawler
is Associate Professor of Sociology at the College of Mount Saint Vincent in New York City. Her first book, *The American Surfer: Radical Culture and Capitalism*, was published by Routledge in 2011. Her work has been published in numerous edited collections, including *Class: The Anthology, The Critical Surf Studies Reader*, and *Southern California Bohemias*. She is on the Editorial Board of the journal *Situations: Project of the Radical Imagination* and is at work on a new book, *Shanty Irish: the Roots of American Syndicalism.*

Nancy S. Love
is Professor of Political Science and Humanities Council Coordinator at Appalachian State University. She received Ph.D. (1984) and M.A. (1981) degrees from Cornell University and an A.B. degree (1977) from Kenyon College. Her recent books include *Trendy Fascism: White Power Music and the Future of Democracy (2016) and Musical Democracy* (2006). https://gjs.appstate.edu/directory/dr-nancy-love.

Stefano Giacchetti
is Assistant Professor of Philosophy at the Rome Center of Loyola University Chicago, and Senior Lecturer at the School of Continuing and Professional Studies of the same university. He has published and presented over 20 articles on, among others, Adorno, Nietzsche, Marx and Schopenhauer. His recent publications include the books (as editor and contributor) *Critical Theory and the Challenge of Praxis: Beyond Reification* (Routledge: 2016) and *Nostalgia for a Redeemed Future* (University of Delaware Press: 2009). Some of his writings have been translated and published in Italian and Portuguese. He is the organizer of the yearly conferences on Critical Theory in Rome at Loyola's Rome Center, and he is member of the editorial board of "Dissonancia: Journal of Critical Theory," and (also as co-founder) of the "Berlin Journal of Critical Theory."

James Meeker
is a Ph.D. candidate in sociology at Kent State University (Ohio, USA). His research interests include hip-hop, inequalities, crime and deviance, and cultural production. He has professional experience producing hip-hop recordings and is a Grammy voting member of The Recording Academy.

Allison Merrick
is Assistant Professor of Philosophy at the California State University, San Marcos. Her main research interests lie in nineteenth-century philosophy, particularly philosophical methodology and moral psychology. In addition to multiple articles and book chapters on Nietzsche's use critique and the genealogical form of inquiry, she has also published work on issues in contemporary biomedical ethics.

Jeremiah Morelock
is a doctoral candidate and teaching fellow in sociology at Boston College. In his research, he analyzes changing themes over time of populism and authoritarianism in popular American science fiction films. He is the editor of *Critical Theory and Authoritarian Populism* (University of Westminster, 2018), and author (with Felipe Ziotti Narita) of the forthcoming book *O Problemo do Populismo* (Paco and Unesp, in press). He has been a guest lecturer at São Paulo State University, where he is an associate researcher for the Postgraduate Program in Public Policy Analysis. He serves as a reviewer for *TripleC: Capitalism, Communication and Critique*, and is founder and director of the recently established Critical Theory Research Network.

John W. Murphy
is Professor of Sociology at the University of Miami, Coral Gables, Florida. He received his Ph.D. degree from Ohio State University. Over the years he has published on a variety of topics, including race relations and medicine. At this time, the focus of his work is the development of community-based projects.

Christine Payne
is an instructor of Women's Studies at San Diego State University. She recently co-edited "Nietzsche and Critical Theory" for a special issue of the journal *Critical Sociology*. She also recently published "Desire and Doubt – The Potentials and the Potential Problems of Pursuing Play" in the *American Journal of Play*. She is currently working on a manuscript where she considers the role that Nietzsche can play in the field of Science and Technology studies in relation to questions of truth and ideology.

Michael J. Roberts
is Professor of Sociology at San Diego State. He is guest co-editor with Christine Payne of the special issue titled "Nietzsche and Critical Theory" for the journal *Critical Sociology* (March 2019). He is also co-editor, with Stanley Aronowitz, of *Class: The Anthology* (Wiley 2018). His book *Tell Tchaikovsky the News: Rock'n'Roll, the Labor Question and the Musicians' Union* (Duke 2014) was

nominated for the Mary Douglas Prize by the Culture Section of the American Sociological Association. His articles have appeared in the journals Critical Sociology, Rethinking Marxism, The American Journal of Play, Sociological Quarterly, and the International Review for the Sociology of Sport. His most recent work is on Baudrillard and the problem of simulated waves in surfing subcultures.

C. Heike Schotten

is Associate Professor of Political Science at the University of Massachusetts Boston, where she teaches political theory, feminist theory, and queer theory. Her new book, *Queer Terror: Life, Death, and Desire in the Settler Colony* (Columbia UP, 2018), uses queer theory and critical indigenous theory to rethink biopolitics in service to challenging the hidden moralism of "terrorism" discourse, Islamophobia, and U.S. Empire. She is the author of *Nietzsche's Revolution:* Décadence, *Politics, and Sexuality* (Palgrave, 2009) as well as many articles and book chapters in Nietzsche studies, political theory, feminist theory, and queer theory.

Daniel Sullivan

is an Assistant Professor of social psychology at the University of Arizona. He has a Ph.D. in Psychology and a B.A. in German Studies. His research concerns cultural differences in individual experiences of suffering and threat. He is the author of *Cultural-Existential Psychology* (2016; Cambridge University Press), which draws extensively on Nietzsche's philosophy.

Bryan S. Turner

is Professor of Sociology and Director of the Institute for Religion Politics and Society at the Australian Catholic University, Honorary Professor and Director of the Centre for Social Citizenship at Potsdam University German, and Emeritus Professor at the Graduate Center at the City University of New York. He is the founding editor of the *Journal of Classical Sociology*. He recently edited the *Blackwell Wiley Encyclopedia for Social Theory* (2018). He was awarded a Doctor of Letters by Cambridge University in 2009 and received the Max Planck Award in social science in 2015.

Gary Yeritsian

is a Ph.D. Candidate in Sociology at UCLA. He is a social theorist and sociologist of media and culture, and his work has been published in *Critical Sociology* and *Journal of Consumer Culture*, among other outlets.

INTRODUCTION

Situating This Volume

Several decades have passed since the Princeton University-based philosopher Walter Kaufmann (1921–1980) began his project of repairing the damaged reputation of the German philosopher Friedrich Nietzsche (1844–1900), an undertaking that was aimed at an Anglo-American audience of academics who lacked adequate translations of Nietzsche's work. Kaufmann's enormous task of translating Nietzsche's oeuvre was motivated by his desire to extricate Nietzsche from the Nazi Party's appropriation that had claimed Nietzsche's work as the philosophical foundation for German fascism (Aschheim 1992). In order to do so, Kaufman sought to cement Nietzsche's status as a legitimate philosopher by situating him as a key contributor to the development of the Existentialist movement of 20th century, Western-European philosophy. A key part of the strategy involved portraying Nietzsche as a thinker relatively unconcerned with politics in the customary sense of the term. In Kaufmann's (1950) words, the "leitmotif of Nietzsche's life and thought" was the "theme of the antipolitical individual who seeks self-perfection far from the modern world" (418).

If Kaufmann could demonstrate – through careful textual interpretations – that Nietzsche should not be considered a political theorist, then one could reasonably claim that the Nazi's had distorted Nietzsche's texts for their own nefarious political intentions. Kaufmann's Nietzsche was a somewhat conventional philosopher, one who remained ensconced within the realms of epistemology, ontology, and aesthetics, separated from the mundane world of everyday life and ordinary politics. In some ways, Kaufmann's strategy has been quite successful, as Nietzsche is now regularly assigned as required reading in American university course offerings on existentialist philosophy, European philosophy of the 19th century, and literary criticism. As Alexander Nehamas (2013) has rightly noted, Kaufmann's efforts "brought about a radical reversal of the popular image of Nietzsche as a ranting, totalitarian anti-Semite and gradually made it possible for philosophers, who had long ago dismissed Nietzsche as a 'poet' or 'prophet,' to take him seriously once again" (v).

While Anglo-American readers of Nietzsche owe a certain debt of gratitude to Kaufmann for the important legacy he left behind, for European intellectuals, artists and activists of the 1950s who were old enough to remember European society, politics and culture prior to the rise of fascism, such an endeavor as Kaufmann's was rather beside the point, since Nietzsche's thought had been appropriated by certain groups on the Left decades before the Nazi Party took power in Germany. In short, Nietzsche's philosophy was widely understood to be rather germane for questions concerning politics and social critique. For example, in Russia, during the years leading up to the Bolshevik revolution, dissident Marxist intellectuals who were critical of the elements of economic determinism found in the writings of the philosopher Georgi Plekhanov (1856–1918) and his followers (including Lenin), formed their own cadre of "Nietzschean-Marxist" intellectuals who sought to steer the culture of the impending revolution away from the reductionist, if not dogmatic Marxism that plagued the intellectual climate of that period (Rosenthal 1986).[1] In Germany during the Weimar period, Nietzsche was widely read by artists leading the Expressionist movement as well as by scores of anarchists, communists and trade union organizers (Taylor 1990; Moore 2004; Yeritsian 2019; Aschheim 1992).[2] The Nietzschean-Marxist intellectual phenomenon of the early decades of the 20th century suggests that the important interpretive question might be how to enlist Nietzsche in the quest for emancipation rather than conclude, as Kaufmann does, that any sort of socio-political reading of Nietzsche is inappropriate and ill-advised.[3]

Most-influential among Nietzschean-Marxist intellectuals of the late Weimar period were the members of the Frankfurt School and founders of Critical Theory. The individuals in the Frankfurt School who were most concerned with Nietzsche's legacy were Max Horkheimer (1895–1973), Theodor Adorno (1903–1969), Herbert Marcuse (1898–1979), Walter Benjamin (1892–1940) and Ernst Bloch (1885–1977). Concerning Nietzsche's relation to Marxist philosophy and sociology, the primary interlocutor for the Frankfurt School was the leading Marxist philosopher and social critic of the early 20th century, the

1 See the chapter by Michael Roberts for more on the Nietzschean-Marxists in pre-Revolutionary Russia.

2 See the essay by Kristin Lawler in this volume for more analysis along these lines.

3 It is important to note that during the early years of the 20th century, radical scholars and activists in the U.S. were also reading and writing about Nietzsche, including, perhaps most importantly, the anarchist-feminist philosopher Emma Goldman (Moore 2004). In addition, as noted by the historian Jennifer Ratner-Rosenhagen, "in the first decades of the century, many of [Nietzsche's] most vocal enthusiasts were socialists" (112). Academics in the U.S. began to lose enthusiasm for Nietzsche, however, beginning with the First World War, as the belligerent posture of Germany led many intellectuals to worry over the political use of Nietzsche for reactionary ends. There were attempts by American intellectuals to clear Nietzsche's name after the Great War, but with the rise of fascism in the 1930s in both Italy and Germany, there was decidedly less enthusiasm for yet another such project, as many intellectuals in the U.S. ceded Nietzsche to the political Right (Ratner-Rosenhagen 2012). In the United States, it was left to Kaufmann to pick up the pieces of Nietzsche's shattered status in the wake of the cultural devastation that followed the rise and collapse of fascist ideology and politics.

Hungarian György Lukács (1885–1971), whose pathbreaking work, *History and Class Consciousness* (1972 [1922]) was a crucial influence on their thinking about the dynamics of the relationship between mass culture and the political economy of late, or "monopoly" capitalism.[4] In particular, the Frankfurt School members were influenced by Lukács' reading of Marx's analysis of commodity fetishism in chapter one of volume one of *Capital* as a means to provide an analysis of culture that was sorely lacking in the official Marxist orthodoxy of the Second International. For Adorno, Horkheimer, and Bloch, the paucity of cultural analysis in orthodox Marxism was precisely the reason to take Nietzsche's critique of bourgeois culture seriously as an indispensable contribution to the Frankfurt School's reconstruction of historical materialism. It is for this reason that Horkheimer, Adorno, Marcuse and Bloch all rebuffed Lukács' (1980) interpretation of Nietzsche as a fascist thinker, an argument that was eventually published in 1950 as *The Destruction of Reason*. The social and political context for the debate over Nietzsche helped to shape the position taken by Adorno and Horkheimer who sharply criticized Lukács' decision to remain loyal to the Communist Party after the failure of the 1956 Hungarian Revolution to challenge the repressive authoritarianism of the Soviet Regime. The debate between Lukács and the Frankfurt School over the status of Nietzsche – a debate that spanned the years between 1938 and 1967, and included other bourgeois philosophers and artists besides Nietzsche – was published in English in the 1970s under the title *Aesthetics and Politics* (Adorno et al. 1977). Here the issue was not - pace Kaufmann - whether Nietzsche was or was not a political theorist. Instead, what was at issue was a distinction made by Benjamin (1968 [1936]) between the fascist rendering of politics as art – i.e. "destruction as an aesthetic pleasure" – and "Communism [which] responds by politicizing art" (242). The question then becomes, does Nietzsche's position on art – for example his analysis of music in *The Birth of Tragedy* – fit Benjamin's definition of fascism? Bloch and Adorno in particular, rejected the argument that Nietzsche's (1967 [1886]) position on aesthetics combined with his (1989

4 For example, the now famous and frequently anthologized 4th chapter of Horkheimer and Adorno's *Dialectic of Enlightenment* titled "The Culture Industry: Enlightenment as Mass Deception," owes much to Lukács' (1972) interpretation of Marx's theory of commodity fetishism in the essay "Reification and the Consciousness of the Proletariat," chapter four of *History and Class Consciousness*. What is referred to as "cultural Marxism" today was made possible, in large part, by the crucially important work of the early Lukács, the period of his writings prior to his acquiescence to Stalinism in the 1930s. During his Stalinist period he publicly rescinded the positions he took in *History and Class Consciousness*. To be fair, there remains much debate about whether he actually accepted his role as a mouthpiece for Stalinism, or if he did so against his will (Pike 1988).

[1887]) critique of science was a recipe for fascism.[5] On the contrary, certain aspects of bourgeois culture that Lukács rejected as reactionary and decadent were viewed by Bloch and Adorno as worth defending as a means to achieve a more meaningful and widespread freedom for all people, including the proletariat (Adorno et al. 1977).[6] In Adorno's (1977) words, "In a highly undialectical manner, the officially licensed dialectician [Lukács] sweeps all the irrationalist strands of modern philosophy into the camp of reaction and Fascism. He blithely ignores the fact that, unlike academic idealism, these schools were struggling against the very same reification in both thought and life of which Lukács was a dedicated opponent" (152). Marcuse, for his part, also defended Nietzsche against Lukács, by arguing that Nietzsche's critique of work and the bourgeois work ethic remains a crucial element for any philosophy seeking the conditions for emancipation. In short, for Marcuse, any social theory that has emancipatory aims must include, if not begin with the demand for the liberation from work. Ironically, repression through the imposition of work is something that the Soviet regime shared with the "free" countries in the capitalist-West. This is precisely why Marcuse turned to Nietzsche for his own particular reconstruction of historical materialism. According to Marcuse (1961),

5 Several of the essays in this volume provide analyses of Nietzsche's position on science, including those by Babette Babich, Daniel Sullivan, Jeremiah Morelock, Christine Payne, Peter Atterton and Michael Roberts. On aesthetics, see the chapter by Tim Berard and James Meeker as well as the chapter by Nancy Love.

6 A good example is the difference between Bloch and Lukács on the significance of the Expressionist movement, which as Taylor (1990) has demonstrated was significantly influenced by Nietzsche and offered an early version of a Left-Nietzscheanism. Bloch viewed the Expressionist movement more favorably than Lukács who dismissed it as an irrational cultural form that at best provided an inadequate resistance to bourgeois decadence and at worst, paved the way to fascism. Bloch, on the other hand, criticized Lukács for being too dogmatic in taking the vulgar Marxist position that "all forms of opposition to the ruling class which are not communist from the outset are lumped together with the ruling class itself." For Bloch, such a point of view was "mechanical" rather than "dialectical" (Adorno et al. 1977: 21). For an excellent treatment of the question of aesthetics and politics in Nietzsche's work see Strong (2012). In Strong's view, Nietzsche's perspective on music provides a glimpse of what an anti-fascist politics would look like. The necessary, if not sufficient condition for such a politics is the prevention or overcoming of *ressentiment* because *ressentiment* is the soil from which fascism flourishes. According to Strong (2012), "Precisely because no words for music will ever be adequate to our experience of it – and, although we always strive to grasp music, we know our inadequacy as long as we do not deny it – does music serve as the model for a community not based on ressentiment" (90). In this volume, see the essays by Berard and Meeker and Nancy Love.

> The assault against 'bourgeois irrationalism' [by Lukács] is particularly illuminating because it reveals the traits common to the Soviet and Western rationality, namely, the prevalence of technological elements over humanistic ones. Schopenhauer and Nietzsche, the various schools of 'vitalism' ... differ and conflict in most essential aspects; however, they are akin in that they explode the technological rationality of modern civilization. They do so by pointing up the psychical and biological forces beneath this rationality and the unredeemable sacrifices, which it exacts from man. The result is a transvaluation of values, which shatters the ideology of progress ... This transvaluation acts upon precisely those values which Soviet society must protect at all cost: the ethical value of competitive performance, socially necessary labor, *self-perpetuating work discipline*, postponed and repressed happiness. (213, emphasis ours)

In hindsight, one can see why an Anglo-American audience was rather receptive to Kaufmann's strategy of portraying Nietzsche as a conventional philosopher rather than a political or social theorist. Left-wing intellectuals in Europe who had appropriated Nietzsche were either murdered under orders of Hitler and Stalin – although for different reasons – or they went underground in exile and resistance. After the war, fascist ideologues in the Nazi Party who had appropriated Nietzsche were, at last, vanquished and discredited. The Allied victory meant that there was an opening for Nietzsche to be considered anew, from the perspective of an American philosopher seeking to bridge the divide between Anglo-American (analytic) and Continental traditions in philosophy.[7] This post-war reconfiguration of politics, so to speak, allowed Kaufmann to step in and reconstruct Nietzsche in an intellectual space that seemed free from dubious political and social interests, allowing Nietzsche to at last find a home among the great thinkers in Western Philosophy.

While Kaufmann was working on his antipolitical reconstruction project, Nietzsche's return to political and social theory was underway in Germany and France once the intellectual Left found an opportunity to reconstitute itself in the late 1940s. In the U.S., Nietzsche would also eventually find a home – again – in American political and social theory during the turbulent era of the 1960s counterculture (Strong, 1996). Kaufmann unintentionally contributed to the

7 While Kaufmann himself was part of the Jewish diaspora that fled Germany for the United States during the war, he was still a teenager when he arrived in the U.S. He went to university and graduate school in the U.S., where he was trained in the analytic tradition of philosophy. This partly explains his difference from the members of the Frankfurt School, who were rather pessimistic regarding American politics and culture, and much more critical of the analytic and positivist traditions in Western philosophy.

return of Left-Nietzscheanism in the sixties because his successful dismantling of fascist readings of Nietzsche both helped create a space for a younger audience to discover the writings of the diaspora of radical intellectuals after the war, and opened the doors to new avenues of thinking about Nietzsche that moved well beyond Kaufmann's own existentialist interpretations as well as those of the original Nietzschean-Marxists of the early 20th century. Perhaps, then, we should view Kaufmann's efforts at creating a clearing – a reset button if you will – in terms of generating the conditions necessary for a flourishing of new interpretations of Nietzsche, including those that do not shy away from a merger of aesthetics and knowledge production with politics, what today we call the field of cultural studies.

Among American scholars, it was left to the generation after Kaufmann to rediscover that Nietzsche was, indeed, a political thinker. Two important developments in American Nietzsche scholarship that were inspired by the politics of the counterculture were the introduction of the post-structuralist Nietzsche to an American audience by David Allison (1944–2016) and the ground-breaking book by Tracy Strong (1975) titled *Friedrich Nietzsche and the Politics of Transfiguration*. Allison's (1977) edited volume, *The New Nietzsche*, helped to familiarize American scholars to the works of the French philosophers of the sixties, including the widely influential thinkers Gilles Deleuze (1925–1995), Jacques Derrida (1930–2004), and Sarah Kofman (1934–1994). The post-structuralist movement in French philosophy in the 1960s provided an alternative to Kaufmann's existentialist reading of Nietzsche, and through the works of Deleuze, Derrida and Michel Foucault (1926–1984) in particular, it provided the intellectual groundwork for more contemporary developments in cultural studies (Schrift 2000), feminist theory (Oliver and Pearsall 1988) queer theory (Butler 1990; Schotten 2019) and critical-race theory (Scott and Franklin 2006). Allison's important post-structuralist intervention in Nietzsche Studies among American scholars included the co-founding of the journal *New Nietzsche Studies* with Babette Babich in 1996. In addition, Babich's (1994) book *Nietzsche's Philosophy of Science* has made an important intervention in the field of science and technology studies, a field that has up until now largely neglected Nietzsche's contributions to the science question (Payne 2018). In the area of political theory, the success of Strong's (1975) book has led to an explosion of interest in Nietzsche as a political theorist, and it is here that the debates about Nietzsche's relationship to the Left have resurfaced to expand upon the older arguments among liberal intellectuals and those to the left of them, regarding the place of Nietzsche in relation to democracy and freedom (Connolly 1992; Hatab 1995; Honig 1993; Villa 2000; Rorty 1989).

While Nietzsche eventually found a home in American political science, via political theory, his work remains on the margins in the field of sociology in the United States (Roberts 2019; Antonio 1995). There has been no equivalent of a Walter Kaufmann or a Tracy Strong in American sociology. Ironically, professional sociologists trained in the U.S. are required to read the work of Max Weber, who was quite public about his own intellectual debt to Nietzsche, but Weber's relationship to Nietzsche remains unknown among sociologists in the U.S. as Nietzsche's texts are not included in the canon of sociological theory constructed by the leading American sociologists (Roberts 2019). To this day, the work of the Frankfurt School remains best example of how to merge the sociological imagination with Nietzsche's perspectivalism, but if it were not for the important contributions of Stanley Aronowitz (1972; 1988; 1990; 1992) and Andrew Arato and Eike Gephardt (1982), the Frankfurt School would have shared Nietzsche's fate of near complete obscurity in American sociology. Several essays in this volume seek to correct this particular problem. In addition, this volume pursues interventions in the fields of queer theory, aesthetics, critical race studies, Marxist cultural studies, political economy, labor history, the field of ludic studies, and science and technology studies. Some of the essays are critical of Nietzsche, while others are more affirmative of the value Nietzsche's perspective in light of the particular areas of intervention under consideration. Others seek to make very limited use of Nietzsche. Hence the subtitle of this volume.

In some ways, the collection of essays here continues the reflection upon the question "why Nietzsche still" that was raised by Schrift (2009) two decades ago. Or rather, we see this volume addressing a slightly different question, which is "why Nietzsche now?" The question raised by Schrift (2009) was grounded in a context where Nietzsche scholars were considering the lasting impact of the post-structuralist version of Nietzsche against claims made by Ferry and Renaut (1997) that Nietzsche's relevance had expired due to what they referred to as the social and political conditions of a "post-postmodern world." In other words, the question back then had to do with the waning influence of the French philosophers of the sixties inside the academy, or rather the alleged waning. We agree with Schrift's (2009) critique of Ferry and Renaut (1997). The prediction made in the 1990s that Nietzsche's presence would fade from the academy and that Left-Nietzscheans were no longer relevant in the aftermath of the fall of the Berlin Wall was a mistake. The stakes are much different now, however, because a decade ago the sudden and dramatic rise of the alt-Right neo-Nazi's in American society and Western Europe was not yet on the horizon. In the United States today, we are faced with a much different political, social and cultural context than that of the 1990s or the 1960s. Unlike the sixties, when the economy was growing and where the New Left was contesting the liberal hegemony of the Democratic Party under the leadership of President Lyndon B. Johnson, capitalism today is in a world-wide structural crisis and authoritarianism is resurgent all over the globe. And unlike the 1990s when it seemed like the capitalist-West was at last triumphant in the era of the dot com bubble, today the promise of freedom and a rising standard of living made by the champions of neoliberalism rings hollow among young people living in an environment of widespread repression unleashed by authoritarian populism and government austerity programs. Left-Nietzscheans of today have not only to contend with their liberal interlocutors from years past, like Kaufman and the followers of Richard Rorty who sought to tame Nietzsche, as it were, in order to make his work more palatable to for a liberal democratic constituency of public intellectuals. In addition, Left-Nietzscheans have to contend with the rise of the alt-Right, and leaders of that movement who are eager to re-enlist Nietzsche as the intellectual voice of fascism (Prideaux 2018).

It seems we are faced with a fork in the road in American society and politics after the economic crash of 2008. On the one hand we have seen the rise of democratic socialism as evidenced by the presidential campaigns led by Bernie Sanders. On the other hand, we are living in the midst of a resurgence of authoritarianism under the Presidency of Donald Trump. Does it seem likely that in 2020, democratic socialism will triumph over authoritarianism? It would certainly be a mistake to reduce our current situation in the United States and other parts of the Western world to a recurrence of the late Weimar period in Germany. Nonetheless, there are some similarities, and again Nietzsche's place at the fork in the road is worth considering carefully. We argue that with the maturation of the field of cultural studies within the context of the crisis in neoliberalism, the time is ripe for asking once again, why Nietzsche? Will the recent attempts by the alt-Right to appropriate Nietzsche for fascism find an audience, or will the Left version of Nietzscheanism that became resurgent in the 1960s win the day? As we struggle to find our way out of the repression of authoritarianism in the context of the accumulation crisis that plagues global capitalism, how can serious reflection upon Nietzsche's work point us toward the path to liberation?

1 Organization of the Book

The following nineteen chapters are divided into four main parts. The first two parts include chapters that appropriate Nietzsche's perspective on aesthetics, morality and politics and deploy them for interventions in a variety of social contexts. The third and fourth parts address issues concerning epistemology, ontology, ethics and pedagogy. The first part, titled "Ressentiment and Redemption: Overcoming the Slave Revolt of Morality, Politics and Aesthetics" begins with C. Heike Schotten's essay "Wounded Attachments? Slave Morality, the Left and the Future of Revolutionary Desire." Rather than labor over a correct interpretation of Nietzsche's own politics – whatever those may have been – Schotten takes for granted that Nietzsche was a conservative thinker committed to social hierarchy, which is why she claims it is "impossible to be a Left-Nietzschean" in the strict sense of the phrase.[8] The question then becomes: can Nietzsche's texts be appropriated for emancipatory purposes? The answer for Schotten is yes, because Nietzsche's critique of slave morality is crucially important for Left-wing social movements and critical theory today. Schotten's provocative intervention reveals how queer praxis pursues Nietzsche's so-called "aristocratic radicalism" (Detwiler 1990) from below. A central aim of Schotten's intervention is an engagement with Wendy Brown's (1995) now famous Nietzschean critique of Left-wing identity politics. While Brown's contribution remains valuable for the insights it made into the conditions where identity politics become reactionary due to an inability to discharge feelings of *ressentiment*,[9] Schotten argues that Brown exaggerates the extent to which *ressentiment* fuels the actually-existing social movements organized around the politics of identity. In other words, while Brown looks at identity politics *as* a kind of slave morality, Schotten looks at how identity politics – in this case queer activism – *performs a critique of* slave morality. In Schotten's words, "Rather than use this critique [of slave morality] to reprimand or discipline the left by blaming oppressed people for their own oppression and/or implying its inevitability due to their failed, weak, or infantile political visions, I suggest instead that Nietzsche's critique of morality be appropriated and re-deployed from *the perspective of* oppressed people(s) so as to make it *useful* for left politics." By looking at how queer identity is both a mark of deviance and a badge

8 Recall Foucault's (1980) claim that "the only valid tribute to thought such as Nietzsche's is precisely to use it, deform it, to make it groan and protest. And if commentators then say that I am being faithful or unfaithful to Nietzsche, that is of absolutely no interest" (53).

9 Brown's (1995) argument is that because the very identities in identity politics – woman, black, etc. – were brought into being by racism and misogyny, that means that said identities can only exist on the basis of a "wounding," to use Brown's term. As a result, the quest to seek redress from the state must fail because in order to receive reparations, one must maintain the injury. In short, there exists within identity politics an investment in the terms and source of their suffering. In this way, Brown reveals how both Left-wing and Right-wing movements can be created and driven by *ressentiment*. Hence the critique of identity politics as a form of slave morality. See Schotten for a more detailed analysis of this critique.

of resistance, Schotten demonstrates how queer praxis frees up the identities from a fixed location on the bottom of the social hierarchy.

Schotten also engages the important and widely influential work of queer theorist Lee Edelman (2004), by revealing how queering strategies should be viewed as an example of the liberatory Nietzschean praxis of anti-morality from below. In Schotten's words, "Just as Nietzsche would reject such redemptive promises as evidence of illness or decline, a queer anti-moralism rejects hopefulness and utopia because they are futurist ideological political projects that secure obedience and social control via the moralized abjection of queer/ed populations." Schotten seeks to include Nietzschean-inspired queer theory as a vital component of a reconstructed critical social theory for our time because, as she argues, it is imperative that we deconstruct the heteronormativity of Left politics.

As in the case with the first chapter by C. Heike Schotten, the following two essays by Doug Kellner and Nancy S. Love also focus on the question of the relationship between morality and politics. Love compares the alt-Right fascists to the Occupy Wall Street movement in order to emphasize the difference between the slave morality of the alt-Right and the master morality, if you will, of the Occupy Movement. Her argument also includes a consideration of how aesthetics mediates the relationship between morality and politics. For Kellner, the focus is on how *ressentiment* fuels reactionary-populism on the Right. In "The Trump Horror Show Through Nietzschean Perspectives," he argues that as we now undergo what he calls the American nightmare of a Trump presidency, we confront the challenges of a divided country with Trump and his often-frenzied followers constituting an authoritarian populist movement under an uninformed and hot-tempered demagogue. Kellner asks, how can the thought of Friedrich Nietzsche help us theorize and overcome the frightening horror show of a Trump presidency? In this chapter, he argues that Nietzsche's concepts of resentment, revenge, the will to power, and the agon as a form of politics can help in analyzing Trump, his followers, and the Trump phenomenon, and thus can explain what he refers to as "the Horror Show of the Trump Presidency."

In her chapter titled "Nietzsche, Adorno and the Musical Spirit of Ressentiment and Redemption," Love considers the question of music in Nietzsche and Adorno in the context of the rise of the alt-Right and the Occupy Wall Street Movement in recent years. As she reveals, new connections between Nietzsche and Nazism have recently been made again among the white-supremacist groups in the United States. While the growth of the alt-Right has been made possible by their successful mobilization of resentment, Love argues against Stefan Dolgert's (2016) plea that the Left should learn from the successes of the

Right and mobilize feelings of *ressentiment*, but for Leftist ends. The idea put forth by Dolgert is that social movements on the Left, like those on the Right, need "enemy-narratives" to achieve their ends, including winning elections. Love argues against this notion by examining the success of a different kind of social movement: namely, the Occupy Wall Street Movement, which as she reveals, "resisted the pressure to transform the moral stance of resentment into the vengeful psychology of ressentiment." Indeed, she goes so far as to refer to Occupy as a Nietzschean social movement of "free spirits," and she insists that we have yet to appreciate the significance and efficacy of this type of social movement on the Left. Love examines how music can play a crucial role in the creation of a non-resentful social movement on the Left that avoids the pitfalls of certain formations of reactionary identity politics, what she calls, following Adorno, a certain kind of "redemption." Music, according to Love, is able to "unsettle linguistic categories and established identities and convey ... unspeakable realities." It is here, in Adorno's critique of identity through music that Love sees promise in the Occupy movement and the myriad of prominent musicians that supported the movement, because music, as Tracy Strong (2012) has argued, can "can serve as a model for a community not based upon *ressentiment*" (90).

In some ways, the three chapters by Schotten, Kellner and Love overlap with Gilles Deleuze's (1983 [1962]) interpretation of Nietzsche where "the Nietzschean notion of the slave does not necessarily stand for someone dominated, by fate or social condition, but also characterizes the dominators as much as the dominated once the regime of domination comes under the sway of forces which are reactive and not active. Totalitarian regimes are in this sense, regimes of slaves, not merely because of the people that they subjugate, but above all because of the type of 'masters' they set up (x)." A critical understanding of this kind of cultural phenomenon is one of the key contributions to critical social theory, because it reveals how the usual Left and Right distinctions that are produced by conventional political discourse are far too simplistic. What the Nietzschean critique provides is another level of distinction, which is the cultural difference between slave morality and master morality[10]. Slave and master, in this Nietzschean sense, do not map directly onto the usual class distinctions made by either orthodox Marxist theory or conventional political discourse, because as Schotten and Love argue, social movements on the bottom, so to speak, may be structurally positioned as oppressed groups, and yet

10 For a more detailed explanation of the terms master morality and slave morality, see the chapter by Schotten.

the cultural politics created by these groups may be an expression of master morality rather than slave morality. In addition, in the passage by Deleuze quoted above, the ruling class may – under certain circumstances – be considered slaves given the kind of culture they propagate and reproduce.[11]

The fourth chapter by James Meeker and T.J. Berard also pursues a Nietzschean analysis of music in relation to cultural politics, but they do so through consideration of the social and cultural context of hip hop. Theirs's is a unique contribution to hip hop studies, being the first to provide a Nietzschean analysis to this particular art form by applying Nietzsche's account of classical Greek tragedy to the hip hop aesthetic that arose from the existential and social conditions of postindustrial decay in the urban environments of the late 1970s. Berard and Meeker provide an analysis of hip-hop culture as a means to demonstrate not only how Nietzsche's work can inform empirical research in the fields of sociology and cultural studies, but also how Nietzsche is a provocative complement to the work of Pierre Bourdieu. Here the focus is on the complimentary contrast between the Marxist analyses of aesthetics that focus upon ideology, co-optation and complicity in reproducing social inequalities and the Nietzschean view on aesthetics as an avenue for affirming life. In an attempt to reveal the limits of Marxist cultural analysis, like that of Bourdieu, Meeker and Berard argue that, "hip-hop is predictably compromised, but also incisively defiant and painfully honest ... [a] challenge is posed for cultural analysis to be critical without being dismissive of existential and aesthetic questions, or blind to the potentials of popular culture."

The final chapter of the first part by Allison Merrick provides a close reading of Nietzsche's *On the Genealogy of Morality* in order to highlight Nietzsche's analysis of economic relations, a relatively neglected topic in Nietzsche scholarship. Merrick reveals how Nietzsche claims, in the first essay, for example, that we know that noble values, as well as the set of values that succeed them, bear some relation to the economic conditions of enslavement (I: 7; I: 10); in the second essay, Nietzsche notably insists we heed the ways in which "the feeling of guilt, of personal obligation" find their origins in the relationships "between buyer and seller, creditor and debtor" (II: 9). Perhaps more pointedly, in the second essay, Nietzsche remarks that it is the complex creditor/debtor relations where "one person first *measured himself* against another." Finally, in the third essay, as Merrick argues, Nietzsche holds that the so-called "blessing of work" and all the "mechanical activity [that] what goes with it – such as

11 In addition to the essays by Schotten and Love, see the chapter by Kristin Lawler for more on the relationship between class and culture. Lawler's focus is on the cultural politics of particular kinds of labor movement organizations.

absolute regularity, punctilious and unthinking obedience, a mode of life fixed once and for all, fully occupied time, a certain permission, indeed training for 'impersonality,' for self-forgetfulness" may very well serve as a balm for excess, unexplained, suffering (III: 18). The primary objective of this essay then is to tease out and put to the forefront these aspects of Nietzsche's investigation into the origins of our moral modes of evaluation and to defend the view that a certain accounting of the adage "Nietzsche's economy," is indeed instructive. Merrick's focus upon Nietzsche's analysis of economic relations provides a good segue into the next part, which is dedicated to the question of Nietzsche's work in relation to Marx and Marxism.

The second part of this volume, titled "On the Advantages and Disadvantages of Nietzsche for Marxist Critique" includes essays for and against the merging of Marxist and Nietzschean analyses. We placed the essays by Ishay Landa and Babette Babich as bookends to this part, for they focus on textual interpretations of Marx and Nietzsche. In between their essays are the chapters by Kristin Lawler and Gary Yeritsian that consider Nietzsche's influence on anarchist and Marxist social movements. Lawler's chapter considers the relation of Nietzsche's thought to the praxis of radical organizations in the early 20th century American labor movement, while Yeritsian considers the student movements of the sixties and the artistic and anarchist movements of the early 20th century. The ongoing issue up for debate among Marxist theorists is whether or not Nietzsche was – to use Ishay Landa's words – "militantly affirmative of capitalism."

We begin the part with Landa's chapter "Marx, Nietzsche and the Contradictions of Capitalism," which, among all the essays in this volume is the most critical of Nietzsche. As a counterpoint to Babich's interpretive intervention (Chapter 9) that reads between Nietzsche and Marx in order to find crucial intersections as a means to expand the liberatory aims of critical theory, Landa sees Nietzsche as perhaps the arch rival for Marxism. For Landa, Nietzsche must be viewed as "the formidable, most versatile and innovative thinker of the bourgeoisie in its defensive phase." It is for this reason that Landa views Nietzsche as the perfect antagonist for Marxist theorists pursuing a critique of bourgeois ideology as part of what Gramsci calls the "war of position," or the struggle for cultural hegemony that precedes any successful political conquest of the state.

Interestingly, Landa (2019) first makes it clear that it is a mistake to claim that Marx neglected cultural analyses in favor of economic ones, and that inversely, it is a mistake to claim that Nietzsche was primarily concerned with culture at the expense of economic phenomena. Landa argues that while both Marx and Nietzsche provide powerful analyses of the relationship between cultural and economic phenomena, they nonetheless remain at odds, for according to Landa, "their respective social vantage-points and political projects ... were fundamentally opposed: Marx envisioned a society overcoming class division, whereas Nietzsche directed all his powers at preventing precisely such an outcome. What Nietzsche in many respects offers us is therefore a Marxist theory with inverted signs." In some ways, Landa's provocative essay is a continuation of Lukács (1980 [1950]) attack on Nietzsche in the *Destruction of Reason*. In addition, the essay here should be read in conjunction with Landa's (2014(a); 2014) previously published critical essays on the French Nietzschean theorist, George Bataille (1994 [1945]). In those essays Landa provides his version of a Marxist critique of the French Left Nietzscheans who provided the groundwork for what would become poststructuralism. Together with the provocative interventions by Jan Rehmann (2007), Landa's work is among the best examples of those Marxists who see Nietzsche as a foe of Marxist critical theory, and therefore the perfect interlocutor for sharpening Marxist critique against the so-called "bourgeois" philosophers, especially Nietzsche. Nietzsche is seen as the predecessor to poststructuralism, and poststructuralism, in turn, is often blamed for creating the cultural environment that has allowed for the rise of the alt-Right fascists; the argument being that the philosophical deconstruction of epistemological and moral foundations has made it impossible to establish right from wrong, leaving us with the no recourse to resist the "might makes right" perspective.[12]

12 It is for this reason that Habermas (1989) refers to the poststructuralists – especially Foucault, Derrida and Deleuze – as "new conservatives." This kind of argument relies on a flawed reading of Nietzsche's concept of "will to power," because it interprets Nietzsche to mean a desire to dominate another. Again, Deleuze's (1983 [1962]) reading of Nietzsche is very instructive on this question. A careful reading of Nietzsche situates the concept of will to power within a context of ethics and ontology in addition to political theory. Failure to do so leads to distortions of Nietzsche. According to Deleuze, "Every time we interpret will to power as 'wanting or seeking power' we encounter platitudes which have nothing to do with Nietzsche's thought. If it is true that all things reflect a state of forces then power designates the element, or rather the differential relationship, of forces which directly confront one another. The relationship expresses itself in the dynamic qualities of types such as 'affirmation' and 'negation.' Power is therefore not what the will wants, but on the contrary, the one that wants in the will. And 'to want or seek power' is only the lowest degree of the will to power, its negative form, the guise it assumes when reactive forces prevail in the state of things ... Nietzsche says that the will to power [in an active, affirmative mode] is not wanting, coveting or seeking power, but only 'giving' or 'creating'" (xi–xii). For more on this reading of the will to power see Chapter 2, "Active and Reactive" in Deleuze (1983 [1962]).

In her chapter titled "Labor's Will to Power: Nietzsche, American Syndicalism and the Politics of Liberation," Kristin Lawler offers an original intervention in critical theory, as her essay is the first to consider the relation of Nietzsche's philosophy to labor movement tactics and culture. In particular, she explores the intersection of Nietzsche's thought with the cultural politics of the Industrial Workers of the World (IWW). She argues against Social Democrats who view Nietzsche as a foe to the cause of emancipation. For Lawler, the issue turns upon the question of culture. In particular she criticizes those on the Social-Democratic Left that claim that a return to class – understood here as an economic category rather than a cultural one – is necessary because questions of culture have been a distraction of sorts that led us astray from the main issue: economic inequality. Lawler refuses to accept this false binary between the cultural and the economic. Lawler begins her analysis with a critique of perhaps the best contemporary version of the Social-Democratic critique of cultural politics in Angela Nagle's best-selling book, *Kill All Normies*. For Nagle, a politics of cultural transgression and anti-moralism – in short Left Nietzscheanism – cannot lead toward emancipation; indeed, such a politics has led to the triumph of fascism rather than liberation. Lawler argues instead that

> with her analysis, Nagle exhorts the left to abandon "the cultural turn" and get back to the business of "class" – which for her seems to be without cultural preferences in general or a desire for freedom in particular. In this essay, I want to use the work of Nietzsche and the early twentieth century labor and cultural politics that it resonates with and in some ways inspired, to argue that the desire for freedom is the essence of any class politics that has a chance of challenging the ascendance of the fascist right, as well as the essence of the kind of labor movement politics that can win in a post-Fordist, post-Keynesian, hyper deregulated economic environment.

For Lawler it is instructive to study the history of the Industrial Workers of the World (IWW) – also known as the Wobblies – who were quite successful in organizing itinerant workers in the early 20th century, due to their unique culture that set them apart from other labor organizations of the same time period, including the American Federation of Labor (AFL). The Wobblies were unique among labor organizations in that they refused to sign labor contracts and they advocated workplace slowdowns and other slacker strategies. What is most important for Lalwer is the anti-work ethos at the center of the culture of the Wobblies. This overlaps significantly with cultural positions taken by Nietzsche. According to Lawler,

> Significantly, a Nietzschean philosophy was present at the creation of the Wobbly culture and tactics of class struggle. And all of it goes to answer the serious question that emerges from a left reading of Nietzsche's work – is the creative, affirmative, vital, free, only the possession of an elite? Or can a subaltern class claim freedom in this sense? I would like to use Nietzsche's work to answer in the affirmative, theoretically and historically, and to make the case that this is only possible when the "sickness" of ascetic-work morality is overcome.

Lawler's focus is upon the labor movement strategy known as syndicalism. What she sees in syndicalism is a certain kind of cultural politics that resonates well with Nietzsche's thought. According to Lawler,

> key here is the 'pathos of distance' with which Nietzsche characterized the original 'noble race' and the values that emerged from their own autonomous perspective. The IWW, especially the migrant 'hoboes' who carried their culture, did create a set of their own, affirmative, vital, and pleasure-oriented values, and disseminated them through songs, stickers, cartoons, posters, newspapers, standup comedy and political and intellectual lectures on soapboxes in urban parks, and an innovative set of linguistic codes that set the counterculture apart.

Lawler's reading of Nietzsche is similar, in some regards, to that of C. Heike Schotten's insofar as both authors seek to demonstrate how Nietzsche's "aristocratic radicalism" (anti-moralism, cultural transgressions) can be pursued from the standpoint of the oppressed.

In his essay "Marxism, Anarchism and the Nietzschean Critique of Capitalism," Gary Yeritsian disagrees with Landa's assertion that Nietzsche was "militantly affirmative of capitalism," arguing instead that Nietzsche offers a uniquely cultural critique of capitalist morality. Yeritsian also focuses on Left-wing social movements that were inspired by Nietzsche, arguing that "we should expand our analytical frame to also encompass the *actual historical reception and appropriation* of Nietzsche's texts." His essay aims at two analytical goals: a reading of Nietzsche in terms of central dimensions of the "artistic critique of capitalism," as theorized by Boltanski and Chiapello; and a connection of that reading to illustrative historical examples of left activists and movements on whom Nietzsche's artistic critique exerted an influence. Yeritsian seeks thus to bring into question the orthodox Marxist reading of Nietzsche – associated with Lukács and Mehring – as a reactionary apologist for imperialism and capitalism. Yeritsian concedes that Nietzsche's political philosophy is explicitly elitist and antidemocratic, and thus in no way mounts a "social critique" of the inegalitarianism and exploitation characteristic of modern class society. However, Nietzsche's opposition to industrial discipline and standardization and his championing of the struggle against generic alienations align him in a profound way with the liberatory impulse of the artistic critique. However, such a reading does not proceed to treat Nietzsche as compatible with the Marxist framework. Rather, the artistic critique found in Nietzsche's work is aligned much more directly with *anarchist* thought and practice, and its subsequent historical impacts and appropriations attest to this fact. Its fundamental neglect of social analysis represents precisely the massive gap that can be "filled" by historical materialism. This complementarity, though, may also work both ways, with the aesthetic concern with liberation helping us to avoid a structuralist Marxism that completely sidesteps questions of human freedom and flourishing.

In her essay "Between Nietzsche and Marx: Great Politics and What They Cost," Babette Babich considers the problem of scholars talking past one another regarding question concerning the intersection – or lack thereof – between Marx and Nietzsche. Her original and provocative intervention situates the Marx/Nietzsche debate within another divide of sorts: namely, the split in the field of philosophy between the analytic and continental traditions. Even within the Marxist paradigm itself, a division exists between analytical Marxists who rely on the techniques of analytical philosophy and rational choice theory like those of G.A. Cohen, John Roemer and Jon Elster, and their continental counterparts like Louis Althusser and the members of the Frankfurt School, who ground their version of Marxist critical theory in the Kantian tradition of critique, which, rather than presuppose reason and the knowing subject, begins with an interrogation of the very possibility of knowledge and its relation to power. For this reason, continental Marxism – for lack of a better phrase – has been more attuned to questions of culture and ideology, whereas the analytic Marxists have been more focused on questions of social structure and measuring instruments that are able to accurately capture the empirical qualities of such structures. According to Babich, the analytic/continental divide in philosophy partly explains why, in Anglo-American cirlces, "Nietzsche is read less as a thinker of the socio-political sphere much less of political economy and certainly not as theorist of science or logic but principally as a critic of morality and religion." This explains, in part, why Nietzschean-Marxist analyses are relatively rare in the Anglo-American context.

Another issue that Babich seeks to address is another kind of division which is within the continental tradition of philosophy. There issue here is: what to do with Hegel? If one were to seek out connections between Marx and

Nietzsche then the figure of Hegel complicates such an endeavor, for clearly Nietzsche's thought is incompatible with the Hegelian tradition in a way that Marx's is not. The French philosophers of the sixties turned to Nietzsche as a means to develop a critical approach to the class relation of master/slave that could serve as an alternative, it not a complement to Alexandre Kojeve's influential reading of Hegel's famous "Lordship and Bondage" section of Hegel's *Phenomenology of Spirit*. The Marxist–Hegelian understanding of the master–slave relation is from the point of view of the slave as someone dominated due to social-structural conditions prevalent in a given socio-economic formation. The Nietzschean configuration of the master-slave relation differs from the Hegelian notion in that the Nietzschean perspective seeks to examine how slave morality comes to be the dominant morality in society. For the philosophers of the sixties like Foucault and Deleuze – as well as the Frankfurt School – what this means is that totalitarian regimes are the regimes of slaves due to the kinds of rulers that come to power.[13] Reading between Marx and Nietzsche can thus be seen as a way to articulate the two different configurations of the master–slave relationship.[14]

Lastly, Babich provides a provocative and original reading of Nietzsche's critique of finance capitalism. Here, we see a side of Nietzsche largely ignored by those critics who claim that Nietzsche was a zealous advocate of capitalism. This is the Nietzsche, who in aphorism 285 of the *Wanderer and His Shadow*, agues that "we must remove from the hands of private individuals and companies all those branches of trade and transportation favorable to accumulation of *great* wealth, thus especially the trade in money – and regard those who possess too much as being as great a danger to society as those who possess nothing." In Babich's words, "The 'trade in money' is the stock market. There is no better indictment of what we call the 1%, or whatever smaller percentage there is to name." Babich's reading between Marx and Nietzsche is a slightly different strategy than that taken by scholars like Michel Foucault or C. Heike

13 One of the main reasons why the Frankfurt School and the French philosophers of the sixties like Foucault Deleuze turned to Nietzsche (and Freud) was because they were seeking to explain how it could be possible that the working-class could come to embrace their own domination rather than fight for their emancipation. In other words, the orthodox Marxist position that the proletariat was destined to liberate humanity never came to pass. On the contrary, in Germany during the 1930s, the proletariat gave the world fascism instead of emancipation. Orthodox Marxist theory was not adequate in explaining how this came to pass.

14 For more on this issue see Chapter 5 of Deleuze (1983 [1962]), titled, "The Overman: Against the Dialectic."

Schotten, who are not concerned with Nietzsche's own politics, or with what Nietzsche's texts "really" mean. What matters for them is what one can do with Nietzsche's texts. While Babich shares their concern with constructing a Left-Nietzscheanism, there remain better and worse interpretations of Nietzsche's texts, and as Babich argues, that does matter. In this way Babich's concern with getting it right – regarding good readings of Nietzsche's texts – overlaps with Deleuze's (1983 [1962]) argument that, "As long as the reader persists in: (1) seeing the Nietzschean 'slave' as someone how finds himself dominated by a master, and deserves to be; (2) understanding the will to power as a will which wants and seeks power; (3) conceiving the eternal return as the tedious return of the same; (4) imagining the Overman as a given master race – no positive relationship between Nietzsche and his reader will be possible" (xii).

The third part of this volume, titled "Beyond Truth and Relativism: Nietzsche and the Question of Knowledge" considers Nietzsche's relation to the science question. The critique of science is, of course, an important component of the framework of critical social theory, especially the question of the relationship between knowledge and power. The first three essays by Michael Roberts, Jeremiah Morelock and Daniel Sullivan consider Nietzsche's relationship to sociology. Unlike political theory, the field of sociological theory, especially in the United States, has yet to engage with the thought of Nietzsche and the Nietzschean tradition. Roberts, Morelock and Sullivan all seek to begin a conversation of how to integrate Nietzsche's perspectivalism with the sociological imagination. The essay by Christine Payne takes a broader approach by looking at Nietzsche's critique of epistemology in relation to Marx's theory of ideology, while Peter Atterton considers a new interpretation of the relationship between Nietzsche's and Darwin's thought.

In his essay "Toward a Gay Social Science," Roberts looks at the unfortunate absence of Nietzsche from sociological theory as it is practiced and reproduced in American sociology. The first part discusses how Talcott Parsons erased the presence of Nietzsche from Weber's work as part of a larger ideological maneuver to provide a theoretical grounding for the belief in American exceptionalism. The second part of the article compares and contrasts Nietzsche to the conventional sociology of Weber and Durkheim in order to demonstrate how Nietzsche's work provides sociologists with valuable material to be used for a critique of conventional sociological theory. American sociology is long overdue for a sustained engagement with Nietzsche. Such an undertaking is particularly relevant for those concerned with the ongoing project of reconstructing a critical social theory that has emancipatory aims. The last section of Roberts' essay considers the significance of the Nietzschean-Marxists in terms of their relationship to the politics of the Russian Revolution.

In the essay "Resuscitating Sociological Theory: Nietzsche and Adorno on Error and Speculations" Jeremiah Morelock argues that sociological theory has backed itself into a corner under both positivist and relativist dogmas. For him, a metatheoretical lens that supports the selective and critical use of multiple perspectives might be helpful. Nietzsche's perspectivalism and Adorno's negative dialectics both point in this direction. While both thinkers are well known for being critical and iconoclastic in their diagnoses of Enlightenment rationality, they also both offer positive depictions of how a liberated and liberating alternate kind of philosophy might operate. In this chapter, Morelock brings together their epistemologies, centering on Nietzsche's theories of error and perspectives, and Adorno's theories of speculation and constellations. This exploration involves two areas of interpretive tweaking. For the first area, Morelock suggests that their epistemologies can be interpreted less as ontological reflections on concrete objects and more as socially motivated metatheories about abstract objects pertaining to society. Second, Morelock argues both theories have Heraclitean conceptions of becoming which include atemporal dimensions.

In his essay "The Science of the Last Man: Nietzsche and the Early Frankfurt School," Daniel Sullivan argues that in their late empirical studies, the Frankfurt School scholars arrived at a diagnosis of how "average" individuals under modern capitalism were able to participate in atrocities such as the Holocaust. This diagnosis resonates strongly with Nietzsche's archetype of the Last Man. Sullivan's aim is to demonstrate how the social scientific methodologies of both Nietzsche and the early Frankfurt School gave them a unique vantage point on this predominant personality type in contemporary culture. Although standard narratives suggest that both Nietzsche and the early Frankfurt School were ultimately hostile to empiricist epistemology, Sullivan contests these accounts by examining three questions: What was Nietzsche's vision for methods at the intersection of philosophy and science? How does this vision relate to the metatheoretical foundations of the Frankfurt School's empirical methodology? And what relevance do this vision and methodology have for the empirical social sciences today? To address these issues, Sullivan compares and synthesizes the writings on social scientific methodology of Friedrich Nietzsche and the early Institute for Social Research (ISR). He then examines how their common assumptions about social science are exemplified in the last major empirical project of the ISR: the *Gruppenexperiment*. Sullivan argues that this neglected vision of empiricism provides a welcome counterpoint to recent developments in the social sciences, and that it granted the ISR empirical insight into a personality type that Nietzsche would have recognized as the Last Man.

In the fourth chapter in this part titled "The Death of Truth – Guilt, Anxiety, Dread, and Hope: Nietzschean Confessions," Christine Payne considers Nietzsche's warnings of a looming epistemological catastrophe as aids for reflecting on the temptation of relativism presented by Nietzsche's own perspectival approach to knowledge. By reading his announcement of the "death of God" through his reflections on the relationship between modern Western science and religion, an understanding of the relationship between Nietzsche's perspectivalism and relativism is clarified. In order to bring into relief both the moments of significant overlap and the even more significant moments of departure that Nietzsche's perspectivalism shares with epistemological relativism, the chapter begins with a consideration of relativism as it manifests in the schools of the Strong Program's Social Studies of Knowledge and in Actor-Network Theory. Between these two approaches to the question of truth, the issues of epistemological and ontological relativism, symmetrical analyses of truth and error, and normatively agnostic evaluations occupy center stage. While Payne does contend that particular elements of Nietzsche's perspectivalism can plausibly be understood to rest comfortably within these relativistic approaches to knowledge, Nietzsche's answer to the question of what grounds knowledge nevertheless moves the issue of relativism away from the realm of the epistemological and toward the realms of the political and the ethical. Approaches to knowledge and to truth rest on historically particular values, desires, and drives – ways of being in the world. Having tracked the potentials and potential pitfalls of perspectivalism against the temptations of relativism, we are lead back to one of the central animating concerns of this work as a whole; namely, the consequences for political imaginations and practices in the face of the deconstruction of traditional understandings of epistemology.

The last chapter in this part is Peter Atterton's "Nietzsche's Anti-Darwinism': A Deflationary Critique." The animal question is on the cutting edge of critical science studies and the anti-humanism of the poststructuralist movement is generally viewed as a precursor to the recent scholarship on this topic.[15] It is in this context that Atterton seeks to make an intervention. Atterton's original and stimulating argument provides a reconsideration of the relationship between Nietzsche's thought and Darwin in order to challenge the poststructuralist interpretation of Nietzsche's philosophy as the forerunner of radical anti-humanism. Atterton himself does not affirm the humanist position. Rather, he starts from the position that the radical ontological distinction between

15 For an excellent example of this provocative, cutting-edge scholarship, see Vanessa Lemm's (2009) *Nietzsche's Animal Philosophy: Culture, Politics and the Animality of the Human Being*.

human and animal is untenable. What Atterton sees in Nietzsche is a contradiction of sorts between deconstructing the human–animal distinction on the one hand, and then reintroducing it through the development of particular concepts. By performing a close reading of Nietzsche's texts Atterton reveals that not only did Nietzsche misinterpret Darwin on several key issues, but also that Nietzsche takes contradictory positions on the human–animal distinction. According to Atterton, Nietzsche learns from Darwin that "there are no essential or absolute differences between humans and (nonhuman) animals," and yet Nietzsche at the same time "reintroduces a teleological and vitalist conception of organisms that Darwin's notion of struggle was precisely meant to leave behind." In short, Atterton uncovers evidence of "Nietzsche's indulging in the vanity that humans are separate from the rest of nature, even as he is in the process of 'placing man back among the animals.'" The consequences of these inconsistencies in Nietzsche's thought are such that Nietzsche is unable to maintain the naturalism that he hoped would overturn Platonism and "provide the antidote to the history of religion and philosophy."

The final part of this volume titled "All-Too-Human: The Question of the Human Condition in Light of Nietzsche," includes chapters that consider a variety of topics that we are referring to broadly as the human condition insofar as each chapter, in its own way, is concerned with specifying the conditions necessary for the flourishing of human life. We lead off this part with the essay "*Genealogy* as a Critique of Racial Narratives and the Loss of Solidarity," by Jung Min Choi and John W. Murphy. In their essay, the authors argue that in recent years individuals and groups have begun to view their identities as narratives, in order to avert the problems associated with essentialism. This maneuver is viewed to be liberating by those who have been marginalized. The problem, however, is that they revel in their own identities and do not appreciate the narratives of others. Social solidarity thus seems to be jeopardized. But borrowing from and extending Nietzsche's anti-essentialist philosophy, this outcome can be averted by recognizing that persons do not create their respective narratives alone; that is, social life is basically an intersubjective affair. When viewed in this way, the construction of narrative identities can support a view of community that does not diminish diversity to secure order. Hence social solidarity can be resurrected.

The next chapter in this part is Dawn Herrera's essay, "Play as a Watchword: Nietzsche and Foucault." Herrera seeks to demonstrate how Nietzsche's importance for Foucault is best clarified by examining the concept of play in the two philosophers. On the one hand, Herrera seeks to expand upon the concept of play that is often taken for granted when considering the work of other poststructuralists influenced by Nietzsche like Jacque Derrida, Gilles Deleuze and Sarah Kofman. Another intervention she makes is to make a distinction between the social science approach, which sees play in terms of the need for social norms to provide a grounding for action, and Foucault's Nietzschean notion of play which emphasizes freedom through transgression of norms.[16] Herrera engages with a perennial objection to Foucault: that his critical project finds totalizing systems of domination everywhere, including the constitution of subjective agency. Herrera suggests that paying attention to Nietzsche's influence on Foucault gives us a better understanding of the critique itself, and how to respond to it. The key to this reading is the notion of play. Both Nietzsche and Foucault envision play as the optimal response to the power-games and foundational contingency that critique reveals. According to Herrera, three themes – the play of force, stylistic play and the play of value creation – assist in foregrounding the importance of play in Nietzsche's work, and in tracing how Foucault adopts this figure and its variations, revealing an overlooked through-line in his trajectory of thought. What remains consistent is the resistance to dogmatic closure.

In his essay, "Critique of Subjectivity and Affirmation of Pleasure in Adorno and Nietzsche," Stefano Giacchetti Ludovisi develops a comparative analysis between Adorno's and Nietzsche's positions in regards to the role of subjectivity. According to Giacchetti Ludovisi, if, on one hand, it is possible to ascertain the affinity of the path followed by these two authors in criticizing "constitutive" subjectivity as the result of a historical process of identification made by rationality, on the other hand the differences among the two perspectives regarding the conclusions achieved by such critique are remarked. The process of the dissolution of subjectivity sustained by Nietzsche is, in fact, in part rejected by Adorno on the basis of a refusal of identifying a principle grounded on passions. Adorno's social critique leads him to the refusal of affirming a principle of pleasure, which is by now reduced to its reified version. The critique of the bourgeois subjectivity leads Adorno to the affirmation of what could be defined as "over-bourgeois"; a form of non-constitutive subjectivity which respects non-identity.

In his essay "Nietzsche and Happiness" Bryan S. Turner makes the case that biographical accounts of Nietzsche's life typically dwell on his personal difficulties and misfortunes. With few exceptions, there is consequently little attention given to the theme of happiness in his work. However, Nietzsche was steeped in classical philosophy and we should therefore not be surprised to discover that the theme of *Eudaimonia* (human flourishing or happiness) runs implicitly through much of his thinking and emerges explicitly in his criticisms

16 For example, see the tradition of sociological theory the stems from the work of Talcott Parsons (1968 [1937]), where the emphasis is upon how social action is made possible by a pre-existing social structure of norms and values.

of English utilitarianism. For Nietzsche, utilitarianism, the sociology of Herbert Spenser, and liberalism more generally were doctrines that were suitable to the "herd." "Greek cheerfulness" emerged through a confrontation with tragedy and suffering. Hence, he made a clear distinction between pleasure, happiness and joy. What he referred to as "English Happiness" was a doctrine of simple pleasures that were suitable for "fattened pigs." While he was clear in his criticisms of English political theory, his attitude to Darwinism was more ambiguous. On the one hand, Darwin's theory of evolution was secular and ruled out any possibility that nature was constructed by some divine plan. On the other, were humans like apes conditioned by elementary needs for food and sex? For Nietzsche strong souls had to rise above animal spirits through a fusion of power and joy. Eudaimonia therefore played an important, if somewhat hidden role, in his revaluation of values in modern societies.

We end the volume with Eve Kornfeld's reflections on teaching Nietzsche. In her innovative intervention that seeks to consider the pedagogical impact of reading Nietzsche, she begins by discussing her experiences with organizing a conversation among Nietzsche scholars as part of her presentation at a conference on Nietzsche. The conversation was aimed at sharing approaches to teaching Nietzsche in a college classroom. For Kornfeld, one issue worth reflecting upon is the transformation that takes place upon reading Nietzsche. Referring to this as a "Nietzschean pedagogy," she reflects upon how students and their professors undergo a certain kind of self transformation when engaging Nietzsche's texts. In Kornfeld's words, "Examining and upsetting relationships of power among more and less dominant students before they could become established in our seminar, then, our Nietzschean pedagogy – supplemented by experiential learning for both active and passive students – stretched everyone's comfort zone and emphasized the group's collective responsibility to engage directly and creatively with the text." One important development, according to Kornfeld was "their struggle with and against Nietzsche enhanced the possibilities for serious engagement in my students' reading and thinking; some expressed a desire to become "free spirits" after discussing Nietzsche." Hence, Kornfeld's description of the process as a "Nietzschean pedagogy." Ultimately, for Kornfeld, what is at stake in the engagements with Nietzsche's texts is the following: "A Nietzschean pedagogy led my students to a difficult and sometimes uncomfortable encounter, but one with tremendous transformative possibilities." Indeed. Is this not, after all, why we read Nietzsche? Not only is important to read Nietzsche in order to make our world a better place to live in; part of creating the conditions for human beings to flourish means first that we must undergo our own personal transformation.

References

Adorno, Theodor, et al. 1977. *Aesthetics and Politics*, edited by Ronald Taylor. New York: Verso Books.

Allison, David B., ed. 1985 [1977]. *The New Nietzsche: Contemporary Styles of Interpretation*. Cambridge, MA: MIT Press.

Antonio, Robert. 1995. "Nietzsche's Anti-Sociology." *American Journal of Sociology* 101(1): 1–43.

Arato, Andrew and Eike Gebhardt, eds. 1982. *The Essential Frankfurt School Reader*. New York: Continuum.

Aronowitz, Stanley. 1992. "The Tensions of Critical Theory," in *Postmodernism and Social Theory*, edited by Steven Seidman and David Wagner. Cambridge, MA: Basil Blackwell.

Aronowitz, Stanley. 1990. *The Crisis in Historical Materialism: Class, Politics and Culture in Marxist Theory*. Minneapolis, MN: University of Minnesota Press.

Aronowitz, Stanley. 1988. *Science and Power: Discourse and Ideology in Modern Society*. Minneapolis, MN: University of Minnesota Press.

Aronowitz, Stanley. 1972. "Introduction," in *Critical Theory: Selected Essays Max Horkheimer*, translated by Matthew J. O'Connell. New York: Continuum.

Aschheim, Steven E. 1992. *The Nietzsche Legacy in Germany, 1890–1990*. Berkeley, CA: Universityof California Press.

Babich, Babette. 1994. *Nietzsche's Philosophy of Science: Reflecting Science on the Ground of Art and Life*. Albany, NY: State University of New York Press.

Bataille, Georges. 1994 [1945]. *On Nietzsche*, translated by Sylvère Lotringer. St. Paul, MN: Paragon House.

Benjamin, Walter. 1969 [1936]. "The Work of Art in the Age of Mechanical Reproduction," in Illuminations: Essays and Reflections, edited by Hannah Arendt and translated by Harry Zohn. New York: Schocken Books.

Brown, Wendy. 1995. "Wounded Attachments," in *States of Injury: Power and Freedom in Late Modernity*, 52–76. Princeton: Princeton University Press.

Butler, Judith. 1990. *Gender Trouble*. New York: Routledge.

Connolly, William E. 1992. *Identity/Difference: Democratic Negotiations of Political Paradox*. Ithaca, NY: Cornell University Press.

Detwiler, Bruce. 1990. *Nietzsche and the Politics of Aristocratic Radicalism*. Chicago: Univesity of Chicago Press.

Dolgert, Stefan. 2016. "The Praise of Ressentiment: or, How I Learned to Stop Worrying and Love Donald Trump." *New Political Science: A Journal of Politics and Culture* 38(3): 354–369.

Edelman, Lee. 2004. *No Future: Queer Theory and the Death Drive*. Durham: Duke University Press.

Ferry, Luc and Alain Renaut. 1997. *Why We Are Not Nietzscheans*, translated by Robert de Loaiza. Chicago: University of Chicago Press.

Foucault, Michel. 1980. "Prison Talk," in *Power/Knowledge: Selected Interviews and Other Writings 1972–1977*, edited and translated by Colin Gordon. New York: Random House.

Habermas, Jurgen. 1989. *The New Conservatism*, edited and translated by Shierry Weber Nicholsen. Cambridge, MA: MIT Press.

Hatab, Lawrence J. 1995. *A Nietzschean Defense of Democracy: An Experiment in Postmodern Politics*. Peru, IL: Open Court Publishing Company.

Honig, Bonnie. 1993. *Political Theory and the Displacement of Politics*. Ithaca, NY: Cornell University Press.

Horkheimer, Max and Theodor Adorno. 2002 [1944]. *Dialectic of Enlightenment*, translated by Edmund Jephcott. Palo Alto, CA: Stanford University Press.

Landa, Ishay. 2019. "The Social Individual and the Last Man: Marx and Nietzsche Agree to Disagree." *Critical Sociology* 45(2): 253–265.

Landa, Ishay. 2014. "Bataille's Libidinal Economics: Capitalism as an Open Wound." *Critical Sociology* 41(4–5): 581–596.

Landa, Ishay. 2014(a). "Bataille: The Master, the Slave, and Consumption." *Critical Sociology* 41(7–8): 1087–1102.

Lemm, Vanessa. 2009. *Nietzsche's Animal Philosophy: Culture, Politics and the Animality of the Human Being*. New York: Fordham University Press.

Lukács, György. 1980 [1950]. *The Destruction of Reason*, translated by P. Palmer. London: the Merlin Press.

Lukács, György. 1972. *History and Class Consciousness: Studies in Marxist Dialectics*, translated by Rodney Livingstone. Cambridge, MA: MIT Press.

Marcuse, Herbert. 1961 [1958]. *Soviet Marxism: A Critical Analysis.* New York: Columbia University Press.

Moore, John, ed. 2004. *I Am Not a Man, I Am Dynamite: Friedrich Nietzsche and the Anarchist Tradition*. Brooklyn, NY: Autonomedia.

Nietzsche, Friedrich. 1989. *On the Genealogy of Morals*, translated by Walter Kaufmann. New York: Vintage Books.

Nietzsche, Friedrich. 1967 [1872, 1886]. *The Birth of Tragedy*, translated by Walter Kaufmann. New York: Vintage Books.

Oliver, Kelly, and Pearsall, Marilyn. 1998. *Feminist Interpretations of Nietzsche*. University Park, PA: The Pennsylvania State University Press.

Parsons, Talcott. 1968 [1937]. *The Structure of Social Action*. New York: The Free Press.

Payne, Christine A. 2018. *Critique Without Foundation: Friedrich Nietzsche and the Social Studies of Science*. Ph.D. Dissertation, University of California, San Diego.

Pike, David. 1988. "The Owl of Minerva: Reappraisals of Georg Lukács, East and West." *German Studies Review* 11(2): 193–225.

Prideaux, Sue. 2018. "Far-Right, Misogynist, Humourless? Why Nietzsche Is Misunderstood." *The Guardian* (October 6, 2018). https://www.theguardian.com/books/2018/oct/06/exploding-nietzsche-myths-need-dynamiting.

Ratner-Rosen, Jennifer. 2012. *American Nietzsche*. Chicago, IL: University of Chicago Press.

Rehmann, Jan. 2007. "Towards a Deconstruction of Postmodernist Neo-Nietzscheanism." *Situations* 2(1): 7–16.

Roberts, Michael J. 2019. "In Search of the Wanderer and Free Spirits: The Ascetic Absence of Nietzsche from American Sociology." *Critical Sociology* 45(2): 167–181.

Rorty, Richard. 1989. *Contingency, Irony, and Solidarity*. New York: Cambridge University Press.

Rosenthal, Bernice. 1986. *Nietzsche in Russia*. Princeton, NJ: Princeton University Press.

Scott, Jacqueline and Franklin, A. Todd., eds. 2006. *Critical Affinities: Nietzsche and African American Thought*. Albany, NY: State University of New York Press.

Schotten, Heike. 2019. "Nietzsche and Emancipatory Politics: Queer Theory as Anti-Morality." *Critical Sociology* 45(2).

Schrift, Alan D., ed. 2000. *Why Nietzsche Still? Reflections on Drama, Culture, and Politics*. Berkeley, CA: University of California Press.

Strong, Tracy B. 2012. *Politics Without Vision: Thinking Without a Banister in the Twentieth Century*. Chicago: University of Chicago Press.

Strong, Tracy B. 1996. "Nietzsche's Political Misappropriation." The Cambridge Companion to Nietzsche, edited by Bernd Magnus and Kathleen Higgins. Cambridge University Press.

Strong, Tracy B. 1988 [1975]. *Friedrich Nietzsche and the Politics of Transfiguration*. Berkeley, CA: University of California Press.

Taylor, Seth. 1990. *Left-Wing Nietzscheans*. Berlin: de Gruyter.

Villa, Dana R. 2000. "Democratizing the Agon: Nietzsche, Arendt, and the Agonistic Tendency in Recent Political Theory." In *Why Nietzsche Still? Reflections on Drama, Culture, and Politics*, edited by Alan Schrift, 224–246. Berkeley and Los Angeles: University of California Press.

Yeritsian, Gary. 2019. "Freedom Above Things: Nietzsche and the Artistic Critique of Capitalism." *Critical Sociology* 45(2).

PART 1

Ressentiment and Redemption: Overcoming the Slave Revolt of Morals, Politics, and Aesthetics

∵

CHAPTER 1

Wounded Attachments?: Slave Morality, the Left, and the Future of Revolutionary Desire

C. Heike Schotten

1 Introduction[1]

Can Nietzsche's work serve as a theoretical or political resource for critical theorists seeking to imagine a better world, an emancipated humanity, or a more just future? Skepticism has historically greeted such a question, as well it might, given Nietzsche's harsh repudiations of human equality, much less any notion of "better" as it had hitherto been imagined or advocated for by modern social movements. A slightly different question, however – one related to, but perhaps also distinct from, the question of Nietzsche's usefulness for critical theory – is the question of his usefulness or appropriability for the left: is there such a thing as a left Nietzscheanism? Is Nietzsche a thinker of the left or capable of appropriation for left political projects and viewpoints?[2]

Answering this question has been something of a cult enterprise within critical and political theory, where various attempts at forming or salvaging a left Nietzscheanism have taken place, whether in the form of agonistic or so-called radical democracy (Brown 2001; Connolly 1992; Hatab 1995; Honig 1993; Villa 2000) or, in one case, ironic liberalism (Rorty 1989). In the following pages, I, too, am going to attempt to offer, if not a left Nietzscheanism, then perhaps what is better called a left Nietzschean critique, one based decisively in queer theory and queer approaches to political theorizing. I actually take it for granted that

1 Parts of this chapter are drawn from Schotten 2018a and Schotten 2018b.

2 There may, in other words, be a distinction between being committed to building a better or more just world and advocating a specifically left or liberatory politics. This is not to say that the latter does not involve the former, but it is to say that the former is compatible with nearly any liberal and "progressive" political position, to the point that even conservatives can (and often do) advocate their positions in the name of progress or improving the world. To be on the left, however, is very specifically to view both individual and social problems as fundamentally questions of group-based oppression, exploitation, and – aspirationally – liberation, questions that are neither addressed nor solved by appeals to progress or betterment simply.

Nietzsche is a conservative thinker but will attempt nevertheless to appropriate his work for left politics on the basis of a re-reading of his critique of slave morality. That re-reading will enact two decisive shifts from previous appropriations: first, it will openly and unqualifiedly advance its interpretation from the perspective of the oppressed, a move of which Nietzsche would of course disapprove (and the place where all too many Nietzsche interpreters falter); and, second, it will centralize the role of *desire* in this perspective-taking in order to articulate the specifically queer character of the left politics I advocate. The result is a formation I call revolutionary desire, which I will suggest is both the animus of left politics and necessarily queer.

To accomplish this, I will rely on an appropriated version of Lee Edelman's work, in particular his *No Future: Queer Theory and the Death Drive* (2004), in order to re-imagine a queer(ed) left politics that opposes morality in a decisively non-hopeful, anti-futurist frame. Throughout, my foil will be Wendy Brown, in particular her famous essay "Wounded Attachments" (1995), which to this day remains a definitive statement of left Nietzschean critique and is still invoked by many as an important and relevant analysis of identity politics. Brown's failures of both imagination and commitment with regard to liberation, however, lead her to defeat a straw version of "identity politics" in the name of an ostensibly Nietzschean freedom that is not, in fact, all that liberatory. By clinging too tenaciously to a narrowly white, Euro-American, class-based version of leftism, Brown abandons the revolutionary desire she otherwise rightly argues is essential to liberation. As such, then, and despite her best intentions, Brown resigns herself to the end of left politics, which she characterizes as an impossible-to-satisfy and therefore ever-thwarted, resentful, moralizing desire.

Yet neither hope nor utopianism are necessary for a functional and vital left politics. Just as Nietzsche would reject such redemptive promises as evidence of illness or decline, a queer anti-moralism rejects hopefulness and utopia because they are futurist ideological political projects that secure obedience and social control via the moralized abjection of queer/ed populations. A successful Nietzschean leftism, therefore, would forgo his love of hierarchy but embrace his critique of morality as a punitive and vengeful will to power that accomplishes its queerphobic goals via dishonesty and projected self-loathing. Anti-moralism thus becomes able to serve liberatory ends. Thus it is not simply Nietzsche who can be marshalled to serve left political projects but, even more so, queer/ness and queer theory itself, which is both essential to left critique and simultaneously a demand that left critique respond to and undertake its own queer politics.

2 Slave Morality

As already noted, in this chapter I take for granted that Nietzsche is a conservative or a thinker of the right. By this I mean that he is a defender of natural(ized), elitist, socio-political hierarchy and understands the emergence of modernity and the enfranchisement of the masses as a direct threat to that hierarchy (Robin 2013).[3] Nietzsche's most extended, explicit reckoning with this commitment occurs in his critical account of slave morality in *On the Genealogy of Morals* (1967 [1887]). A specific rejection of Christianity and its modern derivatives, Nietzsche's critique of slave morality more generally suggests that any repudiation of hierarchy or social stratification must be understood not as

3 Citations are always possible, although as any reader of Nietzsche well knows, providing one or two quickly becomes tendentious since, despite his overall difficulty as a thinker, Nietzsche is nevertheless eminently quotable and his work is easy to cherry-pick. An interpretation of Nietzsche's oeuvre as a whole is therefore necessary to make any particular set of quotations meaningful (hence, see Schotten 2009). This chapter, however, is not an engagement with the question of *if* Nietzsche is a conservative; rather, it is an engagement with the question of if his work can be used to bolster left politics. That this is a question at all suggests there is at least some impediment to its realization; otherwise, there would be no controversy. Moreover, if "conservative" means what I have here defined it to mean, then it is abundantly clear that Nietzsche is a conservative because he is clearly in favor of natural(ized), elitist hierarchies of all sorts (whatever he might call them at any particular moment and however "serious" he may be about implementing them in "real life"). Thus, to claim Nietzsche's conservatism as a premise rather than a conclusion is neither an oversimplification nor an unacknowledged sidestepping of the controversy that has unfolded over this issue within Nietzsche studies over the years. Rather, it is an attempt to take Nietzsche at his word about hierarchy and meaningfully confront it, rather than defer this confrontation endlessly by, say, using his aphoristic style, proto-deconstructionist tendencies, or temporal location in an ostensibly less progressive historical moment to obscure or undermine an otherwise perfectly clear political position. Indeed, the claim that Nietzsche is an advocate of natural(ized), elitist hierarchy (whatever else he may be) remains controversial in some corners of Nietzsche studies only to the extent that such views continue to prove uncomfortable for superficially neutral yet implicitly liberal commentators who would prefer that the study of philosophy or political theory or Great Thinkers in general be separated from ostensibly pettier or more partisan questions of political positionality (this is a particular dilemma for philosophy, the discipline that continues to understand itself as the unvarnished pursuit of truth). Moreover, given that philosophy and political theory have largely resisted the critical epistemological and political challenges of critical race theory, women's/feminist studies, postcolonial studies, critical ethnic studies, and queer studies in their academic institutionalization and professionalization, it may simply be a more general allergy to politically "marked" and/or situated inquiry, rather than any substantial ambiguity on this point in Nietzsche's texts, that makes my otherwise banal statement about his political loyalties seem controversial.

righteousness but rather the vengeful path to power taken by weak and contemptible people who cannot survive or flourish any other way.

In §10 of the first essay of *On the Genealogy of Morals,* Nietzsche claims that the slave revolt in morality is the by-product of persons or groups who have somehow been prevented from acting and must therefore resort to other means in order to live and flourish. Reactive from the outset, then, Nietzsche notes that slave morality always requires a "hostile external world" in order to exist at all; "its action is fundamentally reaction." This reactivity is essentially negative: slave morality says "no" to that hostile external world, to whatever thwarts its own activity and expenditure. The slavish type, then, comes to exist only via reference to an imposed external (set of) force(s) and can only understand and affirm itself through negation of that imposition: "slave morality from the outset says No to what is 'outside,' what is 'different,' what is 'not itself.'" Nietzsche calls this negative reactivity *ressentiment;* its mightiest production and primary weapon is the concept of evil: "picture 'the enemy' as the man of ressentiment conceives him – and here precisely is his deed, his creation: he has conceived 'the evil enemy,' 'the Evil One,' and this in fact is his basic concept, from which he then evolves, as an afterthought and pendant, a 'good one' – himself!" "Evil" is used to (de)limit, judge, and punish those deemed to have brought about the original imposition that has so bitterly limited the activity of the weaker. This production of evil is accomplished via the fabrication of the responsible subject, the notion of an actor with the ability to do otherwise, who thus may be held accountable – and, more importantly, punished – for his deeds. Incapable of acting themselves, impotent to strike back at the aggressors, and condemning the aggressors' imposition as the very definition of evil, slavish types valorize their own weakness and produce the unwieldy apparatus responsible-subject/moral-opprobrium/political-punishment to restrain the activity of the strong. Nietzsche is clear about the effectiveness of this weapon (1967 [1887]: I: 7–8) and equally clear that it is not a weapon the strong deserve to have wielded against them. For imposition is the character of life itself. It is erroneous to think that such fatality comes at one's own expense or vengefully demand that life be otherwise. Rather, "to be incapable of taking one's enemies, one's accidents, even one's misdeeds seriously for very long – that is the sign of strong, full natures in whom there is an excess of power to form, to mold, to recuperate and to forget" (1967 [1887]: I: 10).

Noble morality, by contrast, does not emerge as the result of any necessary relationship to any other person or set of forces. Instead, noble morality is cast by Nietzsche as the anti- or non-morality; it might be characterized as unselfconscious self-affirmation: "the 'well-born' *felt* themselves to be the 'happy'; they did not have to establish their happiness artificially by examining their enemies, or to persuade themselves, *deceive* themselves, that they were happy (as all men of *ressentiment* are in the habit of doing)" (1967 [1887]: I: 10). Unlike the slavishness of slave morality, masters regard encounters with foreign elements as at best unremarkable, at worst a negative confrontation so fleeting or light that it is quickly forgotten or otherwise dispensed with:

> [The noble mode of valuation] acts and grows spontaneously, it seeks its opposite only so as to affirm itself more gratefully and triumphantly – its negative concept "low," "common," "bad" is only a subsequently-invented pale, contrasting image in relation to its positive basic concept – filled with life and passion through and through – "we noble ones, we good, beautiful, happy ones!" When the noble mode of valuation blunders and sins against reality, it does so in respect to the sphere with which it is not sufficiently familiar, against a real knowledge of which it has indeed inflexibly guarded itself: in some circumstances it misunderstands the sphere it despises, that of the common man, of the lower orders; on the other hand, one should remember that, even supposing that the affect of contempt, of looking down from a superior height, *falsifies* the image of that which it despises, it will at any rate still be a much less serious falsification than that perpetrated by its opponent – in *effigie* of course – by the submerged hatred, the vengefulness of the impotent. There is indeed too much carelessness, too much taking lightly, too much looking away and impatience involved in contempt, even too much joyfulness, for it to be able to transform its object into a real caricature and monster. (1967 [1887]: I: 10)

Now, elsewhere I have argued that there is no reason to believe that the slaves of Nietzsche's slave morality are coterminous with any specific oppressed group, nor that the masters of master morality are specifically related to the slaves *as* their oppressors (Schotten 2016). However, the upshot of this analysis is still that orders of rank or hierarchy of any kind are facts of life that only slavish, resentful, weak, and vengeful people seek to undo. Indeed, Nietzsche's critique of slave morality is a critique of both morality and slavishness, which I would suggest are mutually definitionally implicated for him: to be slavish is to be a moralizer, and to moralize is to act like a slave. In either case, one is leveraging an indirect and ignoble form of power – lying, self-hatred, vengefulness – in order to take down those who are somehow "stronger" or "better" by declaring them to be "evil" and deserving of punishment. It is by means of these ignoble practices that the lesser-off, the worse, the weaker, and the undeserving come to dominate and rule. Their foremost aspiration, aside from this very hegemony of course, is punishment of the "evil" ones. Indeed, punishment is slave morality's *raison d'etre*.

This critique seems to be, in its very essence, anti-liberatory. Hierarchy, domination, and exploitation are features of life itself. Any attempt to challenge, resist, undermine, or transform them is not simply hubris; it is contemptible and a form of nihilism. From a Nietzschean perspective, then, any left or liberatory project would constitute a resentful attack not simply on the strong or the exploitative, but in fact on life itself, and would be undertaken only by those unable to cope with or counter the stronger or better forces that naturally and necessarily (if not necessarily intentionally or purposefully) domineer over them. This recalcitrant commitment to naturalized, elitist hierarchy is *the* reason why it is effectively impossible to be a left Nietzschean. It is the philosophical substance behind Nietzsche's seemingly more ambiguous and/or multi-faceted sexist, racist, and Eurocentric remarks, and it was the perpetual stumbling block in the way of any account of "Nietzschean democracy," the production of which was something of a cottage industry in political theory in the 1990s. At some point, however, every one of these efforts had to resort to either tempering democracy with a Nietzschean element, insisting on some form of (sometimes "post-Nietzschean") political agonism or contestation, or else claiming an anti-democratic element as necessary in order for democracy to remain democratic (see e.g. Brown 2001; Connolly 1992; Hatab 1995; Honig 1993; Villa 2000). In other words, Nietzsche's conservative commitment to naturalized, elitist hierarchy proved too formidable to assimilate or overcome; instead, it had to be incorporated into liberatory or left political theory by preserving it as democracy's necessary other or internal challenge.

Perhaps intuiting this root incompatibility, the most influential appropriations of Nietzsche's work for left politics have not attempted such hybrid formations at all, but rather chosen to adopt his conservatism outright and use it instead to critique left politics as itself a form of slave morality. The most famous and definitive version of this argument is still Wendy Brown's widely-cited essay, "Wounded Attachments" (1995b),[4] which offers a Nietzschean critique of identity politics as suffused with resentment and thus incapable of achieving freedom. In this celebrated piece, Brown casts identity politics as

4 Although different versions of it abound, particularly with regard to feminism, which seem to have set an unspoken precedent that only left movements – or only feminism? – should be subjected to this particular analysis, a noteworthy critical consensus that seems to reflect rather than challenge broader conservative and anti-feminist tendencies in academic philosophy and political theory. A more recent version of Brown's critique of feminism as slave morality can be found in Halley 2008; for earlier examples, see Brown 1995a; Conway 1998; Stringer 2000; Tapper 1993.

grounded in "injury." In other words, the "identity" that grounds or serves as the basis of identity politics – for example, race, gender, sexuality, (dis)ability – is understood as having been *brought into being* by racist, sexist, homophobic, or ableist acts of violence, discrimination, and harm. Thus, one's individual "identity" or subjectivity exists only because and insofar as it is wounded or injured. If injury is constitutive of identity, however, then identity politics advocates find themselves in a dilemma. On the one hand, they seek identity-specific redress for their injuries from the state, whether in the form of social welfare policies, affirmative action measures, or anti-discrimination laws. On the other hand, because these identities have been forged in the crucible of injury, identity politics adherents cannot actually attain the redress they seek, because any justification of reparative state policies requires a retrenchment of the very identity that warrants them and thus a reproduction of injury. In order to have the reparation, one needs to maintain the injury, and in fact keep it alive forever. Far from attaining freedom, then, much less freedom from harm, identity politics adherents instead become invested in retaining and perpetuating the very source and terms of their own suffering so that they can justify the reparative policy changes they seek to enact. Identity politics is thus a deeply conservative, even reactionary political formation that seeks to maintain the very structures of oppression that produced the injured *as* injured to begin with:

> [I]n its attempt to displace its suffering, identity structured by *ressentiment* at the same time becomes invested in its own subjection. This investment lies not only in its discovery of a site of blame for its hurt will, not only in its acquisition of recognition through its history of subjection (a recognition predicated on injury, now righteously revalued), but also in the satisfactions of revenge, which ceaselessly reenact even as they redistribute the injuries of marginalization and subordination in a liberal discursive order that alternately denies the very possibility of these things and blames those who experience them for their own condition. Identity politics structured by *ressentiment* reverse without subverting this blaming structure: they do not subject to critique the sovereign subject of accountability that liberal individualism presupposes, nor the economy of inclusion and exclusion that liberal universalism establishes. Thus, politicized identity that presents itself as a self-affirmation now appears as the opposite, as predicated on and requiring its sustained rejection by a 'hostile external world.' (1995b, 70)

Identity politics are thus a kind of moralizing reverse discourse, an anti-liberal political formation that only retains and reproduces liberalism's most toxic formulations. Brown would thus seem to have turned Nietzsche's anti-emancipatory critique of slave morality into a deft tool of left analysis. Nietzsche's denigration of slave morality is not a reprimand of emancipatory social movements but rather a cautionary tale, a warning to the left to guard against political formations that seem liberatory on the surface but are, in fact, resentful and reactionary counterposes that obstruct the left's actual aims.

Unfortunately, there are significant problems with Brown's critique of identity politics as she presents it. First and foremost, it is a real question as to just who or what she is referring. Grace Hong (2015), for example, persuasively argues that Brown overstates the role of injured subjectivity as an animus of 1960s social movements and, specifically, that she overlooks women of color feminism's "alternative notion of subjectivity and community not organized around injury." Hong suggests instead that the politics of resentment Brown charts "became institutionalized" only later, "in the period of containment in the 1970s to the present" (2015: 156). The conservative identity politics formation Brown critiques in "Wounded Attachments," in other words, is actually a by-product of neoliberal retrenchment, rather than a failing of left or of liberatory social movements.[5] This means that Brown is effectively blaming the victim, a criticism that has rightly haunted this essay since its initial publication. As Alexander Weheliye points out, identity politics' alleged attachment to suffering is "less a product of the minority subject's desire to desperately cling to his or her pain but a consequence of the state's dogged insistence on suffering as the only price of entry to proper personhood" (2014: 77). This is an observation one might well have expected Brown to have offered, given her incisive and relentless critique of liberalism in *States of Injury* as anathema to freedom (see e.g. Abbas 2010).

Moreover, as Hong explains, Brown's critique of "identity politics" completely overlooks some of the most influential and defining articulations of identity

5 Elsewhere, Brown notes "the virtual disappearance of the Left in the United States" in the 1980s (2001: 19), which she attributes not so much to the power of neoliberalism but rather to the ineffectiveness of socialism and communism as either political ideologies or the basis for actually existing regimes. In a point that will come up later, however, it is worth noting that while the 1980s in the United States were indeed characterized by the Reagan administration's almost total liquidation of the social safety net and racist imperial foreign policy, they were also a period of resurgence for women of color feminism in the academy and the institutionalization of women's studies and critical ethnic studies, not to mention the influential and wildly effective activist work of ACT-UP, all of which advanced the kind of radical, structural analyses of power that Brown argues the left could no longer muster at this point in the face of, alternatively, the demise of communism or the ascent of poststructuralist philosophy. These may be invisible to Brown however, because, as we will see, for her the left does not really extend much beyond white anti-capitalism.

politics in radical and social movement history; e.g. the Combahee River Collective (CRC) statement, Audre Lorde's work, the groundbreaking women of color feminist anthology *This Bridge Called My Back,* and legal scholar Kimberlé Crenshaw's agenda-setting theorization of intersectionality (and its subsequent uptake in Black and women of color feminisms, both in the academy and in the streets). These versions of identity politics foreground the specificity of Black women's and women of color's experiences of oppression, not in a reactionary celebration of injury or vengeful insistence on punishment, but rather in order to better specify and foreground the oppressions faced by Black women and women of color and queer women of color, oppressions that had been summarily ignored, dismissed, and/or perpetuated by both the male left and white feminism. So, for example, the CRC write powerfully:

> Above all else, our politics initially sprang from the shared belief that Black women are inherently valuable, that our liberation is a necessity not as an adjunct to someone else's but because of our need as human persons for autonomy. This may seem so obvious as to sound simplistic, but it is apparent that no other ostensibly progressive movement has ever considered our specific oppression as a priority or worked seriously for the ending of that oppression. Merely naming the pejorative stereotypes attributed to Black women (e.g., mammy, matriarch, Sapphire, whore, bulldagger), let alone cataloguing the cruel, often murderous, treatment we receive, indicates how little value has been placed upon our lives during four centuries of bondage in the Western Hemisphere. We realize that the only people who care enough about us to work consistently for our liberation are us. Our politics evolve from a healthy love for ourselves, our sisters and our community which allows us to continue our struggle and work. (2017 [1977]: 18)

Such an assertion seems quite far from a reactionary or vengeful attachment to injury. If anything, it seems more akin to the unselfconscious self-affirmation Nietzsche describes as mastery in the *Genealogy*, a robust affirmation of self that requires no reference to a hostile external world for its fulfillment (and indeed, the CRC suggests it is that very hostile external world – and being forced to define themselves in reference to it – that is so toxic for Black women). As well, the goal of this liberatory struggle is not a retrenchment of Black womanhood as injured or oppressed, but rather liberation from the "major systems of oppression" that they famously define as both "interlocking" and the "synthesis" that "creates the conditions of our lives" (2017 [1977]: 15). There is nothing moralizing about such an aspiration, which is neither a resentful nor vengeful retrenchment of the status quo nor an attempt to preserve injured identity.

Ironically, then, although Brown construes identity politics adherents as reactively attached to their own subordination, it is she herself who ends up reiterating the naturalness or necessity of that subordination in her historically ungrounded misrepresentation of identity politics. This becomes evident when "Wounded Attachments" is read in the context of the rest of *States of Injury* as a whole. In the Introduction to the book, for example, Brown suggests that "identity politics" harbors an immature and short-sighted view of the world:

> Ideals of freedom ordinarily emerge to vanquish their imagined immediate enemies, but in this move they frequently recycle and reinstate rather than transform the terms of domination that generated them. Consider exploited workers who dream of a world in which labor has been abolished, blacks who imagine a world without whites, feminists who conjure a world either without men or without sex, or teenagers who imagine a world without parents. Such images of freedom perform mirror reversals of suffering without transforming the *organization of the activity through which the suffering is produced* and without addressing the *subject constitution that domination effects,* that is, the constitution of the social categories, "workers," "blacks," "women," or "teenagers." (1995c: 7, original emphases)

At first glance this passage seems merely to anticipate the fuller argument made later in "Wounded Attachments." Looking more closely, however, and reading both together makes clear that not only has Brown once again misunderstood the liberatory aims of CRC-type identity politics, but also that the real targets of her critical ire in this passage are, in fact, feminist and anti-racist "identity" politics. This is not simply because teenagers are the obvious and noteworthy exception to an otherwise familiar taxonomy of politically oppressed groups (workers, women, Black people), but also because Brown is clear later on in "Wounded Attachments" that identity politics formations are resentful precisely because and insofar as they are not class politics. In other words, largely unremarked but nevertheless central to the argument of "Wounded Attachments" is the old leftist chestnut that identity politics are diversions from "real" politics, which of course only ever means class struggle (1995: 59–61): "what we have come to call identity politics is partly dependent upon the demise of a critique of capitalism and of bourgeois cultural and economic values" (59). Indeed, Brown argues that identity politics obscure the real source of injustice – class domination – and therefore inhibit any political aspirations beyond bourgeois comfort and conformity (60). Thus, she concludes, it is not just the failure of communism or the triumph of (neo)liberalism that are to blame for the foreclosure of a critique of capitalism: it is also identity politics itself (61).

To return, then, to the quote from the Introduction, it is unlikely that Brown is critical of workers who imagine a world without labor, since of course that is the very locus and thrust of left politics and not at all an issue of "identity." Setting teenagers aside as well, then (since there are no known youth identity movements militating for the elimination of parenting as a form of oppression), the only political formations left to worry about in this quotation are anti-racist (identity) politics that imagine "a world without whites" and feminist (identity) politics that imagine "a world without men or without sex." Leaving aside for now Brown's reactionary foreclosure of social justice movements that might complicate, intersect with, or simply extend beyond class politics, it is necessary to pause at this formulation and ask just who, exactly, was advocating for a world without white people – much less a world without men – in 1995? Is this the same "identity politics" Brown critiques in "Wounded Attachments"? Does *any* identity politics, whether a CRC-type argument for Black women's liberation or NAACP lobbying against the death penalty and gerrymandering, really imagine or aspire to a world without white people? We can ask similar questions with regard to feminism: even if one is Catharine MacKinnon – Brown's primary target of critical feminist ire in *States of Injury* – is it really her (or, for that matter, anyone's) feminist aspiration to eliminate men? In whose paranoid political imagination do such specters loom? For whom is the upshot of racial justice organizing and anti-racist protest a world without white people? For whom is the aim of feminist activism the elimination of men, a point of view so powerful that Brown must help warn and guard the left against them?

What is unwittingly revealed here is not simply a surprising anxiety regarding the demise of patriarchy and white supremacy, but also Brown's implicit or unstated concession to Nietzsche's naturalized, elitist hierarchy. That is, embedded in both Nietzsche's critique of slave morality and Brown's critique of identity politics as slave morality, even if not made explicit by either, are the presumptions that those "below" are necessarily weak and this weakness is both necessarily contemptible and somehow deserved. This is why moralism is objectionable to both thinkers: it is a dishonest and meritless (Nietzsche) or reactionary and anti-liberatory (Brown) means by which the subordinate seek to overcome their subordination. For Nietzsche, this moralism has been successful; modernity is effectively the era of slave morality, which has achieved dominance in every arena. For Brown, this moralism is *un*successful because it will necessarily fail in its efforts to redress its constitutive injury. But that lack of success is for the better, since this moralizing by the marginal cannot actually accomplish real freedom. Indeed, for both Nietzsche and Brown, those on the bottom are stuck in their place, somehow lower or weaker, and precisely *because* of the moralizing methods they employ. For Nietzsche, this moralizing is due to its advocates' natural weakness or slavishness. For Brown, this moralism is due to its advocates' immature (teenagers remember), short-sighted, freedom-hating embrace of the very terms of their own subordination. While Brown would likely not say this embrace is natural, she nevertheless provides no other reason as to why it occurs. She is clear that neither liberalism nor neoliberalism, much less the demise of socialism, are to blame for this reactive and reactionary political formation. Unfortunately, then, while it is unlikely that Brown would openly endorse naturalized, elitist hierarchy, her appropriation of Nietzsche's critique of slave morality retains its elitism intact to the extent that she blames identity politics adherents for (remaining attached to) their own injury and suffering. Another way of putting this is to say that Brown fails to clearly distinguish between oppressor and oppressed in her analysis and so ends up using Nietzsche to criticize the oppressed without first identifying them *as* the oppressed, thereby sanctioning (or at least not commenting on) the fact of their subordination, tacitly naturalizing it.[6] Along the way, and as if to dispel any charitable doubts about what she is doing, she reproduces distasteful right-wing canards about the demise of white people, the obsolescence of the male sex, and the militancy of feminists who would destroy all freedom and sexual pleasure if they could.[7]

6 Indeed, part of the problem with identity politics for Brown is "its reproach of power as such" (1995b: 70), which for her is neither marked nor specified in terms of oppression and so is therefore neither objectionable in itself nor an object of critique for her. Thus, throughout *States of Injury*, Brown advocates neither liberatory movements nor liberatory praxis to get free from oppressive structures but rather a left power politics difficult to distinguish from the aspirations to domination and the free marketeering she might otherwise seek to dismantle. Without a critique of oppression as such, however, it is difficult to know how and why the power politics Brown advocates is distinct from a capitalist, neoliberal, or right-wing power politics.

7 In a particularly troubling aside in a later essay on feminism and the decay of revolutionary futurity, Brown names "various feminist nationalisms bound to race and ethnicity" as akin to "lesbian separatism" in their "more conservative *Weltanschauung*" which, she claims, tend "toward the consolidation rather than the disruption of identity, [are] often inward-turning in their politics, less consistently critical of capitalism and liberalism, [and] more inclined toward interest-bound reformism than with propounding a comprehensive vision for society" (2005: 110). In other words, women of color feminisms are *more conservative than* second wave white feminism, insufficiently anti-capitalist, and responsible for the decline of feminist radicalism overall, a truly bizarre reading of history. As is well-known, if anything, it was

It is therefore crucial to acknowledge that, while Nietzsche is surely a critic of morality, he is so from the perspective of those in power – whether we want to call them the oppressors, the ruling class, the "masters," the elite, the great, the few, or what have you. Rather than use this critique to reprimand or discipline the left by blaming oppressed people for their own oppression and/or implying its inevitability due to their failed, weak, or infantile political visions, I suggest instead that Nietzsche's critique of morality be appropriated and redeployed from *the perspective of* oppressed people(s) so as to make it *useful* for left politics. Nietzsche's critique of slave morality is more than simply a claim that the undeserving many have now taken the reins of power to the detriment of the exceptional few. This is, indeed, one thing it claims, and is a by-now familiar articulation of the troubles of the embattled white guy as well as one mainstream explanation for the surprise 2016 presidential election of Donald Trump.[8] However, if Nietzsche is to become useful for left politics, this commitment to elitist hierarchy and consequent complaint about elite beleaguerment in the face of the ascension of the great unwashed are elements of Nietzsche's philosophical and political worldview we are simply going to have to leave behind.

Doing so is entirely possible because Nietzsche rejects not simply the unjustified advancement of modernity's excluded and undeserving masses but also, as Brown rightly recognizes, the *method* by which he argues they have advanced and triumphed. It is their employment of this method that, in his view, redounds back upon them and (further) renders them weak and contemptible. That method is moralism. In Nietzsche's view, the weak or the many or the otherwise undeserving have come to power by transforming the natural, hierarchical order of things into a moral problem of agency, harm, and suffering, a

more that feminisms of all kinds and most anti-racisms were considered inessential "distractions" by socialist organizers in the 1960s and 70s, an attitude that soured women of color on socialism (not to mention white feminism) as their primary *social movement location*, but by no means on anti-capitalism as such (see e.g. Taylor 2017). Moreover, as Deborah King (1988) points out, throughout history it has been white feminism that has followed upon the heels of Black organizing and taken its cues from Black people's freedom movements, so at a minimum Brown's story needs to be reversed; even more so, however, many scholars have argued that it is accommodationist white feminism that should be blamed for the de-radicalization of U.S. feminism overall (see e.g. Mink 1998, and Richie 2012, esp. Chapter 3). Needless to say, Brown does not provide a single example of racial or ethnic feminist "nationalism" here (much less any specific formation of lesbian separatism) to substantiate her point, perhaps because she would be hard-pressed to find one that matched this straw depiction of – and what seems like an outright attack on – women of color feminisms.

8 Thus it may be a better analysis of reactionary conservatism than left-wing identity politics; see e.g. Nealon 2000; Schotten 2016.

fundamentally de-politicizing move that becomes hegemonic by abjecting dissenting positions, existences, and worldviews as evil, irresponsible, immoral, or nihilistic. While Brown understands herself to be arguing against moralism as well (see Brown 2001), she fails to advance this critique from the vantage point of the oppressed, instead echoing Nietzsche's commitment to elitist hierarchy by rebuking the left for its failed and futile critiques of power. My suggestion is that queer theory can better marshal Nietzsche's critique of moralism for left politics than Brown because queer theory's distinctly liberatory character and commitment extends well beyond the narrow parameters of white Euro-American anti-capitalism. While it is true that queer theory has been rigorously critiqued for its own constitutive whiteness, maleness, and bourgeois inclinations, what queer theory as a critical political enterprise shares in common with Nietzsche is the conviction that morality is a political tool by which populations are segregated according to manufactured idealizations of merit or worth in order to stigmatize, demean, ostracize, and punish those deemed undeserving by its measure. This critique has thus simultaneously been used to analyze not simply the oppression of LGBTQ people, but also the operations of racism and racialization, (settler) colonialism, nationalism and empire, ableism and (dis)ability.[9] Rather than employ Nietzsche's critique of morality to defend or uphold a decaying aristocratic order, then, as he himself does, or offer misplaced critiques of social movements for their resentful attachments to their own injury, as Brown does, queer theory instead marshals this critique *on behalf of* queers, an evasive if expansive collection of anti-normal, anti-normative, anti-moral refusers of propriety and its dictates. Rejecting both Nietzsche's view that those on the bottom are by definition contemptible and Brown's subtle acquiescence to this view in her dismissal of left *ressentiment*, queer theory instead champions bottoms and all those *on* the bottom as the abjected dissidents of a stultifying moral order that effectively works to oppress everyone by hegemonically imposing impossible-to-attain ideals regarding the proper, upright, and best way to live. "Queer," then, is simultaneously a mark of abasement and a badge of dissent. It is neither the self-serving sanctity that Nietzsche argues the weak use to compensate themselves for their inevitable failure to win at the game of life, nor a reactionary shoring up of one's own status as injured or oppressed. It is rather an open and radical embrace of the elimination of morality and its array of punitive moralisms once and for all. This makes queerness simultaneously an instantiation of immorality and an emblem of revolt, an emancipatory positioning more

9 See e.g. Abdur-Rahman 2012; Eng, Halberstam and Muñoz 2005; Haritaworn, Kuntsman, and Posocco 2014; Johnson and Henderson 2005; Kafer 2013; Puar 2007; Rifkin 2011.

apposite to left politics than either "Nietzschean democracy" or the accommodationist reprimands of the left that have hitherto been advanced in his name.

3 Queer Theory

For Nietzsche, moralism is a weapon of the weak, and that is how and why it is objectionable. From a queer and/or left perspective, however, moralism is the means by which morality is institutionalized; it is, in other words, the perpetuation of oppression. Indeed, what both Nietzsche and queer theory at its best recognize is that morality and its idealizations *are* politics and in fact serve power's authoritarian function of abjecting all those who fail to comply with its mandates. In Foucaultian language, morality serves the normalizing and disciplinary functions of power, stigmatizing, ostracizing, and punishing some in the name of an abstract and coercive ideal such as the common good, social welfare, the defense of society, or the protection of children.

I have argued elsewhere that the founding moments of queer theory as a field are both fundamentally liberatory and specifically committed to left politics, both in spite and because of the field's initial whiteness (Schotten 2018a; Schotten 2018b). Here, I want to briefly explore another famously white text in queer theory wherein I nevertheless see the liberatory critique of morality unfolding particularly acutely: Lee Edelman's oft-reviled 2004 polemic, *No Future: Queer Theory and the Death Drive.*[10] In *No Future,* Edelman argues that temporality itself is heteronormative, unfolding a linear, teleological progress narrative that demands self-sacrificial anticipation of an ideologically rosy future that, by definition, never arrives. That future, symbolized by an iconographic Child, is innocent, infinitely valuable, and vested with redemptive potential. The future as Child is a future that never ends, a future that never grows up, a future in which life and survival – if not ours alone, then ours in the guise of the species and its future generations – will be preserved to infinity. The impossibility

10 Edelman's work has been rightly criticized for its failure to theorize any other person, position, situation, or identity than that of the white, bourgeois, gay male (the literature here is vast; one emblematic example is Muñoz 2009). These criticisms are not wrong but, as with Nietzsche, they do not exhaust the liberatory or critical potential of their author's work. In Edelman's case, there is actually far less work to do than with Nietzsche to appropriate it for the position and perspective of the oppressed: one need only make this positionality explicit in a way that he declines to do (unlike Nietzsche, who openly embraces naturalized, elitist hierarchy and thus proves far more obstinate). I address this issue extensively in Schotten 2018a, Chapter 4, where I make the case for a liberatory (re-) reading of both Edelman and queer theory and defend it more fully.

of such an achievement is, of course, by both definition and design. Yet futurism obscures this impossibility and secures its own smooth functioning, Edelman argues, via the production of queerness. Queerness designates all those who reject the future or stand in the way of reproduction or refuse to sacrifice their present aims or defer gratification. The fundamental antagonism of social life, in other words, is not class struggle but rather the conflict between the futurist attempt at closure and social meaning-making vs. the destructive antagonism of what Edelman sometimes calls "the negative" and in other places calls "queerness." Regardless, this queer negativity is impossible to definitively vanquish and thus perennially threatens the integrity, wholeness, and persistence of the social, well into the future it coercively envisions for us all.

Now, there is much to be said about Edelman's argument (here only incompletely stated). For the purposes of this chapter, however, what I want to suggest is that a major point of *No Future* is that the future's symbolization in the form of the Child functions to moralize that future, and it is precisely this transformation of a political – and thus contestable – assertion into a moral – and thus incontestable – foundational principle that makes reproductive futurism oppressive. In *No Future,* Edelman argues that "every political vision is *a vision of futurity*" (2004: 13, original emphasis), calling reproductive futurism "the logic within which the political itself must be thought" (2004: 2). Its "presupposition [is] that the body politic must survive" (2004: 3), and although the defense of children and social survival are widely taken to be apolitical, this is precisely what makes them "so oppressively political" (2004: 2). To participate in politics at all, even in protest or dissent, means to "submit to the framing of political debate – and, indeed, of the political field – as defined by the terms of…reproductive futurism: terms that impose an ideological limit on political discourse as such" (2004: 2). The question of the future, Edelman declares, is beyond any pro or con. Whether it is survival or children, the issue of the future is necessarily one-sided and decidedly pro-life. Futurism is the "party line" that "every party endorses" (2002: 182).

Elsewhere I have argued that there is no necessity that the future be symbolized by the Child, and that there are any number of forms the future can take, including among them Christianity, the settler state, the Hobbesian Commonwealth, and U.S. imperialism (Schotten 2018a; Schotten 2015). Indeed, although much attention has been paid to the specifically Childish version of the future Edelman opposes, what too often gets missed is the fact that the particular content of that future is much less important or problematic than the dogmatic insistence on that future's irrefutable *value* and *worth*, an insistence that secures its own hegemony via the exclusion, abjection, and negation of those who deny or defy it. Futurism's oppressiveness, in other words, resides in its totalizing demand that everyone worship at its altar (the altar of, as Edelman puts it elsewhere, the Futurch [2006: 822]) and that anyone refusing refuge in its sanctuary are "whatever a social formation abjects as queer" (Berlant and Edelman, 2014: 29). That altar of futurism symbolizes morality; the abjection of its apostates are the workings of moralism. Indeed, a broader and perhaps more useful designation of reproductive futurism may simply be morality itself, which operates and disperses its punitive effects through the vehicle of moralism. And indeed, as a morality, futurism functions much the same as Nietzsche's ascetic ideal. It is a hegemonic regime of social truth that "permits no other interpretation, no other goal; it rejects, denies, affirms, and sanctions solely from the point of view of *its* interpretation..." (Nietzsche 1967 [1887]: III: 23, original emphasis). Just like the ascetic ideal, futurism allows no other possible interpretation or mode of existence. Any violation of its rules or failure to conform to its dictates entails the visitation of some form(s) of violence, stigma, and punishment, on the grounds that such failures are both intolerable and unthinkable. Like the ascetic ideal, in other words, reproductive futurism – or any other morality – is a regime of truth that exists primarily in order to secure social control and exact punishment as the price of deviance. Edelman's word for this deviance is queerness, and his analysis of the social (re)production of queerness is Nietzschean insofar as it understands morality as a kind of oppression that works to produce resistance to hegemonic social formations as evil, nihilism, or craven wickedness.[11]

Although Nietzsche, in his own analysis in the *Genealogy,* focuses on the punishing effects of morality on the elite few, there is no reason why we cannot re-situate his critique of morality from the terrain of the embattled white guys

11 This is how and why his critique has a liberatory potential that is absent in both Nietzsche and Brown, if for different reasons: "queerness" here is a non-identitarian, structural determination of oppression, not a reified identity category of exclusion and difference. Thus the critique of morality I extract from *No Future* (which Edelman himself may or may not endorse as a reading of his work) is wholly relevant for anti-racist, anti-colonial, and feminist inquiry, especially insofar as white supremacy, (settler) colonialism, and patriarchy are profoundly moralized political formations that abject all resistance and dissent to them as unthinkable, perverse, nihilistic, and evil. Recall the CRC's delineation of the derogatory names and pervasive stereotypes of Black women cited above, or remember the Moynihan Report's disparagement of Black families as enmeshed in a "tangle of pathology," or think of the standard litany of denigrations of liberatory social movements and actors as aggressors, security threats, nature-deniers, infiltrators, abortionists, child-killers, gangs, "thugs," "savages," and "terrorists" – and of course much worse terms I cannot bring myself to reproduce here – all of which, however, effectively mean the same thing: "unthinkable threat to the very social and moral order that renders the world coherent and intelligible, and therefore requiring elimination."

of the world to the situation and perspective of the oppressed. This is what queer theory, in my view, does at its best. Indeed, despite some reticence of the field to explicitly position or understand itself as a tradition of the oppressed (see e.g. Wiegman and Wilson 2015), queer theory is, I contend, a liberatory critical theory to the extent that it understands morality as a form of oppressive power – a kind of Foucaultian biopower, that delineates populations in order to target them for death, and/or a kind of Foucaultian discipline, that normalizes through examination and surveillance in order to produce compliant and docile bodies. This is queerness's specific contribution to critical theory and liberatory politics. Moreover, this contribution is possible because of the field's distinct focus on sexuality and desire. Unlike Nietzsche, who sees morality as the vengeful accomplishment of weak people who resentfully deploy it as and through punishment, Edelman instead argues that futurism becomes hegemonic via the moralization of human existence into a temporal narrative of desire and (dis)satisfaction. Thus, what is distinctive and useful about queer theory for left politics and critical theory is the insistence that desire itself is an arena for the constitution, enforcement, and reproduction of oppression and its subsequent ability to identify morality as a distinct form of oppression.

Reading Edelman in this way aligns him not simply with Nietzsche, a perhaps unlikely forebear of queer theory, but also with Gayle Rubin, whose justly famous 1984 essay, "Thinking Sex: Notes Toward a Radical Politics of Sexuality," is widely considered to have made the 1990s emergence of queer theory possible.[12] It is known for, among other things, a set of charts that visually map the myriad ways that various forms of sexual activity are hierarchized and (de) valued. It is also known for Rubin's indexical listing of the theoretical obstacles that impede the construction of a radical politics of sexuality. These five obstacles are: (1) sexual essentialism (the presumption that sexual desire is an innate, pre-social drive); (2) sex negativity (the belief that sex is dangerous, unhealthy, destructive, or depraved); (3) the fallacy of misplaced scale (the exceptionalizing of sex to the point that it becomes burdened with "an excess of significance"); (4) the domino theory of sexual peril (the fear that sex must be contained or else it will leak out and spread and destroy everything); and (5) the lack of a concept of benign sexual variation (as Rubin puts it, "One of the most tenacious ideas about sex is that there is one best way to do it, and that everyone should do it that way" [1984: 283]). Among other things, these

12 I defend the controversial claim that Nietzsche can be seen as a forebear of queer theory in *Nietzsche's Revolution* (2009); Rubin's iconic "Thinking Sex" (1984) is well-established as having helped inaugurate the field.

five obstacles offer a useful map of the many ways that sex and sexuality are moralized and, in calling for their elimination, Rubin effectively authorizes and demands a strictly political, non-moral(ized) analysis of sex and sexuality. Now, in her essay, Rubin writes in terms of "value," not morality per se, noting the ways that medical, legal, social, and religious discourses classify and rank different forms of sexuality and sexual activity. But she sees clear continuity across these different classificatory and ranking schemes. The common element that gives them their power and coercive force is, I suggest, that of morality. Indeed, it is by now a commonplace that the seemingly more scientific or "objective" categories of pathology and neurosis are medicalizations of formerly moral categories and, as such, carry punitive and normalizing force. And whether religious, scientific, philosophical, or lesbian feminist, Rubin calls all such frameworks for ranking and classifying sex "systems of sexual judgment" (1984: 122). A central premise of Rubin's important essay, then, is that politics and morality are mutually exclusive endeavors, and that we must refuse the moralization of sex and sexuality if it is to remain a site of contestation, interrogation, and dissent, rather than an uncovering of nature, value, or truth.[13] As we know, these latter terms – nature, value, truth – are different modes of insulating otherwise contestable claims from interrogation or critique. Nietzsche argues as much, further instructing that this act of insulation is simultaneously the operation of moralism, which attempts to bypass politics altogether, even as it asserts its own will to power. As Judith Butler similarly pointed out in her early, embattled defense of poststructuralist feminism, the determination that a premise is beyond question because it resides in the realm of nature or truth is a quintessentially political act: "To establish a set of norms that are beyond power or force is itself a powerful and forceful conceptual practice that sublimates, disguises, and extends its own power play through recourse to tropes of normative universality" (1995: 39). Later in this same essay, she argues that "this movement of interrogating that ruse of authority that seeks to close itself off from contest…is, in my view, at the heart of any radical project" (1995: 41).

13 Indeed, part of the controversy of Rubin's essay was its suggestion that feminism was one of the moralized discourses that insulated sex and sexuality from political analysis and inquiry. In a particularly memorable passage, for example, Rubin aligns lesbian feminism with the Catholic Church: "Sounding like the lesbian feminist Julia Penelope, His Holiness explained that 'considering anyone in a lustful way makes that person a sexual object rather than a human being worthy of dignity'" (1984: 298). This episode of the feminist sex wars suggests that queer theory emerges at least in part as a response to and rejection of a specifically left movement that, in and because of its moralism, became a conservative, even reactionary force for women in their sexual lives. In this vein, see also Califia 2002 [1979]; Moraga and Hollibaugh 1992 [1981].

To follow on (the early) Butler and Rubin, then, and also borrow from Rubin's terminology a bit, I want to suggest that queer theory's contribution to left politics is its claim that morality itself is a "vector of oppression" (1984: 293). Recognizing with Nietzsche that all moralities are more or less elaborate systems of punishment and cruelty, Edelman's queer political theory is a critique of oppression insofar as it recognizes the operation of morality as the production of queerness and a reproductive stranglehold on the lives of everyone else. This is why, as Michael Warner observed already in 1993, it cannot be determined in advance who or what queers are or what constituency they name, even as we can be sure that queerness is a radical, indeed "fundamentalist" resistance to the hegemony of the social order. As I have argued here, queerness entails a rejection of moralism and the moralist pieties about survival and preservation of the social order that constitute political, social, and subjective intelligibility. It is no accident, then, that queer theory focuses on and emerges from sexuality, a privileged locus of morality, moralisms, and moral panics of all sorts, as "Thinking Sex" aptly documents. This emergence, however, is also an astute recognition of the political importance of desire and a crucial argument for the foregrounding of desire as integral to liberation and liberatory politics. Because, in the end, politics is not a moral enterprise. Politics is about power: who has it and who does not. What both Nietzsche and queer theory at its best recognize is that morality and its idealizations *are* politics and in fact serve power's authoritarian function of condemning all those who fail to comply with its mandates. Thus morality is never emancipatory – an important reminder the left must heed – but perhaps a Nietzschean critical queer theory actually might be.

4 The Future of Revolutionary Desire

I want to return to one final problem with Brown's critique of identity politics, a problem perhaps external to its Nietzscheanism but not to its dalliance with a kind of moralism of its own. That problem is Brown's insistence on the necessity of utopia or utopian aspirations for left politics (an undeniably futurist argument) simultaneously as she asserts the impossibility of satisfying that utopian desire given its dissolution via the 20th century fall of communism. Far more than identity politics, this is the dilemma that occupies Brown's attention and endures throughout much of her work from *States of Injury* onward, although she articulates it differently at different moments.[14] In "Wounded

14 Despite the long citational life of "Wounded Attachments," Brown made clear only a few years later that she wanted to revise its argument significantly (2001: 22). Even in "Wounded

Attachments," Brown begins to outline this problem by claiming that identity politics cannot construct a future. So mired in its reactionary clinging to its own injured identity, identity politics forecloses the "desire for futurity" essential to freedom projects (1995: 75), a problem that cannot be resolved by "the kinds of ahistorical or utopian turns against identity politics made by a nostalgic and broken humanist Left" (1995: 75–76). This rudimentary articulation of the foreclosure of futurity becomes, in her next book, "a crisis in political teleology" (2001: 22), wherein Brown forthrightly declares that the left is bereft and purposeless in the face of the triumph of capitalism and the foreclosure of any alternatives to it. Here she adapts the argument of "Wounded Attachments" to suggest that left moralism instead emerges in the wake of the fall of the communist bloc and the demise of progress narratives:

> Neither leftists nor liberals are free of the idea of progress in history. Neither can conceive freedom or equality without rights, sovereignty, and the state, and hence without the figures of a sovereign subject and a neutral state. The consequence of living these attachments as ungrievable losses – ungrievable because they are not fully avowed as attachments and hence are unable to be claimed as losses – is theoretical as well as political impotence and rage, which is often expressed as a reproachful political moralism. (2001: 21)[15]

Attachments" itself, she concedes that she may have misconstrued identity politics all along and therefore that the argument of the chapter itself does not hold up: "if I am right about the problematic of pain installed at the heart of many contemporary contradictory demands for political recognition, all that such pain may long for—more than revenge—is the chance to be heard into a certain release, recognized into self-overcoming, incited into possibilities for triumphing over, and hence losing, itself" (74–75). Although this, too, seems like an unlikely reading of the aspirations of "identity politics," it is nevertheless an enormous admission coming at the end of a fairly scathing critique (which she denies is a critique, 55), an admission that allows Brown to conclude that the political task is neither the overcoming of left resentment nor a Marxian-type liberation (since identity politics are not class politics) but rather the construction of "a radically democratic political culture that can sustain such a project in its midst without being overtaken by it, a challenge that includes guarding against the steady slide of political into therapeutic discourse, even as we acknowledge the elements of suffering and healing we might be negotiating" (75). Given that it is Brown herself who has introduced the therapeutic reading of identity politics as a longing for release and self-overcoming, however, one wonders what exactly must be guarded against and by whom.

15 Although in her famous essay, "Resisting Left Melancholy" (1999), Brown offers a more nuanced and sophisticated analysis of this "crisis in political teleology," suggesting that the radicalism of identity politics was blunted by Reagan-Thatcherism and forced the left into a more traditionalist and accommodationist loyal opposition, this analysis does not make it into her other writings and is an outlier in the context of her larger work, which overall is more interested in the collapse of modernity and modern "progress" and the

The left's major problem is thus no longer resentful attachment to injury, but rather the specific philosophical problems of temporality and progress, along with the psychodynamics at stake in the left's desire for and loss of utopia and the grief and rage that accompany these losses (see also Brown, 2005). Indeed, as this problematic develops in Brown's work, it is almost as if utopia becomes the left's own wounded attachment – it is the aspiration that defines the left's identity, but it has become impossible, leaving us stranded on the shores of a broken and futile, if nevertheless wholly necessary sea of desire, an impassable barrier to freedom that we can only contemplate and/or drown ourselves in out of pure sorrow and despair: "We are awash in the loss of a unified analysis and unified movement, in the loss of labor and class as inviolable predicates of political analysis and mobilization, in the loss of an inexorable and scientific forward movement of history, and in the loss of a viable alternative to the political economy of capitalism" (1999: 22).[16] This problem is restated in less lachrymose terms even in Brown's more recent work, wherein she declares that "the Left opposes an order animated by profit instead of the thriving of the earth and its inhabitants," but "it is not clear today how such thriving could be obtained and organized. Lacking a vision to replace those that foundered on the shoals of repression and corruption in the twentieth century, we are reduced to reform and resistance – the latter being a favored term today because it permits action as reaction, rather than as crafting an alternative" (2015: 220).[17]

effects of this on a left almost entirely, in her account, bound up with that version of progress.

16 And indeed, the upshot of this analysis is what Brown calls, borrowing from Benjamin, "left melancholy," a defensive, reactionary, and self-serving shoring up of an exhausted and no-longer-viable identity/politics: "What emerges is a Left that operates without either a deep and radical critique of the status quo or a compelling alternative to the existing order of things. But perhaps even more troubling, it is a Left that has become more attached to its impossibility than to its potential fruitfulness, a Left that is most at home dwelling not in hopefulness but in its own marginality and failure, a Left that is thus caught in a structure of melancholic attachment to a certain strain of its own dead past, whose spirit is ghostly, whose structure of desire is backward looking and punishing" (1999: 26). Arash Davari (2018) extends Brown's notion of left melancholy in his articulation of what he calls "left-liberal melancholy," a political position engendered by the losses of revolutionaries who experience failed revolutions and, as a result, turn to liberal ideals of human rights and American-style "democracy" as more sensible and practical political goals. Davari is clear that this, too, is an ultimately reactionary political position that reinforces U.S. imperialism.

17 Although even here is perhaps a hint of the old Nietzschean analysis, insofar as Brown dismisses "resistance" as "action as reaction," which Nietzsche at least is clear is the behavior of slaves, not of masters. This bereftness of the left, then, continues to render us weak,

Lisa Lowe (2015) has argued that Brown's critique of neoliberalism constitutes a "mourning [of] Western liberal democracy as the only form for imagining 'the political,'" a grief that "universalizes the future of politics across the globe" and "subsum[es] the histories of decolonization in Asia, Africa, Latin America, the Caribbean, and the Middle East to the normative narrative of liberal democracy – even in the critical project of observing how it has been hollowed out while being ideologically touted" (2015: 198n54). Lowe's hunch is not wrong, as Brown explicitly confirms in *Undoing the Demos.* There, she observes that the demise of the left's revolutionary vision is no longer specific to the left anymore, but is rather symptomatic of "a ubiquitous, if unavowed, exhaustion and despair in Western civilization" (2015: 221). No longer a particular or particularly challenging strategic situation, the impossibility of left revolutionary desire *tout court* now signals for Brown the decadence of the West and its civilizational collapse:

> At the triumphal "end of history" in the West, most have ceased to believe in the human capacity to craft and sustain a world that is humane, free, sustainable, and, above all, modestly under human control. This loss of conviction about the human capacity to steer its existence or even to secure its future is the most profound and devastating sense in which modernity is "over." (2015: 221)

Here Brown confirms that her lamentations for the left have been and remain the laments of a rarefied white Euro-American socialist left that already foresaw its own demise with the rise of "identity politics" and the fall of "actually existing" communism. As Lowe correctly points out, Brown's stubbornly north Atlantic geographic focus limits the domain of the political to the liberal democracy of which she is otherwise famous for being so critical; her sorrow over the loss of "alternatives" to it actually shores up its power by naturalizing it as the only possible and foreseeable future for political struggle.[18]

---

contemptible, and without the ability to act or affirm ourselves except in reaction to a "hostile external world."

18 Brown not only ignores anti-colonial and decolonial political criticism and projects, then, but in a strange way actually seems to accept the main contours of conservative and neoconservative claims that the triumph of capitalism and liberal democracy signal the "end of history." Although she may mourn this demise rather than celebrate it, her acceptance of this narrative is noteworthy and, like her disparagement of any politics that is not class politics, largely unremarked in the reception of her work more broadly. (I am grateful to Nicolas Veroli for this astute observation.)

But what if Brown is wrong? Not simply in the racial, geographical, and political narrowness of her political diagnosis and what she very unfortunately both reproduces and laments the loss of under the rubric of "Western civilization," but also in her dogged insistence that a utopian or aspirational futurist vision is essential to left politics? It would seem from Brown's work that the loss of revolutionary futurity leaves us with nothing or, what is the same thing (if not worse), nothing but what Heather Love might call backward feelings – "feelings such as nostalgia, regret, shame, despair, *ressentiment,* passivity, escapism, self-hatred, withdrawal, bitterness, defeatism, and loneliness" (2009: 4). Although in her own work, Love correlates these feelings with "the experience of social exclusion and…the historical 'impossibility' of same-sex desire," she is tracking a similar problematic as Brown in her attempt to document the tension at stake in telling queer history as a story of progress without turning its back on the vast archive of pain, suffering, oppression, and exclusion that constitutes the queer past, a past that is not yet (and may never finally be) over. Although such "negative" affects do, Love admits, pose significant obstacles to political action and also seem to evacuate the present of its ostensibly progressive valence, she nevertheless does not conclude that politics can therefore only flourish or thrive on "positivity." Instead, she encourages the development of a history and a politics of "feeling backward," a timeline and praxis that is neither linear nor futurist nor exclusively focused on a brighter tomorrow. This is a history and politics that does not let us neglect, ignore, or leave behind all of the closeted loves, prematurely ended lives, shame-filled childhoods (and adolescences and adulthoods) – in short, all the failures, disappointments, and self-sabotages – that are part and parcel of queer history and, therefore, essential to any aspiration or vision of queer futurity. This "at times can simply mean living with injury – not fixing it" (2009: 4).

Even more than Love's insistence on the necessity of including the unhappiness of the past in our account of the present, in letting that unhappiness inform how we might think about or imagine the meaning of "progress," is Edelman's even stronger criticism of aspirational futurity. Recall that, for Edelman, futurism's linear temporality is precisely what secures the hegemony of futurism and ensures the (re)production of abjected queerness. This is the operation of moralism as Nietzsche defines it, a reading I have argued can be marshalled for liberatory politics by reading it in conjunction with queer critique. Indeed, if any and all futurity – even left futurity – is already co-opted by the cult of the Child in whose name the future is always wagered and promised, and from which queers are necessarily abjected, then even left, utopian visions remain committed to the ideological operation that endlessly (re)produces abjected queerness. Thus, although Brown is wholly correct that the "desire for freedom" (1995), or the "exuberant critical utopian impulse" (2005: 114), or what I would call "revolutionary desire" is essential to left politics, she is wrong in her assessment that such desire requires a demonstrably desirable and obviously attainable object for its satisfaction. For, what queer theory teaches (and what every queer knows) is that desire all too often simply does not want the right things and that "satisfaction" is not actually all that satisfying.[19] Yet this does not mean that we ever really or finally "finish" with desired objects – much less desire itself – once and for all. In some sense, all these "failures" of desire are what queerness names. Those other fictitious, aspirational notions about desire – that it can and should be for the "right" objects, the attainment of which will make you truly happy, thereby allowing you to move beyond the petty indignities of sex (and gender) and go on and live a meaningful life – are the stories that get told by every authority figure ever, all of whom are actually seeking to order, systematize, predict, and control desire's waywardness in order to secure docility and social control, a disciplinary imperative couched in sanctimony so as to conceal its own will to power. This is not to say that desire is per se liberatory. It is to say, however, that queerness as inappropriate, immoral, unthinkable, impossible, deviant, and/or depraved desire will inevitably be produced by politics' moralizing imperatives, and therefore that liberatory politics cannot do without desire, and even more so without queerness, if it is to resist and surmount this moralism. In other words, the left can and must learn from queers' and queer theory's lessons regarding the futility and reactionary anti-queerness of the moralized insistence on futurity, even when that future is a leftist or utopian one.

Brown is therefore right to see revolutionary desire as crucial to left politics, but she is wrong to think that it is in danger of being extinguished (1995b) or, worse, that it must be "educated" for freedom by the intellectual class (2015: 11). Such elitist, Platonic disciplinarianism is out of place in any liberatory politics that recognizes that (improper) desire lies at the very root of (anti-)moralism and that anti-moralism is crucial to aspirational freedom projects. Left politics is neither dead or dying; nor, moreover, does it reside solely in the domain of Euro-Atlantic class struggle or the morose, impossible refusal of neoliberalism. Rather, its life is and resides in queerness, which is a dissident refusal of and opposition to morality and moralisms of all sorts, which only stigmatize, demean, and destroy freedom. Realizing this requires that we break not simply with outmoded, narrowly socialist versions of the left such as the one Brown advocates, but also its constitutive futurism that dooms queers and queer radicalism to the

19 For a reading of impolitic, inappropriate, failed, and/or futile desire as a (sometimes disavowed) basis of trans*ness, see Andrea Long Chu, "On Liking Women" (2018).

unspeakable domain of negativity and death. It means, in other words, that we must break with the heteronormativity of left politics if we are to engage in a radical praxis that can actually aspire to a liberated world.

References

Abbas, Asma. 2010. *Liberalism and Human Suffering: Materialist Reflections on Politics, Ethics, and Aesthetics.* New York: Palgrave.

Abdur-Rahman, Aliyyah I. 2012. *Against the Closet: Black Political Longing and the Erotics of Race.* Durham: Duke University Press.

Berlant, Lauren, and Lee Edelman. 2014. *Sex, or the Unbearable.* Durham: Duke University Press.

Brown, Wendy. 2015. *Undoing the Demos: Neoliberalism's Stealth Revolution.* Cambridge, MA: Zone Books.

Brown, Wendy. 2005. "Feminism Unbound: Revolution, Mourning, Politics." In *Edgework: Critical Essays on Knowledge and Politics*, 98–115. Princeton: Princeton University Press.

Brown, Wendy. 2001. "Moralism as Anti-Politics." In *Politics Out of History*, 18–44. Princeton: Princeton University Press.

Brown, Wendy. 1999. "Resisting Left Melancholy." *Boundary 2* 26(3): 19–27.

Brown, Wendy. 1995a. "Postmodern Exposures, Feminist Hesitations." In *States of Injury: Power and Freedom in Late Modernity*, 30–51. Princeton, NJ: Princeton University Press.

Brown, Wendy. 1995b. "Wounded Attachments." In *States of Injury: Power and Freedom in Late Modernity*, 52–76. Princeton: Princeton University Press.

Brown, Wendy. 1995c. "Introduction: Freedom and the Plastic Cage." In *States of Injury: Power and Freedom in Late Modernity*, 3–29. Princeton: Princeton University Press.

Butler, Judith. 1995. "Contingent Foundations: Feminism and the Question of 'Postmodernism.'" In *Feminists Theorize the Political*, edited by Judith Butler and Joan W. Scott, 3–21. New York: Routledge.

Califia, Patrick. 2002 [1979]. "A Secret Side of Lesbian Sexuality." In *Public Sex: The Culture of Radical Sex*, 2nd ed. San Francisco: Cleis Press.

Chu, Andrea Long. 2018. "On Liking Women: The Society for Cutting Up Men is a Rather Fabulous Name for a Transsexual Book Club." *n+1* 30 (Winter).

Combahee River Collective. 2017 [1977]. "The Combahee River Collective Statement." In *How We Get Free: Black Feminism and the Combahee River Collective*, edited by Keeanga-Yamahtta Taylor. Chicago: Haymarket Books.

Connolly, William E. 1992. *Identity/Difference: Democratic Negotiations of Political Paradox.* Ithaca, NY: Cornell University Press.

Conway, Daniel W. 1998. "*Das Weib an Sich:* The Slave Revolt in Epistemology." In *Feminist Interpretations of Nietzsche*, edited by Kelly Oliver and Marilyn Pearsall, 252–281. University Park: Pennsylvania State University Press.

Davari, Arash. 2018. "Like 1979 All Over Again: Resisting Left Liberalism among Iranian Émigrés." In *With Stones in Our Hands: Writings on Muslims, Racism, and Empire*, edited by Sohail Daulatzai and Junaid Rana, 122–135. Minneapolis: University of Minnesota Press.

Edelman, Lee. 2006. "Antagonism, Negativity, and the Subject of Queer Theory." In "Conference Debates: The Antisocial Thesis in Queer Theory," edited by Robert L. Caserio. PMLA 121(3): 821–823.

Edelman, Lee. 2004. *No Future: Queer Theory and the Death Drive*. Durham: Duke University Press.

Edelman, Lee. 2002. "Post-Partum." *Narrative* 10(2): 181–185.

Eng, David, Judith Halberstam and José Esteban Muñoz, eds. 2005. "What's Queer about Queer Studies Now?" Special issue of *Social Text* 23(3–4).

Halley, Janet. 2008. *Split Decisions: How and Why to Take a Break from Feminism*. Princeton: Princeton University Press.

Haritaworn, Jin, Adi Kuntsman and Silvia Posocco, eds. 2014. *Queer Necropolitics*. New York: Routledge.

Hatab, Lawrence J. 1995. *A Nietzschean Defense of Democracy: An Experiment in Postmodern Politics*. Peru, IL: Open Court Publishing Company.

Hong, Grace Kyungwon. 2015. *Death Beyond Disavowal: The Impossible Politics of Difference*. Minneapolis: University of Minnesota Press.

Honig, Bonnie. 1993. *Political Theory and the Displacement of Politics*. Ithaca, NY: Cornell University Press.

Johnson, E. Patrick and Mae G. Henderson, eds. 2005. *Black Queer Studies*. Durham: Duke University Press.

Kafer, Alison. 2013. *Feminist, Queer, Crip*. Bloomington: Indiana University Press.

King, Deborah K. 1988. "Multiple Jeopardy, Multiple Consciousness: The Context of a Black Feminist Ideology." *Signs: Journal of Women in Culture and Society* 14(1): 42–72.

Love, Heather. 2009. *Feeling Backward: Loss and the Politics of Queer History*. Cambridge, MA: Harvard University Press.

Lowe, Lisa. 2015. *The Intimacies of Four Continents*. Durham, NC: Duke University Press.

Mink, Gwendolyn. 1998. "Feminists, Welfare Reform, and Welfare Justice." *Social Justice* 21(1): 146–157.

Moraga, Cherríe, and Amber Hollibaugh. 1992 [1981]. "What We're Rollin' Around in Bed With: Sexual Silences in Feminism, A Conversation Toward Ending It." In *The Persistent Desire: A Femme-Butch Reader*, edited by Joan Nestle. Boston: Alyson.

Muñoz, José Esteban. 2009. *Cruising Utopia: The Then and There of Queer Futurity.* New York: NYU Press.

Nealon, Jeffrey T. 2000. "Performing Resentment: While Male Anger; or, 'Lack' and Nietzschean Political Theory." In *Why Nietzsche Still? Reflections on Drama, Culture, and Politics*, edited by Alan D. Schrift, 274–292.

Nietzsche, Friedrich. 1967 [1887]. *On the Genealogy of Morals: A Polemic*, edited and translated by Walter Kaufmann. New York: Vintage.

Puar, Jasbir. 2007. *Terrorist Assemblages: Homonationalism in Queer Times.* Durham: Duke University Press.

Richie, Beth E. 2012. *Arrested Justice: Black Women, Violence, and America's Prison Nation.* New York: NYU Press.

Rifkin, Mark. 2011. *When Did Indians Become Straight? Kinship, the History of Sexuality, and Native Sovereignty.* New York: Oxford University Press.

Robin, Corey. 2013. *The Reactionary Mind: Conservatism from Edmund Burke to Sarah Palin.* Oxford: Oxford University Press.

Rorty, Richard. 1989. *Contingency, Irony, and Solidarity.* New York: Cambridge University Press.

Rubin, Gayle S. 1984. "Thinking Sex: Notes for a Radical Theory of the Politics of Sexuality." In *Pleasure and Danger: Exploring Female Sexuality*, edited by Carole S. Vance. Boston: Routledge.

Schotten, C. Heike. 2018a. *Queer Terror: Life, Death, and Desire in the Settler Colony.* New York: Columbia University Press.

Schotten, C. Heike. 2018b. "Nietzsche and Emancipatory Politics: Queer Theory as Anti-Morality." *Critical Sociology.* DOI: 10.1177/0896920517752071.

Schotten, C. Heike. 2016. "Reading Nietzsche in the Wake of the 2008–09 War on Gaza." In *The Digital Dionysus: Nietzsche and the Network-Centric Condition*, edited by Dan Mellamphy and Nandita Biswas Mellamphy. Brooklyn, NY: Punctum.

Schotten, C. Heike. 2015. "Homonationalist Futurism: 'Terrorism' and (Other) Queer Resistance to Empire." *New Political Science: A Journal of Politics and Culture* 37(1): 71–90.

Schotten, C. Heike. 2009. *Nietzsche's Revolution:* Décadence, *Politics, and Sexuality.* New York: Palgrave.

Stringer, Rebecca. 2000. "'A Nietzschean Breed': Feminism, Victimology, *Ressentiment.*" In *Why Nietzsche Still? Reflections on Drama, Culture, and Politics*, edited by Alan D. Schrift, 247–273. Berkeley and Los Angeles: University of California Press.

Tapper, Marion. 1993. "*Ressentiment* and Power: Some Reflections on Feminist Practices." In *Nietzsche, Feminism and Political Theory*, edited by Paul Patton, 130–143. New York: Routledge.

Taylor, Keeanga-Yamahtta, ed. 2017. *How We Get Free: Black Feminism and the Combahee River Collective.* Chicago: Haymarket Books.

Villa, Dana R. 2000. "Democratizing the Agon: Nietzsche, Arendt, and the Agonistic Tendency in Recent Political Theory." In *Why Nietzsche Still? Reflections on Drama, Culture, and Politics,* edited by Alan Schrift, 224–246. Berkeley and Los Angeles: University of California Press.

Warner, Michael. 1993. "Introduction." In *Fear of a Queer Planet: Queer Politics and Social Theory*, edited by Michael Warner, vii–xxxi. Minneapolis: University of Minnesota Press.

Weheliye, Alexander G. 2014. *Habeas Viscus: Racializing Assemblages, Biopolitics, and Black Feminist Theories of the Human.* Durham: Duke University Press.

Wiegman, Robyn and Elizabeth Wilson E., eds. 2015. "Queer Theory Without Antinormativity." Special issue of *differences: A Journal of Feminist Cultural Studies* 26(1).

CHAPTER 2

The Trump Horror Show through Nietzschean Perspectives

Douglas Kellner

As we now undergo the American nightmare of a Trump presidency, we confront the challenges of a divided country with Trump and his often-frenzied followers constituting an authoritarian populist movement under an uninformed and hot-tempered demagogue. How can the thought of Friedrich Nietzsche help us theorize and overcome the frightening horror show of a Trump presidency? In this paper, I'll argue that Nietzsche's concepts can help in analyzing Trump, his followers, and the Trump phenomenon, and thus can explain the Horror Show of the Trump Presidency.[1]

1 Resentment from Nietzsche through Trump

19th century German philosopher Friedrich Nietzsche believed that all social movements are rooted in the herd psychology of resentment which is directed against superior individuals and classes and the state. In particular, Nietzsche developed a vitriolic attack on the modern state, finding it to be a "new idol" that is "the coldest of all cold monsters," run by annihilators "who continuously lie and relie"; Everything about it is false, "Nietzsche claims (Nietzsche 1954a: 160–163). Nietzsche consistently attacked as well German nationalism, writing": If one spends oneself on power, grand politics, economic affairs, world commerce, parliamentary institutions, military interests – if one expends oneself in *this* direction the quantum of reason, seriousness, will self-overcoming that one is, then, there will be a shortage in the other direction" i.e. culture, art, religion, and the development of personality (Nietzsche 1968: 62). Trump's rabid followers appear to be a variant of Nietzsche's

1 In earlier work (Kellner 2016), I examine how Trump embodies Authoritarian Populism and has used racism, nationalism, xenophobia, and the disturbing underside of American politics to mobilize his supporters in his successful Republican primary campaign and in the hotly contested 2016 general election. In a successor volume, (Kellner 2017a), I discuss how Trump won the 2016 U.S. presidential election and describe the assembling of his administration and the horrors of the first 100 days of Trump's reign.

mass men seething with resentment, while Donald Trump himself is a cauldron of resentment, who has deeply internalized a life-time of deep resentments, and thus is able to tap into, articulate, and mobilize the resentments of his followers, in a way that Democrats and other professional politicians have not been able to do.

Many of Trump's followers deeply resent politicians and the political establishment, and Trump's ability to tout himself as outside of the political system was a major theme of his campaign and an apparently successful way to mobilize voters. Hence, Nietzsche's concept of *resentment* is a key category to help make sense of Trump, his followers, and the ascent of Donald J. Trump to the presidency. To be sure, in *The Genealogy of Morals* Nietzsche uses resentment as a key to explain the origins of other-worldly religious and an idealistic ethics that Nietzsche opposes. In Nietzsche's genealogy, the weak invented religion and morality to temper and control the strong, thus supplanting master morality with slave morality (Nietzsche 1967).

Now before using Nietzsche's categories to interpret and critique Trump further, I want to concede that you can find passages in Nietzsche that valorize, even celebrate, a Trump as well as attack him, as I intend to do. In *Human-All-Too-Human* and other writings Nietzsche makes a distinction between the "noble" and the "base," and describes the noble as those who are sufficiently strong, determined and fearless to "engage in retaliation" when attacked (Nietzsche 1996). This is close to a self-description, or self-conception, of Trump who prides himself as being a tough guy who will engage in retaliation when attacked, hitting his adversary ten times harder, as Trump has bragged on occasion.

However, precisely here Trump opens himself to a Nietzschean critique as well as celebration, for underlying Trump's bold retaliation is a syndrome of malignant narcissism, aggression, and resentment.[2] The following Trump quotes illustrate his malignant narcissism and aggression, and suggest how Nietzsche's concepts of *resentment* and *revenge* can serve as keys to understanding Trump and his followers:

> When somebody challenges you unfairly, fight back—be brutal, be tough—don't take it. It is always important to WIN!
> I think everyone's a threat to me.
> Everyone that's hit me so far has gone down. They've gone down big league.

2 For a Frommian analysis of Trump's malignant narcissism and aggression which I am drawing upon here, see Kellner (2017b).

> I want my generals kicking ass.
> I would bomb the shit out of them.
> You bomb the hell out of the oil. Don't worry about the cities. The cities are terrible.
>
> POGASH 2016: 30, 152, 153

Donald Trump himself is a cauldron of resentment, has deeply internalized a life-time of deep resentments, and thus is able to tap into, articulate, and mobilize the resentments of his followers, in a way that his Republican opponents and then Hillary Clinton, the Democrats and other professional politicians just were not able to. Part of Trump's followers' resentments are resentment of politicians themselves, and Trump's being able to tout himself as being outside of the political system has been a major theme of his campaign and an apparently successful way to mobilize voters. I cannot really psychoanalyze Trump and so I am not sure why he is so resentful, but you could see his resentment throughout the campaign in claims that system was rigged, that women were lying about him when accusing him of sexual assault (although there was an Access Hollywood videotape showing Trump bragging about doing with women exactly what women claimed he did), and that the media were always attacking him and not recognizing his fabulousity, whereas I would argue, Trump would not have had a chance of winning without unparalleled amount of media attention (see Kellner 2017a, 2017b).

To highlight why Trump is so full of resentment, as well as full of other stuff, I want to speculate on how Nietzsche's concepts of resentment and revenge are key categories to explain Trump and Trump's followers and their attachment to him as someone who articulate their resentment and issues and can offer solutions. Let us begin in Marxist fashion with *class resentment*. Trump himself is something of a petite bourgeois who would like to be a haute bourgeois, and has resented his whole life not being recognized in New York society and more broadly in the upper class regions of U.S. society. Part of the reason for his not being accepted in the in-crowd of the rich is his class origins. His grandfather Friedrich Drumpf, an immigrant from Germany who changed his name to Trump when coming to the U.S. in the late 19th century went West to make his fortune and built combination low-rent restaurant-hotel-whore house for miners in San Francisco, Seattle, and then the Artic in the Gold Rush days (Blair 2000).

Don's father Fred built modest housing for workers and the aspiring middle class in Queens and Brooklyn, using post-World War II federal loan programs, and when Donald entered the company in the '70s the Trump organization was hit by federal housing discrimination ordinances, obviously embarrassing for a young guy on the make. Donald went to Manhattan, achieved success, thanks to capital and political connections of his father, and his own connections with the likes of his lawyer Roy Cohen, one of the sleazier figures in U.S. politics who was Trump's first political mentor (Blair 2000).

So Trump's class origins was the first impediment to being accepted in New York society, but his failures in business, particularly the sordidness of failing in the casino business in Atlantic City in the 1990s where he almost went bankrupt and was saved from bankruptcy by a couple of dudes now in his administration like Wilbur Ross, his proposed Secretary of Commerce.[3] Trump's financial fortunes hit the economic slowdown that followed the Reagan orgy of unrestrained capitalism in the late 1980s, and in the 1990s Trump almost went bankrupt. Fittingly, Trump had overinvested in the very epitome of consumer capitalism, buying a string of luxury gambling casinos in Atlantic City. The financial slump hit Trump's overextended casinos, driving him to put them on the market. The banks called in loans on his overextended real estate investments, and he was forced to sell off properties, his yacht and other luxury items. Having temporarily lost his ability to borrow from finance capital to expand his real estate business, Trump was forced to go into partnerships in business ventures, and then sold the Trump name that was attached to an array of consumer items ranging from water to vodka, men's clothes and fragrances (Blair 2000).

Trump's two books *Trump: Surviving at the Top* (1990) and *Trump: The Art of the Comeback* (1997) provide an incisive portrait of the beginning of Trump's business troubles in the late '80s and early '90s, and then his collapse into near bankruptcy and partial comeback later in the decade. It is clear from his books that Trump grossly overextended himself and invested in many dubious projects, such as the three Atlantic City casinos that went bankrupt, or that he was forced to sell. *The Art of the Comeback* drips with venom, resentment, and the spirit of revenge against those bankers who refused to help Trump and pressured him to pay off his loans, as well as others with whom he had conflicts during the decade; revealingly, Trump attacks his tormentors in little vignettes that present his enemies in negative terms, and then he flings a heap of insults upon them, just as he now does to his political opponents. His nastiness and vindictiveness is palpably out of control. He unloads on super lawyer Bert Fields, fires him (Fields said he quit), and concludes: "I think he's highly overrated, and his high legal fees were a continuing source of irritation to me. I continued to use the firm but not Fields" (Trump 1997: 103).

3 On Trump's business investments and history, only partly documented, see Blair (2000), D'Antonio (2015), and Kranish and Fisher (2016).

Interestingly, Wilbur Ross, who Trump nominated to be his Secretary of Commerce, and who is known in financial circles as the "king of bankruptcy," was one of the few financiers to bail Trump out when he was going bankrupt with his Atlantic City casino fiasco in the 1990s. As a side note, I might mention that after these real estate failures, the Trump organization has generally sold his brand to a large number of enterprises who often get the financing and do the work to establish the enterprises, which are branded with Trump's name, but, in fact, his business enterprises, partnerships, and debts are so complex that no one really knows who Trump is beholden to, what the full range of his business empire and debts amount to, or how much he is really worth (O'Brien 2016).

The sources of the *deep resentment of Trump's followers* are manifold. In terms of economics, many people feel that they are screwed over by the system, not recognized, and are angry at those who they see as beneficiaries which Trump has been able to scapegoat as immigrants, people of color, and the elites. His followers are resentful of paying taxes to the state and not having any political power which they believe Trump is giving them. The working class segment of Trump's followers is resentful of not getting adequate recognition and recompense which they believe they are entitled to as workers, supporters of families, and patriots and people, all hoping that Trump will be oriented toward their interests – all dubious hopes but grounded in deep and real resentments.

In his campaign, Trump successfully mobilized specific race, gender, and class resentments which helped him receive enough votes to win the electoral college while losing the popular vote by almost three million votes. In terms of *race resentment*, Trump began his campaign with evocations of armies of Mexicans crossing the border who were criminals, rapists, and would take away American jobs. Working class race resentment was mobilized throughout the campaign with Trump scapegoating immigrants as threats to American jobs and potential sources of terrorism. Here Trump's mobilizing of race resentment against immigrants of color overlaps with his mobilizing of Islamophobia against Muslims who Trump broadly asserted hated Americans (he actually said that Islam is a religion of hate). Further, Trump promised both to keep immigrants from Muslin countries that exhibited terrorism, and to round up and deport illegal immigrants that were deemed threats to Americans in any way.

So, we see that Trump mobilized classic race resentment and scapegoating and Othering of immigrants, people of color, Muslims, and others as threats to (white) America that he would deal with, using violence if necessary; i.e. deportation forces and bombing the shit out of ISIS. Like Hitler and the Nazis and other authoritarian populist movements, Trump also mobilized *class/elite resentment*, specifically against Wall Street, Goldman Sachs, and hedge funds, which had disturbing overtones of anti-Semitism at times. In addition, Trump exploited resentments against corporations that closed down American factories and took jobs to Mexico or other countries. Ironically, Trump did the same thing in his own business enterprises, making deals with companies who used his Trump brand to manufacture a motley array of products, often made in foreign countries, just as he often employed foreign workers, often illegal, to work on his Trump organization construction projects in the U.S., including Trump Towers, which notoriously used illegal Polish workers, some of whom sued him for not paying wages owed, and regularly employed undocumented immigrants in his Florida Mar-a-Lago resort.

Yet Trump the billionaire con was able to associate Hillary Clinton, of middle class origins who had worked her whole life, mostly for public interest and in particular on family and children issues, with Goldman Sachs and other Wall Street venues where she made speeches and received donations. Using classic tropes of anti-Semitism, Trump was also able to associate Clinton with a cabal of global bankers, financiers, corporate moguls, and other sectors of the rich who supposedly financed and controlled her.

This brings us to one of the more invisible but deep-seated resentments that Trump played upon; i.e. *gender resentment*. Working class men resented that they were no longer the sole or major breadwinner of their family, that working and middle-class women were increasingly working, that women were getting more rights, recognition, and power, in part through the efforts of the women's movement and women politicians like Hillary Clinton who had fought for women's issues for decades. The decline of working and middle class male wealth and authority was accompanied by crises of masculinities which men poorly resolved through guns, sports and fight clubs, violence against women and children, drinking and drugs, and other asocial and destructive forms of behavior. For males in crisis, Trump provided a powerful image of the successful man who kept women subservient, and who embodied a powerful, hyper-patriarchal, and successful image of manhood.

Another form of resentment that Trump mobilized is the topic of Katherine Cramer's *The Politics of Resentment* (2016), which through interviews with the people of rural Wisconsin, reveals how her rural subjects felt a deep sense of bitterness toward elites and city dwellers. These rural dwellers felt disrespected, alienated, mistreated by economic and political elites, and ignored by everyone else. Somehow Trump was able to address the alienation and resentment of rural, small town, and other groups of (mostly) white people who were seething with resentment toward the establishment and for whom Trump represented change.

For men and women in crisis, Trump provided a fantasy of a powerful male redemptive figure who was going to solve their problems and "make America great again." Trump's exploitation of *nationalism* and *patriotism* also played on deep resentments that America was in decline, that the Democrats and liberals and women had weakened the United States, and that a strong man would redeem the country and make it great again. Trump was thus able to mobilize an authoritarian populist movement and serve as a powerful demagogue who would draw on a variety of resentments and create a political movement based on fears, anger, and suffering which he claimed he and he alone could address and "make America great again."

Nietzsche, of course, was a sharp critic of German nationalism and Bismarck although another major Nietzschean idea that helps illuminate Trump is Nietzsche's celebration of the self over society, the state, religion, and directing aggression and a *will to power* against a corrupt and decadent establishment. Yet here Trump is arguably more akin to Ayn Rand than Nietzsche. Indeed, it is striking that Ayn Rand is one author who Trump has quote positively and several of his major cabinet appointees are dedicated Randists. According to James Hohmann (2016), "[Rex] Tillerson [Trump's nomination for Secretary of State] and Trump had no previous relationship, but the Texas oilman and the New York developer hit it off when they met face to face. One of the things that they have in common is their shared affection for the works of Ayn Rand, the libertarian heroine who celebrated laissez-faire capitalism." Further: "The president-elect said this spring that he's a fan of Rand and identifies with Howard Roark, the main character in *The Fountainhead*. Roark, played by Gary Cooper in the film adaptation, is an architect who dynamites a housing project he designed because the builders did not precisely follow his blueprints. 'It relates to business, beauty, life and inner emotions. That book relates to … everything,' Trump told Kirsten Powers for a piece in USA Today" (Hohmann 2016).

In addition, "Andy Puzder, tapped by Trump last week to be secretary of labor, is an avid and outspoken fan of Rand's books. One profiler last week asked what he does in his free time, and a friend replied that he reads Ayn Rand. He is the CEO of CKE Restaurants, which is owned by Roark Capital Group, a private equity fund named after Howard Roark. Puzder, who opposes increases in the minimum wage and wants to automate fast food jobs, was quoted just last month saying that he encouraged his six children to read "Fountainhead" first and "Atlas Shrugged" later." Moreover: "Mike Pompeo, who will have the now-very-difficult job of directing the Central Intelligence Agency for Trump, has often said that Rand's works inspired him. 'One of the very first serious books I read when I was growing up was Atlas Shrugged, and it really had an impact on me,' the Kansas congressman told Human Events in 2011."

Hohmann writes further: "Trump has been huddling with and consulting several other Rand followers for advice as he fills out his cabinet. John A. Allison IV, for example, met with Trump for about 90 minutes the week before last. 'As chief executive of BB&T Corp., he distributed copies of *Atlas Shrugged* to senior officers and influenced BB&T's charitable arm to fund classes about the moral foundations of capitalism at a number of colleges,' the Journal noted in a piece about him. 'Mr. Allison's worldview was shaped when he was a college student at the University of North Carolina-Chapel Hill and stumbled across a collection of essays by Ms. Rand'" (Hohmann 2016).

Hence, it is apparent that Trump is not turning just to billionaires and cronies to fill his cabinet and administration, but to a cabal of hardcore Randists, suggesting that *The Virtue of Selfishness* could be the manifesto of the Trump administration. These swamp creature also embody Adam Smith's warning that: "All for ourselves and nothing for other people, seems, in every age of the world, to have been the vile maxim of the masters of mankind" (Smith 1776: Book 3, Chapter 4). So you see that Trump's philosophical and psychological sympathies are more with Ayn Rand than Nietzsche. While Trump and Ayn Rand celebrate the marketplace, for Nietzsche, "all great things occur away from glory and the marketplace: the inventors of new values have always lived away from glory and the marketplace" (Nietzsche 1954b: 79).[4] This is about as strong a Nietzschean denunciation as I can imagine as for Trump the marketplace and glory are all, while Nietzsche finds these idols of modernity hollow and an impediment to higher forms of human beings and social life.

Hence, Nietzsche's concept of the *will to power* also helps elucidate Donald Trump himself. Trump has often said he is not primarily interested in making money, and indeed it is possible that his massive ego and out of control narcissism strives to make deal after deal, leading him to seek the ultimate pinnacle of power, the U.S. presidency. Yet Trump's insatiable drive for power is quite different from Nietzsche's linking of the will to power with the Ubermensch, Nietzsche's ideal of the higher man. For the Ubermensch, the will to power involves self-overcoming and self-transcendence to a higher and better self, which is parallel, curiously and ironically, to the notion of Jihad in Islam. Whereas Jihad for the terrorist is a nihilistic form of destruction parallel to Trump's unbound and nihilistic quest for power, for Nietzsche, or the religious Muslim, Jihad is a form of self-transcendence, over-coming, and transformation.

---

4 Michael Kilivris (2011) notes that Nietzsche refers to manufacturers as "'uninteresting persona,' excluding them from a 'higher race': 'The manufacturers and entrepreneurs of business probably have been too deficient so far in all those forms and signs of a higher race that alone make a *person* interesting.'"

As an aside, I want to suggest that the notion of the will to power and Nietzsche's focus on power may derive from his profound experience of Richard Wagner's music drama. It is well known that Nietzsche worshipped Wagner at one period in his life during his professorship at Basel. While Wagner was in exile in Switzerland, he invited Nietzsche to visit him at his home in Tribschen. Nietzsche's letters and major biographies indicate the rapture in making Wagner's acquaintance and becoming part of Wagner's inner circle. As Wagner planned his return to Germany and construction of a great opera house to perform the cycle of his music dramas, culminating at the time in the *Ring of the Nibelung* which had not yet been performed in its entirety, Nietzsche was closely connected with Wagner and even sent out a fund-raising letter for the Wagner society (Safranski 2002: 135ff).

Nietzsche soon became disillusioned with Wagner and the experience of the Bayreuth Festival, which Nietzsche saw as vulgarized by crass commercialism, superficial societal interactions that failed to appreciate the music and drama, and, in particular, that Wagner himself was coming to characterize the worst features of a vulgar bourgeois German philistine commercialism and narcissism. Yet Nietzsche earlier experienced in ecstatic terms his experience of Wagner's operas, and it is possible that the presentation of power in the Nibelung saga, and especially in the first opera in the saga *Das Rheingold* presents a concept of power that might have influenced Nietzsche's later metaphysical concept of the will to power.

While researching this paper and rereading Nietzsche, I got a DVD set of Wagner's *Ring* and watching *Das Rheingold*, after having read a Nietzsche biography describing his coming to the concept of the will to power (that did not mention Wagner), I noticed in the opera that the key to the saga was the magic ring that would give absolute power to its bearer (a story parallel to Tolkien's *Lord of the Rings* that drew on the same sagas that Wagner drew on, if not Wagner himself), and that when the word Macht! (power) was mentioned in the opera it was intoned with special emphasis and passion and heightened by a powerful Wagnerian leitmotif.

Scholarly studies of Nietzsche always focus on young Nietzsche's attachment to Wagnerian and Wagnerian ideas but claim, like Walter Kaufmann and others, that Nietzsche broke with Wagner and German nationalism and the like and developed his own distinctive philosophy. I am raising the question, however, whether an experience of Wagner's music drama might have involved his later concept of the will to power which is surely one of Nietzsche's most distinctive ideas.

Coming back to Trump, by now it is clear that Trump will use the power of the presidency to augment his own interest and will attack anyone who dares criticize or block him in any way.. Trump may be more interested in the *agonistic drama of power*, rather than sober instrumental and institutional use of presidential power, such as was evident in presidents likes Johnson, Nixon, Clinton, and others. For the early Nietzsche, the *agon*, or contest, was the defining feature of Greek society and culture evident in their poetry festivals, drama competitions, sports contests, out of which the Olympics emerged, and their wars, such as the Peloponnesian war described so well by Thucydides, one of the great historians of power, who may have influenced both Machiavelli and Nietzsche (Nietzsche was a classicist who expressed great admiration for Thucydides and I also wonder if Thucydides had any significant influence on Nietzsche's concept of the will to power, or if there are any Thucydides–Nietzsche studies).

Trump is a creature of the agon, in his daily Twitter wars, his business deals, in the presidential election, and now his presidency which features daily attacks on his opponents via Twitter, or his campaign appearances in which he reveled in the agon against his omnipresent enemies of the media, politicians who defy or criticize him, corporations who do not do his bidding, or random individuals who he chooses to attack if they irritate or agitate his twitchy small twitter finger. To start off his presidency, in a visit to the CIA the day after his inauguration, Trump told an assorted array of CIA people that he was engaged in a "running war against the media" and attacked media presentations of the numbers attending his inauguration in contrast to Obama's inauguration, claiming his was the biggest (but by all metrics it was not), and 200 days into his administration the conflicts and chaos are unending. Trump's agonistic battles, to be sure, do not have the splendor or majesty of Greek or Roman culture, but this form of the use of power, in conjunction with the Trumpworld Reality TV Show that has so far defined and constituted Trump, the Political Spectacle, may well be the form in which agonistic power is expended and deployed in the Trump presidency.

There have been many dangers and unforeseen consequences of a Trump presidency, which has been an American Horror Show that shows signs of continuing to get worse as Trump continues to spiral out of control. In the late 19th century, Friedrich Nietzsche warned of an epoch of *European nihilism* in which all the highest values of preceding civilization would be devalued, and indeed the first decades of the 20th century displayed unparalleled world wars, economic greed and collapse, social chaos and violence, and a nightmarish epoch of history. Since the end of World War II, Western and global societies have undergone a period of expansive, but uneven, economic development, and turbulent processes of democratization countered by forces of reaction and repression, experienced on a global scale in 2011. Has the ascent of Donald

J. Trump brought on an era of barbarism and nihilism that would have even shocked Nietzsche and his modern and postmodern followers? Or will Trump, a man of limited knowledge, experience, and lack of impulse control, careen from scandal to scandal, and finally cascade to eventual downfall that would ignite global Dionysian joy and an explosion of *Frohlichen Wissenschaften* opening the way to an new era of human emancipation and happiness?

Nietzsche was a sharp critic of democracy, but I would argue that Trump could be a *destroyer of U.S. democracy*. Trump himself has run a campaign, and assembled a transition team, cabinet, and administration, that could undermine and even destroy U.S. democracy and diminish the U.S. position in the world. Trump's campaign divided the country with his attacks on Mexicans, immigrants, Muslims, women, the disabled, the media, and whoever dared criticize him. He attempted to destroy his Republican opponents, and then Hillary Clinton, rather than just to beat them, with nasty names, innuendo, personal attacks, and a daily barrage of Twitter insults. Twitter, in Trump's hands, is itself a weapon to undermine democracy which requires dialogue, debate, deliberation, compromise, and consensus. Trump's twitter attacks by contrast polarize, inflame, alienate, and divide.

Having clearly divided U.S. society and polity through his campaign and his transition strategy, Trump is set out to destroy many key elements of the liberal democratic polity that has been developed since the New Deal. Trump's proposed Attorney General Jeff Sessions "was denied appointment as a federal judge in 1986 for a slew of racist comments, including calling the work of the NAACP and ACLU 'un-American.' He has also repeatedly spoken out against the federal Voting Rights Act."[5] Hence, Sessions, could undo decades of progressive civil rights and voting rights legislation, thus weakening the Justice Department.

Trump's proposed Secretary of Education, Betsy DeVos is a sharp critic of public schools who has favored charter schools and vouchers and could undermine the U.S. system of public education that has served us well, despite its flaws, for decades. The environment will be under assault with climate change denier and enemy of environmental regulation, Scott Pruitt appointed to run the Environmental Protection Agency (EPA). With Ben Carson appointed to head the Department of Housing and Urban Development, Trump has chosen someone who has expressed opposition to social safety net programs and fair

5 NAACP statement, November, 18, 2016, cited in Michelle Ye Hee Lee (2016). This article contains a large selection of the Senate testimony on the hearing for a federal judgeship for which Sessions was refused because of his racist actions and comments; as Attorney General, he can now go after his critics and long-time enemies.

housing initiatives and could undermine public housing initiatives and programs. Andrew Puzder, nominated as Trump's labor secretary has been an outspoken opponent of a meaningful increase in the federal minimum wage, and has been a critic of efforts by the Obama administration to update the rules for overtime-pay eligibility (he was forced to drop out of contention). And Rick Perry, a tool of Texas oil interests, named to head Trump's Department of Energy, has called for the elimination of the very department he has been asked to head and generally opposes oil and energy regulation.

Trump's billionaire cabinet, chosen from Goldman Sachs and the Swamps of Wall Street and Big Corporations, will support income tax cuts for the super wealthy, and could dramatically increase income inequality. The rightwing Republicans that serve his administration are deeply committed to destroying the Affordable Care Act and have talked of privatizing Medicare, Social Security, and other government programs. Taken cumulatively, the Trump administration thus constitutes a clear and present danger to U.S. democracy and could seriously weaken the country.

Returning in conclusion to Nietzsche's concept of resentment and revenge, I conclude with a passage from *Zarathustra*: "That man will be delivered from vengeance: that is the bridge to my highest hope, and a rainbow after prolonged storminess" (Nietzsche 1954b). I do not think that Trump, the man of resentment and vengeance par excellence, will ever be delivered from his personality deformations, but we can legitimately hope that someday we may be delivered from the man of vengeance and resentment, and that the American Nightmare and Horror Show will someday be over, sooner rather than later.

References

Blair, Gwenda. 2000. *The Trumps.* New York: Simon and Schuster.

Cramer, Katherine J. 2016. *The Politics of Resentment: Rural Consciousness in Wisconsin and the Rise of Scott Walker.* Chicago: University of Chicago Press.

D'Antonio, Michael. 2015. *Never Enough. Donald Trump and the Pursuit of Success.* New York: Thomas Dunne Books.

Hohmann, James. 2016. "The Daily 202: Ayn Rand-Acolyte Donald Trump Stacks his Cabinet with Fellow Objectivists." *Washington Post,* Dec. 13.

Kellner, Douglas. 2017a. *The American Horror Show: Election 2016 and the Ascendency of Donald J. Trump.* Rotterdam, The Netherlands: Sense Publishers.

Kellner, Douglas. 2017b. "Donald Trump as Authoritarian Populist: A Frommian Analysis." *Logos* 15(2–3) at http://logosjournal.com/2016/kellner-2/ (accessed August 12, 2017).

Kellner, Douglas. 2016. *American Nightmare: Donald Trump, Media Spectacle, and Authoritarian Populism*. Rotterdam, The Netherlands: Sense Publishers.

Kilivris, Michael. 2011. "Beyond Goods and Services: Toward a Nietzsche Critique of Capitalism." *Kritike* 5(2): 26–40.

Kranish, Michael, and Marc Fisher. 2016. *Trump Revealed: An American Journey of Ambition, Ego, Money and Power.* New York: Scribner.

Nietzsche, Friedrich. 1996. *Human, All Too Human: A Book for Free Spirits*, translated by R.J. Hollingdale. Cambridge: Cambridge University Press.

Nietzsche, Friedrich. 1968. *Twilight of the Idols.* New York: Penguin Books.

Nietzsche, Friedrich. 1967. *The Genealogy of Morals*, translated and edited by Walter Kaufmann. New York: Vintage.

Nietzsche, Friedrich. 1954a. *The Portable Nietzsche*, edited by Walter Kaufmann. New York: Viking Press.

Nietzsche, Friedrich. 1954b. *Thus Spoke Zarathustra*, translated by Walter Kaufmann. New York: Random House.

O'Brien, Timothy L. 2016. *TrumpNation: The Art of Being the Donald.* New York: Grand Central Publishing.

Pogash, Carol, ed. 2016. *Quotations from Chairman Trump*. New York: Rosetta Books.

Safranski, Rüdiger. 2002. *Nietzsche: A Philosophical Biography*. New York: Norton.

Smith, Adam. 1776. *Wealth of Nations*. At https://www.marxists.org/reference/archive/smith-adam/...of.../ch04.htm (accessed December 28, 2016).

Trump, Donald J. 2005 [1987]. *The Art of the Deal*, with Tony Schwartz. New York: Ballantine Books.

Trump, Donald J. 1997. *The Art of the Comeback*, with Kate Bohner. New York: Random House.

Trump, Donald J. 1990. *Trump: Surviving at the Top*, with Charles Leehsen. New York: Random House.

Ye Hee Lee, Michelle. 2016. "Jeff Sessions' Comments on Race: For the Record." *Washington Post*, Dec. 2.

CHAPTER 3

Nietzsche, Adorno, and the Musical Spirit of *Ressentiment* and Redemption

Nancy S. Love

1 The Return of "Bad Nietzsche"[1]

I did not expect to revisit the ties between Nietzsche, Marx, and critical theory more than three decades after I first published *Marx, Nietzsche, and Modernity* (1986).[2] Yet the current political context makes this return most relevant. Linkages between Nietzsche and Nazism have resurfaced, despite multiple decades of scholarly attempts to sever them.[3] The rising tide of hate speech and hate crimes in the United States and Europe today (Potok 2017) is partly fueled by a self-proclaimed Nietzschean will to (white) power. The British racist skinhead band Skrewdriver's lead song, "Hail the New Dawn," named after Nietzsche's book, *Morgenröthe: Gedanken über die Moralischen,* continues to sound a clarion call to white supremacists (Donaldson 1984).[4] In his autobiography, Arno Michaelis, a former racist skinhead and lead singer of the white power band, Centurion, writes: "Hearing that song [Hail the New Dawn] enticed me down a path rife with violence, hate, death, and imprisonment that I had narrowly escaped" (2012: 103). Banners displayed recently on many U.S. college and university campuses in conjunction with #ProjectSiege, an initiative of Identity Evropa, a white supremacist hate group, proudly state "A New Dawn is Breaking Rise and Get Active" (Anti-Defamation League 2017; Bawab 2017; Southern Poverty Law Center 2017). William Pierce, former leader of the National Alliance and founder of Resistance Records, once the major distributor of white power music in the US, traces the spiritual roots of his "cosmotheism," a racial religion that stresses the "cosmic stakes of the fight for white survival," to

1 The phrase "bad Nietzsche" comes from Sean Illing 2017. https://www.vox.com/2017/8/17/16140846/nietzsche-richard-spencer-alt-right-nazism.

2 The discussions here of Nietzsche's *Genealogy of Morals* and creditor/debtor relations draw on this earlier work.

3 The now classic example is Walter Kaufmann's *Nietzsche: Philosopher, Psychologist, Anti-Christ*, 1974.

4 The English translation is *The Dawn of Day (or Daybreak): Thoughts on the Prejudices of Morality.*

Nietzsche's philosophy of the will to power. Pierce claims that Nietzsche expressed "the necessity for our race to begin ascending...the Upward Path once again" (Quoted in Strom 2012). Ben Klassen, founder of the World Church of the Creator, invokes Nietzsche to attack Christianity as a religion that denies the natural law of survival of the fittest, espouses life-denying virtues of compassion, equality, and sacrifice, and undermines white racial loyalty, unity, and, most important, pride. He also blames a Jewish media conspiracy for white "brain pollution" and claims "The main problem is to straighten out the White Man's thinking and get him back to sanity" (1973: book 1, chapter 1). Richard Spencer, architect of the alt-right, stated in a recent interview, "You could say I was red-pilled by Nietzsche," a term from *The Matrix*, which refers to a process of awakening and transformation (Quoted in Wood 2017). Spencer praises Nietzsche for his critique of democracy and Christianity, defense of aristocratic values, and embrace of heroic men, such as Napoleon and Wagner (Harkinson 2016). Multiple posts on Stormfront, until recently the major white supremacist website, invoke the Nazi's critique of degenerate music in discussions of how Wagner – unlike Nietzsche – capitulated to the Jews (http://www.stormfront.org). Sean Illing (2017) sums it up best: "'Bad Nietzsche' is back, and he looks a lot like he did in the early 20th century when his ideas were unjustly appropriated by the (original) Nazis."

Let me state clearly up front that Nietzsche's critiques of anti-Semitism and European nationalism provide ample evidence that fascist politics is inconsistent with his philosophical commitments.[5] Yet, once again, scholars must ask: What continues to prompt such readings of Nietzsche's philosophy? Do they arise from the spirit of *ressentiment* he criticized or from something else? The question is particularly vexing today given the prominence of identity politics across the political spectrum. In Breitbart's "An Establishment Conservative's Guide to the Alt-Right," Allum Bokhari and Milo Yiannopoulos (2016) argue that "The politics of identity, when it comes from women, LGBT people, blacks and other non-white, non-straight, non-male demographics is seen as acceptable – even when it descends into outright hatred. Any discussion of white identity, or white interests, is a heretical offence." They and the alt-right, more generally, challenge this perceived double-standard:

5 Nietzsche's sister, Elizabeth Forster-Nietzsche, who married Bernhard Forster, an avowed racial nationalist and anti-Semite, bears primary responsibility for the association of his philosophy with German National Socialism. Although some of Nietzsche's ideas, such as his distinction between master and slave morality, lend themselves to such readings, Nietzsche never intended his philosophy to support fascist regimes. See Yimiyahu Yovel 1994.

> So here is my challenge for progressives, multiculturalists, dynamists, and the like: if your anti-racism is what it claims to be, if it is no more than Voltaire 3.0, why do non-European ethnocentrism and anti-European hostility not seem to bother you in the slightest? Do they maybe even strike you as, um, slightly cool?
>
> YARVIN, quoted in Bokhari and Yiannopoulos 2016

These seem like questions we (anti-racist progressives, broadly defined) should be prepared to answer.

2 From Resentment to *Ressentiment*

To begin, how might we understand Nietzsche on *ressentiment*? I do not linger here on the linguistic differences between Nietzsche's use of the German term, its French original, and the English, resentment, which other scholars have explored at length (Bittner 1994: 127–138). I instead stress structural features of *ressentiment,* articulated so clearly by Scheler, who writes: "The formal structure of *ressentiment* expression is always the same: A is affirmed, valued, and praised not for its own intrinsic quality, but with the unverbalized intention of denying, devaluating, and denigrating B. A is played off 'against B'" (1972: 51). It is well known that Nietzsche's most extensive discussion of *ressentiment* occurs in the three essays of the *Genealogy of Morals.* Although Nietzsche presents different aspects of *ressentiment* in each essay and suggests a developmental relationship between them, they all share the structure Scheler describes. Peter Poellner's comprehensive definition illustrates this structural similarity well:

> 1) *Ressentiment* as Nietzsche presents it…is a psychological condition which has at its core an experience of pain, or discomfort, or frustrated desire. This pain or discomfort…is experienced by the subject of *ressentiment* as caused by other subjects…2) This interpretation of a "not-self" (GM 1: 10) as the cause of one's suffering motivates a negative affective response, resentment in a non-technical, everyday sense—Nietzsche calls it hatred—toward those Others. 3) The original pain and the negative affect towards its presumed cause jointly motivate a desire for mastery or superiority in the subject of *ressentiment*…4) The final element of the dynamic of *ressentiment* is the subject's hitting upon a new evaluative framework that allows him to remove his pain or discomfort by making possible either self-affirmation or mental mastery over the external source of pain.
>
> quoted in ELGAT 2016: 248

I now explore the historical and psychological development of these interrelated aspects of *ressentiment* in greater depth. A developmental analysis, I argue, reveals how Nietzsche's *ressentiment* differs from resentment, and why those differences involve more than linguistics.

In the first essay of the *Genealogy of Morals*, Nietzsche describes how the structural opposition between master and slave morality originates. Unlike the noble type of man, who is self-defining and value-creating, who actively posits himself as good compared to bad, the slave is a reactive type. The slave psyche begins by defining its opposite – the oppressive master – as evil and the qualities which help slaves survive (humility, industry, patience, pity, etc.) as good. In his famous aphorism #260 of *Beyond Good and Evil*, Nietzsche (1966a) encapsulates the contrast: "According to slave morality, those who are 'evil' thus inspire fear; according to master morality it is precisely those who are 'good' that inspire, and wish to inspire, fear, while the 'bad' are felt to be contemptible." Although the slave initially defines an "Other" as the source of "evil," slave morality eventually is internalized through psychological processes that Nietzsche associates with the emergence of political subjects.

The second essay of the *Genealogy of Morals* explains how the origins of political subjects relate to Nietzsche's earlier distinction between master and slave morality. "A conqueror and master race" initially and unconsciously created the state with its laws and, in response, "animal" man learned to control and, most important, internalize his instincts, and became a sovereign individual – calculable, disciplined, and reasonable. Nietzsche says that "In a certain sense, the whole of asceticism belongs here." But only in a certain sense. He distinguishes the conscience (and the subject) from "that other 'somber thing,' the consciousness of guilt, the 'bad conscience'" (1966b: Second Essay, #3–4). Man's initial internalization of his instincts provides the basic template for the bad conscience, but its destructive potential is not actualized until later when ascetic priests take charge. They invent the *bad* conscience, the life-denying internalization of the instincts that typifies slave morality; they forge the links between subjectivity, slave morality, and *ressentiment.*

These ascetic priests are Nietzsche's focus in the third essay. The following passage depicts their role in the history of *ressentiment*:

> Its origin has been briefly suggested...as a piece of animal psychology, no more: there we encountered the sense of guilt in its raw state, so to speak. It was only in the hands of the priest, that artist in guilt feelings, that it achieved form – oh, what a form, 'Sin' – for this the priestly name for the

> animal's 'bad conscience' (cruelty directed backward) – has been the greatest event so far in the history of the sick soul: we possess in it the most dangerous and fateful artifice of religious interpretation. (1966b: Third Essay, #20)

Masters' externalization of their instincts is life-affirming and slaves' internalization of them is life-denying. However, the crucial issue is how – not whether – instincts are internalized. According to Nietzsche, the creation of the conscience and, with it, subjectivity and morality is not itself life-denying. It makes man "interesting" and "promising" by giving him the capacity to create consciously and purposefully as Nietzschean "free spirits" do (1966b: Second Essay, #16). The problem arises when slave morality begins to dominate human history and the state with its laws leads to progressive degeneration of the instincts. Over time even masters learn to feel guilty over what slave moralists deem evil and to deny their instincts for mastery. The ascetic priests triumph by not only redirecting the instincts internally, but also misdirecting them against man's life-affirming instincts.

A further distinction emerges here in the history and psychology of *ressentiment.* Nietzsche holds Christianity and modern science, its secular heir, similarly responsible for the historical triumph of slave morality (Owen 2014; Melnikova 2010). Nietzsche writes: "This pair, science and the ascetic ideal, both rest on the same foundation...on the same overestimation of truth.... Therefore they are necessarily allies, so that if they are to be fought they can only be fought and called into question together" (1966b: Third Essay, #25). Christianity affirms the ascetic values of slave morality as the will of God. Then, modern science in its pursuit of truth destroys all horizons, including belief in God, and renders existence meaningless. In historical succession, Christian faith and scientific truth together undermine the life-affirming creativity of master morality. Eventually, the slaves' loss of agency and sense of powerlessness become the psychological basis for *ressentiment.*

According to David Owen, Nietzsche's history of *ressentiment* involves three (not two) social groups: nobles, priests, and slaves.

> The distinction is, thus, between those subject to "the morality of custom and the social straight-jacket" (everyone) and those definitively locked in the spell of society and peace (priests and slaves). Whereas the warrior-nobles are able to enjoy compensation for the requirements of civilization by exercising their instinct for cruelty outside the bounds of society, the same does not apply to priests and slaves. Hence it is within these

> latter classes of persons that the instinct for cruelty is turned back on itself, vents itself on itself. (2014: 105)

Nietzsche argues that the ascetic priests perform a service by ministering to the slaves' weak(ened) instincts; they give their suffering meaning by attributing blame for it, that is, by assigning a doer (oneself or another) behind the deed. The ascetic priests cannot allow the slaves' *ressentiment* to become politically explosive, however, or it might jeopardize their leadership. Instead, they manipulate the slaves' *ressentiment*, keeping them angry and fearful of others or consumed by self-doubt and guilt, and, in either case, weak and dependent. As Jeremy Engels, sums it up: "The slave morality Nietzsche describes disciplines the herd through the creation of a resentful soul" (2010: 311). Engels concludes that "A resentful soul is easily controlled by an artful leader.... Perpetually reacting, the demos cannot act with deliberation or purpose" (2010: 322).

At this point, it is important to revisit the distinction between *ressentiment* and resentment which many scholars, including Engels, gloss over. In Nietzsche's account, *ressentiment* results from a long history of perceived wrongs and the psychological sense of powerlessness they eventually produce. Elisabetta Brighi contrasts this psychology of *ressentiment* with resentment, a feeling that originates from "situations of injustice" and "always invokes a concept of right and the existence of a moral grievance" (2016: 414). Contra *ressentiment*, resentment is "the guardian of justice" (Brighi 2016: 421). To conflate the two concepts or to reduce resentment to *ressentiment* (as ascetic priests do) denies any possibility of corrective action and, with it, political agency. According to Brighi, "While resentment is understood to denote a legitimate sense of anger, and a desire for justice in the face of an injury, *ressentiment* indicates the pernicious and self-defeating folding-in of this emotion onto itself. *Ressentiment* is suspended, delayed, or botched revenge" (2016: 424). By manipulating the herd with slave moralities, ascetic priests perpetuate *ressentiment* and its preconditions instead of mobilizing resentment into effective struggles against existing injustices.

Ascetics priests are, then, engaged in a very delicate task. The possibility exists that the ascetic priest (leader) will fail and the slaves (people) *ressentiment* will explode. In political terms, Nietzsche's ascetic priests are the demagogues who mobilize populist movements. To return where I began, we might regard Donald Trump as an ascetic priest of authoritarian populism. Trump has taken the "precarity" (Butler and Athanasiou 2013) of middle- and working- class whites, their new status (or lack thereof) as culturally and economically dispossessed and redirected it toward white nationalist identity politics. In doing so, he follows a long line of political leaders who invoke "the wages of whiteness"

(Roediger 1991) to assuage what Richard Sennett and Jonathan Cobb (1993) have poignantly called "the hidden injuries of class." By mobilizing "a kind of moral hierarchy of national and cultural differences," white identity politics mitigates the internalized sense of many poorer whites that they are "nothing special" (Sennett and Cobb 1993: 14). In *The Abolition of White Democracy*, Joel Olson argues that the question "Who *may* be considered white?" has mattered historically, and terribly so (2004: 16–17). Trump's presidential ministry targets "marked" Others – immigrants, Mexicans, Muslims, Native Americans, women – as the cause of white, working-class, male Americans' suffering.

Most important for this Nietzschean critique, Trump invokes the language of creditors and debtors. As we have seen, Nietzsche thinks consciousness was "dearly bought" through cruel punishments for disobedience to social norms. The masterful artists who initially formed man exchanged the creditor's psychic pleasure in inflicting pain for the debtor's infractions of the communal contract. Punishment draws its power "in the contractual relationship between creditor and debtor, which is as old as the idea of 'legal subjects' and in turn points back to the fundamental forms of buying, selling, barter, trade, and traffic" (1966b: Second Essay, #4). Calls to "lock her (Hillary) up," the Obama "birther controversy," the moniker "Pocahontas" for Elizabeth Warren, all feed Trump supporters' sense that these "Others" have stolen their power and privilege, and sullied the U.S. as a white nation. In this exchange economy of contractual agreements, guilty parties, group rights, and legal settlements, Trump's supporters feel that they are the victims of injustice. Theirs is a righteous cause, to retake the(ir) country, to "Make America Great Again."

3 *Ressentiment*, Democracy, and Difference

Democratic theorists have typically been wary of *ressentiment* as a political force, precisely because it springs from this sense of injury that, as Nietzsche warned, can quickly become explosive. The critique of *ressentiment* comes from so-called left Nietzscheans, most famously Wendy Brown. In *States of Injury: Power and Freedom in Late Modernity*, Brown (1995) identified "wounded attachments," an identity politics based on victim status, as constitutive of late capitalist democracies. She worried that democratic citizens fixated on perceived injustices could only build movements, claim rights, and take action by invoking the very terms of their oppression. The likely result would not be real transformation (more on what that might look like later), but a mere inversion of the current oppressive order, that is, a potentially violent acting out of *ressentiment* by poor against rich, black against white, women against men, LGBTQ against Cis-gender, et cetera – and a pyrrhic victory, at best.

As Brown recognizes, the political Right has mobilized *ressentiment* more successfully than the Left, which has typically rejected it as a political strategy. Today, the political Right and, more specifically, the alt right mobilize *ressentiment* using new tactics that many political experts and ordinary citizens have overlooked. This partly explains the surprise of many at the election of Donald Trump as President. According to Kathleen Blee (2002), the new tactics of white supremacy include: apocalyptic images of a global race war; alliances between KKK, Neo-Nazi, and Christian Identity groups; sophisticated use of new technologies, including the Internet; and recruitment strategies focused on so-called vulnerable populations, especially prisoners, teenagers, and women. Online recruiting with memes and music now plays a major role in efforts of the radical right to recruit teens to white supremacy (Love 2017). Richard Spencer has claimed that "we memed alt right into existence," perhaps most famously with Pepe the Frog (Quoted in *Vice News* 2016). The alt right now also has its own soundtrack, "Fashwave," headlined by the band, CyberNazi with its lead song "Galactic *Lebensraum*." According to Reggie Ugwu (2016) of *Buzzfeed*, since Trump's presidential victory, the alt-right has "set its sights on remaking culture consolidating around and promoting a music scene it can call its own." Michael Hann (2016) states that "Fashwave is the music that normalizes fascism, even if coolness is a way away." One fan simply says, "This is celebration music.... We are winning" (Quoted in Ugwu 2016).

I will not repeat my argument in *Trendy Fascism: White Power Music and the Future of Democracy* (2016) here, and only note that the following themes dominate white power song lyrics: enemies of the white nation; epic struggles for survival and founding myths; unemployment and capitalist corruption; government coercion and legal double standards; anti-social behavior; nature worship, environmentalism, and racial religion; male racial warriors and female breeders. The hard-hitting rhythms and sounds of white power music combine with its lyrics to express deep aversions to cultural differences and reveal a deeply rooted pre- or extra-linguistic white collective memory and political imaginary. The founding of American democracy was a racial(ized) project that involved exterminating Native Americans, disenfranchising women, enslaving Africans, and more recently interning Japanese-Americans, deporting Hispanics, and banning Muslims. When this deeper history is acknowledged, the vulnerability of many white citizens to right-wing extremists' messages becomes less surprising. Because the cultural-political roots of liberal democracy include conquest and genocide along with freedom and equality, white supremacists can play to the former. Lest there be any doubt, William Pierce, the former owner of Resistance Records, once the largest distributor of white power music in the United States, confirms the conscious strategy involved here: "Music speaks to us at a deeper level than books or political rhetoric: music speaks directly to the soul. Resistance Records...will be the music of our people's renewal and rebirth" (quoted in Anti-Defamation League 2000).

Most recently, the organizers of the Charlottesville "Unite the Right" rally claimed it was their largest gathering in two decades and part of a plan "slowly [to] unveil a little bit of our power level. You ain't seen nothing yet" (Bacle 2017). Among other purposes, the rally was meant to show that the alt right is more than its internet meme and music scene, that it can mobilize large numbers of people and control public spaces (Bacle 2017). The white supremacists marched through the University of Virginia campus and Charlottesville streets with lit torches and loud chants – "You will not replace us," "Jews will not replace us," and "Blood and Soil." Their tactics were all too familiar. The military and churches have long used chant and drill to promote "muscular bonding," a sense of coordinated group action that neutralizes individuals' sense of physical vulnerability (McNeill 1997). By tapping into primitive brain regions (the amygdala, cerebellum, and hippocampus), chant and drill trigger primal emotions and visceral reactions before the higher brain (cerebral cortex) can receive and process the more complex information necessary to exercise moral judgment. Fight or flight – these primal responses bypass conscious processes of self-reflection and moral judgment.

In a recent article, Stefan Dolgert (2016) argues that was a mistake for the Left to cede *ressentiment* to the political Right and, more specifically, white supremacists. He calls on progressives to recognize that *ressentiment* exists and figure out how they can best use it for change. Dolgert claims that bourgeois subjectivity and so-called negative emotions are the tools that progressives currently have. Citing the revolutions of 1789, 1848, and 1917, among others, he concludes that *ressentiment* has served democratic revolutions relatively well in recent history. Dolgert notes that progressive social movements, such as civil rights, labor, and women's rights have also used *ressentiment* to mobilize supporters. His controversial conclusion is: "We need enemy-narratives to win elections, so let us find some worth targeting." He continues, "Resentment will flow somewhere, regardless of how we chastise or correct it, and if we cannot find a useful outlet for it, then we have no one to blame but ourselves" (2016: 369).

In retrospect, Bernie Sanders' campaign might be understood in these terms. Although Sanders attacked economic elites on behalf of social justice, he and his supporters also crossed over from moral resentment of injustices to *ressentiment* and revenge on multiple occasions. Many pollsters and pundits argued that Sanders and Trump, unlike the more cerebral, policy-wonkish Clinton, mobilized their constituents by appealing to visceral emotions of anger and fear prompted by economic dispossession (Collinson 2016; Long and

Gillpesie 2016). Although Sanders' primary message addressed working class voters' sense of injustice and their actual economic needs, he did willingly enable his supporters' politics of *ressentiment*. For example, when Democratic Chairwoman, Roberta Lange, denied a rule change at the Nevada State Convention and Sanders' supporters disrupted the convention and then harassed her with death threats and personal insults, he did not condemn their actions and instead claimed that *they* had not been treated with "fairness and respect" (Thistlethwaite 2016). Such claims became an increasingly frequent refrain of Sanders and his supporters as the campaign progressed and it became clear that Clinton would receive the Democratic nomination. With tragic irony, Sanders began to resemble Trump; he became another ascetic priest, now ministering to *ressentiment* on the Left. As Rev. Dr. Susan Brooks Thistlethwaite (2016) cautions when discussing political polarization today: "When you mirror your enemy, you become your enemy."

4 Overcoming *Ressentiment*

In closing, I want to turn to another ongoing movement that provides a clearer contrast with the politics of *ressentiment*: Occupy. Occupy Wall Street began on September 17, 2011 in Zuccotti Park in Lower Manhattan and quickly spread to include encampments at public sites in other cities, on college campuses and around the globe. Although the movement was initially very white, it quickly diversified. As Graeber puts it in *The Democracy Project*, "Within a matter of weeks, we were seeing African-American retirees and Latino combat veterans marching and serving food alongside dreadlocked teenagers" (quoted in Quinn 2016: 78). Occupy arguably privileged class over other identity categories, but it also tackled the central issues of neoliberal capitalism: inequality, marketization, criminalization, and unemployment (Quinn 2016). One can certainly see Occupy in Dolgert's terms, as a democratic populist movement of the 99% that successfully constructed the 1% as its enemy and mobilized widespread *ressentiment* against it. Indeed, some like Anthony Fisher (2017), have argued that "the ascendance of Donald Trump finds some of its roots in the Occupy movement.... The Trump train was the xenophobic right-wing offshoot of Occupy's populist rage."[6]

However, I do not think this interpretation recognizes the full import of Occupy. Here I think a Nietzschean perspective again proves useful for understanding how Occupy resisted the pressure to transform the moral stance of

6 For an insightful discussion of the differences between right- and left-wing populism in the Tea Party and Occupy, see Laura Grattan 2016.

resentment into the vengeful psychology of *ressentiment.* Recall that Nietzsche, like Marx, is a critic of the liberal democratic principle of equal right, because to subsume unique individuals under a common standard typifies the *ressentiment* of herd morality. Nietzsche fears that "'equality of rights' could all too easily be changed into equality in violating rights – I mean, into a common war on all that is rare, strange, privileged, the higher man, the higher soul, the higher duty, the higher responsibility, and the abundance of creative power and masterfulness" (1966a: #212). For Nietzsche, the principle of equality is "a will to the denial of life, a principle of disintegration and decay" that leads seemingly inexorably to the last man (1966a: #212).

Without denying Nietzsche's deeply troubling defense of aristocratic values and a master race, might we consider Occupy as a movement of Nietzschean "free spirits" that points beyond bourgeois subjects with their equal rights? Might this be partly why Occupy was so little understood? Recall the frequent laments that Occupy was without plan or purpose. For Nietzsche, purposive production is a reaction to need – whether material or metaphysical. Superabundance rather than hunger, prodigality rather than utility, play rather than work, are primary in life as will to power. Nietzsche regards "'play,' the useless – as the ideal of him who is overfull of strength, as 'childlike'" (1968: #797). In "The Three Metamorphoses," the camel who carries burdens and the lion who resists domination are superceded by the child who is "a new beginning, a game, a self-rolling wheel, a holy 'yes'" (Nietzsche 1977: 140).

For Nietzsche, the problem with capitalism ultimately is not exploitation alone, but vulgar exploitation. He writes, "what the workers see in the employer is usually only a cunning, bloodsucking dog of a man who speculates on all misery.... The manufacturers and entrepreneurs of business probably have been too deficient so far in all those forms and signs of a higher race that alone make a person interesting" (1974: #40). Nietzsche even suggests that capitalists' vulgarity may ultimately be the cause of socialism: "If the nobility of birth showed in their eyes and gestures, there might not be any socialism of the masses" (1974: #40). A higher justice – called mercy – transcends bourgeois rights: "The justice which began with, 'everything is dischargeable, everything must be discharged,' ends by winking and letting those incapable of discharging their debt go free: it ends, as does every good thing on earth, by overcoming itself" (1966b: Second Essay, #10). Mercy transcends the herd's *ressentiment* and its representative, the state with its laws; it is exercised by the privileged, the exceptional, the few "free spirits," who are beyond the law.[7]

7 For a more extensive comparison of Marx's and Nietzsche's critiques of capitalist economics and bourgeois rights, see my 1986 *Marx, Nietzsche, and Modernity,* ch. 5, on which this section draws.

The Occupy movement, I would suggest, raises this question: Is there any reason to associate such gift-giving virtue solely with aristocratic values or might it also serve to ennoble ordinary citizens, perhaps the 99%? Here Scheler's philosophy again becomes relevant. Contra Nietzsche, Scheler argues that "Christian ethics has not grown in the soil of *ressentiment*"; it has been deformed historically to become reactive, guilty, and slavish – "a peculiar sham form of love founded in self-hatred and self-flight" (1972: 125). According to Scheler, Nietzsche was blind-sided by the age of utility and missed the profound difference between democracy as majority rule and the principle of democratic solidarity. Might Occupy represent the ennobling values of the latter, a secular rendition of the Christian injunction to love thy neighbor as thyself?

Here musical experience again becomes an important theme. White power music participates in what Adorno called the "regression of listening" that typifies a commodified, mediated, and stylized mass culture. It reduces unique individuals to stereotypical sameness, and constructs false binaries whether for entertainment or extermination. Yet musical expression can also unsettle linguistic categories and established identities, and convey unspoken and even unspeakable realities. Like Nietzsche, Adorno regards "music [as] a language, but a language without concepts" (2012: 108). For Adorno, music carries the potential for transformation and, with it, redemption – more precisely, redemptive transformation (Babich 2006). It does so by expressing the "necessary failure of identity" and, as I have argued elsewhere, offering the possibility of "becoming sincere" (Love 2016).[8] Adorno writes "Aesthetic identity seeks to aid the nonidentical, which in reality is repressed by reality's compulsion to identity" (Adorno 1977: 4). For Adorno, Schoenberg's 12-tone compositions exemplified this liberatory musical spirit, and he infamously argued that jazz and big band did not.[9] Today new examples are sorely needed.

I want to suggest that the music of Occupy provides an example of how to transform and thereby redeem the spirit of *ressentiment* that marks not only white supremacy, but more generally, identity politics across the political spectrum. Social media and music played central roles in Occupy. Many prominent musicians and others in the music industry from sound engineers to producers stated their support for Occupy with a pledge and website (Cooper 2011). Constant, insistent drumming by a group called Pulse was the earthly heartbeat of Occupy Wall Street. The Occupy soundtrack mirrored the diversity of the

8 In chapter five of Trendy Fascism, I draw on Jurgen Habermas's theory of communicative action to argue that "sincerity" is among the potential outcomes, as well as a precondition, for the redemption of aesthetic-expressive validity claims.

9 It seems important to mention here that Adorno did not blame the masses, but the society that made masses of them.

movement: it had no single anthem; it recognized many genres, performers, songs; it did not court celebrities and superstars, though some joined it; it produced a fundraiser CD with 99 songs, many of them DIY; it embraced a new generation of listeners on social media (Bauder 2011; Boczanowski 2011; Caren and Gaby 2011; McKinley 2011). Occupy Wall Street also affirmed hip-hop culture as part of its challenge to racialized neoliberal capitalism. Although some hip hop artists embrace the "star system" of corporate capitalism and liberal individualism, for Russell Simmons this was not the case. In a letter to Jay-Z, Simmons explained why he chose to amplify Occupy's message with his music:

> So, Jay, here's the deal. You're rich and I'm rich. But, today it's close to impossible to be you or me and get out of Marcy Projects or Hollis, Queens without changing our government to have our politicians work for the people who elect them and not the special interests and corporations that pay them. Because we know that these special interests are nothing special at all. In fact, they spend millions of dollars destroying the fabric of the black community and make billions of dollars in return. If we have to occupy Wall Street or occupy All Streets to change the course of direction of this nation, then we must. We must take our democracy off the market and let the world know that it is no longer for sale! Mic check!
>
> quoted in SIECZKOWSKI 2012

Simmons' frequent visits to Occupy also challenged the "gangsta" image that has haunted hip hop and the binary categories of black and white, poor and rich, criminal and hero, delinquent and intelligent (Quinn 2016; Mubirumsoke 2016). Tom Morello of Rage Against the Machine also questioned the economic "reality" of wealthy, white, males and celebrated another truth in Nietzsche's extra-moral sense – as perspectivism. These and other musicians bridged the gap between their 1% and the 99%, and began to transform the relationship between culture and commercialism.

Although some argue that Occupy failed, Morello thinks its perspectival vision continues to unfold. In a recent interview for *Rolling Stone*, he said:

> The people who were in the streets – whether it was 100,000 people in the streets of Madison, Wisconsin, or the months-long occupation of Zuccotti Park – those people haven't gone away. Their ideas haven't gone away. The mistrust and resentment toward the status quo hasn't gone away. How it manifests itself in the months and years to come will determine the ultimate success or failure of the movement.
>
> quoted in FLANARY 2012

Will the moral resentment that fueled Occupy also eventually become vengeful *ressentiment*? Did the Sanders campaign foreshadow a similar process of devolution for other left-wing movements? For now, it seems crucial to remember that Occupy prefigured a democratic solidarity based on fusion politics rather than identity politics. In Nietzschean terms, Occupy envisioned a future democracy "for all and for none." Or, as Angela Davis put it in more traditional terms: "the Occupy movement's exhilarating potential lies in forging a unity that can make a new majority of the old minorities" (quoted in Quinn: 78).

Finally, regarding Breitbart's questions with which I began, "bad Nietzsche" has returned due to a spirit of *ressentiment* that today increasingly spans the political spectrum, rather than any unfortunate ideas Nietzsche articulated. In contrast, Occupy demonstrated that progressive anti-racism is not about European versus non-European ethnocentrism and anti-European hostility, and it prefigured far more than being "cool." It showed how resentment over pervasive injustices can transform itself into a new spirit of justice beyond the law. We (anti-racist progressives) should call on that spirit to return to politics today.

References

Adorno, Theodor. 2012. "Music and Language." In *Quasi Una Fantasia: Essays on Modern Music*, translated by Rodney Livingstone. London and New York: Verso.

Adorno, Theodor. 1977. *Aesthetic Theory*, translated by Robert Hullot-Kentor. Minneapolis, MN: University of Minnesota.

Anti-Defamation League. 2017. "Identity Evropa." Anti-Defamation League. https://www.adl.org/resources/profiles/identity-evropa.

Anti-Defamation League. 2013. "Deafening Hate: The Revival of Resistance Records." Anti-Defamation League. https://www.adl.org/news/article/deafening-hate-the-revival-of-resistance-records.

Babich, Babette. 2006. "The Genealogy of Morals and Right Reading: On the Nietzschean Aphorism and the Art of the Polemic." In *Nietzsche's On the Genealogy of Morals, Critical Essays*, edited by Christa Davis Acampora, 177–190. Lanham, MD: Rowman & Littlefield.

Bacle, Ariana. 2017. "Charlottesville Episode." *Vice News Today*, Aug. 15. http://ew.com/tv/2017/08/15/vice-news-tonight-charlottes-ville-episode/.

Bauder, David. 2011. "Occupy Wall Street: Music Central to Protest." *The Huffington Post*, Nov. 13. http://www.huffingtonpost.com/2011/11/13/occupy-wall-street-music_n_1091176.html.

Bawab, Nashwa. 2017. "Appalachian State Students Greeted by White Supremacy Banner." *USA Today: College*, Aug. 24. http://college.usatoday.com/2017/08/24/appalachian-state-students-greeted-by-white-supremacy-banner/.

Bittner, Rudiger. 1994. "Ressentiment." In *Nietzsche, Genealogy, Morality: Essays on Nietzsche's Genealogy of Morals*, edited by Richard Schacht, 127–138. Berkeley, CA: University of California Press.

Blee, Kathleen. 2002. *Inside Organized Racism: Women in the Hate Movement.* Berkeley, CA: University of California Press.

Boczanowski, Zosia. 2011. "The Occupy Movement and Music." *Music Business Journal.* December. http://www.thembj.org/2011/12/the-occupy-movement-and-music.

Bokhari, Allum, and Milo Yiannopoulos. 2016. "An Establishment Conservative's Guide to the Alt-Right." *Breitbart News*, March 29. http://www.breitbart.com/tech/2016/03/29/an-establishment-conservatives-guide-to-the-alt-right/.

Brighi, Elisabeth. 2016. "The Globalisation of Resentment: Failure, Denial, and Violence in World Politics." *Millennium: Journal of International Studies* 44(3): 411–432.

Brown, Wendy. 1995. *States of Injury, Power and Freedom in Late Modernity.* Princeton, NJ: Princeton University Press.

Butler, Judith, and Athena Athanasiou. 2013. *Dispossession: The Performative in the Political – Conversations with Athena Athanasiou.* Cambridge, UK: Cambridge University Press.

Caren, Neal, and Sarah Gaby. 2011. "Occupy Online: Facebook and the Spread of Occupy Wall Street." Unpublished manuscript.

Collinson, Stephen. 2016. "How Trump and Sanders Tapped America's Economic Rage." *CNN*, March 9. http://www.cnn.com/2016/03/09/politics/sanders-trump-economy-trade/.

Cooper, Leonie. 2011. "Musicians in Support of Occupy Movement Launch Website." *NME*, Nov. 21. http://www.nme.com/news/music/lou-reed-48-1273766.

Dolgert, Stefan. 2016. "The Praise of *Ressentiment*: Or, How I Learned to Stop Worrying and Love Donald Trump." *New Political Science: A Journal of Politics and Culture* 38(3): 354–369.

Donaldson, Ian Stuart. 1984. "Hail the New Dawn." On *Hail the New Dawn.* Rock-O-Rama Records RRR 046. 33 1/3 RPM.

Elgat, Guy. 2016. "How Smart (and Just) Is Ressentiment?" *The Journal of Nietzsche Studies* 47(2): 247–255. http://o-muse.jhu.edu/article/623769.

Engels, Jeremy. 2010. "The Politics of Resentment and the Tyranny of the Minority: Rethinking Victimage for Resentful Times." *Rhetoric Society Quarterly* 40(1): 303–325.

Fisher, Anthony L. 2017. "Occupy, 6 Years Later." *The Week*, Sept. 15. http://theweek.com/articles/724178/occupy-6-years-later.

Flanary, Patrick. 2012. "Tom Morello Leads Occupy Wall Street Anniversary Concert." *Rolling Stone*, Sept. 17. http://www.rollingstone.com/music/news/tom-morello-leads-occupy-wall-street-anniversary-concert-183226.

Grattan, Laura. 2016. *Populism's Power: Radical Grassroots Democracy in America.* New York, NY: Oxford University Press.

Hann, Michael. 2016. "'Fash-wave' Synth Music Co-opted by the Far Right, Fascist Bloggers and Musicians Have Expressed Their Liking For an 80s Obsessed Variant of Instrumental Electronica." *The Guardian,* Dec. 14. https://www.theguardian.com/music/musicblog/2016/dec/14/fashwave-synth-music-co-opted-by-the-far-right.

Harkinson, Josh. 2016. "Meet the White Nationalist Trying to Ride the Trump Train to Lasting Power, Alt-right Architect Richard Spencer Aims to Make Racism Cool Again." *Mother Jones,* Oct. 27. http://www.motherjones.com/politics/2016/10/richard-spencer-trump-alt-right-white-nationalist.

Illing, Sean. 2017. "The Alt-Right Is Drunk on Bad Readings of Nietzsche. The Nazis Were Too." *Vox,* August 17. https://www.vox.com/2017/8/17/16140846/nietzsche-richard-spencer-alt-right-nazism.

Klassen, Ben. 1973. *Nature's Eternal Religion.* Lighthouse Point, FLA: Church of the Creator.

Kaufmann, Walter. 1974. *Nietzsche: Philosopher, Psychologist, Anti-Christ.* Princeton, NJ: Princeton University Press.

Long, Heather, and Patrick Gillpesie. 2016. "Why Americans Are So Angry in 2016." *CNN Money,* March 9. http://money.cnn.com/2016/03/09/news/economy/donald-trump-bernie-sanders-angry-america/index.html.

Love, Nancy S. 2017. "Back to the Future: Trendy Fascism, the Trump Effect, and the Alt-Right." *New Political Science: A Journal of Politics and Culture* 39(2): 263–268.

Love, Nancy S. 2016. *Trendy Fascism: White Power Music and the Future of Democracy.* Albany, NY: State University of New York Press.

Love, Nancy S. 1986. *Marx, Nietzsche, and Modernity.* New York, NY: Columbia University Press.

McKinley, James, C. Jr. 2011. "Occupy Wall Street Protest Lacks an Anthem." *New York Times,* Oct. 18. http://www.nytimes.com/2011/10/19/arts/music/occupy-wall-street-protest-lacks-an-anthem.html.

McNeill, William H. 1997. *Keeping Together in Time: Dance and Drill in Human History.* Cambridge, MA: Harvard University Press.

Melnikova, Eva. 2010. "Nietzsche's Morality of Ressentiment." *Filosof* (Fall): 4–13.

Michaelis, Arno. 2012. *My Life After Hate.* Milwaukee, WI: Authentic Presence Publications.

Mubirumsoke, Mukasa. 2016. "Rapping Honestly: *Nas,* Nietzsche, and the Moral Prejudices of Truth." *The Journal of Speculative Philosophy* 30(2): 175–203.

Nietzsche, Friedrich. 1977. *Thus Spoke Zarathustra: A Book for All and For None.* In *The Portable Nietzsche,* translated and edited by Walter Kaufmann, 103–439. New York, NY: Penguin Books.

Nietzsche, Friedrich. 1974. *Gay Science,* translated by Walter Kaufmann. New York, NY: Random House.

Nietzsche, Friedrich. 1968. *The Will to Power*, translated and edited by Walter Kaufmann and R.J. Hollingdale. New York, NY: Random House.

Nietzsche, Friedrich. 1966a. "Beyond Good and Evil." In *Basic Writings of Nietzsche*, translated and edited by Walter Kaufmann, 179–436. New York, NY: Random House.

Nietzsche, Friedrich. 1966b. "The Genealogy of Morals." In *Basic Writings of Nietzsche*, translated and edited by Walter Kaufmann, 437–600. New York, NY: Random House.

Olson, Joel. 2004. *The Abolition of White Democracy*. Minneapolis, MN: University of Minnesota Press.

Owen, David. 2014. *Nietzsche's Genealogy of Morals*. New York, NY: Routledge.

Quinn, Eithne. 2016. "Occupy Wall Street, Racial Neoliberalism, and New York's Hip-Hop Moguls." *American Quarterly* 68(1): 75–99.

Potok, Mark. 2017. "The Radical Right was More Successful in Entering the Political Mainstream Last Year than in Half a Century. How Did it Happen?" *Intelligence Report*, Feb. 15. https://www.splcenter.org/fighting-hate/intelligence-report/2017/year-hate-and-extremism

Roediger, David R. 1991. *The Wages of Whiteness: Race and the Making of the American Working Class*. London and New York: Verso.

Scheler, Max. 1972. *Ressentiment*, translated by William H. Holdheim. New York, NY: Schocken Books.

Sennett, Richard, and Jonathan Cobb. 1993. *The Hidden Injuries of Class*. New York, NY: Alfred A. Knopf.

Sieczkowski, Calvin. 2012. "Russell Simmons on Jay-Z Occupy Wall Street Diss: 'Right 99 Times, But This Ain't One.'" *HuffPost*, Sept. 9. https://www.huffingtonpost.com/2012/09/12/russell-simmons-jay-z-occupy-wall-street-response_n_1876907.html.

Southern Poverty Law Center. 2017. "Identity Europa and Arktos Media – Likely Bedfellows." *Hatewatch*, Sept. 26. https://www.splcenter.org/hatewatch/2017/09/26/identity-evropa-and-arktos-media-%E2%80%94-likely-bedfellows.

Strom, Kevin Alfred. 2012. "I Remember Dr. Pierce." *National Vanguard*, August 13. http://nationalvanguard.org/2012/08/i-remember-dr-pierce/.

Thistlethwaite, Rev. Dr. Susan Brooks. 2016. "Our Dangerous Politics of Resentment." *The Blog, HuffPost*, May 19. https://www.huffingtonpost.com/rev-dr-susan-brooks-thistlethwaite/our-dangerous-politics-of_b_10055136.html.

Ugwu, Reggie. 2016. "How Electronic Music Made by Neo-Nazis Soundtracks the Alt Right, 'Fashwave': The Sound of Young White Nationalism." *Buzzfeed News*, Dec. 13. https://www.buzzfeed.com/reggieugwu/fashwave?utm_term=.boAgvKxbe#.haDQWgKjv.

Vice News. 2016. "The Face of the Alt Right: Richard Spencer on White Nationalism." Dec. 10. https://news.vice.com/story/we-memed-alt-right-into-existence-our-extended-interview-with-richard-spencer-on-white-nationalism.

Wood, Graeme. 2017. "His Kampf: Richard Spencer Is a Troll and an Icon for White Supremacists. He Was Also my High-School Classmate." *The Atlantic*, June. https://www.theatlantic.com/magazine/archive/2017/06/his-kampf/524505.

Yovel, Yimiyahu. 1994. "Nietzsche, the Jews, and Ressentiment." In *Nietzsche, Genealogy, Morality: Essays on Nietzsche's Genealogy of Morals*, edited by Richard Schacht, 214–246. Berkeley, CA: University of California Press.

CHAPTER 4

Hip-Hop as Critical Tragic Realism: Cultural Analysis beyond Irony and Conflict

James Meeker and T.J. Berard

> Science rushes headlong, without selectivity, without 'taste' at whatever is knowable, in the blind desire to know all at any cost. Philosophical thinking, on the other hand, is ever on the scent of those things which are most worth knowing, the great and the important insights.
>
> NIETZSCHE, *Philosophy in the Tragic Age of the Greeks* (1994 [1894]: 43)

∵

1 Introduction: The Privileging of Conflict in Cultural Analysis[1]

A history of cultural analysis in the 20th century could be expected to chart a fascinating but ominous path from a largely anthropological and conservative focus on integration and consensus to a much more interdisciplinary and much more cynical focus on phenomena such as ideology, hegemony, identity politics, and the cultural economy of status distinctions. Obviously the Critical Theory of the Frankfurt School was pivotal in this development, integrating the economic concerns of Marxism with the social-psychological worries of Freud's later writings and the incisive and pessimistic interpretive macro-sociology of modernity and rationalization bequeathed by Max Weber. Other notable neo-Marxists in the broad tradition of critical cultural analysis would include Lukács, Gramsci, and Althusser, among many others. The Birmingham School in the U.K. contributed prominently to neo-Marxist, critical cultural studies,

1 A portion of this essay was previously published in Roberts (2019). Smaller portions, especially overviewing Nietzsche's scholarship on tragic culture and Bourdieu's critique of culture, have drawn directly or indirectly from Berard (1999). The authors acknowledge gratefully the support of Michael Roberts.

but the "critical" went without saying in cultural studies by this time. By the end of the twentieth century, arguably the most influential figures in the critical analysis of culture were two icons of late twentieth century French social theory, Bourdieu and Foucault, both of whom certainly drew in part from Critical Theory and cultural Marxism but deserve to be understood as initiating their own traditions of social critique. Bourdieu has been especially influential with respect to the analysis of culture *per se*, with his attention to such phenomena as artistic production and tastes and especially status distinctions and the role of cultural capital in social reproduction, i.e. the perpetuation of inequality.

Throughout this development of critical cultural analysis, our understanding of the dark side of culture improved immeasurably by engaging with concepts from false consciousness through propaganda and the culture industry to misrecognition and symbolic violence. But these remarkable insights developed from particular and pointed attention to the development of social critique, arguably at the expense of other scholarly values and virtues, such as the stubborn empiricism of Max Weber and the philosophical depth of Friedrich Nietzsche. Seminal insights from both Weber and Nietzsche were certainly drawn upon in subsequent cultural analysis, however the keen development of critical vision in cultural analysis was not and perhaps could not have been accompanied by the advocacy of objectivity and empiricism in social science which were hallmarks of Weber's thought even in his sobering, disenchanting studies of capitalism and bureaucracy. Similarly, the incisive focus of critical theories of culture was not and really could not have been accompanied by the existential and aesthetic sensibilities which informed Nietzsche's thought from his classicist (and somewhat Romantic) interest in Greek tragedy to his creative cynical virtuosity in *Thus Spake Zarathustra* (1985 [1883–1891]).

Storey has tried to suggest diplomatically, avoiding an ascription of orthodoxy in cultural studies, that "'Culture' in cultural studies is defined politically rather than aesthetically" (1996: 2). Cultural studies could be conceived as addressing high culture, understood primarily as elitist, and popular culture, understood largely as uncritical: the source of distractions or confusions, and an increasingly important segment of the capitalist economy. When cultural forms or subcultural forms *are* critical, culture becomes actively embroiled in economic and political conflict, rather than quietly reflecting it, rationalizing it and reproducing it, but whether culture is overtly politicized or not, it is understood primarily in relation to economic and political interests.

Where does all this leave twenty-first century cultural theory? Has the *Kulturpessimismus*[2] characteristic of Nietzsche, Simmel and Weber been concentrated, politicized, adopted and adapted and updated so well through

2 On the remarkable phenomenon of *Kulturpessimismus* and its significance for modern social thought, see e.g. Kalberg (1987).

international dissemination and engagement with world war, post-colonial strife, mass media, racial division and gender inequality that every case and every pattern is understood through a theoretical prism of domination, exposé and resistance? What room is there left in cultural studies and cultural theory for being surprised or disappointed – genuinely schooled – by the facts of a recalcitrant, often inconvenient and endemically complex reality, the way that Weber envisioned social science and higher education to work? What room might be left to earnestly, respectfully consider existential and aesthetic themes of creativity, meaning, interpretation, coping, transfiguration and transcendence … the possibility of literally *sublime* human activity and experience beyond partisan concern with subliminal meanings and sublimated struggles? Are principled concerns with empiricism, existentialism and aesthetics even valid commitments for theorists, or are they the self-defeating distractions of naïve or neo-conservative colleagues who would unwittingly or maliciously undermine the projects of critical theory and progressive politics?

Perhaps these questions are not susceptible to definitive answers, but these are arguably foundational questions for contemporary cultural studies and social theory, and pivotal for understanding their future possibilities. In that spirit it is worth attending to such theoretical considerations, critically considering recent trends in cultural critique not only with reference to foci and insights, but with reference to alternative models of cultural inquiry, and with consideration to the heuristic value of different models in relation to actual cultural phenomena.

In what follows, Pierre Bourdieu will be considered as exemplary of contemporary cultural critique, and an alternative approach to cultural phenomena will be suggested with reference to Friedrich Nietzsche, and to a lesser degree Max Weber. Three thematic foci will be irony, conflict, and tragedy in the analysis of culture. Bourdieu's and Niezsche's approaches to culture will be surveyed with reference to these focal concerns and also explored with a consideration of an iconic contemporary cultural phenomenon, hip-hop.

2 Irony

Not just critical analyses of culture, but many academic and scientific and professional analyses of cultural phenomena, try to simultaneously distinguish themselves from and illuminate common sense and lay perspectives in a manner that can be referred to as ironic, ironical or ironicizing.[3] The irony is both methodological and epistemological.

3 The reference to irony is not meant primarily as a reference to literary or aesthetic interests, but meant to refer to a variety of rhetorical epistemological device, as the term has been used

Methodologically, the irony involves a type of skepticism of the way culture is (thought to be) understood by natives, by laypersons, by the "folks" who provide the grist for the mill of specialized knowledge and expertise. This skepticism is partly expressed in philosophies of science and in analytic methods which emphasize exploring underlying forces or general patterns unknown to natives, rather than simply describing and explicating natives' commonsense knowledge, vernacular skills, subjective experiences and intentions and the like. A famous example would be Durkheim's programmatic preference for explaining suicide in terms of demographic data rather than by reading suicide notes or interviewing family (Durkheim 2002 [1897]; cf. Atkinson 1978). Distinctions between objective and subjective are often deployed for advantage in methodological debates for these reasons. Structural(ist) analysis and functional(ist) analysis have provided very influential, overlapping illustrations of irony in social thought. The distinction between latent functions and manifest functions, which might be viewed specifically as an innovation that Merton provided to Parsonian structural functionalism (Merton 1968 [1949]), actually suggests a methodological premise which is surprisingly widespread, that scholars need to go beyond considering what social phenomena are commonly thought to do or to be about, using specialized training to uncover obscure truths about the functioning of social systems. Much Critical Theory could be likened to a structural (dys)functionalism along these lines.

Epistemologically, the irony involves a type of invidious status politics (an epistemological politics), where the expertise of the experts is relationally conceptualized, understood in relation to others' relative lack of knowledge, lack of training, lack of reflection, lack of critical thinking, lack of abstraction, and lack of objectivity. In other words experts are understood in relation to natives who are in varying degrees and in varying ways uninformed, unskilled, unreflective, uncritical, myopic and subjective. As Garfinkel suggested, the members of a culture are often understood by credentialed social thinkers as cultural dopes (Garfinkel 1967; Lynch 2012).

---

e.g. in ethnomethodology, especially by Pollner (see e.g. 1987), referring to qualities of some accounts of social affairs that undermine other accounts, as the accounts by a police officer and by somebody ticketed by the officer might each fault the other, disjunctive account in traffic court. Competing accounts can be cast as mistaken, subjective, impaired by a poor vantage point or faulty memory, self-interested, etc. Similarly, in addressing issues of collusion or complicity retrospectively observable between colonized and colonizers, Webber and Lynd observe that irony can refer "to the effects of re-reading what an earlier ehnographer, chronicler, artist, or writer once thought was a rather transparent sort of discursive, analytical or aesthetic project," finding unintended, perhaps discrediting, meaning or significance (Webber and Lynd 1996: ix).

It might be best to consider cultural understanding along a continuum, from blind, obfuscating, reactionary dopery to maximal mastery of the best vantage examined with the benefit of methods and knowledge which are simultaneously highly specialized but also rigorously interdisciplinary, with a very respectable scope. Marx could suggest that the proletariat was best positioned to understand capitalism, while privately understanding that his colleague Engels did rather well despite his privileged social position, perhaps even better than a random proletarian plucked from a shop floor or a mine. Standpoint theories of this kind, beginning with Marx, generally suggest that one group has a superior if not unique access to understanding by virtue of a social position that provides simultaneously a better vantage point on oppressive social relations and a direct interest in seeing a social system in precisely this manner. Implicitly, however, there is the awkward but crucial question of whether those who buy and buy into standpoint theory texts might at least partially overcome their epistemological handicaps.

Standpoint theories might be seen as more explicit, reflective varieties of very common theoretical tendencies to offer some form of self-credentialing paired with some form of ironic downgrading of alternative views. Karl Mannheim (2015 [1929]) offered one famous formulation of this in his discussion of the intelligentsia, with his contention that free-floating intellectuals were, by virtue of their relative transcendence of class and a weakening of traditional status distinctions through education, capable of greater understanding of society than those with more determined or partial perspectives. At the extremes we find critical scholars dismissed as unscientific, and positivist scholars dismissed as dogmatically *scientistic*, ideologically transfixed by the status quo, hesitant to evaluate, and at best incrementalist in their anti-septic policy prescriptions. From those who champion objectivity to those who espouse particular(ist) critical perspectives – and those who do both – a dual, invidious concern with credentialing and irony is a pervasive pattern. As Lynch points out, Garfinkel's objection to ironically treating cultural members as dopes was itself an ironic reference to conventional sociological theorizing (2012: 223) from someone who recommended explicating members' commonsense knowledge and practical skills.

Whether the natives are cultural dopes or not, it is of foundational importance to acknowledge the widespread *assumption* that the natives are dopes, that their understandings and accounts should be disregarded or reinterpreted. This assumption is subject to debates that go to the heart of social thought and social science. The implications extend to debates including whether or how scholarship should be critical, whether or how scholarship should be empirical, whether the scope of inquiry should be macro or micro, whether the methods should be quantitative or qualitative, whether inquiry needs to be historical or not, comparative or not, whether the goal is to transcend subjectivity or topicalize subjectivity, whether explanation should be deterministic or voluntaristic, and how structure is related to agency. Whether cultural analysis is ironic or not, and in what manner it is or is not, is a question that ramifies in all these directions.

3 Conflict

A great deal has been written about conflict theories of society, a very broad umbrella term which can cover Critical Theory and other neo-Marxist social thought, critical race theory, feminist scholarship, queer theory, and post-colonial scholarship. These traditions of inquiry overlap typically in conceptualizing the units of analysis as conflicting or competing groups (classes, races, sexes, etc.), emphasizing the illumination and critique of oppressive social relations between these units, and endorsing in some manner (sometimes rather muted) the goals of resistance and liberation. In many cases there can also be an emphasis on a systems analysis of society, in which conflicting groups are relationally bound to each other in a system understood in terms of institutionalized oppression or the dynamics of group conflict, providing us with social systems characterized in terms of capitalist society and capitalist world system, patriarchal society, white supremacy, hetero-normativity.

Just as conflict has become a privileged concern in social theory, culture has become a privileged concern in conflict theories. One might say that from the *Communist Manifesto* to Weimar Germany, conflict theorists were optimistic about working through culture towards liberatory ends, especially by raising (working) class consciousness in preparation for the transcendence of capitalist class relations. The Frankfurt School in the 1930s Germany has a pivotal significance in intellectual history, one that can largely be attributed to overlapping interests between Horkheimer, their founder, and Erich Fromm, their social psychologist. At that historical juncture, culture started to be understood not in terms of its transforming potential but as a conservative, literally *retarding* historical force. As Fay suggests, the revolutionary attitude collided with stubborn questions of tradition and identity (1987: 159–164).

Since the 1930's Critical Theory concerns over the authoritarianism of the German working class (see e.g. Berard 2013), and through the tremendous expansion of conflict-theoretical sensibilities as they were adapted to the analysis of race relations and gendered inequality and beyond, one can speak of a dual-faced conception of culture. Culture now can progressively look forward but too often does not; one face of culture provides the potential to critically understand and resist oppressive social relations, whereas the other face of culture, generally the one staring back at theorists, generally reflects and reinforces structured inequality. This is much as it was originally understood in Marx's early base-superstructure analogy, even if concessions of partial autonomy for the superstructure are now almost obligatory.[4] The original base-superstructure model needs to be understood today, in light of the 20th century development of social psychology broadly construed, as not only treating the *cultural corpus* and *cultural institutions* reductively as having primarily ideological significance, but also *subjectivity*. Subjectivity in much of the most sophisticated critical scholarship has become the final mechanism for ideological domination, or at best a resource which might offer meaningful resistance after a rare form of self-critique (reflexive, critical practices of the self) not unlike deconstruction.

4 Ignorance and the Unconscious: Relating Irony and Conflict

The themes of irony and conflict arguably should be discussed together as they are explored with reference to a particular author, tradition of inquiry, or cultural phenomenon. The reason for this is fairly simple; in cultural analysis it is often the case that the underlying reality escaping the understanding of the natives, often conscripting them in their own subordination, is the underlying reality of conflict. The irony often consists of just this: the cultural theorist is generally analyzing a culture understood to lack a popular understanding of oppressive social relations, or to lack a popular understanding of effective mobilization, and therefore to be engaged in a macro-social, intergenerational pattern of unwitting self-sabotage. Culture is therefore understood to be crucially important, and yet epiphenomenal in relation to structural inequalities. Its content is deserving of the most serious attention, but only in conjunction with specialized theoretical tools such as concepts of *ressentiment*, false consciousness, ideology, hegemony, propaganda, mass society, culture industry, consumerism, co-optation, ethnocentrism, stereotypes, prejudices, biases, authoritarianism, nationalism, racism, sexism, xenophobia, nativism, anti-Semitism,

4 Harris (1980: 51–56; 70–75) offers a brief survey of issues involved in the base-superstructure analogy in cultural materialism. Peters suggests that a broader understanding of an "ontological complicity" between "social and symbolic structures," visible in the thought of Kant and Durkheim, in Marxist thought undergoes a twist by which symbolic structures become "masked forms of domination" (2014: 140).

Islamophobia, symbolic violence and misrecognition. By such means culture is understood to deserve serious analytic attention, but *ironic* attention.

Central to many of these lines of cultural critique are implicit assumptions of ignorance and explicit references to the unconscious, including not just the psycho-analytic conception of the unconscious but extending extremely widely to include Giddens' practical consciousness and Bourdieu's *habitus*, not to mention popular and influential terms such as unconscious bias. While it is not professionally acceptable to claim that the natives are ignorant, one really does not see critical analyses treating the natives as well-informed.[5] Ever since the authoritarian character failed to realize his true class interests in 1930's Germany, culture and the unconscious have been the two theoretical devices most relied upon to explain the gap between the structural and political insights of the critical theorists, on the one hand, and the actual beliefs and values of critically important but disappointing demographic groups, on the other hand.

In recent generations, related innovations relate to individual reflexivity and collective biases. A lack of reflexivity is in important ways functionally or ideologically comparable to both ignorance and to the operation of unconscious drives and distortions, however a lack of reflexivity implies the presence of conscious but uncritical thinking and thoughts, rather than an absence of content or hidden content. A further theoretical device of increasing importance might be called constructions of *collective* unconscious, such as seems to be implied in notions of institutional racism or the white "racial frame," whereby subjective deficits and biases are – more or less – attributed to collectives such as macro-social institutions or macro-social groups. These claims are certainly similar to older class-analytic concerns with e.g. the authoritarianism of

5 An exception would be cases like standpoint theory where some rather common ascribed minority characteristic (esp. an oppressed racial or sexual identity) is suggested to be linked to some epistemological advantage. However even in these cases the attribution of a standpoint to a huge and inevitably diverse minority group is not meant as an empirical claim amenable to testing by interviewing people or observing people. The only way a claim of a shared standpoint between Blacks or between women (or even between African-American women) could be reconciled with the observable diversity of expressions and behavior would be to have recourse to something like an unconscious knowledge which is being heeded when people live up to the collective norms expressed by a standpoint theorist, and not heeded when they fall short. In other words standpoint theories on their face are extremely liberal in widely attributing knowledge and other virtues among a minority group, but generally without claiming that any particular knowledge or virtue can be attributed to group members as an empirical matter. What is required then is something like a collective consciousness which can be either conscious or unconscious, not necessarily observable but nevertheless attributable.

certain classes or class segments, but decidedly less empirical, more holistic and essentialistic.

5 Irony and Conflict in Bourdieu's Cultural Analysis

Bourdieu's analysis of culture is provided in a substantial *oeuvre*. His works on culture have a noteworthy breadth and density, however a central concern remains the reproduction and *seeming legitimation* of economic inequalities through cultural distinctions, ranging from institutional credentials such as educational attainment, to aesthetic tastes (e.g. oil paintings or tattoos), and preferred leisure activities (e.g. golf or boxing). A crude summary would have it that economic capital enables the cultivation of cultural capital (such as formal qualifications, skills, respectable judgment, sophisticated disposition) and social capital (advantageous contacts and networks). Social and cultural capital, perceived as meritorious in the distribution of social positions (primarily salaried positions, but also honorific and political statuses), lead directly and indirectly to further income, wealth and power. In this way inequalities of economic capital are reproduced from generation to generation, but in a manner ostensibly driven by qualifications and consistent with democratic norms. Shorter still: class-based cultural distinctions enable the invidious intergenerational laundering of economic capital and the perpetuation of class divisions which are based much more on (sublimated) class conflict than merit.

While these points are certainly subject to debate, two of the widespread conclusions about Bourdieu's work are, first, that it is a masterful exploration of the subtle intergenerational interplay between economic stratification and cultural distinctions, and, second, that it is ultimately deterministic and reductionistic. Bourdieu's determinism and reductionism turn out to be intimately related to the analytic deployment of irony. Peters argues there is a need to "bridge the gap between the 'pessimism of the intellect' that marks [Bourdieu's] portrayal of the (lack of) reflexive capabilities of the lay agent, on the one hand, and the 'optimism of the will' infused in the critical program of reflexive sociology, on the other" (2014: 124, 144). Bourdieu certainly addresses questions of praxis, seemingly suggestive of a respect for human agency, but in a decidedly "structural praxeology" (2014: 125), in the sense that "the very cognitive and practical capabilities which agents continually invest in the practices that produce and reproduce the social world carry the undeniable marks of their socialization within the structures of this same world" (2014: 128).

In both respects Bourdieu's contributions can be likened to the longstanding neo-Marxist proclivity to focus in very serious and illuminating ways on cultural phenomena, while retaining and reproducing the notion that ultimately culture is significant as an epiphenomenal superstructure to be evaluated as either more or less effective in legitimating (or perhaps undermining) socio-economic hierarchies – usually legitimating rather than undermining. Bourdieu's analysis is certainly unique in important ways, but in ways which remain consistent with broad patterns of deterministic and reductionistic explanation in neo-Marxist critiques of capitalist societies.

Bourdieu's notion of *fields* is certainly an important, overarching concern. According to Bourdieu, the social world can be conceptualized as a "whole universe of economies, that is, of fields of struggle differing both in the stakes and the scarcities that are generated within them and in the forms of capital deployed in them" (1990a: 51). This understanding of society is conducive to respecting that fields associated with e.g. education, visual arts, and music each have distinctive economies, each partially autonomous from all other fields, including the economic field. However, Bourdieu also insists that struggles within these many fields, such as those between competing aesthetics, should be interpreted in relation to a broader or more fundamental reality of class conflict (see e.g. 1993: 57, 94–96, 120). Struggles over distinctions, credentials, and resources within specialized fields often involve varieties of symbolic capital, or capital that is "unrecognized as capital and recognized as legitimate competence, as authority exerting an effect of (mis)recognition" (1986: 245, 255; 1989: 21; 1993: 75).

The notion of fields, combined with conceptualizations of different forms of capital, deserves recognition as providing a sophisticated, illuminating model of multi-dimensional social conflicts in which an omni-relevant field of class inequalities exerts an indirect, refracted (Bourdieu 1993: 164, 182) influence over other fields. These other fields, including art and music, are at least semi-autonomous with respect to class divisions, but often perceived or misrecognized as being autonomous, and therefore become much more effective at legitimating the inequalities which they generally reproduce, indirectly.

Irony and conflict can be seen to be fundamental to Bourdieu's cultural analysis repeatedly, and in many different manifestations. Among these, it should be appreciated that processes of conflict, competition and invidious distinction are suggested to be central dynamics in social fields generally, not just in economics and politics, but in such fields as law and education and the arts. The irony comes in largely because semi-autonomous fields, including fields of cultural production and consumption, are *misrecognized* as autonomous fields. This asserted misrecognition simultaneously suggests an endemic ignorance about the role of cultural activities, values and institutions in society, and an unwitting complicity or collusion in the reproduction of capitalist class relations. Such misrecognition and complicity extend to those groups which are most marginalized and exploited, and may also extend to those who perceive themselves to be critical thinkers, to enjoy personal autonomy from economic and political struggles, or to be engaged with informed resistance against the status quo.

This irony is critically addressed, for example, in Grattan's discussion of Bourdieu's pessimism in relation to social protest. She writes,

> ...when resistance is coupled with eviscerated capacities for critique and reform, it registers as reactionary backlash or fails to break the surface of social life. Bourdieu is skeptical that anything more than reaction or fantasy can come from people who suffer daily exposure to the 'inert violence' of economic and social structures.... In Bourdieu's words: 'The populist illusion which is nowadays nourished by simplistic rhetoric of "resistance" tends to conceal one of the most tragic effects of the condition of the dominated – the inclination to violence that is engendered by early and constant exposure to violence.' [Bourdieu 1997: 232–233] Reactionary populism thus mimics state violence, yet their bellicose visage and pitch restores the sheen of neoliberalism as the rational future of democracy.
>
> GRATTAN 2012: 205

It should be noted here that Bourdieu's reference to tragic effects on the dominated serves to express pity, and in such a manner that underestimates the role of culture in adapting to violence. Grattan suggests in turn that democratic theorists usually worry about Bourdieu's excessive pessimism, his deterministic tendencies, and his "myopic vision of everyday practice, which on the one hand, remains tone deaf to the quotidian capacities of bodies and speech, and on the other, misses the more reflexive rituals through which groups and movements countertrain subjective dispositions and sensibilities" (2012: 205). Grattan suggests constructively that the habitus "also generates the dispositions and practices that make up our basic defenses against social disintegration, and that equip us with subversive dispositions ... we need to preserve its democratic resources, and countertrain its reactionary impulses" (2012: 206).

In all of this it needs to be remembered that Bourdieu's causal link between the structures of capitalist class relations and the social practices which reproduce them is a theoretical construct according to which individuals are motivated by internal but socially determined assemblages of largely unconscious dispositions – the *habitus*. The concept of habitus, while ostensibly a virtuoso answer to the dualism of objectivism and subjectivism, ultimately reproduces cultural materialism in a misrecognized form with much additional – but still reductionist – attention to culture and agency. Rather than truly synthesizing the subjective with the objective, we could speak of the habitus' articulation within social fields as involving the interplay of "two objective structures: the one in which he agent was socialized and which is sedimented in the matrix of structured dispositions of the agent's body and mind, on the one hand, and the one in which the agent is acting, on the other" (Peters 2014: 142). Similar to objections raised against Foucault, Peters remarks of Bourdieu's model of subjects that "it depicts human beings" as "…wordly, all too worldly, molded in their personalities' most intimate territories by social-historical determinations which are not of their choosing, as Marx would say, but end up objectivated in their very subjectivities" (Peters 2014: 139).

This co-opted habitus is not Bourdieu's habitus, which has ostensibly been checked and balanced to the degree that is humanly possible, but the habitus which Bourdieu would ironically attribute to virtually everyone else to explain how and why it is that cultural values and practices generally can be understood as mechanisms for the unknowing, largely unintentional, often counter-intuitive and frequently self-harming reproduction of inequality. The indebtedness to ironic notions of the unconscious should be clear. Griller suggests that Bourdieu presupposes "a theory of practice that tells him that unconscious *habitus* interacts with field to produce unconscious strategies that determine behavior…" and through a habitus which, in the case of dominated subjects, "legitimizes their dominated status" (2000: 197). Noting the irony here, Griller writes that "Bourdieu's attempt to bridge the gap between structure and practice through unconscious dispositions … puts the ethnographic observer above, epistemologically, that which he observes" (2000: 202). Griller then ironically notes that Bourdieu "unintentionally reinvents all over again the anthropologist's gaze, looking at the practice of unconscious natives, knowing better than they the sources of their behavior because he is a scientist, because he is reflexive, something they cannot be without his help" (2000: 203). With all his attention to subjectivity, it is not clear that his subjectivity is a meaningful subjectivity, and Bourdieu's "theory of practice must be deemed a failed attempt to revive the subject in objective sociology" (2000: 203).

The flip side of the ironic emphasis on unconscious dispositions is the programmatic praise of analytic reflexivity. Kauppi suggests that Bourdieu attaches to the reflexive researcher the status of a "Romantic hero, who liberates him/herself from the chains of preconceptions and illusions" rationalizing a demand for the legitimacy of his project, which can be likened to Plato aspiring to lead the way out of the cave of shadows (2000: 230).

The extensive reliance upon theoretical constructs of unconscious subjective content notably renders Bourdieu's ironic critique vulnerable to the ironic critique of Karl Popper, who influentially suggested that psychoanalyis – and by implication much social thought dependent upon social-psychological diagnoses of *unconscious* delusions and programming, falls on the wrong side of his demarcation criteria for scientific scholarship.[6]

Bourdieu's conceptualization of the habitus, similar to notions of institutional racism and a white racial frame, also suggests that an individual's habitus is not individual, but reflective of group position in the context of classes and fields. The concept of habitus therefore overlaps to some degree with discredited historical notions of group mind and contemporary critical notions of unconscious mental traits collectively attributed on the basis of membership in a social group, usually cognitive deficits attributed in an essentializing, stereotyping manner to dominant or majority groups.

6 Irony and Conflict in Nietzsche's Cultural Analysis

Certainly a great deal could be said about Nietzsche's contributions to social critique, including cruelly ironic observations and abundant concern for manipulative and underhanded machinations of power within the cultural realm. While his social criticism is brilliant and unique, and a very early and influential example of ideology critique, it is also true that there is now an over-abundance of incisive social criticism in modern social thought, and Nietzsche's critical contributions have already been taken up by prominent social critics in many ways, as well as admirably surveyed by legions of Nietzsche scholars. In other ways, including Nietzsche's service as a prophet for secularism, his contributions have a much more historical than contemporary significance.

Arguably two of Nietzsche's most distinctive contributions to cultural analysis are his method of genealogical critique and his insights on the importance of aesthetics, including tragic aesthetics. Of these, the method of genealogical critique, later adopted by Foucault (see e.g. Foucault 1984 [1971]), is arguably his most influential contribution to cultural criticism, while the concern for aesthetics is arguably the most noteworthy contribution to a broader and

6 Analytic dependence upon attributions of unconscious attributes generally runs up against the criterion of falsifiability which many respect as necessary for empirical scholarship. The problem of unfalsifiability in Bourdieu's theory of practice is suggested by Griller when he characterizes it as an epistemology (which, like a paradigm, is a different animal than the kind of theory Bourdieu claimed to be providing) and notes that one cannot really "demonstrate the nonexistence of unconscious dispositions" (2000: 207 f 21).

(somewhat, relatively) more appreciative, constructive cultural analysis. A discussion of genealogical critique will be followed by attention to Nietzsche's more neglected interest in tragic culture.

Genealogy, as its name would suggest, has an important historical dimension to it, an empirical grounding of sorts, but in Nietzsche's hands genealogy becomes a method of critique, picked up later by Foucault for exactly that purpose. Leiter compares genealogy to pedigree, conventionally understood as roughly synonymous, implying however that the point of genealogy for Nietzsche is something like the *deconstruction* of a pedigree (2002: 165–166). A genealogy reveals its object to have more complicated origins than is conventionally understood, and therefore to have multiple possible evaluations (Leiter 2002: 167–173). For example, Nietzsche suggests in his *Genealogy of Morals* (1967a [1887]) that Western morality largely originates in three psychological traits which considered together are rather debasing: "*ressentiment* ... internalized cruelty ... the will to power" (Leiter 2002: 173). Genealogy provides essentially a soured origin story in order to create critical space in which to re-evaluate conventional, contemporary authorities. As Leiter suggests (2002: 176), the critical goal of genealogy is much like the paradigmatic critical goal of dispelling false consciousness.

Solomon rightly observes that genealogy may have a stronger dimension of psychological diagnosis than historical research. Nietzsche's historical account could be "very condensed and rather mythic," whereas the driving interest is in challenging "the motives and mechanisms underlying that history and evolution" (Solomon 1994: 96), placing something of a "collective *ad hominem* argument at the center of moral philosophy" (Solomon 1994: 97). But in either sense, as an historical or as a psychological calumny, a genealogy provocatively and smartly suggests that the underlying realities of contemporary values or institutions are deeply discrediting.

Arguably the most central feature of genealogical critiques is that they or their authors themselves need only a modest pedigree to be effective, perhaps a respectable faculty appointment, or a reputation as a noteworthy author – just enough of a pedigree to acquire an audience. Historically and psychologically speaking they may proffer quite arguable interpretations, and yet still have exactly the desired critical effect. The point is not to establish a new truth or a new consciousness, but to cast doubt upon established conventions of belief and valuation. For this, what is most relevant is effective rhetorical presentation of historical (and implicitly social-psychological) narratives of origins and evolutions which are plausible enough to gain an audience.

This feature of genealogical critique is arguably most central for primarily two reasons. *First*, the logic of genealogical critique is anti-foundationalist (see e.g. Owen 1994: 146–150) not only in questioning the foundations of established social institutions, practices, beliefs and values, but also in claiming and needing no foundation for itself – no authority, no external vantage point, no answers for questions raised or substitutes for undermined structures of collective life. As Conway suggests, "Nietzsche is therefore warranted in claiming for his genealogies a validity relative to the authoritative interpretations they discredit and supplant" (1994: 318). Genealogies are tools for ironic social commentary which themselves provide only minimal, difficult foothold for effective counter-argument. Genealogies can be criticized as historically invalid, nihilistic, or even – very ironically – as neo-conservative in their effect, but such arguments are much better at blocking the ascension of new orthodoxies than warding off uncertainty and doubt about previous *doxa* (cf. Bourdieu 1977: 159–171). If defenses against genealogical critique have become relevant, then the genealogy has already succeeded.

Closely related to this first point, *secondly*, the logic of genealogical critique is one of immanent criticism or internal critique (see e.g. Conway 1994; Owen 1994: 82–83; Leiter 2002: 174–176), involving the exploitation of tensions or contradictions among others' foundational commitments, similar to the Marxist notion of contradictions in capitalism but rather more idealist and interventionist. In this manner values are turned against values, as a commitment for truth can be turned against mythical conceptions, attention to consistency can problematize inconsistencies, renewed considerations of virtue can be mobilized against pettiness.

The conflicts that receive Nietzsche's sustained attention are conflicts between values, conflicts in which life-affirming virtues and wisdom struggle against countervailing developments by which stunted souls would turn base instincts such as *ressentiment* into a universal moral code. In such conflicts genealogy figures as the primary analytic device for offering ironic accounts of the humble, humbling origins at the foundations of the cultural phenomena in question.

7 Tragedy in Nietzsche's Thought

Nietzsche is often understood as the theorist of the will to power, as an elitist early critic of modern mass society and mass culture, and as a uniquely critical intellect and crucially important precursor to lines of critical social analysis running (partly through Max Weber) to the Frankfurt School and to Foucault. Nietzsche is also, however, recognized for his relevance to existentialist thought, for his sober and sobering explorations of the death of God and the implications for morality and ethics in the modern world, and perhaps to a lesser degree for his aesthetics, including early insights and interests in Greek tragedy. It is in these latter respects that Nietzsche arguably still has something rather innovative to contribute to cultural analysis, something neglected in the almost unrelenting pessimism of the Frankfurt School, and largely neglected in Foucault with the partial exception of his important, late concern with aesthetics.

It should be noted that aesthetics, including an appreciation for tragic sensibilities in arts and culture, is a potential source of meaning and guidance unlike many of the cultural moorings challenged (if not outright undermined) in the modern period by relativism and secularism and historicism and social critique. Aesthetics are in many ways unlike supernatural beliefs, moral codes, and ideologies. Aesthetics are also not nearly so stipulative or vulnerable to skepticism as are the grand theories of justice, morality or society that some theorists have offered as if to rebuild where previous structures have been undermined. The importance of aesthetics for Nietzsche's entire philosophy, including his ethics, have been subject to a variety of rewarding commentaries (e.g. Winchester 1994; Sleinis 1994: 123–150; Berkowitz 1995: 44–66); it is in any case firmly established in the Nietzsche literature, if not more widely understood. It is certainly appropriate to consider in much greater depth the potential contributions of cultural analyses that can find insight and wisdom and agency within cultural phenomena – as is true of Nietzsche's aesthetic observations – rather than minimizing their agency, their creativity, their validity, and ultimately perhaps their very humanity.

Nietzsche began his career as an academic classicist, and his significance for contemporary social thought was already, remarkably, clearly signaled in an early work on Pre-Socratic Greek culture. According to Nietzsche in *The Birth of Tragedy*, the fundamental quality of this culture was its tragic nature. This tragic culture, he suggested, comprised two complementary traits. First, this culture admitted that destruction, absurdity, horror and misfortune were inevitable features of human life. Second, this culture used art to allow its members to view these features of existence at a distance, to see them as aesthetically meaningful, thereby to modify and defy "nauseous thoughts about the horror or absurdity of existence" (1967b: 60), but without becoming dogmatic or supernatural.

Culture can therefore be an affirming resource without dependence upon vulnerable fabrications subject to becoming inhuman (reified) and eventually revealed to be all too human. By means of these two movements, the admission of man's existential predicament and the adoption of an aesthetic disposition towards life, art makes life possible and worth living (1967b: 41), and in a manner that is suggested to have an integrity lacking in many cultural crutches. This is true whether, in any particular case, art performs this function by means of distancing the individual from the unfortunate aspects of life (1967b: 34–35), by means of overcoming, transfiguring or defying these aspects of life (1967b: 70, 140), by means of veiling and withdrawing them from sight, or by means of the truly tragic task of drawing man's attention to the larger patterns of "eternal life" which "abides through the perpetual destruction of appearances" (1967b: 61, 140) and lies behind the ugliness and disharmony of life (1967b: 141). Nietzsche conceives of art, then, as a creative complement, consummation and justification of existence that seduces man into a continuation of life (1967b: 43, 52, 118).

While tragedy is not a common theme in cultural studies, its importance has not been completely neglected. In evaluating the impact of Nietzsche's *Birth of Tragedy*, Burnham and Jesinghausen (2010: 155) suggest that it is "is one of the most important and interesting books ... from the second half of the 19th century, on a par with, for example, Nietzsche's own *Zarathustra*, Darwin's *Origin of Species* (1859), Marx's *Capital* (1867–1894) or, right at the end of the century, Freud's *Interpretation of Dreams*."

Independent of Nietzsche's legacy, Raymond Williams suggested it is important to consider at least the possibility of tragedy "...when we see mourning and lament, when we see men and women breaking under their actual loss ... where the suffering is felt, where it is taken into the person of another, we are clearly within the possible dimensions of tragedy" (1966: 47). Moreover, Williams suggests that to generally deny tragic meaning to ordinary suffering, "all that suffering which is part of our social and political world," rests in part on a neglect of human agency (48–49). Williams argues that a general neglect to consider tragedy implicates a type of elitism as well as a type of alienation; "The definition of tragedy as dependent on the history of a man of rank was ... an alienation: some deaths mattered more than others, and rank was the actual dividing line" (49). He suggests moreover that the "extension of the tragic category" to the middle class was a significant moment in modern cultural history (49). Nevertheless, and perhaps most importantly, Williams notes a tendency in modern social thought, including revolutionary thought, to neglect tragedy, a tendency that has a strange overlap with the elitism of traditions in the tragic genre. Similarly, Orr intimates that there may be a social geography to tragic realism in modern fiction, noting that tragic meaning is disproportionately recognized in rural and maritime settings, largely ignoring urban culture and working-class life (Orr 1977: 189–191). Williams observes, "The idea of tragedy, in its ordinary form, excludes especially that tragic experience which is social, and the idea of revolution, again in its ordinary form, excludes especially that social experience which is tragic" (1966: 64).

While Nietzsche's aesthetics were generally elitist and usually very individualistic, his interest in tragic culture stands out as his most Democratic acknowledgement that a life-affirming aesthetics could be generalized to a cultural phenomenon. This is part of his complex legacy. While Owen suggests that "Nietzsche's legacy lies in the degree to which his thought enables individuals to confront and overcome nihilism in their everyday lives, to mount 'local rebellions' against nihilism, and to achieve a measure of maturity" (1994: 83), Nietzsche's legacy is much broader. Nietzsche's legacy should be evaluated in part by considering whether his writing enables cultural studies to understand and appreciate how cultural forms can avoid or transcend nihilism and embody the maturity to acknowledge the worst and to persevere with authenticity and artfulness.

8 The Applicability of Bourdieu and Nietzsche to the Subaltern and Subcultural

In considering hip-hop by reference to Bourdieu's cultural sociology, there are virtues as well as difficulties in extending this type of analysis to a cultural form associated with a minority group in a different society than the ones Bourdieu himself studied. There are many indications of Bourdieu's relevance, and some concerns over potential applications and the way applications may be attempted.

Shusterman suggests Bourdieu may have been wrong "to universalize from the French case" (2015: 440), and that "American culture (despite its stubborn social inequalities) might provide a promising context in which popular art (in some of its exciting new hybrid forms such as hip-hop) could indeed claim aesthetic validity and genuine artistic status" (2015: 441). However, while Bourdieu often suggested that aesthetic merit and artistic status were related to marginal positions within privileged strata, his cultural analysis is much more amenable to ironic readings of cultural production, especially in popular culture, than to acknowledging artistic validity and authenticity. Shusterman's reference to American popular culture seems to have met with the following response:

> One cannot, at the same time, denounce the inhuman social conditions of existence imposed upon proletarians and subproletarians, especially in the black ghettoes of the United States ... and credit the people placed in such situations with the full accomplishment of their human potentialities, and in particular with the gratuitous and disinterested dispositions

> that we tacitly or explicitly inscribe in notions such as those of 'culture' or 'aesthetics.'
>
> BOURDIEU 1990b: 387–388, quoted in SHUSTERMAN 2015: 441

While it should be conceded that living in conditions of poverty, marginalization, and insecurity are not conducive to maximizing human potentialities, this quote also clearly suggests an ironic elitism (oddly reminiscent of Mannheim's problematic notion of the free-swimming intellegentsia) that is decidedly *not* predisposed to acknowledge cultural or aesthetic validity within marginalized minority subcultures. The skepticism concerning the capacities of the most disprivileged should also be understood as a more concentrated form of a cynicism which is in any case rather broad in scope. Grattan notes that Bourdieu holds a very critical view of the "methodological volunteerism and optimism which define the populist vision of the 'people' as a site of subversion, or at least 'resistance'" (Bourdieu 1997: 231 in Grattan 2012: 196). It is therefore crucial to consider irony as well as conflict as sensitizing concepts in the extension of Bourdieu's analysis to any subaltern cultural or subcultural forms.

Similarly, Hanchard writes of a misrecognition of black agency in Wacquant's work, with particular reference to his analysis of African American athletes, quoting Wacquant as arguing "Athletes do not move people and provide a new vision of the world ... They are not *other-worldly*, they are *this-worldly. They are not violators of tradition but expressions of it; not innovators but ritualists. This is particularly true of African-American culture and history...*" (Wacquant 1996: 27, quoted in Hanchard 2003: 24; italics added by Hanchard). Hanchard notes ironically that, although "Bourdieu and Wacquant have forged their scholarly and political reputations, in part, on their proximity and intimacy with subaltern populations" ... "their objects of study and critique ... (actual people and movements) are remarkably inorganic" (2003: 25–26). Persons of African ancestry in the Americas are portrayed as static; "They do not have multiple roles or multi-faceted identities, or serve as cultural producers or political actors outside a Dahrendorfian 'incumbency of social role'", thus minimizing their complexity and dynamism and minimizing the presence of progressive values (Hanchard 2003: 26). Hanchard ironically likens this tendency to cultural imperialism, one which may be blind to "forms of culture and politics" which are not already familiar.

In considering the application of Nietzsche's cultural observations to hip-hop, obviously one difficulty is that hip-hop is radically different from Greek tragedy, and German icons such as Goethe and Wagner. One challenge is to keep in mind both Nietzsche's underlying appreciative interests, and the ironic concern that the dis-privileged are liable to try to turn weakness and vices into virtues, perhaps even try to tarnish the powerful with guilt.

9 The Cultural Phenomenon of Hip-Hop

Theoretical elaboration, exegetical works and literature surveys are valuable elements in cultural studies, including much of Bourdieu's works and works addressing Bourdieu, but it is crucial for cultural analysis as a whole to remain engaged with real cultural phenomena, and to allow data or performance to prompt refinements, elaborations, and sometimes retractions to even the smartest abstractions. Whether culture serves to dominate or to empower are questions amenable to research, scholarship involving "vigilance and attention to the details of the production, distribution and consumption of culture" (Storey 1996: 6). So too should scholarship enable us to see in particular groups, regions, genres, and generations, whether culture serves only political roles, or perhaps has much broader significance. Hip-hop is a fascinating case to consider in this light.

The term hip-hop refers to uniquely African American cultural practices and beliefs encompassing a wide range of artistic and social behaviors (Kitwana 2005; Keyes 2002). Initially emerging from the 1970's New York City black community, hip-hop has become a worldwide subcultural phenomenon (Watkins 2005). In general, hip-hop represents a stylized expression of the African American experience and consists of musical forms, urban dance styles such as breakdancing or "popping and locking," clothing styles, urban art typically referred to as graffiti, as well as a complex code of normative behaviors and attitudes (Persaud 2006; Kitwana 2002). Historically, hip-hop served as an evolution of earlier types of African American culture ranging from soul music, club dancing, competitive street performance, and disc jockeying, and drew influence as well from the black consciousness movements of the mid-Twentieth Century (Rose 2008; Hess 2005; Keyes 2002). Owing to its origins in New York City, and further developments in major metropolitan areas such as Los Angeles, Chicago, or Atlanta, hip-hop is heavily informed by the urban African American reality characterized by racial discrimination, lack of economic mobility, social marginalization, community disorganization, and being subject to institutional and street violence (Collins 2006; Kitwana 2005; Keyes 2002). Consequently, hip-hop has become a cultural vehicle in which African Americans are able to articulate social commentary regarding their condition as a racially marginalized group (Kelley 1994), create feelings of belonging and racial authenticity (Jackson 2001), and mount cultural resistance towards what are viewed as oppressive, racialized norms of American society (Best and Kellner 1999).

While hip-hop consists of many different types of artistic and cultural forms it is perhaps most recognized for its various musical styles such as rap, new soul, Afro-pop, or various derivatives combining earlier black musical forms with a hip-hop sensibility (Collins 2006; Persaud 2006). As a commercial music genre hip-hop is lucrative, equaling or exceeding albums sales by competing musical styles such as pop or rock music (Clay 2003; Hess 2005). Like other forms of successful music genres, hip-hop has been highly commercialized by the professional music industry and is therefore widely available to the general public, making its subject matter and lyrics particularly fruitful for conducting cultural analysis (Asante 2008; Watkins 2005). This is especially true of hip-hop, as musical forms often have a "structural resonance" (Middleton 1990: 9) allowing marginalized groups such as African Americans to reveal existing power relations and inequalities in society. Consequently, cultural phenomena such as hip-hop can be thought to express subcultural resistance to the prevailing social order, viewed by many African Americans as being racially oppressive and politically marginalizing (Keyes 2002; Clinton 1990; Clark et al. 2006 [1971]). As Hebdidge (1979) observes, disenfranchised groups such as African Americans typically develop cultural practices in opposition to mainstream, dominant codes, particularly if the prevailing social organization is viewed as unjust and unfair (Sykes 1958). In this way hip-hop can be understood as a forum in which African Americans are able to create their own cultural opposition against a hostile and exclusionary racial landscape (Trondman et al. 2011; Clark et al. 2006 [1971]). These elements, when taken in tandem, provide an avenue towards understanding adaptations, discursive moves, and objections that characterize artistic forms such as hip-hop as noteworthy dimensions of the African American experience.

On the other hand, while hip-hop provides a means for African Americans to comment on a racially oppressive society, the lyrical themes and imagery of hip-hop are not exclusively confined to resisting the dominant culture. Instead, hip-hop exists in a complex relationship with the mainstream culture, being capable of *reproducing*, as well as resisting, aspects of the dominant social order (Hebdidge, 1979). Consequently, hip-hop should be understood as a subculture that simultaneously accepts and rejects dominant cultural norms rather than a "contraculture" (Yinger 1960: 625) in conflict and opposition with the surrounding dominant culture. In other words, hip-hop both *resists* and *reproduces* aspects of the dominant culture. Owing to its particular formation and position in society, hip-hop consists of unique cultural formulations and homologies that are cultural reflections of the lived realities of African Americans and therefore are exclusive to hip-hop (Trondman et al. 2011; Asante 2008; Willis 1978). These homologies, singular to hip-hop, nevertheless reproduce in their own fashion problematic mainstream cultural values.

Critiques concerning the negative messaging and tensions within hip-hop have existed almost since the beginning of the genre (Collins 2006). Rebollo-Gil and Moras (2012) observe that the negative messaging, such as the sexual objectification of women or the veneration of criminality, are routinely ignored in favor of the more positive political commentary and cultural resistance of hip-hop. Applying Bourdieu's model results in more critical attention.

10 Irony and Conflict: Latent and Manifest Conflict in Hip-Hop

In cultural analysis hip-hop is often credited with giving voice to African Americans as an oppressed racial minority as well as criticizing historic systems of white supremacy. While it is certainly true that many hip-hop artists feature themes of resistance against the prevailing social order, these themes are often found alongside or in contradiction to messages that reinforce or reproduce non-racial structural inequalities. For example, while virtually all African American hip-hop artists address racial inequality or aspects of white supremacy, themes that rally against discrimination are often found alongside anti-Semitic, anti-Asian, misogynist or homophobic messages (Baldwin 1999; Best and Kellner 1999). Furthermore, hypersexualized depictions of black women, termed "hip hop pornography," traverse shaky territory between strategies of radical self-expression, commercialized misogyny, and capitalist exploitation (Rebollo-Gil and Moras 2012; Miller-Young 2008).

Another seemingly contradictory theme in hip-hop centers on economic inequality. On one hand, many hip-hop artists condemn economic inequality, call attention to the plight of the black urban poor, and offer sustained critiques of the capitalist system for its abuses and transgressions against the black community. On the other hand however, hip-hop also tends to valorize materialistic wealth and conspicuous consumption in a fashion that undermines the implicit racial justice project that is relatively consistent across hip-hop genres, artistic forms, and lyrics. What are cultural analysts to make of the incongruity between these contradictory themes in hip-hop?

Fortunately, Bourdieu provides some resources for unpacking and analyzing these nuanced themes in hip-hop music. Most generally, Bourdieu's work suggests the central importance of analyzing culture in the context of class structures and the reproduction of class relations, recognizing the semi-autonomous nature of cultural fields and the ways in which they can manifest structural determinants in a refracted manner, and similarly emphasizing ideological phenomena of misrecognition and symbolic violence. More particularly, what in many cases are conceived of as subcultural forms or critical movements can be illuminated by conceiving them as cultural expressions of marginalized field positions, often associated with strategies for increasing cultural distinction among those compensating for relative deficits in other forms of capital. Bourdieu generally approached such issues in terms of "opposing poles of the field of the dominant class" (1984: 283) or the dominated fractions of the dominant class in relation to the dominant fraction of the dominant class (1984: 286), with additional consideration for succession struggles within fractions of the dominant class (1984: 295). However, Bourdieu's concepts and arguments, as related to practices of distinction, have been extended by others into various genres of popular culture. Prior, for example, suggests such extension in discussing the incorporation of Bourdieu within British cultural sociology (2011: 129–130).

Consequently, Bourdieu's cultural sociology enables us to see within cultural innovations refracted or vestigial, miscrecognized and burdensome cultural baggage, complementing more conventional interpretations emphasizing cultural resistance. Hip-hop does not need to represent either cultural domination or a complete break from American culture – instead, hip-hop simultaneously reproduces and opposes various aspects of the dominant, largely white, culture. Therefore, it is hardly surprising that hip-hop generally tends to support the acquisition of material wealth and the tenets of the "American Dream" (Merton 1938). Furthermore, given the prevalence of male domination throughout the history of the United States, the presence of hypermasculinity and sexual discrimination within hip-hop is generally aligned with American cultural practices, arguably even more so with subcultural emphases among the working class and the poor. Lastly, discrimination towards other racial, religious, or ethnic minority groups generally follows a similar social pattern that is consistent with white dominance. Of course, the tension between resisting anti-black racism while contributing messages that reproduce discrimination against Jews, Asians, Hispanics, or other marginalized groups is highly problematic.

Hip-hop as a cultural phenomenon can therefore be analyzed both in terms of misrecognition and resistance. The concept of misrecognition applies to themes and messages that are supportive of dominant ideological tendencies in mainstream culture. The category of resistance collects together cultural messages and themes that oppose or undermine ideological tendencies in the dominant United States culture, challenging racism, classism, sexism, or other structural inequalities. Furthermore, misrecognition and resistance can both be discussed in terms of latent and manifest forms, with misrecognition generally serving latent functions. Resistance will often serve manifest functions, at least for those resisting – and manifest dysfunctions for conservative critics – however forms of resistance certainly vary in their degrees of reflexivity, strategy and intentionality. One way to gauge the relative strengths of such theories is to suspend theoretical disbelief and listen to the people in question.

Hip-hop, like many emergent musical forms largely aimed at young audiences, places value on rebellious and anti-authoritarian topics. These resistance messages are manifestly intentional and directed by the artists as evidenced by Public Enemy (1990) famously directing African Americans to "…fight the powers that be!" Figures of authority are often targets of criticism in hip-hop, particularly politicians and law enforcement officers, both of whom are characterized as corrupt, racist, and personally impotent outside of a system of white supremacy.

Legendary gangsta rappers N.W.A. (1988) describe police officers as being "…punk[7] motherfucker(s) with a badge and a gun…. waiting to get shot." Continuing that sentiment, The Geto Boys (1990) claim that: "…the average cop with a badge is a bitch, back in high school they used to get their fucking ass kicked." Commenting on the apparently unchecked power of the police, KRS-One (Boogie Down Productions 1989) wonders "who will protect us from you [the police]?" since the history of policing in America is "…killin' blacks and calling it the law." Racially motivated police brutality, long a subject in hip-hop, is also addressed, as Lakim Shabazz (1990) describes how: "The brother stopped, threw his hands in the air and he still got shot." Other artists indicate that the police are resentful of successful black persons, such as Kool Moe Dee's (1987) account that he is giving the police "…fits" because he is a "…young brother in a Benz [Mercedes Benz], legit [legitimately]" without selling or using drugs.

Other authority figures, such as politicians, are also frequent subjects of resistance for hip-hop artists. Politicians are typically portrayed as being self-serving elites that are disinterested in the social problems of racial minorities, as Willie D points out that politicians are focused only on "…schemin' for power" (The Geto Boys 1990). Directly addressing George W. Bush's Vice-President Richard Cheney, and his financial connections to the Haliburton corporation, Immortal Technique (2003) claims that: "colonialism is sponsored by corporations, that's why Haliburton gets paid to rebuild nations." United States presidents are often targeted by hip-hop artists for criticism, particularly conservative

7 Prison slang for persons that submit to stronger prisoners, often for sex; considered an insult as punks are the lowest status members of the prisoner hierarchy.

politicians viewed as supporting policies and viewpoints hostile to the black community. For example, rapper Paris (1992) released a track critical of then-President George H.W. Bush entitled "Bush Killa" in which the artist fantasizes about assassinating the president, hoping that he: "...think(s) about what he done us [the black community] when he lay to waste." In his controversial track "Reagan," Killer Mike (2012) accuses the president of using The War on Drugs as a tool of urban genocide against the black community, stating that conservative politicians "...only love the rich, and how they loathe the poor," concluding with the sentiment that he is: "...glad Reagan [is] dead!" However, criticism leveled against politicians is not restricted to a single political party, as Kendrick Lamar (2015) equates political parties to rival gangs, suggesting that there "...ain't nothing new but a flu of new Demo-Crips and Re-Bloodlicans.[8] Red State versus a blue state, which one you governin'?" Here, Kendrick Lamar views United States politics as a self-serving regime of power that is indifferent to the concerns of African Americans.

Manifest anti-racist themes are among the most common themes of resistance in hip-hop music. The theme of resistance against racism continues to be active today, as Common (2016) declares that the African American community is: "...staring in the face of hate again, the same hate they say will 'Make America Great Again'..." and that "For America to rise, it's a matter of Black Lives." Thematically, hip-hop often criticizes the default social structure as being one of white supremacy, as Chuck D (Public Enemy 1991) wryly quips that "...these days you can't see who's in cahoots [with white supremacy] because now the KKK wears three-piece suits." Calling attention to the past-in-present realities of systematic racism, rapper Lupe Fiasco (2012) states: "...now I can't pledge allegiance to your flag, cause I can't find no reconciliation with your past when there was nothing equal for my people in your math, you forced us in the ghetto and then you took our dads." Here, Lupe Fiasco comments on the systems of racial exclusion, first through legal segregation and the more recent hyper-policing and mass incarceration resulting from The War on Drugs, that have made the black community wary of American society.

In general, hip-hop is critical of the United States' history of racial violence directed at African Americans, as Rick Ross (The Game 2014) comments on the police killing of Michael Brown stating that his death was "...another soul stole by the system, black men, we pay the toll. The price is your life, Uncle Sam [the United States] want a slice." Further commenting on the violence in the United States, The Roots (2004) declare that the dominant white culture "...only

8 Portmanteau of the Crips and Bloods street gangs and the Republican and Democratic Party names.

wanna see us [black males] occupying a coffin." Regarding the value of African American men, hip-hop artist J. Cole (2014) bemoans the lack of positive black role models in American society unless they "…dribble or … fiddles with mics."[9] However, the recognition of racial injustice can serve as an influence for activism. Influenced by his grandmother's and mother's experience with racial segregation in the Jim Crow south, Kanye West (2004) writes: "At the tender age of six [my mother] was arrested for the sit-ins, and with that in my blood I was born to be different." In this example Kanye West indicates that racial discrimination faced by his family members informs his perspective, and consequently his artistic message of resistance against systems of racism.

While manifest resistance themes are prevalent in hip-hop, particularly against racial discrimination, the genre commonly displays latent messages that reaffirm and reproduce other types of inequality, particularly class or gender disparities. These themes that reproduce structural inequality are often unrealized by the artist, and therefore can be understood as misrecognition, as serving latent functions, that potentially undercut the resistance themes present in hip-hop. Perhaps one of the most routine categories of misrecognition in hip-hop is materialism, especially materialism that attempts to convey higher status based on wealth, as AZ (Nas 1994) plainly declares: "…a person's status depends on salary." Simlarly, Big L (2000) declares: "I'm gettin' stacks [of money] while you askin' people: 'do you want fries with that?'" The focus on material wealth is one of the earliest themes explored in hip-hop, as foundational rappers Run-DMC (1984) exclaim: "money is the key to end all your woes, your ups, your downs, your highs, and your lows—won't you tell me [the] last time love bought your clothes?" because, after all "…life is a gamble, we scramble for money" (Mobb Deep 1995).

The manner that wealth is acquired, either legitimately or illegitimately, is inconsequential – the important thing is to be *Paid in Full* as Eric B. and Rakim (1987) describe robbery where: "this is a hold up … nothing move but the money." In parallel with the values of Protestant capitalism (Weber 2010 [1904/1905]) hip-hop artist Slug (2001) declares that "…time is money, every moment is costly," further emphasizing the underlying, misrecognized capitalist values that often accompany materialistic themes in hip-hop. Lastly, the money fetish trope remains common in hip-hop, particularly since materialistic wealth is often related to sexual prowess, as Notorious B.I.G. (1997) informs us that if you are broke, "…girls won't date you." Confirming this relationship between financial and sexual success, Big L. (1995) writes: "If you don't got ends you won't be gettin ' no skins; and if you don't got money, you won't scoop a honey…"

9 That is, unless they are professional basketball players or famous hip-hop artists.

While valorization of materialistic success is a mainstay in hip-hop lyrics, in recent years there has been significant resistance towards the so-called "American Dream" among more socially conscious artists. Far from being "cultural dopes," most hip-hop artists are hyper-aware of the workings of capitalist relations, as O.C. (Show & A.G. 2007) relates that in America "...everything has a price..." and that under capitalism "...it's all about paper – everything has a fee in the land of the free." Further criticizing the dominant economic system, Ras Kass (Semi Hendrix 2015) observes a relationship between conservative politics, capitalism, and racial discrimination, writing: "They say the richest 400 Americans make more than the other 180 million combined. If that sounds fair then you are out of your mind. So fuck a Republican, I'm out on my grind [working, making money] because being poor, being black and Latino's a crime." When calling in to question the black community's focus on materialism Dead Prez (2008) asks whether African Americans would "...rather have a Lexus or justice? A dream or some substance? A Beemer [BMW], a necklace, or freedom?" Comparatively, in the track "New Slaves" (2013) rapper Kanye West critiques the African Americans' focus on material items that display wealth and status, claiming "...all you blacks want all the same things."

In addition to questioning the dominant cultural values of the American Dream the value of material success can be downplayed in favor of developing an identity outside of the capitalist system of production and consumption. For example, Nas (2012) narrates: "I know you think my life is good 'cause my diamond piece, but my life has been good since I started finding peace," conveying the sentiment that he failed to find happiness and contentment through material success. Some hip-hop artists broadcast anti-materialist messages, such as Guru's (Gang Starr 2003) "Peace of Mine" in which he raps: "my sense of self and my mental health is much more powerful than any hint of wealth." Socially conscious rapper KRS-One (KRS-One, Kanye West, and Nas 2007) rejects the dominant cultural value that wealth and self-respect are related, indicating that he has "...no jewels on my neck. Why? I don't need 'em, I got your respect." More radically, O.C. (1994) claims that he would "...rather be broke and have a whole lot of respect..." in pursuit of his own anti-materialist principles.

Resistance against materialism is not restricted to criticizing the world external to hip-hop. Many artists have leveled criticism at the materialism within hip-hop and the music industry. For example, PMD (1994) sought to distance hip-hop music from materialism, insisting that artists focus on political and social commentary versus seeking material or status rewards, stating the proper course was to: "...save the temptation, money, keep the limos 'cause that's not hip-hop, that's a fashion show." Some artists yearn for the early years of hip-hop prior to the involvement of corporate music labels and the focus on commercially lucrative gangsta rappers that promote negative stereotypes of African Americans. Immortal Technique (2001) asks: "What the fuck happened to reality-spitting rhyme sayers? These days, everybody trying to be a thug or a player. Where did all the real motherfuckers go in the game? Bring back the break dancers and graffiti writers with fame." Dissatisfaction with the music industry is not new, particularly since hip-hop artists contend that corporate labels' only focus is on record sales and not improving the social conditions for the African American community. Commenting on this issue Cormega (2014), when discussing the music industry, states: "this is a business, they don't care about your lyrics.... controversy sells, so they support conflict" because this "...makes more profit."

In a shocking display of self-criticism Jay-Z (2003) claims that he avoided writing socio-political lyrics in his music and "...dumbed down for my audience to double my dollars..." even though "...truthfully, I wanna rhyme like Common Sense,[10] but I did five mil [million dollars] and ain't been rhyming like Common since." The necessity to sell records for the music industry is a focal concern for most hip-hop artists because "...if your album sell slow, bet you'll get dropped quick"[11] (Cormega 2014). However, despite the danger of career failure KRS-One (Boogie Down Productions 1990) maintains that he is "...the manifestation of study, not the manifestation of money" and that he "advance[s] through thought" instead of defining his self-worth on records that are "...manufactured and bought." In other words, KRS-One rejects the corporatized aspects of the music industry and instead focuses on the intellectual and political message within his music.

Bourdieu's ironic emphasis, extended in application to hip-hop, helps contextualize such issues as materialism, racism, sexism and homophobia, and also to link hip-hop practices with concerns for distinction, career, and corporate profits. Bourdieu's emphasis on conflict can help sensitize us to the importance of observing within hip-hop a wide variation between the uncritical and the critical, although recognizing critical aspects of hip-hop also involves a break with Bourdieu's pessimism about the critical potential of popular culture and especially marginalized subcultures among the poor.

11 Tragedy: Troubles, Coping and Perseverance in Hip-Hop

The theme of tragedy within hip-hop can encompass a wide range of attitudes and emotions concerning the difficulty and absurdity of life commonly faced

10 A rapper famous for his controversial progressive and anti-racist lyrical themes.

11 Get dropped – lose your recording contract, as in "dropped from the label."

by African Americans, particularly those residing in racially segregated neighborhoods characterized as the inner city. Thus, we should consider whether, through consumption or production of hip-hop, the inevitable and imminent challenges of the urban African American experience can be partially mitigated or transformed in a life-affirming manner.

Many hip-hop artists focus on the suffering and deprivation of inner city life with references to the challenges of living within an ethnic ghetto. It is not always clear that addressing such themes provides solace or affirms life, however the simple fact that these realities are taken up and respected as themes in hip-hop invites comparisons to tragic realism in other cultural genres. This is especially appropriate to consider when concerns for insecurity, suffering, and death are addressed as subcultural experiences separate from references to social divisions of class or race which would resonate more with themes of social activism than tragedy.

In one of the earliest hip-hop songs Grandmaster Flash and the Furious Five (1982) describe the ghetto as a place with "broken glass everywhere, people pissin' on the stairs, you know they just don't care" and where "junkies in the alley" are waiting "...with a baseball bat." Rapper Treach (Naughty by Nature 1991) warns outsiders to avoid the ghetto "...'cause you wouldn't understand the ghetto—so stay the fuck out of the ghetto!" When addressing ghetto life during a guest appearance on The Game's (2005) song "Hate It or Love It" rapper 50Cent warns listeners that there "...ain't nothing good in the hood, I'd run away from this bitch and never come back if I could."

The corrupting environment of the ghetto is frequently a topic in hip-hop, as Eric B. and Rakim (1990) claim that: "...you can hear the seven sins blowin' through the ghetto wind." B-Real (Cypress Hill 2001) raps "I lost my innocence at birth..." and suggests that through the influence of older, more established criminals his mind became filled with "deadly rituals... nothing spiritual." MF Grimm (Copywrite 2010) relates his circle of friends' life course from innocence to criminality stating that: "we went from candy bars, to handle bars, to hangin' in bars, to being behind bars." The endemic poverty of inner city life is pointedly, yet comically, addressed by DMX (1993), claiming that: "Times are hard in the ghetto, I gotta steal for a living; eating turkey-flavored Now & Laters for Thanksgiving." Narrating his early life as a child of the ghetto G.Dep (2001) claims that everyday he "...had a cigarette for breakfast ... cried for my lunch and sleep for dinner." Co$$ (2011) affirms that, for him "...pain took the softness away and left the hard half." Some hip-hop artists even credit personal suffering with providing their identity, as Pusha T (2013) forcefully proclaims: "This is my time, this is my hour. This is my pain, this is my name, this is my power." 50Cent (2003) further acknowledges the difficulty of life, concluding that "...life is hard, it'll leave you physically, mentally, and emotionally scarred."

Distrust and violence among African Americans are further themes relating to the negative environment of the ghetto. Wariness of persons within the black community is a common hip-hop theme because: "Nowadays you gots ta' walk the streets and watch your back, 'cause brothers with the gats [handguns] don't be knowin' how to act" (Shyheim 1994). The threat of violence is omnipresent within the ghetto, as Masta Ace (1995) describes being: "...surrounded by psychopathic little fellas, ghetto [dwellers], with ammunition in their [cellars]." Furthermore, due to the increased police presence as a result of The War on Drugs, duplicity and betrayal lurk around every corner of the ghetto so one cannot "...be too safe, 'cause niggas is two-faced" even though cooperating with the police as a "snitch" is a "lifetime scar" (Jay-Z 1998).

At face value it would appear that these dire accounts of African American life in the ghetto would only reinforce the negative for listeners of hip-hop. However, Nietzsche's observations on tragic culture suggest that aesthetic depictions of common troubles may result in an affirming transformation. A tragic aesthetic acknowledgement of troubles in hip-hop may promote resilience in the face of adversity. Hip-hop clearly is not about wallowing in self-pity, so it deserves careful consideration why the difficulties of the African American experience are such central themes.

While there are numerous examples of negative depictions of African American life in hip-hop, many artists also present more positive or nuanced messages within their lyrics. Oftentimes these lyrics could be said to tragically extol a sense of perseverance and persistence in the face of adversity. Thematically, many hip-hop songs acknowledge that suffering exists alongside good fortune.

In hip-hop music perhaps one of the most well-known examples of navigating a tragic existence is Ice Cube's (1992) "It Was a Good Day" where the author relates the details of an uncharacteristically positive day in which "...nobody I know got killed in South Central L.A." and in which he "...didn't even have to use my AK [AK-47 assault rifle]." Ice Cube (1992) further relates how unusual this is by claiming that the day before "...them fools tried to blast me." Despite enjoying the company of friends, playing dominos, and watching *Yo!* MTV *Raps* on television, Ice Cube (1992) wonders: "...will I live another 24 [hours]?" When asked about his motivations for writing "It Was a Good Day" Ice Cube explained: "...there's been the riots [the 1992 Los Angeles riots], people know I will deal with that ... But I rap all this gangsta stuff—what about all the good days I had?" (Odell 2005). While Ice Cube admits that his daily life did not involve using firearms he was otherwise "...near enough to that world to write about it" (Odell 2005). The now legendary song "It Was a Good Day" (Ice Cube 1992) reminds listeners to enjoy the pleasures of the present, despite being surrounded by a hostile and uncertain existence. Similarly, Jay-Z (1998) characterizes ghetto life as uncertain and in a constant state of flux, explaining that it is: "...funny what seven days can change" since "...it was all good just a week ago."

The balance between the positive and negative aspects of life is observable in hip-hop, perhaps communicated most directly in 50Cent's (2003) "Many Men (Wish Death)" in which he observes that: "sunny days wouldn't be special if it wasn't for rain. Joy wouldn't feel so good, if it wasn't for pain." Continuing this theme golden age rapper Scarface (2002) also invokes a weather metaphor, explaining that: "...though the sun is shining, there's a cloud in the sky lettin' me know that any moment there could be rain, and as beautiful as life is, there still can be pain." In the face of challenges hip-hop conveys that it is important to remain steadfast and "...be grateful for blessings..." so as to "...keep your essence" (2Pac 1995). Finally, hip-hop listeners are further reminded that beauty exists in the midst of the tragedy of ghetto life because even "...the sunset looks beautiful over the projects..." (Mobb Deep 1999). MC Lyte (1991) instructs that: "Some type of grief you must experience in order to appreciate happiness, 'cause if you are always satisfied life will just pass you by, you would have never tried." Here, MC Lyte (1991) acknowledges the contrast between misfortune and fortune, concluding that struggling against adversity is not only life-affirmative, but actually constitutes an authentic life. Additionally, owing to existential uncertainty, one should "...never question when you get the blessings, so don't get vexed when your life is stressed" (Shad 2010). Despite the suffering of life, Joe Budden (2010) reminds listeners to appreciate their current standing, warning: "...whatever you goin' through, could always be much worse—don't make a mistake, mistakin' your blessings for a curse." This is important because "...pessimism is an emotion, not a philosophy... Knowing what's wrong doesn't imply that you are right" (Immortal Technique 2009).

Hip-hop also frequently acknowledges the benefits of overcoming suffering. For example, Talib Kweli (2000) makes the Nietzschean observation that adversity engenders strength, stating: "a flower that grow[s] in the ghetto know[s] more about survival than the one from the fresh meadows." Here, Kweli (2000) reframes the harshness of living in the ghetto as a vehicle for developing personal fortitude; furthermore, individuals having grown up in that environment have a cause for celebration in having survived through such a difficult environment. Echoing this sentiment, AZ (Nas 1994) instructs his listeners to keep the "...street ghetto inside us, 'cause it provides us with the proper insight to guide us." Furthermore, harnessing strength in the face of adversity can be seen as a type of self-empowerment, as Ray West and OC (2014) relate that: "...life is love, heartache, and strain—yet the strength to overcome it all keeps me sane." Accepting that tragedy is part of life, Jay-Z (1996) advises: "...in order to survive [you] got to learn to live with regrets." In its ideal form pain can be understood as a force that must be transcended to reach a higher understanding, as Talib Kweli (2000) notes that he "...speak[s] the love language" whereas persons that "...don't love themselves ... speak from pain and anguish." However, transcendence beyond a painful existence is not guaranteed – sometimes the mere hope for a better life can provide motivation, as 2Pac (Digital Underground 1991) explains how he "...can't live with the negative and ghetto pains..." but he has "...faith, that's all it takes to get to where we're going" to reach a more peaceful, fulfilling existence.

While themes of coping and persistence are present in hip-hop lyrics, consuming and producing hip-hop music has its own intrinsic rewards through enjoyment of the medium. After all "art is essentially *affirmation, blessing, deification of existence...*" (Nietzsche 1968 [1888]: 434); music "...is required for pleasure..." because "...without music life would be an error" (Nietzsche 2005: 160). Hip-hop, along with many other cultural forms, can be appreciated for circumventing or allaying sobering truths.

There are many examples of hip-hop being celebrated as pleasant, perhaps particularly as a strategy to sidestep negative life experiences. Aptly named Tragedy Khadafi (2001) relates: "See, my Mom chose dope, my Pop chose the pipe, so I rhyme like a triple beam balance in life." Tragedy Khadafi here relates how he turned to hip-hop to alleviate the anxieties associated with his disappointing upbringing. Similarly, Common (2000) indicates that hip-hop allows him to "...escape through rhythms in search of peace and wisdom." The sentiment that hip-hop provides vital enjoyment is a common theme, as Digable Planets (1993) assert they "...live to love and we love to rock mics [perform hip-hop]." Veteran rapper Chuck D (Public Enemy 2012), when reflecting on the difficulties and disappointments of his personal life, takes strength from the fact that he: "...never, ever stopped that real hip-hop" and concludes with his music he has "...got it all." As perhaps the ultimate tribute to the power of hip-hop, rap artist Ka (2013) equates his musical career to a type of salvation when he sings: "The mic and I are like staff and shepherd." The theme of hip-hop being driven by a spiritual force also surfaces in the song "Ghetto Gospel" (2Pac 2004): "If I upset you, don't stress. Never forget that God isn't finished with me yet. I feel his hand on my brain, when I write rhymes I go blind and let the Lord do His thang." If there is a type of salvation involved, it is an inner-worldly salvation through activity of aesthetic value, not an other-worldly salvation predicated on an afterlife, or divine judgment.

Arguably, ironically, any cultural activity that helps marginalized groups to cope with suffering and insecurity, or to let off steam prior to their liberation, might be characterized as a type of defeatist accommodation. However, consideration of the content of hip-hop lyrics and interviews with hip-hop artists should lead one to a broader, more balanced understanding, one which sees much more than the symbolic activity of cultural dopes.

12 Conclusion

The ultimate value of different traditions of cultural analysis should arguably be considered in a broad context including their influence and the judgments of critical commentators, but also alternative theoretical perspectives, and heuristic value for examining specific empirical phenomena.

Bourdieu's contributions to social theory have clearly led to tremendous insights about matters including the reproduction of inequality in class societies and inter-relations between what can be called the economic and the cultural fields of society. With respect to culture specifically, his scholarship has greatly illuminated socio-economic interests and stakes in cultural institutions of education and the media as well as the arts. In these respects his impact has been truly distinctive, but also largely in keeping with pervasive concerns across critical scholarship – broadly conceived – for perhaps four generations now. While critical scholarship, to varying degrees, still holds out a hope of contributing to the dissemination of critical thinking, offering probing investigations of critical relevance, cultivating reflexive awareness, and advancing progressive causes, such has arguably not been its primary achievement, especially in scholarship and academia. It might be said that critical theories have primarily succeeded at cultivating a sophisticated cynicism about the ways in which culture can obfuscate, rationalize and perpetuate contingent and unnecessary structural injustices at the foundation of modern society. Culture thereby frustrates progress towards progressive ideals rather than facilitating transformative understanding and a world-historical improvement of social conditions and social relations. This variety of insight has a pivotal practical significance, but the pivot has yet to occur and does not appear to be coming anytime soon.

Bourdieu has done a tremendous service to the understanding of culture by teasing out the connections between, on the one hand, the cultural distinctions and tastes which often command our respect and inspire much of our commitments and our consumerism, and on the other hand the sordid realities of ideological manipulation and economic domination. His work is illuminating, but perhaps only insofar as he engaged with a disenchanting line of criticism in which everything must be revealed to be profane or vulgar (Maton 2005; cf Bourdieu 1984: 510–512), and even religion is reduced to a crass, redundant field within a conflict-ridden class system (Willey 2016).[12] A charitably balanced review would have it that this disenchanting reductionism reflects a strategic and provisional analytic focus (Maton 2005) rather than a stunted vision or a principled objection to an ultimately broader understanding, but in any case Bourdieu's model of culture is in a fundamental sense *partial* in a manner that is not only profaning, but dehumanizing.

Nietzsche is a familiar reference, but it is also true that his significance for social thought today is commonly overlooked, and even some of those who draw from him might not be as eager to reference him as they are with other figures who are more contemporary or who were much more conventional academic authors, who were much more successful at training junior colleagues, perhaps forming schools or founding institutions. The reputations of other famous figures in modern social thought also, generally, were not subjected to remarkable patterns of intellectual misappropriation, contortion, and ensuing slander which started with problematic custodial arrangements and intellectual property rights during Nietzsche's long period of mental incapacity and terminal illness, and got worse as the German nationalist ideology of the late 1800s – which so influenced his brother in law – later fed into German National Socialism in the 1930's.

Nietzsche had a remarkable skill at using historical analysis both to suggest inspiring potentials for human culture, as with his analysis in *The Birth of Tragedy*, and his "On the Uses and Disadvantages of History for Life" (in Nietzsche 1983 [1874]: 57–123), and to suggest all-too-human origins behind cultural authorities, including supernatural beings and moral codes, as with his *Genealogy of Morals*. The latter method was taken up very famously and to great effect by Foucault in his critiques of modern penality and later in his works on sexuality, both of which explore in a way the colonization of subjectivity by discourses of power, ultimately re-evaluating the modern experiences of self and governance.

The disenchanting, cynical dimensions to the genealogical analyses of both Foucault and Nietzsche are related indirectly but in the most crucial manner to their interests in aesthetics. Aesthetics hold out the promise of meaningful evaluation, arguably extending even to the realm of ethics (see e.g. Winchester 1994) at a time when traditions and institutions of evaluation have seen their authority questioned in light of scientific discoveries, globalization and

12 Consider the following quote from Bourdieu in Shusterman (2015: 453–454): "Sociology unveils the self-deception, the collectively entertained and encouraged lying to oneself which, in every society, is at the foundation of the most sacred values and therefore, of all social existence" including "the cult of art and science" (Bourdieu 1990b: 188).

cultural relativism, historicism, secularization ... and critical cultural analyses. More importantly, aesthetics not only involves meaningful interpretation and evaluation – attributes it shares with traditional authorities and also critical theories – but also can have a robust affirmative dimension which cannot be reduced to one half of an invidious distinction, as high culture is defined relative to low culture, high-brow relative to low-brow, and the distinctive is defined relative to the passé, the cliché, the mass-produced, the plebian.

Compared to critiques provided in 20th century critical analyses, Nietzsche was comparably incisive and effective in his withering analysis of Christian history and morality, and modern Western culture more generally. However, Nietzsche has bequeathed to us much more than critical studies. His writings are themselves in many cases artistic achievements, in his prose analyses as well as in his fictional narrative of Zarathustra and his mastery of the aphoristic form. But most importantly, Nietzsche saw much more to culture than conflict, intrigue, sordid interests and veiled violence. Nietzsche's probing, heretical cynicism of the most valued cultural inheritance of Western civilization achieved an absolutely world-historical significance, however culture for Nietzsche also was a field of human experience with agency, creativity, beauty, virtuosity, and hope, a field of human experience inevitably engaged with universal aspects of human existence, and capable at least occasionally of remarkable authenticity and affirmation of life.

Nietzsche therefore engaged questions of meaning and value with incredible respect even if he was unsatisfied with available answers. In the sociology of religion, such issues have been addressed partly in terms of the problem of theodicy (e.g. Weber 1964 [1922]; Berger 1969), however for Nietzsche the problem of theodicy had two analogues, one being the problem of Christianity, which was subjected to genealogical critique, and one being the problem of identifying life-affirming cultural forms which could provide wisdom and resilience without falsifying the human condition. Tragedy was the earliest and most collective illustration of such a life-affirming cultural form.

There are many interests at work in cultural analysis, of which critique is seemingly dominant. However, following Max Weber, another important interest is in valid interpretive understanding, or adequacy at the level of meaning. Following Nietzsche, a further potential interest is to showcase through historical examples life-affirming figures and cultural forms. Hip-hop, as one important example of cultural phenomena among an indefinite number of others, can certainly be understood better, following Bourdieu, with reference to strategies of distinction, symbolic violence, relations between economic and social and cultural forms of capital, fields of production and consumption structured by class relations, and references also to dispositions and tastes which often enough lead the dispossessed and the marginalized to engage in practices putting them on a trajectory whereby their past becomes the future. But hip-hop can be observed to be more than that, if one is open to discovering more than that, open to recognizing within a culture the phenomena of human understanding, agency, creativity, forms of survival and perseverance that amount to more than social reproduction, a will to life that transcends concerns of social position and social mobility ... forms of affirmation neither restricted to the self-satisfaction of elites nor reducible to ideological misrecognition ironically attributed to the masses.

Theorists of culture, especially now given the resources of poststructuralist and post-modern social thought, have at their disposal enough ironic devices and techniques of academic argument and critical interpretation not only to reveal corrupting or conservative ideological dimensions in every last corner of human culture and subjectivity, but also to de-certify each other in an endless regress of penetrating critical cross-fire.[13] A belated consideration of Nietzsche's more appreciative observations concerning culture could salvage the kind of insight Nietzsche recommended as an advantage of history for life. Ironic critique neglects aspects of human culture which, if acknowledged by critics, would help restore the role of humanism and optimism in cultural analysis,[14] and without tying these to elaborate and inherently self-important

13 Even if some theorists and theories might somehow avoid being down-graded on the basis of an author's sex, gender, race, religion, nationality, language, disciplinary training, occupation, philosophy of science, methodological skills, and politics, there are still such concerns as internal distortions of motivation and understanding which, following Freud's notion of the unconscious, can be alleged by ironic psychological and social-psychological attributions, and then Bourdieu's ironic structural determinants of human judgment and interests, and Foucault's ironic co-optations of human subjectivity extending even to problematization and politicization of the pursuit of truth, and the prospect of having one's positions critically interrogated to the point of deconstruction, following Derrida, and the objection from ethnomethodologists that critical scholars trade uncritically in vernacular skills which they will not acknowledge or study. There is also a formidable range of troubling logical and epistemological objections relating to such faults and fallacies and follies as reification and hypostatization, the genetic fallacy, the ecological fallacy, anthropomorphism of human ideations and human aggregates, objectivism, subjectivism, determinism, naivete, scientism, Utopianism, reductionism, essentialism, tautological reasoning, teleological explanation, self-contradiction, opacity, elitism, apologetics, going Native, arm-chair theorizing, navel-gazing, lack of historical vision, lack of reflexivity, failure of sociological imagination, and allowing ordinary language to go on holiday to the point of terminal conceptual confusion. There are also Popper's demarcation criteria, suggesting in part the wonderfully inescapable irony that only falsifiable claims should be taken seriously in social science; if a claim is not subject to disproof it cannot be empirically grounded.

14 Fay discusses, for example, what he describes as a humanist, secularized variant of estrangement theory, which suggests "an enlarged view of the possibilities of human power

projects of grand theory. The point is not that we should replace critical theories with complacency theories,[15] but rather that critical theories have never and cannot be allowed to ever monopolize determinations of cultural value and validity. Like literary criticism, cultural critics need to be able to offer critique, even radical critique, without scorching the earth or playing Noah in the Flood. Given the absence of any Archimedean point allowing an omniscient and unassailable vantage upon cultural phenomena, it is worth reconsidering the intellectual virtues of humility and appreciation even as we remain certain that social relations can and should be transformed, and that viable progress requires not just structural change but critical engagement with the confusion and prejudice which prevent structural change.

References

Note: Artist stage names are alphabetized by first name.

2Pac. 2004. "Ghetto Gospel." On *Loyal to the Game* [CD]. Amar Entertainment/Interscope Records.

2Pac. 1995. "Me Against the World." On *Me Against the World* [CD]. Out Da Gutta Records/Interscope/Atlantic Records.

50Cent. 2003. "Many Men (Wish Death)." On *Get Rich or Die Tryin'* [CD]. Shady/Aftermath/Interscope/Universal Records.

Asante, Molefi. 2008. *It's Bigger than Hip-Hop: The Rise of the Post-Hip-Hop Generation.* New York: Saint Martin's Press.

Atkinson, J. Maxwell. 1978. *Discovering Suicide: Studies in the Social Organization of Sudden Death.* New York: Palgrave Macmillan.

Baldwin, Davarian L. 1999. "Black Empires, White Desires: The Spatial Politics of Identity in the Age of Hip Hop." *Black Renaissance* 2(2): 138–159.

---

and human reason to deal with the problems of human life … humans are not only capable of understanding who they are and what they need, they are further capable of organizing their affairs on the basis of this understanding so as to produce a satisfying existence" (1987: 20). This can be contrasted with an arguable optimistic undercurrent in Bourdieu's work, by which sociology "frees us by *freeing us* from the illusion of freedom" (Bourdieu 1990b: 28; quoted and italics added in Peters 2014: 141).

15 As Shusterman rightly observes, "There is merit in Bourdieu's critique of the cognitive limits of aesthetic experience in its subjective and religiously romantic mode of immediacy" (2015: 448). However the fact that aesthetic experience has limits does not necessitate that it be treated dismissively, in a reductive, minimalist manner (2015: 451–453). As Prior suggests, the point should be to go beyond determinism without falling into a micro-aestheticism or aesthetic individualism, to move *past* theoretical imperialism rather than from one form to another (2011: 134).

Berard, Tim J. 2013. "Under the Shadow of the Authoritarian Personality: Elias, Fromm, and Alternative Social Psychologies of Authoritarianism." In *Norbert Elias and Social Theory*, edited by Francois Depelteau and Tatiana Landini, 209–243. New York: Palgrave MacMillan.

Berard, Tim J. 1999. "Dada Between Nietzsche's *Birth of Tragedy* and Bourdieu's *Distinction*: Existenz and Conflict in Cultural Analysis." *Theory, Culture & Society* 16(1): 141–165.

Berger, Peter L. 1969. *The Sacred Canopy: Elements of a Sociological Theory of Religion*. Garden City, NY: Doubleday.

Berkowitz, Peter. 1995. *Nietzsche: The Ethics of an Immoralist*. Cambridge, MA: Harvard University Press.

Best, Steven, and Douglas Kellner. 1999. "Rap, Black Rage, and Racial Difference." *Enculturation* 2(2): 1–23.

Big L. 2000. "Holdin' it Down." On *The Big Picture* [CD]. Rawkus/Flamboyant Entertainment.

Big L. 1995. "No Endz, No Skinz." On *Lifestylez Ov Da Poor & Dangerous* [CD]. Columbia Records.

Boogie Down Productions. 1990. "Original Lyrics." On *Edutainment* [CD]. Jive/RCA Records.

Boogie Down Productions. 1989. "Who Will Protect Us from You?" On *Ghetto Music: The Blueprint of Hip Hop* [CD]. Jive/RCA Records.

Bourdieu, Pierre. 1997. *Pascalian Meditations*, translated by Richard Nice. Stanford, CA: Stanford University Press.

Bourdieu, Pierre. 1993. *The Field of Cultural Production: Essays on Art and Literature*, edited by Randal Johnson. New York: Columbia University Press.

Bourdieu, Pierre. 1990a. *The Logic of Practice*, translated by Richard Nice. Stanford, CA: Stanford University Press.

Bourdieu, Pierre. 1990b. *In Other Words: Essays towards a Reflexive Sociology*, translated by Matthew Adamson. Stanford, CA: Stanford University Press.

Bourdieu, Pierre. 1989. "Social Space and Symbolic Power." *Sociological Theory* 7(1): 14–25. Translated by Lois J.D. Wacquant.

Bourdieu, Pierre. 1986. "The Forms of Capital." In *Handbook of Theory and Research for the Sociology of Education*, edited by John G. Richardson, article translated by Richard Nice. New York: Greenwood.

Bourdieu, Pierre. 1984. *Distinction: A Social Critique of the Judgment of Taste*, translated by Richard Nice. Cambridge, MA: Harvard University Press.

Bourdieu, Pierre. 1977. *Outline of a Theory of Practice*, translated by Richard Nice. New York: Cambridge University Press.

Burnham, Douglas, and Martin Jesinghausen. 2010. *Nietzsche's Birth of Tragedy: A Reader's Guide*. New York: Continuum.

Clark, John, Stuart Hall, Tony Jefferson, and Brian Roberts. 2006 [1971]. "Subcultures, Cultures, and Class." In *Resistance through Rituals: Youth Subcultures in Post-War Britain,* second edition, edited by Stuart Hall and Tony Jefferson, 3–59. Abingdon: Routledge.

Clay, Andreanna. 2003. "Keepin' It Real: Black Youth, Hip-hop, and Black Identity." *American Behavioral Scientist* 46(10): 1346–1358.

Clinton, Sanders. 1990. "'A Lot of People Like It': The Relationship Between Deviance and Popular Culture." In *Marginal Conventions: Popular Culture, Mass Media, and Social Deviance*, edited by Clinton Sanders, 3–13. Bowling Green, Ohio: Bowling Green State University Popular Press.

Co$$. 2011. "Pot Ash." On *Before I Awoke* [CD]. Tres Records.

Collins, Patricia Hill. 2006. *From Black Power to Hip-hop: Racism, Nationalism, and Feminism.* Philadelphia, PA: Temple University Press.

Common. 2016. "Letter to the Free." On *Let's Get Free.* [CD].

Common. 2000. "The 6th Sense." On *Like Water for Chocolate* [CD]. MCA Records.

Conway, Daniel W. 1994. "Genealogy and Critical Method." In *Nietzsche, Genealogy, Morality: Essays on Nietzsche's On the Genealogy of Morals*, edited by Richard Schacht, 318–333. Berkeley, CA: University of California Press.

Copywrite. 2010. "Three Story Building." On *The Life and Times of Peter Nelson* [CD]. Man Bites Dog Records.

Cormega. 2014. "Industry." On *Mega Philosophy* [CD]. Slimstyle Records.

Cypress Hill. 2001. "Bitter." On *Stoned Raiders* [CD]. Columbia Records.

Dead Prez. 2008. "Hip-Hop." On *Let's Get Free* [CD]. Loud/Columbia/Relativity Records.

Digable Planets. 1993. "Where I'm From." On *Reachin' (A New Refutation of Time and Space)* [CD]. Pendulum/Elektra Records.

Digital Underground. 1991. "The DFLO Shuttle." On *Sons of the P* [CD]. Tommy Boy/T.N.T. Recording.

DMX. 1993. "Born Loser." On Born Loser [CD Single]. Ruffhouse Records.

Durkheim, Emile. 2002 [1897]. *Suicide: A Study in Sociology*. Second edition. Routledge.

Eric B. and Rakim. 1990. "In the Ghetto." On *Let the Rhythm Hit 'Em* [CD]. MCA Records.

Eric B. and Rakim. 1987. "Paid in Full." On *Paid in Full* [CD]. 4th & B'way/Island Records.

Fay, Brian. 1987. *Critical Social Science.* Ithaca, NY: Cornell University Press.

Foucault, Michel. 1984 [1971]. "Nietzsche, Genealogy, History." In *The Foucault Reader,* edited by Paul Rabinow, 76–100. New York: Pantheon.

Game, The. 2014. "Don't Shoot." On *Don't Shoot* [CD Single]. Digital Release.

Game, The. 2005. "Hate It or Love It," in *The Documentary.* G-Unit/Aftermath/Interscope.

Gang Starr. 2003. "Peace of Mine." On *The Ownerz* [CD]. Virgin/EMI Records.

Garfinkel, Harold. 1967. *Studies in Ethnomethodology*. Englewood Cliffs, NJ: Prentice Hall.

G.Dep. 2001. "Everyday." On *Child of the Ghetto* [CD]. Bad Boy Records.

Geto Boys, The. 1990. "City Under Siege." On *The Geto Boys* [CD]. Def American/Warner Brothers Records.

Grandmaster Flash and the Furious Five. 1982. "The Message." On *The Message* [CD]. Sugar Hill Records.

Grattan, Laura. 2012. "Pierre Bourdieu and Populism: The Everyday Politics of Outrageous Resistance." *The Good Society* 21(2): 194–218.

Griller, Robin. 2000. "The Return of the Subject? The Methodology of Pierre Bourdieu." In *Pierre Bourdieu*, Vol. 1., edited by Derek Robbins, 187–208. London: Sage.

Hanchard, Michael. 2003. "Acts of Misrecognition: Transformational Black Politics, Anti-Imperialism and the Ethnocentrisms of Pierre Bourdieu and Loic Wacquant." *Theory, Culture & Society* 20(4): 5–29.

Harris, Marvin. 1980. *Cultural Materialism: The Struggle for a Science of Culture*. New York: Random House.

Hebdidge, Dick. 1979. *Subculture: The Meaning of Style*. London and New York: Routledge.

Hess, Mickey. 2005. "Metal Faces, Rap Masks: Identity and Resistance in Hip-hop's Persona Artist." *Popular Music and Society* 28(3): 297–311.

Ice Cube. 1992. "Today Was a Good Day." On *The Predator* [CD]. Priority/EMI.

Immortal Technique. 2009. "Mistakes." On *The 3rd World* [CD]. Viper Records/Fontana.

Immortal Technique. 2003. "Cause of Death." On *Revolutionary Volume 2* [CD]. Viper Records/Fontana.

Immortal Technique. 2001. "Revolutionary." On *Revolutionary Volume 1* [CD]. Viper Records/Fontana.

J. Cole. 2014. "January 28th." On *2014 Forest Hills Drive* [CD]. Roc Nation/Dreamville/Columbia Records.

Jackson, John. 2001. *Harlemworld: Doing Race and Class in Contemporary Black America*. Chicago, IL: University of Chicago Press.

Jay-Z. 2003. "Moment of Clarity." On *The Black Album* [CD]. Roc-A-Fella/Def Jam.

Jay-Z. 1998. "A Week Ago." On *Volume 2… Hard Knock Life* [CD]. Roc-A-Fella/Def Jam.

Jay-Z. 1996. "Regrets." On *Reasonable Doubt* [CD]. Roc-A-Fella/Priority Records.

Joe Budden. 2010. "Welcome to Real Life." On *Mood Muzik 4: A Turn for the Worst.* [CD]. eOne Music/22 Entertainment.

Ka. 2013. "Peace Akhi." On *Night's Gambit* [CD]. Ironworks.

Kalberg, Stephen. 1987. "The Origin and Expansion of *Kulturpessimismus*: The Relationship Between Public and Private Spheres in Early-Twentieth-Century Germany." *Sociological Theory* 5: 150–164.

Kanye West. 2013. "New Slaves." On *Yeezus* [CD]. Roc-A-Fella/Def Jam.

Kanye West. 2004. "Never Let Me Down." On *The College Dropout* [CD]. Roc-A-Fella/Def Jam.

Kauppi, Niilo. 2000. "Scientific Practice and Epistemological *a Priori*: Durkheim, Mauss, Levi-Strauss, Bourdieu." In *Pierre Bourdieu*, Vol. 1., edited by Derek Robbins, 229–243. London: Sage.

Kelley, Robin. 1994. *Race Rebels: Culture, Politics and the Black Working Class*. New York: Free Press.

Kendrick Lamar. 2015. "Hood Politics." On *To Pimp a Butterfly* [CD]. Top Dawg/Aftermath/Interscope Records.

Keyes, Cheryl. 2002. *Rap Music and Street Consciousness*. Urbana and Chicago, IL: University of Chicago Press.

Killer Mike. 2012. "Reagan." On R.A.P. *Music* [CD]. Williams Street Records.

Kitwana, Bakara. 2005. *Why White Kids Love Hip-hop: Wankstas, Wiggers, Wannabes, and the New Reality of Race in America.* New York: Civitas Books.

Kitwana, Bakara. 2002. *The Hip-Hop Generation: Young Blacks and the Crisis in African American Culture.* New York: Perseus Books Group.

Kool Moe Dee. 1987. "They Want Money." On *Knowledge is King* [CD]. Jive/RCA Records.

KRS-One, Kanye West, and Nas. 2007. "Classic (Better Than I've Ever Been)." On *Classic (Better Than I've Ever Been).* [Digital Download] Nike.

Lakim Shabazz. 1990. "No Justice No Peace." On *The Lost Tribe of Shabazz* [CD]. Tuff City.

Leiter, Brian. 2002. *Nietzsche on Morality*. New York: Routledge.

Lupe Fiasco. 2012. "Strange Fruition." On *Food and Liquor II: The Great American Rap Album Part 1* [CD]. 1st & 5th/Atlantic Records.

Lynch, Michael. 2012. "Revisiting the Cultural Dope." *Human Studies* 35: 223–233.

Mannheim, Karl. 2015 [1929]. *Ideology and Utopia: An Introduction to the Sociology of Knowledge*, translated by Louis Wirth and Edward Shils. Eastford, CO: Martino Fine Books.

Masta Ace. 1995. "Maintain." On *Sittin' on Chrome 12* [CD]. Delicious Vinyl.

Maton, Karl. 2005. "The Sacred and the Profane: The Arbitrary Legacy of Pierre Bourdieu." *European Journal of Cultural Studies* 8(1): 101–112.

MC Lyte. 1991. "Search 4 the Lyte." On *Act Like You Know* [CD]. First Priority Music.

Merton, Robert K. 1968 [1949]. *Social Theory and Social Structure*. Enlarged edition. New York: Free Press.

Merton, Robert K. 1938. "Social Structure and Anomie." *American Sociological Review* 3: 672–682.

Middleton, Richard. 1990. *Studying Popular Music*. Philadelphia, PA: Open University Press.

Miller-Young, Mireille. 2008. "Hip-Hop Honeys and Da Hustlaz: Black Sexualities in the New Hip-Hop Pornography." *Meridians* 8(1): 261–292.

Mobb Deep. 1999. "Streets Raised Me." On *Murda Muzik.* [CD]. Loud/Columbia Records.

Mobb Deep. 1995. "Eye for an Eye (Your Beef is Mines)." On *The Infamous* [CD]. Loud Records.

Nas. 2012. "Loco-Motive." On *Life is Good* [CD]. Def Jam.

Nas. 1994. "Life's a Bitch (Featuring AZ)." On *Illmatic* [CD]. Columbia Records.

Naughty by Nature. 1991. "Everything's Gonna Be Alright." On *Naughty by Nature* [CD]. Tommy Boy Records.

Nietzsche, Friedrich. 2005. *The Anti-Christ, Ecce Homo, Twilight of the Idols, and Other Writings.* Translated by Judith Norman. New York: Cambridge University Press.

Nietzsche, Friedrich. 1994 [1894]. *Philosophy in the Tragic Age of the Greeks*, translated by Marianne Cowan. Washington, DC: Regnery.

Nietzsche, Friedrich. 1985 [1883–1891]. *Thus Spoke Zarathustra: A Book for Everyone and No One*, translated by R.J. Hollingdale. New York: Penguin.

Nietzsche, Friedrich. 1983 [1873–1876]. *Untimely Meditations*, translated by R.J. Hollingdale. New York: Cambridge University Press.

Nietzsche, Friedrich. 1968 [1888]. *The Will to Power*, translated by Walter Kaufmann and R.J. Hollingdale. New York: Vintage.

Nietzsche, Friedrich. 1967a [1887/1908]. *On the Genealogy of Morals* and *Ecce Homo*, edited and translated by Walter Kaufmann. New York: Vintage.

Nietzsche, Friedrich. 1967b [1872/1888]. *The Birth of Tragedy* and *The Case of Wagner*, edited and translated by Walter Kaufmann. New York: Vintage.

Notorious B.I.G. 1997. "Long Kiss Goodnight." On *Life After Death* [CD]. Bad Boy Records/Arista.

N.W.A. 1988. "Fuck tha Police." On *Straight Outta Compton.* Ruthless Records/Priority.

O.C. 1994. "Time's Up." On *Word... Life* [CD]. Wild Pitch Records.

Odell, Michael. 2005. "The Greatest Songs Ever! It Was a Good Day: How Did Ice Cube Go From Parental-Advisor Poster Boy to Family-Friendly Movie Star? By Showing His Cuddly Side." *Blender.* Accessed by archive at Wayback Machine: https://web.archive.org/web/20071013131651/http://www.blender.com/guide/articles.aspx?id=1988.

Orr, John. 1977. *Tragic Realism & Modern Society: Studies in the Sociology of the Modern Novel.* Pittsburgh, PA: University of Pittsburgh Press.

Owen, David. 1994. *Maturity & Modernity: Nietzsche, Weber, Foucault and the Ambivalence of Reason.* New York: Routledge.

Paris. 1992. "Bush Killa." On *Sleeping with the Enemy* [CD]. Scarface Records.

Persaud, Jerry. 2006. "The Signature of Hip-hop: A Sociological Perspective." *International Journal of Criminology and Sociological Theory* 4(1): 626–647.

Peters, Gabriel. 2014. "Explanation, Understanding and Determinism in Pierre Bourdieu's Sociology." *History of the Human Sciences* 27(1): 124–149.

PMD. 1994. "Shade Business." On *Shade Business* [CD]. RCA Records.

Pollner, Melvin. 1987. *Mundane Reason: Reality in Everyday and Sociological Discourse*. New York: Cambridge University Press.

Prior, Nick. 2011. "Critique and Renewal in the Sociology of Music: Bourdieu and Beyond." *Cultural Sociology* 5(1): 121–138.

Public Enemy. 2012. "Everything." On *The Evil Empire of Everything* [CD]. Enemy Records/Spit Digital.

Public Enemy. 1991. "Rebirth." On *Apocalypse '91... The Enemy Strikes Black* [CD]. Def Jam/Columbia Records.

Public Enemy. 1990. "Fight the Power." On *Fear of a Black Planet* [CD]. Def Jam/Columbia Records.

Pusha T. 2013. "King Push." On *My Name is My Name* [CD]. Good Music/Def Jam.

Ray West and OC. 2014. "Gotta Luv It." On *Ray's Café* [CD]. Red Apples 45.

Rebollo-Gil, Guillermo, and Amanda Moras. 2012. "Black Women and Black Men in Hip Hop Music: Misogyny, Violence and the Negotiation of (White Owned) Space." *The Journal of Popular Culture* 45(1): 118–132.

Roberts, Michael, and Christine Payne, eds. 2019. "Nietzsche and Critical Theory." Special Issue. *Critical Sociology* 45(2).

Roots, The. 2004. "Guns are Drawn." On *The Tipping Point* [CD]. Geffen/Interscope.

Rose, Tricia. 2008. *The Hip-hop Wars: What We Talk About When We Talk About Hip-hop – And Why It Matters*. New York: Basic Books.

Run-DMC. 1984. "It's Like That." On *Run-DMC* [CD]. Profile/Arista.

Scarface. 2002. "What Can I Do?" On *The Fix* [CD]. Def Jam South/Def Jam Records.

Semi Hendrix. 2015. "Stone Cold Hustler." On *Breakfast at Banksy's* [CD]. Mello Music Group.

Shad. 2010. "Rose Garden." On *TSOL* [CD]. Black Box/Decon.

Show & A.G. 2007. "Land of the Free." On *Live Hard* [CD EP]. D.I.T.C. Records.

Shusterman, Richard. 2015. "Pierre Bourdieu and Pragmatist Aesthetics: Between Practice and Experience." *New Literary History* 46: 435–457.

Shyheim. 1994. "On and On." On *AKA The Rugged Child* [CD]. Virgin/EMI Records.

Sleinis, E.E. 1994. *Nietzsche's Revaluation of Values: A Study in Strategies*. Chicago, IL: University of Illinois Press.

Slug. 2001. "They're All Gonna Laugh @ You." On *Lucy Ford: The Atmosphere EP* [CD]. Rhymesayers Entertainment/Fat Beats.

Solomon, Robert C. 1994. "One Hundred Years of *Ressentiment*: Nietzsche's *Genealogy of Morals*." In *Nietzsche, Genealogy, Morality: Essays on Nietzsche's On the Genealogy of Morals*, edited by Richard Schacht, 95–126. Berkeley, CA: University of California Press.

Storey, John. 1996. *Cultural Studies & the Study of Popular Culture: Theories and Methods*. Athens, GA: University of Georgia Press.

Sykes, Gresham. 1958. *The Society of Captives: A Study of a Maximum Security Prison.* Princeton University Press.

Talib Kweli. 2000. "Love Language." On *Trains of Thought: Reflection Eternal Album* [CD]. Rawkus Records.

Tragedy Khadafi. 2001. "Permanently Scarred." On *Against All Odds* [CD]. Gee Street/V2/BMG Records.

Trondman, Mats, Lund, Anna, and Lund, Stefan. 2011. "Socio-Symbolic Homologies: Exploring Paul Willis' Theory of Cultural Forms." *European Journal of Cultural Studies* 14(5): 11–26.

Wacquant, Loic. 1996. "From Charisma to Persona: On Boxing and Social Being." In *The Charisma of Sport and Race*, 23–34. Berkeley, CA: Doreen B. Townsend Center for the Humanities.

Watkins, Craig. 2005. *Hip-hop Matters: Politics, Pop Culture, and the Struggle for the Soul of a Movement.* Boston, MA: Beacon Press.

Webber, Sabra J., and Margaret R. Lynd, eds. 1996. *Fantasy or Ethnography? Irony and Collusion in Subaltern Representation.* Papers in Comparative Studies 8, Ohio State University.

Weber, Max. 2010 [1904/1905]. *The Protestant Ethic and the Spirit of Capitalism.* Revised 1920 edition, translated by Stephen Kalberg. Oxford University Press.

Weber, Max. 1964 [1922]. *The Sociology of Religion*, translated by Ephraim Fischoff. Boston, MA: Beacon Press.

Willey, Robin D. 2016. "Liminal Practice: Pierre Bourdieu, Madness, and Religion." *Social Compass* 63(1): 125–141.

Williams, Raymond. 1966. *Modern Tragedy.* Stanford, CA: Stanford University Press.

Willis, Paul. 1978. *Profane Culture.* London: RoutledgeFalmer.

Winchester, James J. 1994. *Nietzsche's Aesthetic Turn: Reading Nietzsche after Heidegger, Deleuze, Derrida.* Albany, NY: State University of New York Press.

Yinger, Milton. 1960. "Contraculture and Subculture." *American Sociological Review* 25(5): 625–635.

CHAPTER 5

Nietzsche's Economy: Revisiting the Slave Revolt in Morals

Allison Merrick

It is beyond dispute that in some sense or other Nietzsche (2005) seeks, *inter alia*, to engender a "*revaluation of all values*" (IV: 1). *On the Genealogy of Morality*, a work he describes in his autobiography (2005) as "three decisive preliminary studies…for a revaluation of all values," (III: 8) contains, arguably at least, Nietzsche's account (1997) of one such successful "*conceptual transformation*" (I: 4) – "that slave revolt in morality" – which he claims has "two thousand years behind it and which we no longer see because it – has been victorious" (I: 7). But however incisive such events in the history of morality may be, it remains a point of contention what role, if any, economy plays in such re-evaluative projects (cf. Andrew 1995; McCarthy 1994; Shapiro 1994; Shapiro 1991).

Indeed, many commentators have castigated Nietzsche for a "lack of concern for social and economic questions" (Löwith 1965: 176) or, for what very well might amount to the same thing, "his insufficient analysis of the socio-economic conditions of production" (Spiekermann 1999: 229). A point made clearer, some have found, by means of a tidy comparison: "whereas Marx focuses solely on the economic factors driving social change, Nietzsche focuses solely on the philosophical and religious ones" (Katsafanas 2016: 208). To put it another way, Nietzsche's re-evaluative project (2005), which may create the space for a "Yes-saying without reservation, even to suffering, even to guilt, even to everything that is questionable and strange in existence" (III: 2), hits only philosophical and religious notes, not economic ones. So, if claims like these are right, it may seem strange to then place the notion of "economy," however broadly interpreted or applied, at the fore of our analysis of this crucial text. But that is just what I seek to do in this essay.

This move may lose its initial air of eccentricity if we return again to *On the Genealogy of Morality* and note the following moments: in the First Essay, for example, we know that that noble values, as well as the set of values that succeed them, bear some relation to the economic conditions of enslavement (I: 7; I: 10); in the Second Essay Nietzsche notably insists that we heed the ways in which "the feeling of guilt, of personal obligation" find their origins in the relationships "between buyer and seller, creditor and debtor" (II: 9), or perhaps more pointedly, there too in the Second Essay, he remarks that it is the complex creditor/debtor relations where "one person first *measured himself* against another"; finally in the Third Essay he holds that the so-called "blessing of work" and all the "mechanical activity" that goes with it – such as absolute regularity, punctilious and unthinking obedience, a mode of life fixed once and for all, fully occupied time, a certain permission, indeed training for 'impersonality,' for self-forgetfulness, for '*incuria sui*' – may very well serve as a balm for excess, unexplained suffering (III: 18).

The primary objective of this essay then is to tease out and bring to the fore these aspects of Nietzsche's investigation into the origins of our moral modes of evaluation and to defend the view that a certain accounting of the idea "Nietzsche's economy," is indeed instructive. Towards such an end, this paper has the following form: first, I raise the preliminary issue: namely, what might be meant by "Nietzsche's economy"? I review four possible candidates before making the case that the best approach is to heed the ways in which the complex economic relations of creditor/debtor characterize subjectivity. Finally, I attempt to lend credence to this interpretation by revisiting what Nietzsche (2005) labels that "countermovement" – "the great rebellion against the dominion of *noble* values" (III: 8) – and offer a couple of examples of how economic relations might very well engender modes of subjectivity.

1 Nietzsche's Economy

So, what is it that we are attempting to get at via the notion of "Nietzsche's economy"? There appear to be at least five ways in which such a question, preliminarily at least, has been, or at least might be, answered.

First, it can refer to Nietzsche's use of key concepts, "exchange, credit, debit, sacrifice, labor, possession, expenditure, surplus, measuring, weighing, evaluating," which might very well, and when taken together, serve to represent his economic philosophy (Shapiro 1991: 39; cf. Sedgwick 2007: x). The upshot of such a view is that it may help us to see clearly the ways in which "economic notions are at work in all human endeavors" (Sedgwick 2007: x), a point which ostensibly is on offer in Section 8 of the Second Essay of *On the Genealogy of Morality* where Nietzsche remarks: "Setting prices, determining values, contriving equivalences, exchanging – these preoccupied the earliest thinking of man to so great an extent that in a certain sense they constitute thinking *as such*…" (II: 8). On the face of it, at least, this account looks plausible for how it can demonstrate that the notions are ubiquitous both in the work of Nietzsche and, further, "in all human endeavors" (Sedgwick 2007: x).

But despite this initial promise, this interpretation is not strict enough to be ultimately helpful for our purposes. The worry, plain enough, is that in focusing on Nietzsche's use of terms that bear some relation to the realm of economy it still remains unclear that these notions are squarely *economic* in kind. So, for example, it may be apparent to many that "surplus" is undeniably an economic notion, but there are times when Nietzsche uses it to refer to something that is not fiscal in kind (2005 III: 1). But there is more. It also seems to reify our concepts in a way that Nietzsche repeatedly warns against. As early as *The Wanderer and his Shadow* Nietzsche contends:

> The word 'revenge' is said so quickly it almost seems as if it could contain no more than one conceptual and perceptional root. And so, one continues to strive to discover it: just as our economists have not yet wearied of scenting a similar unity in the word 'value' and of searching after the original root concept of the word. As if every word were not a pocket into which now this, now that, now several things at once have been put! (1996: 33)

If our notions make sense, which is to say gain their meanings, only within systems of purposes or evaluative frameworks, then we would do better to investigate those structures, rather than paying heed to the concepts themselves. And, this is a point Nietzsche underscores at the center of *On the Genealogy of Morality* when he explores the various systems of purposes which the concept of punishment was made to serve – punishment as deterrence, as festival, as a mode of repayment, and so forth (II: 13). So, if the meaning, the purpose, is indeed "fluid"; if our concepts "possess not in fact one meaning but a whole synthesis of 'meanings,'" if something like this actually captures Nietzsche's point that our concepts make sense only in terms of the systems of purposes which they serve, then we at least have *prima facie* grounds for resisting this account (II: 13).

But, it might be said, in an effort to rehabilitate such an argument, that we can work by way of a kind of cumulative characterization to form what might be Nietzsche's general theory of economics. And such a reprisal, I take it, is amply nuanced to provide the contours of our second contender. So, can we combine such economic notions to form a general theory? To be sure, Nietzsche certainly weighs in on a number of economic themes: he has views about the mechanization of labor (2001 I: 42, 2001 III: 188); the importance of leisure and idleness (2001 IV: 329); and finally, in his notebooks he predicts that: "common economic management of the earth…will soon be inevitable" (1968: 866). Yet, there is not a set of squarely economic principles, which may be said to reasonably connect each of these disparate elements.

But, if it is nevertheless true, and I think it is, that Nietzsche puts to use concepts that are at least "economically inspired," then at this juncture we would do well to say a bit more about how this might be the case in a way that is coherent enough to make our category both conceptually meaningful and practically useful (Sedgwick 2007: x). And this means turning our attention to the third of our interpretive options, which maintains that what Nietzsche offers us is an economic representation of ideas. So, for example, Robert Solomon has suggested that it may be plausible to think that Nietzsche has an "'economic' model of emotions" (Solomon 2003: 84). Solomon puts the point in this way:

> An emotion is an investment, an investment in how things are or could be, and as such it incurs costs and aims at benefits. Thus, we can understand the difference between life-enhancing and life-stultifying passions as the difference between wise and stupid economics, between enriching the future or squandering it away by getting wholly caught up in past offenses and injustices. That is why ... resentment ... is the very paradigm of a life-stultifying emotion.
>
> SOLOMON 2003: 84

The outline of such a picture is clear enough. But it does not help us directly. The reason, of course, is that even a cursory reading of the Second Essay of *On the Genealogy of Morality* seems to make plain that in attempting to make clearer the origins of personal obligations, for instance, Nietzsche is not talking about buyers and sellers or creditors and debtors in a solely figurative sense (II: 8). So, even if Solomon is right about Nietzsche on emotions, which incidentally I do not think he is for reasons I make clearer in a moment, it seems evident that a suitable proposal for our purposes would require accounting for such moments in a way that indeed does justice to, and heeds the tenor of, Nietzsche's thought when he seems to be concerned with the actual material condition in which humans have found themselves, namely, and in isolating that Second Essay, asymmetrical creditor/debtor relations.

The fourth candidate captures those attempts to systematize Nietzsche's philosophy, by trading in, for want of a better expression, the economy of his thought. The most well-known candidate in this regard is surely Deleuze's *Nietzsche as Philosopher* in which he attempts to make clearer the "active/reactive" register by which we can account for a number of key themes at once: the "will to power," the "eternal return," and the push towards a revaluation of values.[1] And we can surely note that in places Nietzsche indeed gives us such an

1 Others have suggested that the key may be the "economy of decadence," which at once explains both the "decline of modernity" (Conway 1996: 94) and the truth of Christian morality (Conway 1996: 188).

impression. He talks of "the overall economy of mankind" (2002: 62) or how things appear "from the heights and in the sense of a great economy" (2005, 1; 2001 I: 1; 2005 IV). But equally worth bearing in mind is what Nietzsche actually tells us about those concepts that are, supposedly at least, housed singly on either side of such a register.

To make such a case we need only focus on that seemingly quintessentially reactive emotion of "*ressentiment*" to undermine the interpretive work that the easy register – active/reactive – is meant to do (cf. Staten 1990: 16).[2] The standard interpretive strategy regarding *ressentiment* is to make plain that it falls on the "reactive," slavish side of things. An approach bolstered, no doubt, by Nietzsche's (1997) claim that ressentiment, if "it should appear in the noble man, consummates and exhausts itself as immediate reaction, and therefore does not *poison*" (I: 11). On the face of it, this could mean that there are two types of *ressentiment* – an active, as it were, noble mode, which is immediately discharged, and a slave form, which is pent-up for it cannot be expressed externally. But, as Henry Staten, among others, has pointed out: "in the second essay vengefulness *as such* (not merely repressed vengefulness) is numbered among the reactive feelings" (1990: 17). So, even if this does not serve as a decisive refutation of the "economy of thought" position, it does enough, I think, to displace the notion that such an interpretation will be immediately and obviously helpful for our purpose.

If what I have said so far is right then, each of these interpretations of "Nietzsche's economy" seems to be disqualified, albeit for different reasons. The first treads too loosely on seeming "economic" notions, without paying sufficient attention to the ways in which our concepts come nestled in systems of purposes, a point that incidentally, Nietzsche (1997) insists, failed to draw the appropriate attention from all those "naïve genealogists of law and morals" (II: 13). The second fails by over-determining Nietzsche's project, while the third and fourth neglect the tenor of key arguments (cf. 2002: 246).

My account, by contrast, with a nod to the Greek etymology of the term (*oiko*) that denotes the management of the household, places the structural elements of Nietzsche's position at the core.[3] To put it another way, and to return again to Section 8 of the Second Essay of *On the Genealogy of Morality* where Nietzsche remarks: "Setting prices, determining values, contriving equivalences, exchanging – these preoccupied the earliest thinking of man to

2 In a similar vein Nietzsche notes "the problem of *the noble ideal itself*... – just think what a problem that is: ... this synthesis of *the inhuman* and *the overhuman*" (*GM* I: 16).

3 We might push the notion further, as some have done, to "there is only one thing that we really care about from the heart – bring something home" (P: 1; cf. Conway 1996)

so great an extent that in a certain sense they constitute thinking *as such…*" (II: 8), what we are concerned with under the banner of "Nietzsche's economy" then are the ways in which certain relations, such as that of the creditor–debtor, typify subjectivity (cf. Diprose 1993). So understood this account offers a useful corrective to those alternative explanations that focus on the figurate aspects of Nietzsche's prose that we just reviewed: instead, we are interested in the actual economic relations that engender certain modes of life, particularly asymmetrical creditor/debtor relations, which, for the purposes of this essay, are what constitute "Nietzsche's economy" (cf. Staten 1990: 5).

2 Revisiting the Slave Revolt in Morals

The conclusion just noted may gain some strength if we return to *On the Genealogy of Morality* and take care to note the ways in which certain subjectivities and modes of life are produced. We can do this through two references.

The first takes us to "the oldest and most primitive personal relationship … between buyer and seller, creditor and debtor," (II: 8) that fundamental social relation in which, Nietzsche tells us, "it was here that one person first encountered another person; one person first *measured himself* against another" (II: 8), and in so doing we can pose the question: how might such relations engender forms of subjectivity? One way in which we might shape an answer to this question is to focus on what it means to serve as a "creditor" or a "debtor" and note that it is here, amidst such relations, that Nietzsche maintains "*promises* were made; it was here that memory had to be *made* for those that promised" (II: 5). So, in tying these threads together we have a preliminary answer to our question: the complex economic relations of creditor/debtor form subjects; those that are able to make promises; those that may "stand security" for themselves into the uncertain future (II: 3); those that can repay according to "the idea that every injury has its *equivalent* and can actually be paid back, even if only through the *pain* of the culprit" (II: 4). So, the self gains a place in the world through such complex creditor-debtor relations.

The mode of agency that emerges, here, in this "contractual relationship," amidst the "fundamental forms of buying, selling, barter, trade, and traffic," is one in which the doer has yet to be separated from their deed (II: 4). Such that if, for instance, the debtor cannot repay, "with money, land, possessions of any kind" and the creditor receives "a recompense in the form of a kind of *pleasure*" (II: 5), the debtor may find that, as Nietzsche notes: "here something has unexpectedly gone wrong," *not* "I ought not have done that." They submitted to punishment as one submits to an illness or to a misfortune or to death, with that stout-hearted fatalism without rebellion" (II: 15). So, it seems, central to this form of agency is the idea of fate (cf. Owen 1995: 56).

But, however this might be, there is another dimension of Nietzsche's account that is worth shaping in a bit more detail. And this requires us to return to the First Essay. This aspect seeks to make clearer the ways in which our capacities for agency are themselves shaped by and through historical processes. Key to Nietzsche's argument, I submit, is the claim that such capacities are interwoven with particular forms of life such that particular conceptions we may have about ourselves are themselves products of a long history, which includes, of course, economic relations.

In the First Essay Nietzsche (1997) argues that a certain "type of man," the downtrodden, "*needs* to believe in a neutral independent 'subject,' prompted by an instinct for self-preservation and self-affirmation in which the lie is sanctified...the sublime self-deception that interprets weakness as freedom, and their being thus-and-thus as a *merit*" (I: 13). Under the conditions of a "hostile external world" the slaves were "natures that are denied the true reaction, that of deeds, and compensate themselves with an imaginary revenge" (I: 10). So this version of self-understanding is the result of a "struggle between power-complexes" (II: 11). Thus, Nietzsche's argument reveals the necessity of the revolt in morality – or, as David Owen neatly puts it: that "*anyone* placed in the position of the slave class would be compelled to engage in the kind of imaginary revenge that they accomplish as a necessary condition of making sense of themselves as agents whose agency is intrinsically valuable" (Owen 2007: 79). It is, on Nietzsche's (1997) account, the only way in which "'the slaves' or 'the mob' or 'the herd' or whatever you like to call them" (I: 9) can achieve a form of "self-preservation and self-affirmation" (I: 13) given their historical and economic circumstances. So this form of self-understanding is linked to relations of power and conditions of enslavement.

3 Conclusion

By way of conclusion let me note that this paper has sought to clarify the status of the notion of "Nietzsche's economy." Indeed, if the arguments of this paper have been compelling, then it may be said to cogently refer to the ways in which such complex relations may be said to characterize subjectivity. My argument for this conclusion hangs on the two examples from *On the Genealogy of Morality* where something like this may be plausibly said to be on offer.

Yet, open still is the question concerning what insights, if any, this may have for times like ours. And adding some contours to this could very well be the subject of another essay.

References

Andrew, Edward G. 1995. *The Genealogy of Values: The Aesthetic Economy of Nietzsche and Proust.* London: Rowman & Littlefield.

Conway, Daniel. 1996. *Nietzsche and the Political.* New York: Routledge.

Diprose, Rosalyn. 1993. "Nietzsche and the Pathos of Distance." In *Nietzsche, Feminism, and Political Theory*, edited by Paul Patton, 1–26. New York: Routledge.

Katsafanas, Paul. 2016. *The Nietzschean Self: Moral Psychology, Agency, and the Unconscious.* Oxford: Oxford University Press.

Löwith, Karl. 1965. *From Hegel to Nietzsche.* London: Constable.

McCarthy, George. 1994. *Dialectics and Decadence: Echoes of Antiquity in Marx and Nietzsche.* Lanham, MD: Rowman & Littlefield.

Nietzsche, Friedrich. 2005. *The Anti-Christ, Ecce Homo, Twilight of the Idols and Other Writings*, translated by C. Diethe. Cambridge: Cambridge University Press.

Nietzsche, Friedrich. 2002. *Beyond Good and Evil*, translated by J. Norman. Cambridge: Cambridge University Press.

Nietzsche, Friedrich. 2001. *The Gay Science*, translated by Josefine Nauckhoff. Cambridge: Cambridge University Press.

Nietzsche, Friedrich. 1997. *On the Genealogy of Morality*, translated by C. Diethe. Cambridge: Cambridge University Press.

Nietzsche, Friedrich. 1996. *Human, All Too Human: A Book for Free Spirits*, translated by R.J. Hollingdale. Cambridge: Cambridge University Press.

Nietzsche, Friedrich. 1968. *The Will to Power*, translated by Walter Kaufmann and R.J. Hollingdale. New York: Vintage Books.

Owen, David. 2007. *Nietzsche's Genealogy of Morality.* Stocksfield : Acumen.

Owen, David. 1995. *Nietzsche, Politics and Modernity: A Critique of Liberal Reason.* London: Sage.

Sedgwick, Peter R. 2007. *Nietzsche's Economy: Modernity, Normativity and Futurity.* Basingstoke: Palgrave Macmillan.

Shapiro, Gary. 1994. "Debts Due and Overdue: Beginnings of Philosophy in Nietzsche, Heidegger, and Anaximander." In *Nietzsche, Genealogy, Morality: Essays on Nietzsche's* Genealogy of Morals, edited by Richard Schacht, 358–375. Berkeley: University of California Press.

Shapiro, Gary. 1991. *Alcyone: Nietzsche on Gifts, Noise, and Women.* Albany: State University of New York Press.

Solomon, Robert. 2003. *Living with Nietzsche: What the Great Immoralist Has to Teach Us*. Oxford: Oxford University Press.

Spiekermann, Klaus. 1999. "Nietzsche and Critical Theory." In *Nietzsche, Theories of Knowledge, and Critical Theory: Nietzsche and the Sciences I*, edited by Babette Babich, 225–242. Dordrecht/Boston/London: Kluwer Academic Publishers.

Staten, Henry. 1990. *Nietzsche's Voice*. Ithaca, NY: Cornell University Press.

PART 2

On the Advantages and Disadvantages of Nietzsche for Marxist Critique

∵

CHAPTER 6

Marx, Nietzsche, and the Contradictions of Capitalism

Ishay Landa

1 Introduction

Karl Marx and Friedrich Nietzsche have a lot in common in their basic vision of modernity. It is mistaken, for example, to assume that Nietzsche was interested chiefly in ethical and cultural matters, as opposed to Marx's supposed fixation on the economic 'base.' Nietzsche's whole notion of culture was predicated upon a keen appreciation of the indispensable role of economic arrangements, particularly of the hierarchical division of labor, in sustaining all culture, while Marx, for his part, was deeply concerned about the fate of civilization. Their respective social vantage-points and political projects, however, were fundamentally opposed: Marx envisioned a society overcoming class division, whereas Nietzsche directed all his powers at preventing precisely such an outcome. What Nietzsche in many respects offers us is therefore a Marxist theory with inverted signs.[1]

No comprehensive comparison of these two immensely complex and influential philosophers is possible here, of course. But if we have to zoom in on the most important feature they have in common, it is useful to foreground the fact that both Marx and Nietzsche were thinkers of the contradiction: contradictions and dealing with contradictions was absolutely central to their thought. Yet to this the caveat must be added that Marx was a conscious thinker of the contradiction, a dialectician, so he came closer to mastering contradictions, or was at least disposed to thinking them through systematically. For Marx, furthermore, contradictions were celebrated as the prime agent of *change*, impelling a revolutionary forward *movement*. This indispensable insight about the inextricable linkage between contradiction, motion and change was inherited from the Hegelian dialectic, and it might be helpful to recall Hegel's original emphasis on this point:

1 A portion of this essay appeared in Landa (2019).

> Something moves, not because at one moment it is here and at another there, but because at one and the same moment it is here and not here, because in this "here," it at once is and is not. The ancient dialecticians must be granted the contradictions that they pointed out in motion; but it does not follow that therefore there is no motion, but on the contrary, that motion is *existent* contradiction itself.
>
> HEGEL 1969: 440

Nietzsche was no less preoccupied with contradictions and in fact often seemed content to give the impression that he was toying with contradictions, turning his entire oeuvre into a site of hectic ping-pong movement between wildly conflicting statements and affirmations, wearing masks, asserting supposed Truths only to demolish them shortly thereafter, etc. This is Nietzsche in the familiar guise of the forefather of postmodernist irreverence. What is absent, however, in Nietzsche's contradictions is precisely the key notion, for Hegel and Marx, of forward movement. For this, Nietzsche substitutes an element of stasis, of contradictions resisting any prospect of sublation.

This contradictory basis they have in common means that it is not very helpful to approach Marx and Nietzsche with an eye to straightforward definitions, for these are likely to mislead us. Even as they will capture some truth, they will tend to efface the contradiction. The simplest and apparently unproblematic epithets – for example, 'Marx was revolutionary,' 'Nietzsche was a defender of the status quo' – will fall short of the mark.

2 Marx and the Social Individual

Take Marx, to begin with. Possibly the safest way to define Marx would be as 'a revolutionary anti-capitalist.' Yet, as is well known, Marx had a lot of *positive* things to say about capitalism and the bourgeois mode of production, on whose productive and dynamical prowess he showered effusive praise in *The Communist Manifesto*, which was repeated in later works such as the *Grundrisse* and *Capital*, where one frequently reads of capital's 'civilizing aspects,' its 'civilizing mission,' its 'historic mission,' and so on and so forth. While this is common knowledge relatively few commentators have attempted to pursue this and ask what exactly Marx had meant when affixing the adjective 'civilizing' to capitalism. One common way of coming to terms with such utterances – apart from skipping over them with embarrassed silence – is to see them as reflections of Marx's weak side: he was after all a child his time, a Victorian, and therefore could not but have shared some of the common beliefs and prejudices of the age, such as faith in the progressive march of history, a celebration of productivism, or a Promethean view of human empowerment. Probably the pithiest formulation of that critique, although one which would have Marx's thought discredited entirely, is Michel Foucault's famous jibe that 'Marxism exists in nineteenth-century thought like a fish in water: that is, it is unable to breathe anywhere else' (Foucault 1994: 262).

Taking issue with such assumptions, I will argue that Marx held these beliefs to a large extent *against* the spirit of the age. The second half of the 19th century was not, after all, the classical age of the belief in progress – that was rather the 18th century, finding its unsurpassable formulations in Turgot and Condorcet. The more the 19th century unfolds, in fact, and especially following the traumatic revolutionary wave of 1848, the belief in progress wanes, and disillusion and doubt increasingly set in. This is a time of deeply pessimist innovations when ideologies of fall and decline, cultural, social, and racial, start to incubate which will fully mature towards the end of the century and in the first half of the 20th century. In 1852, the first edition of Count Gobineau's *Essai sur l'inégalité des races humaines* is published, representing a major instance of conservative lament over the alleged deterioration of the social stock in a Europe which seems to be rapidly succumbing to democracy. But even in liberal circles the mood is far from buoyant. Consider J.S. Mill's morose diagnosis of massified modernity:

> [T]he general tendency of things throughout the world is to render mediocrity the ascendant power among mankind. In ancient history, in the middle ages, and in a diminishing degree through the long transition from feudality to the present time, the individual was a power in himself [...]. At present individuals are lost in the crowd. In politics [the] only power deserving the name is that of masses, and of governments while they make themselves the organ of the tendencies and instincts of the masses.
>
> MILL 1998: 73

Modernity is regarded by Mill as a progressive *retrogression* of the individualistic spirit, and his ideal of individualism lies in the *past*. His narrative is an inversion of conventional Whig history: individualism, that hallowed liberal tenet, was at its peak in ancient history and in the middle ages; from then on, up to 'the present time,' is a sad story of individual disempowerment, narrowing of personal initiative, and the rise of collectivism. Mill warns against the crippling collectivism sweeping over England and the prospect of Chinese-like stagnation; only the reemergence of genuine, towering individuals which once have made England great might 'prevent its decline' (Mill 1998: 78–79). There is thus little trace of a stout Victorian faith in progress in *On Liberty*, written in 1859.

At almost exactly the same time (1857–1858), and also in England, Marx is tackling the same phenomena from a very different vantage-point, in the *Grundrisse*. Instructively, Marx's understanding of individualism forms nearly the converse of Mill's. To be sure, Marx is a biting detractor of the notion that free-market capitalism signifies the free development of individuals, let alone the historical peak in the unfolding of individualism. This notion is deconstructed already in the *Manifesto*, where, against the bourgeois catchwords of 'individualism' and 'culture,' it is asserted that, 'in bourgeois society, capital is independent and has individuality, while the living person is dependent and has no individuality,' and that the 'culture, the loss of which [the bourgeois] laments, is, for the enormous majority, a mere training to act as a machine' (Marx and Engels 2005: 62, 64). Ten years later, the insistence that bourgeois individualism is a sham is repeated almost verbatim: 'It is not individuals who are set free by free competition; it is, rather, capital which is set free' (Marx 1993: 650). 'This kind of individual freedom,' Marx adds shortly thereafter (652), is 'the most complete suspension of individual freedom, and the most complete subjugation of individuality under social conditions which assume the form of objective powers, even of overpowering objects – of things independent of the relations among individuals themselves.'

Even as Mill and Marx criticize modern individualism, their premises are diametrically opposed. Mill is concerned by the alleged disappearance of the genius, the unique individual vanquished by the masses, whereas Marx is indifferent to the fate of the purported genius, and laments instead the subjugation of ordinary people, the way they are systematically prevented from developing their individualities. But the contrast between their respective outlooks goes deeper still: given their antagonistic social perspectives, they must also take a completely different view of the state of individualism in the past and of its future prospects. Since Mill essentially defends the ruling classes, it is natural that he should wistfully evoke those past epochs when the chasm between the individuals of the elite and the masses was much wider. In his account, capitalist modernity stands accused for empowering the masses. And it is precisely in that sense that Marx is driven to *defend capitalist modernity*, albeit at all times dialectically. If modern individualism, for Marx, is profoundly insufficient and underdeveloped, this is true *only* when measured up against the yardstick of absolute human potential, to be further developed in the communistic future. Compared with *the past*, the bourgeois order signifies a great qualitative *advance* in individualism. Marx's position is worth quoting at some length:

> Universally developed individuals [...] are no product of nature, but of history. The degree and the universality of the development of wealth where *this* individuality becomes possible supposes production on the basis of exchange values as a prior condition, whose universality produces not only the alienation of the individual from himself and from others, but also the universality and the comprehensiveness of his relations and capacities. In earlier stages of development, the single individual seems to be developed more fully, because he has not yet worked out his relationships in their fullness, or erected them as independent social powers and relations opposite himself. It is as ridiculous to yearn for a return to that original fullness as it is to believe that with this complete emptiness history has come to a standstill.
>
> MARX 1993: 162

Individualism, indeed, is an upshot of bourgeois modernity, a corollary of bourgeois relations of production and exchange. The task for the future is to build on the emerging *universality* of the individual, while combating her present *alienation*. One must fiercely criticize individualism as presently exists, but to lament the historical decline of individualism makes no sense (apart from an ideological and functional sense, obviously). Notice how the following, renowned passage from the *Grundrisse*, forms the negative image of the historical portrait drawn in *On Liberty*:

> The more deeply we go back into history, the more does the individual, and hence also the producing individual, appear as dependent, as belonging to a greater whole: in a still quite natural way in the family and in the family expanded into the clan [*Stamm*]; then later in the various forms of communal society arising out of the antitheses and fusions of the clan. Only in the eighteenth century, in "civil society," do the various forms of social connectedness confront the individual as a mere means towards his private purposes, as external necessity. But the epoch which produces this standpoint, that of the isolated individual, is also precisely that of the hitherto most developed social (from this standpoint, general) relations. The human being is in the most literal sense a political animal,[2] not merely a gregarious animal, but an animal which can individuate itself only in the midst of society.
>
> MARX 1993: 84

2 'A political animal' appears originally in Greek.

Mill wishes to arrest history: shield the individual from massification, limit democracy, etc. Marx, on the contrary, urges history to *go further*. The cause of individualism can be served only by allowing history to run its course. Whereas Mill, and later Nietzsche in a still more emphatic and undiscriminating way, denounces modernity as the era of the herd-animal, Marx, in a notable passage, argues that modernity is an individualistic *disbanding* of the herd:

> [H]uman beings become individuals only through the process of history. He appears originally as a *species-being* [*Gattungswesen*], *clan being, herd animal* [...]. Exchange itself is a chief means of this individuation [*Vereinzelung*]. It makes the herd-like existence superfluous and dissolves it.
>
> MARX 1993: 496

Where the likes of Mill, Tocqueville and Nietzsche fear collectivism, Marx identifies the promise of what he calls 'the social individual.' In marked contrast to notable future Nietzscheans such as Max Weber and Werner Sombart, who idealized earlier stages of capitalist production and invested them with all sorts of ethical and spiritual advantages,[3] the emergence of the social individual envisaged by Marx, while a mere embryonic phenomenon to be fully materialized in the future, is unthinkable without the thorough socialization of production brought about by properly modern, large-scale industry:

> In this transformation, it is [...] the appropriation of his own general productive power, his understanding of nature and his mastery over it by virtue of his presence as a social body – it is, in a word, the development of the social individual which appears as the great foundation-stone of production and of wealth. The *theft of alien labour time, on which the present wealth is based*, appears a miserable foundation in face of this new one, created by large-scale industry itself.
>
> MARX 1993: 705

Mass production, for Marx, was demeaning but also potentially emancipating: it propelled the socialization of work to a degree never before imagined, up to the point where no longer the isolated individual creates but society, society becoming the individual. In that regard, too, capitalism was sowing – '*malgre lui*,' against its intentions – the seeds of the future.[4] Paradoxically, Marx, the

3 See, for example, Weber (2002); Sombart (2003 [1913]: 201–202).
4 For a useful definition of this 'objective socialization of production' see Mandel (1978: 595).

most trenchant critic of capitalism, was much more *sanguine* about the future of 'civilization' than most of his pro-capitalist bourgeois counterparts. And not merely on account of his faith in the imminent proletarian revolution which will brush aside bourgeois society and its iniquities. It is important to acknowledge the full import of the fact that for Marx the prime revolutionary force in bourgeois society, and *in many ways against* it, is 'the living contradiction,' capital itself (Marx 1993: 421). These insights were later integrated into Marx's mature argument, unfolded in *Capital*. I provide just two examples:

> Modern industry never views or treats the existing form of a production process as the definitive one. Its technical basis is therefore revolutionary, whereas all earlier modes of production were essentially conservative. [...] [L]arge scale industry, through its very catastrophes, makes the recognition of variation of labour and hence of the fitness of the worker for the maximum number of different kinds of labour into a question of life and death. [...] That monstrosity, the disposable working population held in reserve, in misery, [...] must be replaced by the individual man who is absolutely available for the different kinds of labour required of him; the partially developed individual, who is merely the bearer of a specialized social function, must be replaced by the totally developed individual [...].
>
> MARX 1990: 617–618

This 'transformation,' Marx adds immediately, 'has developed spontaneously from the foundation provided by large-scale industry.' Similarly, in the third volume of *Capital*, Marx emphasizes that it 'is one of the civilizing aspects of capital that it extorts this surplus labour in a manner and in conditions that are more advantageous to social relations and to the creation of elements for a new and higher formation than was the case under the earlier forms of slavery, serfdom, etc.' (Marx, 1991: 958). Significantly, in the very next page of this edition, Marx goes on to delineate the move form a realm of necessity to a realm of freedom. Capitalism points, and actively moves, beyond itself. Marx sticks to a progressive philosophy of history not because he was a Victorian at heart but because he glimpsed in it the overcoming of Victorianism:

> [I]t is evident that the [...] the abundant development of the social individual –that the development of the productive forces brought about by the historical development of capital itself, when it reaches a certain point, suspends the self-realization of capital, instead of positing it.
>
> MARX 1993: 749

This understanding of capitalism as preparing the ground for a higher form of individualism, is merely one of many aspects in which Marx reveals himself far more appreciative of the possibilities of progress contained within, and by capitalism, than most bourgeois thinkers. Alternatively put, they realize such possibilities as keenly as he does, but *fear* their emancipatory and subversive nature. They, too, can perceive the contours of the realm of freedom outlined at the historical horizon and, for that very reason, being not progressive but conservative, they turn their back on history, idealize pre-history, or think how to forestall the coming of utopia, launch a *counter*-movement of one sort or another. Many of Marx's contemporaries turned *against progress* not because it failed to keep its promise of greater equality to the masses, but because it seemed to be delivering just that. Two such notable contemporaries were Edgar Allan Poe and Charles Baudelaire, who were amongst the earliest and staunchest critics of progress. To Poe, democracy signified the ignominious rule of the mob while Baudelaire (1972: 193), discussing Poe's work, once called progress 'that grand heresy of decrepitude.' But let us now turn to another great critic of progress: Friedrich Nietzsche.

3 Nietzsche's Noisy Quietism

Nietzsche was the formidable, most versatile and innovative thinker of the bourgeoisie in its defensive phase. He was acutely aware of the profound transformations, both revolutionary and evolutionary, that society was going through, and of the contradictions which underlay them. These contradictions, in turn, impelled the contradictions in his own writings.

On the one hand, Nietzsche emerges as a quintessentially conservative thinker, resisting the tides of change, shoring up the status quo. This is the Nietzsche who throughout his writings, with relentless repetitions and in a myriad of slightly-altered formulations, had advanced the idea that any attempt to challenge the present socioeconomic hierarchy and transcend it would be 'life-denying' 'unnatural,' 'world-slandering,' etc. 'All ideals are dangerous,' he once maintained, 'because they debase and brand the actual' (Nietzsche 1968: 130).

But why, from a Nietzschean perspective, should 'the actual' *not* be debased and branded? After all, was not Nietzsche supposed to be committed, rather, to an iconoclastic devastation of all systems, lending his irreverent skepticism to a *demolition* of all actualities? This is the Nietzsche who philosophizes with a hammer, frontally assaulting the status quo, the 'radical' Nietzsche, whose 'libertarian magic' had appealed to so many people on the left, deeply affecting 'Socialism, anarchism, feminism, the generational revolt of the young' (Aschheim 1994: 6).

It is tempting to see in this patent contradiction a confirmation of Nietzsche as a playful thinker, shifting and restless, defying the laws of philosophical and logical gravity, whose mission is to deflate all Truths and destabilize all systems.[5] Arguably more productive, however, is to see Nietzsche as a *static thinker*, facing *a reality in motion*. Being, as Marx (1993: 706) put it, 'the moving contradiction,' capitalism was dragging Nietzsche along. So if you wanted to defend the status quo, preserve hierarchy, prevent revolution, you could not afford to just stand still. The status quo itself was changing, was dynamic, and pointed towards a new society and the social individual. So in order to stay put, Nietzsche was forced to become, to apply a later term, a conservative revolutionary, like many of his most salient 20th-century right-wing successors, such as Oswald Spengler or Ernst Jünger. That straightforward conservatism had become unfeasible, was admitted by Nietzsche when he whispered – note the intimacy! – 'In the ear of conservatives':

> What was formerly not known, what is known today or could be known – a *reversion*, a turning back in any sense and to any degree, is quite impossible. [...] [E]ven today there are parties whose goal is a dream of the crabwise *retrogression* of all things. But no one is free to be a crab. There is nothing for it: one *has* to go forward, which is to say *step by step further into décadence* (– this is *my* definition of modern 'progress'...).
>
> NIETZSCHE 1990a: 108

The paradoxical essence of Nietzsche's radical stasis might be captured by Lampedusa's immortal turn of phrase from *Il Gattopardo*: 'Se vogliamo che *tutto* rimanga come è, bisogna che *tutto* cambi' [if we want everything to remain as it is, everything must change].

On the one hand, Nietzsche was militantly affirmative of capitalism. He envisioned human society as inexorably enacting the universal, competitive struggle for existence of nature, engulfed in a blind, perpetual collision of forces and wills. This incorporated the tragic substratum of Schopenhauer's philosophy, yet Nietzsche discarded his former masters' resigned pessimism in favor of an affirmation of 'Promethean' heroism. This grand activity remained tragic and circular, offering no final redemptive vista, yet through it those human beings could experience sublimity who were bold enough to embrace, rather than deny, the cosmic tragedy. To be sure, throughout his career Nietzsche maintained that only a small minority of human beings could actually

5 Which is how postmodernist interpreters typically construe him. For classic examples see, Derrida (1986) and White (1990).

muster the spiritual resources needed to unflinchingly accept the tragic view of the world and revel in it, a manly, aristocratic élite, whereas the masses cannot but take a 'womanish flight from all that was grave and frightening,' opting instead for a 'senile and slavish enjoyment of life and cheerfulness' (Nietzsche 1999: 57). And at least to begin with such an opposition was also rendered in terms of the difference between the virile Aryans and the mendacious, moralistic Semites. As Nietzsche affirmed in the same book, *The Birth of Tragedy* (1999: 50), 'What distinguishes the Aryan conception is the sublime view that *active sin* is the true Promethean virtue; thereby we have also found the ethical foundation of pessimistic tragedy, its *justification* of the evil in human life.' The valiant 'reflective Aryan,' in contradistinction to the timorous Semite, is able to come to terms with the 'curse in the nature of things, […] the contradiction at the heart of the world,' and make them his own (51):

> The double essence of Aeschylus' Prometheus […] could therefore be expressed like this: 'All that exists is just and unjust and is equally justified in both respects.'
>
> That is your world. That you call a world.

It should not be thought that such 'Prometheanism' was reserved to spiritual and artistic pursuits, shunning political and, especially, economic matters. Far from it, Nietzsche's tragic vision of the world centrally included the fundamental institutions of capitalism, whose operations, too, were sanctified as integral to the Dionysian, afflicted-cum-magnificent reality, and postulated as eternal and inevitable.[6] Private property, to begin with, Nietzsche (1968: 77) justified in the following terms:

> But there will always be too many who have possessions for socialism to signify more than an attack of sickness – and those who have possessions are of one mind on one article of faith: 'one must possess something in order to be something.'

Directly continuing, Nietzsche went beyond a mere confirmation of private property, and ontologized accumulation, too:

> But this is the oldest and healthiest of all instincts: I should add, 'one must want to have more than one has in order to become more.' For this

6 For my interpretation of Nietzsche's essential commitment to capitalism see more in Landa (2007). The present discussion of Nietzsche partly draws on materials which were first published in this book.

> is the doctrine preached by life itself to all that has life: the morality of development. To have and to want to have more – growth, in one word – that is life itself.

Nietzsche here made capitalism practically interchangeable with life. Exploitation, to complete the picture, he deemed no less rooted in life, forming a biological compulsion beyond the reach of history and impervious to any conceivable social transformation:

> [L]ife itself is *essentially* appropriation, injury, overpowering of the strange and weaker, suppression, severity, imposition of one's own forms, incorporation and, at the least and mildest, exploitation [...]. 'Exploitation' does not pertain to a corrupt or imperfect or primitive society: it pertains to the essence of the living thing as a fundamental organic function, it is a consequence of the intrinsic will to power which is precisely the will to life.
>
> NIETZSCHE 1990b: 194

The basic algorithm of capitalism, conceived indeed as a ruthless and competitive system, Nietzsche (1968: 164) enshrined as 'the grand economy, which cannot do without evil.'

On the other hand, however, capitalism terrified Nietzsche, and this precisely because he shared something of Marx's dialectical vision of capitalism, albeit in a highly abstract form. It is useful, when reading the following passage, to bear in mind how the developments which filled Nietzsche with deep pessimism and distrust of the future, were a source of hope for Marx:

> What I relate is the history of the next two centuries. I describe what is coming, what can no longer come differently: *the advent of nihilism*. This history can be related even now; for necessity itself is at work here. [...] For some time now, our whole European culture, has been moving as toward a catastrophe, with a tortured tension that is growing from decade to decade: restlessly, violently, headlong, like a river that wants to reach the end, that no longer reflects, that is afraid to reflect.
>
> NIETZSCHE 1968: 3

That is why Nietzsche is compelled to instigate a countermovement, promote a radical 'reevaluation of all values,' and preach the overman, all in order to somehow change the tide of historical development. This consciously counterhistoric commitment has received a powerful earlier expression in Nietzsche's youthful treatise *On the Uses and Disadvantages of History for Life* (1874). In direct polemics against Hegelianism, Nietzsche extols 'the great fighters *against history*,' those heroic individuals who dare to defy the laws of history. Any possible virtue, for Nietzsche (1997: 106), 'becomes a virtue through rising against the blind power of the factual and the tyranny of the actual and by submitting to laws that are not the laws of the fluctuations of history. It always swims against the tides of history.' It will be recalled, in passing, how this very same author, who is here combating 'the tyranny of the actual,' elsewhere inveighed precisely against those who 'debase and brand the actual.' The contradiction is clarified, however, once it is born in mind that in the present case Nietzsche combats 'the actual' as that which is in the process of *becoming*, brought along by the current of history. In the former case, he defended 'the actual' precisely as the present state of things, threatened by historical developments. Nietzsche's moments of optimism tellingly draw on the anticipation of a successful *derailing* of history. As in *Ecce Homo*:

> A tremendous hope speaks out of this writing. [...] Let us look a century ahead, let us suppose that my *attentat* on two millennia of anti-nature and the violation of man succeeds. That party of life which takes in hand the greatest of all tasks, the higher breeding of humanity, together with the remorseless extermination of all degenerate and parasitic elements, will again make possible on earth that *superfluity of life* out of which the dionysian condition must again proceed.
>
> NIETZSCHE 1992: 51–52[7]

Paradoxically, Marx, the revolutionary, never pretended to be able to change history singlehandedly, nor did he wish to derail it; he expressly disowned the notion that communism aims to reshape reality in agreement with some ideal or moral system; his goal was rather to assist the revolutionary transformation which is already in the making.[8] It was Nietzsche, the conservative, who was forced to plan an *attentat*, and elsewhere likened himself to a dynamite.

In a sense, Nietzsche was yearning for a capitalism that will no longer be 'a moving contradiction,' a static one, that will not lead towards transcendence. The doctrine of 'eternal recurrence' gave expression to this hope. For Georg Lukács, this was 'the pith of Nietzschean philosophy,' whose key social purpose was to deny 'that history could produce anything that was new in principle (such as socialism after the class society),' and provide the 'decisive counter-idea

7 I have changed the translation of *Vernichtung* from 'destruction,' to 'extermination.'

8 Cf. Marx and Engels (2005: 59).

to the concept of becoming. This counter balance was needed because Becoming cannot give rise to something new' (Lukács 1952). Since Lukács's critique of Nietzsche's 'indirect apologetics of capitalism' has itself been the target of harsh criticism ever since the publication of the *Destruction of Reason*, notably by a condescending Adorno (1980), it might be useful to recall that long before Lukács Walter Benjamin had reached rather similar conclusions: 'The notion of eternal return appeared at a time when the bourgeoisie no longer dared count on the impending development of the system of production which they had set going' (Benjamin 1999: 117). While doubtlessly far more indebted than Lukács to the German romantic tradition, including its Nietzschean variant,[9] Benjamin was also quite clear on Nietzsche's affinities with both capitalism – 'The Paradigm of capitalist religious thought is magnificently formulated in Nietzsche's philosophy' (Benjamin 1996: 289) – and imperialism.[10]

Nietzsche's theories offered the paradox of a noisy and frenzied quietism. Capitalism was affirmed mythopoeically but, crucially, without its transformative and self-destructive side. In 1886, approximating the zenith of his philosophical career, Nietzsche looked back at his first book, *The Birth of Tragedy*, and saw behind this early effort the bold celebration of a new, amoral artist-god. It so happens, that this artist-god is uncannily analogous to the classical Marxist description of capitalism, containing all its crucial contradictions – save one:

> Indeed, the whole book acknowledges only an artist's meaning (and hidden meaning) behind all that happens – a "god," if you will, but certainly only an utterly unscrupulous and amoral artist-god, who frees himself from the dire pressure of fullness and *over-fullness*, from suffering the oppositions packed within him, and who wishes to become conscious of his autarchic power and constant delight and desire, whether he is building or destroying, whether acting benignly or malevolently. The world as the release and redemption of god, *achieved* at each and every moment, as the eternally changing, eternally new vision of the most suffering being of all, the being most full of oppositions and contradictions, able to redeem and release itself only in *semblance*.
>
> NIETZSCHE 1999: 8

9 See, for an extended discussion, McFarland (2013).

10 See, for a brief statement, Benjamin (1999: 117). For two detailed expositions on Nietzsche's affinity and support for imperialism, see Domboswky (2014) and Conway (2002).

Does not Nietzsche inadvertently or covertly provides us here with a description/celebration, of capitalism, with its abounding power to 'build and destroy,' its restless, frenzied 'eternal changing,' its circular crises of 'fullness and over-fullness,' and its inner 'oppositions and contradictions' which it is able to solve 'only in semblance'? The crucial contradiction that is missing, of course, is the one involving *self*-destruction. Capitalism should be allowed to destroy everything but not prove to be the grave digger of the bourgeoisie. In this way, the unpleasant vicissitudes of capitalism could be presented to modern humans as divine and awe-striking; the working of an artist-god was supposed to be evident precisely in the chaotic arbitrariness of this mode of production, in its uncontrollability, periodic circular crises and disregard for human needs.

Such a reading of Nietzsche as apologizing for capitalism might be criticized for taking too much of a poetic license in its approach to a passage which, after all, does not directly engage economics. And it certainly differs from the conventional exegetic wisdom that would have us believe that Nietzsche was a thinker fundamentally aloof from worldly concerns and certainly not interested in justifying a system as vulgar as capitalism. Such common views, however, disregard Nietzsche's strong interest in socio-economic matters and the fact that he was fairly well read in contemporary literature dealing with political economy; indeed, while he may not have read Marx's writings directly, he knew of Marx's economic and political theories from several sources, some of which have discussed and cited Marx extensively, and in one of which he had even underlined Marx's name.[11] Hence the frequent economic overtones of Nietzsche's rhetoric, even when writing on seemingly metaphysical or cultural matters, should by no means be neglected or considered merely fortuitous.[12] Take the following sentence where Nietzsche affirms that 'in order for there to be a broad, deep, fertile soil for the development of art, the overwhelming majority has to be slavishly subjected to life's necessity in the service of the minority [...]. At their expense, through their extra work, that privileged class is to be removed from the struggle for existence, in order to produce and satisfy a new world of necessities.' The striking resemblance to the socialist, indeed Marxist vocabulary, the talk of the 'extra work' [Mehrarbeit] extracted from the workers, is not a fluke but stems from his specific opposition to socialist theories.

11 For details see Brobjer (2002). For a very useful discussion of Nietzsche's familiarity with political economy and his indirect dialogue with Marx see Nicolás González Varela's insightful and detailed discussion and analysis (2010).

12 For an insightful discussion of the significance of economics within Nietzsche's theories of *Bildung*, and the way key economic tropes such as circulation, debt and exchange inform even some of Nietzsche's most metaphysical ideas, see Cooper (2008).

The same mythopoeic reflection of capitalism is found elsewhere. Consider the last section of *The Will to Power*, a highly charged passage (1885) from which I extract just a few sentences:

> And do you know what 'the world' is to me? Shall I show it to you in my mirror? This world: a monster of energy, without beginning, without end; [...] out of the play of contradictions back to the joy of concord, [...] blessing itself as that which must return eternally [...]: this, my *Dionysian* world [...], without goal, unless the joy of the circle is itself a goal, unless a ring feels good will toward itself [...].
>
> NIETZSCHE 1968: 549–550

Nietzsche's yearning is again for a status quo which is really static, or rather utterly dynamic, but in a circular way. As beautifully put by Tony McKenna (2013: 403), Nietzsche's vision centers on the proposition of 'a revolution without revolution, an event risen from a never ending historical slip-stream in which everything is flux but nothing is change.' Robert Wicks' is also right in pointing out the way that Nietzsche, objectively, apologizes for the deficiencies of the present social system; the author, moreover, usefully juxtaposes such apologia with the Hegelian and Marxist critical and transformative project. 'Nietzsche,' he writes, 'did not glorify the world in the socially and morally traditional manner of Hegel or Marx, for he did not envision a heaven on earth where justice and peaceful community would prevail. Nietzsche's aesthetic glorification involved taking what appears to be a disappointingly imperfect, mediocre and mundane situation and reinterpreting it as a sublime situation' (Wicks 2005: 116). Similarly, Stephen Houlgate perceptively compared Nietzsche's understanding of tragedy with that of Hegel and found it lacking since, unlike Hegel who drew from the fate of the tragic hero a lesson about the need to transform social relations, Nietzsche eschewed any such prospect, and instead used the hero to justify the status quo. 'Nietzsche,' wrote Houlgate (1986: 216), 'does not tie tragic suffering directly to human responsibility, so the individual does not feel the tragic destructiveness of life as essentially his own, but always "overcomes" it, covers it up or pushes it away in the very act of affirming it.' This leads the author to the conclusion that, for Nietzsche, 'tragedy celebrates the heroism of confrontation' (Houlgate 1986: 218).

The fact should not be overlooked that Nietzsche in the passage quoted above does not simply claim to reflect cosmic and social realities such as they actually are or necessarily must be. Quite the contrary, he virtually admits that this is the world and society as *he* would like them to be, that he is presenting us with an ideal, rather than a fact: 'what "the world" is *to me*,' 'Shall I show it to you in *my mirror,*' '*my* Dionysian world,' etc. Nietzsche advanced a political project which was meant to counter the way the world, in his estimation, was *actually* shaping up. Nor was Nietzsche's vision truly atheistic. It was not the case that there was no longer a divine authority to which agonizing humanity could turn in its distress. In the new myth that Nietzsche sought to inculcate, god was not really dead; it was *god himself,* rather, who lavishly inflicted all sorts of misery on humanity to satisfy his artistic impulses. However, since Nietzsche was well aware that his 'amoral artist-God,' his 'Dionysos,' was by no means omnipotent, he prompted human beings to actively assist him in preserving the sand-like instability and precariousness of their social ground: 'If the individuals are to become stronger, society must remain in *a state of emergency,* always in the expectance of great variations: lead a *continually provisional existence.*' (Nietzsche 1988, vol. 9: 426) The ultra capitalist commitment behind these words is thrown into a strong relief once it is taken into account that they were written in polemics against none other than Herbert Spencer, the very coiner of 'the-survival-of-the-fittest' catchphrase, whose position Nietzsche nonetheless deemed too utilitarian and heedful of society, weakening individual competition, and hence leading to 'humanity's decline.'

This furnishes another example of how Nietzsche's contradictions differ from Marx's. Like Marx, Nietzsche was highly ambivalent about capitalism. Yet he rejected precisely those elements and patterns of development characteristic of capitalism which pressed beyond it or, at the very least, seemed destined to transform capitalism into a far more egalitarian and peaceful system. Nietzsche's contempt at utilitarianism as decadent was therefore an attempt to neutralize what was considered the decaying element in bourgeois culture and politics, which may eventually eat into the foundations of the class system and veer towards democracy and socialism. In other words, Nietzsche rebuked the bourgeoisie for *not being capitalistic enough,* or, interchangeably, for being capitalistic on account of the wrong, practical, comfort and safety-seeking reasons.[13] Utilitarianism, according to Nietzsche, was merely a democratic prelude to socialism, as attested to particularly by its emphasis on 'the happiness of the greatest number.' In that respect Nietzsche's cultural critique of philistine bourgeois complacency and timidity was broadly anticipative of, indeed was often directly emulated by such proto-fascist thinkers as Tommaso Marinetti,

13 Michael Kilivris (2011) is therefore right to claim that Nietzsche was in many respects anti-capitalist, but wrong to conclude from this that he cannot therefore be regarded 'a bourgeois ideologue.' On the contrary, it was precisely as a bourgeois ideologue that Nietzsche was repelled by certain aspects of capitalism and driven to embrace a neo-aristocratic stance.

who protested against the 'timid clerical conservatism symbolized by the bedroom slippers and the hot water bottle,' favoring instead the heroic hygiene of war (in Joll 1973: 127); or Vilfredo Pareto, who found that the liberal institution of democracy is conducive to the survival of *the weakest*: 'Going along to the polling station to vote is a very easy business, and if by so doing one can procure food and shelter, then everybody – especially the unfit, the incompetent and the idle – will rush to do it' (in Joll 1973: 130–131).

4 The Task of the Last Human

Nietzsche's problem, of course, was the mismatch between his ideal of the capitalist 'joy of the circle' and contemporary reality, where the world appeared dangerously close to breaking out of what many had experienced as a vicious, rather than a joyous circle; that the social individual was knocking on the door.

In order to try and preempt any such possibility he attempted to dystopianize the social individual by rewriting him disparagingly as 'the Last Human.' Instead of leading humanity to new cultural summits, modernity signifies a social and economic leveling down, the formation of a mass society at the heart of which stands

> the most contemptible human: and that is the Last Human. [...] The earth has become small, and upon it hops the Last Human, who makes everything small. His race is as inexterminable as the flea; the Last Human lives longest. [...] Nobody grows rich or poor anymore: both are too much of a burden. Who still wants to rule? Who obey? Both are too much of a burden. No herdsman and one herd.
>
> NIETZSCHE 1969: 45–46[14]

The Last Human epitomizes the nightmare of social subversion, an egalitarian dystopia, consisting of increased consumption and mass happiness – Zarathustra says that the Last Humans 'still work, for work is entertainment. [...] They have their little pleasure for the day and their little pleasure for the

14 Here and in the next citation I occasionally depart from Richard J. Hollingdale's translation, consulting the original German. The Last Humans are usually rendered the Last Men in English, yet this is problematic, since the German term is the gender neutral *Mensch*, encompassing both men and women. In reality, in view of their alleged deterioration and loss of vigor, the Last Humans – in Nietzsche's terms – can be said to be more womanly and effeminate than virile.

night: but they respect health. "We have discovered happiness," say the Last Humans and blink' (Nietzsche 1969: 47).

And, at bottom, are not the Last Human and the social individual one and the same individual, regarded from the opposing sides of the social and ideological divide? What in Marx is affirmed as a positive vision of the future, when a multi-faceted, highly socialized and creative human being will come into her own, capable of various enjoyments and having multiple free time at her disposal, is scoffed at by Nietzsche as a plebeian elimination of excellence, heroism, and everything that makes life worthwhile. In general, from a Nietzschean perspective the gains of the social individual are dismissed or ridiculed. For example, the fact that knowledge is held in common and is collectively accumulated through time, absorbing the formidable efforts and contributions of multiple individuals, was both taken for granted and saluted by Hegel and Marx. For Hegel, famously, 'what in former ages engaged the attention of men of mature mind, has been reduced to the level of facts, exercises, and even games for children; and, in the child's progress through school, we shall recognize the history of the cultural development of the world traced, as it were, in a silhouette' (Hegel, 1977: 16). From a Nietzschean vantage-point, however, such diffusion of knowledge arouses indignation, and is construed as the thankless usurpation of the works of geniuses by undeserving masses. 'Just look at these superfluous people!' sneers Zarathustra: 'They steal for themselves the works of inventors and the treasures of the wise: they call their theft culture – and they turn everything to sickness and calamity' (Nietzsche 1969: 77). Reading a Nietzschean-inspired communist like Alain Badiou (2002: 70), for example, one gets the impression that this process has something scandalous about it: '[I]t is the eternal destiny of the most astonishing mathematical inventions to wind up in college textbooks.'[15] Where else, one is tempted to ask, should they wind up?

Given Nietzsche's agonistic scheme, in which one person's gain cannot but be another's loss – for 'person' one might just as well read 'class' here – widespread excellence and horizontally distributed knowledge are discredited as 'mediocrity' and the rule of the herd. Hence Nietzsche's profound suspicion of, often outright hostility, to universal education, which he associated with creeping Hegelianism, socialism and worse. 'Universal education,' he averred early on (1871), 'is but a preparatory stage of communism. Education is so weakened that it can no longer bestow any privileges. Least of all is it a means against communism. Universal education, i.e. barbarism, is the precondition of communism.' (Nietzsche 1988, vol. 7: 243) Significantly, Nietzsche goes on to

15 For my view of Badiou as indebted to Nietzsche, see Landa (2013).

lament the way universal education breeds the consumerism of the Last Humans – without using the exact term, which he coined much later – a mass hedonism which he associates, furthermore, with the demands of Lassalle. The socialist agitator is accused of having taught the common people that 'having no needs is the greatest infelicity,' and instilling them with a lust for 'luxury and fashion' as opposed to *Kultur*. This explains, for Nietzsche, the pernicious tendency of the workers' educational associations to 'generate needs.' (Nietzsche 1988, vol. 7: 243) The multiplication of state educational institutions and their inclusion of wider sections of the population Nietzsche diagnoses as the result of fear of 'the aristocratic nature of real education' (Nietzsche 1988, vol. 1: 710).

To be sure, in his criticism of the educational system of the triumphant Second Reich, Nietzsche had also pointed out many of the limitations of this system, notably its serviceability to the state and to commercial purposes. Consider the following passage from *Schopenhauer as Educator* (1874), where the detrimental cultural and educational effect of '*the greed of the money – makers*' is denounced:

> [A]s much knowledge and education as possible, therefore as much demand as possible, therefore as much production as possible, therefore as much happiness and profit as possible – that is the seductive formula. Education would be defined by its adherents as the insight by means of which, through demand and its satisfaction, one becomes time-bound through and through but at the same time best acquires all the ways and means of making money as easily as possible. The goal would then be to create as many current human beings as possible, in the sense in which one speaks of a coin as being current [...].
>
> NIETZSCHE 1997: 164

These are problems which continue to vitiate education under capitalist states to our days, when the scope of free inquiry is narrowed, and the very legitimacy of the humanities is questioned under pretexts of lack of practicality and profitability, to say nothing of the charges of *counter*-productive, critical thinking. This might convey the impression that Nietzsche can serve as an ally of the humanities in the struggle against 'instrumental reason' and many scholars have indeed pursued such reasoning (for a recent example, see Church [2015] especially Chapter 5, dealing with 'The Education to Culture'). Such readings, however, typically downplay, when they not outright obliterate, the profoundly conservative wider context in which Nietzsche's defense of 'culture' was embedded, and the way it was conceived first and foremost to buttress social and cultural hierarchies. What ultimately concerned Nietzsche, in other words, was not to defend culture from oppressive capitalism but rather from the oppressed masses. 'If culture were really left to the discretion of the people,' he made clear during the same, early period, in the essay *The Greek State*, 'the cry of pity' would tear 'down the walls of culture; the urge for justice, for equal sharing of the pain, would swamp all other ideas' (Nietzsche 1994: 178–179). A closer scrutiny of Nietzsche's critique of the commercialization and standardization of education reveals that it is primarily a critique of its *democratization*. Standardization and instrumentalization of the masses cannot form Nietzsche's true grievance with capitalist education for two simple reasons: he assumes, complementarily if incoherently, that (1) the broad masses are by their very nature irretrievably mediocre and 'current,' and hence cannot really be turned into such by bad education, and (2) that their mediocrity, far from being lamentable, is actually salutary and indispensable for the proliferation of genuine culture and the ascendancy of 'the genius,' and must therefore be deliberately encouraged and inculcated. The late Nietzsche (1968: 462) thus writes, for instance, that 'A high culture can stand only upon a broad base, upon a strong and healthy consolidated mediocrity [...]. The power of the middle is, further, upheld by trade, above all trade in money: the instinct of great financiers goes against everything extreme,' and elsewhere assures his readers (1990b: 193) that 'the essential thing in a good and healthy aristocracy is [...] that it does *not* feel itself to be a function (of the monarchy or of the commonwealth) but as their *meaning* and supreme justification – that it therefore accepts with a good conscience the sacrifice of innumerable men who *for its sake* have to be oppressed and reduced to imperfect men, to slaves and instruments.'

Universal education is thus ultimately criticized by Nietzsche not on account of its serviceability to capitalism but, on the very contrary, because it mounts a formidable challenge to capitalism and the entire class system. As Nietzsche averred in a polemic against socialism from 1877, by spreading education among the masses, the workers, becoming spoiled and refined, can no longer perform their preordained tasks: 'Since a great deal of hard and coarse work must be done, people must be preserved who can perform them [...]. Once the need and refinement of a higher education penetrates the working class, it can no longer do such work, without inordinately suffering from it' (Nietzsche 1988, vol. 8: 481). Again, Nietzsche is bemused and disturbed by the moving contradiction embodied in capitalism: the very effort to instrumentalize the masses dialectically breeds their restlessness. Nietzsche would like to secure the former requirement, which he regards as the pre-condition for all high culture, but eschew the latter, disturbing by-product. 'These are ill-fated times,' he lamented in *The Greek State* (1994: 177), 'when the slave [...] is stirred up to think about himself and beyond himself! Ill-fated seducers who have destroyed the slave's state of innocence with the fruit of the tree of knowledge!' In short, 'If one wills an end, one must also will the means to it: if one wants slaves, one is a fool if one educates them to be masters' (Nietzsche 1990a: 106). The fundamental problem for the philosopher is thus not the instrumentalization of education under capitalism but precisely the democratization that threatens to bring such instrumentalization to an end.[16]

A similar contradiction underpins Nietzsche's critique of 'the coldest of all cold monsters': the state (Nietzsche 1969: 75). This is another element that was seized upon by many protective readers to vouch for Nietzsche's 'anarchist,' and 'anti-totalitarian' spirit. Yet in truth Nietzsche's fierce opposition to 'the new idol' was restricted to the state as an expression of a Hegelian, democratic and popular spirit, dedicated to promoting the welfare of the masses. As Zarathustra (1969: 76) proclaims, 'Many too many are born: the state was invented for the superfluous!' and in 1872, in explicit polemics against Hegel's view of the state as an 'ethical organism,' Nietzsche discards the ideal of a democratic state and pits against it a defiantly aristocratic alternative:

> For what purpose does the state need such an excessive number of institutions of education, of teachers? For what purpose this broadly-based education and enlightenment of the people? Because the true German spirit is hated, because the aristocratic nature of real education is feared, because one wishes to drive the great individuals to self-ostracism; one plants and nurtures the pretention of education in the multitude, since one seeks thereby to evade the severe and hard breeding of great leaders, persuading the mass that it will find its own way.
>
> NIETZSCHE 1988, vol. 1: 710

Nietzsche thus rejects the state only inasmuch as it has fallen under the sway of the masses; he opposes it to the extent, indeed, that it is construed as a *new* idol, materializing the 'modern ideas' he viscerally despises of democracy, popular sovereignty, and egalitarianism. The state as an *old* idol, however, whose purpose is to produce 'the genius' by using the masses as tools, Nietzsche ardently promotes as an antidote to modern degeneration. This happens with

16 For a detailed exploration of Nietzsche's approach to the question of education see the excellent and comprehensive study of Nietzsche's political thought, soon to appear in English, by Losurdo (2004) as well as Chapter 5 of González Varela's no less impressive book (2010), incisively analyzing the early Nietzsche's 'reactionary' ideas for future education.

great clarity in *The Greek State*, where Nietzsche derives from the politics of antiquity – freely interpreted, certainly – a counter-democratic social model. The following passage, written in 1871, should serve as a sobering reminder for those wishing to present Nietzsche as a principled enemy of authoritarianism and state coercion. It begins, notably, with a critique of capitalism as *a vehicle of egalitarianism*, a force whose social and cultural implications are radical. The contradictions of capitalism and its partially revolutionary thrust are again borne out by Nietzsche's analysis:

> If I point to the use of revolutionary ideas in the service of a self-seeking, stateless money aristocracy as a dangerous characteristic of the contemporary political scene, and if, at the same time, I regard the massive spread of liberal optimism as a result of the fact that the modern money economy has fallen into strange hands, and if I view all social evils, including the inevitable decline of the arts, as either sprouting from that root or enmeshed with it: then you will just have to excuse me if I occasionally sing a paean to war.
>
> NIETZSCHE 1994: 184

Against the incipient 'revolt of the masses' – to borrow José Ortega y Gasset's famous 20th-century term, itself centrally inspired by his readings of the German thinker – Nietzsche then recommends a revival of the state of antiquity, establishing a system in which the masses will be drilled into both labor and military discipline:

> [T]hrough war, and in the military profession, we are presented with a type, even perhaps the *archetype of the state*. Here we see as the most general effect of the war tendency, the immediate separation and division of the chaotic masses into *military castes*, from which there arises the construction of a 'war-like society' in the shape of a pyramid on the broadest possible base: a slave-like bottom stratum. The unconscious purpose of the whole movement forces every individual under its yoke [...]. In the higher castes, it becomes a little clearer what is actually happening with this inner process, namely the creation of the *military genius* – whom we have already met as original founder of the state.

The ancient ideal of the promotion of the genius, Nietzsche concludes, should be placed at the heart of the modern state project, displacing the masses into a wholly subservient position, and demonstrating the vacuity of such endemic modern catchphrases as 'dignity of man' and 'dignity of work.' 'But what I have demonstrated here,' Nietzsche counters (1994: 185), 'is valid in the most general sense: every man, with his whole activity, is only dignified to the extent that he is a tool of genius, consciously or unconsciously.' His reading of Plato reassures Nietzsche, as he wishes to reassure his readers grappling with modern politics, that the *state of the masses* must be superseded by the *state of the genius*: 'The actual aim of the state, the Olympian existence and constantly renewed creation and the preparation of the genius, compared with whom everything else is just a tool, aid and facilitator, is discovered here through poetic intuition and described vividly.'

Nietzsche's mythic dichotomy of the genius vs. the masses, applied across all domains – social, cultural and educational – serves as a useful way of discrediting the advances and achievements of democratic society and presenting its results as somehow depressing, gray, and shorn of genuine value. Yet it conceals the anxious deference to rigid class barriers and the privileges they confer and safeguard; the attack on general mediocrity in the name of the putative excellence of the solitary genius in fact rests on the *reactive* idea that the genius can only shine so bright as long as the masses remain dull enough to serve as its backdrop. Paradoxically, the genius, far from being a self-made individual, rising on account of his formidable gifts, requires the drilling and suppressing of the whole of society, a coordinated work of breeding and discipline: consider the revealing phrase used in *Schopenhauer as Educator*, again carrying economic overtones: 'the production of genius' (Nietzsche 1997: 164). Hence the admittance, de facto, that without mediocrity – artificially produced and enforced – the genius cannot prosper: for 'high culture,' as will be recalled, 'can stand only upon a broad base, upon a strong and healthy consolidated mediocrity.' According to the Nietzschean logic, if taken to its ultimate conclusions, in a classroom with one reasonably clever and knowledgeable student and 19 illiterates one finds – *a genius*; a classroom, by contrast, with 20 highly intelligent and learned students, of roughly the same talents, presents us with the sorry spectacle of – *mediocrity*. An illustration of this vantage-point can be gleaned from an instance of popular Nietzscheanism, *The Incredibles*, that won the Oscar for best animated picture of 2004. A specimen of the vast genre of 'superhero' tales, which by its very nature is close to the Nietzschean thematic, the film tells the story of a middle-class family of superheroes, father, mother, and their three little kids, all in possession of remarkable innate super powers, distinguishing them from the multitude. The story's villain is Syndrome, a minute and resentful guy, who yearns to be a superhero himself but possesses no 'super' gifts. All he has is the ability to invent advanced technology which gives him a semblance of super-heroism. Terribly jealous of the family for their enjoyment of the real thing, he captures them and threatens to 'sell my invention so that everyone could be superhero. Everyone can be super. And when everyone's super – no one will be!' (Bird 2004) This neatly captures the fear that capitalism-cum-socialism will democratize excellence, distribute it amongst the mass, and thereby eliminate it.

5 Conclusion

While the Last Human was meant to ridicule the rise of the social individual, the social individual, in turn, can help us to see the Last Human in a very different light. The Last Human and the social individual are both contradictory and complementary, in that their true meaning emerges at best when they are brought together. It may be apposite to end by juxtaposing two famous statements by Marx and Nietzsche. 'Communism,' Marx wrote in 1844, 'is the riddle of history solved, [das aufgelöste Rätsel der Geschichte] and it knows itself to be this solution' (Marx 1974: 348). Forty-one years later, Nietzsche wrote: 'do you want a *name* for this world? A *solution* for all its riddles? [Eine Lösung für alle ihre Rätsel?] *This world is the will to power – and nothing besides!*' (Nietzsche 1968: 550).

References

Adorno, Theodor. 1980. 'Reconciliation under Duress.' In *Aesthetics and Politics: Debates Between Bloch, Lukacs, Brecht, Benjamin, Adorno*, edited by Fredric Jameson, 151–176. London and New York: Verso.

Aschheim, Steven E. 1994. *The Nietzsche Legacy in Germany 1890–1990*. Berkeley, CA: University of California Press.

Badiou, Alain. 2002. *Ethics. An Essay on the Understanding of Evil*. London and New York: Verso.

Baudelaire, Charles. 1972. *Selected Writings on Art and Artists*. Cambridge: Cambridge University Press.

Benjamin, Walter. 1999. *The Arcades Project*. Cambridge, MS, and London: Belknap University Press.

Benjamin, Walter. 1996. *Selected Writings: Volume 1, 1913–1926*. Edited by Marcus Bullock and Michael W. Jennings. Cambridge, MA and London: Belknap Press.

Bird, Brad. 2004. *The Incredibles* [motion picture]. Emeryville, CA: Pixar Studios.

Brobjer, Thomas H. 2002. 'Nietzsche's Knowledge of Marx and Marxism.' *Nietzsche-Studien*, 31: 298–313.

Conway, Daniel W. 2002. '*Ecce Caesar*: Nietzsche's Imperial Aspirations.' In *Nietzsche, Godfather of Fascism? On the Uses and Abuses of a Philosophy*, edited by Jacob Golomb and Robert S. Wistrich, 173–195. Princeton, NJ: Princeton University Press.

Cooper, Ian. 2008. 'Nietzsche, Money and *Bildung*.' In *Nietzsche, Power and Politics: Rethinking Nietzsche's Legacy for Political Thought*, edited by Herman W. Siemens and Vasti Roodt, 605–628. Berlin, New York: Walter de Gruyter.

Church, Jeffrey. 2015. *Nietzsche's Culture of Humanity: Beyond Aristocracy and Democracy in the Early Period*. Cambridge: Cambridge University Press.

Derrida, Jacque. 1986. 'Interpreting Signatures (Nietzsche/Heidegger): Two Questions.' *Philosophy and Literature* 10: 246–262.

Dombowsky, Don. 2014. *Nietzsche and Napoleon: The Dionysian Conspiracy*. Cardiff: University of Wales Press.

Foucault, Michel. 1994. *The Order of Things: An Archaeology of the Human Sciences*. New York: Vintage.

González Varela, Nicholás. 2010. *Nietzsche contra La Democracia: El pensamiento político de Friedrich Nietzsche, 1862–1872*. Barcelona: Montesinos.

Hegel, Georg Wilhelm Fredrich. 1977. *Phenomenology of Spirit*. Oxford: Oxford University Press.

Hegel, Georg Wilhelm Fredrich. 1969. *Hegel's Science of Logic*. New York: Humanity Books.

Houlgate, Stephen. 1986. *Hegel, Nietzsche and the Criticism of Metaphysics*. Cambridge: Cambridge University Press.

Joll, James. 1973. *Europe Since 1870: An International History*. London: Penguin.

Kilivris, Michael. 2011. 'Beyond Goods and Services: Toward a Nietzschean Critique of Capitalism.' *Kritike* 5(2): 26–40.

Landa, Ishay. 2019. 'The Social Individual and the Last Human: Marx and Nietzsche Agree to Disagree.' *Critical Sociology* 45(2): 253–265.

Landa, Ishay. 2013. 'True Requirements or the Requirements of Truth? The Nietzschean Communism of Alain Badiou.' *International Critical Thought* 3(4): 424–443.

Landa, Ishay. 2007. *The Overman in the Marketplace. Nietzschean Heroism in Popular Culture* Lanham, MD: Lexington.

Losurdo, Domenico. 2004. *Nietzsche, il ribelle aristocratico*. Torino: Bollati Boringhieri.

Lukács, György. 1952. 'Nietzsche as Founder of Irrationalism in the Imperialist Period.' In *The Destruction of Reason*. https://www.marxists.org/archive/lukacs/works/destruction-reason/ch03.htm. Accessed 15 July 2016.

Mandel, Ernst. 1978. *Late Capitalism*. London and New York: Verso.

Marx, Karl. 1993. *Grundrisse*. London: Penguin.

Marx, Karl. 1991. *Capital. Volume 3*. London: Penguin.

Marx, Karl. 1990. *Capital. Volume 1*. London: Penguin.

Marx, Karl. 1974. *Early Writings*. London: Penguin.

Marx, Karl, and Friedrich Engels. 2005. *The Communist Manifesto*. Chicago, IL: Haymarket.

McFarland, James. 2013. *Constellation: Friedrich Nietzsche & Walter Benjamin in the Now-Time of History*. New York: Fordham University Press.

McKenna, Tony. 2013. 'Method in the Madness: Three Moments in Nietzsche's Philosophy—An Exposition.' *Critique: Journal of Socialist Theory* 41(3): 391–409.

Mill, John S. 1998. *On Liberty and Other Essays*. Oxford: Oxford University Press.

Nietzsche, Friedrich. 1999. *The Birth of Tragedy and Other Writings*. Cambridge: Cambridge University Press.

Nietzsche, Friedrich. 1997. *Untimely Meditations*. Cambridge: Cambridge University Press.

Nietzsche, Friedrich. 1994. *On the Genealogy of Morality*. Cambridge: Cambridge University Press.

Nietzsche, Friedrich. 1992. *Ecce Homo*. Harmondsworth: Penguin.

Nietzsche, Friedrich. 1990a. *Twilight of the Idols and The Anti-Christ*. Harmondsworth: Penguin.

Nietzsche, Friedrich. 1990b. *Beyond Good and Evil*. Harmondsworth: Penguin.

Nietzsche, Friedrich. 1988. *Sämtliche Werke. Kritische Studienausgabe in 15 Einzelbänden*. Berlin and New York: Walter de Gruyter.

Nietzsche, Friedrich. 1969. *Thus Spoke Zarathustra*. Harmondsworth: Penguin.

Nietzsche, Friedrich. 1968. *The Will to Power*. New York, NY: Vintage.

Sombart, Werner. 2003 [1913]. *Der Bourgeois. Zur Geistesgeschichte des modernen Wirtschaftsmenschen*. Berlin: Duncker & Humblot.

Weber, Max. 2002. *The Protestant Ethic and the 'Spirit' of Capitalism and other writings*. London: Penguin.

White, Alan. 1990. *Within Nietzsche's Labyrinth*. London and New York: Routledge.

Wicks, Robert. 2005. 'Nietzsche's "Yes" to Life and the Apollonian Neutrality of Existence.' *Nietzsche-Studien* 34: 100–123.

CHAPTER 7

Labor's Will to Power: Nietzsche, American Syndicalism, and the Politics of Liberation

Kristin Lawler

1 Introduction: The Political Stakes of Nietzsche

At this writing, it is fifty years since the world-shaking countercultural rebellions of 1968 and we live in the wake of the brutal reaction to them. Since then, the transgressive attitude toward authoritarian, ascetic moralism that the movements of the 60s and the zeitgeist they shaped and enacted has, sadly, not fared very well. In the U.S., a proto-fascist right wing has come out of the shadows and uses the discourse of freedom – free speech, cultural transgression – to enact a rapacious pro-corporate, anti-worker and environment, nationalist, revanchist agenda, and to revel openly in the aggressiveness that has always accompanied the oppression of the workers of the world.

Perhaps not surprisingly, then, many on the left who would oppose this oppression have come to see precisely the liberatory cultural transgression of that explosive period as among their enemies. Nowhere is this clearer than in the phenomenon of Angela Nagle's 2017 analysis of the alt-right, *Kill All Normies*. In her bestselling work, Nagle dives deep into the murky toxic waters of the internet to map the racist, xenophobic, misogynist "alt-right" and the Trump ascendance it prefigured and created, and to find its roots in just the kind of transgressive anti-moralism that characterized the counterculture of the post WWII period and the postmodern, deconstructive, chaotic sensibilities that emerged out of it. Nagle's book was widely read, publicized, and discussed, and has in many left circles put the nail in the coffin of the idea that the politics of cultural transgression and anti-moralism could constitute a road to mass liberation.

Nagle, like many left cultural conservatives before her, rightly identifies the work of Nietzsche as the furnace fueling both the politics of countercultural transgression and of a postmodern deconstruction of the discourses that previously organized social life. For her, the latter tendency ultimately wound up in a moralistic politics of race, gender, and sexual identity (as against the Marxist metanarrative of the emancipatory destiny of the proletariat) and "calling-out" culture the inevitable reaction to which, she claims, was an aggressive white male nationalism that refused the guilt that said white males were supposed to feel in the face of the oppressions of women and people of color and that was inspired by the oppressive moralism of the former tendency.

In Nagle's telling, the amoral aggressiveness of the alt-right was both a reaction to and a product of the Nietzschean rejection of civilized values. With her analysis, Nagle exhorts the left to abandon "the cultural turn" and get back to the business of "class" – which for her seems to be without cultural preferences in general or a desire for freedom in particular. In this essay, I want to use the work of Nietzsche and the early twentieth century labor and cultural politics that it resonates with and in some ways inspired, to argue that the desire for freedom is the essence of any class politics that has a chance of challenging the ascendance of the fascist right, as well as the essence of the kind of labor movement politics that can win in a post-Fordist, post-Keynesian, hyper deregulated economic environment.

•••

To her credit, Nagle does identify Nietzschean transgression as "politically fungible" and potentially available to many groups for whom another world might be possible, but ultimately makes the case that it (along with the carnivalesque celebrated by Bakhtin and the "revolution in everyday life" of Vaneigem and the French Situationists of the 1960s, the Marxist cultural politics of Gramsci and the Birmingham School, as well as Bataille and pretty much all postmodern theorists of liberation) in the last instance, has accrued to the aggressiveness of the proto-fascist.

According to Nagle:

> Nietzsche, one of the main thinkers being channeled by the rightist chan [brutally aggressive online forums] culture knowingly or otherwise, argued for transgression of the pacifying moral order and instead for a celebration of life as the will to power [Nagle 2017: 34] … just as Nietzsche appealed to the Nazis as a way to formulate a right-wing anti-moralism, it is precisely the transgressive sensibility that is used to excuse and rationalize the utter dehumanization of women and ethnic minorities in the alt-right online sphere now. The culture of transgression they have produced liberates their conscience from having to take seriously the potential human cost of breaking the taboo against racial politics that has held since WWII. The Sadean transgressive element of the 60s, condemned by conservatives for decades as the very heart of the destruction of civilization, the degenerate and the nihilistic, is not being challenged by the

> emergence of this new online right. Instead, the emergence of this new online right is the full coming to fruition of the transgressive anti-moral style, the final detachment from any egalitarian philosophy of the left or Christian morality of the right. (39)

This pessimistic stance is certainly understandable in a moment in which the proto-fascist right has emerged from the shadows, taken the gloves off, and seems to be appealing to large swaths of the American population (and not just the affluent and super rich to whom the classic Republican pro-corporate anti-regulation policies championed by the Trump administration along with its hateful white nationalism, obviously appeals). But in this essay I will challenge the political direction coming out of Nagle's analysis, shared widely on the social democratic part of the left that is beginning to get some traction electorally – that is, that we need to abandon the politics of culture and get back to the business of egalitarianism and the working class.

Nagle cites the approving stance of right wingers like Milo Yannopoulis and Andrew Breitbart toward a Gramscian politics of cultural transformation – in Breitbart's famous words, "politics is downstream from culture" – to argue for abandoning them altogether. We all live in the world of Altamont and *Fight Club* now – so what begins as transgressive liberation can only end in the liberation of aggression. Thus, this logic goes, those who would arrest and reverse the trend toward the social brutalization of masses of people in the neoliberal era of capital, need to abandon cultural politics in favor of economic egalitarianism.

This argument is, however, not so new as Nagle's breathless fans might imagine. Culturally conservative leftists like Christopher Lasch (1979) have been making it, in fact, since the uprisings of the nineteen sixties and even earlier, since the liberatory modernism of the turn of the twentieth century infused the labor movement itself with a very Nietzschean transgressive cultural politics. In fact, the early 20th century left-popular movements – followed then, too, by the rise of a hard-right, xenophobic, racist reaction of respectable eugenicists and redneck Klansmen – brought together the "real" class politics of labor with the cultural politics of modern, individualist, Nietzschean liberation far more than did the sixties reverberation of it since by the post WWII period, much of the labor movement had been institutionalized within the state both structurally and culturally.

During the pre WWI heyday of the Industrial Workers of the World, "serious" socialist leaders like Daniel DeLeon, head of the Socialist Labor Party, decried the cultural politics of the iconic, countercultural hoboes within the IWW, a radical group of mostly male migrant workers who deployed direct action tactics, engaged in free speech fights around public assembly and discourse, and lived (and celebrated) a relatively debauched lifestyle of riding the rails and occupying "jungles" and "main stems" outside cities.[1] DeLeon and the socialists were ultimately defeated within the IWW in their battle to "civilize" the "bummery" – in DeLeon's description, those who would rather sing "Hallelujah I'm a Bum" than "The Marseillaise" and who are always likely to "throw a bomb" – but the battle itself was, in Mike Davis's (1975) analysis of the IWW, prefigurative of what he calls the "left-right" split in American labor going forward. Importantly, it was over the question of sabotage – the labor movement tactic least friendly to institutions and most resonant with the irresponsible refusal of work discipline that I will highlight in this essay – that formed the fault lines of this split more than anything.

•••

The major question then as now is the one that Wilhelm Reich posed in 1933: what are the cultural and libidinal politics that explain why the downwardly mobile turn to the authoritarianism of the right rather than to the potentially more liberatory vision of the left (Reich 1970 [1933])? For him, the answer lies both in the realities of sexual repression as well as the fear and ambivalence about freedom from it that is seeded by the family structure. The question of freedom is both economic and cultural, a matter of body and psyche, and a failure to address it fully just leaves its allure and its dangers out there, creating mass psychic material available to be mobilized by proto-fascist forces.

Central here is the simple psychoanalytic insight that Eros is the only force strong enough to bind back aggressiveness. And it is from this basic insight that a politics of liberation, a Nietzschean politics, must be engaged. Nagle, heir to the left cultural conservatives of intellectual history, mentions Freud in the same breath as her first Nietzsche citation: "Today, the appeal of [Nietzsche's] anti-moralism is strong on the alt-right because their goals necessitate

1 This essay will focus on the mostly male and largely Irish and Irish-American hoboes who rode the rails in the Western U.S. during the first two decades of the twentieth century. But elsewhere (Lawler, forthcoming) I address the female counterparts of these itinerant radicals in the West – women who were also of Irish lineage, who also lived out a transvaluation of the morality of the day, and who moved to places where the supply of their labor was scarce and thus highly compensated; that is, the prostitutes and madams of the era. Highly Nietzschean characters, these women were some of the first to own property independently and to be armed so that they could defend it from potential predators. They were also some of the most generous welfare capitalists of their day.

the repudiation of Christian codes that Nietzsche characterized as slave morality. Freud, on the other hand, characterized transgression as an anti-civilizational impulse, as part of the antagonism between the freedom of instinctual will and the necessary repressions of civilization" (Nagle, 2017: 39).

Nagle is with Freud in the last instance, agreeing that instinctual freedom ultimately destroys society because it unleashes aggressiveness. And although the postmodern moment that really began with the work of Nietzsche (and his reception among postwar French theorists like Deleuze, Foucault, and Derrida) rejects psychoanalytic theory and practice on just the grounds for which Nagle approvingly cites it, there is another, liberatory version of psychoanalytic theory that is actually the lens through which we must read Nietzsche's emancipatory vision if we are not to leave the politics of freedom to the right and its ugly orgy of aggressiveness. There are, let's not forget, other kinds of orgies.

I refer to the make-love-not-war hippie social theory of Herbert Marcuse, which is of course an heir to the work of Reich. It has certainly fallen out of favor these days, but given that the left's counter cultural politics have been arguably its greatest and most long lasting source of victory in the US, it might be a good idea to dust it off. Marcuse's psychoanalytic theory, like that of Wilhelm Reich, points to the axis on which the politics of liberation can indeed be "fungible" – that is, can accrue to the aggressiveness of authoritarian politics or to the libidinal freedom of emancipatory ones. This axis is the fundamental question of work.

2 Aggression, Repression, and Freedom

Although Freud's discovery of the unconscious made it possible for early moderns to think seriously about questions of repression and freedom, Freud was of course not unambiguously liberationist. For him, sexual repression is painful but ultimately necessary to inhibit the aggressive drive that, if freed, would make all civilized social life impossible. Marcuse, reading Freud through a Marxist lens, looks around at a mid twentieth century "civilized" world and sees a surplus of aggression, violence, and cruelty, along with sublimations and more bald repressions, everywhere. So what went wrong? In his 1955 work, *Eros and Civilization,* he identifies a dangerous dynamic whereby Eros undergoes not only the repression made necessary by the "reality principle," that allows us to get out of each other's pants for a minute and get some food, but a surplus-repression that functions to turn the body from an instrument of pleasure and intercourse with nature and one another, into an instrument of alienated labor under what he calls the "performance principle."

Under this, the historically specific reality principle of capitalism, Marcuse says, Eros undergoes such an intense level of repression that it becomes unable to hold back or "bind" aggressiveness – and Freud clearly posits Eros as the only force with this capacity. In a sense, the only thing stronger than hate is love, and when love, or libido, is so intensely repressed in modern society (so that people can work), hate and aggressiveness are unleashed on a disastrous scale. Far more than aggression, it is sexuality that suffers such brutal repression in modern society, and it is sexuality that threatens to explode through not society itself, but modern, rational, repressed, capitalist society.

For Marcuse, only a liberation from the surplus repressions of capitalist society – the "freedom" to work or starve – can offer the possibility of overcoming the aggressiveness unleashed by all the ways in which the primitive desires for pleasure are denied. Work is the most central of these, and in fact it grounds all the others. Thus, those who would oppose today's fascist threat cannot win by attempting to contain the liberation of instinct represented by the rise of the angry right and the predecessors of its reactionary impulse. Instead, the answer to the rise of authoritarianism and nationalism can only be more freedom, of the libidinal variety. If libido is the only thing strong enough to dissolve aggressiveness, and repression of libido is the main source of aggressiveness, then libidinal repression in the unpleasures and unfreedoms of work is precisely what an antifascist politics must oppose.

Although Marcuse did speak approvingly of Nietzsche's "affirmation of the life instincts," Nietzsche is generally not considered a hippie philosopher. Just as Nietzsche is so often associated with Nazism, his work is often read as advocating not just freedom but especially the freedom of the will to dominate another, cruelly and aggressively – as a social theory for assholes. Much of this interpretation is a misreading: his Nazi sister's publication of his notes for *The Will to Power* was a dishonest interpretation, he was a scathing critic of nationalism,[2] his notion of the "Aryan" included the Celt, the Indian, and the Persian, and his deconstruction of slave morality argued not for the oppression of the subaltern but for a transvaluation of values and the generation of a culture and a society that would no longer produce slavish and resentful people. Most important, as Michael Roberts (2016) demonstrates comprehensively in his essay, *The Twilight of Work*, Nietzsche is unequivocal in his disparagement of modern work and the work ethic and his celebration of leisure and the virtues of idleness.

Nietzsche certainly is no enemy of the free expression of aggressiveness and the sadistic pleasures that come with it. But I want to argue that the kind of

2 See especially Nietzsche (2010, V: 377).

aggressiveness exhibited by the fascist and proto-fascist right is exactly the opposite of the unrestrained and joyful freedom and even aggression that Nietzsche's work celebrated. And that his stance against both ascetic moralism and resentment prefigures precisely the kind of anti-work cultural politics that are the only potentially effective solution to the recurring problem of the ascendance of authoritarian personalities. In fact, I want to argue that Nietzsche advocated primarily *not* for an other-centered focus on the pain of another but in favor of the "pathos of distance" of the aristocratic soul, which is just the opposite of the kind of aggressiveness that white nationalist ressentiment enacts and which is actually the fuel for the ability to walk away, to detach, from an oppressive situation.

As I hope to demonstrate, this detachment is the essence of the syndicalist labor tactic of sabotage and especially of the American *ubermenschen* known as hoboes who were its most iconic practitioners. The wild, itinerant, ever militant hoboes of the Industrial Workers of the World were the single most influential figures on the development of American counterculture. Nietzschean sensibilities were in fact present at the creation of this profoundly influential brand of emancipatory labor politics, broadly referred to as syndicalism.

Syndicalism is far more an agitational strategy than a political theory, and there are many different ideas of what exactly syndicalism is and how it differs from industrial unionism. There are several clear varieties but the essence remains: a focus on power vis a vis the employer at the point of production; an effort to control the supply of labor to increase workers' leverage; sabotage or striking on the job; spontaneity, a refusal to sign contracts or to engage in electoral politics; the doctrine of tainted goods whereby goods from struck shops or ports would not be touched by any worker; and the sympathetic and eventually general strike. Importantly, the direct action of syndicalism is opposed to the statist orientation of socialism and social democracy. But more than anything, I want to argue, this kind of emancipatory labor politics is rooted in precisely the pathos of distance that Nietzsche says characterizes the noble and in a cultural transvaluation of the ascetic, other-centered morality of the modern age.

3 American Syndicalism

The strain of American emancipatory labor politics that resonated through the twentieth century to the counterculture originated in the "American syndicalism" of the IWW. Although syndicalism and sabotage are generally associated with the French labor movement, according to Brissenden's (1919) history of the Wobblies:

> the main ideas of IWWism... were of American origin, not French, as is commonly supposed...it was only after 1908 that the *syndicalisme revolutionnaire* of France had any direct influence on the revolutionary industrial unionist movement here. Even then it was largely a matter of borrowing such phrases as *sabotage, la greve perlee* (go-slow), etc. The tactics back of the words sabotage and 'direct action' had been practiced by American working men years before those words ever came into use among our radical unionists.
>
> BRISSENDEN 1919: 4

The IWW was born of several historical tendencies. One is pointed out by Mike Davis in his classic *Radical America* essay: the Taylorist logic of efficiency that was coming to dominate production around the turn of the 20th century (and that, Taylor's own work [1911] makes clear, was a response to constant and longstanding worker irresponsibility, inefficiency, and insubordination). Also, majorities of factory workers (including in munitions factories) in the Mid-Atlantic and Northeast as well as coal and metal miners and workers in timber and other raw materials in the west, were Irish, shaped by the syndicalist "new unionism" of the Irish labor movement as well as early Irish anti-landlord folk traditions of revolt used by miners involved with the militant secret society, the Mollie Maguires.

There was also certainly a French influence. Legendary organizer for the Western Federation of Miners (another IWW precursor, formed by the Irish miners who'd been Mollies in Pennsylvania and then headed out west to the silver and copper mines) and the IWW, and proponent of sabotage, Big Bill Haywood, famously said, "when we strike now, we strike with our hands in our pockets." Haywood spoke often of his trip to France and how the officially syndicalist French union, the CGT, had inspired him. Daniel Colson (2004) has noted the influence of Nietzsche on the development of the French labor movement, especially on the CGT's formative precursor *Bourses du Travail*, hiring halls with "liberatory study groups" that often read Nietzsche. What is far more obscure is the independent relationship between the ideas of Friedrich Nietzsche and the hoboes of the western IWW. It is rarely pointed out that this American syndicalist tradition is so resonant, historically and analytically, with the work of Nietzsche. It was clearer to people at the time.

According to a 1912 IWW pamphlet, *How Capital Has Hypnotized Society*, "it is just as imperative that the working class create its own civilization, its own morals, ethics, religion, and industrial and economic order, as it was that the capitalist class should." And *Direct Action* (an Australian IWW paper which reprinted the HCHS pamphlet) explained its adaptation of Nietzschean philosophy:

"Nietzsche had shown the way for the favored few; it was necessary to do likewise for the many, to teach the masses 'the will to power.' The weakness of labor organizations lay in the psychology of the units, therefore Nietzsche was badly needed to clarify the workers' vision, to transvalue all capitalist values, thus rejuvenating the ranks of labor with a new hope and a definite goal" (quoted in Burgmann 1998: 132).

4 An Antiwork Culture

Wobblies were the first Americans to be called "slackers" and were relentlessly repressed as such. In fact, the Palmer Raids were also known at the time as the "slacker raids" – a series of WWI-era searches, arrests, mass trials, and convictions led by the organization that would become the FBI (and its special agent in charge, J. Edgar Hoover) – and which aimed to destroy the IWW explicitly. This was the moment that the term "slacker" came into common parlance, as a word for a draft dodger and on-the-job saboteur. The Wobblies refused both to fight in what they saw as a war to save a brutal exploitative British empire as well as to submit to capitalist work-discipline.

Although their resistance to work is generally seen among labor historians as the reason for the intense repression of the IWW, it seems likely that the group's Irish roots among miners, dockworkers, and, importantly, munitions workers, and their at times active sabotage of the Allied war effort, had more to do with it. Of course, the two – anti-imperialism and anti-capitalism – are closely related, and Nietzsche had a well known and powerful impact on Ireland's two most important nationalist anti-imperialist writers, Yeats and Joyce, and thus on the Irish revolutionary spirit – but that's another story.

In any case, refusing to internalize bourgeois ideology about nation, work, and life, the Wobblies in the west collectively lived an alternative set of social relations centered around common public spaces and common pool resources. Disparaged in the popular press as meaning "I Won't Work" and "I Want Whiskey," the IWW was the only major American union consistently devoted to an anti-productivist logic, one that roundly rejected capitalist work and the ideology that sees it as a social or moral good. According to historian Franklin Rosemont, chronicler of the IWW's "Revolutionary Working Class Counterculture" and member of the editorial collective of the new left journal *Radical America*:

> In bright contrast to the AFL unions, which were glad to settle for "a Fair Day's Wage for a Fair Day's Work," Wobblies developed a critique not only of the work ethic but also of work itself…Wobblies knew too much

> about work to be 'workerist.' Their constant emphasis on shortening the hours of labor; their defense of "The Right to Be Lazy" (the title of a popular pamphlet by Marx's son-in-law, Paul Lafargue [published by the IWW]) and even their advocacy of "sabotage," in the original sense of the word – signifying slowdowns on the job and other forms of workplace malingering – suffice to distinguish them from the middle-class Socialist and Communist intellectuals who so often glorified the misery known as work.
>
> ROSEMONT 2003: 455–456

And they made the case in song, in art, in soapbox oratory and stand up comedy. The IWW produced some of the most memorable and influential pieces of radical American culture: from the song, *Hallelujah I'm a Bum* to the sabotabby, wise to the politics of labor supply, exhorting workers to "slow down, the job you save may be your own," to the Mr. Blockhead cartoons mocking squares who internalize capitalist ideology, the Wobblies, especially the hobo migrant workers in the west, crafted an anti-work, anti-responsibility, pro-freedom ethic out of the folk culture and resistance of workers themselves. The content of these cultural productions never centered on the boss or resentment toward the powerful; the idea behind it all was much more to get free from oppressive people and situations. To always seek out the most advantageous situation, to enjoy life; this is not often the way Nietzsche's will to power is understood, but in the *Genealogy* he refers to it as the "instinct for freedom" (1967, II: 18) and this, I want to argue, points to the most politically important use of his work.

5 Walking Away: Distance, Transvaluation, and Power

I want to demonstrate in this essay that the anti-work cultural politics of the IWW, and the way they manifested in struggles with employers during the pre-WWII period, were of a piece with the emancipatory anti-asceticism of Nietzsche. Key here is the "pathos of distance" with which Nietzsche characterized the original "noble race" and the values that emerged from their own autonomous perspective. The IWW, especially the migrant "hoboes" who carried their culture, did create a set of their own, affirmative, vital, and pleasure-oriented values, and disseminated them through songs, stickers, cartoons, posters, newspapers, standup comedy and political and intellectual lectures on soapboxes in urban parks, and an innovative set of linguistic codes that set the counterculture apart.

This pathos of distance that I argue is present in hobo cultural creations manifested in their labor movement tactics as well, which are best understood through the lens of Albert O. Hirschman's classic work, *Exit, Voice, and Loyalty* (1970). For Hirschman, power can be gained within an unequal relationship through loyalty, through democratic participation, or through the exit door (or the threat of leaving). The logic of exit as a strategy for leverage or power was deployed by the hoboes and by the larger Wobbly-labor counterculture often in the practice of hopping a freight train in search of a more favorable labor market. Wherever jobs were in short supply and there was a worker surplus, desperation would follow. As they had since the late 19th century start of a widespread institution of wage labor and thus the employer's need for a regularized labor supply, the police and state authorities worked to keep workers in their places and thus at the mercy of employers. A large part of hobo life consisted in outwitting railroad "bulls" and local police trying to keep them off the trains, in one place, and thus unable to exit.

Another characteristic tactic used by the hoboes in particular and the IWW more generally to gain leverage and power was the use of sabotage, or the "conscious withdrawal of the workers' industrial efficiency," (Flynn 1917) as a main tactic. In exhortatory pamphlets Wobbly intellectuals encouraged workers to "slacken up" their efforts on the job as a means to gain leverage with respect to employers. This slow down – also known as striking on the job – and the transvaluation of Protestant work values that fuels it is, was widely lamented by bourgeois ideologists of the time, profoundly "irresponsible," just as was the hobo practice of up and leaving a job or a location when it stopped being any good.

The refusal to sign contracts, another characteristic of the IWW's version of syndicalism, is also an iteration of the pathos of distance and the culture of freedom that was the hoboes' affirmative creation. All of it characterizes a Nietzschean refusal of the responsible-subject identity that grounds the asceticism of the bourgeois work ethic. And all of it was geared *both* to building working class power *and* to a joyous present oriented life in the moment. The second, in fact, is precisely what generates the first.

Significantly, a Nietzschean philosophy was present at the creation of the Wobbly culture and tactics of class struggle. And all of it goes to answer the serious question that emerges from a left reading of Nietzsche's work – is the creative, affirmative, vital, free, only the possession of an elite? Or can a subaltern class claim freedom in this sense? I would like to use Nietzsche's work to answer in the affirmative, theoretically and historically, and to make the case that this is only possible when the "sickness" of ascetic-work morality is overcome since bad conscience, guilt, and slave morality are, in Nietzsche's theory as well as in German critical theory more generally, products of pain and repression.

6 The Pathos of Distance

Early in the *Genealogy of Morals*, Nietzsche (1967) describes the original, autonomous, life-affirming, value-creating distance of the noble (and, I am arguing here, of the working-class counterculture of the Wobblies) as against the other-centered moralizations of the slave:

> …in this theory the source of the concept 'good' has been sought and established in the wrong place: the judgment 'good' did not originate with those to whom 'goodness' was shown. Rather it was 'the good' themselves, that is to say, the noble, powerful, high-stationed and high-minded, who felt and established themselves and their actions as good, that is of the first rank, in contradistinction to all the low, low-minded, common, and plebian. It was out of this *pathos of distance* that they first seized the right to create values and to coin names for values… the lordly right of giving names extends so far that one should allow oneself to conceive the origin of language itself as an expression of power on the part of the rulers… it follows from this origin that the word 'good' was definitely *not* linked from the first and by necessity to 'unegoistic' actions as the superstition of these genealogists of morality would have it. Rather it was only when aristocratic value judgments *declined* that the whole antithesis 'egoistic' 'unegoistic' obtruded itself more and more on the human conscience… [now this equivalence between moral and unegoistic] already rules today with the force of a "fixed idea" and brain-sickness. (I: 2)

When he talks about the "noble mode" of valuation, whereby those with the power and distance from the other to name values in the image of their own preferences, Nietzsche also valorizes the spontaneous, the open, the free – the not ensnared, not caught up in the other. The ability to forget, to walk away, to let things roll off your back like water, to not take things, especially enemies, seriously for very long: "such a man shakes off with a *single* shrug many vermin that eat deep into others…" (I: 2).

The pathos of distance is the lens through which the free person sees the unfree or unfortunate. Unlike slave morality and *ressentiment*, it actually cares very little for the other – no hard feelings, but no guilty, seething, resentful feelings either. It is the root of the power to name things and especially to name values in the image of what is good for you. It is a cultural detachment that I would like to argue is the essence of the ability of subaltern classes to be part of a transvaluation of the work ethic and all slavish, ascetic morality.

Wild, debauched, the hoboes of the early 20th century were class radicals, but of a unique type. A far more Nietzschean type than many socialists of the day, who were far more interested in replacing bourgeois rule than with overturning it. The Wobblies sought not to rule but to be emancipated from being ruled. Walking away from an oppressive situation is a liberating and healthy strategy for freedom, and in the hoboes' labor market strategy (explicitly about controlling labor supply, a fact often forgotten now) we can see the "pathos of distance" with which Nietzsche characterized the original "noble race" and the values that emerged from their own autonomous perspective.

In one of many iterations of the characteristic IWW theme of sabotage, the hoboes moved on freight trains, countering the capitalist move to extract labor power efficiently from a captive workforce, sabotaging the very tools, the railroads, created to generate greater and greater profits. Their mobility generated a spontaneity to their politics – when free workers' spaces created in parks and other public places were being repressed by local police, a call would go out in the *Industrial Worker* ("CALLING ALL FOOTLOOSE REBELS") for fellow workers to spontaneously flood the town and fill the jails to make police work impossible.

These itinerant workers, who actively battled the police and the bosses at every turn, were the quintessential bad subjects.[3] They spoke a lingo that few outsiders understood. They were known only by their nicknames. They skipped town when they felt like leaving. They refused to sign labor contracts, using direct action and sabotage to affect wages and working conditions and eschewing the "responsibility" not to disrupt production once an agreement with the boss had been made. They were neither identifiable, dependable, nor authentic, as one of their favorite aspects of the main stems and jungles where they made their temporary homes was precisely the anonymity they enjoyed there

3 Etienne Balibar's political positioning of the "bad subject" in terms of Louis Althusser's Lacanian deconstruction of the subject of ideological interpellation is highly resonant with the American hobo, whose experience was locatable only at the margins of official texts and at the margins of society, disturbing both: in his words, Althusser "implicitly asks how we should think the 'real,' which in the well-known Lacanian scheme, forms the third pillar of the explanation of the unconscious...what then, constitutes the *positivity* of the real, the correlate of the *materiality* of the imaginary? The suggestion is made on the text's horizon, but here too, in very enigmatic fashion, that this question can probably not be divorced from the question of the bad subject, the one who does not manage to go all by herself, or who resists interpellation." (Balibar 2014: xvii).

and thus the tall tales of the road that they could perform. They created a unique, affirmative culture and more than anything, their culture valued freedom, from work and from the related repressions of the state and of the family. They celebrated the refusal of work openly, singing "Hallelujah I'm a Bum" and celebrating a transvaluation of the work ethic that I argue is central to a syndicalist labor politics of direct action.

7 The Question of Work

Of course, Max Weber (1992) was Europe's most important theorist of the relationship between suffering and repression, ascetic culture and capitalism, and the resonances between Nietzsche and Weber on the question of work are striking. Weber demonstrates historically what Nietzsche claims theoretically: that the instrumental attitude to time and the lifeworld that characterizes work and the cold dominating logic of capital has its roots in Puritan shame and self-hatred.

Given the deeply ascetic Puritan cosmology, in which the divine and the natural were separated by an "unbridgeable gulf," any expression of a natural or spontaneous desire or emotion was seen as a sign of damnation. Work functioned as an approved ascetic technique both to keep desires at bay and to rationally order a post-Eden world always susceptible to wildness, chaos, sin. So just as in Nietzsche's analysis, the spontaneous, pleasure and present oriented experience is opposed to the rational, the calculating, the instrumental, the ascetic, all of which Weber links with the Protestant work ethic and thus with the cultural basis of capitalism itself.

For Weber, the asceticism of the work ethic is of a piece with the broader iron cage of instrumental rationality in the modern west. This resonates with Nietzsche's critique of instrumentality, as well as with the denunciation of *ressentiment*, since Nietzsche calls the reformation (for Weber, the cultural source of the iron cage) a "*ressentiment* movement" and posits cruelty as the essence of the Gods of the reformation – "merely consult Calvin and Luther" (II: 7).

In both Max Weber and in Nietzsche, the fundamental relationship between economics and culture, particularly morality, is front and center: in Nietzsche, moral discourses of fairness, justice, responsibility, rights, all had their origin in the notion that "everything has its price, all things can be paid for, not because we are free but because we are measurable against one another," because all singularity can be analyzed according to a rational grid. The grid fixes, locates, equalizes, hypostatizes a multiplicity and flow that, in Nietzsche's conception of freedom, always opposes it. And the center of the grid is – as Althusser's

(1971) psychoanalytic and structuralist Marxist work shows as well – the responsible subject, the one who "works all by himself."

8 Promises and Pain: The Subject

In contrast to the irresponsible spontaneity of the IWW hobo, being an animal bred "*with the right to make promises*" is for Nietzsche (1967) the "real problem regarding man." Nietzsche opposes to this another "force, that of *forgetfulness.* Forgetting is no mere *via inertiae* as the superficial imagine; it is rather an active and in the strictest sense positive faculty of repression… there could be no happiness, no cheerfulness, no hope, no pride, no *present,* without forgetfulness." But where "promises are made," "Man himself must first have become *calculable, regular, necessary,* even in his own image of himself, if he is to be able to stand security for *his own future,* which is what one who promises does!" (II: 1).

The conscience of a promising, calculable subject, one who can sign contracts and stand by them, is predicated in Nietzsche, as in Freud, on an internalization of aggression that is blocked from being released: "all instincts that do not discharge themselves outwardly *turn inward* – this is what I call the *internalization* of man: thus it was that man first developed what was later called his 'soul'" (II: 16).

Promises, responsibility, contracts are the currency of those who would make man (and nature) unitary, ruled by a sovereign, and calculable. And they were born from repression just as they make its continuation possible.

> This precisely is the long story of how *responsibility* originated. The task of breeding an animal with the right to make promises evidently embraces and presupposes as a preparatory task that one first *makes* men to a certain degree necessary, uniform, like among like, regular, and consequently calculable…with the aid of the morality of mores, and the social straitjacket, man was actually *made* calculable. If we place ourselves at the end of this tremendous process, where the tree at last brings forth fruit…we discover that the ripest fruit is the *sovereign individual…* [the subject who can stand by his word] even in the face of adversity. (II: 2)

This subject, this repressed being that has come to "rage against itself" becomes the bearer of the responsibility of the work ethic, the central morality of bourgeois society. Nietzsche lays out how the ascetic ideal and its priests "precipitate this via a different *training* against states of depression which is at any rate easier: *mechanical activity*. It is beyond doubt that this regimen alleviates an existence of suffering to a not inconsiderable degree: this fact is today called, somewhat dishonestly, 'the blessings of work.'"

He goes on: "Mechanical activity and what goes with it – such as absolute regularity, punctilious and unthinking obedience, a mode of life fixed once and for all, fully occupied time, a certain permission, indeed training for 'impersonality,' for self-forgetfulness, for 'incuria sui' – how thoroughly, how subtly the ascetic priest has known how to employ them in the struggle against pain!" (III: 18) Just as in Weber's (1992) story of the pastors who advised their flock to work hard (and take cold showers, among other ascetic techniques) to alleviate their psychic suffering, we see that in dealing with sufferers the priest made them "see benefits and a relative happiness in things they formerly hated..." that is, especially, work.

So, in all this (very German) social theory, aggressiveness that is thwarted from its original object is redirected back to its origin and taken up by the predictable, calculable subject who can be then counted on to make and honor promises to do what is "right" – that is, to work. But we must remember that the origin of aggressiveness directed outwards is the first installment of libidinal repression – the first "no." According to Marcuse, modern technology has made a serious reduction of working hours and thus of libidinal repression, not only possible but necessary. If we continue with the surplus repression of the capitalist performance principle or work ethic, libido will continue to be hyper-repressed and thus generative of more aggression and more guilt. If, instead, we become more free, there will be less aggression unleashed *and* internalized into guilt, bad conscience, and the asceticism of the slave morality that glorifies the "blessings of work."

9 A Postmodern Politics

One of the most important aspects of the IWW (a practice that began with the prefigurative organization, the WFM) was its refusal to sign contracts. They did not make promises. In this model of shop floor labor relations, conflicts get worked out day to day, based on the relation of forces at the time. The labor side works to keep those forces in labor's favor (by eliminating scabs, controlling labor supply, and by generating solidarity via speeches, songs, and person to person organizing). Essentially, a labor contract is a voluntary holding back, a promise not to use your power even when you have it – like at the busy time when your walking away from your responsibilities could do the most damage.

In the *Genealogy,* the strong and powerful have no need for contracts: "The man who can command, who is by nature a 'master'... what has he to do with making contracts? We do not negotiate with such beings... these men, these born organizers, have no idea what guilt, responsibility, and consideration are. In them that fearsome egotism of the artist is in charge..." (II:17). In Nietzsche's mythical telling, these "masters" were predators and thus subordinated their prey and generated in them the aggression that became internalized as bad conscience. But if, as I argue we should, we bracket the equation between predation and freedom, and even between predation and the free expression of aggression, what remains is the point that those with power have no need for contracts or the subjectivity or calculability that underlies contractual obligations. This is what is foundational to a Nietzschean labor movement politics: the organizing for power that allows for a life lived spontaneously and fully, even forgetfully, in the present.

Once a contract is signed by the representative of the collective worker, this representative has responsibility for enforcing it – that is, for disciplining those who would strike during its course or refuse to follow the agreed upon rules. In this way, the American syndicalism of the IWW, rooted in that of an earlier generation of miners, is an imminent critique of representation akin to Nietzsche's. Syndicalism is always considered the least theoretical of all left politics, far less than anarchism, with which it is frequently associated. The tag of antitheoretical comes partly because syndicalism does not attempt to *represent* the movement of the working class. It is a logic of pure, spontaneous action – economic resistance and cultural production, not a representation of the working class in the form of an analytical treatise or of a union official. It is made up of direct action at the point of production, and non-representational – that is, political and liberationist – art and literature.

The very figure of the working class in syndicalist politics, in fact, is a critique of identity and especially of identity based on work or the job. This is especially true within the IWW's American syndicalism, which mounted a militant critique of the AFL idea that the worker's interests would inevitably line up with their job, or even with having a job at all. The IWW organized the unwaged and the waged, the migratory and the local, and its workers were the original precariat. The syndicalist model is a critique of a sovereign political identity, one that can, like legitimate union leaders who sign contracts and make agreements, ultimately discipline its wilder internal forces, which is precisely what the subject does to the wild internal forces of the person in order to discipline them into a unitary, consistent identity.

A Nietzschean, postmodern critique of the subject refuses its totalizations, deconstructs its fictions of truth and falsity and points instead to a *partial* evaluation, from a position within (and not above or outside of) a differential state of forces. In the *Genealogy of Morals*, Nietzsche (1967) urges us to:

> ...be on guard against the dangerous old conceptual fiction that posited a 'pure, will-less, painless, timeless knowing subject'; let us guard against the snares of such contradictory concepts as 'pure reason,' 'absolute spirituality,' 'knowledge in itself,': these always demand that we should think of an eye that is completely unthinkable, an eye turned in no particular direction, in which the active and interpreting forces through which alone seeing becomes seeing *something*, are supposed to be lacking; these always demand of the eye an absurdity and a nonsense. There is *only* a perspective seeing, *only* a perspective 'knowing,' and the *more* affects we allow to speak about one thing, the *more* eyes, different eyes, we can use to observe one thing, the more complete will our 'concept' of this thing, our 'objectivity,' be. But to eliminate the will altogether, to suspend each and every affect, supposing we were capable of this – what would this mean but to *castrate* the intellect? (III: 12)

It is his advocacy of this kind of partial knowledge that makes Nietzsche the root of the postmodern deconstruction of enlightenment metanarratives of truth and history that critics of postmodernism like Angela Nagle see as the destruction of the ground of "real" politics, but that links him with the kind of emancipatory labor movement that explicitly refuses a politics based on the integrity of a responsible, fully interpellated, subjectified subject.

In a Nietzschean framework, as well as within the syndicalist politics of direct action, the movement of the working class does not need an abstract subject; it is one with its own action, a product of the will that is an inevitable characteristic of its position in a relation of forces and not of a working-class subject identity in the driver's seat:

> A quantum of force is equivalent to a quantum of drive, will, effect – more, it is nothing other than precisely this very driving, willing, effecting, and only owing to the seduction of language (and of the fundamental errors of reason that are petrified in it) which conceives and misconceives all effects as conditioned by something that causes effects, by a 'subject,' can it appear otherwise. For just as the popular mind separates the lightning from its flash and takes the latter for an *action*, for the operation of a subject called lightning, so popular morality also separates strength from expressions of strength, as if there were a neutral substratum behind the strong man, which was *free* to express strength or not to

> do so. But there is no such substratum; there is no "being" behind doing, effecting, becoming: "the doer" is merely a fiction added to the deed – the deed is everything... (1:13)

10 Labor's Will to Power

The labor and cultural politics I point to in this essay do not deploy any kind of stable subject identity – of the worker who signs a name to a contract or as a citizen in a state with rights and responsibilities. Hoboes were famous for never giving their real names and only going by playful nicknames. And these original American syndicalists were exiles who rode the rails and worked in liminal unconventional spaces like docks and mines and forests. They had no interest in the state (they were in fact mostly anti-imperialist resisters and considered enemies of the state), only in the differential relations between boss and worker and cop and worker, generally in flux moment to moment. The Nietzschean, and Wobbly, power analysis replaces one whereby the traditional subject with agency (ostensibly held by those at the top of the social hierarchy only) acts on its counterpart, the passive object of that agency, with a decentered terrain whereby forces come up against each other with differential power.

Politically, then, a Nietzschean sensibility never moves to identify the sovereign and try to replace it, with socialist or social democratic electoral victories or with worker's control of production. Those moves reproduce the repression – of chaos, wildness, the Dionysian – by which the rational subject, either individual or state, is constituted. It is not surprising, then, that the Wobblies in their "irresponsible" use of sabotage, or work slowdowns, as well as their refusal to fight in a nationalist war, or to link their identity with the state, were subjected to the most massive state and employer repression that American society has ever seen. Both the Espionage Act and the nationwide legal injunctions against "Criminal Syndicalism" were invented for them. And this is why the more electoral and civility minded socialists of their day broke decisively with and actually worked to repress their politics – Wobblies were not looking to replace the boss or the nation but to oppose it; not looking to rule or to manage, but to be powerful and free.

The syndicalist model, thus, is a model of action based on the strategic analysis of the state of forces at all times. In Deleuze's (1983) *Nietzsche and Philosophy*, he lays out this kind of power analysis: "Nietzsche is most misunderstood in relation to the question of power. Every time we interpret will to power as 'wanting or seeking power' we encounter platitudes which have nothing to do with Nietzsche's thought. If it is true that all things reflect a state of forces then power designates the element, or rather the differential relationship, of forces which directly confront one another" (xi). Under capitalism, the space in which the two forces, capitalist and worker, come up against each other is the point of production. Thus, labor's will to power is precisely direct action at the point of production.

The IWW is of course well known for its advocacy of the idea of the One Big Union (OBU). But this concept is also far more resonant with a decentered Nietzschean power analysis than is generally understood. The One Big Union idea has actually nothing to do with a unitary apparatus, a union in the traditional sense of a legal representative authorized to represent its official members, to which all workers would belong. Instead, OBU referred to the viral, sympathetic strike: the spread of spontaneous shutdowns, slowdowns, and sabotage, like wildfire, from one shop to another. According to Irish syndicalist organizer Jim Larkin's "doctrine of tainted goods," (for our purposes, Larkinism in the UK, new unionism, and syndicalism generally refer to the same industrial logic) workers organized in solidarity would not touch, especially on the docks, cargo that was coming from a struck shop or port, until the workers there won their demands.

This union model is not "legitimate" or "organized" but instead spontaneous and viral; its fuel is not an institution but a culture, of solidarity; and it is multiple and horizontal by nature and functions to enact a refusal of work that spreads, eventually leading to a revolutionary general strike. Contracts, although capable of protecting workers in times of poor leverage, only held them back when they were powerful. Most important, the promises of calculability and responsibility in the contract restrict the freedom and power of exit that were central to the hobo culture and to their labor market strategy, aimed at keeping the supply of workers in any one place low relative to capitalist demand. It is a labor strategy that mobilizes the selfish desire for freedom rather than – as so many early 20th century socialists did – moralizing about how irresponsible it is.

Reactionary, authoritarian politics are rooted in the resentment that characterizes slave morality – the idea (usually imaginary) that someone is getting something that we do not have drives the slavish desire to humble them. This is what the white nationalist and fascist reaction to the gains of the civil rights movement and the liberatory politics of the counterculture, in the context of a neoliberal capitalist era characterized by austerity, insecurity, and downward mobility, is made of. To be fascist is to be the complete opposite of what Nietzsche defines as the freedom of the noble, even in its aggressive form. Because for the free, aggression takes the form of competition and sport, that which gives pleasure, far more than in the desire to murder, rape, pillage, destroy, actions which are characterized not by freedom, selfishness, and the pathos of distance, but by a slavish obsession with an other which *must be destroyed.*

Unmasking the so-called morality of authoritarianism is more important than ever as the ascendant proto-fascist right talks freedom but actually espouses the most ressentiment-fueled, other-centered, moralistic and punitive logic imaginable. A bold politics of liberation has always been the only effective way to oppose authoritarianism. Free spontaneity is the polar opposite of the modern rationality that, as Max Weber makes indelibly clear, is all about the discipline and repression of the work ethic and the forms of responsibility and accountability central to it. If capital's cultural logic is instrumental and ascetic, what opposes it is a countercultural logic – a Dionysian, rock and roll refusal of work and affirmation of the vital forces of pleasure, creativity, and love. When the roots of American counterculture were planted by hoboes and modernists around the turn of the twentieth century, its proponents understood clearly its Nietzschean origins.

11 Labor and Liberation: American Nietzsche

Given all these connections, it is not surprising that Nietzsche had an independent influence and resonance with American liberatory labor politics, via the anarchism of Emma Goldman, via the organizers and intellectuals who formed such a large part of the IWW's American syndicalism, and via the modernist intellectual currents swirling around American radicalism in the early twentieth century.

Emma Goldman, one of the twentieth century's greatest Americans and anarchists, is the best known of these linkages. Of course, the combination of Nietzsche's dismissals of anarchism itself with his quite anarchistic views have contributed to volumes of debates. But one thing is clear: Goldman's ideas were a key conduit for Nietzsche's liberatory vision to link up with the labor movement and the libidinal culture that, as she made indelibly clear, had to be its foundation. Although the twenty plus lectures she gave on Nietzsche between 1913 and 1917 were, tragically, lost forever after the offices of her paper, *Mother Earth,* were confiscated by police during the same WWI anti-sedition raids that ultimately destroyed the IWW, the evidence that does remain shows that Goldman was particularly concerned to correct the misreadings of Nietzsche prevailing in her day, long before the Nazis got a hold of him.

Goldman recognized her own liberatory anarchism in Nietzsche's work – the power of the creative, the individual, the will; the fusing of form and substance in political discourse, common to his work and to hers; and the necessity for a transvaluation of values to fuel the kind of direct action that is the product of the will to freedom and not of a subjected being. But most of all, Goldman's interpretation of the *ubermensch* was a democratic one, and she understood the "aristocratic" sensibilities for which Nietzsche is often misinterpreted, the pathos of distance that allows the affirmative and independent creation of values, as being potentially available to all:

> Friedrich Nietzsche, for instance, is decried as a hater of the weak because he believed in the *ubermensch*. It does not occur to the shallow interpreters of that giant mind that this vision of the *ubermensch* also called for a state of society which will not give birth to a race of weaklings or slaves.
>
> quoted in Starcross 2004: 33–34

This is in many ways a very American idea – that aristocratic power and pleasure could be the province of the many, and not just the few. And that individual freedom was, although predicated on social transformation, ultimately more important than the imperatives of the collective:

> Friedrich Nietzsche called the state a cold monster. What would he have called the hideous beast in the garb of modern dictatorship? Not that government had ever allowed much scope to the individual; but the champions of the new State ideology do not grant even that much. "The individual is nothing," they declare, "it is the collectivity which counts." Nothing less than complete surrender of the individual will satisfy the insatiable appetite of the new deity.
>
> quoted in Starcross 2004: 35

This is a Nietzschean anarchism critical of both imperialism and state socialism. Goldman's work was so popular (and so threatening to its nationalist, newly imperialist war effort that the U.S. government deported her) largely because it resonated so deeply with a particularly American form of individualism and libertarianism: a politics she shared with her friend Elizabeth Gurley Flynn and the Wobbly hobo free speech fighters that they both publicly joined and defended.

Nietzsche was so central for Goldman that she recounted in *Living My Life* (2006 [1931]) the story of the night she ended it with her then-lover because he did not understand or care for Nietzsche and thus could not possibly understand her.

Later, she found a more suitable partner in Dr. Ben Reitman, among whose feats of cultural organizing included Chicago's Washington "Bughouse" Square and the Dil Pickle Club, radical and democratic spaces of art, politics, and intellectual life, where open air lectures on Nietzsche and Stirner, among other modernist philosophers, were common and where Wobblies and hoboes congregated.

Reitman was shaped by Nietzsche's work as well; in one of many stories of the way that Nietzsche's work made its way into early 20th century cultural and political radicalism, novelist, chronicler and proponent of bohemian Greenwich Village sexual freedom Henry Miller tells a story of his taking a trip to San Diego in 1913. It coincided with one of the pitched hobo free speech battles there: in response to the incendiary speech of the radical soapbox orators, street riots, vigilante mobs, and mass jailings ensued. In the midst of the chaos, Miller attended a speech by Emma Goldman that he says changed his life; after the speech he approached her "consort" Reitman, from whom he bought a copy of Nietzsche's *Anti-Christ* and Max Stirner's *The Ego and His Own*. (According to Miller's biographer Robert Ferguson [1991 (1980)], all this probably actually happened in San Pedro.) More important, "Reitman cross-examined Henry carefully before letting him have the books, fearing that he might be an agent provocateur." Here was further proof for Miller of the explosive social power of the word, written or spoken – an explosive character enacted by Nietzsche's texts and not just described – and it was then that he decided to work exclusively as a writer pushing the boundaries of art and sexual liberation.

Miller remained close to the IWW and political radicals throughout the 1910s, frequenting Mabel Dodge Luhan's storied weekly Greenwich Village salon with writers, artists, and activists like Big Bill Haywood (who reportedly was never comfortable in the crowd) and John Reed. Emma Goldman was a habitué of the salon as well. Luhan wanted explicitly to make a cultural intervention into political life and, according to Rosenhagen, gave IWW organizer Frank Tannenbaum a copy of Nietzsche to "bolster his political will" as he served a year in prison for his labor movement activity.

The Nietzschean influence on Henry Miller was evident too in what Jennifer Ratner-Rosenhagen calls his "idolization" of the West Indian radical Hubert Harrison, founding father of the "New Negro" movement – cultural, internationalist, characterized by militant refusal of racist discipline and, significantly, allied with the anti-imperialism of Irish nationalists in the United States. It was the left wing of what became known as the Harlem Renaissance, and in Ratner-Rosenhagen's work on the American intellectual and cultural reception of Nietzsche, she points out the ways in which Harrison, the "Father of Harlem Radicalism" "drew on Nietzsche's philosophy as he hammered out his own...

Harrison discovered in Nietzsche a model of the freelance, freethinking, autonomous intellectual he aspired to become" (Ratner-Rosenhagen 2012: 156).[4]

Harrison was one of many links between the intellectual ferment of the early twentieth century and the labor radicalism of that time, editing *The Masses* briefly, publishing in the IWW's *International Socialist Review*, and organizing an open-air street corner university in Harlem as well as working with Marcus Garvey to found the United Negro Improvement Association (Perry 2010). Significantly, Harrison lectured frequently at the Ferrer Center, an educational institution that was part of the Modern School movement, a free school that Ratner-Rosenhagen characterizes as a "hothouse of American Nietzscheanism" where Emma Goldman and other intellectuals with a libertarian bent often lectured. It was also a hothouse of Irish American anti-imperialist and pro-labor radicalism, run by Harry Kelly and often headlined by Elizabeth Gurley Flynn, one of sabotage's most eloquent proponents.

This "hothouse of Nietzscheanism" was also a base of operations for the American syndicalism of the IWW and its allies – Mexican revolutionaries, free speech fighters, strikers, especially those associated with the IWW (Paterson, Ludlow, Lawrence, and the unemployed movement of 1913–1914). The IWW and revolutionary syndicalism were among the common topics of discussion and debate, along with psychoanalysis, sex, poetry, art, literature, and the theater. Ferrer School members and friends were the New Yorkers who took in the children of the Paterson and the Lawrence IWW strikers so that the workers could fight the bosses there without the worry and conservatism that comes with parental responsibility.

According to Paul Avrich (2005):

> In an age of industrial violence, anarcho-syndicalism exerted a powerful appeal among Ferrer Center adherents, with its uncomplicated philosophy of action and uncompromising opposition to capitalism. Two of the first American books on revolutionary syndicalism were written by Ferrer Center regulars, *The New Unionism* by Andre Tridon and *Syndicalism in France* by Louis Levine. Tridon and Levine also delivered lectures and led discussions on the subject, together with Bill Shatoff, Bill Haywood, Carlos

4 Harrison was explicitly a Nietzschean; much of the flowering of black culture and politics during the early twentieth century implicitly resonated with Nietzsche's critique. Zora Neale Hurston, for instance, once said: "Sometimes, I feel discriminated against, but it does not make me angry. It merely astonishes me. How can any deny themselves the pleasure of my company? It's beyond me." A better example of Nietzsche's aristocratic pathos of distance would be difficult to find (Hurston 2000: 117).

> Tresca, and Flynn. *The Modern School* magazine reported that syndicalists and labor militants were "familiar figures at our center."
>
> AVRICH 2005: 133

Avrich goes on to describe how in 1912 the Syndicalist Educational League was established at the center and led by Hippolyte Havel and Harry Kelly, center directors. The aim was to spread "the idea of Syndicalism, Direct Action, and the General Strike among the organized and unorganized workers of America." Its program "echoed the preamble of the IWW constitution" ("the working class and the employing class have nothing in common"), stating that "economic compromises with capital are based on the fundamental fallacy of the identity of interests between master and slave, and are detrimental to the cause of labor." The League also exhorted workers to stay clear of the ballot box and stick with the antagonistic logic of direct action.

Significantly for the cultural analysis of class politics that emerges from a Nietzschean read, Ferrer radicals Gurley Flynn and Harrison both refused to pit the liberation of women or of blacks against that of the class as a whole. And Harrison, like Flynn, saw the tactic of sabotage and the anti-work demand for shorter hours – less time spent in alienated labor, both for mass worker leverage and because work under capitalism is unpleasant and oppressive and ought to be resisted – as key to the liberation of the working class as a whole as well as its subaltern members.

Driven by this, Harrison took sides in the intra-left battle mentioned earlier between the direct actionists and saboteurs of the IWW and the more "respectable" (and far less Nietzschean) socialists who saw victory not in fighting power but in taking it, not in escaping from rule – freedom – but in ruling. Harrison recognized that most blacks in the U.S. could not vote and thus the electoral strategies pursued by the Socialist Party were limited. In "The Negro and Industrial Socialism" (2001 [1914]) he argued for a politics of direct action at the point of production, where "even the voteless proletarian can in a measure help toward the final abolition of the capitalist system" because they still have "labor power-which they can be taught to withhold" and they can organize themselves "at the point of production" and "work to shorten the hours of labor, [and] to raise wages..." (Harrison 2001 [1914]: 76). He noted that the Western Federation of Miners had done this and had successfully won the eight-hour workday "without the aid of the legislatures or the courts" (or, as we have noted here, contracts). He was also a featured speaker (and the only black speaker) at the IWW's 1913 Paterson silk strike, with Haywood, Flynn, and others, and he publicly defended Haywood against attack by the right wing of the Socialist Party on the issue of sabotage.

And in fact only Haywood spoke in defense of the "Negro Question" at the 1912 convention of the party, where all other delegates either ignored the question or supported the statement that came out of the convention, which has been called one of the most "rabidly racist sentiments in the history of the American left." Harrison ended his involvement with the party soon after, and he continued to support the tactics of direct action and sabotage. By that time, Haywood too had been kicked out of the party for his open advocacy of the "guerrilla warfare" of sabotage.

12 Jack London and the Hobo *Ubermenschen*

The American writer whose life and work has been most closely associated with Nietzsche was Jack London, yet another modernist radical associated with the Ferrer School. London lectured at the Ferrer Center frequently during his time in New York City and, like Harrison and Haywood, fought on the left of the Socialist Party until his departure from it. London's Nietzschean sensibilities were part and parcel of his celebration of that iconic American rebel, the hobo. And Nietzsche's pathos of distance was, without a doubt, the most prominent characteristic of London's depiction of the hobo.

It is precisely in London's hobo material that we can see most clearly how a Nietzschean individualism can link up with a labor politics oriented not to morality, justice, or responsibility, but to freedom. London clearly saw the hobos as the vanguard of what Nietzsche called the pathos of distance. In his portrayal of skilled hobos in 1902's *Rods and Gunnels*, their rebellious lawlessness resonates with Nietzsche's idea of the noble races, those who create their own values:

> They [skilled hobos] are ... the *blond beasts*[5] of Nietzsche, lustfully roving and conquering through sheer superiority and strength. Unwritten is the

5 The blond beast is one of the more problematic aspects of London's appropriation of Nietzsche – and of Nietzsche (1967) himself, who says: "One cannot fail to see at the bottom of all these noble races the beast of prey, the splendid blond beast prowling about avidly in search of spoil and victory...in contrast to the tame man, the hopelessly mediocre and insipid man ..." (I: 11).

Although "blond beast" was, according to Walter Kauffman, mistranslated as "teutonic blond beast" by Francis Goiffing in the *Portable Nietzsche*, it was not a white supremacist term, as so many on today's proto-fascist right misread it. Given that in Nietzsche's day, the term "Aryan" that he uses to talk about a race of masters, referred to Indians, Persians, and, as he explicitly links them together in the *Genealogy*, Celts, Kauffman's assertion that the blond beast simply referred to the lion, the king of the jungle, and as easily could have been a panther, a black beast, is one easy out.

> law they impose. They are the Law, the Law incarnate. And the underworld looks up and obeys. They are not easy of access. They are conscious of their own nobility and treat only with equals.
>
> quoted in FONER 1947: 42

According to John Lennon (2007), a chronicler of London who was highly critical of the

competitive individualism on the railroad boxcars:

But London was arguably a real racist, writing explicitly anti-Japanese material during the war and saying in no uncertain terms, "I am a white man first and then a socialist." Also, he was a fan of Herbert Spencer and Charles Darwin and for a time applied "survival of the fittest" ideas to race. However, the relationship between his Nietzscheanism and his racism is not as clear as it might seem, since London also, in his time in Hawaii among the surfers of Waikiki, writes glowingly of the majestic natives in "blond-beastly" language, calling the native sport of surfing "a royal sport for the natural kings of earth." Lest it be unclear who these natural kings were, London describes one of them:

And suddenly, out there where a big smoker lifts skyward, rising like a sea-god from out of the welter of spume and churning white, on the giddy, toppling, overhanging and downfalling, precarious crest appears the dark head of a man. Swiftly he rises through the rushing white. His black shoulders, his chest, his loins, his limbs – all is abruptly projected on one's vision. Where but the moment before was only the wide desolation and invincible roar, is now a man, erect, full-statured, not struggling frantically in that wild movement, not buried and crushed and buffeted by those mighty monsters, but standing above them all, calm and superb, poised on the giddy summit, his feet buried in the churning foam, the salt smoke rising to his knees, and all the rest of him in the free air and flashing sunlight, and he is flying through the air, flying forward, flying fast as the surge on which he stands.

He is a Mercury – a brown Mercury. His heels are winged, and in them is the swiftness of the sea. In truth, from out of the sea he has leaped upon the back of the sea, and he is riding the sea that roars and bellows and cannot shake him from its back. But no frantic outreaching and balancing is his. He is impassive, motionless as a statue carved suddenly by some miracle out of the sea's depth from which he rose. And straight on toward shore he flies on his winged heels and the white crest of the breaker. There is a wild burst of foam, a long tumultuous rushing sound as the breaker falls futile and spent on the beach at your feet; and there, at your feet steps calmly ashore a Kanaka, burnt golden and brown by the tropic sun. Several minutes ago he was a speck a quarter of a mile away. He has 'bitted the bull-mouth breaker' and ridden it in, and the pride in the feat shows in the carriage of his magnificent body as he glances for a moment carelessly at you who sit in the shade of the shore. He is a Kanaka – and more, he is a man, a member of the kingly species that has mastered matter and the brutes and lorded it over creation..." (London 1923: 75–78).

London wrote in similarly glowing terms about the majesty of Jack Johnson, so although he can certainly be accused of a romanticizing primitivism, his interpretation of Nietzsche's blond beast and aristocratic race of nobles had nothing to do with blood and soil white nationalism.

> As Jack London's writings, along with many hobo autobiographies, indicate, there was a real sense of pride resulting from outwitting and tricking the bulls, whose job was specifically to ensure that the 'bo stayed off the train. Although London put his physical self in much danger when "catching out," his movements were no longer subject to the same regulations as those who were "riding the cushions." Unlike these passengers who had to accept the rules of the railroad company when they bought their tickets, London did not have an assigned seat, nor had he exchanged money for the ride…Being a part of this elite group of hobos…allowed London to place himself as both the dispenser and the very embodiment of the law, thus transcending any feelings of inferiority.
>
> LENNON 2007: 15

For London, the hobo's invisibility was the key to playing by their own rules: as Lennon puts it,

> that he was invisible to those who were searching for him was, in fact, the very thing that made him part of the nobility of the underworld. He was a success, a "lord and master," only if he *perfected his ability to disappear*. Those "gay-cats" and inexperienced rail riders that London so despised would eventually be seen and caught by the bulls, but the "profresh" would remain undetected and ride wherever they wished. Instead of reading his invisibility and hiding as a mark of weakness, London wore them as badges of honor.
>
> LENNON 2007: 15, emphasis mine

The spirit of freedom that made London such a romantic character followed him until his death at forty from a morphine overdose. He remained a socialist his whole life even after he bitterly quit the Socialist party over what he saw as their misguided, bourgeois, tame, and doomed desire to take electoral power. He remained a lifelong direct actionist and a critic of left-electoral politics. Like Emma Goldman and Hubert Harrison, his Nietzschean anti-capitalism insisted on individual freedom as something that could not be given up in the course of collective struggle and that indeed would be the product of it.

According to Foner,

> the fact that so much of the Nietzschean philosophy, emphasizing as it did an aristocracy of supermen who would dominate the ordinary run of human beings, and flaunting its detestation of socialism and trade unionism, went counter to his socialist convictions did not bother Jack London.

> He took those aspects of Nietzsche which appealed to him and which he could, in his own fashion, reconcile with Marxism. After all, why could not the supermen work to bring about a system under which the average man would be benefited? 'Why should there be one empty belly in all the world,' he wrote in the essay *Wanted: A New Law of Development,* when the work of ten men can feed a hundred? What if my brother be not so strong as I? He has not sinned. Wherefore should he suffer hunger – he and his sinless little ones? *Away with the old law*. There is food and shelter for all, therefore let us all receive food and shelter.
>
> FONER 1947: 35, emphasis mine

Most of London's biographers point to the Nietzscheanism of the way in which he described his own youthful experiences with tramping and contrast it with the militant socialist he later became, and in "How I Became a Socialist," he outlines the way one led to the other. In London's own telling, he had to leave behind the Nietzschean philosophy of his young tramping days when those days showed him how brutal the world could be to the worker. However, his socialism never really lost its Nietzschean cast: in London's words, "The first principle of the socialist movement," he wrote, is "selfishness, pure, downright, selfishness" (quoted in Raskin 2006).

Still, London does recount a transformation from Nietzschean to socialist:

> I was a rampant individualist. It was very natural. I was a winner... I could see myself only raging through life without end like one of Nietzsche's *blond beasts*, lustfully roving and conquering by sheer superiority and strength. As for the unfortunates, the sick, and ailing, and old, and maimed, I must confess I hardly thought of them at all... I was proud to be one of nature's strong-armed noblemen.
>
> quoted in FONER 1947: 363

However, he goes on to say that "my joyous individualism was dominated by orthodox bourgeois ethics" until he embarked on tramping, "this new *blond-beast* adventure" which showed him a different world and:

> I found myself looking upon life from a new and totally different angle... I found there all sorts of men, many of whom had once been as good as myself and just as *blond-beastly*; sailor-men, soldier-men, labor-men, all wrenched and distorted and twisted out of shape by toil and hardship and accident...[ending] there before my eyes in the shambles at the bottom of the Social Pit.
>
> quoted in FONER 1947: 364

As Nels Anderson (1923) lays out in his classic Chicago School ethnography *The Hobo* (and as Ben Reitman's own migrant worker typology makes clear), there were in fact different varieties of migrant workers at the turn of the 20th century. Some were more wild and free; others were more desperate. Jack London was among the former, which Anderson calls "Hobohemia" to refer to the group as well as their bohemian, communal "jungles" and "main stems" and those who he saw moving down into the Pit were in the second group. Importantly, both groups together constituted the "footloose rebels," of the IWW and fought in the hobo free speech battles as well as the labor struggles of the early 20th century. And significantly, both groups rejected the work ethic as an oppressive value that could only accrue to the benefit of the capitalist.

In fact, the key moment in "How I Became a Socialist" is when London comes to see that it is precisely work itself that turns the wild and free beings into the downtrodden ones, and that threatens even him – young, strong, full of life – with sliding into the Social Pit. It is here, indeed, that London lays out a clear refusal of the work ethic:

> There and then I swore a great oath. It ran something like this: *All my days I have worked hard with my body, and according to the number of days I have worked, by just that much am I nearer the bottom of the Pit. I shall climb out of the Pit, but not by the muscles of my body shall I climb out. I shall do no more hard work, and may God strike me dead if I do another day's hard work with my body more than I absolutely have to do.* And I have been busy ever since running away from hard work.
>
> quoted in FONER 1947: 364

So, it is really not Nietzschean individualism and transvaluation of ascetic slave morality that London turns away from when he embraces socialism – his remained a profoundly individualistic socialism that, like the anarchism of Emma Goldman, insisted on vitality and pleasure as central to revolution. It is the fact that capitalism itself, and especially work under capitalism, destroys the conditions under which people can flourish and be free. London's whole iconic essay can be read as his turning to socialism as a turn away from the work ethic (and later, his resignation from the Socialist Party can be read as his coming to understand that the party was not the enemy of work, responsibility, or sovereignty).

Thus, although scholars like Foner (1947) and Katherine Littell (1977) see a radical break between London's early Nietzscheanism and later class-struggle radicalism, I argue that he leaves behind not his focus on individual freedom and autonomy, but his valorization of work. Reading London this way allows us to revisit the Nietzscheanism of his hobo tales in *The Road* and see its continuity with his socialism – a socialism that ended, as it did for Haywood and Harrison, in a break with the Socialist Party over what can be described as the battle between syndicalist, antagonistic direct action and the bourgeois respectability of electoral socialism.

In fact, his socialism, bringing together of the work of Marx and Nietzsche, exemplified the kind of politics that the IWW espoused. He was not only close to the IWW (the IWW published a number of his works), but he also, like them, insisted (in numerous speeches and political treatises) on class struggle and antagonism as the essence of capitalism and on direct action at the point of production as the only way that the working class could fight capital effectively.

After years of battling within the socialist movement for more working-class militancy and rebellion, more open contempt for the bourgeoisie and less bourgeois civility and electoral strategy, he finally left the Socialist Party shortly before his death. His 1916 resignation letter began: "Dear Comrades. I am resigning from the Socialist Party because of its lack of fire and fight, and its loss of emphasis upon the class struggle." He says: "Trained in the class struggle... I believed that the working class, by fighting, by never fusing, by never making terms with the enemy, could emancipate itself. [But] the whole trend of Socialism in the US during recent years has been one of peaceableness and compromise..." (Foner 1947: 123).

The ending of his resignation letter shows that he never lost his Nietzscheanism, and that his remained a radical and militantly left wing interpretation of his philosophy (even if he had disavowed him from time to time): "My final word is that liberty, freedom, and independence are royal things...If races and classes cannot rise up and by their own strength of brain and brawn, wrest from the world liberty, freedom, and independence, they never in time can come to these possessions...and will be what they have always been in the past... inferior races and inferior classes" (Foner 1947: 124).

He'd given up socialism as useless – the movement had not heeded the lesson of his novel *The Iron Heel*, which speculated a future society in which weak tepid socialists with failed electoral strategies had been brutally and finally defeated by the capitalists, who were always willing to fight with the gloves off. Importantly, London was also like Nietzsche in that he saw the written word as more than a representation: it was an intervention. Socialism was part and parcel of his literary art, and vice versa. For him as for Nietzsche, form and content were not separate. According to one biographer: "He thought of rhetoric as an art, and propaganda as an art, and socialism as an art, too. An author who cared about language, and the sound of words, and about the felicities of style and form, he refused to crank out books with simple socialist sermons, or to deliver speeches with clichés about oppression" (Raskin 2006).

13 Claiming the Instinct for Freedom

The anarchist, the black liberationist socialist; the theorist of sabotage and transvaluation; and the chronicler of the quintessential American *ubermensch*, the hobo: Goldman, Harrison, Flynn, and London provide direct links between the American modernism suffused with Nietzschean sensibilities and the most vibrant and militant tradition in the history of the American labor movement. This tradition, of direct action fueled by a transvaluation of the Protestant work ethic and geared toward greater individual freedom in everyday life, is the soul of the institutions of the movement, unions. Without this soul, the union form is vulnerable and crumbles under attack. This attack is central to contemporary politics, and I propose that the answer is not to work to defend decaying structures but to fire up the spirit that animated them: solidarity. To the IWW and syndicalism in general, if you have solidarity, you do not even need a union (this is essentially what the One Big Union idea was).

This is why it is so important that the affirmative, vitalist, value creating ethic of the Nietzschean not be ceded to the ressentiment-fueled revanchist hard right. They are polar opposites. Americans are culturally libertarian, as the culture warriors of the 1910s and 60s understood clearly, and as Ratner-Rosenhagen (2012) argues, Nietzsche's sensibilities have been a central part of American culture for over a century.

Nietzsche is punk rock, his poetry not representative but an explosive intervention, and just as fascists were attracted to the liberated aggressiveness of punk, the *Daily Stormer* types have wanted the contested Nietzsche for their own for a long time now. But just as antifascists beat back the fascists at concerts in the 1970s, directly refused them the territory of punk, liberationists who understand that freedom augurs far more than the liberation of cruel desires must do the same thing now. We do not fight authoritarian white nationalism by posing as morally superior but by engaging in the kind of pure power politics that can really win; that is, the politics of freedom and pleasure.

These are the forces that are stronger than aggressiveness and that can counter the subjection, resentment, and authoritarianism that emerges from the austerity and repression that capitalism's neoliberal era has made commonplace. This is how we ought to read the emancipatory politics of Nietzsche, and how he has been read by some of the most important forces in the history of American radicalism.

As the IWW and its precursors understood clearly, refusing to flood the market with labor is the key to working class power. And countercultural worker militancy, among Wobblies, hippies, and others, shows us that in the struggle to restrict labor supply, that is, reduce hours and thus raise wages, a liberatory culture is labor's strongest and most resilient weapon. It inspires collective action and it is inherently solidaristic. Anti-work counterculture (that is, an anti-ascetic transvaluation of values) has fueled the most militant moments of the American labor movement, and it has been the most influential, because it speaks to what is truly essential in the class struggle. These radical cultural politics live on, (even as we've all been relentlessly sped up over the past decades), in the subterranean desires and practices of the American worker. They remain available to be mobilized by a labor movement reinvigorated with its own best, most solidaristic, most militant, and most life-affirming history.

Part of this history is the story of American labor radicals' reception of Nietzsche and their recognition of the deep resonance between Nietzsche's philosophy and the syndicalist essence of the American labor movement. It is high time to reclaim this tradition of American (and international) labor – of refusing work and transvaluing ascetic moralism especially around work and austerity – and we cannot see our way clearly if we leave the insights and inspiration of Friedrich Nietzsche to the history and politics of the right.

References

Althusser, Louis. 1971. "Ideology and Ideological State Apparatuses." In *Lenin and Philosophy and Other Essays*. London: New Left Books.

Anderson, Nels. 1923. *The Hobo: The Sociology of the Homeless Man*. Chicago: University of Chicago Press.

Avrich, Paul. 2005. *The Modern School Movement: Anarchism and Education in the United States.* New York: AK Press.

Balibar, Etienne. 2014. "Althusser and the 'Ideological State Apparatuses.'" In *On the Reproduction of Capitalism*, by Louis Althusser, vii-xviii. London and New York: Verso.

Brissenden, Paul. 1919. *The IWW: A Study of American Syndicalism.* New York: Russell and Russell.

Burgmann, Verity. 1998. *Revolutionary Industrial Unionism: The Industrial Workers of the World in Australia.* New York: Cambridge University Press.

Colson, Daniel. 2004. "Nietzsche and the Libertarian Workers' Movement." In *I Am Not a Man, I Am Dynamite! Friedrich Nietzsche and the Anarchist Tradition*, edited by John Moore with Spencer Sunshine. New York: Autonomedia.

Davis, Mike. 1975. "The Stopwatch and the Wooden Shoe: Scientific Management and the Industrial Workers of the World." *Radical America* 9 (January–February): 69–95.

Deleuze, Gilles, 1983. *Nietzsche and Philosophy.* New York: Columbia University Press.

Ferguson, Robert. 1991 [1980]. *Henry Miller: A Life.* New York: W. W. Norton and Company.

Flynn, Elizabeth Gurley. 1917. *Sabotage: The Conscious Withdrawal of the Workers' Industrial Efficiency*. Chicago: IWW Publishing Bureau.

Foner, Philip. 1947. *Jack London, American Rebel: A Collection of His Social Writings, Together with an Extensive Study of the Man and His Times.* New York: Citadel Press.

Goldman, Emma. 2006 [1931]. *Living My Life, Vol. I.* New York: Penguin Classics.

Harrison, Hubert. 2001 [1914]. "The Negro and Industrial Socialism." In *A Hubert Harrison Reader*, edited by Jeffrey B. Perry, 76. Middletown, CT: Wesleyan University Press.

Hirschman, Albert O. 1970. *Exit, Voice, and Loyalty: Responses to Decline in Firms, Organizations, and States.* Cambridge: Harvard University Press.

Hurston, Zora Neale. 2000. "How it Feels to be Colored Me." In *The Best American Essays of the Century,* edited by Joyce Carol Oates. New York: Houghton Mifflin.

Lasch, Christopher. 1979. *The Culture of Narcissism.* New York: W. W. Norton and Company.

Lennon, John. 2007. "Can a Hobo Share a Box-Car?" *American Studies* Winter: 5–30.

Littell Katherine M. 1977. "The 'Nietzschean' and the Individualist in Jack London's Socialist Writings." In *American Studies*, 309–323. Stuttgart: J.B. Metzler.

London, Jack. 1907. *The Road.* New York: Macmillan.

London, Jack. 1923. *The Cruise of the Snark.* New York: Macmillan.

Marcuse, Herbert. 1955. *Eros and Civilization: A Philosophical Inquiry into Freud.* Boston: Beacon Press.

Nagle, Angela. 2017. *Kill All Normies: Online Culture Wars from 4chan and Tumblr to Trump and the Alt-Right.* New York: Zero Books.

Nietzsche, Friedrich. 2010. *The Gay Science.* New York: Knopf Doubleday.

Nietzsche, Friedrich. 1967. *On the Genealogy of Morals.* New York: Random House.

Perry, Jeffrey. 2010. *Hubert Harrison: The Voice of Harlem Radicalism.* New York: Columbia University Press.

Raskin, Jonah. 2006. "Jack London, Burning Man: Portrait of an American Socialist." *Socialism and Democracy* 19(2). http://sdonline.org/38/jack-london-burning-man-portrait-of-an-american-socialist/. Accessed August 1, 2018.

Ratner-Rosenhagen, Jennifer. 2012. *American Nietzsche.* Chicago: University of Chicago Press.

Reich, Wilhelm. 1970 [1933]. *The Mass Psychology of Fascism.* New York: Farrar, Strauss, and Giroux.

Roberts, Michael. 2016. "Twilight of Work: The Labor Question in Nietzsche and Marx." *Critical Sociology*. https://doi.org/10.1177/0896920516681427.

Rosemont, Franklin. 2003. *Joe Hill: the IWW and the Making of a Revolutionary Working Class Counterculture*. New York: PM Press.

Starcross, Leigh. 2004. "Nietzsche was an Anarchist." In *I Am Not a Man, I Am Dynamite! Friedrich Nietzsche and the Anarchist Tradition*, edited by John Moore with Spencer Sunshine. New York: Autonomedia.

Taylor, Frederick. 1911. *Principles of Scientific Management*. New York: W. W. Norton.

Weber, Max. 1992. *The Protestant Ethic and the Spirit of Capitalism*. New York: Routledge.

CHAPTER 8

Marxism, Anarchism, and the Nietzschean Critique of Capitalism

Gary Yeritsian

[W]e need all exuberant, floating, dancing, mocking, childish, and blissful art lest we lose our *freedom above things* that our ideal demands of us....

FRIEDRICH NIETZSCHE, *The Gay Science* (1974)

1 Introduction[1]

A rich tradition within Marxist thought has looked down upon Friedrich Nietzsche as a reactionary defender of domination and inequality. Georg Lukács' *The Destruction of Reason* (1980) is one standard point of reference. Lukács concedes Nietzsche's rhetorical and literary brilliance, but ultimately deems him a reactionary whose ostensibly unsystematic thought conceals an underlying ideological alignment with capitalism and imperialism. For Lukács, this is part of the wave of irrationalist post-Hegelian German thought – much of which is oriented around a quasi-heroic *Lebensphilosphie* – that would culminate in the hideous ideology of the Nazi regime. Moreover, Nietzschean philosophy represents, on this reading, an all-out assault on the Marxian concerns with equality and historical progress, reflecting the unease of socially detached intellectuals with the supposedly homogenizing tendencies of modern democracy: "The fight against democracy and socialism, the imperialist myth and the summons to barbarous action are intended to appear as an unprecedented reversal, a 'transvaluation of all values,' a 'twilight of the false gods'; and the indirect apologetics of imperialism as a demagogically effective pseudo-revolution" (Lukács 1980: 321). The outwardly "revolutionary" appearance of Nietzscheanism, then, is just that, an appearance, cloaking a reactionary defense of social stratification.

This reading of the Nietzschean oeuvre dates back to the writing of German Social Democratic Party theoretician Franz Mehring, who also linked Nietzschean ideas to alienated and disgruntled segments of the petty bourgeoisie: "Nietzscheanism is a healthy guzzle for the *literatis vulgaris*, one which ...

1 Portions of this essay were previously published in Yeritsian (2018).

provides a thrill and allows one to play a little *Sturm und Drang*, but ... enables them under every circumstance to feast from the fleshpots of capitalism" (quoted in Aschheim 1992: 43–44). It provides such intellectuals with a seemingly radical and uncompromising mode of thought that simultaneously confirms their cultural elitism and justifies their social privilege. As historian Steven Aschheim (1992) comments, the standard Marxist line at the turn of the century considered Nietzschean thought to be a kind of pseudo-radicalism that, while indulging in pseudo-revolutionary rhetorical flourishes, failed in any significant way to critique capitalism or class society. On the contrary, for Mehring, Lukács, and others, Nietzsche's thought explicitly sanctioned social hierarchy and domination and was therefore fundamentally reactionary.

In retrospect, this was not an entirely tendentious reading of Nietzsche. His philosophy naturalizes and justifies exploitation and domination of the many by the few, linking them to a vitalist ontology, as when he writes in *Beyond Good and Evil*, "'Exploitation' does not belong to a corrupt or imperfect and primitive society: it belongs to the *essence* of what lives, as a basic organic function; it is a consequence of the will to power, which is after all the will of life" (1966: 259). Nietzsche, then, has a tendency to biologize inequality and domination, foreclosing any possibility of their overcoming. Several recent commentators have drawn upon this stream in Nietzschean thought in interrogating its specifically *political* ramifications and bringing into question whether it contained proto-Nazi undercurrents.

As Mark Warren points out in *Nietzsche and Political Thought* (1988), the Nazi appropriation of Nietzsche, while clearly distorted, was not entirely a *mis*-appropriation, given the undeniable affinities between aspects of Nietzsche's thought and Nazi ideology, most notably his vision of the mastery exercised by a cultural elite over the common herd. Similarly, Bruce Detwiler notes that Nietzsche's "talk of master races and supermen, his occasional advocacy of breeding experiments, his praise of war and destruction, his willingness to discourse on the positive value of cruelty, his professed 'immoralism,' his radical elitism, and his denigration of compassion and rationalism all become rather ominous when given a political cast" (1990: 2). Along these lines, the recent effort by students to launch a "Nietzsche Club" at University College London aroused controversy – and was even banned – because of its far-right leanings, with publicity posters proclaiming, "Equality is a false God," and denouncing "political correctness" (Hines 2014).

At the same time, many commentators have pointed to the internal tensions that characterize Nietzsche's body of work, the availability to interpreters and commentators of many contrary readings. The lack of systematicity of his thinking and his reliance on aphoristic and oracular discourses leave space, as is the case for much of Continental philosophy, for diverse readings and appropriations. For Karl Jaspers (1997: 10, 222), "self-contradiction is the fundamental ingredient in Nietzsche's thought"; Jaspers links this to Nietzsche's implicit anti-humanism, his critique of the notion of a "self-identical" ego incapable of self-contradiction. Perhaps Nietzsche's philosophy is better likened to an intellectual "game" rather than a system. Lukács' seems to err in reading into Nietzsche's work a reactionary systematicity that it lacks. Historian Seth Taylor notes that, for different readers, "[Nietzsche] was at once a materialist and an antimaterialist, at once an individualist and the prophet of the dissolution of individualism in dionysian ecstasy, at once a social activist and an aesthete frowning down on German society" (1990: 27).

Indeed, it is important not to limit ourselves, in understanding the import of Nietzsche's thought, to textual hermeneutics. Rather we should expand our analytical frame to also encompass the *actual historical reception and appropriation* of Nietzsche's texts. Indeed, in the immediate aftermath of Nietzsche's death, he was primarily received as a forward-looking, radical thinker rather than as a conservative or a reactionary, his work compared by conservatives to Marxism in terms of its potential threat to the existing social order. As Aschheim remarks vis-à-vis turn of the century German Nietzscheans, "Far from representing the reactionary ... sectors of society they were characteristically emancipationist... Socialism, anarchism, feminism, the generational revolt of the young – these were all touched by the libertarian magic of Nietzsche" (1992: 6; see also Thomas 1983). It was the *libertarian* spirit in Nietzsche, then, which was picked up by readers – and seems to explain, it must be suggested, the continuing rediscovery of Nietzsche on the part of adolescents – and which particularly influenced the cultural and political avant gardes of the period.

In the spirit of hermeneutic openness described by Jaspers, Taylor, and other commentators, and in light of the diverse modes of historical and theoretical reception of his work exemplified by its initial emancipationist influence, this essay proposes a reading of Nietzsche that is partially at odds with the orthodox Marxist one. I will argue that Nietzsche represents the "artistic critique of capitalism," with its emancipatory project of aesthetic liberation. This represents a progressive potentiality within Nietzsche that Lukács and Mehring fail to recognize. However, such a reading does not proceed to treat Nietzsche as an unavowed Marxist. Rather, the artistic critique found in Nietzsche's work is aligned much more directly with *anarchist* thought and practice, and its subsequent historical impacts and appropriations attest to this fact. Its fundamental neglect of social analysis represents precisely the massive gap that can be "filled" by historical materialism. This complementarity, though, may also work both ways, with the aesthetic concern with liberation helping us to avoid a structuralist Marxism that completely sidesteps questions of human freedom and flourishing.

This distinction between the social and artistic critiques of capitalism derives from French sociologists Luc Boltanski and Eve Chiapello's *The New Spirit of Capitalism* (2007). The artistic critique overlaps significantly with "romantic anticapitalism," without necessarily implying the nostalgia that is central to most forms of the latter (Sayre and Löwy note, "The Romantic soul longs ardently to return home, and it is precisely this *nostalgia* for what has been lost that is at the center of the Romantic anti-capitalist vision" [1984: 56]; also see Lukács [1980: 341–342]). For Boltanski and Chiapello, unlike the *social* critique of capitalism, which targets inequality and exploitation and is oriented fundamentally around material egalitarianism, the *artistic* critique focuses on the ways in which the system produces soulless rationalization and alienation and thwarts autonomy and expression. The social critique aims at security, the artistic critique at freedom.

On Boltanski and Chiapello's account, the artistic critique developed initially among nineteenth-century bohemians. As they write, it is

> based upon a contrast between attachment and detachment, stability and mobility... On the one hand, we have the bourgeoisie, owning land, factories and women ... and thereby condemned to meticulous forethought, rational management of space and time, and a quasi-obsessive pursuit of production for production's sake. On the other hand, we have intellectuals and artists free of all attachments, [who] made the absence of production (unless it was self-production) and a culture of uncertainty into untranscendable ideals.
>
> BOLTANSKI and CHIAPELLO 2007: 38

The artistic critique, then, arose as a response to capitalist rationalization, appealing to a humanism that was seen to be threatened by the rise of industrial power and discipline. Its fundamental impulse is toward a kind of liberatory escape from the strictures that hinder the possibility of genuine creativity and expression.

In its late-nineteenth and twentieth century development, the artistic critique drew on and combined influences ranging from Marx and Freud to Surrealism and, indeed, Nietzsche (Boltanski and Chiapello 2007: 170). It inspired many of the movements of the 1960s in the advanced capitalist countries, most notably the rebellion of May 1968 in France, and has been central to the development of contemporary feminist, environmentalist, and anti-racist politics. Critics of orthodox Marxism often lean on some dimension of the artistic critique in championing the more humanist texts of the early Marx or in advocating a greater engagement on the part of Marxist theory with questions of identity, ecology, and difference (see Sim 2013).

The remainder of this essay will develop the connection between Nietzsche and the artistic critique both theoretically and historically. Theoretically, I will illustrate how Nietzsche's thought exemplifies several key dimensions of the artistic critique. Historically, I will offer a number of instances of left-wing movements that were influenced by his artistic critique. I will at the same time underline the basically *anarchist* orientation of these movements, even if Nietzschean inspired thinkers and activists originally sprung up in socialist organizations and struggles. By way of conclusion, I will remark upon both the deficiencies of Nietzschean thought and what contributions the latter can offer to Marxist and critical theory.

2 Nietzsche and the Artistic Critique

A central dimension of the artistic critique as developed by Boltanski and Chiapello is the critique of industrial discipline: "the duration of work, enslavement to factory discipline, and meagre pay no longer allow for the realization of a properly human existence, which is precisely defined by self-determination and a multiplicity of practices" (2007: 427). Such discipline reduces the subject's spatial and temporal freedom, enclosing her in a workplace for the majority of her waking life and imposing a strict rationalization aimed at the maximization of efficiency. This aspect of the artistic critique has informed worker demands for a reduction of the working week and day, such that "existence could once again find expression in activities other than waged work" (Boltanski and Chiapello 2007: 427). It was also central to the May 1968 upsurge, as students and skilled employees in particular increasingly resisted the imposition of Fordist discipline in the workplace.

This line of critique resonates with the Nietzschean critique of work, as described by Michael Roberts (2016). Nietzsche described industrial work as a form of enslavement, denouncing it in aphorism 18 of the third essay of *On the Genealogy of Morals* as "[m]echanical activity and what goes with it – such an absolute regularity, punctilious and unthinking obedience, a mode of life fixed once and for all, *fully occupied time*" (1989: 134). One would be hard pressed to distinguish this passage in any significant way from the account of "estranged labor" found in Marx's *Economic and Philosophic Manuscripts*, e.g. "labor is *external* to the worker … he does not affirm himself but denies himself … does not develop freely his physical and mental energy but mortifies his body and ruins his mind" (1988: 72). Roberts points to similar passages in *The Gay Science*, *Twilight of the Idols*, *Daybreak*, and other texts, noting that, for Nietzsche, "an ample amount of free time is the principal condition for the good life, because leisure makes possible the cultivation of the human being through the pursuit of aesthetic activity" (2016: 3). Thus Nietzsche advocates a distance from economic production and its rationalizing imperatives, and values in its stead the free enjoyment of aesthetic activity.

The second aspect of the artistic critique of interest here is the critique of standardization or massification, by which Boltanski and Chiapello mean the "loss of difference between entities, whether these are objects or human beings" (2007: 439). This encompasses an opposition to both industrial mechanization, with its rationalizing rhythms and mass production of identical goods, and to the massification of increasingly conformist human beings, who are in turn more and more vulnerable to elite control and manipulation. Per the artistic critique, mass production makes for the following: "The lack of difference concerns the proliferating objects that fill the lived world: cotton fabrics, furniture, knick-knacks, cars, household appliances, and so on… In another respect, however, each is utterly identical to all the others in the same series" (Boltanski and Chiapello 2007: 439). The corollary to this is human *massification*, through the routines both of production and consumption. With respect to consumption, effective marketing amounts to the colonization of individual desire: "my desire for some particular object and someone else's desire for an identical object belonging to the same series" (Boltanski and Chiapello 2007: 439). With respect to production, individual human workers are utterly replaceable, especially on the Taylorist assembly line.

The logic extends to other domains of social life: the interchangeability of infantry fighters in mass warfare; the disappearance of the individual within the democratic crowd; the loss of the capacity for free thought on the part of the totalitarian subject; and the indoctrination by media of the passive consumer. The key Frankfurt School treatises, *Dialectic of Enlightenment* and *One-Dimensional Man*, place front and center this dimension of the artistic critique (Boltanski and Chiapello 2007: 441). In the former, Horkheimer and Adorno (2002: 136) condemn the obliteration of difference by the late capitalist culture industry: "The most intimate reactions of human beings have become so entirely reified, even to themselves, that the idea of anything peculiar to them survives only in extreme abstraction." In the latter, Marcuse (2002) diagnoses the late capitalist absorption of previously radical social forces, presenting an "opposition between a free consciousness, capable of knowing its own desires, and the man of 'advanced industrial civilization,' 'cretinized' and 'standardized' by mass production and 'comfort,' rendered incapable of acceding to the immediate experience of the world, wholly subject to needs manipulated by others" (Boltanski and Chiapello 2007: 441).

This aspect of the artistic critique contrasts a tragic authenticity with the inauthenticity of a life characterized by seriality and conformism:

> On the one hand, then, we have the human being who, accepting her "facticity" and "contingency," courageously faces up to the "anxiety" of "being for herself" … On the other hand, we have the one who, fleeing anxiety by becoming submerged in everyday "banality," takes refuge in "chatter," as a debasement of speech, and allows herself to be entirely determined by others.
>
> BOLTANSKI and CHIAPELLO 2007: 440

As is clear, many of the philosophical reference points in Boltanski and Chiapello's account of the artistic critique are bound up with the existential thematics of Sartre, Camus, and Heidegger.

Nietzsche's critique of mass culture is especially relevant with regard to the problems of standardization and massification (see Kellner 1999). Nietzsche viewed the state as a "cold monster" securing its domination over the people with the help of the press. In the section "On the New Idol" of *Thus Spoke Zarathustra*, Nietzsche advocates a withdrawal from the state and mass society: "Their idol smells foul to me, the cold monster… Smash the windows instead and leap into the open! … where the state ends, only there begins the human being who is not superfluous" (2006: 36) As Kellner (1999) remarks, "mass politics led to herd conformity, the loss of individuality, and mass manipulation and homogenization." Analogously, Nietzsche's critique of Christianity was precisely that it was bound up with the logic of massification, inculcating in its subjects a "slave morality" that deprived them of the capacity for free action and expression. In aphorism 235 of *Human, All Too Human*, he claims that Jesus Christ "promoted the stupidifying of man, placed himself on the side of the poor in spirit and retarded the production of the supreme intellect" (1996: 112). Ultimately, for Nietzsche (1989), the Judeo-Christian tradition exalts the lowly, weak, and common, at the expense of the noble and powerful few.

More broadly, mass culture exercises a homogenizing influence, sapping people of energy, creativity, and individuality. Kellner (1999) highlights the specifically vitalist aspect of this analysis, noting that Nietzsche's "assault on religion, morality, mass culture, and the banality of modern societies is thus unleashed from the standpoint of an ideal of the free and uninhibited flow of life energies, an unrestrained expression of instinctual powers." Those few who do retain their expressive and instinctual vitality are analogous to the figure in

Boltanski and Chiapello who boldly accepts his agency in the face of the radical contingency and groundlessness of existence.

The members of the herd, on the other hand, are those caught up in banality and chatter, completely determined by the social structures that surround them. Nietzsche's term for this figure of conformity is the Last Man: "No shepherd and one herd! Each wants the same, each is the same, and whoever feels differently goes voluntarily into the insane asylum" (2006: 10).

What of the response to industrial discipline and the loss of difference? Here Boltanski and Chiapello develop the most important feature of the artistic critique, namely the overarching struggle against what they term "generic alienations." "Specific alienations" refer to oppression or disadvantage inflicted on a particular social category: "these are specific to a group or category unjustly suffering oppression which other groups do not suffer" (2007: 433). Some straightforward examples include the exploitation of labor by capital, the oppression of marginalized racial groups by privileged ones, and the domination of women by men. The struggle against generic alienations refers, by contrast, to

> emancipation from all forms of necessity, whether these derive from settlement in a social environment stabilized by conventions (e.g. membership of a nation), or are inherent in inscription in an objective world (ties of filiation, type of work performed presupposing a specific skill), or the possession of a particular body (impossibility of being everywhere at once, age- or sex-related determinations).
>
> BOLTANSKI and CHIAPELLO 2007: 433

The distinction calls forth association with Camus' definition of "metaphysical rebellion" in *The Rebel*: "The slave protests against the condition in which he finds himself within his state of slavery; the metaphysical rebel protests against the condition in which he finds himself as a man" (1991: 23). Boltanski and Chiapello include in this category the valorization of uncertainty; the cultivation of a multiplicity of identities; and the call for a freedom from endowments, debts, or life plans derived from or imposed by others:

> Viewed thus, liberation is predominantly conceived as setting free the oppressed desire to be someone else ... to be who one wants to be, when one wants it. This leaves open the possibility of a multiplicity of identifications adopted in the way one adopts a look and, consequently, of escaping identitarian affiliation to a nation, region, ethnicity, and especially ... the family.
>
> BOLTANSKI and CHIAPELLO 2007: 434

The struggle against generic alienations amounts to the demand for a total liberation that resonates deeply with Nietzsche's call for unbounded creative proliferation. As he declares in aphorism 107 of *The Gay Science*, "we need all exuberant, floating, dancing, mocking, childish, and blissful art lest we lose our *freedom above things* that our ideal demands of us…" (1974: 164). The notion of "freedom above things" is especially important here – it suggests a project of liberation from all forms of external determination. As Kellner (1999) comments, Nietzsche's free individual must be liberated from "societal determinism" in all of its forms, including "morality, religion, and society and free to fully develop one's own potentialities." Aesthetic creation is crucial insofar as art, per aphorism 853 of *The Will to Power*, is the "real task of life": "Art and nothing but art! It is the great means of making life possible, the great seduction to life, the great stimulant of life" (Nietzsche 1968: 452).

Moreover, the anti-humanist dimension of Nietzsche precisely points to the opening up of the subject toward Boltanski and Chiapello's "multiplicity of identifications." According to aphorism 490 of *The Will to Power*, "The assumption of one single subject is perhaps unnecessary; perhaps it is just as permissible to assume a multiplicity of subjects, whose interaction and struggle is the basis of our thought and our consciousness in general? … *My hypotheses*: (sic) The subject as multiplicity" (1968: 270). Similarly, in *Ecce Homo* (1989), he refers to the multiplicity of his philosophical and discursive styles, a la the "self-contradiction" pointed to by Jaspers; as Sooväli (2015: 437) comments, "the whole of Nietzsche's work – that is, his different styles, voices, philosophical perspectives etc – testifies to the irreducible multiplicity of the subject."

Ultimately, Nietzsche counterposes to the Last Man the figure of the self-creating "sovereign individual" (1989); per aphorism 335 of *The Gay Science*, "We … *want to become those we are* – human beings who are new. unique, incomparable, who give themselves laws, who create themselves" (1974: 266). Such a figure aims, precisely, at emancipation from all forms of external necessity.

3 Historical Reference Points: Nietzsche's Influence on Radical Critics of Capitalism

Having noted these precise affinities between Nietzsche and features of the artistic critique as articulated by Boltanski and Chiapello, I now move on to illustrate the historical influence of these aspects of Nietzsche's critique on the diverse contexts represented by three left-wing cultural and political movements:

avant-garde and anarchist circles in prewar Germany, Situationism in May 1968 in France, and American anarchism.

As Seth Taylor argues in *Left-Wing Nietzscheans* (1990), the pre-war German Expressionist circles around the periodicals *Der Sturm* and *Die Aktion*, which brought together left-wing intellectual critics of Wilhelminian Germany, were influenced by Nietzsche's critique of German culture. *Die Aktion*, the more political of the two, announced in its first issue that it "favors, without taking the part of a particular political party, the idea of a great German left. *Die Aktion* wants to promote the imposing thought of an organization of the Intelligentsia and would like to restore once again the long forbidden word *Kulturkampf* to its old glamor" (Taylor 1990: 48). In this way, the journal linked politics and culture, and its writers viewed Nietzsche as in line with a broad-based Enlightenment tradition as against the narrowness of Prussian nationalism. This provincial and militarist nationalism they saw as arising from primarily cultural rather than structural forces, in particular the philistinism of the mass man who represented social, religious and political conservatism, as opposed to the individual who represents will and *Geist* – a la Nietzsche's *freie Geist* – in his opposition to established law, morality, and tradition. It bears mentioning that the Expressionists constituted a cultural rather than a political movement, and their deepening engagement with practical politics during and after the First World War also brought with it a reorientation from Nietzsche toward Marx (Taylor 1990: 59).

Young radicals within the German Social Democratic Party at the time, however, sought to integrate Nietzsche *with* Marx. While Nietzscheanism was never a mainstream tendency within the political life of the party, these young members, referred to as the *Jungen*, were, in the words of historian Steven Aschheim,

> attracted to Nietzsche partly because of his devastating indictment of the status quo and partly because he provided a counter-language, a rhetoric of total regeneration and vision of the New Man which could channel the revolutionary impulse, while at the same time keeping the content of that impulse vague, indeed open and unclassifiable.
>
> ASCHHEIM 1992: 166

The *Jungen* argued that Nietzschean ideals could be rendered "universal property" – that ordinary workers could become "new men" given the increased freedom and leisure time under socialism. Their critique was prescient insofar as it targeted the bureaucratism and conservatism of the Party, both in terms of its organizational structure and its vision of the future – they aimed to inject into this a dose of voluntarism, in the sense of a greater concern with individual freedom and human action. The *Jungen* were clearly motivated by a libertarian, anarchist impulse that became more conscious and explicit over time. As historian R. Hinton Thomas remarks, "Before Erfurt [a Party congress and program] they had been revolutionary social democrats rather than anarchists. Thereafter they were essentially anarchists" (1983: 15). Indeed, Nietzsche's thought was also influential for those more unequivocally in the anarchist camp, for whom its voluntarism and anti-statism belied Nietzsche's avowed antipathy toward anarchism.

In analogous fashion to the *Jungen* and the anarchists, the French student and worker uprising of May '68 incorporated libertarian and cultural concerns into its radical politics. Inasmuch as students, intellectuals, and professionals were central players in the movement, they were motivated by an artistic critique of alienation and unfreedom. Activists rebelled against the stultifying economic, political, and educational bureaucracies characteristic of what Boltanski and Chiapello (2007) refer to as the "second spirit of capitalism," namely the Fordism of the postwar period (just as the counterculture in the United States was launching its own attack on mainstream institutions [see Sennett 2006]; also see [Zhao 1998] on the "Nietzsche fever" among radical Chinese students in the 1980s).

The intellectual influence of Nietzsche on the 68ers was mediated by the Situationists, who played an active role in the university occupations and street protests. One reference point in this mediation was the theoretical work of Henri Lefebvre, active with the Situationists in the early 1960s, who argued for a strong compatibility between the existentialist thematics in Nietzsche and Marx's account of alienation (Schrift 2014). Arising from avant-garde cultural circles, the Situationists saw as their project the resistance to what leading theoretician Guy Debord referred to as the "society of the spectacle": "The spectacle is the moment when the commodity has attained the *total occupation* of social life" (1983: 42). The commodity spectacle engendered a dull, conformist society, rendering individuals incapable of creativity and self-expression. The Situationists thus aimed to inject into Marxist theory and practice – the mainstream manifestations of which were primarily oriented around the *social* critique of capitalism – a deeper engagement with the *artistic* critique, through a concern with alienation, desire, aesthetics, and freedom. As Steven Best and Douglas Kellner write, "Whereas Marxism focused on the factory, the Situationists focused on the city and everyday life, supplementing the Marxian emphasis on class struggle with a project of cultural revolution and the transformation of subjectivity ... and the constitution of liberated zones of desire" (1997: 81).

Crucially, Situationist practice was infused with a "Nietzschean vitalism... which attempts to enhance, intensify, and increase life energies against the banal death culture of the existing society" (Best and Kellner 1997: 92). This concern with vitality and expression resonated in many of the myriad examples of street art and graffiti from May 1968. Nietzschean themes proliferate, including the critique of Christianity and asceticism; an emphasis on dynamism, spontaneity, and action; antipathy toward mere "adaptation" and survival, tantamount to conformity to a life-denying culture and society; and an opposition to cultural philistinism. Moreover, they point to the possibility of a socialization or democratization of the Nietzschean figure of the master. What follow are several illustrative examples of May 1968 graffiti (cited in Knabb 2006), one of which notably quotes directly from Nietzsche himself:

> [1] If God existed it would be necessary to abolish him.
> [2] The enemy of movement is skepticism. Everything that has been realized comes from dynamism, which comes from spontaneity.
> [3] Culture is an inversion of life.
> [4] Beautiful, maybe not, but O how charming: life versus survival.
> [5] We must remain 'unadapted.'
> [6] The tears of philistines are the nectar of the gods.
> [7] In a society that has abolished every kind of adventure the only adventure that remains is to abolish the society.
> [8] 'You must bear a chaos inside you to give birth to a dancing star.' (Nietzsche)
> [9] We will have good masters as soon as everyone is their own.

The libertarian spirit on display in these slogans calls forth association with the turn of the century German anarchists and points to the influence exerted by Nietzsche's thought on twentieth-century *American* anarchism, illustrated here by reference to activist-intellectuals Emma Goldman and Murray Bookchin. In the early 1900s Goldman gave many lectures on Nietzsche and offered his books for sale through her journal *Mother Earth* (Radical Archives 2010). Against those who viewed Nietzsche as fundamentally elitist, she argued that he called for an aristocracy of the spirit rather than one based on blood or wealth. She was influenced by Nietzsche's critique of morality as an instrument of social control. As she stated in her lecture, "Victims of Morality" (Goldman 1913: 6), "Though Morality may continue to devour its victims, it is utterly powerless in the face of the modern spirit, that shines in all its glory upon the brow of man and woman, liberated and unafraid." And she argued that part of the reason class society persisted was that ordinary people clung to their masters and to their own subjugation, caught up in the spirit of mass conformity.

As Jennifer Ratner-Rosenhagen (2012) points out in her book on the American receptions of Nietzsche, Goldman and other critical American intellectuals saw his ideas as a weapon against the lingering strains of Puritanism in American thought and culture, especially as regards Puritan sexual ethics. Nietzschean libertarianism urged people to think, to go beyond conventional wisdom and morality, to liberate themselves, in the words of Goldman, from "man-made law" and "truth grown false with age" (Ratner-Rosenhagen 2012: 178). By contrast, ordinary people remained victims of slave morality, as manifest in the frenzy of patriotism that arose amidst America's entry into World War I. As Ratner-Rosenhagen (2012: 179) recounts, "[Goldman] insisted that patriotism was another manufactured notion of affiliation and obligation that turned one's homeland into a sentimental idol while demanding that the individual submit his labor, if not his life, for the state's aggrandizement." Goldman's activism against the war then, was colored with Nietzschean influence, and she paid a steep price for her agitation: arrest and deportation.

A later American anarchist activist and intellectual, Murray Bookchin, while very critical of "lifestyle anarchism" that was divorced from class (see Bookchin 1995), urged that anarchist class politics be supplemented with a concern with agency and freedom: "workers must see themselves as human beings, not as class beings; as creative personalities, not as 'proletarians,' as self-affirming individuals, not as 'masses'" (Bookchin 1974). Central to this, for Bookchin, was the critique of industrial discipline: the "economic component must be humanized precisely by bringing an 'affinity of friendship' to the work process, by diminishing the role of onerous work in the lives of producers, indeed by a total 'transvaluation of values' (to use Nietzsche's phrase) as it applies to production and consumption as well as social and personal life" (Bookchin 1974). Bookchin, like the German *Jungen* and anarchists, aimed to open up the category of overman to ordinary people, as when he described one Spanish anarchist leader as "an admirer of Nietzschean individualism, of the superhombre to whom 'all is permitted'" (Sunshine 2005). It is the way in which such Nietzschean concepts as "transvaluation of values," "overman," and the struggle against "slave morality" point to an emphasis on action, expression, individuality, and liberation – crucial reference points for the artistic critique – that was especially picked up on by the American anarchists.

4 Conclusion

This essay has aimed at two analytical goals: a reading of Nietzsche in terms of central dimensions of the "artistic critique of capitalism," as theorized by

Boltanski and Chiapello; and a connection of that reading to illustrative historical examples of left activists and movements on whom Nietzsche's artistic critique exerted an influence. I sought to thus bring into question the orthodox Marxist reading, associated primarily with Lukács and Mehring, of Nietzsche as a reactionary apologist for imperialism and capitalism. Certainly, Nietzsche's political philosophy is explicitly elitist and antidemocratic, and thus in no way mounts a "social critique" of the inegalitarianism and exploitation characteristic of modern class society. However, Nietzsche's opposition to industrial discipline and standardization and his championing of the struggle against generic alienations align him in a profound way with the liberatory impulse of the artistic critique.

This liberatory impulse has been picked up on historically by Left Nietzschean activists, especially anarchists. The corrective they apply to it is precisely to supplement its artistic critique with a social dimension and thereby divest it of its aristocratic elitism, to recognize, as Max Horkheimer did in a 1942 exchange among Frankfurt School exiles in Los Angeles, Nietzsche as an enemy of bourgeois decadence and conformism. As Horkheimer stated, "Beneath [Nietzsche's] seemingly misanthropic formulations lies ... not so much this [elitist] error but the hatred of the patient, self-avoiding, passive and conformist character at peace with the present" (quoted in Wiggershaus 2001: 145). On Horkheimer's reading, in the society of the future, the potential represented by the figure of the *Übermensch* would be open to all.

But this is only part of the picture. The Nietzschean concern with agency and liberation can itself serve as an important corrective to the tendencies within Marxism toward economism and a deterministic structuralism. This was, I would suggest, what Theodor Adorno meant in the same exchange when he distinguished Marx from Nietzsche insofar as Nietzsche is concerned with the "totality of happiness incarnate" (Wiggershaus 2001: 147).

It is this brand of "essentialist" and "static" Marxism (Roberts 1995) that is on display in large sections of Lukács' *Destruction of Reason* (1980) – for example, in his close adherence to the model of base and superstructure and in his very binaristic rejection of most forms of allegedly bourgeois thought. A similar error is made by Marxists associated with the World Socialist Web Site like David North, whose recent book on the "pseudo-left" (2015) represents a polemical assault on the Frankfurt School and other philosophically inspired variants of Marxist theory. North, echoing the tone and style of Lukács, writes,

> [T]he connection has become much clearer between the reactionary pseudo-left politics of the middle class and the theories of Nietzsche, Brzozowski, Sorel, De Man, the Frankfurt School and the many forms of

> extreme philosophical subjectivism and irrationalism propagated by postmodernists (Foucault, Laclau, Badiou et al.). Pseudo-left politics – centered on race, nationality, ethnicity, gender, and sexual preference – has come to play a critical role in suppressing opposition to capitalism, by rejecting class as the essential social category and emphasizing, instead, personal "identity" and "lifestyle."
>
> NORTH 2015

North, like other Marxists of decidedly orthodox hue, wants to turn back the clock, refusing to take into account significant shifts in the nature of capitalism that have taken place since the heyday of classical Marxist thought. Those changes have included, among countless other phenomena, the proliferation of consumer society, the rise of the service sector, the sharpening of ecological crises and struggles, and the rise of new social movements fighting for racial and gender equality. To pretend that none of these developments has been of real significance and instead call for a single-minded theoretical and political orientation toward the master category of Class smacks of the worst sort of dogmatism, especially when combined with denunciations of laudable organizational efforts like Greece's Syriza and France's New Anticapitalist Party as "pseudo-left."

By contrast to this dogmatic rejectionism, critical theorists must engage meaningfully with the ways in which Marxist thought has been hybridized with other intellectual traditions in the context of transformations within global capitalism. Like the other philosophical tendencies that have exerted an influence on twentieth- and twenty-first century Marxism – including psychoanalysis, existentialism, and post-structuralism – Nietzsche's artistic critique of capitalism should be approached not as an irredeemable ideological opponent, but sympathetically, in terms of its potential to enrich liberatory theory and practice.

References

Aschheim, Steven E. 1992. *The Nietzsche Legacy in Germany: 1890–1990*. Berkeley, CA: University of California Press.

Best, Steven, and Douglas Kellner. 1997. *The Postmodern Turn*. New York, NY: Guildford Press.

Boltanski, Luc, and Eve Chiapello. 2007. *The New Spirit of Capitalism*. London and New York: Verso.

Bookchin, Murray. 1995. "Social Anarchism or Lifestyle Anarchism: An Unbridgeable Chasm." Available at https://theanarchistlibrary.org/library/murray-bookchin-social-anarchism-or-lifestyle-anarchism-an-unbridgeable-chasm. Accessed Sept. 24, 2017.

Bookchin, Murray. 1974. "Introductory Essay." *The Anarchist Collectives: Workers' Self-Management in the Spanish Revolution, 1936–1939*, edited by Sam Dolgoff. Available at https://theanarchistlibrary.org/library/sam-dolgoff-editor-the-anarchist-collectives#toc3. Accessed Sept. 24, 2017.

Camus, Albert. 1991. *The Rebel: An Essay on Man in Revolt*, translated by Anthony Bower. New York, NY: Vintage.

Debord, Guy. 1983. *Society of the Spectacle*, translated by Fredy Perlman. Detroit, MI: Black & Red.

Detwiler, Bruce. 1990. *Nietzsche and the Politics of Aristocratic Radicalism*. Chicago, IL: University of Chicago Press.

Goldman, Emma. 1913. *Victims of Morality and the Failure of Christianity: Two Lectures*. New York, NY: Mother Earth.

Hines, Nico. 2014. "University College London's Nietzsche Club is Banned." *The Daily Beast*. Available at http://www.thedailybeast.com/university-college-londons-nietzsche-club-is-banned. Accessed Sept. 19, 2017.

Horkheimer, Max, and Theodor Adorno. 2002. *Dialectic of Enlightenment: Philosophical Fragments*, translated by Edmund Jephcott. Stanford, CA: Stanford University Press.

Jaspers, Karl. 1997. *Nietzsche: An Introduction to the Understanding of His Philosophical Activity*, translated by Charles F. Wallraff and Frederick J. Schmitz. Baltimore, MD: Johns Hopkins University Press.

Kellner, Douglas. 1999. "Nietzsche's Critique of Mass Culture." *International Studies in Philosophy* 31(3): 77–89.

Knabb, Ken. 2006. "May 1968 Graffiti." In *Situationist International Anthology*, edited by Ken Knabb. Berkeley, CA: Bureau of Public Secrets. Available at http://www.bopsecrets.org/CF/graffiti.htm. Accessed Sept. 24, 2017.

Lukács, Georg. 1980. *The Destruction of Reason*, translated by Peter Palmer. London: The Merlin Press.

Marcuse, Herbert. 2002. *One-Dimensional Man: Studies in the Ideology of Advanced Industrial Society*. New York, NY: Routledge.

Marx, Karl. 1988. *Economic and Philosophic Manuscripts of 1844*, translated by Martin Milligan. Amherst, NY: Prometheus Books.

Nietzsche, Friedrich. 2006. *Thus Spoke Zarathustra*, translated by Adrian Del Caro. New York, NY: Cambridge University Press.

Nietzsche, Friedrich. 1996. *Human, All Too Human*, translated by RJ Hollingdale. New York, NY: Cambridge University Press.

Nietzsche, Friedrich. 1989. *On the Genealogy of Morals* and *Ecce Homo*, translated by Walter Kaufmann and R.J. Hollingdale. New York, NY: Vintage Books.

Nietzsche, Friedrich. 1974. *The Gay Science*, translated by Walter Kaufmann. New York, NY: Vintage Books.

Nietzsche, Friedrich. 1968. *The Will to Power*, translated by Walter Kaufmann and R.J. Hollingdale. New York, NY: Vintage Books.

Nietzsche, Friedrich. 1966. *Beyond Good and Evil: Prelude to a Philosophy of the Future*, translated by Walter Kaufmann. New York, NY: Vintage Books.

North, David. 2015. *The Frankfurt School, Postmodernism and the Politics of the Pseudo-Left: A Marxist Critique*. Oak Park, WI: Mehring. Sections available at https://www.wsws.org/en/articles/2015/07/21/dnbo-j21.html. Accessed Sept. 24, 2017.

Radical Archives. 2010. "Emma Goldman's 'Mother Earth' & Nietzsche." Available at https://radicalarchives.org/2010/02/12/mother-earth-sells-nietzsche/. Accessed Sept. 24, 2017.

Ratner-Rosenhagen, Jennifer. 2012. *American Nietzsche*. Chicago, IL: University of Chicago Press.

Roberts, Michael. 2016. "Twilight of Work: The Labor Question in Nietzsche and Marx." *Critical Sociology*. https://doi.org/10.1177/0896920516681427.

Roberts, Michael. 1995. "Rereading Marx and Nietzsche." *Rethinking Marxism* 8(1): 100–111.

Sayre, Robert, and Michael Löwy. 1984. "Figures of Romantic Anti-Capitalism." *New German Critique* 32: 42–92.

Schrift, Alan D. 2014. "French Nietzscheanism." In *Poststructuralism and Critical Theory's Second Generation*, edited by Alan D. Schrift, 19–46. New York, NY: Routledge.

Sennett, Richard. 2006. *The Culture of the New Capitalism*. New Haven, CT: Yale University Press.

Sim, Stuart. 2013. *Post-Marxism: An Intellectual History*. New York, NY: Routledge.

Soováli, Jaanus. 2015. "Gapping the Subject: Nietzsche and Derrida." In *Nietzsche and the Problem of Subjectivity*, edited by João Constâncio, Maria João Mayer Branco, and Bartholomew Ryan, 436–453. Boston, MA: de Gruyter.

Sunshine, Spencer. 2005. "Nietzsche and the Anarchists." Available at https://radicalarchives.org/2010/05/18/nietzsche-and-the-anarchists/. Accessed Sept. 24, 2017.

Taylor, Seth. 1990. *Left-Wing Nietzscheans: The Politics of German Expressionism, 1910–1920*. New York, NY: de Gruyter.

Thomas, Richard Hinton. 1983. *Nietzsche in German Politics and Society: 1890–1918*. Dover, NH: Manchester University Press.

Warren, Mark. 1988. *Nietzsche and Political Thought*. Cambridge, MA: MIT Press.

Wiggershaus, Rolf. 2001. "The Frankfurt School's 'Nietzschean Moment.'" *Constellations* 8(1): 144–147.

Yeritsian, Gary. 2018. "Freedom Above Things: Nietzsche and the Artistic Critique of Capitalism." *Critical Sociology*. https://doi.org/10.1177/0896920517750743.

Zhao, Dingxin. 1998. "Ecologies of Social Movements: Student Mobilization during the 1989 Prodemocracy Movement in Beijing." *American Journal of Sociology* 103(6): 1493–1529.

CHAPTER 9

Between Nietzsche and Marx: "Great Politics and What They Cost"

Babette Babich

> The machine accommodates itself to the weakness of the human being in order to make the weak human being into a machine.
>
> MARX

•••

> As at all times, so now too, men are divided into the slaves and the free; for he who does not have two-thirds of his day to himself is a slave, let him be what he may otherwise be: statesman, businessman, official, scholar.
>
> NIETZSCHE

•••

> The world in which, spiritually and intellectually, we live today is a world bearing the imprint of Marx and Nietzsche.
>
> MAX WEBER[1]

∴

1 Nietzsche and Marx: Left and Right Readings

The past century has seen a tradition of scholars talking past one another on Nietzsche and Marx. To be sure, this has a number of causes – and the current essay does not aspire to wave them all away – but the most important of these is *equivocation* especially the equivocation interior to professional philosophy

1 Cited by Eduard Baumgarten (1964: 554f) and Caygill (1993: 190), etc.

as such.[2] Hence, and apart from disciplinary differences in political theory/ social economics, political/comparative sociology, ethnography, intellectual history, etc., philosophy as such breaks down, mostly, into *analytic* kinds, including what analytic philosophers name "continental," by which is *not meant* the traditional continental philosophy of the sort one might have read in Derrida or Gadamer or Baudrillard but *analytically styled version of 'continental philosophy'*, articulated in analytic or standardized mainstream terms with respect to conventionally "continental" names like Nietzsche (and Husserl and Heidegger) and to a lesser degree – and this may be instructive – Marx, Adorno, etc. For this reason (among others), Nietzsche is not read as a thinker of the socio-political sphere much less of political economy and certainly not as theorist of science or logic but as a critic of morality and religion. This limitation is in spite of his own absorption with questions of logic, science, and epistemology, including questions of method, especially regarding the study of Greek antiquity, including history.

Even when Nietzsche happens to be read *socio-politically*, it is atypical (this does not mean that this never happens, only that it is an exception when it does) to take him as a political thinker of the left. There are important socio-historical reasons for this in the wake of two world wars, both of which have been connected to Nietzsche. If the first world war was journalistically dubbed "Nietzsche's war,"[3] still more important would be the ongoing effects of the second world war, particularly the declared influence of Nietzsche on National Socialism – rekindled in recent years by the scandal of Anti-Semitism in connection with Heidegger's Black Notebooks.[4] Discussion of Nietzsche and Marx is complicated by the post-war division of Germany into two parts – intriguingly varying the geographic schematism of the analytic/continental divide – and in consequence by the geographical circumstance setting Nietzsche at the mercy of ideological denunciation in the former DDR.[5] This is not to say that there were no scholars in the West who read Nietzsche,[6] even indeed and in connection with

2 See, for example, Babich (2018), and, including a review of social economic citation practice, Babich (2017a).

3 See for an overview, Tracy B. Strong, "Introduction" (Strong 2009: xi–xxiii). See also, Salter (1917).

4 See e.g. in descending order (and the list can be expanded), Bull (2016), Losurdo (2014), and Rayman (2015).

5 See, just to begin, as I will return to this point below, Busch (2000).

6 Well known would be Alfred Schmidt and Hans Heinz Holz in addition to Reinhart Maurer, Renate Reschke, Steffen Dietzsch, and Holz's student Rüdiger Schmidt-Grépalý. See on Holz, Hermand (1978). In the DDR, see Pepperle (1986), to which came the rather indignant re

critical theory, such as Reinhart Maurer and, more recently, Martin Saar, but it can be hard today to see the scope of Nietzsche resistance in the post-war Bundesrepublik Deutschland – and no small part of that resistance had to do with regarding Nietzsche as, at least, an educational "danger."[7] But the circumstance of ongoing anxiety on the side of West German philosophy, not least Habermas who famously declared Nietzsche no longer "contagious" only to modify that assessment a bit later,[8] but also Ernst Tugendhat (who took care to urge that we remain suspicious of Nietzsche) (Tugendhat 2000), came just at a time when German philosophy was struggling to import as much as possible of the analytic philosophical mainstream into the German academy. The resounding success of this analytic project in Germany (as in France and elsewhere) has not helped Nietzsche's cause.[9] Nietzsche has not fared much better on the international left, consequent to his repudiation as prophet of irrationalism,[10] following Georg Lukács along with Habermas and other representatives of the Frankfurt school (Habermas 1968, 1985). Thus scholars who undertake to read Nietzsche *and* Marx (or even to "*reread* Nietzsche and Marx") (Roberts 1995), have their work cut out for them: where are they to begin? If, as Aristotle argued,

sponse by Harich (1987). The phenomenon was at the time sufficiently remarkable that an article about it made the *New York Times* (Binder 1987). For a useful discussion with many details on just one aspect of an arguably still to be researched academic chapter, see Reschke's (2009) retrospective. For a more mainstream account within philosophy and analytic history of ideas proper (only consider the press), see Golomb and Wistrich (2009) as well as, of course, Aschheim's (1994) now standard: *The Nietzsche Legacy in Germany: 1890–1990*.

7 See Rodden (2008) for a description of the furor surrounding the re-opening of the Nietzsche Archive in 1991, which as I was in Weimar then myself, was really more a matter of bringing Nietzsche back into mainstream discussion, complete with a front-page proclamation in *Die Zeit* "The Banished One is Back!" Rodden is not concerned with Marx as such, except to emphasize the shift as one from one ideology to (perhaps and not in fact as it turned out) another Nietzsche über Marx (Rodden 2008). On the side of critical theory, see for an overview, Maurer (1981–1982) and see, ostensibly dedicated to a discussion of the subject of its title, my book *Nietzsches Wissenschaftstheorie* (Babich 2015d), but offering an elaboration of Maurer's thinking on scientific and Marxist Critical Theory (Maurer 2015).

8 See for discussion the contributing essays included in Babich (2004).

9 Indeed, Nietzsche studies have, if anything, lost institutional support in recent years (this is not the same as saying that no one wants to study him and it certainly does not mean that no one writes books and articles on his thought: instead what is meant is that few university posts are held by scholars specifically dedicated to his work, especially scholars with formations in philosophy rather than literature).

10 See Lukács (1953, in English as of 1980) as well as Lukács (1982 [1933]). For a contemporary expression, see Wolin (2004).

citing an already older convention in Greek antiquity, the beginning is (almost) everything: the point of departure determines what can and cannot be said just as it determines what is and is not seen.

2 Reading Epigraphs

Here, we consider the epigraph (although, as Weber emphasizes, to quote Günther Anders, the most important bits are found in the notes "Das Wichtigste steht natürlich in den Anmerkungen" [Anders 1980: 14]). And if this essay has epigraphs from all three, it is common for readings between Nietzsche and Marx to begin with an epigraph from Max Weber,[11] a sub-industry of its own,[12] or Paul Ricoeur or Michel Foucault.

Thus Alfred Schmidt's *History and Structure* features an epigraph comprised of, not merely a line or two, but an entire aphorism from Nietzsche.[13] In addition we may speak of those influenced by Nietzsche such Günther Anders, in addition to Max Horkheimer and Theodor Adorno. As Gillian Rose offers the acute observation, oddly unobserved by other scholars, that quite in spite of

11 Thus Caygill's (1993: 189) epigraph to his chapter "The Return of Nietzsche and Marx." Weber's citation had also served as epigraph to Nancy Love's *Nietzsche, Marx, and Modernity* (1986), and Mike Roberts duly cites Love's epigraph to prefix his own "Rereading Marx and Nietzsche" (Roberts 1995: 100). Kostas Axelos (1966 [1961], in English, 2017) carefully details the origin and more specific context of the quote as point of departure for the inaugural chapter of *Einführung in ein künftiges Denken: Über Marx und Heidegger*. Note here that Wolfgang Müller-Lauter's (1960) own account is relevant for Axelos' reading. See further Müller-Lauter (2000), and see especially Müller-Lauter's introduction (2000: 26ff. and 154ff.), and not less his reference, key and critical, to Alexander Schwan (1987). See Duk-Yung Kim (1995: 87), following, as everyone follows, Eduard Baumgarten (1964: 554f., note 1). See also Wilhelm Hennis (1987).

12 The wide differences between Weber and Marx have long been noted, see: Birnbaum (1953), but their themes overlap in part, and thus comparisons are both inevitable and fruitful. See the comparison offered by the Nietzsche scholar, Karl Löwith (1982), and note Bryan Turner's (1993: 1–32) useful preface to the new edition reissued in 1993 by Routledge in addition to Turner's "Max Weber and the Spirit of Resentment: The Nietzsche Legacy," (2011) along with, in Italian, Giuseppe Antonio Di Marco (1984) in addition to, to touch the tip of an iceberg of readings, Anthony Giddens (1970) as well as Robert Eden's *Political Leadership and Nihilism* (1984), among related studies and for a recent monograph, Derek Sayer (2015).

13 Nietzsche, "*The Possibility of Progress*" from *Human, All too Human*, §24 featured in Alfred Schmidt (1981).

Adorno's retention of a "Hegelian vocabulary – subject, object, mediation – his reception of Hegel's philosophy is structured by his reception of Nietzsche's philosophy as well as that of Marx" (Rose 1978: 55).[14]

Another approach reviews both Nietzsche and Marx as students of Classical Philology.[15] In addition, the term "classical" has a more conventional, i.e. 19th century sense and thus the late Marshall Berman draws on Goethe. Günther Anders likewise draws on Goethe's *Zauberlehrling* [Sorceror's Apprentice] as incipient techno-critique. In a more American variation upon the same technical focus, Berman refers to Goethe's Faust, including comic book depictions of Superman (not without some imprecision) in *All That is Solid Melts into Air* where Nietzsche also makes occasional cameos.[16] Caped crusader of all things American, qua television and film ideal beyond his comic book beginnings, Superman may be with us always, symbolizing the cargo-cultic enthusiasms of the transhumanists together with the popular vision of the overman (Babich 2015b; 2012: 158–159).

Nietzsche is also essential in Jacob Taubes' recollection of his reading of Karl Löwith *From Hegel to Nietzsche* as Nietzsche read his Schopenhauer (the Augustinian resonances are deliberate and thus – if Hadot is right – to be treated with some reservation), at the moment of its 1941 publication in Zürich (both the date and the locus matter for this revelation) (Löwith 1967). In Taubes' preface to *Ad Carl Schmitt*, he explains:

> It was like scales falling from my eyes as I grasped the line that Löwith traced from Hegel via Marx and Kierkegaard to Nietzsche. Everything I had read or heard so far about the spiritual and intellectual history of the nineteenth century seemed at once stale and irrelevant. It became clear to me that "whoever has tested the depths of European thinking from 1830 to 1848 is as well-prepared as can be for what is today emerging both in East and in West."
>
> TAUBES 2013: 2

14 More recondite and conceptually agile commentators to Giorgio Agamben (who worries about Nietzsche in terms of eternal recurrence and thence to Marx) or, Friedrich Kittler or Peter Sloterdijk.

15 I discuss this as part of my discussion of Nietzsche and Epicurus (Babich 2019) and see, extremely wide ranging, Waite (1996).

16 See the first part of Berman (1988 [1982]). For a discussion of Nietzsche and Superman and pop culture, foregrounding film and television, see Babich (2015b). For a more recent resumption of this move, see Ishay Landa's (2007) discussion of market capitalism and pop culture in his *The Overman in the Marketplace: Nietzschean Heroism in Popular Culture*.

The Löwith-Effect culminating in Nietzsche (who, as if for the sake of this effect, dies on cue in 1900), speaks in the subtitle: *The Revolution in Nineteenth Century Thought*. Löwith's 1941 focus on 1830–1848, the years formative for the young Marx, underscores the eclipse of "the world of Goethe and Hegel" (Löwith 1967). The insight lent Taubes a dissertation (in this section of his book, Löwith adumbrates a detailed outline of eschatology in the context of world history) (Löwith 1967: 29–49). Löwith's reading offers a very German and very systematic assessment of the revolutionary reading of the 19th century: as Löwith articulates "The Problem of Bourgeois Society" – from Rousseau to Nietzsche no less –, before going on to "The Problem of Work," "The Problem of Education," "The Problem of Man," and (thus its appeal to Taubes) "The Problem of Christianity." If a single thought might be drawn from this tour through the century that, arguably, continues to frame our own, it might be Löwith's Hegelianism, parsing and reflecting the synthetic move, the inclusive choosing between two opposed claims, in this case: articulated by the relation between the Third Reich (by no means decided at the time of writing) and its description as "the 'fulfilment' of Nietzsche" (Löwith 1967: 198). The balance indicates, on the one hand, the significance of Heidegger for Löwith as well as, on the other, the extent to which Löwith's historical sensibility exceeds Heidegger's.

As Löwith reflects on this constellation:

> no one who takes Nietzsche's work seriously or 'expounds' it can fail to recognize that Nietzsche is alien both to the 'national' and to the 'social,' just as, on the other hand, the spirit of Beyreuth is related to the instincts of more than Bismarck's Reich. To see the abyss which separates Nietzsche from latter-day prophets, it suffices to read his writings against Wagner and his remarks on the Jewish question and the converse question of what is 'German,' without editing or excerpting.
>
> LÖWITH 1967: 198

We know these deflective movements but Löwith insists as well on the converse claim:

> This does not contradict the obvious fact that Nietzsche became a catalyst of the 'movement,' and determined its ideology in a decisive way. The attempt to unburden Nietzsche of this intellectual 'guilt,' or even to claim his support against what he brought about is just as unfounded as the reverse effort to make him an advocate of a matter over which he sits in judgment.
>
> LÖWITH 1967: 198

In this way, Löwith's dialectical tension highlights the difficulty faced by those who seek to situate Nietzsche on the right and on the left.

Alasdair MacIntyre reflects on this tension between right and left Nietzscheans well before recent economic events and also before the current emigration crisis, in his 1984 *After Virtue* (MacIntyre 1984). Elsewhere I have pointed to the significance of MacIntyre's book as it falls into two parts, with a disjunction in the title of the central chapter, "Nietzsche *or* Aristotle?," and given the emphatically disjoint/conjoint title of its last chapter: "After Virtue: Nietzsche *or* Aristotle, Trotsky *and* St. Benedict" (MacIntyre 1984: 109ff. and 256ff., respectively). Noting the "Weberian managerial forms of our culture," MacIntyre invokes Nietzsche's "prophetic irrationalism" to be found in right and left varieties, and this is the neatness of MacIntyre's argument, "insofar as contemporary Marxism is Weberian in substance we can expect prophetic irrationalisms of the Left as well as of the Right" (MacIntyre 1984: 114).[17]

But even with such an authority as MacIntyre, robustly "Left Nietzscheans" turn out to be rare – MacIntyre names Kathryn Pyne Parsons, Tracy Strong, and Jim Miller – especially if one means to look to Marx.[18] Thus there is – just as Löwith already observed – no gainsaying the spirit of the popular conviction that Nietzsche must be arraigned on the right: a "forerunner" of fascism.[19] For Löwith, the effort to set Nietzsche down on either side "must crumble before the historical insight that 'forerunners' have ever prepared roads for others which they themselves did not travel" (Löwith 1967: 198).[20]

There is a good deal more besides: thus I already mentioned the Black Notebooks, where Nietzsche is named, in no good spirit, a proto-Heidegger (Beiner 2018), or: perhaps more dissonantly, as some sort of precursor to Ayn Rand (who did not like him),[21] or, still more mysteriously, a fan of exploitation, and thus of the entrepreneurial spirit and all its works (Babich 2017d; Kline 1969;

17 Note that MacIntyre does not detail names on the right (legion, one supposes), but only on the left (1978). I cite parts of Strong's (1999 [1975]) discussion of Nietzsche and Marx, which Strong, like MacIntyre, advances in connection with Weber. See also Caygill.

18 It is for this reason that Geoff Waite, after retracing the so-called Nietzsche-cult (Ferdinand Tönnies), speaks of factions or remnant splinters – "Left-Nietzschoids" – to highlight a clearly divided aspect on the left. See Waite (1996: 139–166).

19 See Wolin (2004) and see too the phrase given in quotes by Robert C. Holub (2015: 213).

20 The historical tension is more comprehensive than can be considered here, but Löwith goes on the reflect that "As antagonist to Bismarck and to Wagner, he moved within the circumference of *their* 'will to power,' and even his timeliness in the Third Reich rested upon the fact that it was the heir of the Second" (Lowith 1967: 198–199).

21 See for a discussion, Stephen R.C. Hicks (2009) and Lester Hunt (2016).

Polyakova and Sineokaya 2017). These are caricatures although substantive scholarship is sometimes expended upon such assays and these are all the more important as analytic (which is to say the majority of currently conventional philosophic) readings of Nietzsche likewise favour such caricatures, sometimes in seeming good conscience. More esoterically, with its own strengths/pitfalls, some read Simmel along with a more complicated discussion of so-called "Austrian sociology,"[22] and there is a (still unreceived) reflection on Nietzsche and economics authored by German scholars post the unification of Germany at the end of the last century (Backhaus and Drechsler 2003). Related reflections inspire a number of popular leftist take-downs of Nietzsche, most conspicuously because baldly titled, Malcolm Bull's *Anti-Nietzsche*. If this is by no means a serious reading of Nietzsche (in contrast with Simmel and given his influence on Weber himself),[23] there is also basic anti-socialism, anti-crowdism, anti-populism, which is why, more respectably, Luc Ferry and Alain Renaut could edit a collective volume, decades ago now, *Why We Are Not Nietzscheans* (Ferry and Renaut 1997). Nietzsche's influence continues in a French context, adumbrated via Heidegger as Kostas Axelos argues (and as one may also read in part in Michel Foucault and certainly Jean Baudrillard), with Jacques Derrida and Gilles Deleuze, who in an oft-cited note in *Negotiations* reflects on identifying as a Marxist – *nota bene*, not a Nietzschean and the difference is profoundly salutary –

> Felix Guattari and I have remained Marxists, in our two different ways, perhaps, but both of us. You see, we think any political philosophy must turn on the analysis of capitalism and the ways it has developed. What we find most interesting in Marx is his analysis of capitalism as an immanent system that's constantly overcoming its own limitations, and then coming up against them once more in a broader form, because its fundamental limit is capital itself.
>
> DELEUZE 1995: 171

To be sure it has been claimed Deleuze's reading of Marx is imbued with his Nietzsche (Krtolica 2012), but this can obscure the force of this reflection,

---

22 See Simmel (1896) as well as, if not specifically in relation to Marx, Simmel (1907). Also see Solms-Laubach (2012). On Nietzsche and Simmel see, again, Rose (1978).

23 There are a number of recent "returns" to Simmel, but see, including a discussion of Nietzsche and Marx, Leck (2000). For the connection with Weber, see Schluchter (1995).

especially in connection with other French thinkers on Marx where the connection with Nietzsche can be less secure.[24]

Deleuze's definition of capitalism as "an immanent system that's constantly overcoming its own limitations, and then coming up against them once more in a broader form, because its fundamental limit is capital itself" is key (Deleuze 1995: 171). The insight recurs in Alain Badiou, Slavoj Žižek, David Harvey, Thomas Picketty and others. It is the reason one must continue to think through Marx – this is why the simplistic notion that one can switch out Nietzsche for Marx, whereby Nietzsche would be "in," Marx "out," as an already cited account of 1991 Germany related the impression, falls as short as Habermas's famous claim that "*Nietzsche is no longer contagious*" (Habermas 1999: 209). At stake is the point Deleuze emphasizes in speaking of capitalism's immanence: we do not see it, as Anders will emphasize, as I note below, referring to the globality that is nature and history: the immanent continues apart from us, and so abject is the contingent character of this immanence, very potentially without us.

For his part, arguably the most influential in generic discussion of Nietzsche and Marx, Michel Foucault is master of the mélange *an sich*: mixing discussion of Marx-Nietzsche-Freud so thoroughly that none of these, perhaps with the exception of Freud, is distinguishable (Foucault 1990). In addition, one might name Paul Virilio in addition to Henri Lefebvre's *Hegel, Marx, Nietzsche* (1996 [1975]).[25] Reinhold Grimm (1983) reminds his readers in his closing contribution to a 1977 conference on Nietzsche and Marx of the importance of Italian names so often neglected.[26] Grimm, who writes on Nietzsche, rightly foregrounds Mazzino Montinari, who co-edited with Giorgio Colli the critical edition of Nietzsche's works and I myself will return to Montinari below.

24 See further, Beaulieu (2009).

25 In addition, to go beyond French (and above German) names, there would be Antonio Gramsci, Domenico Losurdo, Giorgio Agamben, just to note authors who read between Nietzsche and Marx, naming both Nietzsche and Marx in their writings, there is of course very importantly, Gianni Vattimo. See, for example, Vattimo's (2009) "Nihilism as Emancipation." Vattimo places weight on both Nietzsche and Marx with Heidegger, and this can also be seen in Axelos and others, as a kind of fulcrum. See most recently, Vattimo and Zabala (2011). And see too the contributions to Sylvie Mazzinie and Owen Glyn-Williams, eds. (2017).

26 Grimm's apothegm, political "theatricality" refers to Castri, Artaud, and Brecht but he also mentions Shakespeare's *Lear* and, in passing, Charles Laughton's "sympathetic" film portrayal of Galileo, alluding to André Glucksmann's *Les Maitres penseurs* and Bernard Henry-Levy, whereby whether the motif is "silence" (socialism) or "terrorism" (Marxism), the conjunction Nietzsche and Marx rules them all.

The lines to be drawn are those between those who wish to appropriate Nietzsche for a progressive and yet emphatically "rational" (meaning 'mainstream') politics and those who wish to keep to the rigors of Hegel and then there are those who insist upon the (revolutionary) dimensions of Marx himself.[27] The complexities to be added to this are all the details of Nietzsche's "theory of knowledge" as Habermas edited a collection of these writings, encouraged by – as Jacob Taubes told me, with all *gravitas*, that this was anything but Habermas' own initiative – the collective suggestion of Hans Blumenberg, Theodor Adorno and Taubes himself.[28]

Nietzsche is *not* an irrationalist (even if it is fun to think he is), and this recognition undermines many Marxist accounts that take this supposition as their point of departure. Much rather, Nietzsche is a philosopher who underlines philosophy's fixation on the ideal of knowledge as salvific illusion, beginning with Socrates and Plato and Aristotle and culminating in Descartes and Kant, a philosopher keen to examine logic and language and mathematics and concepts, and who looks to the natural sciences not as ultimate resort but just for the sake of understanding this latest, and as he named it, *best* instance of the ascetic ideal: our 'new religion.'[29]

3 Critique and the Antiquated Human: Changing the World in the Age of Digital Media

Günther Anders, who remains famous mostly for having been Hannah Arendt's ex-husband or Walter Benjamin's cousin, rather than, as he should be celebrated, for having penned one of the most critically theoretical and enduringly relevant analyses of modern technology, features an epigraph in his 1980 book, *The Antiquatedness of Humanity Volume* II, *On the Destruction of Life in*

27 I discuss as one of these thinkers, who for his part *does not* discuss Nietzsche, the late Marxist thinker Robert Kurz in "Tools for Subversion: Illich and Žižek on Changing the World" (Babich 2017e).

28 Habermas himself is a far more complicated case. See the contributions to Babich (2004) as well as to Babich (1999a), the first of a two-volume collection on *Nietzsche and Science*, incited but not in praxical fact co-edited by the Marxist philosopher of science, Robert S. Cohen who collected all the royalties on the co-edited volumes we published.

29 It is thus worth noting that the most revolutionary readings of Nietzsche are those that consider Nietzsche and the sciences. Cf. Reinhard Löw (1984) in addition to the readings of natural scientists such as the chemist, Alwin Mittasch, for a discussion including a review of Nietzsche's radicalization of Kant and his theory of science, see Babich (1994), the updated German edition (Babich 2010), and Babich (1999b).

the Era of the Third Industrial Revolution, glosses Marx's great challenge to philosophers:

> It isn't sufficient to change the world. That we do anyway. And to a great extent this goes on even apart from what we do. We have to interpret this change as well. And indeed, in order to change this. In order that the world not continue to alter itself apart from us. And not, ultimately, in a world lacking us.
>
> ANDERS 1980: 6

The back reference – and we *always* need a back reference when reading Anders's apothegms – is Nietzsche's own provocation with respect to the world, just where there are, for Nietzsche, "no facts," "only interpretations."[30] In *Beyond Good and Evil*, Nietzsche addresses physics as such as little "more than a world-interpretation [*Welt-Auslegung*] and arrangement [*Zurechtlegung*] of the world," (Nietzsche, *Jenseits von Gut und Böse*, §14; KSA 5: 28) in a chained array of reflections in which he indicts the same physicists themselves for their weak interpretative skill [the German is a little harsher: *schlechte Interpretations-Künste*] which Nietzsche proceeds to read in socio-political terms as the desire to reduce everything, including nature itself, to our own level. Thus Nietzsche claims that we consider something "known" when we have merely translated it from its proper sphere, alien and strange as that remains, into terms familiar to us. This translation is a "humanization" whereby we also assume uniformity beginning with our own sphere which we proceed to assume to extend without exception to the furthest corner of the universe itself, which *physis*, which "nature" is thereby held to be, decreed to be, just as subject to the same rules and regulations we happen to know: "Above all, equality before the law, – nature has it not otherwise and no better than we ourselves" which is for Nietzsche to be just as indicted as the political ethos of atheistic anarchy: "'*Ni dieu, ni maître*'... and what is more: 'Up with natural law'!" (Nietzsche, *Jenseits von Gut und Böse*, §22; KSA 5: 37).

Truth might not be worth more than appearance (this is for Nietzsche no more than a "moral prejudice)," but Nietzsche asks, "Why could the world which is of any concern to us – not be a fiction?" Here after pointing out that we insist on regularity according to a scheme that matches our environment, be it a matter of laws or the anti-thesis of the same in the political spirit of atheistic

---

30 I talk about this in Babich (1994), attesting to Nietzsche's hermeneutic methodology. For a discussion of hermeneutics and science, see Babich (2015c) as well as in this same connection (and collection): Babich (2015a).

revolution, whereby the latter nonetheless insists on the reign of natural law (once again: "*Hoch die Naturgesetze*"), to conclude "Granted this too is only interpretation – and you will be eager enough to raise this objection? – now, all the better.–" (Nietzsche, *Jenseits von Gut und Böse*, §22; KSA 5: 37).

Nietzsche's reflections on interpretation unnerve the ruling cadre of analytic readers, from Maudemarie Clark to Brian Leiter and their dutiful followers in the current generation. The problem concerns the lack of the same facts Nietzsche says we have not got, to which must also be accounted a decided absence of "truth" and any access to it (Nietzsche challenges both Plato and Aristotle on the matter, followed by Descartes, Spinoza, and Kant, disposing of Hegel in passing in his essay on the use and inconveniences of history). Mark Warren, in a context referring to both Ricoeur and Weber, reflects that not only are we concerned to evaluate Nietzsche's claims in terms of knowledge and interests, à la Habermas, but we assume still more fundamentally "that it is possible and necessary to develop a defensible theory of truth that underwrites both explanation and evaluation of ideologies" (Warren 1984).

Anders' epigraph remains difficult for scholars to interpret (or coopt which also hinders the reception of his work), yet hopefully the above explication of Nietzsche on world interpretation may at least serve to underline that reading between Nietzsche and Marx is as inescapable as is the challenge to change our own lives accordingly and so that, this is the naturalistic reflex, given what the world (and not only the natural world as this is also an industrial-political realm to boot) can do to us, we might hope to see our human, all too human legacy remain. If, given the limitations of his reception, Anders wrote under a dark star – *nomen est omen* – it is important to recall that Anders is fairly unique as a scholar. Not merely broad in his concerns, Anders very conscientiously writes, like Adorno, *post* Auschwitz, but also (and fewer follow him here): *post* Hiroshima, and (with still fewer echoes): *post* Chernobyl. In all this, like Nietzsche, Anders insists on thinking this through to what Nietzsche called the "last consequences."

More cannot be needed to justify the claim, as Max Weber observes, that Nietzsche and Marx may be viewed as an intellectual touchstone:

> The probity of a contemporary intellectual, especially a contemporary philosopher, can be measured by their attitude toward Nietzsche and Marx.[31]

31 Max Weber, cited by Eduard Baumgarten (1964: 554f., note 1; Hennis 1987) and Howard Caygill (1993: 190).

Speaking to our deepest, our best instincts in philosophy, we can live more authentic, better lives in our own hearts and for our own souls (Nietzsche) and do so in fairness and justice with one another (Marx), so that my flourishing is not (as it often is in capitalist and generically competitive societies) a matter of someone else's pain, languishing, failure.

4 Media Archaeology and Decay

Our society seems the fulfillment of the sick or "decadent" society Nietzsche analyses in his 19th century, highlighting the sickness of our abandonment to work (and its alienation) (Krtolica 2012; Roberts 2016) and not less our dedication to cultural distraction or entertainment (and its alienation). Thus if the Canadian political theorist of media and economy, Dallas Smythe anticipated (converged with) some of Jean Baudrillard's complaints, paralleling Anders and Adorno's insights on the "culture industry" which we today designate with the neutered name, "media," sometimes further neutralized as "digital media," the tactic seems to underscore the virtuosity of the virtual, the very media Smythe described as the "blind spot of Western Marxism" (Smythe 1977). Marxism (and it is not alone) would thereby be subject to the same *scotosis* – to use a modern Thomist term, likewise coined by a Canadian.[32]

Our lives could not be more effectively mediated via advertising, what we call "news" – both true and "false" – what Adorno described as "standardized ubiquity," and what its major proponent, Edward Bernays, characterized as "crystallizing" the currents of our opinions, judgments, thinking,[33] and, as omnipresent, effectively invisible in our lives.[34] In the course of the writing of *The*

32 The term is deployed by Bernard Lonergan and includes Freudian elements as a subsection of what he calls "Dramatic bias" (as one can desire insight, one can also desire darkness): "Fundamentally, the scotosis is an unconscious process. It arises not in conscious acts but in the censorship that governs the emergence of psychic contents. Nonetheless, the whole process is not hidden from us" (Lonergan 1958 [1957]: 191). In the following section, entitled "Repression," Lonergan explains that "The scotosis is an aberration, not only of the understanding, but also of the censorship" (Lonergan 1958 [1957]: 192).

33 The referent here is to Bernays (1923). See for a recent discussion, Wimberley (2017). See too for a connection with Adorno often left out in accounts of Bernays, Babich (2014). The best discussion remains Ellul (1973). For a recent discussion, see Wollaeger (2008). See too, as a pendant in sociological discourse to the philosopher, Jason Stanley (who writes on propaganda) and Julian Baggini (on truth), Fuller (2018).

34 In a footnote, citing Baran and Sweezey's *Monopoly Capitalism*, Smythe (1977: 26) meditates upon the extraordinary cost of advertising (and presumptive profit margin): "reporting a reported $13 million advertising budget which produced $16 million in drug store

Hallelujah Effect which took the current author in the writing of it to sociological studies of music (Babich 2016b), phenomenologically articulated both in the field (Bennett's [2017 (1980)] *On Becoming a Rock Musician*, a book about what its title proclaims) as well as forbiddingly high theory (Adorno's little understood [2006; see Babich 2014 and 2016b] *Current of Music*, a study of radio developed under the auspices of the federally instigated Princeton Radio Project), I noted the relative denial on the part of political theorists, sociologists, media theorists, and even psychologists (but not marketing psychologists), etc., who preferred instead to insist on the impotence of advertising (no matter whether called branding or priming) as a mechanism to actually sell anything, rather as if advertisement somehow failed to "work."[35] By contrast, the Frankfurt School focuses on little apart from advertising and its effects (Horkheimer and Adorno 1972; Marcuse 1991).[36] Anders for his part might be argued as preempting a number of media theorists in his reflection on how the consumer manages, all by him or herself – that solitude being key for Anders – to create him or herself in the image of mass consumption: a homeworker on him or herself as consumer.[37] Marxists still attend the mechanical process that would be "history" to do the work which leaves propaganda and its effects "on men's minds" as Jacques Ellul (1973) speaks of these, to mere "consciousness" raising.[38] But if we have learned anything from the culture of exposing our imprinting, be it via Kalle Lasn[39] or the exceedingly mainstream conventions of Noam Chomsky and Edward S. Herman, it is that items brought to consciousness seem to show little more than the tremendous versatility of co-option, usurpation, rebranding, and remix.

How then, read *between* Nietzsche and Marx? If Anders argues in his critique of Heidegger that there is attention paid to neither hunger nor to sex in

sales, expressed in wholesale prices, to which they say: 'Allowing for a handsome profit margin,' which of course is added to selling as well as production cost, it seems clear that the cost of production can hardly be more than a minute proportion of even the wholesale price." See Horkheimer and Adorno as well as Baudrillard but also the late Marxist Robert Kurz. See, again, for some of these notions, my contribution to a collection dedicated to the notion of hermeneutic Marxism, in the spirit of Gianni Vattimo (Babich 2017e).

35 See for further discussion and additional literature, again, Babich (2014) and Babich (2017e).

36 I am not focusing here on Chomsky as his work routinely seems to capitulate to mainstream lines of thinking and thus limits itself.

37 See my reflection on Anders and Heidegger: Babich (2013).

38 With social media for distraction on every level, at every moment, these stakes have only been increased and here I mention Kittler, among others like Schmidt-Grepaly and Sloterdijk.

39 See in particular Lasn's (2000) *Culture Jam* as well as the parodic Adbusters gloss magazine he introduced and, most recently, and explicitly, Lassn (2012).

Being and Time as little as Heidegger attends to a practical focus on economic affairs despite his focus on very worldly "cares," Nietzsche's own reading on related topics, if exempt from the same reproof – Nietzsche emphasizes our preoccupation with the market and with money above all –, can likewise seem oblique.[40]

Bracketing the absurd question, although it continues to be exhumed from time to time – was Nietzsche or was he not a philosopher? – there is also the sheer volume and diversity of his work, just as one may point to the same, vastly more extensive, in the case of Marx. How, again, and given this range, is one to say in either case just what it was that they maintained?

Nietzsche writes in his *Human, All Too Human* on the general disjoint intersection between men of the world, actively or practically engaged in worldly activities and the so-called "higher pursuits." Instead, Nietzsche writes

> They are active as officials, businessmen, scholars, that is to say as generic creatures, but not as distinct individual and unique human beings… One ought not to ask the cash-amassing banker, for example, what the purpose of his restless activity is: it is irrational. The active human being rolls as the stone rolls, in obedience to the stupidity [*Dummheit*] of mechanics.
>
> NIETZSCHE, *Menschliches, Allzumenschliches* I, 283; KSA 2: 281

It is arguable that the convergence between Nietzsche and Marx's views of labor may be traced to their original study of antiquity, where as Nietzsche writes in a reflection on "leisure and idleness" to which we will return, the noble ethos was opposed to work and "The slave used to work, oppressed by the feeling he was doing something contemptible [*dass er etwas Verächtliches tut*]: 'doing' itself was contemptible. 'Nobility and honor are attached solely to *otium* and *bellum*,' that is the ancient prejudice" (Nietzsche, *Die fröhliche Wissenschaft*, §329; KSA 3: 557). A good deal of this ancient conviction is found in Marx's own esteem for free time or leisure for the sake of full or complete humanity.

Thus, if Marx can argue that "the whole of society must fall apart into the two classes – the property-owners and the property workers" (Marx 1975, *Economic and Philosophical Manuscripts 1844*, "Estranged Labor": 270), he highlights (as Nietzsche likewise does for his own part, as Günther Anders will later do) the extent to which, in the most literal terms, "Labor's realization is its objectification" (Marx 1975: 272). To this same degree,

40 Anders (1980: 18) emphasizes that the professional philosopher seems to specialize in laying claim to the right to say what ought and ought not be counted as philosophy.

> Just as he estranges his own activity from himself, so he confers upon the stranger an activity which is not his own. ... The relationship of the worker to labor creates the relationship to it of the capitalist (or whatever one chooses to call the master of labor).
>
> MARX 1975: 279

For this reason, and although

> private property appears to be the reason, the cause of alienated labor, it is rather its consequence, just as the gods are originally not the cause but the effect of man's intellectual confusion.
>
> MARX 1975: 279–280

Only because of this can Marx argue that

> Communism, as fully developed naturalism, equals humanism, and as a fully developed humanism equals naturalism; it is the genuine resolution of the conflict between men and nature and between man and man.
>
> MARX 1975, *Economic and Philosophical Manuscripts 1844*, "Private Property and Communism": 296

5 Religion, Gold-Lust, and the Conciousness-Deadening Virtue of Work

Instructively, at his emancipatory beginning of the third book of *The Gay Science*, Nietzsche begins by reflecting "God is dead"; noting that, "given the fashion of humanity, there must yet be expected for thousands of years that there will be caves in which his shadow will be shown" (Nietzsche, *Die fröhliche Wissenschaft*, §108; KSA 3: 467). As Nietzsche goes on in the following cautionary aphorism to emphasize, after reflecting contra the Timean and teleological theory of the cosmos, as against the Copernican, Newtonian, Laplacean, mechanistic conception – "none of our aesthetic and moral judgments apply to it" – to argue for *nothing* but consummate necessity: "there is nobody who commands, nobody who obeys, nobody who trespasses. Once you know that there are no purposes you also know that there is no accident" (Nietzsche, *Die fröhliche Wissenschaft*, §109: 468). It is in this sense that Nietzsche uses the same language we found in Marx above, asking "When may we begin to 'naturalize' humanity in terms of a pure, newly discovered, newly redeemed nature?" (Nietzsche, *Die fröhliche Wissenschaft*, §109: 469).

In the fourth book, Nietzsche makes one of his few references to America and thus to the social and political circumstances of 1882 – and *The Gay Science* is Nietzsche's most Emersonian book, explicitly so as he begins with an epigraph, in German rhyming, from Emerson: "To the poet, to the philosopher, to the saint, all things are friendly and sacred, all events profitable, all days holy, all men divine" (Emerson 1970: 8).[41] Relevant in the current context is the aphorism entitled "Leisure and idleness" where Nietzsche offers a (very German) reflection on Native Americans via Lamarckian metonymy transmitted to their usurpers:

> There is something of the American Indians, something of the ferocity peculiar to the Indian blood, in the American lust for gold; and the breathless haste with which they work – the distinctive vice of the new world – is already beginning to infect old Europe with its ferocity, spreading mindlessness like a blanket. Even now one is ashamed of resting, and prolonged reflection almost gives people a bad conscience. One thinks with a watch in one's hand, even as one eats one's midday meal while reading the latest news of the stock market … Living in a constant chase after gain compels people to expend their spirit to the point of exhaustion in continual pretense and over reaching and anticipating others. Virtue has come to consist in doing something in less time than someone else.
>
> NIETZSCHE, *Die fröhliche Wissenschaft*, §329; KSA 3: 556

If Anders, whom we cited above, made Nietzsche's observation here "one lives as if one always might 'miss out on something'" in Anders' analysis of the modern solitary manufacture of oneself as consumer in the image of all other consumers in his *The Antiquatedness of Humanity* (Anders 1980),[42] it is this same

41 Nietzsche's version is suitably epigraphic and recognizably Stoic: [*Dem Dichter und Weisen sing alle Dinge befreundet und geweiht, alle Erlebnisse nützlich, alle Tage heilig, alle Menschen göttlich.*] It has been argued, somewhat misleadingly, that Nietzsche takes the title of his text from Emerson's New England transcendentalism/idealism, as Walter Kaufmann cites Emerson as proclaiming, "we were made for another office, professors of the Joyous Science" (Kaufmann 1974: 9). But this New World academic association compels one to miss Nietzsche's references to the science that was his own proper formation – i.e. classical philology – and his 1886 appended subtitle "*la gaya scienza.*" Thus I argue that Nietzsche returns to the themes of his first book on tragedy in *The Gay Science*. See on Nietzsche and the Provençal troubadours' "gay science," Babich (2006) as well as, with reference to lyric poetic form, Babich (2016d).

42 Parts of this text can be found in English translation together with valuable accompanying reflections in Müller (2016). See, too, for discussion, Babich (2013).

point that makes Nietzsche's observations seem prophetic in our age of internet absorption and social media distraction: "If sociability and the arts still offer any delight, it is the kind of delight that tired, work-weary slaves, devise for themselves" (Nietzsche, *Die fröhliche Wissenschaft*, §329; KSA 3: 557).

For Marx, the parallel fit into his analysis of technology, the Industrial Revolution that Anders' counted off as having seen no less than *two* subsequent turns in our age (we are, he argued in the midst of the third, and a case could be made that in the age of social media relentlessly polishing the product of ourselves, perfecting our curated repetition of everyone else's "news" (both what we take to be authorized and what we take to be "fake") the age of likes and retweets, we have entered, to continue Anders' count, the fourth industrial age), renders the worker not merely adjunct to the machine but an appendage of capital. This is the dialectical paradox of joblessness and it is the reason we insist on believing that what is good for the industrialist, the banker, the capitalist, is good for the worker. This is not an esoteric claim: "The worker has become a commodity, and it is a bit of luck for him if he can find a buyer. And the demand on which the life of the worker depends, depends on the whim of the rich and the capitalists" (Marx 1975, *Economic and Philosophic Manuscripts of 1844*, "Wages of Labor": 235). To this extent, and famously if not always perspicuously analyzed, as we read in the *Communist Manifesto*, the worker becomes "an appendage of the machine" (Pelz 2016). Everything that has to do with the relation between technology and capital is involved in this. And we have trouble understanding this to the extent that we remain, to vary the sense but not the force of Nietzsche's "too pious," committed to the ideal of science, and thereby to the ideal of techno-neutrality.

If, to repeat the first epigraph above, Marx writes that the "machine accommodates itself to the weakness of the human being in order to make the weak human being into a machine" (Marx 1978, *Economic and Philosophic Manuscripts of 1844*: 95), in *Capital*, Marx emphasizes the inevitable complexity of this coordination to the extent that the worker must serve, at whatever level of specialization – and note that this includes both blue collar work, classical labor, as it includes white collar work, laborers bound to the machine in deeper and deeper ways as only a very few scholars of our digital era have adverted to this,[43] and including, in case university professors had not noticed (and few

43 See Germaine (1993) more broadly with respect to technology as well as more recently with reference to the digital: (Berry 2014; Dyer-Witheford 2015; Koloğlugil 2015) in addition to, more nuancedly, more complicatedly, again, Waite's *Nietzsche's Corps/e*, especially

have, with the marked exception of Kittler and his heirs who are busy covering up the radical force of Kittler's insights [Kittler 1999]), the internet both as locus of dissemination and distraction and not less the 'digital' as formative of thought and expression. Thus Marx writes,

> in place of the hierarchy of specialized workers that characterizes manufacture, there appears in the automatic factory a tendency to equalize and reduce to an identical level every kind of work that has to be done by the minders of the machines.
>
> MARX 1977, *Capital*: 545

Many authors read between Marx and Nietzsche with respect to labor or else religion. It seems plain that Marx converges most with Nietzsche in his analysis of the ascetic ideal of capitalism, especially at the level of the worker: (and maybe this is all we need to explain the connection to Weber) as the more quotidian contradictions of capitalism: "Political economy, this science of wealth, is therefore simultaneously the science of denial, of want, of thrift, of saving" (Marx 1978, *Economic and Philosophic Manuscripts of 1844*: 95). Speaking of the idolization of the ideal of saving for the worker classes, the incentive to save

> actually reaches the point where it spares man the need of either fresh air or physical exercise. This science of marvelous industry is simultaneously the science of asceticism, and its true ideal is the ascetic but extortionate miser and the ascetic but productive slave.
>
> MARX 1978, *Economic and Philosophic Manuscripts of 1844*: 95

In fact, the asceticism of which Nietzsche himself speaks in *On the Genealogy of Morals* becomes the abstemiousness that will later be diagnosed, given its plain Calvinistic tonality, as the *spirit of Protestantism* in Weber to quote Marx:

> The less you eat, drink, and read books, the less you go to the theatre, the dance hall the pub, the less you think, love, theorize, sing, paint, fence, etc., the more you save – the greater becomes your treasure which neither moths nor dust will devour – your capital.
>
> MARX 1978, *Economic and Philosophic Manuscripts of 1844*: 95–96

---

the chapter, a bit ahead of its time in terms of readerly enthusiasms, albeit spot-on, Bladerunner style, "*Transformismo* from Gramsci to Dick, or the Spectacular Culture of Everyday Life" (Waite 1996: 339–390).

The same imperative to store up riches for the beyond, that is: rather than to enjoy them to save or reserve them for a time and a space beyond all time and space is, of course, Nietzsche's ascetic ideal: economic advice for the poor.

6 Becoming Marx, Becoming Nietzsche

I have been quoting Marx, early and late, Nietzsche too. And elsewhere, I have sought to explicate Heidegger's hermeneutic and historically material argument that an author's work so far from being divisible into separate categorizations (early, middle, late) is much rather to be understood (we are speaking of authors after all) as epiphenomena of the effects of publication, what Gadamer duly analyzes as the *Wirkungsgeschichte* of a text. Thus when the *1844 Manuscripts* first appeared, as Tracy Strong has pointed out, 'good,' i.e. exemplary Marxists, could dismiss these as 'not really' Marx, this is the Althusserian claim as it is also Leninist convention – what did it matter what a young man who was not yet Marx thought? The controversy has been widely discussed,[44] but it matters all the more when transposed into a Heideggerian, hermeneutic perspective (and given the Black Notebooks themselves, Heidegger himself would prove the best exemplification of his own claim), as an author undergoes a sea-change when the *Nachlass* appears, and if the claim applies in the case of both Nietzsche and Marx, Heidegger himself instantiated the poet Hölderlin along with no one other than Hegel.

I argue that for Heidgger, the effect of the *Nachlass* brings a certain and specific and hermeneutically significant *Nachtraglichkeit* to work (Babich 2016a), which backwards working changes not only the author's reception, but the work itself, a signal "fusion" in Gadamerian terms, of horizons.[45] Where Nietzsche for his part has yet to be integrated into the texts named the *Nachlass* writings, texts including *The Will to Power* and thus the texts that constitute the greater part of what has led scholars to associate Nietzsche with fascism, it is unlikely that Lukács could have claimed (as he did) a direct link between

44 See for a recent overview: Musto (2015).

45 To certain extent, this has become a hermeneutic commonplace, evident not least in the transformation of Heidegger scholarship by the publication of the *Beiträge* and the Black Notebooks, both of these complete with editorial interventions, in the case of Friedrich von Hermann who in a fashion that the editors of the *Will to Power* would have endorsed, shifted entire sections from the start of the *Beiträge*, to serve as closing chapter to the same, and without touching the text as such, Peter Trawny whose editorial intervention served as introduction, setting tone of the reception of the Black Notebooks from the start. See Babich (2016a).

Hitler and Nietzsche,[46] were the main text available to him *The Birth of Tragedy* or even *Thus Spoke Zarathustra*, as opposed to the *Will to Power*.[47]

Thus one can read Heidegger (complete with the political fortunes of his reception if one likes) as a fulcrum to access Nietzsche with respect to Marx. Certainly, as noted, Kostas Axelos does this or one can use, as a kind of lever, as Caygill does, the language of return,[48] or else "rhythm,"[49] this last a term with ambiguities tied to the Weberian dimensions of the ethos or spirit of the West, but also with regard to Mauss and Bataille. As is evident in the subtitle of Bataille's book on Nietzsche, "The Will to Chance," and not less Derrida, ways to see commerce as well as the "general economy" in a Nietzschean light are key.[50]

Indeed, one of my Berlin teachers, Wolfgang Müller-Lauter, who by no means incidentally began as a Heidegger scholar but not less critically on the personal level as an émigré to Berlin when I first met him in 1984, from East Germany. The Weimar born Müller-Lauter shows the importance of Marxist themes in Nietzsche by adverting as few do to Nietzsche's reading of Emmanuel Hermann, noting Nietzsche's "numerous underlinings as well as marginal notes" in Hermann's *Kultur und Natur. Studien im Gebiete der Wirthschaft*. Readers today can benefit from Müller-Lauter's instructive engagement in this context, that is, in a politico-economic spirit, with Pierre Klossowski's *Nietzsche et le circle vicieux* (Müller-Lauter 1999: 175). Again, it can be plain that we remain in need of a reading – which is precisely to say that scholars today

46 See Lukács (1954) as well as his patently titled *Der deutsche Faschismus und Nietzsche, Schicksalswende* (Lukács 1948) in addition to an informative reading by András Gedö (1988). There are to be sure other approaches: Schmidt (1982) and Harich (1987: 101ff.)

47 It makes a difference that in many political readings of Nietzsche, it is not his own works as he himself published these but the non-book (compiled, literally for the sake of profitability and understandable as that may have been for the financial survival of his family, quite for the sake of marketability, that editors put together in his name after his death and steadily expanded until it had attained a certain size/gravity, in subsequent editions), that makes all the difference. See Babich (2009).

48 This emphasis is already patent in Caygill's (1993) title: "The Return of Nietzsche and Marx."

49 To this extent, as Lefebvre already along with Caygill has noted, rhythm makes a return, almost as constant as the eternal readings of Nietzsche's time atom fragment in Löschenkohl (2008: 16f.) as well as, in addition to Joan Stambaugh's work on Nietzsche, Miller (2012) and, among others, da Silva (2009).

50 See Bataille (2005). Cf. Müller-Lauter, who himself thanks Hubert Treiber in "Die Ökonomie in Natur und Gesellschaft. Nietzsche und Emanuel Hermann," in his book *Nietzsche-Interpretationen, Bd. 2, Über Freiheit und Chaos* (Müller-Lauter 1999: 173ff.). Müller-Lauter himself cites Klossowski (1969; in English as Klossowski 1987). And see for valuable discussions of Nietzsche and economics, again, the contributions to Backhaus and Drechsler (2003).

need to advert to past readings, political, sociological, and philosophical of Nietzsche's *economics*.[51]

Still by adverting to such an array of disparate readings (and calling for their amplification) there is the equivocation I began by noting. How ought one read between the disciplines and over time, as disciplines change, on the theme of Nietzsche and Marx? My friend, Thomas Brobjer, rightly observes, historically speaking, that quite in spite of the fact that Nietzsche would have had the opportunity to read neither Marx nor Engels, he would have been aware of their work and influence. Brobjer thus refuses Mazzino Montinari's hermeneutically informed (and rigorously Marxist) claim in his book, *Reading Nietzsche*, where Montinari sets Nietzsche between a Nazi or right-political reading and a typically leftist reading, i.e. between Alfred Baeumler and Georg Lukács (Montinari 1982). If Brobjer for his part does not advert to the complexity of this particular constellation (the first sections of the current chapter were dedicated to indicating some of this) he is concerned to engage the implication of Montinari's assessment (as Brobjer hardly denies the claim) that Nietzsche "never read a line of Marx or Engels, and did not even know the word 'Marxism' or 'historical Materialism' [...]!" (Brobjer 2002: 299).[52]

But here, after noting above Müller-Lauter's own attention to the complex of concerns that must face us when reading *between* Nietzsche and Marx in Nietzsche's own day and not less given the contraversions of Nietzsche's claims, not a dialectic but adumbrated through contradiction, paradoxical plays, textual shadows, and provocation, it is essential to foreground rigorous hermeneutic sensibility, and just this Brobjer overlooks, which we may read in Montinari:

> The socialism of which Marx speaks, existed at the time – *as theory* – solely in London, with Marx and Engels. Nietzsche himself knew at most – do consider the political limitations of academics of the day! – neither national socialism à la Lassalle nor indeed the democratic phrases concerning equality, roughly through the political agitations of Eisenacher. [...] As nuanced und complicated as the problematic of equality was for Engels und Marx, so simplified and reduced to propagandistic effect was agitation – to be sure on very understandable grounds – for the then practicing socialists in Germany and Europe. But it was only the latter that Nietzsche would have known, and not even that accurately!
>
> MONTINARI 1982: 201–203[53]

51 See here, again, and for a beginning, the contributions to Backhaus and Drechsler (2003).

52 See also Brobjer (1999).

53 See on Nietzsche and the notion of equality in the context of critical theory, Babich (2016c).

It is instructive to note, which is also why it matters to emphasize the *published* and the *unpublished* works of an author, as these works are part and parcel of critical *editions*. And editions have editors: indeed they only come to stand as they do in consequence of these often overlooked names. To this same degree, historically considered, it was this insight and its sensibility and sensitivity that made it possible for Montinari together with Giorgio Colli in the era of the DDR to bring out a critical edition of Nietzsche's Works: the KGW and the KSA, and not less the letters as well.

By hermeneutic contrast, Brobjer's approach to source scholarship, although dependent on such editions, is limited by its own intent to reporting on which books Nietzsche owned and what books he might have otherwise had access to (libraries and such). Brobjer's source critical point turns in the same spirit as that already noted in evidence in Müller-Lauter's reading and which one can also find in Karl Schlechta among others. Key to source scholarship is its obliquity. In the process, Brobjer relates the generalities of Nietzsche's familiarity with Friedrich Albert Lange (Jörg Salaquarda also tells us this as does, in an Anglophone context, George Stack [1983]), in addition to Eugen Dühring,[54] and August Bebel along with Nietzsche's reflections on the relation between socialism and the "woman question," where Brobjer's best note is, perhaps, the observation regarding Leopold Jacoby's *Die Idee der Entwicklung*, where we read that "Nietzsche had underlined the name Karl Marx in pencil in his copy of the book" (Brobjer 2002: 311).[55]

Montinari finds the conclusions to be drawn from reading in and through the traces that remain in Nietzsche's library "doubtful,"[56] but Brobjer focuses on just such readings, as he was not as concerned as Montinari was with hermeneutic philology as such. For Brobjer, who is in this sense the pioneer of today's word-frequency "scholarship" (although Brobjer himself far exceeds its current expressions), it will be the numbers that are the most significant. How many times does a particular word appear? Thus Brobjer,

54 Thus Montinari (1982: 201) distinguishes: "Von Marx kannte Nietzsche höchstens den Namen, wenn er wirklich den ganzen Wälzer von Eugen Dühring, Kritische Geschichte der Nationalökonomie und des Socialismus, gelesen haben sollte – was trotz des Vorhandenseins dieses Werkes in seiner Bibliothek sehr zweifelhaft ist."

55 I think we are persuaded here by analogy and the comfort of noting that Nietzsche proceeds as we ourselves do.

56 Cf. by contrast, "Nietzsches Bibliothek" in Montinari (1982: 201).

already undertaking digitally archaeological assays of the literature, tells us, for example that as of 2002 between 18 and 22 titles on Nietzsche and Marx were to be found in the secondary literature und that the name of Marx was, according to Brobjer's own investigation, a theme in no less than 13 of Nietzsche's own books. To be sure, we will never know with any certainty whether the fact that Marx played a given role in this or that book which Nietzsche possessed or to conclude that Nietzsche himself might taken account of this, or indeed whether he read the book or whether he held the reference to be meaningful or not. Here the issue is what we can conclude from the sheer fact of possession alone.

For example, consider the famous book collection, as an image of this has made the rounds on the internet, belonging to the late Karl Lagerfeld (relevant not only for its iconic value but also because Lagerfeld undertook to reissue all the books Nietzsche published in his lifetime, as Nietzsche himself published them) (Peck 2011) but just where it is impossible that Lagerfeld would himself have read all of them. The same reservation may be made with respect to the library of any academic.[57] Brobjer himself arguably would agree with just this hermeneutic differentiation all the while refusing Nietzsche's own claim to have read only "sparely." According to Brobjer – this is the substance of his research as a whole – Nietzsche had read extensively. But what Nietzsche means by his own claim, which hardly contradicts Brobjer, is that to read, really to read a text is a substantive, repetitive, undertaking. This is the meaning of hermeneutics as Gadamer and Vattimo speak of this: it is what Nietzsche named philology.

57 To be sure, this is second-hand knowledge at best – *and at its best.* This is how much scholarship works. We academics can thus take ourselves to know our colleagues' work without reading anything they have written and make judgments on them, voting on promotion and writing reviews. Like the German song parodist (not a little dependent on the great Tom Lehrer), Georg Kreisler's 1959 "Der Musikkritiker," found it most expedient "not to listen to" the music, a similar tactic seems to work for reviewers of collective volumes, who comment on a series of books, often exceeding thousands of pages, in a short essay, less for nefarious but human, all too human reasons: the reviewer, having projects and concerns of his or her own, quite as evidenced in the review, skims the book's opening lines, here and there, and in the case of book collections this cursory practice is more worrisome, discussing only a few chapters. If Nietzsche himself suffered from such academic silencing or eclipsing, he had no aversions to practicing it for his own part. See his complex discussion of David Strauss.

7 Readings and "Re-readings" of Nietzsche and Marx: Getting beyond Suspicion and Return

Reflecting in 1976 on "Marx, Nietzsche and Freud" in reflecting on philosophy and rhetoric (Ijsseling 1976), Samuel Ijsseling identifies the problem of connecting Nietzsche and Marx by pointing to the rhetorical. What is at stake here may be difficult to see after an interval of forty years, as Ijesseling begins with Karl Löwith's then-recent (1972) observation that Nietzsche would be more celebrated in France (the reference is to the famous Cerisy-la-Salle conference) than in Germany. Today and to be sure: Nietzsche and Marx (and Freud) are freely traded at every level, like academic baseball cards, from beginner to advanced.

If one of the most careful meditations of this question is Caygill's (1993) "The Return of Nietzsche and Marx," beginning with the obligatory conjunction and disjunction – *and* vs. *or*[58] as we also saw the importance of the same with reference to MacIntyre's *After Virtue* – in terms of both history and political party line(s), left and right, it is compounded by the ongoing division of intellectual labor in a Germany that has yet to see the fusion of these historically complicated and world-politically fraught horizons. Part of the reason for Caygill's perspicuity is his sympathy for the same French thinkers who see no reason to choose between these two thinkers and to this we may add Caygill's Kantian approach to the question.[59] Other readers tend to filter their readings of Nietzsche and Marx through Hegel and I have already mentioned the dominant analytic orientation of the Anglophone tradition.

Here I agree with Caygill who reads between

> 'crisis-as-condition' and 'crisis-as-decision' as the crisis of the Kantian autonomous, legislative subject of modernity. This is the subject which would give itself its own laws, the subject for whom the claims of traditional

58 "the energy that motivates the profound reflections upon the question of the relation between Nietzsche *and* Marx is the same that drives it into the impasse of the choice between Marx *or* Nietzsche" (Caygill 1993: 189).

59 By contrast, though this is surely used by his exclusive focus on Russian Marxism, George L. Kline reads between his reading of Nietzsche and Marx by delivering himself of one erroneous judgment after another: "Nietzsche, like Marx, is a decisively post-Hegelian thinker. Both thinkers place primary emphasis upon human history, although both – in clear opposition to Hegel – stress future, not past, history," before offering a clinching misreading of Nietzsche's second *Untimely Meditation*: "The 'disadvantage' which Nietzsche sees in a hypertrophied historical consciousness is that the 'dead' weight of the past stifles present cultural creativity" (Kline 1969: 166).

> values have been stripped of their legitimacy by the 'critical tribunal', who is free but nevertheless subjected, one who is dissatisfied and locked into oppressive and exploitative relations of its own making.
>
> CAYGILL 1993: 191

Tracy Strong, in the chapter, "Who is Dionysian? The Problem of the Immoralist" – and note here that the subtitle, despite the force of the title in this case is more important – contends that one may parallel the logic of Nietzsche's analysis of slavely moraline value culture – whereby the highest values necessarily devalue themselves, claiming that

> the position is no different from that of Karl Marx, who saw bourgeois civilization creating the conditions of its own destruction. Contrary to Marx, Nietzsche saw no logic inherent in the process of self-destruction which guaranteed the change from the period of the 'morality of mores' to the present stage and no logic that might ensure that the end of this stage correspond with the beginning of a new one. For Marx, the world of proletarian socialism was the death of the bourgeois world that had spawned it; for Nietzsche, there is no reason to assume that the end of Christian morality might be anything but frustration.
>
> STRONG 1999 [1975]: 109

Between Caygill and Strong, as between Müller-Lauter and Brobjer, Ijsseling and Löwith, it can seem that every effort to read between Nietzsche and Marx must come to grief on the problem of their intersection. There would seem to be no *there* there. Thus we have noted above that Marxist appraisals of Nietzsche cannot but be critical on several levels, here we may count in left readings of Nietzsche like Caygill and Strong and Axelos still more classically, even when articulated from the side of sympathy (Cacciari 1976: 56ff.; Gedö 1988; Harich 1987; Lambrecht 1988; Lukács 1954; 1948; Schmidt 1982).

Thus I began by noting the conviction on Nietzsche's part that labor of *any kind*, in the service of *anything*, be it the state or the church or one's "job," just to the extent that such labor is independent of one's own spirit, is effective enslavement. It is for this reason that Nietzsche tells us in *The Gay Science* that the Greeks retained a secret "suspicion" that many more were slaves in fact than tended to be assumed. The insight is of course of the essence of Stoicism, it shows Nietzsche's debt to antiquity and the same time it is the key to his articulation of and analysis of modern asceticism as Nietzsche traces this in his account of master and slave morality. Indeed, for both Nietzsche and for Marx, if you did not have your day, your time, your life, to yourself, if you were thus as a laborer, alienated from yourself, you were a slave. If Marx writes more powerfully about the contradictory character of this relation, whereby one creates oneself as a worker:

> Thus through estranged labor man not only creates his relationship to the object and to the act of production as to powers [*Menschen*] that are alien and hostile to him; he also creates the relationship in which other men stand to his production and to his product, and the relationship in which he stands to these other men.
>
> MARX 1975, *Economic and Philosophic Manuscripts 1844*, "Estranged Labor": 279

Nietzsche already emphasizes the effect of the mechanical agency undermining one's own spirit and mind

> As at all times, so now too, human beings are divided into the slaves and the free; for one who does not have two-thirds of his day to himself is a slave, whatever one may otherwise be: statesman, businessman, official, scholar.
>
> NIETZSCHE, *Human, All too Human*, §283

The "work" of the workers, which Nietzsche also in his first book identifies as the very metaphysical *comfort* of earthly consonance, induced by nothing other than the earthly deities of technoscience and its devices, i.e. as he says "the God of the machines and smelting forges," which he immediately explicates, in beautifully Goethian tones no less, "i.e., those spirits of nature recognized as being in the service of a higher egoism and applied forces, that believe in a correction of the world through knowledge, in a life led by science" (Nietzsche, *The Birth of Tragedy*, §17). If that faith in a life directed by or led in accord with the "spirit of science" has been with us, according to Nietzsche, since Plato and his promotion of the Socratic vision of a life improved by reason and reason alone, we are today as Nietzsche argues, quite in the position of really being able to live such a life: what Plato and Socrates dreamt in their philosophies, we meet in heaven very literally (we "fly") and earth (this would be Faust's first spirit). Thus we *live* the gifts of 19th century techno-science. But techno-science is a capitalist's dream, that is what Nietzsche foregrounds as the mechanism for killing the individual's heart or spirit and mind ("*Herz und Kopfkapital*" in the language of *Human, All Too Human*, and by time Nietzsche gets to *The Genealogy of Morals* he will simply speak of the deadening effects of any kind of "*mechanical activity*").[60]

60 Cf. Müller-Lauter 1999, 164ff. and Babich 2017b.

Folk today wonder if there might not be a right reading of Nietzsche to match left Nietzschean accounts, and that makes everyone nervous just to the extent that a right reading of Nietzsche is also dangerously close to national socialist or fascist readings and one assumes that that might be the Nietzsche of self-realization or capitalist self-promotion. After all: if Nietzsche criticizes altruism *and* pity as he seemingly does and if Nietzsche criticizes the notion of equality, as he surely does, together with his criticisms of the socialism of his day, what connection is there between Nietzsche and Marx?

And to be sure, when it comes to extant readings between Nietzsche and Marx – and there are far fewer of these than there might be (indeed a quick survey of the literature shows more scholars dedicated to reading Nietzsche and Foucault, or Deleuze, or Rousseau or even Montaigne) – we are either in Althusser's words, which is exactly not to say that Althusser was concerned with Nietzsche, *For Marx*, or *For Nietzsche*. We have our man when we approach such a reading between. Thus, we are hoist on the schema of "suspicion" as we recall that Ricoeur expresses this, repeating Nietzsche's own repetition of another's insinuation, as his writings were designated as such by others, just as he took over for himself the description offered in a review of one of his books, "I am dynamite."[61]

At stake here is a kind of playing with questioning, Nietzsche's positing of questions after oneself, for the sake of, as Nietzsche writes at the start of *The Gay Science* that no one yet has had the courage heretofore to manage to laugh at oneself as one would need to laugh out of, the entire truth. The question of distance is also one that frames not only Nietzsche's reference to his sardonic master of parody, the 2nd century C.E. Syrian, Lucian, but also the first lines of his "On Truth and Lie in an Extra Moral Sense." How can we come to see ourselves? Where will we have to stand?

Here we may recall the urging that speaks in the first lines of the General Rules of the first meeting of the Workingmen's Association in London in 1864 of the 1st International:

> That the emancipation of the working classes must be conquered by the working classes themselves, that the struggle for the emancipation of the working classes means not a struggle for class privileges and monopolies, but for equal rights and duties, and the abolition of all class rule…
>
> MARX 1984, "Provisional Rules of the Association": 14[62]

61 I discuss this in several loci. See too the discussion in Allison (2001).

62 [*dass die Emanzipation der Arbeiterklasse durch die Arbeiterklasse selbst erobert werden muss; dass der Kampf für die Emanzipation der Arbeiterklasse kein Kampf für*

This is articulated in Marx's own opening address when he emphasizes the workers themselves, closing with the key words: "Proletarians of all countries, unite!"

This is the imperative and socialism (and communism) come to stand or fail to do so in its wake. Thus Hal Draper in 1966 emphasizes that despite an understandable, perhaps human, all too human desire to have socialism handed to one, via going to the polls (we note the current political enthusiasm for voting) or by legislative decree, the sole way to any socialist result has to be the approach from below. As Draper explains,

> The heart of Socialism-from-Below is its view that socialism can be realized only through the self-emancipation of activized masses in motion, reaching out for freedom with their own hands, mobilized 'from below' in a struggle to take charge of their own destiny, as actors (not merely subjects) on the stage of history.
>
> DRAPER 1966: 58

•••

Nietzsche himself means critique as questioning, and questioning for Nietzsche requires method and dedication to what Nietzsche called science [*Wissenschaft*], which for him had to be put in question as such and in order to be science. Such Nietzschean critique entails that one risks the effort of suspicion, the questioning that puts the questioner himself or herself in question, questioning the subject, taking a glance, as Axelos argues, behind the mask, reflecting on what it is to be the mask, yet this often means that rather than Nietzsche we are reading (as a previous generation read) a certain Freud or else Foucault or Deleuze rather than Nietzsche himself.

The same argument structure can work, whether pro or con, for Nietzsche and Marx – where we assume that Marx being right, Nietzsche in order to be right, must think as Marx does and hence the challenge for us is to go into the bushes and find a Tübingen style synthesis, rightly or wrongly. Or if we for some reason fantasize that capitalism is a good thing (and I cannot imagine, after Greece, and after the current insanity in the U.K. with Brexit and the U.S., given Trump and his socialism for billionaire's tax reform, after Obama's mandatory health insurance for the sake of the insurance industry reform, that anyone

Klassenvorrechte und Monopole ist, sondern für gleiche Rechte und Pflichten und für die Vernichtung aller Klassenherrschaft.]

could wish to argue this), we can do the math to have Nietzsche come out in favour of capitalism and banking.

Above, I cited Jacob Taubes' account of the startling effect of Löwith's constellation as this brings Nietzsche less as what Habermas regarded as a turntable, a repeating recursion characteristic of the cult figure, than lynchpin. For this account, one needs the emphasis as Gillian Rose offers this in her own reading of Adorno that puts Nietzsche at the center. But such a center is unsettling – this is the author who tells us, does he not, that what is missing in our theory is nothing other than the facts: *gerade Thatsachen* – thus we scholars prefer the mainstream account.[63]

For his part, and this is where the reference to reason and to science betrays the Marxist, Lukàcs quite intended to bury Nietzsche as irrationalist, which means that Lukàcs subscribed to the same materialist idealization of science that characterizes most of us today, analytic philosophers and sociologists, political intellectual and television science personages and so on, but which fetishization did not characterize Nietzsche.

In another mode, I might have begun by reading between Feuerbach and Nietzsche to allow me to articulate standard and standardizing critiques of religion, as it is Feuerbach's critique that echoes in both Nietzsche and Marx.[64] But here if one may point to atheism, a word on the way to nihilism as Nietzsche highlights this enticement–legacy-entanglement of the enlightenment at the end of his *On the Genealogy of Morals*, the other side of the problem is the counterweight of *Diesseitigkeitsdenken* contra the *Jenseitsdenken* of another era, enthroned today in the prominence of today's humanism, foregrounded in transhumanist readings of Nietzsche. No one wants to die, everyone believes in the central importance of every Peter and Paul, to vary Nietzsche's reflections in the same locus.

To this end, the concern when it comes to Nietzsche and Marx ought to be a matter of economics and not less of autonomy: who do you serve? Your vanity? Corporate fantasy as this drives your every move on social media, Facebook,

63 This is Weber, the go-to socio-political name. Thus even if and other readers of Weber who read Nietzsche like Robert Eden, David Owen, Mark Warren, and, of course, Tracy Strong, it is important to add, immediately, that these are not the names of famous Marxists, and then we are spun back to the other side of the prevailing wind, via Adorno and Horkheimer, along with Lukàcs and Habermas, along with, as my reference to Axelos already indicates, Heidegger but also, and here it begins to get hard, Adorno, once again, and Günther Anders, as well as Peter Sloterdijk and to this I would add Dominque Janicaud along with Müller-Lauter and Gadamer.

64 See for a start, Bernoulli (1908). Extensive documentation following the first world war may be found in and through Krummel (2006) but see too Strong (2009).

Twitter, Google searches? Or are you otherwise a slave (to the church, to your profession, to your family, to your belly and its desires)? For Nietzsche, as he argued that this would also be the case for the Greeks, fair pay for fair work would still leave you as much a slave as someone forced to work for too little compensation or someone not paid at all.

We cannot read either Nietzsche or Marx as long as our concern is to be – as Nietzsche indicted his Christian – "well-paid." As long as our concern is, as it is, the concern of capital, with capital, for capital, we are caught in the same immanence noted by Deleuze. And to this extent we can be for neither Marx nor Nietzsche.

8 *Ressentiment* and Its Discontents: "Great Politics" vs. "Great Wealth"

We are well into the concluding third part of this essay, which final section includes three further moments. Note, to summarize, that Nietzsche saw through the power of *ressentiment* as this spoke in socialist movements of his day, movements of economic justice and the fight for equality, valuation, rights, remuneration. Marx saw the oppression along with the contradictions of the same. If many argue that they shared a common sensibility in their perception of the cultural role of religion – this is a good Weberian insight – others claim this as redemptive commonality, or even perhaps, because I would like to use his word and see its promise more fully realized, if Tracy Strong, say, could be lured to write more specifically than he has on the intersection between Nietzsche and Marx, foregrounding the term he uses, specifically: *transfiguration*, the difference between Nietzsche and Marx is arguably a matter of Nietzsche's positive antipathy to Hegel. Thus if one can say, as Nietzsche himself said, without Hegel, no Darwin, one can also argue, without Darwin, no dialectical materialism in Marx.

Marx needs Hegel. It is this need Nietzsche manages not to have for his own part, an independence frustrating generations of poststructuralist and deconstructionist and postmodern French scholars, along with, think of Schacht and Pippin, many analytic Nietzscheans. Thus Nietzsche skips Hegel without missing him and more significantly: without reinventing him. Yet we today have never needed Marx more, as Žižek insists and rightly so. Where Žižek is less useful, it is where he systematically overlooks (but he has so much company in so doing) why and just how very much we still need Nietzsche.

But the problem of course is that reading between two authors is always a non-dialectical exercise however much one may assume that one can come to a synthesis. And here, the very Hegelian *Aufhebung* needs if ever it did, not the

Suabian parsing of the meaning of *Aufhebung*, including the notion of reserving or "saving" or retaining some part for later use. This is of course the common slant and we read between two thinkers all the time, very often solving the problem by smuggling in a third (what about Bruno Bauer or Feuerbach, or Lange, and so on).

Nietzscheans, and I am one, tend to find Nietzsche in everything they do. Marx is faulted for missing what such readers favour, and Marxists for their own part and quite expectedly do the same, if the same is that much worse inasmuch as good Marxists (here they resemble mainstream analytic Nietzsche scholars) know who is right and who is wrong.

8.1 *"The European Human Being and the Destruction of Nations"*

In the context of a reading between Nietzsche and Marx, the question posed by Nietzsche's aphorism in *Human, All Too Human*, "The European Human Being and the Destruction of Nations" describes such an all-too-human theme that it has the force of a prophecy. Surely Nietzsche is anticipating Brexit, even if he would seem to be, and here I bring my last and final reflection, namely with regard to technology, *anticipating* the migrant crises all over Europe and in Israel/Palestine and with a savagely punitive policy of child incarceration, the U.S.

Nietzsche, for all his emphasis on homelessness, is not an advocate of the local, the fixed. Instead, and Nietzsche himself lived his life in this way, one oneself has to move in the world, away from the world. The abyss that looks back into you means that there is no way to stay in place and transcend what is around you.

From the moment that Marx made the machine and the technology of capitalist society responsible for alienation and announced the self-transformation of the capitalist system into a socialist system – it does not matter whether correctly or incorrectly – he also affirmed the dialectical overthrow precisely with respect to technology as such. As Günther Anders has it, where the ideological is already part and parcel of modern technology, we ourselves are effectively a "post-ideological era." Everything we need of ideology is already in the products we use, the technology we use.

As opposed to Taubes' reading of Löwith cited at the outset of this essay above, Anders emphasizes less the shift back before Goethe and Hegel, the key difference would be for Anders that material difference made by the first World War, as he observes that names like Marx and Nietzsche but also Kierkegaard and Feuerbach were routinely missing in university philosophy. Anders served already as a youth, barely more than a boy, in WWI and was marked by the violence which he encountered in a less elegiac mode than Jünger would celebrate as the glory of combat, the soldier, Marinetti-esque beauty, but bodily, and broken.

In this spirit of bodily default and defect, Anders wrote two complicated studies of what he called first the "second" (Anders 1956) and then the "third industrial revolution." (Anders 1980) Here it is essential to emphasize that counting to three is always instructive. For us, to read between Nietzsche and Marx we need to review the very specifically 19th century technology that concerned both Nietzsche and Marx.[65] This is the technology of the railroad, but not less the printing press – thus media – and also the telegraph/telephone.

Thus, the complexity of this 19th century tends to escape us not least because we are convinced that things are utterly "different now" – we today, thanks to the internet can get the news any time we like. Thus we tend not to be conscious of what print technology already made possible in the 19th century, where early morning, mid-morning, and late morning editions of the paper were routine affairs, as were 4-time and sometimes more frequent daily post and other deliveries (Kroker 2004).[66]

8.2 *Nietzsche and Socialism*

I have mentioned and will again return to the relevance of specifically 19th century technologies. But here, it may be worth turning to Nietzsche's *Human, All Too Human*, the same book from which the Marxist historian, Alfred Schmidt cites (as his own epigraph): on *The Possibility of Progress*. Here Nietzsche, self-referentially, reflects:

> When a scholar of the ancient culture forswears the company of men who believe in progress, he does quite right. For the greatness and goodness of ancient culture lie behind it, and historical education compels one to admit that they can never be fresh again; an unbearable stupidity or an equally insufferable fanaticism would be necessary to deny this.
>
> NIETZSCHE, *Menschliches, Allzumenschliches*, §24; cited in Schmidt 1981: xxx

65 See for a usefully comprehensive discussion of Nietzsche and technology, i.e. specifically the 19th century technology that concerned both Nietzsche and Marx, McGinn (1980). Similarly, McGinn also places a particular lens in front of his Nietzsche as well who turns out to be, unsurprisingly, an individualist who recommends a kind of Epicurean retreat. Nonetheless McGinn's reflections on Nietzsche's urging that Europe as a whole migrate in order to avoid the depredations of technicized existence, all the way up and all the way down, do not fall all-too-short. See too, albeit only with spare references to Marx, Strong (2002).

66 Though Kroker is quite good on the political economy of technology, via Marx, the reading is hampered by the insistence on "hyper-nihilism" which is not entirely fair to what is going on in Nietzsche: "Nietzsche is the anti-Christ of digital being" (Kroker 2004: 22). Probably not but see the contributions to Mellamphy and Melamphy (2016).

This aphorism appears in the first section, *Of First and Last Things*. But it is more common to look ahead to the section, *A Glance at the State*, as this is relevant to the current theme. Here scholars typically dive into Nietzsche's complicated reflection, penultimate in this penultimate section, *Great Politics and What They Cost* (Nietzsche, *Menschliches, Allzumenschliches* I, §481; KSA 2: 314–316). I have elsewhere written on the difficulty of the notion of "greatness" here but it continues to be read as just a grand affair, rather as Socrates tells us at the outset of the *Republic* and as if what were at stake were merely a matter of scale, majuscule, writ large (Babich 2017b).

To approach this it may be helpful to return to the beginning of the section as Nietzsche titles his first aphorism in *A Glance at the State*: "Permission to speak! [*Um das Wort bitten*]" (Nietzsche, *Menschliches, Allzumenschliches* I, §438; KSA 2: 285). The language is that of those who stand, not quite as Hölderlin's Scardanelli, the *Untherthan*, but precisely *zum Befehl*. This is the language of the "military school of life" as this made so much impact on Nietzsche that he invokes this military school to preface his first book when he reissues that same book, as we have already noted that Nietzsche made a habit of writing and rewriting his books, with his famously decisive, "*Versuch einer Selbstkritik*," in Sils Maria in late summer, 1886.

Nietzsche's "Attempt at a Self-Critique," sways between the modern, self-referred sense of self-appraisal, assessment, an examination of conscious intentions, and the Kantian critique of the First Critique that also concerned Nietzsche in *The Birth of Tragedy*, a book in which, so he tells us he is the first to propose not the Jewish problem, not the Catholic problem as he does elsewhere and we can add the German problem if we like (Nietzsche himself always added the woman problem) and not even the Greek problem but "science for the first time conceived as a problem, as questionworthy [*fragwürdig*]" (Nietzsche, *The Birth of Tragedy, Self-Critique*, §2). I mention this not merely because science is always on my mind, along with truth, and reason, and logic, but also because Nietzsche is not simply touching on essay after essay in nine intervals in *Human, All Too Human*. His is a scientific concern, which for the Nietzsche who worried about the *unscientific* danger corresponding to the triumph of method over science, would not, as such, entail a methodological reflection. And thus we can remember that the 1886 "Attempt" recalls the contextualization of his first book during the very battle for the soul of what would become the spirit of the good European, the era of "the Franco-Prussian war of 1870/71," written "as the thunder of the battle of Wörth was rolling over Europe" (Nietzsche, *The Birth of Tragedy, Self-Critique*, §2). In his introductory paragraph, Nietzsche manages to add a fair amount of personal detail, speaking of his health: "slowly convalescing from an illness contracted at the front"

(Nietzsche, *The Birth of Tragedy, Self-Critique*, §2), "as the peace treaty was being debated at Versailles," and, again of his location, "under the walls of Metz," as well as "the art form of pessimism" and whether this is "*necessarily* a sign of decline, decay, degeneration, weary and weak instincts?" especially considered "among us, 'modern' human beings and Europeans." I am citing all of this to situate a consideration of this first aphorism of the penultimate section of the first book of *Human, All Too Human* where Nietzsche observes in the very first line that "The demagogic character and the intention to appeal to the masses is at present common to all political parties…" (Nietzsche, *Human, All Too Human* I, §438; KSA 3: 285). Nietzsche's point is that this cannot but transform all political principles in the image of the masses. Considering the state of politics today, again: Nietzsche seems to be a card-reader, certainly *as if* he speaks directly to us, his readers, speaking to the concerns of our day, up to the minute, just to paint such "Alfresco-Dummheiten" on the proverbial wall.

Nietzsche proceeds to talk, in succession, of nobility (Nietzsche, *Human, All Too Human* I, §440), subordination as I have already mentioned this (Nietzsche, *Human, All Too Human* I, §441), and "Conscript armies" [*Volksheere*] (Nietzsche, *Human, All Too Human* I, §442; KSA 3: 288), he separates ideal talk and ideal predictions to draw parallels from the same historical science that was his own philological science: "But as the Greeks once waded in Greek blood, so Europeans now do in European blood"[67] anticipating the substance of his later reflections on the spirit- and heart-capital that is the ultimate tribute of what he goes on to describe as "Great politics" here writing that

> and it is always the most highly cultivated, those who guarantee a good and abundant posterity, who are sacrificed in relatively the largest numbers: for they stand in the van of the battle as the commanders and on account of their superior ambition expose themselves most to danger.
>
> NIETZSCHE, *Human, All Too Human* I, §442; KSA 3: 288

Nietzsche's point sediments into his analysis of the revaluation of values as the tactic of slave morality and its triumphs, not as conclusion but engine. As he writes, "Against war it can be said: it makes the victor stupid, the defeated malicious. [*Zu Ungunsten des Krieges kann man sagen: er macht den Sieger dumm, den Besiegten boshaft.*]" (Nietzsche, *Menschliches, Allzumenschliches* I, §444; KSA 3: 289). Because Nietzsche is taking the longer, historical view, he is able to point to an outcome at once disturbing and provocative if still promissory: "through producing these two effects it barbarizes and therefore makes more

67 [*Aber wie die Griechen in Griechenblut wütheten, so die Europäer jetzt in Europäerblut*].

natural; it is the winter or hibernation time of culture, mankind emerges from it stronger for good and evil" (Nietzsche, *Menschliches, Allzumenschliches* I, §444; KSA 3: 289).

The conjunction, "gut *und* böse" is what matters: thus humanity "first becomes" as he will write in *On the Genealogy of Morals*, "interesting." Here we read Nietzsche's critique of both princes *and* statesmen, socialism *and* revolution, and business interests always in the first line. On socialism, the subtlety of Nietzsche's critique routinely goes without remark as we seem, with no justification whatever, hellbent in remaking Nietzsche in the image of either fascism or capitalism, neither of which he would support or defend. The problem with socialism is that one has to assume to begin with that "it is *really* the rebellion of those who have been oppressed and held down for millennia against their oppressors…" (Nietzsche, *Menschliches, Allzumenschliches* I, §446; KSA 3: 290).

If Nietzsche repeats the standard Marxist point that socialism will acquire "rights" only if war appears to be imminent, his point calls for a different sensibility inasmuch as in each case what is at work is the "calculation," to use his term, of personal advantage. It is this calculus which effects the slave revolt in values and every other revolution the world has ever seen: thus socialism never emerges, as what emerges in its stead follows from power rather than justice, as the title of the aphorism indicates: *A question of power, not justice*:

> Socialism will acquire rights only if war appears to be imminent between the two powers, the representatives of the old and the new, but prudent calculation of possible advantage and preservation gives rise to the desire on the part of both parties for a compact. Without a compact no rights. Up to now, however, there has in the said domain been neither war nor compacts, and thus no rights, no 'ought,' either.
>
> NIETZSCHE, *Menschliches, Allzumenschliches* I, §446; KSA 3: 290

And no socialism either.

Hence when Nietzsche goes on in a later aphorism to reflect on *Property and Justice* (Nietzsche, *Menschliches, Allzumenschliches* I, §452; KSA 3: 293–294) he will argue that what is needed is what will *not* be forthcoming. Not only is will to power to be found at every level, among the weakest who hope to inherit nothing less than the earth (or at least an eternity of bliss), but also among the strongest, among masters as much as among slaves. Thus, and sheerly historically, this is not the non-history of *On the Genealogy of Morals*, which was after all, a matter of philology, i.e. what things are called, Nietzsche here reminds us, as he will also observe of the will to power of the weakest in his *Zarathustra*, that the "disposition to injustice inhabits the souls of the nonpossessors too, they are no better than the possessors and have no moral prerogative over them, for their own ancestors were at some time or other possessors" (Nietzsche, *Menschliches, Allzumenschliches* I, §452; KSA 3: 294). To this end, Nietzsche calls for something still unrepresentable to this day (Žižek calls it the "impossible," it is a Lacanian thing): "the sense of justice must grow greater in everyone, the instinct for violence weaker" (Nietzsche, *Menschliches, Allzumenschliches* I, §452; KSA 3: 294). The problem is that even justice, perhaps especially *justice*, is a weasel word, equivocation once again: meaning one thing to one person and one thing to another, thus the call for what Nietzsche later calls "the extremest terrorism [*den äussersten Terrorismus*]" (Nietzsche, *Menschliches, Allzumenschliches* I, §473; KSA 3: 307) on behalf of the ideal of the social, contravening the point between abating the instinct to violence and enhancing that of the sense of "justice."

Suffice it to say that Nietzsche reflects a genealogy of sentiments contra political theoretical phantasms, here invoking "Rousseau's superstition, which believes in a miraculous primeval but, as it were, buried goodness of human nature and ascribes all the blame for this burying to the institutions of culture in the form of society, state and education" (Nietzsche, *Menschliches, Allzumenschliches* I, §463; KSA 3: 299; cf. the conclusion of §452).

If the problem is the pursuit of bliss as the all-too-American calculation of advantage or pursuit of happiness, Nietzsche reminds us that "an age of happiness [*Ein glückliches Zeitalter*] is quite impossible, because human beings want only to desire it, but not to have it" (Nietzsche, *Menschliches, Allzumenschliches* I, §471; KSA 2: 361). Accordingly, he can go on to explain, the "destiny of the human is designed for happy moments – every life has them –, but not for happy ages" (Nietzsche, *Menschliches, Allzumenschliches* I, §471; KSA 2: 361).

A reflection on religion and government (Nietzsche, *Menschliches, Allzumenschliches* I, §472; KSA 2: 302ff.) would require more than one study of its own and Nietzsche dedicates two books, *Beyond Good and Evil* and an entire, if polemical, sequel to this juncture: *On the Genealogy of Morals*. Here it will have to be enough simply to point to it.

8.3 *Nomadic Life*

These reflections permit us to look at the European human being as well as the abolition of nations as Nietzsche lists the human condition of the state of modern Europe:

> rapid changing of home and scene, the nomadic life now lived by all who do not own land – these circumstances are necessarily bringing with them a weakening and finally an abolition of nations, at least the

> European: so that as a consequence of continual crossing a mixed race, that of European man, must come into being out of them.
>
> NIETZSCHE, *Human, All Too Human* I, §475; KSA 2: 309

Let us look at how the aphorism begins as it refers to the very 19th century technologies mentioned above and indeed in the full complexity of that same technological constellation, the vehicle or medium of intellectual culture: "Trade and industry, the post and the book-trade, the possession in common of all higher culture," to which he adds travel – we can think of rail and other forms of transport, enabling the "rapid changing of home and scene," followed by its direct or most immediate concomitants: migrant work forces, who move and live for the sake of, and in search of, remunerative employment, once again as relevant: "the nomadic life now lived by all who do not own land [*Nomadenleben aller Nicht-Landbesitzer*]" (Nietzsche, *Human, All Too Human* I, §475; KSA 2: 309).

For Nietzsche, all of this would be and should be seen as so many preconditions of the EU *avant la lettre*,

> – these circumstances are necessarily bringing with them a weakening and finally a destruction of nations, at least the European: so that as a consequence of continual crossing a mixed race [*eine Mischrasse*], that of European human, must come into being out of them.
>
> NIETZSCHE, *Human, All Too Human* I, §475; KSA 2: 309

The "good European" is a consequence of both economic politics and politics of technology as quite explicit forces of miscegenation. Thus Nietzsche can argue, contra what one might otherwise say, that is: *auf gut deutsch* and with respect to everything that belongs to the traditional ideal of the Good German: "one should not be afraid to proclaim oneself unashamedly as good Europeans and actively to work for the amalgamation of nations" (Nietzsche, *Human, All Too Human* I, §475; KSA 2: 309).

This discussion as already noted is articulated in immediate proximity to "the entire problem of the *Jews*" and in turn with the theme closest to Nietzsche himself, such that "the ring of culture that now unites us with the enlightenment of Graeco-Roman antiquity remains unbroken," a connection permits Nietzsche to argue that it is ultimately the dynamic working of Judaism between Orientalizing and Occidentalizing forces that "in a certain sense means making of Europe's mission and history a *continuation of the Greek* [*Fortsetzung der griechischen*]" (Nietzsche, *Human, All Too Human* I, §475; KSA 2: 311).

If Nietzsche were here simply making a plea for a connection between Athens and Jerusalem, calling for a new Germany as a kind of New Greece that would be a fairly familiar trope, running from Winckelmann to Eliza Butler's *Tyranny of Greece over Germany* (as Roger Scruton [2017] characterizes the lineage as somehow disposing of Nietzsche) but the question of the relation must be rethought altogether (given the complexities Nietzsche brings to a philological discussion of Greece).[68] In this case, the complex truth of war with which Nietzsche begins this section – once again, we recall: *permission to speak!* – is also how Nietzsche draws the section to an end and it is from this juncture that we may return to the aphorism, *Great Politics and What They Cost.*

I suggested that it is common enough to suppose Nietzsche an advocate of what he named "great politics." Yet his invocation of the term is complicated. Thus we read his closing aphorism beyond the economic costs of war and the individual injury to body and spirit of those conscripted armies earlier mentioned, emphasizing the terrible tribute sacrificed to "this coarse and gaudy flower" which is to say, the obsession with the "nation" and not less with its generic concerns quite as opposed to the individual as such. Henceforth, what preoccupies each individual will no longer be the life interests and passions of that given individual (irrespective of talent and genius, disposition and love) but a new set of personal concerns, namely "questions and cares of the public weal" [*Fragen und Sorgen des öffentlichen Wohles*]. (Nietzsche, *Human, All Too Human* I, §475; KSA 2: 315).

This, so argues Nietzsche, "almost with necessity" engenders "a spiritual impoverishment and enfeeblement and a diminution of the capacity for undertakings demanding great concentration and application" (Nietzsche, *Human, All Too Human* I, §475; KSA 2: 315). Instead of thinking and talking about philosophy or the meaning of life, life and death, love and death, the spirit of philological science, the spirit of music, of stars and ancient ritual cults, or plants and food and what have you, individual interests vary, we increasingly talk politics as if it were our own ownmost concern. The point is hard to make: we are sure that the political *is* our ownmost concern by which concern we mean not that we are affected by it as we surely are but that we are to express an opinion on it and debate this opinion on Facebook and Twitter.

To understand what Nietzsche is getting at one might include Nietzsche's generic denigration of journalism, our conviction that the affairs of others are our own affairs, this is the basis of social media and social networking but it is also the ground in which *ressentiment* grows. Thus Nietzsche asks whether sacrificing the many and varied concerns of the individual as such is *worth* it in

68 See on Winckelmann and Nietzsche, Babich (2017c).

the end, and he asks this contrary-to-fact question, whereby the major concern of each and every individual in a nation henceforth corresponds to nothing but the concerns of that nation and its ambition to be top nation – think here of the world cup – as he writes parenthetically: "(which is, after all, apparent only in the fear of other states for the new colossus and in the more favourable terms for trade and travel extorted from them)" (Nietzsche, *Human, All Too Human* I, §481; KSA 2: 315). Here, if anywhere, we might find Nietzsche's version of the Brexit question.

9 Conclusion: The Price of "Great Politics" and "Great Wealth"

We have read through the section *A Glance at the State*, and the significance of Nietzsche's reflection on "Great Politics and What They Cost." In the later written section, *The Wanderer and His Shadow*, first written in 1880, and added along with a collection of aphorisms as Volume II to the edition of *Human, All Too Human* published in 1886, it is plain that we are for Nietzsche hardly beyond Plato, who for his part retains a sense of justice and concern for the predations of violence, as we recall that Plato says at the start of the *Republic* that to the extent that one desires and organizes society for the sake of the proliferation of various and sundry pleasures, those of the rich, and presupposing the abundances of advantaged culture, one will, as Plato has his Socrates say, be compelled to go to war for the sake of obtaining and securing such luxuries or conveniences. Simultaneously, or from the other side of the many for whom such pleasures will never be really at hand, is born the pressure, and we may be facing just these pressures at the moment, that grows from the need for a bloody revolution. Plato argues that states that live in such economic tension also live as divided nations, with armies effectively garrisoned within the state: *the dispossessed*. Thus Nietzsche will speak of those with no property as being as dangerous to the state and civic society as those with too much.

When it comes to war, whether to obtain an advantage from one's neighbor or when it comes to revolution, the problem, as Nietzsche also pointed out, is the tremendous amount of bloodshed for an end as often confused as perverted. This is one of the reasons Nietzsche, when he reflects on the French Revolution, chooses not for Rousseau and his rhetoric much less the consequences of that rhetoric for the terror, but and much rather for Goethe.

If both Engels and Marx refer to Goethe and thus the connection with technology, so too does Günther Anders. But it is the way that Anders makes this transition that brings in at least an allusion to Nietzsche where Anders muses that, like Taubes one might say, he originally meant to take up the theme of "religion" but found himself compelled to change his title to "The Transmuted Sorceror's Apprentice" [*Der verwandelte Zauberlehrling*].

What compelled Anders' attention was the shift of the locus of production from the outside world of the factory, the farm, what have you, to what Anders analysed as the world transfigured, the world on the screen, television, today we ought to add, our cellphones and the like: as phantom and matrix. The Nietzschean resonance is to the beginning of *Beyond Good and Evil*, where Anders speaks of what technology brings home, Nietzsche speaks of our treasure: where our heart finds us. For Anders, what is instructive is the flight away from the world effected in the same instance as the world is brought to us, delivered as phantom, on our screens. The example Anders takes for this is religion and without tucking a tiny essay on "Nietzsche, Marx, Religion" into my conclusion, it is essential to reflect on the cargo-cult but also mystical element that has always been part of technology. Thus Anders reflects on the delivery of the mass to the masses, on TV. To this day, delivered into "the comfort of your living room" one can tune into a religious service, a megachurch, a born-again preacher preaching not merely the New Testament but (never forget the cargo cult) tricks for becoming the elect of this world, with all the blessings of worldly riches.

In the *Wanderer and his Shadow*, Nietzsche asks *Can property be reconciled with justice?*, invoking the socialist ideal of "Equal Allotment of Land," where he immediately points to the troubles that follow, not merely a matter of resentment and chaos – "One digs up morality when one digs up boundary stones." – not merely the noisome affair of theft and appropriation (and reappropriation: where does one stop?) but also the community and generation of tradition. But what is instructive is that Nietzsche does not end there. And if technology has changed in the 20th and 21st century, the reason Deleuze could say that he would have to remain a Marxist is because capital changes with the same transitions and transformations.

For Nietzsche and I think he gets here at the real problem of capitalism today and that is already evident in the digital realm, information age, big data, bubbles and crashes, arguing that if there is to be such a thing as "a more moral" kind of property, that will have to be a smaller kind than the juggernaut of possession and indeed specifically capital speculation, already well at work in Nietzsche's day. Thus he argued:

> We must keep open all the paths to the accumulation of *moderate* wealth through work, but prevent the sudden or unearned acquisition of riches; we must remove from the hands of private individuals and companies all those branches of trade and transportation favorable to accumulation of

> *great* wealth, thus especially the trade in money – and regard those who possess too much as being as great a danger to society as those who possess nothing [*die Zuviel- wie die Nichts-Besitzer*].
>
> NIETZSCHE, *The Wanderer and his Shadow*, §285; KSA 2: 681

The "trade in money" is the stock market. There is no better indictment of what we call 1%, or whatever smaller percentage there is to name. And the one who poses this indictment is the same author who tells us, and the Trump–Clinton battle in the U.S. was the most recent instauration of this as it was really the tale of the dispossession of Bernie Sanders' bid for the presidency: "All political powers nowadays try to exploit the fear of socialism in order to strengthen themselves" (Nietzsche, *The Wanderer and his Shadow*, §292; KSA 2: 684). For Nietzsche, even the success of such a bid – socialism installed – contains the seeds of its own destruction, and as soon as a certain redistribution of wealth is effected one as swiftly "*forgets* socialism like an illness one has recovered from."

This seems to echo a certain course of a certain history – but that history proceeds and today we still need to think *between* Nietzsche and Marx.

References

Adorno, Theodor W. 2006. *Current of Music: Elements of a Radio Theory*. Frankfurt: Suhrkamp.

Allison, David B. 2001. *Reading the New Nietzsche: The Birth of Tragedy, The Gay Science, Thus Spoke Zarathustra, and On the Genealogy of Morals*. Lanham, MD: Rowman & Littlefield Publishers.

Anders, Günther. 1980. *Die Antiquiertheit des Menschen. Zweiter Band. Über die Zerstörung des Lebens im Zeitalter der dritten industriellen Revolution*. Munich: C.H. Beck.

Anders, Günther. 1956. *Die Antiquiertheit des Menschen. Über die Seele im Zeitalter der zweiten industriellen Revolution*. Munich: C.H. Beck.

Aschheim, Steven E. 1994. *The Nietzsche Legacy in Germany: 1890–1990*. Berkeley: University of California Press.

Axelos, Kostas. 2017. *Introduction to a Future Way of Thought: On Marx and Heidegger*, edited by Stuart Elden. London: Meson Press.

Axelos, Kostas. 1966 [1961]. *Einführung in ein künftiges Denken: Über Marx und Heidegger*. Berlin: de Gruyter.

Babich, Babette E., ed. 2019. "Epicurean Gardens and Nietzsche's White Seas." In *Epicurus and Nietzsche*, edited by Vinod Acharya and Ryan Johnson. London: Bloomsbury.

Babich, Babette E., ed. 2018. "Philosophy Bakes No Bread." *Philosophy of the Social Sciences* 48(1): 47–55.

Babich, Babette E., ed. 2017a. "Are They Good? Are They Bad? Double Hermeneutics and Citation in Philosophy, Asphodel and Alan Rickman, Bruno Latour and the 'Science Wars.'" In *Das Interpretative Universum*, edited by Paula Angelova et al., 259–290. Würzburg: Königshausen & Neumann.

Babich, Babette E., ed. 2017b. "Auf dem Weg zur Großen Politik. 'Der europäische Mensch und die Vernichtung der Nationen." *Phainomena. One hundred per cent* xxvi, 102–103 (November 2017): 31–50.

Babich, Babette E., ed. 2017c. "From Winkelmann's Apollo to Nietzsche's Dionysus." In *Winkelmanns Antike*, edited by Renate Reschke, 167–192. Berlin: de Gruyter.

Babich, Babette E., ed. 2017d. "Querying Nietzsche's Influence and Meaning Today." In *Фридрих Ницше: наследие и проект.* М.: Культурная революция, / *Friedrich Nietzsche: Heritage and Prospects*, edited by Ekaterina Polyakova and Yulia Sineokaya, 391–406. Moscow: LRC Publishing House.

Babich, Babette E., ed. 2017e. "Tools for Subversion: Illich and Žižek on Changing the World." In *Making Communism Hermeneutical: Reading Vattimo and Zabala*, edited by Sylvie Mazzinie and Owen Glyn-Williams, 95–111. Frankfurt am Main: Metzler.

Babich, Babette E., ed. 2016a. "Heidegger's Black Night: The *Nachlass* and Its *Wirkungsgeschichte*." In *Reading Heidegger's Black Notebooks: 1931–1941*, edited by Ingo Farin and Jeff Malpas, 59–86. Cambridge: MIT Press.

Babich, Babette E., ed. 2016b. *The Hallelujah Effect: Music, Technology, and Performance Practice.* London: Routledge.

Babich, Babette E., ed. 2016c. "Towards Nietzsche's 'Critical' Theory – Science, Art, Life and Creative Economics." In *Nietzsche als Kritiker und Denker der Transformation*, edited by Helmut Heit and Sigga Thorgeirsdottir, 112–133. Berlin: de Gruyter.

Babich, Babette E., ed. 2016d. "Nietzsche's Archilochus." *New Nietzsche Studies* 10(1/2): 133–170.

Babich, Babette E., ed. 2015a. "Friedrich Nietzsche." In *Blackwell Companion to Hermeneutics*, edited by Niall Keane, 366–377. Oxford: Wiley-Blackwell.

Babich, Babette E., ed. 2015b. "Friedrich Nietzsche and the Posthuman/Transhuman in Film and Television." In *The Palgrave Handbook of Posthumanism in Film and Television*, edited by Michael Hauskeller et al., 45–53. London: Palgrave/Macmillan.

Babich, Babette E., ed. 2015c. "Hermeneutic Philosophy of Science." In *Blackwell Companion to Hermeneutics*, edited by Niall Keane, 492–505. Oxford: Wiley-Blackwell.

Babich, Babette E., ed. 2015d. "*Nietzsches Wissenschaftstheorie*." *New Nietzsche Studies* 9(3–4): 193–226.

Babich, Babette E., ed. 2014. "Adorno's Radio Phenomenology: Technical Reproduction, Physiognomy and Music." *Philosophy and Social Criticism* 40(10) (Oct.): 957–996.

Babich, Babette E., ed. 2013. "O, Superman! or Being Towards Transhumanism: Martin Heidegger, Günther Anders, and Media Aesthetics." *Divinatio* 36 (autumn–winter): 83–99.

Babich, Babette E., ed. 2012. "Politics and Heidegger: Aristotle, Superman, and Žižek." *Telos* 161: 141–161.

Babich, Babette E., ed. 2010. *Nietzsches Wissenschaftsphilosophie: Die Wissenschaft unter der Optik des Künstlers zu sehn, die Kunst aber unter der des Lebens.* Oxford: Peter Lang.

Babich, Babette E., ed. 2009. "Nietzsche's Will to Power: Politics and Destiny." In *Friedrich Nietzsche*, edited by Tracy B. Strong, 282–296. London: Ashgate.

Babich, Babette E., ed. 2006. "Gay Science: Science and *Wissenschaft, Leidenschaft* and Music." In *Companion to Nietzsche*, edited by Keith Ansell-Pearson, 97–114. Oxford: Blackwell.

Babich, Babette E., ed. 1999b. "Nietzsche's Critical Theory: The Culture of Science as Art." In *Nietzsche, Theories of Knowledge, Critical Theory*, edited by Babette Babich, 1–24. Dordrecht: Springer Netherlands.

Babich, Babette E., ed. 1994. *Nietzsche's Philosophy of Science: Reflecting Science on the Ground of Art and Life.* Albany: State University of New York Press.

Babich, Babette E., ed. 2004. *Nietzsche, Habermas, and Critical Theory*. Amherst, New York: Prometheus/Humanity Books.

Babich, Babette E., ed. 1999a. *Nietzsche, Theories of Knowledge and Critical Theory: Nietzsche and the Sciences* I. Dordrecht: Springer Netherlands.

Backhaus, Jürgen, and Wolfgang Drechsler, eds. 2003. *Friedrich Nietzsche: Economy and Society.* Dordrecht: Kluwer.

Bataille, Georges. 2005. *Nietzsche und der Wille zur Chance. Atheologische Summe* III. Berlin: Mathes & Seitz.

Baumgarten, Eduard. 1964. *Max Weber: Werk und Person.* Tübingen: Mohr.

Beaulieu, Alain. 2009. "Gilles Deleuze's Politics." In *Gilles Deleuze: The Intensive Reduction*, edited by Constantin V. Boundas, 204–217. Cambridge: A&C Black.

Beiner, Ronald. 2018. *Dangerous Minds: Nietzsche, Heidegger, and the Return of the Far Right.* Philadelphia: University of Pennsylvania Press.

Bennett, H. Stith. 2017 [1980]. *On Becoming a Rock Musician.* New York: Columbia University Press.

Berman, Marshall. 1988 [1982]. *All That is Solid Melts into Air.* Toronto: Penguin.

Bernays, Edward L. 1923. *Crystallizing Public Opinion.* New York: Boni and Liveright.

Bernoulli, Carl Albrecht. 1908. *Franz Overbeck und Friedrich Nietzsche.* Jena: Eugen Diederichs.

Berry, David. 2014. *Critical Theory and the Digital.* London: Bloomsbury.

Binder, David. 1987. "See East Berlin Journal; Strange Bedfellows: Marxists Embrace Nietzsche." *New York Times*, Nov. 28.

Birnbaum, Norman. 1953. "Conflicting Interpretations of the Rise of Capitalism: Marx and Weber." *The British Journal of Sociology* 4(2): 125–141.

Brobjer, Thomas H. 2002. "Nietzsche's Knowledge of Marx." *Nietzsche-Studien* 31(1): 298–313.

Brobjer, Thomas H. 1999. "Nietzsche's Knowledge, Reading, and Critique of Political Economy." *Journal of Nietzsche Studies* 18 (Fall): 56–70.

Bull, Malcolm. 2016. "Great Again." *London Review of Books* 38(20): 8–10.

Busch, Ulrich. 2000. "Friedrich Nietzsche und die DDR." *UTOPIE kreativ* 118: 762–777.

Cacciari, Massimo. 1976. *Krisis.* Milano.

Caygill, Howard. 1993. "The Return of Nietzsche and Marx." In *Nietzsche, Feminism and Political Theory*, edited by Paul Patton, 189–203. London: Routledge.

da Silva, Ada Albuquerque. 2009. "Redemptive Narratives in Marx and Nietzsche." *intersections* 10(2): 151–159.

Deleuze, Gilles. 1995. *Negotiations*, translated by Martin Joughin. New York: Columbia University Press.

Di Marco, Giuseppe Antonio. 1984. *Marx, Nietzsche, Weber. Gli Ideali Ascetici tra Critica, Genealogia, Comprensione.* Naples: Guida.

Draper, Hal. 1966. "The Two Souls of Socialism." *New Politics* 5(1) (Winter): 57–84.

Dyer-Witheford, Nick. 2015. *Cyber-Proletariat: Global Labour in the Digital Vortex*. London: Pluto Press.

Eden, Robert. 1984. *Political Leadership and Nihilism: A Study of Weber and Nietzsche.* Tampa, FL: University Press of Florida.

Ellul, Jacques. 1973. *Propaganda: The Formation of Men's Attitudes*, translated by Konrad Kellen. New York: Vintage.

Emerson, Ralph Waldo. 1970. *The Journals and Notebooks, Vol* VIII*: 1841–1843*, edited by William H. Gilman and I.E. Parsons. Cambridge: Harvard University Press.

Ferry, Luc, and Alain Renaut, eds. 1997. *Why We Are Not Nietzscheans*, translated by Robert de Loaiza. Chicago: University of Chicago Press.

Foucault, Michel. 1990. "Nietzsche, Freud, Marx." In *Transforming the Hermeneutic Context*, edited by Gayle L. Ormiston and Alan D. Schrift, 59–67. Albany, NY: State University of New York Press.

Fuller, Steve. 2018. *Post-Truth: Knowledge as a Power Game.* London: Anthem Press.

Gedö, András. 1988. "Marx oder Nietzsche? Die Gegenwärtigkeit einer beharrenden Alternative." *Deutsche Zeitschrift für Philosophie* 9: 787ff.

Germaine, Gil. 1993. *Discourse on Disenchantment: Reflections on Politics and Technology.* Albany: State University of New York Press.

Giddens, Anthony. 1970. "Marx, Weber, and the Development of Capitalism." *Sociology* 4(3): 289–310.

Golomb, Jacob, and Robert S. Wistrich. 2009. *Nietzsche, Godfather of Fascism?: On the Uses and Abuses of a Philosophy.* Princeton: Princeton University Press.

Grimm, Reinhold. 1983. "Dionysos und Sokrates: Nietzsche und der Entwurf eines neuen politischen Theaters." In *Karl Marx und Friedrich Nietzsche*, edited by Reinhold Grimm and Jost Hermand, 152–171. Bodenheim: Athenaeum.

Habermas, Jürgen. 1999. "On Nietzsche's Theory of Knowledge: A Postscript from 1968." In *Nietzsche, Theories of Knowledge, and Critical Theory: Nietzsche and the Sciences: 1*, edited by Babette Babich, translated by James Swindal, 209–223. Dordrecht: Kluwer.

Habermas, Jürgen. 1985. "Eintritt in die Postmoderne: Nietzsche als Drehscheibe." In *Philosophischen Diskurs der Moderne*, 104–129. Frankfurt am Main: Suhrkamp.

Habermas, Jürgen. 1968. "Nachwort." In *Erkenntnistheoretische Schriften*, Friedrich Nietzsche, 237–261. Frankfurt am Main: Suhrkamp.

Harich, Wolfgang. 1987. "Revision des marxistischen Nietzsche-Bildes?" *Sinn und Form* 39(5): 1018–1053.

Hennis, Wilhelm. 1987. "Die Spuren Nietzsches im Werk Max Webers." *Nietzsche-Studien* 16: 382–404.

Hermand, Jost. 1978. "Paroxysmen eines Neinsagers?: Zum Nietzsche-Bild von Hans Heinz Holz." In *Karl Marx und Friedrich Nietzsche: 8 Beiträge, 136–151.* Königstein: Athenäum-Verlag.

Hicks, Stephen R.C. 2009. "Egoism in Nietzsche and Rand." *The Journal of Ayn Rand Studies* 10(2): 249–291.

Holub, Robert C. 2015. *Nietzsche's Jewish Problem: Between Anti-Semitism and Anti-Judaism.* Princeton: Princeton University Press.

Horkheimer, Max, and Theodor W. Adorno. 1972. *Dialectic of Enlightenment*, translated by John Cumming. New York: Herder and Herder.

Hunt, Lester. 2016. "Ayn Rand's Evolving View of Friedrich Nietzsche." In *A Companion to Ayn Rand*, edited by Allan Gotthelf and Gregory Salmieri, 343–350. Hoboken, NJ: Wiley.

Ijsseling, Samuel. 1976. "Marx, Nietzsche and Freud." In *Rhetoric and Philosophy in Conflict*, 92–102. The Hague: Nijhoff.

Kaufmann, Walter. 1974. "Translator's Introduction." In *The Gay Science*, Friedrich Nietzsche. New York: Random House.

Kim, Duk-Yung. 1995. "Nietzsche und die Soziologie: Georg Simmel und Max Weber." *Jahrbuch für Soziologiegeschichte*: 87–121.

Kittler, Friedrich A. 1999. *Gramophone, Film, Typewriter*, translated by Geoffrey Winthrop-Young and Michael Wutz. Stanford: Stanford University Press.

Kline, George L. 1969. "'Nietzschean Marxism' in Russia." In *Demythologizing Marxism*, edited by Freddie Adelmann, 166–183. The Hague: Nijhoff.

Klossowski, Pierre. 1987. *Nietzsche and the Vicious Circle*, translated by Daniel Smith. Chicago: University of Chicago Press.

Klossowski, Pierre. 1969. *Nietzsche et la Circle Vicieux.* Paris: Mercure de France.

Koloğlugil, Serhat. 2015. "Digitizing Karl Marx: The New Political Economy of General Intellect and Immaterial Labor." *Rethinking Marxism: A Journal of Economics, Culture & Society* 27: 123–137.

Kroker, Arthur. 2004. *The Will to Technology and the Culture of Nihilism: Heidegger, Nietzsche and Marx.* Toronto: University of Toronto Press.

Krtolica, Igor. 2012. "Deleuze, entre Nietzsche et Marx: l'histoire universelle, le fait moderne et le devenir-révolutionnaire." *Actuel Marx* n° 52(2) (*Deleuze/Guattari*): 62–77.

Krummel, Richard Frank. 2006. *Ausbreitung und Wirkung des Nietzscheschen Werkes im deutschen Sprachraum bis zum Ende des Zweiten Weltkrieges.* Berlin: de Gruyter.

Lambrecht, Lars. 1988. "Nietzsche und die deutsche Arbeiterbewegung." In *Bruder Nietzsche?*, 91–118. Düsseldorf: Schriften der Marx-Engels-Stiftung.

Landa, Ishay. 2007. *The Overman in the Marketplace: Nietzschean Heroism in Popular Culture.* Lanham, MD: Lexington Books.

Lasn, Kalle. 2012. *Meme Wars: The Creative Destruction of Neoclassical Economics.* New York: Seven Stories Press.

Lasn, Kalle. 2000. *Culture Jam.* New York: Quill.

Leck, Ralph M. 2000. *Georg Simmel and Avant-Garde Sociology: The Birth of Modernity, 1880–1920.* Amherst, NY: Humanity Books.

Lefebvre, Henri. 1996 [1975]. *Hegel, Marx, Nietzsche ou le royaume des ombres.* Paris: Casterman.

Lonergan, Bernard. 1958 [1957]. *Insight: A Study of Human Understanding.* New York: Philosophical Library.

Löschenkohl, Birte. 2008. "Die ewige Widerkunft des G-W-G'. Marx' Spuren in Nietzsches Werk." In *Nietzsche – Philosoph der Kultur(en)*, edited by Andreas Urs Sommer, 161–172. Berlin: De Gruyter.

Losurdo, Domenico. 2014. "The Black Notebooks Aren't All That Surprising." *The Guardian*, March 19.

Love, Nancy. 1986. *Nietzsche, Marx, and Modernity.* New York: Columbia University Press.

Löw, Reinhard. 1984. "Die Aktualität von Nietzsches Wissenschaftskritik." *Merkur* 38: 399–409.

Löwith, Karl. 1982. *Max Weber and Karl Marx*, translated by H. Fantel. London: Harper Collins.

Löwith, Karl. 1967. *From Hegel to Nietzsche: The Revolution in Nineteenth Century Thought*, translated by David E. Green. New York: Doubleday.

Lukács, György. 1982 [1933]. *Wie ist die faschistische Philosophie in Deutschland entstanden? Wie ist die faschistische Philosophie in Deutschland entstanden?* (*Veröffentlichungen des Lukács-Archivs aus dem Nachlass von Georg Lukács*), edited by Lazslo Szilaki. Budapest: Akadémiai Kiadó.

Lukács, György. 1954. *Die Zerstörung der Vernunft.* Berlin: Altbau Verlag.

Lukács, György. 1953. *Die Zerstörung der Vernunft: Der Weg des Irrationalismus von Schelling zu Hitler*. Berlin: Aufbau Verlag.

Lukács, György. 1948. *Der deutsche Faschismus und Nietzsche, Schicksalswende.* Berlin: Altbau Verlag.

MacIntyre, Alasdair. 1984. *After Virtue.* Notre Dame, IN: University of Notre Dame Press.

Marcuse, Herbert. 1991. *One Dimensional Man.* Boston: Beacon Press.

Marx, Karl. 1984. *Collected Works*, with Friedrich Engels, vol. 20. New York: International Publishers.

Marx, Karl. 1978. "Economic and Philosophical Manuscripts 1844." In *The Marx-Engels Reader*, edited by Robert C. Tucker, 66–125. New York: W.W. Norton.

Marx, Karl. 1977. *Capital*, translated by Ben Fowkes. New York: Vintage.

Marx, Karl. 1975. "Economic and Philosophical Manuscripts 1844," with Friedrich Engels. In *Collected Works*, Vol. 3. New York: International Publishers.

Maurer, Reinhart. 2015. "Zu Babette Babich, Nietzsches Wissenschaftsphilosophie." *New Nietzsche Studies* 9(3–4): 193–226.

Maurer, Reinhart. 1981–1982. "Nietzsche und die Kritische Theorie." *Nietzsche-Studien* X–XI: 34–58.

Mazzinie, Sylvie, and Owen Glyn-Williams, eds. 2017. *Making Communism Hermeneutical: Reading Vattimo and Zabala.* Frankfurt am Main: Metzler.

McGinn, Robert E. 1980. "Nietzsche on Technology." *Journal of the History of Ideas* 41(4) (Oct.–Dec.): 679–691.

Melamphy, Dan, and Nandita Biswas Mellamphy, eds. 2016. *The Digital Dionysus: Nietzsche & the Network-Centric Condition.* New York: Punctum Books.

Miller, Elaine P. 2012. "Saving Time: Temporality, Recurrence and Transcendence in de Beauvoir's Nietzschean Cycles." In *Beauvoir and Western Thought from Plato to Butler*, edited by Shannon M. Mussett and William S. Wilkerson, 103–124. Albany: State University of New York Press.

Miller, James. 1978. "Some Implications of Nietzsche's Thought and Marxism." *Telos* XXXVII: 22–41.

Montinari, Mazzino. 1982. *Nietzsche lesen.* Berlin: de Gruyter.

Müller, Christopher John. 2016. *Prometheanism: Technology, Digital Culture and Human Obsolescence.* Lanham: Rowman & Littlefield.

Müller-Lauter, Wolfgang. 2000. *Nietzsche-Interpretationen, Volume 3*. Berlin: de Gruyter.

Müller-Lauter, Wolfgang. 1999. *Nietzsche-Interpretationen, Bd. 2, Über Freiheit und Chaos.* Berlin: de Gruyter.

Müller-Lauter, Wolfgang. 1960. *Möglichkeit und Wirklichkeit bei Martin Heidegger*. Berlin: de Gruyter.

Musto, Marcello. 2015. "The 'Young Marx' Myth in Interpretations of the Economic–Philosophic Manuscripts of 1844." *Critique: Journal of Socialist Theory* 43(2): 233–260.

Nietzsche, Friedrich. 1980a. *Menschliches, Allzumenschliches* [*Human, All Too Human*]. KSA, vol. 2. Berlin: de Gruyter.

Nietzsche, Friedrich. 1980b. *Jenseits von Gut und Böse*. KSA, vol. 5. Berlin: de Gruyter.

Nietzsche, Friedrich. 1980c. *Die Geburt der Tragödie*. [*The Birth of Tragedy*]. Berlin: de Gruyter.

Nietzsche, Friedrich. 1980d. *Die fröhliche Wissenschaft*. [*The Gay Science*]. KSA, vol 3. Berlin: de Gruyter.

Peck, Tom. 2011. "Thus Spoke Lagerfeld: Design-Guru Goes Back to Nietzsche." *Independent*, May 12.

Pelz, William A. 2016. "Becoming an Appendage to the Machine." In *A People's History of Modern Europe*, 52–63. London: Pluto Press.

Pepperle, Heinz. 1986. "Revision des marxistischen Nietzsche-Bildes? Vom inneren Zusammenhang eines fragmentarischen Philosophie." *Sinn und Form* 5: 934–969.

Polyakova, Ekaterina, and Yulia Sineokaya, eds. 2017. *Фридрих Ницше: наследие и проект*. М.: Культурная революция, / *Friedrich Nietzsche: Heritage and Prospects*. Moscow: LRC Publishing House.

Rayman, Joshua. 2015. "Heidegger's 'Nazism' as Veiled Nietzscheanism and Heideggerianism: Evidence from the Black Notebooks." *Gatherings: The Heidegger Circle Annual* 5: 77–92.

Reschke, Renate. 2009. "Nietzsche Stand wieder zur Diskussion. Zur Marxistischen Nietzsche Rezeption in der DDR der Achtziger Jahre." In *Ausgänge: zur DDR-Philosophie in den 70er und 80er Jahren*, edited by Hans-Christoph Rauh and Hans-Martin Gerlach, 203–244. Berlin: Links Verlag.

Roberts, Michael. 2016. "Twilight of Work: The Labor Question in Nietzsche and Marx." *Critical Sociology*. https://doi.org/10.1177/0896920516681427.

Roberts, Michael. 1995. "Rereading Marx and Nietzsche." *Rethinking Marxism: A Journal of Economics, Culture & Society* 8(1): 100–111.

Rodden, John. 2008. "Zarathustra as Educator: The Nietzsche Archive in German History." In *The Holocaust and the Book: Destruction and Preservation*, edited by Jonathan Rose, 213–265. Amherst: University of Massachusetts Press.

Rose, Gillian. 1978. *The Melancholy Science: An Introduction to the Thought of Theodor W. Adorno*. London: Macmillan.

Salter, William M. 1917. "Nietzsche and the War." *International Journal of Ethics* 27(3): 357–379.

Sayer, Derek. 2015. *Capitalism and Modernity: An Excursus on Marx and Weber*. London: Routledge.

Schluchter, Wolfgang. 1995. "Zeitgemäße Unzeitgemäße: Von Friedrich Nietzsche über Georg Simmel zu Max Weber." *Revue Internationale de Philosophie* 49, no. 192(2) *Max Weber* (June): 107–126.

Schmidt, Alfred. 1981. *History and Structure: An Essay on Hegelian-Marxist and Structuralist Theories of History*, translated by Jeffrey Herf. Cambridge, MA: MIT Press.

Schmidt, Rüdiger. 1982. *Ein Text ohne Ende für den Denkenden.* Königstein/Ts: Forum Academicum.

Schwan, Alexander. 1987. "Zeitkritik und Politik in Heideggers Spätphilosophie." In *Heidegger und die praktische Philosophie*, edited by Annemarie Gethmann-Siefert and Otto Pöggeler, 93–107. Frankfurt am Main: Suhrkamp.

Scruton, Roger. 2017. *The Ring of Truth: The Wisdom of Wagner's Ring of the Nibelung.* London: Penguin.

Simmel, Georg. 1907. *Schopenhauer und Nietzsche: Ein Vortragszyklus.* Leipzig: Duncker and Humblot.

Simmel, Georg. 1896. "Friedrich Nietzsche: Eine moralphilosophische Silhouette." *Zeitschrif für Philosophie und philosophische Kritik* 2: 202–215.

Smythe, Dallas W. 1977. "Communications: Blindspot of Western Marxism." *Canadian Journal of Political and Social Theory/Revue canadienne de theorie politique et sociale* 1(3) (Fall/Automne): 1–27.

Solms-Laubach, Franz zu. 2012. *Nietzsche and Early German and Austrian Sociology.* Berlin: de Gruyter.

Stack, George J. 1983. *Lange and Nietzsche.* Berlin: de Gruyter.

Strong, Tracy B. 2002. "Love, Passion, and Maturity: Nietzsche and Weber on Science, Morality, and Politics." In *Confronting Mass Democracy and Industrial Technology: Political and Social Theory from Nietzsche to Habermas*, edited by John P. McCormick, 15–42. Durham: Duke University Press.

Strong, Tracy B. 1999 [1975]. *Nietzsche and the Politics of Transfiguration.* Bloomington, IL: University of Illinois Press.

Strong, Tracy B., ed. 2009. *Friedrich Nietzsche.* Farnham, UK: Ashgate.

Taubes, Jacob. 2013. *To Carl Schmitt: Letters and Reflections*, translated by Keith Tribe. New York: Columbia University Press.

Tugendhat, Ernst. 2000. "Der Wille zur Macht. Macht und Anti-Egalitarismus bei Nietzsche und Hitler – Einspruch gegen den Versuch einer Verharmlosung." *Die Zeit*, Sept. 14.

Turner, Bryan. 2011. "Max Weber and the Spirit of Resentment: The Nietzsche Legacy." *Journal of Classical Sociology* 11(1): 75–92.

Turner, Bryan. 1993. "Preface." In *Max Weber and Karl Marx*, Karl Löwith, 1–32. New York: Routledge.

Vattimo, Gianni. 2009. "Nihilism as Emancipation." *Cosmos and History: The Journal of Natural and Social Philosophy* 5(1): 20–23.

Vattimo, Gianni, and Santiago Zabala. 2011. *Hermeneutic Communism: From Heidegger to Marx.* New York: Columbia University Press.

Waite, Geoff. 1996. "Left-Nietzschoids, Right-Nietzscheans." In *Nietzsche's Corps/e: Aesthetics, Politics, Prophecy, Or, The Spectacular Technoculture of Everyday Life*, 139–166. Durham: Duke University Press.

Warren, Mark. 1984. "Nietzsche's Concept of Ideology." *Theory and Society* 13(4): 541–565.

Wimberley, Cory. 2017. "The Job of Creating Desire: Propaganda as an Apparatus of Government and Subjectification." *Journal of Speculative Philosophy* 31(1): 101–118.
Wolin, Richard. 2004. *The Seduction of Unreason: "Intellectual Romance" from Nietzsche to Postmodernism*. Princeton: Princeton University Press.
Wollaeger, Mark. 2008. *Modernism, Media, and Propaganda: British Narrative from 1900 to 1945*. Princeton: Princeton University Press.

PART 3

Beyond Truth and Relativism: Nietzsche and the Question of Knowledge

∵

CHAPTER 10

Toward a Gay Social Science: A Nietzschean-Marxist Alternative to Conventional Sociological Theory

Michael Roberts

The historic destiny [of capitalism] is fulfilled as soon as … labour in which a human being does what a thing could do has ceased.

KARL MARX, *The Grundrisse*

•••

Let us look one another in the face. We are Hyperboreans.

NIETZSCHE, *The Anti-Christ*

∴

1 Introduction[1]

For conventionally trained sociologists in the United States, Nietzsche remains marginal to the discipline in spite of the fact that the work of Max Weber and his American followers enjoyed a certain dominance over sociological theory in the U.S. between the 1930s and 1960s (Horowitz 1964).[2] Weber was quite

1 A portion of this essay was previously published in Roberts (2019).

2 Of course, Durkheimian functionalism and symbolic interactionism have also had a significant place in the conventional-professional training of American sociologists. For the purposes of this essay, by "conventional sociology" I mean the works of sociologists whose empirical investigations are informed by the theoretical frameworks constructed by Weber and/or Durkheim. Löwith (1993) refers to Weberian sociology as "bourgeois" sociology, since a major task of the Weberian tradition – especially in the U.S. – after Weber's death has been the attempt to discredit Marxist theory and politics (Stammer 1971). By "critical sociology," I mean sociological analyses that use the Marxist paradigm – often in conjunction with feminist theory and critical race theory – as an alternative to the Weberian and Durkheimian frameworks. Although I prefer the term "conventional" to "bourgeois" sociology, I am in agreement with how Löwith (1993) sees the main difference between the two paradigms as

public about his intellectual debt to Nietzsche – and Marx for that matter – but this detail is not well-known among professional sociologists in the U.S. (Antonio 1995).[3] The absence of Nietzsche in American sociology is partly the result of the widespread influence of Talcott Parsons and his particular interpretation and translation of Weber's texts that erased the presence of Nietzsche in Weber's work (Roberts 2019).[4] Of course, Parsons' construction of structural-functionalist theory also included a particular interpretation of Durkheim. In the case of Durkheim, it is perhaps understandable that his American followers would know relatively little about Nietzsche, since Durkheim, unlike Weber, had very little to say about Nietzsche. It was a much different

---

one that turns on the understanding of sociology's relationship to capitalism. Unlike critical sociology, conventional sociology affirms capitalism as preferable to the socialism despite Parsons' claims to be "value neutral" in his sociological analyses. The issue is what, exactly, is meant by "socialism." I consider this issue in more detail throughout this essay. There was a significant challenge to Weberian and Durkheimian hegemony in the 1960s when Marxist sociologists provided alternative theoretical paradigms in the wake of the social movements of the 1960s that threw conventional sociology into a temporary crisis due to a lack of adequate theoretical tools to make sense of the social and political turmoil that characterized the sixties (Gouldner 1970). Weber returned to dominance in the American sociology after the fall of the Berlin Wall (Antonio 2005). Today, however, as capitalism is in crisis all around the world, the search for a new critical paradigm is once again underway in sociology.

3 According to Weber, "One can measure the honesty of a contemporary philosopher in his posture toward Marx and Nietzsche. Whoever does not admit that he could not perform the most important parts of his own work without the work those two have done swindles himself and others. Our intellectual world has to a great extent been shaped by Marx and Nietzsche" (quote appears in Mitzman 1969: 182).

4 For example, toward the end of Weber's *Protestant Ethic and the Spirit of Capitalism*, Parsons chose to use the English phrase "last stage" rather than "last men," in his now controversial translation of Weber's classic text. Weber himself was clearly borrowing the phrase "die letzten Menschen" from Nietzsche's (1969) *Thus Spoke Zarathustra*, but this was lost on generations of sociologists trained in the U.S. thanks to Parsons' widespread influence upon American sociology. Nietzsche used the phrase "last men" to indicate a certain nihilism that follows in the aftermath of the rise of science and the displacement of the Christian world view by the Enlightenment. Parsons, on the other hand, did not share either Nietzsche's or Weber's critical view of science. For more on this issue, see Peter Baehr's introduction to his more recent and accurate translation of Weber (2002 [1905]). The other key text where Weber (2004 [1917]) makes use of Nietzsche's phrase "last men" is in the essay, "Science as a Vocation." There Weber writes, "a naïve optimism has led people to glorify science, or rather the techniques of mastering problems of life based on science, as the road to happiness. But after Nietzsche's annihilating criticism of those 'last men' who have discovered 'happiness' I can probably ignore this completely" (2004 [1917]: 17). Unfortunately, Parsons transforms Weber's critique of the value of science into a question of methodology, a how-to rather than a question of *what value*. American sociology has a long tradition of reifying if not celebrating science rather than critically reflecting upon its methodologies and the social conditions whereby facts are produced (Burris 2007).

situation in Europe. It is interesting to note that at roughly the same time that Parsons was beginning his ascent within professional sociology in the U.S., critical social theorists like Georges Bataille began working on innovative articulations of Durkheim with Nietzsche (Riley 2005).[5] Meanwhile, other critical theorists in France like Henri Lefebvre were seeking to make room for Nietzsche within the Marxist paradigm (Lefebvre 2003a), an effort that was in direct opposition to György Lukács (1980 [1950]), who sought to purge Nietzsche from Critical Theory.[6] In Lefebvre's words,

> If there was anyone who wanted to 'change the world' it was Nietzsche. Protests and challenges to the status quo are fired off [by Nietzsche] in all directions. Individual life and lived experience reassert themselves against political pressures, 'productivism' and economism. When it is not putting one policy in opposition to another, protest finds support in poetry, music and the theatre, and also in hope and expectation of the extraordinary: the surreal, the supernatural, the superhuman.
>
> LEFEBVRE 2003b: 43

Critical sociologists in the U.S. are perhaps more aware of Nietzsche's influence upon modern and postmodern social theory than their conventional counterparts, but Marxists have remained split over the value of Nietzsche's contributions as well as the intellectual movements inspired by him like post-structuralism and postmodernism (Harvey 1991). In short, conventional sociologists in the U.S. have not sought an engagement with Nietzsche, while many critical sociologists tend to see Nietzsche as a foe, along lines similar to that of Lukács (1980 [1950]), who reads Nietzsche as a political reactionary, opposed to the emancipatory aims of critical sociology (Landa 2019).

---

5 Bataille's critical appropriation of Durkheim is sometimes referred to as a "renegade Durkheimianism" for the attempt to use Durkheim as a way to not only describe the processes of transgressing social norms, but perhaps more importantly because Bataille was an advocate of transgression, something that Durkheim himself would not approve given his more conservative orientation- relative to Bataille. For these reasons, Bataille was a major influence on the Left-Nietzscheans of the 1960s like Michel Foucault and Gilles Deleuze.

6 This attempt failed, as the founders of Critical Theory (also known as the "Frankfurt School"), including Theodor Adorno, Max Horkheimer, Herbert Marcuse, – and to a lesser extent – Ernst Bloch and Walter Benjamin, broke with Lukács over the question of Nietzsche (Adorno et al. 1977). In short, while the early Lukács (author of the now classic text *History and Class Consciousness*) had a profound influence over the entire project of Critical Theory, his later attempt to purge Nietzsche was dismissed by the Frankfurt School on the grounds that Lukács lost whatever independence he once had from Stalin (Aronowitz 2013).

In the following pages I make an intervention into this context by making a case for Nietzsche through revealing how his work lends itself to a critique of conventional sociology *and* orthodox Marxism, both of which downplay the importance of aesthetics in what we call the good life, due to what Arendt (1958) refers to as the "glorification of labor." By reading Nietzsche alongside of Durkheim and Marx in order to reveal how Marx has more in common with Nietzsche than Durkheim, I show how Nietzsche offers valuable insights into the problems of morality and work. I hope to also pique the interests of conventionally-trained sociologists who read Durkheim, by revealing an alternative way of looking at morality. By "gay" social science I do not mean to directly refer to sexual identities and politics.[7] Following Walter Kaufmann (1950), who was Nietzsche's main English translator, I am using "gay" social science in the sense of a "cheerful" social science, with an emphasis on aesthetic play and the defiance of convention. In Kaufmann's (1974) words, the term gay "suggests Nietzsche's 'immoralism' and his 'revaluation of values'" (5). Elsewhere, Nietzsche (1967) explains his point of view in the following words: "to look at science in the perspective of the artist, but at art in that of life" (Attempt at Self-Criticism: 2).

Cheerfulness, then, has an aesthetic dimension to it, and as I will argue below, all three theorists under consideration in this essay understand art and play (leisure) as being fundamentally opposed to work and labor. Thus, an analysis of the relationship between aesthetics and work will be one main focus of this essay. As I will demonstrate, Durkheim takes a position against art, whereas Nietzsche and Marx affirm art along the lines of Nietzsche's (1967) claim that "the world is *justified* only as an aesthetic phenomenon" (Attempt at Self-Criticism: 5). I refer to this important difference between conventional and critical (gay) sociology as the distinction between asceticism (self-denial and hostility toward life) and aestheticism (playfulness and an affirmation of life and pleasure). I run these differences through close readings of particular texts of the three theorists under consideration.

I begin with a comparison of Durkheim and Nietzsche on the topics of morality and aesthetics and then move into a comparison of Nietzsche and Marx on the labor question. I argue that the problem of morality is essentially a labor question, and because of this, any critical sociological project that has emancipation from oppressive moral and economic systems as its aim must also question the value of work and the work ethic. Here I emphasize Marx's argument that the liberation from work is the necessary if not sufficient condition

7 For the relationship between Nietzsche and queer theory see the important and provocative work of Heike Schotten (2019).

to achieve Nietzsche's aim of transfiguring Western morality, what he calls going "beyond good and evil" in order pursue an aesthetic rather than moral mode of living. In short, the pursuit of art – as the necessary if not sufficient condition of the good life – begins where work ends. Secondly, the emancipatory aims also require us to make a connection between the labor question and the question concerning science. With this in mind, I include an analysis of the contrasting – and sometimes similar – views on science found in Durkheim, Marx and Nietzsche. The aim here is to provide an alternative to conventional sociological analyses of science which remain bereft of any concern for emancipation.

I conclude the essay with a discussion of the death and rebirth of Nietzschean-Marxism through an examination of the fate of Russian intellectuals who attempted to fuse Nietzsche with Marx during the years leading up to and during the Bolshevik Revolution and following that, a brief consideration of particular Western Marxists like Henri Lefebvre and Theodor Adorno who sought to revive the initial attempts at such a synthesis. Any attempt to contribute new content to a critical sociology requires an understanding of similar efforts made in the past. Here too I consider the debate over aesthetics, although in the context of competing revolutionary intellectuals, including Leon Trotsky and A.A. Bogdanov among others. In sum, I seek to find common ground between Marx and Nietzsche in the effort to add a few stones to a reconstituted foundation for a contemporary critical sociology that seeks an intervention into the current context of economic crisis that constitutes global capitalism in the neoliberal era. Overcoming a culture that celebrates labor and uncritically worships science are the necessary, if not sufficient conditions for creating a new way of life beyond the taken-for-granted capitalist-postmodernity that we presently experience. A gay social science, then, has such an overcoming as one of its principal aims.

2 A Nietzschean Critique of Conventional Sociology

A good place to start an analysis of Nietzsche's relationship to conventional sociology is with the figure of Immanuel Kant. For Durkheim and Weber, as well as Nietzsche, Kant provides a touchstone from which they all develop their own perspectives. In the *Elementary Forms of Religious Life*, Durkheim (1995) seeks to solve certain problems in Kantian epistemology by moving the forms of intuition and categories of understanding out of the Kantian transcendental structure of the mind and into social forms, creating the perspective in sociology that we call "the sociology of knowledge." In this way,

Durkheim breaks with a particular reification of the knowing subject in the Cartesian epistemological tradition: what Cartesian and Kantian epistemology assume, Durkheim seeks to explain. In terms of *ontology*, however, Durkheim remains an orthodox Kantian because he assumes certain features of the human condition that need historical explanation. In short, Durkheim ultimately reifies the Western subject: "Man." A particular ontological perspective grounds Durkheim's view of morality and this is where Nietzsche parts ways with Durkheim's Kantianism (more on this below). Weber shares the Kantian perspective with Durkheim in spite of the fact that we tend to polarize Weber and Durkheim in our conventional-professional sociological training when we view Weber in terms of "methodological individualism," and Durkheim in terms of the primacy of "social facts." A closer examination of Nietzsche helps us reveal how both Durkheim and Weber (conventional sociologists) remain rooted in orthodox Kantianism.

In terms of theoretical differences involving the methods of historical research, Weber's version of historical-comparative sociology diverges sharply from that of another disciple of Nietzsche, Michel Foucault. Whereas the methodology of Weber's "cultural science" presupposes a transcendental, meaning-giving subject, much in the same way as Kant (1998), Foucault, following Nietzsche's (1989) genealogical critique of Kant's transcendental subject, analyzes the histories of the formation of said subject, rather than take the subject, *a priori*, as simply given (Foucault 1984; Dean 1994: 71). And where Weber's (2002 [1905]) pessimism sees only an "iron cage," or "a shell as hard as steel" at the end of the project of modernity, Foucault's (1984) genealogical approach to the history of modernity goes in the opposite direction, seeking to reveal *contingency* rather than determinism in history. Compare Weber (2002 [1905]): "when asceticism moved out of the monastic cells and into working life ... it helped build the mighty cosmos of the modern economic order ... Today this mighty cosmos *determines*, with *overwhelming coercion*, the style of life not only of those directly involved in business but of every individual who is born into this mechanism" (120, emphasis mine) to Foucault:

> Criticism is no longer going to be practiced in the [Kantian] search for formal structures with universal value, but rather as an historical investigation into the events that have led us to constitute ourselves ... In that sense, this criticism is not transcendental, and its goal is not that of making a metaphysics possible: it is genealogical in its design ... this critique will be genealogical in the sense that *it will not deduce from the form of what we are what it is impossible for us to do and to know*; but it will separate out, from the *contingency* that has made us what we are, *the possibility of*

> *no longer being, doing, or thinking what we are, do, or think* ... The critical ontology of ourselves has to be ... conceived as ... a philosophical life in which the critique of what we are is at one and the same time the historical analysis of the limits that are imposed on us and an *experiment* with the possibility of *going beyond* them ... I do not know whether it must be said today that the critical task still entails faith in the Enlightenment; I continue to think that *this task requires work on our limits*, that is, a patient labor giving form to our impatience for liberty.
>
> FOUCAULT 1984: 46, 50, emphasis mine

In these particular examples, it would seem that Foucault's analyses are closer in spirit to Nietzsche than Weber's, insofar as whatever pessimism that Nietzsche expressed about modernity, his genealogical analyses did not close off the possibility for the radical transformation of everyday life. It is for this reason that critical theorists like Marcuse (1974), Bloch (1991; 1986 [1938]), Lefebvre (2003a) and Foucault (1984) find elements in Nietzsche's diagnoses of modernity that lend themselves to a critical-social theory that has emancipatory aims: in short, the study of the contingent formation of moralities and subjectivities in history reveals that the horizon remains open for us to become something new while overcoming that which we have become. This perspective provides an alternative to conventional sociology in terms of methods and aims. The Kantian quest for what Foucault calls "formal structures with universal value," is shared by the founders of conventional sociology, including Weber, Durkheim and Parsons, all of whom seek to deduce what we *cannot* do or know from the *form* of what we are. In a manner similar to Kant (1998 [1789]), who sought to uncover the conditions that make knowledge possible in order to find and enforce the boundaries of what reason should be allowed to do, conventional-bourgeois sociology seeks to locate and enforce limits – for knowledge and for action – rather than advocate the transgression of them in the quest for freedom. Parsons goes so far as to throw the very *possibility* of freedom in doubt when he places the word free inside scare quotes in the following passage: "In a completely 'free' orientation relationship ego is free," writes Parsons (1951). "But here we are talking about social structures. It is taken for granted that social structure through institutionalization places *limits* on the range of legitimized orientation of an actor in a given status of ego (139, emphasis mine). In other words, conventional sociology takes social structures as the object of analysis for sociological theory, and thereby "takes for granted" the impossibility of freedom, because whatever it is that actors in the social system are able to do is deduced from the [reified] form of the social system.

We can see Kantianism in Durkheim (1984) as well, whose sociology becomes ontology with statements like the following: "in reality our capacity for happiness is very restricted ... Not without reason does human experience see the *aurea mediocritas* as the condition of happiness ... we understand what *limits* happiness: it is the constitution of man [sic] himself" (181–183, emphasis mine). In this passage Durkheim takes "Man" for granted, without any historical context. Nietzsche finds Christian morality lurking inside such statements as these that claim to be scientific. In other words, conventional sociologists in the Durkheimian tradition unconsciously code their normative view – in this case the affirmation of the value of mediocrity – in the language of science. Nietzsche (1968) argues that "everywhere the Christian-nihilistic value standard has to be pulled up and fought under every mask; e.g., in present-day sociology" (I: 51). Although Nietzsche was responding to the sociology of Hebert Spencer, his critique applies equally well to functionalism in the tradition of Durkheim and Parsons. Durkheim's notion that the golden mean or the "moderate course" is the condition of happiness is for Nietzsche, an unconscious expression of the herd instinct, which places a value upon mediocrity. Here Nietzsche seeks to provide an explanation for that which Durkheim takes for granted. According to Nietzsche (1968):

> Even the ideals of science can be deeply, yet completely unconsciously influenced by decadence: our entire sociology is proof of that. *The objection to it is that from experience it knows only the form of decay of society, and inevitably it takes its own instincts of decay for the norms of sociological judgment.* In these norms the life that is declining in present-day Europe formulates its social ideals ... The herd instinct, then – a power that has now become sovereign ... the value of the units determines the significance of the sum. – Our entire sociology simply does not know any other instinct than that of the herd, i.e., that of the sum of zeroes ... where it is *virtuous* to be zero.
>
> I: 53, emphasis mine

What does Nietzsche mean by decay? Nietzsche's focus is upon how all perspectives are grounded in life, and life can be either ascending (healthy) or descending (sick). In short, cultural expressions – including science – are firmly rooted in material conditions. For Nietzsche, European culture remained mired in sickness in spite of whatever cultural achievements followed from the Enlightenment and the rise of science.[8]

8 I will elaborate on this below by arguing that the bourgeois-work ethic is a sign of sickness in the Nietzschean sense.

While Nietzsche might seem like an elitist when he uses terms like "herd," a better way to frame Nietzsche's intervention is through asking questions like: Why do we persist in mediocrity? Or, from what perspective can one claim that it is virtuous to be zero? A main concern for Nietzsche is the way in which the Enlightenment has contributed to the liquidation of individuality and particularity, the denial of difference as such. Durkheim's emphasis on the notion of equilibrium in his functionalist theoretical framework and his dogmatic assertion that happiness is found in mediocrity is one such example of this phenomenon. As Deleuze argues,

> What Nietzsche attacks in science is ... the scientific mania for seeking balances, the *utilitarianism* and *egalitarianism* proper to science. This is why his whole critique operates on three levels; against logical identity, against mathematical equality and against physical equilibrium. *Against the three forms of the undifferentiated* ... What is the significance of this tendency? In the first place, it expresses the way in which science is part of the *nihilism* of modern thought. The attempt to deny differences is part of the more general enterprise of denying life, depreciating existence and promising it a death.
>
> DELEUZE 1983: 45

What does it mean to say that science – both natural and social – denies life? For Nietzsche science partakes in the Christian denial of life because both perspectives invent another world in *opposition* to this one that we live in: for Christianity it is heaven, for science it is "truth." Nietzsche explains how science fails to make a break from Christian morality and metaphysics in the text *Gay Science*, where he (1974) writes,

> This unconditional will to truth – what is it? ... One does not want to allow oneself to be deceived because one assumes that it is harmful, dangerous, calamitous to be deceived. In this sense, science would be a long-range prudence, a caution, a utility; but one could object in all fairness: How is that? Is wanting not to allow oneself to be deceived really less harmful, less dangerous, less calamitous? What do you know in advance of the character of existence to be able to decide whether the greater advantage is on the side of unconditionally mistrustful or of the unconditionally trusting? ...'Will to truth' does *not* mean 'I will not allow myself to be deceived' but – there is no alternative – 'I will not deceive, not even myself'; *and with that we stand on moral ground.* For you only have to ask yourself carefully, 'Why do you not want to deceive?' especially if it should seem – and it does seem! – as if life aimed at semblance, meaning error,

> deception, simulation, delusion, self-delusion, and when the great sweep of life has always shown itself to be on the side of the most unscrupulous *polytropoi*. Charitably interpreted, such a resolve might perhaps be a quixotism, a minor, slightly mad enthusiasm; but it might also be something more serious, namely, a principle that is hostile to life and destructive. – Will to Truth' – that might be a concealed will to death … No doubt, those who are truthful in that audacious and ultimate sense that is presupposed by the faith in science thus *affirm another world* than the world of life, nature and history; and insofar as they affirm this 'other world' – look, must they not by the same token negate its counterpart, this world, *our* world? – But you will have gathered what I am driving at, namely, that it is still a *metaphysical faith* upon which our faith in science rests – that even we seekers after knowledge today, we godless anti-metaphysicians still take our fire too, from the flame lit by a faith that is thousands of years old, that Christian faith which was also the faith of Plato, that God is the truth, that truth is divine.
>
> V: 344

Here we see why Nietzsche views modernity as a sign of decay. The Enlightenment has not made good on its promise of emancipation because it harbors an unconscious death drive – an issue that Freud took up in *Beyond the Pleasure Principle*. According to Nietzsche, modern science, by inventing a "true world" in opposition to this world, slanders and devalues the material world in much the same way as Platonism and Christianity. Nietzsche was not opposed to scientific activity as such, but rather the particular cultural context of scientific practices that remain unexamined.[9] The "true" world created by modern science – what Marcuse (1982) refers to as Galileo's "mathematization of nature" – is a version of Plato's idealism that constructs an unchanging, stable realm of *Being* – what Plato calls the "forms" that can only be accessed through philosophical reflection upon ideas – as opposed to the material world of *Becoming* that eludes the grasp of reason due to how our senses are fooled by semblance, simulation, deception, etc. It is a moral point of view, according to Nietzsche, that places a greater value on the ideal world – or "true" world – while denigrating the material world, "our" world as something we must escape. Such a morality is at the basis of the destructive elements made manifest in the modern era. As I will discuss below, the "metaphysical faith" that Nietzsche identifies in modern science is also present in the modern social science of Durkheim.

9 For the best treatment of Nietzsche's relationship to science see Babich (1994) and Payne (2018).

Nietzsche sought to analyze social and cultural phenomena in terms of whether or not they indicate an ascending or descending life (decay). Those who are not free and *who cannot act*, become resentful (reactive), and develop a negative perspective upon life. As a way to cope with their suffering, they create an imaginary afterlife where they will eventually find happiness. A particular mode of being in the world gives rise to a certain valuation of life. A descending life (sickness) finds expression in attitudes that negate the material world, including the human body. In order to make such diagnoses of society – determining whether it is sick (decaying) or healthy – Nietzsche sometimes referred to himself as a physician of culture (Ahern 1995). A main sickness in society that Nietzsche seeks to overcome is the ailment of asceticism, the hatred of the body and sexual desire that has its roots in the ancient history of Christian morality and which eventually led to the period of nihilism that Nietzsche claims is characteristic of modernity after the triumph of Enlightenment over Christianity. Hatred of the body and of life more generally, creates the conditions for a deadly and destructive politics.

In the history of the development of Western morality, the key figure for Nietzsche is the ascetic priest who redirects the resentment of those who suffer back onto the sufferers themselves, creating what Nietzsche (1989) calls the "bad conscience" a concept later re-signified by Freud as the superego. Rather than discharge their resentment – through a political and cultural revolution for example – slaves are encouraged by the ascetic priest to internalize resentment and blame *themselves* for their suffering (original sin). One of Nietzsche's (1989) main concerns is what happens when resentment become creative, that is to say, when resentment gives birth to particular values that form a system of morality. According to Nietzsche (1989) this negative view upon life – what he calls slave morality – eventually became the *dominant* perspective in society at large thanks to the work of the ascetic priest over many centuries. This is why Nietzsche (1989) makes the ironic claim that after Christian morality achieved cultural hegemony, it is the strong who must now be defended against the weak; the "strong" are those who affirm life and refuse to conform to the dominant-ascetic morality. This is a focus on culture rather than structure, because in the era of modernity, those in structural positions of power over others perpetuate the deadly culture of slave morality. Fascism and white supremacy more generally would be an example of how resentment and slave morality can generate a deadly, life-denying form of politics (Nealon 2000). A key feature of slave morality for Nietzsche is the seeking out of scapegoats, an Other that is to blame for why we suffer. In today's reactionary political discourse in the U.S., the so-called "immigrant" plays this role. In short, slave morality has its origins in structural relations of power and domination – unfree labor – but it eventually developed into *the* dominant cultural form that now seems to have a life of its own, so to speak, independent of its origins in the ancient, material-structural relations of master and slave. This is a crucial point to make because as Deleuze (1983) argues,

> this shows the extent to which the Nietzschean notion of the slave does not necessarily stand for someone dominated, by fate or social condition, but also characterizes the dominators as much as the dominated once the regime of domination comes under the sway of forces which are reactive and not active. Totalitarian regimes are in this sense regimes of slaves, not merely because of the people that they subjugate, but above all because of the type of "masters" they set up. (x)

According to Nietzsche (1989), the ascetic priest is the one who is "filled with a profound disgust at themselves, at the earth, at all life" (III: 11). The cultural hegemony achieved by the figure of the ascetic priest involves the prescription of work as a means to cope with the suffering that follows from looking into the horror and absurdity of existence. Suffering is an existential condition, but we also compound suffering by pursuing an ascetic mode of life where we deny ourselves pleasure, especially sexual pleasure. Hatred and anger are amplified by asceticism, so the priest must find some way to control such anger and frustration. The ascetic mode involves various techniques and practices that aim to make us numb to suffering, by releasing us from the burden of unsatisfied desire that stirs inside of us. Work is perhaps the most common of such techniques. In aphorism 18 of the third essay in the *Genealogy of Morals*, Nietzsche (1989) writes that

> 'mechanical activity' is a kind of 'training' that 'alleviates' an existence of suffering to a not inconsiderable degree: this fact is today called, somewhat *dishonestly*, 'the blessing of work' ... Mechanical activity and what goes with it – such an absolute regularity, punctilious and unthinking obedience, a mode of life fixed once and for all, fully occupied time ... how thoroughly the ascetic priest has known how to employ them against pain! When he was dealing with sufferers of the lower class, with work-slaves or prisoners ... he required hardly more than a little ingenuity in name-changing and re-baptizing to make them see benefits and a relative happiness in things they formerly hated [work].
>
> III: 18, emphasis mine

Convincing the "lower class" – or working class – to see benefits in work, something that under other circumstances they would not do, is a major aspect of what Nietzsche means by the trans-valuation of values that took place between antiquity and modernity. The ancient Greeks de-valued work, while affirming the value of leisure. With the rise of the work ethic in modernity, we see an inversion of these values.[10] The affirmation of work is a major feature of what Nietzsche means by the ascent of slave morality and the overthrow of master morality (more on this below).

The question of "name-changing" by the figure of the ascetic priest is addressed by Nietzsche in the first essay of *Genealogy of Morals*, where he conducts an historical etymology (genealogy) of two ideal types of value binaries: "good/bad" and "good/evil." The first pairing is the perspective of the master, and the second pairing is the perspective of the priest, which attempts to *represent* the interests of slaves. From the point of view of master morality, "good" is associated with happiness and "signifies one who *is*, who possesses reality, who is actual and true" (I: 5). Elsewhere Nietzsche characterizes "aristocratic value judgments" in master morality as flowing from "an abundant, even overflowing health, together with ... vigorous, free, joyful activity" (I: 7). What is of particular importance for this essay is Nietzsche's (1989) philological analysis of the various definitions of "bad" from the perspective of master morality. "Bad," in the ancient tongue, means simultaneously: "unlucky," "oppressed by toils," "cowardly," "woeful," "unfortunate" and "toilsome" (I: 11). Toil, labor, work, etc.: these conditions and activities give content to the term "bad" from the perspective of those who are free from such toil. We might think of master morality as the point of view of the traditionally defined leisure class who escape work by means of their wealth, but I also think that bohemian types who reject the work ethic and affirm a leisurely lifestyle full of artistic activities also express a particular version of master morality in spite of not being wealthy. After all, Nietzsche himself was not an independently wealthy individual.

This enquiry points to work as the necessary if not sufficient condition for the development of the unhappy, or "bad conscience." According to Nietzsche (1989):

> The judgment 'good' did not originate with those whom 'goodness' was shown! Rather it was 'the good' themselves, that is to say, the noble, powerful ... who felt and established themselves and their action as good ... in contradistinction to ... the common and plebian. It was out of this *pathos of distance* that they first seized the right to create values and to coin names for values ... (I: 2)

10 For more on the analysis of the rise of the bourgeois work ethic see Weber (2002 [1905]) and Scheler (1994 [1914]).

The expression "pathos of distance" should be understood to mean the phenomenological difference between leisure and work, for it is in the sphere of leisure that we experience health and happiness in free, joyful activity, that which provides us the capacity to create values and give names. Cultivation of the human being begins where necessary work ends. The one who *is*, the "possessor of reality" is the one whose lived experience is inside the realm of leisure.

For those who are unable to act freely because they are "oppressed by toils," life is given a negative evaluation. "A condemnation of life by one who is alive is, in the end," writes Nietzsche (1997), "just a symptom of a particular kind of life ... A judgment made by which kind of life? ... the answer: declining, weakened, tired and condemned life" (Morality as Anti-Nature: 5). Toil and travail is that which explains, in part at least, the conditions for a declining, tired and weakened life.[11] Nietzsche argues that an active bad conscience *can* overcome feelings of resentment – which are feelings of hostility toward the world accompanied by a feeling of powerlessness – but when the ascetic priest appropriates such feelings and redirects them back onto the slave, self-overcoming (the process of *discharging* resentment) mutates into self-hatred which results from an endless feedback loop of resentment directed against the self.

The "good/evil" binary is an inversion of the "good/bad" binary and issues forth out of the priestly organization and interpretation of resentment. According to Nietzsche (1989) it was the priest who,

> Dared to invert the aristocratic value-equation (good = noble = powerful = happy ...) and to hang on to this inversion ... saying 'the wretched alone are the good; the poor, important, lowly alone are the good; the suffering, deprived, sick ... alone are pious ... blessed by God – and you, the powerful and noble, are on the contrary the evil, the cruel ... the godless to all eternity. (I: 7)

What accounts for this inversion? For Nietzsche the answer lies in the condition of impotence. "It is because of their impotence," writes Nietzsche (1989), "that hatred grows to monstrous and uncanny proportions, to the most spiritual and poisonous kind of hatred. The truly great haters in world history have

11 In some cases, work actually kills. In Japan, they use the word "Karoshi" for death from over work. The term does not refer to death caused by accidents at work, or to dangerous jobs. Rather, the term refers to normal, regulated work under modern, safe conditions. Too much of work without rest, even in a cubicle with ergonomic chairs and keyboards, can cause death, usually from heart failure brought on by exhaustion caused by lack of sleep (Reuters 2016).

always been priests" (I: 7). Nietzsche's main concern is with how much damage has been done by slave morality once it becomes *the* dominant morality in society, irrespective of class or status positions. With what does this have to do with the conventional sociology of Emile Durkheim?

3 The Aesthetic vs. Ascetic Mode of Life

For starters, Nietzsche's analysis of the labor question is at odds with Durkheim's. Nietzsche (1989) emphasizes the *unfreedom* of work as the basis for the development of the unhappy consciousness (bad conscience), while Durkheim (1984) celebrates work as the means to find happiness and he even goes so far as to recommend limiting the amount of education that workers should receive so that they do *not* develop a taste for an aesthetic mode of life outside of work, which would provide an alternative to a moral, or ascetic mode of life (307–308). When Nietzsche (1989) says that one of the historic tasks of the ascetic priest has been to get slaves (workers) to "see benefits and happiness in things [work] they formerly hated" he may as well have been talking about Durkheim. Consider the following passage from Durkheim (1984) who considers the problem of workers being reduced to "lifeless cogs" in the division of labor:

> Occasionally the remedy [for alienated labor] has been proposed for workers, that besides their technical and special knowledge, they should receive a general education [liberal arts]. But assuming that in this way some of the bad effects attributed to the division of labor can be redeemed, it is still not a means of preventing them … Moreover, who can fail to see that that these two types of existence [work and leisure] are too opposing to be reconciled or to be lived by the same man! If one acquires the habit of contemplating *vast horizons*, overall views, and fine generalizations, one can no longer without impatience allow oneself to be confined within the narrow limits of a specialized task.
>
> 307, emphasis mine

What then, does Durkheim propose as the solution to the problem of alienated labor if not an increase in leisure time (the vast horizon) and a decrease in work time? The solution for Durkheim is not more leisure time. Rather, Durkheim's solution is to restructure the workplace so that workers can find happiness and satisfaction at and in work; in other words, to have them see benefits in things they formerly hated. "What resolves this contradiction," writes Durkheim (1984), "is the fact that, contrary to what has been said, the division of labor [work] does not produce these consequences [destruction of the mind] through some imperatives of its own nature, but only in exceptional and abnormal circumstances" (307). Thus, if the division of labor develops "normally" no workers would be alienated because "normally the operation of each special function demands that the individual should be not closely shut up in it, but should keep in constant contact with neighboring functions, becoming aware of their needs and changes that take place in them, etc." (308). In short, if workers interact more, then, somehow, they will not feel like cogs in a machine, but rather like "living cells" in a "living organism." In this "normal" organization of work, the worker "feels that he is of some use. For this he has no need to take in very vast areas of the social horizon; it is enough for him to perceive *enough of it* to understand that his actions have a goal beyond themselves. Thenceforth ... however *uniform* his activity may be, it is that of an intelligent being, for he knows that his activity has a meaning" (308, emphasis mine). The solution, then, involves *limiting* what workers are allowed to experience. There is only so much of the social horizon (art and aesthetic pleasure) that should be given to workers, and it is up to sociologists like Durkheim to make that decision for them. Here we see the Kantian morality in Durkheim's perspective where he seeks to locate limits for behavior and then enforce those limits rather than transgress them.

Against Durkheim, the aesthetic mode of life is precisely what Nietzsche advocates. For Nietzsche (1967) art is crucially important because it "makes life possible and worth living" (1). Nietzsche was interested in examining the Greek culture of antiquity because the Greeks had a different way of dealing with, and giving meaning to, suffering. The difference is that the ancients found a way of dealing with suffering that did not negate life, unlike the Christian-moral perspective. Nietzsche (1967) notes that, "the Greek knew and felt the horror of existence" (3). The question becomes, what do we make out of that horror or what kind of meaning can we give to suffering? One option is the road taken by Schopenhauer who argued that because the world is characterized by endless strife, we must attempt to remove ourselves from it through restricting or repressing our will (desires). The aim of such an ascetic mode of life is the achievement of a more tranquil state of mind.

Nietzsche of course goes in the other direction, toward affirming the will. Nietzsche (1967) reveals the aesthetic solution to this problem when he writes, "When the danger to his will is greatest, *art* approaches as a saving sorceress, expert at healing. She alone knows how to turn these nauseous thoughts about the horror or absurdity of existence into notions with which one can live: these are the *sublime* as the artistic taming of the horrible, and the *comic* as the artistic discharge of the nausea of absurdity" (7). Most important for Nietzsche is that the aesthetic response to suffering was developed such that art became a means for "seducing one to a *continuation* of life" (3, emphasis mine), rather than a denial of life, which is the ascetic solution to such problems. When Nietzsche speaks of the "danger to the will," he is indicating his break from Schopenhauer who sought out "will-less knowing" as the path to bliss if not happiness. In short, Nietzsche is arguing against what he sees as the "Buddhistic negation of the will," (7) a view which contrasts sharply with Durkheim, who sides with Schopenhauer on the necessity to negate desire in order to find peacefulness of mind (Mestrovic, 1988). "Freedom consists," writes Durkheim (1974) "in the deliverance from blind unthinking forces [desire]" (72). In this way, Durkheim construes desire as if it were a tyrant that exists in us, an insatiable monster that causes us to suffer. The best way to confront that suffering is to desire *less* from life. To do that, however, Durkheim (1974) argues that we need the help of the major institutions in society like the school, the workplace, the church and the family, because on our own, we are incapable of controlling our desires. For Durkheim, to continually want more than what society can offer leads to morbidity. Durkheim never considers the possibility of less work in an environment of abundance, an issue I return to in my consideration of Marx below. By asking less from life and advocating the denial of pleasures, we see how Durkheim's sociology is an example of what Nietzsche means by making "a virtue out of being zero."

Durkheim (1984) follows in the tradition of Platonism insofar as he poses art as a problem. "Too much artistic sensibility," writes Durkheim (1984), "is a sign of sickness that cannot be generalized without danger to society" (185). Durkheim uses the same set of terms in his analysis as does Nietzsche – that is to say the difference between morality and aesthetics – where pursuing one means the reduction or abandonment of the other. The main difference is that Durkheim advocates morality (asceticism) *against* an aesthetic mode of life. For Durkheim, the danger posed by art to society results from the desire of the "ploughman," (worker/slave) who might, after being exposed to art, prefer play over work. Durkheim is primarily concerned with what might happen if suddenly workers decide they would rather pursue aesthetic activities than work. What, then, would happen to social order? How would the necessary work get done if nobody wants to do it after being exposed to art? For Durkheim (1984),

> it is true that aesthetic ... activity, because it is not regulated, appears free of any constraint or limitation. Yet in reality it is closely circumscribed by activity [work] that is properly of a *moral* kind ... If we expend too much of our strength upon what is superfluous, we have not enough left to do

> what is needful. When too large a share is given to the imagination in morality, obligatory tasks are neglected. Any discipline must needs appear intolerable when one has grown *over-accustomed to acting without rules* ... The need to play, to indulge in acting without any purpose and for the pleasure of so doing *cannot be developed beyond a certain point without detaching oneself from the serious business of life* ... The ploughman, *if he is at one with the conditions of his existence*, is and must remain, shut off from aesthetic pleasures which are normal with the man of letters.
>
> 184 and 185, emphasis mine

Precisely. The question for both Marx and Nietzsche would be: how can we detach ourselves from the serious business of life (work/morality) so that we can pursue artistic activity (freedom)? For Durkheim such an aim is an impossibility. It follows then, that the main issue for sociologists in the Durkheimian tradition is to find ways to make sure that the "ploughman," or factory worker, is always "at one with their existence," never desiring anything more than a life of perpetual work. Durkheim sets the bar very low in terms of what a worker can expect from life. Perhaps Nietzsche might agree that slaves cannot indulge in aesthetic activity without posing a threat to social order, but at least Nietzsche (1997) recognizes workers for what they are under the conditions of capitalism: namely, "slaves" (Raids of an Untimely Man: 40). Durkheim, on the other hand, must construe workers as individuals who are able to find meaning and happiness in work, so long as work is "normally" organized on a "spontaneous" basis. I say that Durkheim must do so because he claims that his aims are the "perfection" of individuals and an end to the social conditions that "degrade" human beings. By "spontaneous" division of labor, Durkheim means a social environment where all individuals are allowed to freely gravitate toward the job that is a best match with their "capacities." Because Durkheim believes in such a thing as "natural" inequality, his task is to make sure that social inequality perfectly matches natural-born inequality, and then, under those conditions, we will have arrived at a "just" society. Today, we refer to this ideology as meritocracy. This is another way in which Durkheim situates himself in the tradition of Platonism, because in spite of being against slavery, caste and class systems, Durkheim still seeks to create the "just" society, one that is characterized by each individual being in their proper place in the social hierarchy. Some people are born to be "workers" and others are born to be "men of letters."

If nothing else, at least Nietzsche is honest about what work is under capitalism.[12] To expect, as Durkheim does, that anyone should find happiness within

12 It should be noted that neither thinker is able to fully imagine an alternative to work for those that suffer the burden of toil, unlike Marx who argues that automation – as a

such a limited horizon of existence is problematic to say the least. In short, for Durkheim, the job of the professional sociologist is to find the most efficient means of "shutting off aesthetic pleasures" to and for the working class. On the other hand, what I am referring to as a gay social science would take Durkheim's notion of "acting without rules and purpose" as its object of inquiry, seeking – in a post-Kantian manner – the conditions of possibility for such action: namely, how is it possible to live a life beyond repressive norms, what Nietzsche refers to as going "beyond good and evil?" The contrast in how Durkheim and Nietzsche situate themselves in the context of Western thought after Kant turns upon how to interpret the phenomenon that Durkheim calls "acting without rules."

Nietzsche's emphasis on the aesthetic mode of life takes its cue from Kant's (2000 [1790]) third critique, the *Critique of Judgment*, where Kant is concerned with aesthetics: beauty, freedom, and purposeless activity. In the third *Critique*, Kant raises the question of the free play of imagination – the very imagination that Durkheim poses as a threat to social order in the passage above. Durkheim's sociology, on the other hand, is situated firmly within Kant's first and second critiques, where the focus is upon, first: the possibility of knowledge about nature: i.e. science (*Critique of Pure Reason*) and second: the necessity of morality (*Critique of Practical Reason*). In the first *Critique*, Kant (1998 [1789]) defines the faculty of judgment as the "capacity to subsume [particulars] under rules, that is, to distinguish whether something falls under a rule" (268). Here the imagination is not free, but rather it is governed by the principles of the faculty of understanding. In order for science to proceed along the lines of obtaining apodictic knowledge, particulars must be subsumed under universal concepts which are already given, *a priori*, as it were. In science, the objects of cognition are made possible by preexisting concepts that are universal in the faculty of understanding: i.e. causality. But in the realm of aesthetics, cognition is not a concern. The task of the third *Critique* considers a very different kind of question: namely, how it is that in the activity of reflection upon the beautiful, the faculty of judgment is in search of a universal for given particulars; universals in this context are *not* given *a priori*, and therefore a certain kind of freedom becomes possible. In other words, this kind of reflection points toward the possibility of acting in the *absence* of an external moral force or metaphysical principles. Neither moral obligation nor the necessity of the laws of nature

capitalist response to the labor movement – has at least the potential to free workers from labor and allow them to enter the sphere of leisure where aesthetic activity reigns supreme. This can only be achieved, however, if workers are able and willing to fight a reduction of working hours through direct action, including most importantly, strikes. Against Durkheim, Marx presents us with a vision for how workers are indeed able to and should "detach themselves from the serious business of life" (more on this below).

applies to the realm of aesthetic activity. For Nietzsche (1967) this is "a realm of wisdom from which the logician is exiled" (93).

For Kant (2000 [1790]), an example of particulars that exist without *a priori* universal concepts would be music, because music does not represent anything. According to Kant, music – what he refers to as a phenomenon "without a text" – is an example of what he calls "free beauty" because it "presupposes no concept of what the object ought to be" (114). In other words, music is "not attached to a determinate object in accordance with concepts regarding its end, but [music is] free and pleases for [itself]" (ibid.). What is ultimately at stake here – for the purposes of this essay – is an alternative basis for forming a human community. Rather than seek to unite people as a moral community as Durkheim does through an emphasis upon coercion, an aesthetic context provides the means by which human beings create meaningful relationships based upon free activity rather than obligation and duty. How is such an aesthetic type of community possible? According to Kant (2000 [1790]),

> First, one must be fully convinced that through the judgment of taste (on the beautiful) one ascribes the satisfaction in an object *to everyone*, yet without grounding it in a concept ... Thus there can be no rule in accordance with which someone could be compelled to acknowledge something as beautiful ... One wants to submit the object to his own eyes, just as if his satisfaction depended on sensation; and yet, if one then calls the object beautiful, one believes oneself to have a universal voice, and lays claim to the consent of everyone. (99–101)

In short, there is a radical difference between the context of work (duty, obligation, repression of desires) and the context of art (freedom and pleasure) and it follows that the kinds of relationships that people form with one another vary significantly due to being based upon these radically different social contexts.

Nietzsche – and Marx – speculate upon these profound differences in the question concerning the quality and form of human relationships. Nietzsche in particular sees music as a way to find commonality with others that is not coerced or made possible through duty and/or resentment. Indeed, Nietzsche (1967) is at his most democratic in his discussion of music[13] found in the *Birth of Tragedy*, where he argues that,

13 For a thorough analysis on this point see the excellent and provocative reading of Nietzsche's *Birth of Tragedy* by Tracy Strong (2012: 57–90).

> The Greek man of culture felt himself nullified in the presence of the satyric chorus; and this is the most immediate effect of the Dionysian tragedy, that the state and society and, quite generally, the gulfs between man and man give way to an overwhelming feeling of unity leading back to the very heart of nature. The metaphysical comfort – with which, I am suggesting even now, every true tragedy leaves us – that life is at the bottom of things, despite all the changes of appearances, independently powerful and *pleasurable*- this comfort appears in the incarnate clarity in the chorus of satyrs, a chorus of natural beings who live ineradicably, as it were, behind all civilizations and remain eternally the same, despite the changes of generations and the history of nations.
>
> 7, emphasis mine

Nietzsche argued that music provides an opportunity for people to open up as it were, and free themselves from a fixed identity that is opposed to an Other. Such a fixed identity is the hallmark of *ressentiment*. The feeling of ecstasy one experiences – in the Greek tragedy for example – creates the possibility of being outside or alongside of one's self through the process where an audience member is "nullified in the presence of the satyric chorus." Fixed identities, on the other hand, are the product of *ressentiment,* created within the context of work, duty and obligation, and for that reason they can never provide the grounds for a community of free people.[14] To return to the question of transgressing limits that Foucault emphasizes in the passage near the beginning of this essay, Nietzsche (1967) finds in the music festival an escape from the drudgery of work in the mundane everyday world that threatens to suck the life out of workers, or "folk" as Nietzsche refers to them. In this way, the pursuit of aesthetics is an example of the transgression of limits that Foucault advocates, a pursuit which aims at liberation. According to Nietzsche (1967),

> For the rapture of the Dionysian state with its annihilation of the ordinary bounds and limits of existence contains, while it lasts, a lethargic element which all personal experiences of the past become immersed.

14 Nietzsche's description of "the giving way to an overwhelming feeling of unity" through the experience of music is interpreted by Strong (2012) in the following manner: "It is in the nature of the experience of music that all words must fail to account for it and, nevertheless, it is in the nature of music to want to acquire form, to be spoken of, it is, thus, also in the nature of music to want to ground a particular community ... For Nietzsche, music provides access to the realm about which one can only remain silent, about which we must nonetheless speak, while recognizing that every word is an injustice and never final – perhaps a good basis for a democratic culture" (85, 89).

> This chasm of oblivion separates the worlds of everyday reality and the Dionysian reality. But as soon as this everyday reality re-enters consciousness, it is experienced as such, with nausea: as ascetic, will-negating mood is the fruit of these states. (7)

This distinction that Nietzsche refers to as the "chasm of oblivion" that "separates the everyday reality (work) and Dionysian reality (music festival)" is shared by Marx (1992a) who refers to this distinction as the difference between "work time" and "life time" (377). This is also the point at which Lefebvre (2014 [1947, 1981]) seeks to merge Marx with Nietzsche when he demands that we must have a radical transformation of everyday life in addition to the traditional Marxist demand that workers seize the means of production (more on this issue below). It is not enough to change the ownership of the means of production. All is lost without a radical transfiguration of everyday life world beyond the confines of work and morality. As Durkheim correctly points out, the necessity of morality is indeed a labor question, *but if automation of the labor process means that there is – potentially – much less work to do, then what have we to do with morality?* I return to this question in my analysis of Marx and Nietzsche in part two and three below.

Like Nietzsche, Durkheim's functionalism is also frequently understood in metaphorical terms as the perspective of a physician, insofar as functionalism views society as if it were an organism like a human body. The sociologist's role in the functionalist framework is to provide diagnoses for society, using particular criteria to judge whether or not it is sick, what Durkheim refers to as the condition of "abnormality." But the criteria that Durkheim and Nietzsche use in order to offer such diagnoses are add odds, because what Durkheim would consider "healthy" and "normal" about society, is precisely what Nietzsche would diagnose as a sickness. This difference can be explained by looking at how it turns upon the question of asceticism, or self-denial, what Durkheim (1972) refers to as the need to "limit the passions" in order to find happiness (176). Thus, while Nietzsche is quite critical of asceticism, Durkheim affirms it. The kind of sickness that Nietzsche seeks to cure – the hatred of the body – is exemplified by Durkheim's (1961) statement that "we must see people as they are … in their ugliness and wretchedness – if we want to help them" (271–272). What makes people ugly, and how exactly do we help them? For Durkheim, the ugliness is found in the body, in our passions. Therefore, to help people, Durkheim advocates that certain institutions in society must help the individual free themselves from their own desires and escape our bodies. Here we see the secularization of Christian morality in the social sciences as the conventional-bourgeois sociologist steps into the shoes of the ascetic priest. In short, science – in this case social science – remains rooted in the ascetic ideal. The act of limiting and denying the outward expression our passions is precisely what Nietzsche considers a symptom of an illness. In aphorism 11of the *Genealogy*, Nietzsche (1989) writes,

> Read from a distant star, the majuscule script of our earthly existence would perhaps lead to the conclusion that the earth was the distinctively *ascetic planet*, a nook of disgruntled, arrogant, and offensive creatures filled with a profound disgust at themselves, at earth, at all life, who inflict as much pain on themselves as they possibly can out of pleasure ... For consider how regularly and universally the ascetic priest appears in almost every age ... he prospers everywhere; *he emerges from every class of society* ... an ascetic life is a self-contradiction: here rules a *ressentiment* without equal, that of an insatiable instinct and power-will that wants to become master not over something in life but over life itself, over its most profound, powerful, and basic conditions: here an attempt is made to employ force to block up the wells of force; here physiological well-being is viewed askance, and especially outward expression of this well-being, beauty and joy; while pleasure is felt and *sought* in ... decay, pain ... self-mortification, self-flagellation, self-sacrifice. All this is in the highest degree paradoxical: we stand before a discord that wants to be discordant, that *enjoys* itself in this suffering and even grows more self-confident and triumphant the more its own presupposition, its physiological capacity for life *decreases*.
>
> III: 11, second emphasis mine

When Nietzsche asks us to consider how the ascetic priest appears regularly in every age, he is, in part, arguing that (conventional) sociology is but one example of the modern-scientific appropriation and expression of asceticism. In this way, Nietzsche's "genealogy" of morals is a critical alternative to Durkheim's "science" of morals because not only does Nietzsche provide a critique of asceticism that saturates classical sociology – with the important exception of Marx! – but also because he provides a way for finding contingency and the possibility of freedom where conventional sociology finds inertia, limits and the necessity of self-denial. Nietzsche should, therefore, find a home in the critical sociology that rejects Kantian universalism and morality. The very notion of "critique" which grounds what we call "critical" sociology is a concept that changes its orientation as it travels from its Kantian origins through Marx to Nietzsche.

4 Nietzsche's Critique of Work and the Bourgeois Work Ethic

In the *Gay Science*, Nietzsche (1974) offers one of his most profound ruminations upon the virtues of leisure and idleness. He does so by means of lamenting the damage that has been done as a result of the peculiarly American (Puritan) obsession with work for the sake of being busy. In the *Gay Science*, Nietzsche writes,

> If sociability and the arts still offer any delight, it is the kind of delight that slaves, *weary of their work*, devise for themselves. How frugal our educated people ... have become regarding 'joy'! How they are becoming increasingly suspicious of all joy! More and more, work enlists all good conscience on its side; the desire for joy already calls itself a 'need to recuperate' and is becoming ashamed of itself. 'One owes it to one's health' – that is what people say when they are *caught* on an excursion into the country. Soon we may well reach the point where people can no longer give in to the desire for a *vita contemplativa* (that is, taking a walk with ideas and friends) without self-contempt and a bad conscience. Well, formerly it was the other way around: it was work that was afflicted with the bad conscience. A person of good family used to *conceal* the fact that he was working if need compelled him to work. Slaves used to work, oppressed by the feeling that they were doing something contemptable.
>
> IV: 329, first and third emphasis mine

In this passage, Nietzsche offers a broad definition of "slaves" to include the "educated." How can he do that? It turns on the question of how our modern culture values work and turns "leisure" into a means for more work rather than remain an end in itself: in short, the perspective of slave morality transforms "leisure" into "need to recuperate." Another important question that Nietzsche seeks to examine is: how has it come to be that we moderns – as opposed to the ancients – feel *guilty* about our desire for joy and free time? Why do we need to make up an excuse – for example, walking is an exercise that improves our health and therefore increases our productivity while at work – for why we enjoy taking a leisurely stroll in nature?

The critique of work and the work ethic is found throughout Nietzsche's texts. In *The Will to Power* (1968) Nietzsche identifies "overwork," as "our modern vice" (I: 73) and in the *Genealogy of Morals* (1989) he refers to work as a "disgrace" (III: 9). Taking a walk with ideas, according to Nietzsche, requires a particular pace to everyday life, one that we should refer to as a leisurely lifestyle. Indeed, an ample amount of free time is the principal condition for the good life, because leisure makes possible the cultivation of the human being through the pursuit of aesthetic activity, what Foucault refers to as the practice of making your life a work of art. Nietzsche's text *Twilight of the Idols* (1997) was originally titled, "A Philosopher's Idleness." In the first draft of the text the opening epigram reads, "Idleness is the start of all philosophy. Is philosophy then – a sin?" One is tempted to reply on the behalf of modern individuals: "yes." Think of the platitude we have heard countless times: namely, the question, "What can you do with a philosophy degree?" The transformation of education from an end in itself (antiquity) to a means toward an end (modernity) is another aspect of what Nietzsche refers to as the triumph of slave morality. For the ancients, the notion that one should have an education in order to get a job would have been considered a degradation of the academy and an anathema to cultured sensibilities.

Elsewhere in the same aphorism, Nietzsche attacks the American "breathless haste with which they work," for "infecting" the old world. He laments that "now one is ashamed of resting, and prolonged reflection almost gives people a bad conscience." The uniquely American phrase, "rather do anything than nothing" is blamed by Nietzsche for creating a barrier to "all culture and good taste." About education in relation to leisure, Nietzsche (1997) argues that,

> The whole system of higher education in Germany has lost what is most important: the *end*, as well as the *means* to the end. The fact that education, *cultivation* is itself the goal – and *not* 'the Reich' ... this has been forgotten ... the 'main question': *which* profession, *which* calling? – Human beings of a higher type, if I may say so, don't like 'callings' ... They have time, they take their time, they don't think at all about getting 'done' – at the age of thirty, when it comes to higher culture, one is a beginner, a child.
>
> What the Germans are Missing: 5

Shall we consider Nietzsche an elitist on account of remarks like these that affirm what he calls human beings of a "higher type?" Is this what critics on the Left mean, in part, when they say that Nietzsche was an advocate of class domination? Critics of Nietzsche overlook his important critique of the work ethic when they claim that Nietzsche desired a political system based upon social domination (Appel 1999; Habermas 1990 [1985]). Rather, I agree with Emma Goldman, who argued that Nietzsche's "aristocracy was neither of birth nor of purse; it was of the spirit" (Moore 2004: 31). This means that consciousness cannot be reduced to one's economic status/class. One can be wealthy, and yet take the point of view of slave morality and *vice versa*. Goldman's interpretation can be seen in Nietzsche's emphasis on education as *cultivation* rather than as an instrument of the state, or as a means to get a job. There are passages in Nietzsche's texts, however, that lend themselves to an interpretation that frames Nietzsche in opposition to Marxist-influenced critical theory and politics. For example, in *Twilight of the Idols* Nietzsche (1997) writes,

> *The question of the working class* ... I just cannot see what one wants to do with the European worker now that one has made a question out of him .... What has one done? [One] has destroyed the very basis of the instincts thanks to which a worker becomes possible as a class, becomes possible for *himself*. One has made the worker eligible for military service, one has given him the right to unionize, the right to vote: so no wonder that today the worker already experiences his existence as a crisis ... But what does one *will*? If one wills to have slaves, one is a fool to educate them to be masters.
>
> Raids of an Untimely Man: 40

It is interesting to note that Nietzsche recognizes workers under a capitalist system for what they are: namely, unfree (slaves). In this way, Nietzsche penetrates the bourgeois ideology which claims that capitalism is made possible by the universal freedom of all individuals interacting in a marketplace. But does the passage above indicate that Nietzsche himself is *unequivocally* in favor of creating and reproducing a working class to serve a master class? Perhaps not.

In other texts, Nietzsche advocates for workers to become "masters" of themselves by throwing off the chains that form workers into a class. In a section called "the impossible class" within the text *Daybreak*, Nietzsche (2003) broadens his conception of slaves to include all those who do *not* resist work. Any individual who embraces hard work for the sake of being "productive" affirms the culture of slave morality, which is expressed through the priestly manipulation of the feeling of *ressentiment*. "Poor, happy and independent," writes Nietzsche (2003), "these things can go together; Poor, happy and a slave! – These things can also go together" (III: 206). How is it possible for a worker (slave) to be happy? Only when they "do not feel it in general a *disgrace* to be thus used, and *used up*, as part of a machine" (III: 206). The question then becomes, under what conditions are workers able and willing to resist work, that is to say, how can we shed light upon the conditions where workers *do* feel it a disgrace to be used up as a means to an end, or as a part of a machine? This would entail shaking off the cultural hegemony of slave morality and the work ethic in regard to the labor question. I return to this question below on my discussion of Marx.

This conception of slavery described by Nietzsche was a central theme of the radical plank of the labor movement in the early 19th century, when the transition to the wage system at the beginning of the Industrial Revolution was seen as a dire threat to freedom and independence. It was not until after the Civil War that more than half of all working people in the U.S. worked for a wage. Prior to that, most workers were either skilled artisans (master craftsmen) working in the guild system, or yeoman farmers, indentured servants or slaves. Radicalized artisans who opposed the demise of the guild system referred to factory work as "wage slavery" (Wilentz 2004). Today, receiving wages for work has been normalized. Working for wages or for a salary is no longer understood as being "used" because the inversion of values regarding work is more or less complete, save for important pockets of counter-cultural resistance to the global-capitalist system in movements like Occupy Wall Street and the struggle against austerity policies in Europe. In addition, large numbers of workers in the U.S. still report dissatisfaction with their jobs (Adams 2014), a phenomenon Nietzsche would understand quite well.

This is not the case, however, among those who claim to *represent* workers – in a manner that overlaps with the figure of the ascetic priest. For example, the AFL-CIO released an organizing video recently on their YouTube channel (AFL-CIO Now) that extols the virtues of work, claiming that work gives people "pride and purpose" ("America Wants to Work," 2012). The labor movement leadership in the U.S. today has virtually reversed its point of view since the late 19th century when May Day was established as a holiday by workers to celebrate the virtues of *less* work and *more* leisure through the fight for the 8-hour workday (Roediger and Foner 1989). Historians of the American Labor Movement have demonstrated that not only have rank and file workers had to struggle against employers in order to achieve their aims. They've also had to fight against their own leadership since the passage of the National Labor Relations Act of 1935. Often times, employers rely upon union officials to enforce work discipline upon their constituents, because labor leaders are obligated by labor contracts to serve as a second layer of management on top of workers (Cutler 2004).

Central to capitalist ideology is the notion that not only does work have intrinsic value; but that the accumulation of wealth, increases in wages and salary are all seen as indications of success in terms of an achievement of a "higher" station in life. Nietzsche (2003) rejects such notions and advocates a resistance to capitalism when he writes,

> To the devil with the belief that higher payment could lift from them [workers] the essence of their miserable condition – I mean their impersonal

> enslavement! To the devil with the idea of being persuaded that an enhancement of this impersonality within the mechanical operation of a *new society could transform the disgrace of slavery into a virtue*! To the devil with setting a price on oneself in exchange for which *one ceases to be a person and becomes part of a machine*! [...] What you ought to do, rather, is to hold up to them the counter-reckoning: how great a sum of inner value is thrown away in pursuit of this external goal! *But where is your inner value if you no longer know what it is to breathe freely...?*
>
> III: 206, emphasis mine

In the same passage, Nietzsche (2003) attacks socialism for being part of the same machinery that animates capitalism. Capitalism and socialism – while seemingly mortal enemies in the quest to define modernity – actually share important cultural values. What capitalism and socialism share is the affirmation of work, what Nietzsche refers to as the "disgrace" of transforming "slavery [work] into a virtue." Then what is to be done?

Nietzsche does not have a road map *per se*, but he does make it clear that any attempt to resist capitalism requires the rejection of the capitalist-work ethic and the self-overcoming of workers as a class. The continuation of the passage above reads,

> If on the other hand, you have always in your ears the flutings of the Socialist pied-pipers whose design is to enflame you with wild hopes? [...] Better to go abroad, to seek to become master in new ... regions of the world and above all become master over [yourself]; to keep moving from place to place for just as long as any sign of slavery seems to threaten [you]. All this rather than further endure this indecent servitude, rather than to go on becoming soured and malicious and conspiratorial! This would be the right attitude of mind: the workers of Europe ought henceforth to *declare themselves as a class a human impossibility* ... they ought to inaugurate within the European beehive an age of a great swarming-out such as has never been seen before ... to protest against the machine, against capital, and against the choice now threatening them of being compelled to become either the slave of the state or the slave of the party of disruption.
>
> III: 206, emphasis mine

Nietzsche has two problems with "socialism." The first issue is that Nietzsche is troubled by a politics of leveling down that he sees in some versions of socialism. In in *Twilight of the Idols*, he (1997) paraphrases this perspective as "'I'm a lowlife, you should be one too': on this logic revolutions are built" (Raids of an Untimely Man: 34). Nietzsche's criticism of the politics of leveling down resonates nicely with Marx's (1992b) critique of "crude communism," where he argues, "this [crude] communism ... negates the personality of man in every sphere ... the crude communist is merely the culmination of ... envy and [a] desire to level down on the basis of a *preconceived* minimum" (346). Furthermore, for both thinkers, it is not enough to focus on questions of distribution, what Hannah Arendt (1958) refers to as "the social question." It is crucially important to focus on the possibility of abundance in a post-scarcity environment, and both Nietzsche and Marx make precisely that point. Certain versions of socialism, on the other hand make an end out of the question of distribution and seeks the liberation *of* work, not the liberation *from* work (more on this below). Where does this analysis lead in terms of a relationship with Marx' writings?

5 Marx's Analysis of the Fight for Shorter Hours of Work

Nietzsche's talk of workers being cogs in the machine of the capitalist system certainly resonates with Marx, but Marx's discussion of the problem of work also echoes Nietzsche. The cultural distinction between leisure and work, including the contempt for the latter was, for *both* Nietzsche and Marx, rooted in the culture of antiquity and each of the thinkers, in their own way, approved of the ancient mode of drawing a line in the sand between work and leisure, where it was understood that leisure is to be valued over work (Aristotle 1984). In volume 3 of *Capital* Marx (1993a) describes the difference between work and leisure in the following way:

> The realm of freedom really begins only where labor determined by necessity and external expediency ends; *it lies by its very nature beyond the sphere of material production proper.* Just as the savage must wrestle with nature to satisfy his needs, to maintain and reproduce his life, so must civilized man ... This realm of natural necessity expands with his development, because his needs do too; but the productive forces to satisfy these needs expand at the same time. Freedom, in this sphere, can consist only in this, that socialized man ... governs the human metabolism with nature ... bringing it under their collective control instead of being dominated by it as a blind power; *accomplishing this with the least expenditure of energy* ... But this *always remains* a realm of necessity. The true realm of freedom, the development of human powers as an *end in itself,*

> begins beyond it ... *The reduction of the working day is the basic prerequisite.*
>
> 958–959, emphasis mine

First, Marx argues that capitalism is *already* moving toward the abolition of work through the relentless application of technology to the labor process. For example, in the *Grundrisse,* Marx (1993b) argues that the "historic destiny" of capitalism will be fulfilled when,

> the productive powers of labor, which capital incessantly whips onward with its mania for wealth, and of the sole conditions in which this mania can be realized, have flourished to the stage where the possession and preservation of general wealth require lesser labor time of society as a whole, and where the laboring society relates specifically to the process of its progressive reproduction, its reproduction in a constantly *greater abundance*; hence where *labor in which a human being does what a thing could do has ceased.*
>
> 325, emphasis mine

What alienated work activity would be left to overcome or transform, once we reach a point where machines replace human labor? One has only to look at the automobile and mining industries to see that Marx was correct in his assessment that within the capitalist mode of production, the tendency of development moves in the direction of replacing humans with robots in the workplace. This tendency pervades all modes of work under capitalism (Aronowitz and DiFazio 2010).

Secondly, Marx argues that it is the activity of the labor movement which ultimately drives the expansion of automation in the workplace. The "mania" for more wealth which drives the automation of the workplace is a complex dynamic according to Marx, where under particular conditions, automation as a practice *of* capitalists is understood as a response *to* workers who refuse work through the epic struggle for the eight-hour work day and the two-day weekend that took place during the second half of the 19th and early part of the 20th centuries. It is important to note that during the 19th century and early 20th century, workers in the U.S. worked six days a week and 10, 12, sometimes 14 hours a day. Historically, when workers have been successful in achieving shorter hours of work, not only do they receive more leisure time, which is an end-in-itself, but in addition, shorter hours of work drives down unemployment, which in turn puts upward pressure on wages. When the workers who have jobs dramatically reduce the hours that they work, it forces employers to hire new workers in order to tackle all the tasks that still need to be completed in the workplace. The workers who significantly reduce their time at work effectively create jobs for those who are unemployed. By working less, workers earn more in wages because low unemployment translates into higher wages. Thus the fight for less work is both a means and an end. It is a means to gain leverage for workers in their negotiations with capitalists and an end, in so far as less work translates into more leisure (McNeill 1886).

A feedback loop then emerges where capitalists eliminate expensive workers with machines, which drives up unemployment and pushes wages down, but then workers respond by fighting *once again* for shorter hours of work as a means to decrease unemployment and drive wages back up *once more,* and so on and so on. What I am describing here is not a utopian form of thinking. On the contrary the dynamic I am describing is based on actual events in the history of the U.S. labor movement (Roediger and Foner 1989). The struggle for less work and more leisure is what Marx meant, in concrete terms, by the phrase "class struggle." The conflict is over the length and intensity of the working day. This analysis constitutes the middle sections of *Capital Volume 1*, where Marx (1992a), argues,

> The shortening of the working day creates, to begin with, the subjective condition for the condensation of labor, i.e. it makes it possible for the worker to set more labor-power in motion within a given time. *As soon as that shortening becomes compulsory*, machinery becomes in the hands of the capitalist the objective means, systematically employed, for squeezing more out of labor in a given time. This happens in two ways: the speed of the machines is increased, and the same worker receives a greater quantity of machinery to supervise ... *Improved construction of the machinery is necessary* ... since the legal limitation of the working day *compels* the capitalist to exercise the strictest economy in the cost of production.
>
> 536, emphasis mine

In this passage, Marx demonstrates that when workers are successful in their attempts to institutionalize fewer hours of work – either through laws passed by governments or through labor contracts or both – then capitalists have an incentive to automate with "improved machinery." If capitalists are unable to force workers to work longer, harder and faster, then the only alternative to boost productivity in the workplace is to automate. Marx's analysis of this dynamic was based upon his studies of the history of the working day in both the U.K. and the U.S. According to Marx (1992a),

> Capital's tendency, *as soon as the prolongation of the hours of labor is once and for all forbidden*, is to *compensate* for this by ... converting every improvement in machinery into a more perfect means for soaking up labor-power. There cannot be the slightest doubt that this process must soon lead *once again* to a critical point at which a further reduction in the hours of labor will be inevitable ... The rapid advance of English industry between 1848 and the present time, i.e. during the period of the 10-hour working day, surpasses the advance made between 1833 and 1847, during the period of the 12-hour working day, by far more than the latter surpasses the advance made during the half century after the first introduction of the factory system, i.e. during the period of the unrestricted working day.
>
> 542, emphasis mine

Marx's empirical studies of the history of the working day demonstrate how advances in labor-saving technology exist in inverse relation to the successful fight for less work. As working hours *decrease*, advances in labor-saving technologies *increase*. The faster the rate at which working hours are forced down translates into relatively more productive and more efficient forms of labor-saving technologies. Labor-saving technology is most sophisticated and most productive within a context where the reduction of working hours increases in rapidity. The struggle for shorter hours of work also leads in the direction of material abundance and the creation of a post-scarcity society because of the enormous leap in levels of productivity made possible by labor-saving technology.

We see in the analysis provided by Marx in both the *Grundrisse* and in *Capital* that the fight for shorter hours of work transforms both the organization of the workplace and everyday life; indeed *life* becomes possible for the first time when workers enter the realm of freedom, what Marx (1992a) calls "life-time" as opposed to "work-time" (377). The only way that workers can resist the attempts by capitalists to shorten their life-span by working them to death is to resist work.

In the section known as the "fragment on machines" in the *Grundrisse*, Marx makes it clear that the sphere of aesthetic activity expands for the worker once s/he *steps to the side* of the production. According to Marx (1993b),

> Capital ... quite *unintentionally* ... reduces human labor, expenditure of energy to a minimum. *This will redound to the benefit of labor and its condition of emancipation* ... The surplus labor of the mass has ceased to be the condition for the development of general wealth, just as the non-labor of the few, for the development of the general powers of the human head.

> With that, production based upon exchange value breaks down ... *The free development of individualities*, and hence not the reduction of necessary labor time so as to posit surplus labor, but rather the general reduction of the necessary labor of society to a minimum, *which then corresponds to the* ***artistic*** *... development of the individuals in the time set free*, and with the means created, for all of them ... Wealth is not command over surplus labor time ... but rather *disposable time outside that needed in direct production*, for every individual and the whole society.
>
> 701, 705–706, emphasis mine

What Marx means by the phrase "surplus labor" is the amount of time workers spend creating value beyond the point at which employers break even, in terms of production costs. In other words, once workers produce enough commodities – objects or services – the value of which covers all the expenses of the capitalist(s), then the amount of work they continue to perform above and beyond that cut-off point becomes surplus, or profit for the company. The time before that cut-off point is referred to by Marx as "necessary labor time," which is the amount of time that is necessary for workers to produce enough value to allow the employer to cover all of the costs of production. It is in the interests of capitalists to reduce, as much as possible, the necessary labor time performed by workers, so that more profit can be created by workers during surplus labor time. It is up to workers themselves how this dynamic plays out, since whenever they are successful in achieving higher wages and shorter hours of work, they increase the amount of necessary labor time relative to surplus labor time, which in turn provides the capitalist with the incentive to further automate.

The irony is that in their drive to reduce necessary labor time, capitalists are creating – by accident – the conditions for a post-capitalist/post-work society because capitalism *depends* on the difference between necessary labor time and surplus labor time as the condition which make the system possible in the first place. But if capitalists continue to automate the workplace, there is the possibility of approaching the point where necessary labor time becomes so small a quantity that it has no significant relation to surplus labor time, which is what Marx is referring to in the passage when he says that "production based upon exchange value breaks down." The very existence of capitalism, according to Marx, depends upon the difference between necessary and surplus labor time, but in the elimination of workers from the production process, capitalists also eliminate the condition for creating such a distinction.

Lastly, in contrast to Durkheim, Marx (1993b) argues that, "labor cannot become play" (712). For Marx, the fight for shorter hours of work, and the widespread automation that capitalists deploy in response to recalcitrant workers opens up the door to a new way of life *after* work for all people, not just the lucky few. It remains a question for history whether or not we can step through that door. Here we see Marx lines up with Nietzsche and against Durkheim insofar as he affirms the aesthetic mode of existence over a moral (ascetic) mode of existence. What then of historical attempts at merging Marxist with Nietzschean theoretical perspectives and political practices?

6 The Death and Rebirth of Nietzschean-Marxist Theory

Today, the notion of a left-wing reading of Nietzsche is largely associated with the work of the French philosophers of the sixties including Michel Foucault and Gilles Deleuze (Rehmann 2007), who turned to Nietzsche in order to develop a particular kind of Left politics that can be, in part, understood as a version of Left-libertarianism that is perhaps best represented by the Anarchist readings of Nietzsche (Moore 2004). Less well-known is the appropriation of Nietzsche by Marxist intellectuals who were politically active in the Bolshevik Revolution, inside Lenin's inner circle before Lenin ostracized them. This unique collection of intellectuals was part of a much larger period of cultural flourishing and artistic freedom in the Soviet Union that marked the years between 1917 and 1924 (Steinberg 2002). Nietzsche was widely read and discussed by Russian intellectuals in the years leading up to the Bolshevik Revolution. Unfortunately, the freedom that was unleashed by the revolution was short-lived. As part of a larger crackdown upon countercultural and left-libertarian tendencies, Lenin ordered the removal of Nietzsche's books from libraries and union halls, and in some cases sanctioned the public burning of Nietzsche's texts (Rosenthal 1986). Most of the Nietzschean-Marxist intellectuals were eventually murdered by Stalin (Steinberg 2002; Kline 1969). These inimitable intellectuals – who Lenin disapprovingly dubbed the "God-builders" for their attempts to create a new proletarian culture after the death of God – included Stanislav Volski, real name Andrei Vladimirovich, (1890–1936), Anatoli Vasilyevich Lunacharsky (1875–1933), A.A. Bogdanov, real name Alexander Aleksandrovich Malinovski (1873–1928), V.A. Bazarov (1874–1939) whose real name was Vladimir Aleksandrovich Rudnev, and the famous working-class writer, and founder of Socialist Realism in literature, Maxim Gorky (1868–1936). Gorky's popular hobo characters – the "super tramp" (*über*-brodiag) and "super hobo" (*über*-bosiak) – were based upon Nietzsche's (1969) *Thus Spake Zarathustra*.

The phrase "God-building" was used to capture Luncharsky's notion that "Man does not need God, he himself is God. Man is a God to man. He does not need personal immortality since his immortality is the life of the species and hope is an eternal victory of life over dead elements, of higher forms over lower ones" (Williams 1980: 393). A main argument for the Nietzschean-Marxists was that any ideology, including orthodox Marxism, should be viewed as a useful political *myth* rather than true doctrine as pursued by the so-called "scientific" socialists of the day. The perspective also relied upon a utopian vision of the future, where workers would create their own distinctive culture, encompassing a new art and a new science grounded in art.

These peculiar revolutionary intellectuals sought to fuse Nietzsche with Marx for four interrelated reasons. First, they opposed the economic determinism and teleology that characterized the perspective of Georgi Plekhanov (1856–1918), considered the "father" of Russian Marxism and who was also the primary influence upon Lenin's theoretical orientation. Economic determinism was a larger problem that plagued the intellectual leaders of the Second International, including Karl Kautsky (1854–1938), who together with Plekhanov laid the groundwork for what we call today "orthodox Marxism," as opposed to the more open-ended, and less dogmatic form of critical theory advanced by the Frankfurt School (Aronowitz 1990). Years later, Stalin would use the determinist viewpoint as an excuse for his atrocities when he claimed that he was not to blame for the violence, as he was fulfilling his historic destiny. Nietzsche proved to be an antidote to economic determinism for the "God-builders" as they sought to emphasize the role of individuals making revolutionary change, much in the sense of Marx's claim that individuals and classes make history, although seldom as they choose.

Secondly, Nietzsche was appropriated to counter the fetishism of duty and obligation, notions that were at the core of the authoritarian discourse used by Lenin, Stalin and their followers. *Here the emphasis was upon viewing morality as a form of oppression rather than as the basis for social justice.* Christian morality in particular, with its negative view of the body and sexual desire, together with its patriarchal despotism was a main target for Nietzschean-Marxists, for if a revolution focused only upon the transfer of the ownership of the means of production at the expense of these oppressive cultural factors, then such a revolution was doomed to fail. Bogdanov and Bazarov in particular were concerned with liberating the individual from coercive norms that create oppressive forms of morality. They made a distinction between "coercive norms," which are exempt from criticism and compel the individual without reason (authoritarianism) and "expediency norms," which in the words of Bazarov are instrumental and serve as the "means for attaining the joys of life" (Kline 1969: 180). Nietzsche's influence can be seen in Bazarov's lashing out against the "sodden, dull, self-satisfied moral systems through which life appears in the most desolate light ... Life, it may be, appears a hopelessly vulgar thing precisely because it is viewed through the dim glass of moral norms ... To seize life's mystery, one must revolt against norms as such" (Kline 1969: 180). Nietzsche would gain popularity again in the 1960s counterculture in the West for much the same reason. In short, Nietzsche was appropriated as an ally against the authoritarianism that would ultimately betray the promise of the Bolshevik Revolution.

Third, almost all of the Nietzschean-Marxists were sympathetic to syndicalism in opposition to the socialists who excluded the anarcho-syndicalists from membership in the Second International. The syndicalist position emphasizes the use of the strike weapon, with a focus upon waging class struggle at the point of production through worker self-activity rather than seeking power through parliamentary means, which was the main strategy of the Social Democrats in both Germany and Russia, including Lenin himself. The syndicalist view is that any state seeking to represent the interests of workers will eventually end up seeking its own interests and/or the interests of a ruling elite at the expense of workers. This was also the view of Nietzsche (2003: III, 206). The Nietzschean-Marxists took Nietzsche's demand for workers to "declare themselves as a class a human possibility" to be an integral component of his larger project of creating the cultural figure of the "overman" who would signal the overcoming of the last man, who is understood as a bridge to a better form of life beyond both the repressive morality (authoritarianism) of Christianity and the pervasive nihilism that follows from the death of God and the rise of science. The Nietzschean-Marxist interpretation of Nietzsche's "overman" included overcoming the bourgeois work ethic as a cornerstone of a new, post-revolutionary culture.

The split between the Second International and the anarcho-syndicalists eventually manifested itself as the distinction between *authoritarian* socialism and *libertarian* syndicalism respectively. Anarcho-syndicalism was at the peak of its influence in 1907, when leaders of the movement held their international meetings in Paris of that year. It was shortly after that when Plekhanov and later Lenin would view syndicalism as the main opposition to their hegemony over the European Left (Williams 1980). This split between socialists and syndicalists also resulted – tragically – in the murder of Rosa Luxemburg, an act that was ordered by Friedrich Ebert, the leader of the Social Democratic Party of Germany (SPD). Ebert ordered the fascist group known as the Freikorps to carry out the assasination. The Freikorps would later provide the basis for the rise of Hitler and the Nazi party (Theweleit 1987). In spite of Kautsky's split from Lenin over the tactics of that latter in the invasion of Georgia, the German SPD was no less authoritarian than the Bolsheviks. Authoritarianism and economic determinism saturated the perspectives of both

German and Russian versions of socialism in the early years of the 20th century, evidenced by the fact that both sought the destruction of anarcho-syndicalism (see the chapter by Kristin Lawler in this volume for more on this particular issue).

Lastly, the Nietzschean-Marxists were major players in the debate over the role of culture and art in revolutionary strategies. The main split here was between Bogdanov, who argued that "Art … is a most powerful weapon for the organization of collective forces and, in a class society, of class forces," and Trotsky who argued that the "place of art is in the rear of the historic advance" of the revolution (McClelland 1980). The former view saw the need for immediate and dramatic cultural changes in order for the proletariat to develop the form of consciousness needed for a successful revolution. Such a new culture was necessary for individuals to break out of the authoritarianism and destructive resentment that often plague the culture of revolutionary movements. The second view, that of Trotsky, was that a massive build-up of the economy and industrial infrastructure was the first priority for the revolution, and unfortunately this entailed the hierarchical rationalization of the production process as a means toward the ultimate end of a successful political revolution. This perspective became known as "war communism," and it demanded extreme sacrifices without regard for the welfare of workers (McClelland 1980). For Trotsky and his followers in the race to industrialize the Soviet Union, a focus on art and the development of a proletarian culture seemed a luxury that revolutionaries could not afford. Instead, both Trotsky and Lenin sought to make use of the authoritarian-capitalist methods of factory production that were based upon Frederick Winslow Taylor's "scientific management," which viewed workers as mere instruments in the process of production (Braverman 1974; Traub 1978). This perspective was at odds with Lunacharsky's view that a broad, liberal arts educational program – rather than a narrow vocational curriculum – was crucial to the successful process of building the foundations for a socialist society. One wonders how different things would have been in the Soviet Union – indeed for the world itself – if the Nietzschean-Marxists had not perished in the Gulags and the Holocaust. As I have sought to reveal, the repression of workers was advocated by both conventional sociologists like Durkheim – who himself was a social democrat of sorts – and orthodox Marxist revolutionaries like Trotsky and Lenin during the early years of the 20th century. This similarity is often obscured by the ways in which professional sociologists are trained, especially those trained in the United States. Conventional training in professional sociology in the U.S. tends to polarize Durkheim and orthodox Marxism, but in terms of politics, the two converge around the development of Social Democracy.

Another key problem for the Nietzschean-Marxists was the question of science and its relation to power on the one hand, and resistance to domination on the other. The labor question once again provides the framework for the critical analysis of science. After the earliest attempt to merge Marx with Nietzsche in Russia failed when Stalin purged the Nietzschean-Marxists from the inner circle of Bolshevik intellectuals (Steinberg 2002), and the Nazi Party vanquished the German Left, Nietzsche's presence as a political philosopher for the Left all but disappeared. The intellectual tradition remained alive only among a few isolated enclaves, including a small portion of the diaspora of Jewish intellectuals, including most importantly, the key figures of the Institute for Social Research in Frankfurt, Germany, or as they are more commonly known, the Frankfurt School of Critical Theory. Important members included Max Horkheimer, Theodor Adorno, and Herbert Marcuse, who was a student of Martin Heidegger prior to Heidegger's joining the Nazi Party. There were also important figures who were loosely affiliated with the Institute for Social Research, like Walter Benjamin, Siegfried Kracauer, and especially Ernst Bloch (1986 [1938]), who, together with Adorno, was perhaps the most ardent defender of Nietzsche among the diasporic, intellectual-Left during the 1930s and 1940s. Other important figures in the Frankfurt School included Friedrich Pollock, Leo Lowenthal, Otto Kirchheimer and Franz Leopold Neumann.[15] With the exception of Walter Benjamin, who committed suicide in France while trying to elude the Gestapo, most of the members of the Frankfurt school were able to escape the Nazi's by fleeing to the United States. The Frankfurt School would eventually earn notoriety among European intellectuals after the war for their creative articulation of the works of Marx, Nietzsche, Weber, Freud and Lukács that became their hallmark for merging sociology with philosophy. The interdisciplinary endeavor that we call critical theory today has its roots in the innovative work of the Frankfurt School.[16]

There were also important Left-philosophers who fought against the Nazi's as members of the French Resistance to the Vichy regime during the war, including the philosopher of science, Georges Canguilhem – Michel Foucault's primary mentor[17] – Georges Bataille, and Henri Lefebvre, the most prominent

15 For an excellent history of the Frankfurt School and their efforts to create a new research paradigm that merged sociology with philosophy, see Martin Jay's *Dialectical Imagination* (1996).

16 Nietzsche's work has since provided opportunities to expand critical theory well beyond the Marx–Nietzsche–Freud nexus into areas like poststructurualism, postcolonial theory, critical race theory, feminist and queer theory.

17 In the introduction to Canguilhem's (1991 [1966]) *The Normal and the Pathological*, Foucault writes, "Nietzsche said that truth was the most profound lie. Canguilhem, who is at

Marxist philosopher in France. When Lefebvre arrived at the Sorbonne in the 1920s to study philosophy, he joined a proto-existentialist study group with other young radicals with the aim of conducting close readings of Nietzsche's texts, an endeavor that eventually led him to reconfigure the base/superstructure model in Marxist theory that had been the subject of serious criticism among Western Marxists due to Stalin's attempt to codify "dialectical materialism" as a "science of the history of society" that was modeled upon the then-perceived level of accuracy and certainty achieved in the natural sciences. This kind of conceptual maneuver that Stalin referred to as the "world outlook of the Marxist-Leninist Party" made "dialectical materialism" a closed theoretical system and a dogma.[18] Lefebvre's first book on Nietzsche was published in 1939

once close to and far away from Nietzsche, would say perhaps that on the enormous calendar of life, it is the most recent error; he would say that the true-false division and the value accorded truth constitute the most singular way of living which could have been invented by a life which, from its furthermost origin, carried the eventuality of error within itself. Error for Canguilhem is the permanent chance around which the history of life and that of men develops" (22–23). The connection to Nietzsche can be found in aphorism 4,the section titled, "The Prejudices of the Philosophers" in *Beyond Good and Evil*, where Nietzsche (1966 [1886]) remarks, "we are fundamentally inclined to claim that the falsest of judgments (which include the synthetic judgments *a priori*) are the most indispensable for us; that without accepting the fictions of logic, without measuring reality against the purely invented world of the unconditional and self-identical, without a constant falsification of the world by means of numbers, man could not live – that renouncing false judgments would mean renouncing life and a denial of life. To recognize untruth as a condition of life – that certainly means resisting accustomed value feelings in a dangerous way; and a philosophy that risks this would by that token alone place itself beyond good and evil" (12).

18 Stalin argued that "scientific socialism" would provide a solid foundation for an error-free approach to policy decisions, since it was claimed that the Communist Party had achieved a "scientific" understanding of the "laws of motion" – akin to gravity in physics – in human history and society. In this way, Stalin could claim that all his decisions were determined by abstract forces that shape history – destiny, if you will. Furthermore, if consciousness could be explained in terms of a reflection theory – where ideas and culture are reduced to products of material determinants and structural location in the economy – then the CP could claim that they understood the conditions that made bourgeois culture "false," and therefore lacking in value relative to the "true" perspective of the CP. Of course, Marx himself was not a determinist, nor a positivist. Instead, he spoke of "tendencies" in capitalist development rather than strict "laws of motion" and more importantly, in texts like the *18th Brumaire of Louis Bonaparte*, he argues that people, rather than abstract forces, make history. Although the outcomes of attempts to shape history are always indeterminate. In short, Marx emphasized accidents and contingencies in human history – just as Nietzsche did – rather than necessity and determinism, ala orthodox Marxism. In his letter to Joseph Bloch in 1890, Engels (1978 [1890]) argued "history is made in such a way that the final result always arises from many individual wills, of which each again has been made what it is by a host of particular conditions of life. Thus, there are innumerable

and represents one of the best early attempts at fusing Marx with Nietzsche as a means to drive a wedge between Stalin's dogma and Marx's own texts.[19] It was written and published simultaneously with another book titled *Dialectical Materialism*, which was an explicit attack upon Stalin's interpretation of historical materialism. Lefebvre intended to provoke the Communist Party by giving his book the same title as Stalin's previously published text.

Lefebvre (2014 [1947, 1981]) was also among the first intellectuals in France to critically engage the work of Heidegger in his 3-volume masterpiece, *The Critique of Everyday Life*, a work which spanned the years between 1947 and 1981. After being introduced to Heidegger by Jean Wahl, Lefebvre's project of articulating Heidegger's ontological investigations into the conditions which give rise to the "inauthentic" life with Marx's theory of alienation emerged from his reading of *Being and Time*, especially the sections where Heidegger (1996 [1927]) offers a phenomenological treatment of the "dullness" everyday life, a topic that had long been neglected by Western philosophers (339).[20] Lefebvre was drawn to Heidegger's analysis of everyday life in order to further reconfigure the theoretical framework of historical materialism that he began with his reading of Nietzsche. He did so by arguing that everyday life should be understood not as a subsystem within the social system – ala Talcott Parsons' structural functionalism – but as the base in the mode of production. In addition to his critique of Parsons' sociology, Lefebvre directed his intervention once more against the crude base/superstructure model in orthodox Marxism that views the superstructure in terms of a mechanistic reflection theory, where the forces and relations of production in the economic base determine

---

intersecting forces, and infinite series of parallelograms of forces which give rise to one resultant – the historical event. This may again itself be viewed as the product of a power which works as a whole, *unconsciously* and without volition. For what each individual wills is obstructed by everyone else, and what emerges is something that no one willed" (761).

19 In Lefebvre's (1991 [1974]) words, his project was one of conducting a "confrontation between the most powerful of 'syntheses' – that of Hegel – and its radical critique; this critique is rooted on the one hand in social practice (Marx), and on the other hand in art, poetry, music and drama (Nietzsche) – and rooted, too, in both cases, in the (material) body" (406).

20 The key section in Heidegger (1996 [1927]) is chapter IV of Division Two titled, "Temporality and Everydayness." Heidegger uses the term "everydayness" to reveal the conditions where *Dasein* (Being-with-others) develops an "inauthentic" form of existence by becoming lost in the "They" – the indeterminate "Man." Authenticity, on the other hand, is a way of being-in-the-world where one is not lost in the "neuter" of the "They-self." Lucien Goldmann has demonstrated that Heidegger's notion of inauthenticity owes much to Lukács concept of reification in *History and Class Consciousness*, but unlike Heidegger, Lefebvre had not read Lukács before developing his own concept of everyday life.

the form and content of the political and cultural institutions in the superstructure. "Daily life cannot be defined as a 'sub-system' within a larger system," writes Lefebvre (2014 [1947, 1981]),

> On the contrary: it is the 'base' from which the mode of production endeavors to constitute itself as a system, by programming the base. Thus, we are not dealing with the self-regulation of a closed totality. The programming of daily life has powerful means at its disposal: it contains an element of luck, but it holds the initiative, has the impetus at the 'base' that makes the edifice totter. Whatever happens, *alterations in daily life will remain the criterion of change.*
>
> 717, emphasis mine

Rather than understanding everyday life as part of the superstructure that reflects the economic base, or as a layer between the state and the economic infrastructure – i.e. "civil society" – for Lefebvre, everyday life – here understood in terms of alienation – is the basic mode of being in capitalist and state socialist societies. The experience of alienation is not exclusive to the workplace; in saturates all spheres of social life. Appropriating Heidegger's ontological position, Lefebvre argued that the lived experience in the social world is *constituted* by alienation, but unlike Heidegger, Lefebvre relies upon an historical and sociological analysis rather that an ontological explanation of the phenomenon when he argues that alienation is made possible by the colonization of everyday life ("programming") by the state and by economic relations. Such programming is the primary means by which monopoly, or "late" capitalism is reproduced.

For Lefebvre, what this means is that if we do not change the social and cultural forms of everyday life, revolution is relatively meaningless; merely changing the ownership of the means of production, as in the case of the Soviet Union, is not enough. In other words, any attempt at emancipatory change must make its intervention in the sphere of everyday life, which is why Lefebvre argued that alienation persisted inside the state-socialist countries, the so-called "really existing" socialist societies like the USSR, where workers remained under the yoke of oppression after the revolution.[21] The most significant avenues for radically

21 A good example of this problem is Lenin's application of the capitalist principles of scientific management – developed by the American engineer Frederick Winslow Taylor as a means to more thoroughly control and discipline workers – to the factories inside the USSR. A change in the ownership of the means of production did nothing to change everyday life of workers in the USSR, because work in Soviet factories was just as oppressive and alienating as work inside the factories of the capitalist economies. At one point,

transfiguring everyday life are (1) the significant reduction – if not elimination – of the amount of time we spend working so that we can engages in artistic activities, (2) the abolition of the patriarchal-authoritarian family, and (3) the liberation of sexuality. In order to achieve these ends, according to Lefebvre, we need a critical reflection upon the cultural conditions that escape the inquiries of orthodox Marxism. In the Soviet Union under Stalin, repetitive everyday life – authoritarianism, monotony and routine at work and outside of work – was preserved, and desire was once again relegated to dream work, since life under such conditions life is bereft of pleasure. "The full-blown conception of the revolution," writes Lefebvre (1991 [1974]), "has to compete with a variety of corruptions, among them economistic and productivistic interpretations and *versions founded on the work ethic*. The maximal version derives directly from Marx and his project of a total revolution entailing the end of the state, of the nation, of the family ... and to the central idea of an *ever-greater automation of the productive process* and the related notion of the production of a space that is different" (392, emphasis mine). The production of a different social space would entail the expansion of artistic activities like "poetry and music" (Lefebvre 1991 [1974]: 392). Hence, Lefebvre's turn toward Nietzsche. It was for these reasons that Lefebvre was expelled from the French Communist Party in 1958, an event that he later described as "self-expulsion" on the grounds of "ideological deviations" from the party line.

Lenin was opposed to Taylorism – which was characterized by stop-motion studies of the worker's body that approached the human body as an instrument to be manipulated by scientific experiments – but he later changed his mind. There was an important debate about scientific management that took place in the Soviet Union between those who were in favor of its implementation, led by Alexi Gastev, and a group that called itself the "Time League" that opposed such implementation. While Gastev and his followers attempted to make the case that the implementation of scientific management was in the "objective" interests of Soviet workers, the Time League argued instead that unpleasant work should be automated (Heideman 2015). Thus, the question was where to focus the application of scientific knowledge: upon the human body – understood as a machine of sorts – or upon the designs and creations of machines that would free workers from being themselves interpellated as machines. The Time League took its perspective from Marx's (1993b [1858]) famous passage on the "Fragment of Machines" in the *Grundrisse* (701–714), where he argues the automation of work – which is *already* taking place under capitalist conditions – should be encouraged so that workers can be liberated from work and have more time for artistic activities. In order for workers to take advantage of such developments, Marx (1993a: 959) argued that a coherent strategy for the reduction of the working day was the basic prerequisite. In other words, the fight for shorter hours of work must be continuous driving force that compels the capitalist class to further automate the production process to the point at which the conditions for a fully-automated post-capitalist society becomes possible. I covered this issue in more detail in a part three of this essay.

One of Lefebvre's (1991 [1974]) central theoretical developments that was influenced by Nietzsche was his notion of an "Anti-Logos," the particular practices that resist the domination by the Logos: defined here as technocratic knowledge that achieves domination through the scientific manipulation and systematization of everything. Logos provides the content for the "programming" of everyday life (717). "On the side of Logos," writes Lefebvre (1991 [1974]), "is rationality, constantly being refined and constantly asserting itself in the shape of organizational forms ... On this side of things are ranged the forces that aspire to dominate and control space: business and the state ... the family, 'the establishment,' ... corporate and constituted bodies of all kinds" (392).[22] On the other hand,

> thanks to the potential energies of a variety of groups capable of diverting homogenized space to their own purposes, a *theatricalized or dramatized* space is liable to rise. Space is liable to be *eroticized and restored to ambiguity*, to the common birthplace of needs and desires, by means of music, by means of differential systems and valorizations which overwhelm the strict localizations of needs and desires in spaces specialized either physiologically (sexuality) or socially (places set aside, supposedly, for pleasure). An unusual struggle, sometimes furious, sometimes more low-key, takes place between the Logos and the Anti-Logos, these terms being taken in their broadest possible sense – the sense in which Nietzsche takes them.
>
> 391, emphasis mine

An example of the eroticization of social space for the Lefebvre is the festival, especially the music festival. The festival, "is the day of excess. Anything goes ... [it is an] enormous orgy of eating and drinking – with no limits, no rules ... the

22 These passages are drawn from Lefebvre's (1991) *Production of Space*, which has had a tremendous influence on the fields of geography and urban studies. Lefebvre examines how space is never simply "there." Rather, space is socially produced, and the spatial relations that are developed under capitalist conditions eventually take on a life of their own, so to speak, which in turn, contributes to the reproduction of the social relations of domination; in other words, a social form of inertia is made possible by habitual activities among the masses that compel the individual along, a phenomenon that Heidegger refers to as the loss of Dasein into the abstract "They." This aspect of Lefebvre's work is well-known and much emulated in urban studies and geography (see the work of David Harvey as one such example). I do not intend to discuss Lefebvre's influence on these fields, as much has already been done in this regard. Rather, I focus upon how Nietzsche's influence on Lefebvre has yet to be adequately explored by American-trained urbanists, geographers, political theorists and sociologists.

festivities would end in scuffles and orgies" (2014 [1947, 1981]: 222). Lefebvre refers to such festivals as "moments" that intervene and transform the dullness of everyday life, because the festival "[gives] rein to all the desires which had been pent up by collective discipline and the necessities of everyday work" (2014 [1947, 1981]: 222). The emphasis on the festival in Lefebvre is appropriated in part, from a reading of Francois Rabelais' (2006 [1564]) novel *Gargantua and Pantagruel*, but also from Nietzsche's (1967 [1872]) *Birth of Tragedy*, where Nietzsche has much to say about aesthetics and music in the context of the Dionysian festival and its relationship to the "nausea" experienced in everyday life.

Although Jean-Paul Sartre may have enjoyed more international fame as a radical French Philosopher, it was Lefebvre, along with Canguilhem and Georges Bataille, who did the most to integrate the works of Nietzsche and Heidegger with the concerns of the intellectuals on the French Left. Lefebvre was a harsh critic of Sartre's existentialist reading of Heidegger, leading Sartre (1992 [1943]) himself to later modify, if not abandon his humanist-existentialist reading of Heidegger that defined his early work, *Being and Nothingness*. Sartre's later works that tempered existentialism with historical materialism, including *Search for a Method* (1968 [1957]) and the *Critique of Dialectical Reason* (2004 [1960]) were made possible, in part, by Lefebvre's influence. In addition, Lefebvre's (2009 [1940]) blistering critique of Soviet Marxism shared the concerns of the Frankfurt School that Stalin posed a serious threat to the aims of the independent Left in Europe and that certain elements of bourgeois culture under attack in the Soviet Union were worth defending. For Lefebvre, critical engagement with the thought of Nietzsche and Heidegger was necessary in order to ensure that Marxist theory did not stagnate and ossify into an orthodoxy like that of Plekhanov, Karl Kautsky and the leaders of the Second International. What we today refer to as "Western Marxism" – some might even say a "postmodern Marxism" – is the collective attempt to preserve Marxist theory as an *open framework*, able to unfold in different directions as historical changes in cultural and political conditions transform the context for critique (Carver 1998; Ryan 1982). It is precisely here that an engagement with Nietzsche is most fruitful, as his is among the most anti-systematic forms of thought in the Western philosophical tradition.

While much has been said about Lefebvre's problematic "humanism" by the Althusserian school, it would be a mistake to view Althusser's (2006 [1965]) contribution to the deconstruction of the "humanist" subject as closer to the concerns of the poststructuralists than Lefebvre's work. Unlike Althusser, Lefebvre was not a systematic thinker, and because Lefebvre was much more critical of an adherence to "scientific truth" than the structuralists of the

Althusserian school, his work remains perhaps more compatible with most of the aims of poststructuralism. For example, a favorite text of Lefebvre's was Nietzsche's (1979 [1873]) essay "On the Truth and Lies in a Nonmoral Sense." According to Lefebvre (1991 [1974]),

> Let us now consider a seminal text of Nietzsche's on language, written in 1873 ... In Nietzschean thought ... meta- is understood in a very radical manner ... words as such are already metaphoric and metonymic for Nietzsche ... Words themselves go beyond the immediate, beyond the perceptible – that is to say, beyond the chaos of sense perceptions and stimuli ... The words of ... language are simply metaphors for things. The concept arises from an identification of things which are not identical – i.e. form metonymy. We take language for an instrument of veracity and a structure of accumulated truths. In reality, according to Nietzsche, it is a 'mobile army of metaphors, metonyms, and anthropomorphisms – in short, a sum of human relations, which have been enhanced, transposed, and embellished poetically and rhetorically, and which after long use seem firm, canonical, and obligatory to a people' ... A society is a space and an architecture of concepts, forms and laws whose abstract truth is imposed on the reality of the senses, of bodies, of wishes and desires. (138–139)

What is at stake here, with the phenomena of metaphor and metonymy is that a gap exists between the sign and the signified, a gap which can become the terrain of class struggle, where the struggle is a cultural struggle over meaning. Lefebvre's appropriation of Marx's analyses of "abstract labor" and the critique of exchange value is here grafted onto Nietzsche's analysis of language in order to develop a new theory of power. "The shift from one to the other [sign and signified]," writes Lefebvre (1991 [1974]), "seems simple enough, and it is easy for someone who has the words to feel that they possess the things those words refer to. And, indeed, they do possess them up to a certain point – a terrible point" (135). Why terror according to Lefebvre?

> As a vain yet also effective trace, the sign has the power of destruction because it has the power of abstraction – and thus also the power to construct a new world different from nature's initial one. Herein lies the secret of the Logos as foundation of all power and all authority; hence too the growth in Europe of knowledge and technology, industry and imperialism. (135)

Lefebvre's work demonstrates a unique articulation of Marxist and poststructuralist theory because he was a careful reader of both Marx and Nietzsche.[23] As was the case with the Frankfurt School, the contributions that Bataille, Canguilhem and Lefebvre made to critical theory would not gain widespread recognition until after the war, when their work would have an enormous influence on the French critical theory of the sixties, including poststructuralism. The critique of "scientific socialism" by Nietzschean-Marxist critics like Lefebvre eventually led to a critical reflection upon science itself. The Frankfurt School were among the first to launch such an endeavor.

Fortunately for us today, the members of the Frankfurt School kept very busy while in exile during the war years, producing some of most creative and influential works of critical scholarship that revealed Nietzsche's unique significance for political and social theory. Horkheimer and Adorno's (2002 [1944]) now famous *Dialectic of Enlightenment*, written in the mid-1940s while in exile in Southern California, relied upon Nietzsche in order to argue that the emancipatory aims of the Enlightenment were ironically betrayed by the very means that were intended to realize them: namely, science. For Nietzsche, science had yet to free itself from moral judgments that it inherited from

23 It is ironic that the Marxist geographer David Harvey (1991), one of Lefebvre's principle champions, declared war on the poststructuralists on the grounds that the move to poststructuralist and postmodern theory entails an abandonment of the critique of capitalism. We now know that this was never the case, as Derrida (1994 [1993]), Deleuze (1995) and Foucault made it clear that they never jettisoned Marxist theory. Rather, they grafted the work of other theorists onto it. Perhaps Foucault (1991 [1981]) said it best when he claimed "For many of us young intellectuals, an interest in Nietzsche or Bataille didn't represent a distancing of oneself from Marxism or communism. Rather, it was almost the only path leading to what we, of course, thought could be expected of communism" (50–51). Harvey (1991), on the other hand, concurs with Habermas that the poststructuralists should be understood as "defeatists" and "relativists" because of their critique of language and of the Enlightenment notions of universality as well as any "unified representation of the world" (52). As an alternative to Lefebvre's and the poststructuralist emphasis on the relationship between language and domination, Harvey takes sides with Habermas' view of language where, "the dialogical qualities of human communication in which the speaker and hearer [are engaged] are *necessarily oriented to the task of reciprocal understanding*. Out of this, Habermas argues, consensual and normative statements do arise, thus grounding the role of universalizing reason in daily life" (52, emphasis mine). Precisely, but Harvey misses the point. Habermas' (1990 [1985]) project still relies – just like the Enlightenment figures he defends – upon *coercing* individuals to recognize one another through the imposition of norms and morality. But as Schotten (2019) convincingly argues, "morality is never emancipatory." Hence the value of Nietzsche for any critical theory that has emancipatory aims. For more on this issue, see the chapter by Heike Schotten in this volume. For a different version of the Marxist criticism of Nietzsche, see the chapter by Ishay Landa in this volume.

Christianity. The asceticism of Christian morality, which for Nietzsche contains a profound hostility towards life, remains unconscious in the scientific world view. "Residues of Christian value judgments are found everywhere in ... positivistic systems" (1968: 7). For the Frankfurt School this phenomenon – hostility toward life – has disastrous potential. As Nietzsche (1989) argues,

> an ascetic life is a self-contradiction: here rules a *ressentiment* without equal, that of an insatiable instinct and *power-will that wants to become master not over something in life but over life itself*, over its most profound, powerful, and basic conditions: here an attempt is made to employ force to block up the wells of force.
>
> 118, second emphasis mine

It was Nietzsche's argument that a certain "power-will ... wants to become master over life itself," combined with his inquiry into the "will to truth" as a "concealed will to death" that inspired Horkheimer and Adorno (2002 [1944]) to evaluate the discontinuity between the aims and the results of the Enlightenment. How was it possible that the Enlightenment carried its opposite within it?

The Frankfurt School's Nietzschean analysis of the relationship between science and domination has yet to be given full consideration within the field of Science and Technology Studies (STS), an interdisciplinary field of inquiry that has its roots in sociology.[24] Science and Technology Studies, as a distinct field of sociological inquiry, arose, in part, out of Robert Merton's, "sociology of science" (1973, 1970 [1938]) which partially explains the absence of Nietzsche's influence, since Nietzsche is ignored by professional sociologists in the United States (Antonio 1995) who to this day remain loyal to Merton's (1963) insistence that sociological inquiries must not pursue research questions that are informed by any questions which go beyond the "middle range"; the argument being that research must be conducted along the lines of "verifiable" data, excluding, by definition, any form of speculative thought that might point to production in general or social relations taken as a whole.[25] According to Adorno

24 For more on the relationship between Nietzsche and the field of Science Studies, see Payne (2018).

25 See also Aronowitz (1988), who claims that "because of his [Merton's] invocation that propositions refer to an empirical frame of reference subject to confirmation or information, we are advised to say nothing of such phenomena as ... the totality of social structures" (275). The notion of "totality" here is not something static, nor something "outside" or "above" individuals as understood by Durkheimian "realists." Rather, the critical-Marxist notion of "totality" of the whole is meant to refer to an historical-cultural context

(1976), however, sociology "does not have unqualified data at its disposal but only such data as are structured through the context of societal totality" (106).[26] Adorno's perspective here is considerably influenced by Nietzsche's analyses of the intimate relationship between knowledge and power and his claim that there are not facts *per se*, only interpretations. "Against positivism which halts at phenomena – 'There are only facts' – I would say: No, facts is precisely what there is not, only interpretations. We cannot establish any fact 'it itself': perhaps it is folly to want to do such a thing … In so far as the word 'knowledge has any meaning, the world is knowable; but it is interpretable otherwise, it has no meaning behind it, but countless meanings. – 'Perspectivalism.' It is our needs that interpret the world" (Nietzsche 1968: 265). Needs, of course, are also socially mediated.

Equally important for Adorno, such an attitude as that taken by Merton reduces the professional sociologist to a "salaried employee" as opposed to the independent scholar (Adorno 2000 [1968]: 21). In conventional sociology today, methodological procedures take precedence over substantive issues and the

---

that makes it possible for particular phenomena to appear, what Heidegger (1977) refers to as a "mode of revealing." For example, as Aronowitz (1988) argues, "a worker operating a drill press makes a hole, but it must be pointed out that the drill press is a design that presupposes a division of labor marked by increased specialization" (188). It is also important to note that Merton's sociology of science did not aim to explain the possibility of the truth-content of scientific knowledge, only the organization of the social institutions external to it. Such an aim restricts itself to explaining how false claims are possible. In Merton's framework, sociology is relegated to a supplementary role: the task is to explain how social conditions get in the way of or distort particular scientific pursuits. Since "truth" is understood to simply exist – as opposed to it being produced – only false claims need to be explained, and for Merton, the job of the sociology of science is to specify what conditions create the best external (social) environment for the pursuit of science free from external constraint.

26 Adorno (1976) argues further that "Societal totality can no more be detached from life, form the co-operation and the antagonism of its elements than can an element be understood merely as it functions without insight into the whole which has its source in the motion of the individual himself. System and individual entity are reciprocal and can only be apprehended in their reciprocity. Even those enclaves, survivals from previous societies, the favorites of a sociology … become what they are only in relation to the dominant totality from which they deviate. This is presumably under-estimated in the present most popular conception, that of middle-range theory" (107). Adorno's concept of "totality" differs from that of Hegel, which rightfully came under criticism by poststructuralists. Rather, Adorno's project is a "negative" dialectics that does not reify the "presence" of the whole, but like Derrida, emphasizes the "absent-presence" of Being. As Rose (2014 [1978]) argues, Adorno "stressed the necessity of understanding social phenomena form the perspective of 'totality,' yet denied the possibility of ever grasping the 'totality'" (10). See Adorno (2007 [1966]).

relevance of the subject matter. What this means for Adorno is that in the research conducted by conventional sociologists we tend to learn more about the measuring instruments than we do about substantive issues and the objects under consideration. "This has given rise," writes Adorno (2000 [1968]) "to the countless studies which simply apply any existing instruments of research over and over again, or which apply the same instruments to different problems or areas of subject matter; and then, if all really goes well, they may refine or modify the research instrument" (20). Under these conditions, professional sociologists become mere technicians available for hire, applying their research methods to any topic that is chosen by powerful institutional actors that use the accumulation of knowledge to further their particular interests. What then is the alternative for Adorno? Following Nietzsche's lead, Adorno seeks to pursue a different kind of sociology, one that can rescue an aesthetic mode of experience from the norms of everyday life that habituate us to routine. Such a meta-critique involves reflection upon the procedures of positivism where the concept of experience is placed in the extreme foreground – "halting before the facts" – as Nietzsche would say. "On the one hand ... experience of something new, which has not existed before, is hardly possible in the world in which we live," writes Adorno. On the other hand, "science, by the system of rules it imposes on knowledge, no longer permits such experience. It might be said that what I am attempting to set out here is something like the basic principles of a rebellion of experience against empiricism" (Adorno 2000 [1968]: 51). Such a rebellion is a crucial component of what I am referring to as a gay social science.

Of course, STS also has roots in European sociology, in the tradition known as the "Sociology of Knowledge." The founding texts in this tradition are Durkheim's (1995 [1912]) *Elementary Forms of Religious Life* and Karl Mannheim's (1936 [1929]) *Ideology and Utopia*. Adorno, informed by Nietzsche's analysis of nihilism, was very critical of both these traditions. According to Adorno (1967), "the sociology of knowledge expounded by Karl Mannheim has begun to take hold in Germany again. For this it can thank its gesture of innocuous skepticism. Like its existentialist counterparts, *it calls everything into question* and *criticizes nothing*" (37, emphasis mine).[27] More recent sociological analyses

27 In *Dialectic of Enlightenment*, Horkheimer and Adorno (2002 [1994]) say the following about Durkheim's sociology of knowledge, which seeks to find the obligatory character of truth in authority, which is a social category: "Even the deductive form of science mirrors hierarchy and compulsion. Just as the first categories represented the organized tribe and its power over the individual, the entire logical order, with its chains of inference and dependence, the superordination and coordination of concepts, is founded on the corresponding conditions in social reality, that is, on the division of labor. Of course, this

scientific knowledge like that of David Bloor (1991) which relies upon Durkheim, and Bruno Latour's (1988) *Science in Action*, which is a particular appropriation of Heidegger's (1977) *Question Concerning Technology*, remain in the quagmire of relativism,[28] something Nietzsche (1969 [1883]) himself would have condemned as the product of the nihilism of the "Last Men." Ironically, conventional sociologists who frequently claim Max Weber as one of their own – due to a misunderstanding that views Weber's intervention in sociology as a clean break from historical materialism – have neglected Weber's (2004 [1917]) classic essay, "Science as a Vocation," which provides a preliminary appropriation of Nietzsche's position on science for the field of sociology. Consider this passage from Weber (2004 [1917]) which has yet to be appreciated by the purveyors of mainstream sociological analyses of science:

social character of intellectual forms is not, as Durkheim argues, an expression of solidarity but evidence of the impenetrable unity of society and power. Power confers increased cohesion and strength on the social whole in which it is established. The division of labor, through which power manifests itself socially, serves the self-preservation of the dominated whole. But this necessarily turns the whole, as a whole, and the operation of its immanent reason, into a means of enforcing the particular interest. Power confronts the individual as the universal, as the reason which informs reality ... What is done to all by the few always takes the form of subduing of individuals by the many: the oppression of society always bears the features of oppression by a collective" (16).

28 On Latour's appropriation of Heidegger, see Riis (2008). Latour (1988) makes a point to mock his critics and affirm his lack of concern with politics – questions of power and domination as they relate to science – when he taunts his critical interlocutors in the following imaginary exchange: "But I'd rather anticipate the objection of my (semiotic) reader: 'What do you mean social?' it indignantly says. 'Where is capitalism, the proletarian classes, the battle of the sexes, the struggle for emancipation of the races ... the strategies of wicked multinational corporations, the military establishment, the devious interests of professional lobbies ... All these elements are social, and this is what you did *not show* with all your texts, rhetorical tricks and technicalities!' I agree, we saw noting of that sort" (62). In this way, Latour situates himself within conventional sociology that has a long tradition of removing any sense of power and conflict from the concept "social." Of course, Heidegger did have politics in a way the Latour does not. Latour's appropriation of Heidegger has to do with ontological questions rather than political ones, which begs the question about how to separate out politics from ontology. There are also important differences between Latour and Bloor, as Latour is very critical of Bloor's orthodox Durkheimian perspective which looks to a reified notion of *the* "social" as a transcendental cause that makes knowledge possible. For Latour, Bloor's reliance upon Durkheim's notion of the "social" is a form of metaphysics. What Bloor and Latour have in common, however, is their desire to remain apolitical, which is why I refer to them as conventional sociologists. Finally, it is important to note that Bloor and Latour are not "conventional" in the sense of epistemology, as they obviously break from the positivism that characterizes a particular tradition in Anglo-American sociology that no longer exercises the hegemony over the field that it once did in previous generations.

> a naïve optimism had led people to glorify science, as the road to *happiness*. But after Nietzsche's annihilating criticism of those 'last men' who 'have discovered happiness,' I can probably ignore this completely. After all who believes it – apart from some overgrown children in their professional chairs or editorial offices? (17)

This is not to suggest that the members of the Frankfurt School were uncritical of Weber. Max Horkheimer revealed the limits of Weber's contribution to the development of Critical Theory when he remarked upon Talcott Parson's (1971) essay titled, "Value-Freedom and Objectivity" at a conference celebrating the centenary of Weber's birth. According to Horkheimer (1971),

> I learnt about value-freedom in Max Weber's sense of the word when I was a student of his in 1919. Like many of my comrades I was deeply interested in understanding the Russian Revolution. In 1917 the Bolsheviks had been the first to call a halt to the war with their cry of 'Peace and Bread!' Thus, it appeared that backward Russia was to devote her energies not to final victory but to setting up a better society. The question for us was to understand what these events signified for world history, what attitudes peoples of the West, particularly Germany, should take to them. *Was it possible to strengthen the positive impulses of the process and limit the negative ones, to avoid radical isolation and retrogression into a new and dangerous nationalism?* The politically alert were already aware of the first signs of a development in Russia towards Stalinism, and in Germany to National Socialism. Max Weber lectured on the Soviet system. The auditorium was crowded to its doors, but great disappointment followed. *Instead of theoretical reflection* and analysis, which, not only in posing the problem, but in every step of thinking would have led to a reasoned structuring of the future, *we listened for two or three hours to finely balanced definitions of the Russian system, shrewdly formulated ideal types, by which it was possible to define the Soviet order. It was all so precise, so scientifically exact, so value-free that we all went sadly home.* (51, emphasis mine)[29]

29 As is the case with Nietzsche, there are divergent interpretations of Weber. What the Frankfurt School appreciated in Weber was his critique of science as the means to acquire happiness and the condition he calls "disenchantment" that follows from the triumph of science over religion. As the quote above states, the Frankfurt School thinkers were very critical of the American attempt – under the influence of Talcott Parsons – to remove Weber's critique of science in order to make Weber amenable to what they viewed as the naïve empiricism of American sociology, which remains hostile to philosophical investigations

Concerning Nietzsche's relation to Marxist philosophy, the primary interlocutor for the Frankfurt School was György Lukács, whose pathbreaking work, *History and Class Consciousness* (1972 [1922]) was a crucial influence on their thinking about the dynamics of the relationship between mass culture and the political economy of mature, or "monopoly" capitalism.[30] After the rise of Stalin and Hitler, however, Horkheimer, Adorno, Marcuse and Bloch all broke with Lukács (1980 [1950]) over his interpretation of Nietzsche as a fascist thinker, an argument that was eventually published in 1950 as *The Destruction of Reason*. The Frankfurt School also criticized Lukács decision to remain loyal to the Communist Party after the atrocities of the Gulags were made public upon the death of Stalin.[31] The debate between Lukács and his one-time progeny over the status of Nietzsche – a debate that spanned the years between 1938 and 1967 and included other "bourgeois" philosophers and artists besides Nietzsche – was published in English in the 1970s under the title *Aesthetics and Politics* (Adorno et al. 1977). According to Adorno (1977) "in a highly undialectical manner, the officially licensed dialectian [Lukács] sweeps all the irrationalist strands of modern philosophy in the the camp of reaction and Fascism. He blithely ignores the fact that, unlike academic idealism, these schools were struggling against the very same reification in both thought and life of which

that do not shy away from speculative thinking. Another example of important differences in the German and American readings of Weber is the contrast between Parsons and Karl Löwith, which highlights the difference between American sociological inquires which attempt to spurn philosophy, and continental versions of sociological inquiry that do not. Unlike Parsons, Löwith (1993) finds profound similarities between Weber and Marx when he says: "as a critical analysis of human economy and society, such an inquiry will at the same time be guided by an 'idea' of man, which is *distinct from the factual situation*. One must ultimately refer back to this idea of man if the 'sociological 'investigations of Weber and Marx are to be understood in their fundamental and radical significance. 'To be radical is to grasp things by the root. But for man the root is man himself.' The radically this-wordly [sic] view of man expressed here is a presupposition for both Marx and Weber" (42–43, emphasis mine).

30 For example, the now famous and frequently anthologized 4th chapter of *Dialectic of Enlightenment* titled "The Culture Industry: Enlightenment as Mass Deception," owes much to Lukács' (1972 [1922]) analysis of Marx's theory of commodity fetishism in the essay "Reification and the Consciousness of the Proletariat," chapter four of *History and Class Consciousness*.

31 According to Adorno (1997) Lukács "acquiesced in the communist custom and disavowed his earlier writings [*The Theory of the Novel*]. He took the crudest criticisms from the Party hierarchy to heart, twisting Hegelian motifs and turning them against himself; and for decades on end he labored in series of books and essays to adapt his obviously unimpaired talents to the unrelieved sterility of Soviet claptrap, which in the meantime had degraded the philosophy it proclaimed to the level of a mere instrument in the service of its rule" (151).

Lukács too was a dedicated opponent" (152). Here the issue was not – *pace* Kaufmann (1950) – whether Nietzsche was or was not a political theorist, but rather what was at issue was a distinction made by Benjamin (1969 [1936]) between the fascist rendering of politics as art – "destruction as an aesthetic pleasure" – and "Communism [which] responds by politicizing art" (242). Bloch and Adorno rejected the argument that Nietzsche's (1967 [1886]) position on aesthetics in *Birth of Tragedy* combined with his (1989 [1887]) critique of science as nihilism in *Genealogy of Morals* leads to a fascist outcome.[32] On the contrary, for both Bloch and Adorno, certain aspects of "bourgeois culture" were viewed as worth defending as a means to achieve a more meaningful and widespread freedom for all people, including the proletariat (Adorno et al. 1977).[33] Years later, Marcuse (1958) relied heavily upon Nietzsche in his critique of "Soviet Marxism," reviving, in part, the project begun decades earlier by the Nietzschean-Marxists of the pre-Revolutionary era. Marcuse's (1958) *Soviet Marxism* was also written in response to Lukács' (1980 [1950]) attack upon Nietzsche's so-called "irrationalism." According to Marcuse (1958),

> The assault against 'bourgeois irrationalism' is particularly illuminating because it reveals the traits common to the Soviet and Western rationality, namely, the prevalence of technological elements over humanistic ones. Schopenhauer and Nietzsche, the various schools of 'vitalism' ... differ and conflict in most essential aspects; however, they are akin in that they explode the technological rationality of modern civilization. They do so by pointing up the psychical and biological forces beneath this rationality and the unredeemable sacrifices, which it exacts from man. The result is a transvaluation of values, which shatters the ideology of progress ... This transvaluation acts upon precisely those values which Soviet society must protect at all cost: the ethical value of competitive performance, socially necessary labor, *self-perpetuating work discipline, postponed and repressed happiness*.
>
> 228–229, emphasis mine

In short, like Kaufmann, the members of the Frankfurt School argued that Nietzsche cannot be interpreted as an advocate of fascism, but unlike Kaufmann,

32 Several of the essays in this volume provide analyses of Nietzsche's position on science, including those by Babich, Sullivan, Morelock, Payne, Atterton and Roberts.

33 For an excellent treatment of this topic see Strong (1988). In this volume, see the essay by Meeker and Berard.

they insisted that Nietzsche should be understood as a political thinker.[34] And yet, for Adorno, Horkheimer and Bloch, Nietzsche was more than a political theorist, narrowly defined.

The adjective "critical" in the Critical Theory of the Frankfurt school indicates that the aims of the Frankfurt school were to merge descriptive analyses with normative ones. When they founded the Institute for Social Research in 1923, what set them apart was their insistence on not removing philosophy from the social sciences. Historically, it has been the norm for modern scholars – especially in the Anglo-American tradition – to separate social science, which attends to descriptive and explanatory analyses from political theory, a branch of philosophy that operates within the normative dimension. Adorno and the members of the Frankfurt school refused this division of labor in the quest for knowledge about the human condition. According to Rose (2014 [1978]), "Adorno opposed the separation of philosophy from sociology since it amounted, in his opinion, to the separation of substantial issues from the development of methodology and empirical techniques … [furthermore] 'method' means for him the relation between ideas and the composition of texts. It does not mean devising procedures for applying theories" (16). Most relevant for this volume is Rose's (2014 [1978]) claim that "much of Adorno's critique of philosophy and of sociology is drawn from his reception of Nietzsche's philosophy" (15).

Unfortunately for sociologists in the Anglo-American orbit, there have not yet been any intellectuals able to successfully argue for Nietzsche's relevance to the discipline in the way that Kaufmann was able to do so in the field of professional philosophy in the U.S. While the Frankfurt School itself remains marginal to professional sociology in the U.S., in Continental Europe, they, like Nietzsche, are widely read and included as mandatory reading in the training of professional social scientists (Rose 2014 [1978]). As I have attempted to show, Nietzsche made a crucial contribution to the concerns of critical-social theory. While it is of course important to scrutinize Nietzsche's views on socialism and democracy, it is also the case, as Max Horkheimer made clear, that his criticisms of socialism were based upon his exposure to the particularities of the German Social Democrats, and the Second International, *not* to Marx himself. Nietzsche did not, according to Horkheimer, "so badly misjudge the Social Democrats" (quote appears in Aschheim 1994: 187). All of the shortcomings

34 For some, the position on Nietzsche within Critical Theory has come full circle, as Jurgen Habermas (1990 [1985]), Adorno's former student and the heir to Frankfurt School Critical Theory, has sought to banish Nietzsche from Critical Theory. For a thorough critique of Habermas' position on Nietzsche see Babich (2004).

that we have come to identify in orthodox Marxism – the authoritarianism, economic determinism, the teleological perspective on history, the lack of attention to culture – were precisely the criticisms that Nietzsche made about the "scientific socialists" of his day. If socialism is on the rise again today, as it seems to be after the rise of Bernie Sanders and his followers, we should, as critical sociologists, not forget our past. To shape the socialism of today, we must to learn from the mistakes that gave rise to authoritarian versions of socialism in the past. A crucial aspect of this task is to affirm the importance of aesthetics in both our sociological analyses of modernity and in our practical politics. In this way, we cannot avoid engaging with Nietzsche and the Left-Nietzschean traditions among generations past. To create a new paradigm for critical sociology – what I am referring to as a gay social science – the task is to break from conventional sociology in order to specify the conditions for the possibility of acting without rules in a post-work society.

References

Adams, Susan. 2014. "Most Americans are Unhappy at Work." *Forbes Magazine*, June 20. http://www.forbes.com/sites/susanadams/2014/06/20/most-americans-are-unhappy-at-work/#5db74fc5862a. Accessed June 2, 2016.

Adorno, Theodor. 2007 [1966]. *Negative Dialectics*, translated by E.B. Ashton. New York: Continuum.

Adorno, Theodor. 2000 [1968]. *Introduction to Sociology*, translated by Edmund Jephcott. Palo Alto, CA: Stanford University Press.

Adorno, Theodor. 1989. "Society," translated by Fredric R. Jameson. In *Critical Theory and Society*, edited by Stephen Eric Bronner and Douglas Kellner, 267–275. New York: Routledge.

Adorno, Theodor. 1983 [1967]. "Sociology of Knowledge and Its Consciousness." In *Prisms*, translated by Shierry Nicolsen Weber and Samuel Weber. Cambridge, MA: MIT Press.

Adorno, Theodor. 1976. "On the Logic of the Social Sciences." In *The Positivist Dispute in German Sociology*, translated by Glyn Adey and David Frisby, 105–122. London: Heinemann.

Adorno, Theodor, Walter Benjamin, Ernst Bloch, Bertolt Brecht, and Georg Lukács. 1977. *Aesthetics and Politics*, edited by Ronald Taylor. London and New York: Verso.

Ahern, Daniel R. 1995. *Nietzsche as Cultural Physician*. University Park, PA: Pennsylvania State University.

Althusser, Louis. 2006 [1965]. *For Marx*, translated by Ben Brewster. London and New York: Verso

Antonio, Robert J. 2005. "Max Weber in Post WWII US and After." *Etica & Politica/Ethics & Politics* 7(2): 1–94.

Antonio, Robert J. 1995. "Nietzsche's Anti-Sociology." *American Journal of Sociology* 101(1): 1–43.

Appel, Fredrick. 1999. *Nietzsche Contra Democracy*. Ithaca and London: Cornell University Press.

Arendt, Hannah. 1958. *The Human Condition*. Chicago, IL: University of Chicago Press.

Aristotle. 1984. *The Complete Works of Aristotle: The Revised Oxford Translation*. Princeton, NJ: Princeton University Press.

Aronowitz, Stanley. 2013. "Lukács' Destruction of Reason." In *Lukács Reconsidered*, edited by Michael J. Thompson. New York: Bloomsbury Academic.

Aronowitz, Stanley. 1990. *The Crisis in Historical Materialism*. Minneapolis, MN: University of Minnesota Press.

Aronowitz, Stanley. 1988. *Science as Power: Discourse and Ideology in Modern Society*. Minneapolis, MN: University of Minnesota Press.

Aronowitz, Stanley, and William DiFazio. 2010. *The Jobless Future*. Minneapolis, MN: University of Minnesota Press.

Aschheim, Steven E. 1994. *The Nietzsche Legacy in Germany, 1890–1990*. Berkeley, CA: University of California Press.

Babich, Babbette E. 1994. *Nietzsche's Philosophy of Science: Reflecting Science on the Ground of Art and Life*. New York: Columbia University Press.

Babich, Babbette E., ed. 2004. *Habermas, Nietzsche and Critical Theory*. Amherst, NY: Humanity Books.

Bataille, Georges. 1994 [1945]. *On Nietzsche*. Translated by Sylvère Lotringer. St. Paul, MN: Paragon House.

Bauer, Karin. 1999. *Adorno's Nietzschean Narratives: Critiques of Ideology, Readings of Wagner*. Albany, NY: State University of New York Press.

Benjamin, Walter. 1969 [1936]. "The Work of Art in the Age of Mechanical Reproduction." In *Illuminations*, translated and edited by Hannah Arendt. New York: Schocken Books.

Bloch, Ernst. 1991. *Heritage of Our Times*, translated by Neville Plaice and Stephen Plaice. Cambridge: Polity Press.

Bloch, Ernst. 1986 [1938]. *The Principle of Hope: Volume One*, translated by Neville Plaice, Stephen Plaice, and Paul Knight. Cambridge, MA: MIT Press.

Bloor, David. 1991. *Knowledge and Social Imagery*. Chicago, IL: University of Chicago Press.

Braverman, Harry. 1974. *Labor and Monopoly Capital*. New York: Monthly Review Press.

Burris, Val. 2007. "Fordism and Positivism in U.S. Sociology." *Social Science History* (31)1: 93–105.

Canguilhem, Georges. 1991 [1966]. *The Normal and the Pathological*, translated by Carolyn R. Fawcett. New York: Zone Books.

Carver, Terrell. 1998. *The Postmodern Marx*. University Park, PA: Penn State University Press.

Cutler, Jonathan. 2004. *Labor's Time*. Philadelphia, PA: Temple University Press.

Dean, Mitchell. 1994. *Critical and Effective Histories: Foucault's Methods and Historical Sociology*. New York and London: Routledge.

Deleuze, Gilles. 1995. *Negotiations 1972–1990*, translated by Joughin, Martin. New York: Columbia University Press.

Deleuze, Gilles. 1983. *Nietzsche and Philosophy*, translated by Hugh Tomlinson. NY: Columbia University Press.

Derrida, Jacques. 1994 [1993]. *Specters of Marx*, translated by Peggy Kamuf. New York: Routledge.

Durkheim, Emile. 1995 [1912]. *Elementary Forms of Religious Life*, translated by Karen Fields. New York: The Free Press.

Durkheim, Emile. 1984. *The Division of Labor in Society*, translated by W.D. Halls. New York: The Free Press.

Durkheim, Emile. 1974. *Sociology and Philosophy*, translated by D.F. Pocock. New York, NY: The Free Press.

Durkheim, Emile. 1972. *Selected Writings*, edited by Anthony Giddens. Cambridge: Cambridge University Press.

Durkheim, Emile. 1961. *Moral Education*, translated by Everett K. Wilson and Herman Schnurer. New York: The Free Press.

Engels, Friedrich. 1978 [1890]. "To Joseph Bloch." In *The Marx-Engels Reader*, second edition, edited by Robert C. Tucker, 760–765. New York: W. W. Norton & Company.

Foucault, Michel. 1991 [1981]. *Remarks on Marx: Conversations with Duccio Trombadori*, translated by James R. Goldstein and James Cascaito. New York: Semiotext(e).

Foucault, Michel. 1984. "What is Enlightenment." In *The Foucault Reader*, edited by Paul Rabinow, 32–50. New York: Pantheon Books.

Gouldner, Alvin W. 1970. *The Coming Crisis of Western Sociology*. New York: Basic Books.

Habermas, Jurgen. 1990 [1985]. *Philosophical Discourse of Modernity*, translated by Frederick G. Lawerence. Cambridge, MA: MIT Press.

Harvey, David. 1991. *The Condition of Postmodernity*. New York: Wiley-Blackwell.

Heidegger, Martin. 1996 [1927]. *Being and Time*, translated by Joan Stambaugh. Albany, NY: State University Press of New York.

Heidegger, Martin. 1977. *The Question Concerning Technology*, translated by William Lovitt. New York: Harper Torchbooks.

Heideman, Paul. 2015. "Technology and Socialist Strategy." *Jacobin*, April 7. https://jacobinmag.com/2015/04/braverman-gramsci-marx-technology. Accessed February 2, 2019.

Horkheimer, Max. 1971. "Discussion on Value-Freedom and Objectivity." In *Max Weber and Sociology Today*, edited by Otto Stammer, translated by Kathleen Morris, 51–53. New York: Harper & Row.

Horkheimer, Max, and Theodor Adorno. 2002 [1944]. *Dialectic of Enlightenment*, translated by Edmund Jephcott. Palo Alto, CA: Stanford University Press.

Horowitz, Irving Louis. 1964. "Max Weber and the Spirit of American Sociology." *Sociological Quarterly* 5(4): 344–354.

Jay, Martin. 1996. *The Dialectical Imagination: A History of the Frankfurt School and the Institute of Social Research, 1923–1950*. Berkeley, CA: University of California Press.

Kant, Immanuel. 2000 [1790]. *The Critique of Judgment*, edited by Paul Guyer, translated by Paul Guyer and Eric Matthews. Cambridge, UK: Cambridge University Press.

Kant, Immanuel. 1998 [1789]. *The Critique of Pure Reason*, translated and edited by Paul Guyer and Allen W. Wood. Cambridge: Cambridge University Press.

Kaufmann, Walter. 1974. "Translator's Introduction." In *The Gay Science*, Friedrich Nietzsche, 3–31. New York: Vintage Books.

Kaufmann, Walter. 1950. *Nietzsche: Philosopher, Psychologist, Anti-Christ*. Princeton, NJ: Princeton University Press.

Kline, George. 1969. "'Nietzschean Marxism' in Russia." In *Demythologizing Marxism: A Series of Studies on Marxism, The Boston College Studies in Philosophy*, Volume II. Boston College, Chestnut Hill.

Landa, Ishay. 2019. "The Social Individual and the Last Human: Marx and Nietzsche Agree to Disagree." *Critical Sociology* 45(2).

Latour, Bruno. 1988. *Science in Action*. Cambridge, MA: Harvard University Press.

Lefebvre, Henri. 2014 [1947, 1981]. *Critique of Everyday Life*, translated by John Moore. London and New York: Verso.

Lefebvre, Henri. 2009 [1940]. *Dialectical Materialism*, translated by John Sturrock. Minneapolis: University of Minnesota Press.

Lefebvre, Henri. 2003a. *Nietzsche*. Paris: Editions Syllepse.

Lefebvre, Henri. 2003b. *Key Writings*, edited by Stuart Elden, Elizabeth Lebas, and Eleonore Kofman. New York and London: Continuum.

Lefebvre, Henri. 1991 [1974]. *The Production of Space*, translated by Donald Nicholson-Smith. Oxford: Blackwell.

Löwith, Karl. 1993 [1932]. *Max Weber and Karl Marx*, translated by Hans Fantel. New York: Routledge.

Lukács, György. 1980 [1950]. *The Destruction of Reason*, translated by Peter Palmer. London: The Merlin Press.

Lukács, György. 1972 [1922]. *History and Class Consciousness: Studies in Marxist Dialectics*, translated by Rodney Livingstone. Cambridge, MA: MIT Press.

Mannheim, Karl. 1936 [1929]. *Ideology and Utopia*, translated by Louis Wirth. New York: Harvest Books.

Marcuse, Herbert. 1982. "On Science and Phenomenology." In *The Essential Frankfurt School Reader*, edited by Andrew Arato and Eike Gebhardt. New York: Continuum.

Marcuse, Herbert. 1974. *Eros and Civlization*. Boston, MA: Beacon Press.

Marcuse, Herbert. 1958. *Soviet Marxism: A Critical Analysis*. New York: Columbia University Press.

Marx, Karl. 1993a. *Capital: Volume 3*, translated by David Fernbach. New York: Penguin.

Marx, Karl. 1993b. *Grundrisse*, translated by Martin Nicolaus. New York: Penguin.

Marx, Karl. 1992a. *Capital: Volume 1*, translated by Ben Fowkes. New York: Penguin.

Marx, Karl. 1992b. *Early Writings*, translated by Rodney Livingston. New York: Penguin.

McClelland, James C. 1980. "Utopianism versus Revolutionary Heroism in Bolshevik Policy: The Proletarian Culture Debate." *Slavic Review* 39(3): 403–425.

McNeill, George E. 1886. *The Labor Movement: The Problem of Today*. Boston, MA: A.M. Bridgman & Co.

Merton, Robert. 1973. *The Sociology of Science*. Chicago, IL: University of Chicago Press.

Merton, Robert. 1970 [1938]. *Science, Technology and Society in Seventeenth-Century England*. New York: Howard Fertig, Publisher.

Merton, Robert. 1963. "On Sociological Theories of the Middle Range." In *Social Theory and Social Structure*. Glencoe, IL: The Free Press.

Mestrovic, Stjepan G. 1988. "The Social World as Will and Idea: Schopenhauer's Influence on Durkheim's Thought." *The Sociological Review* 36(4): 674–705.

Mitzman, Arthur. 1969. *The Iron Cage*. New York: Grosset and Dunlap.

Moore, John, ed. 2004. *I Am Not a Man, I Am Dynamite: Friedrich Nietzsche and the Anarchist Tradition*. Brooklyn, NY: Autonomedia.

Nealon, Jeffrey T. 2000. "Performing Resentment: White Male Anger; or, 'Lack' and Nietzschean Political Theory." In *Why Nietzsche Still?*, edited by Alan D. Schrift, 274–292. Berkeley, CA: University of California Press.

Nietzsche, Friedrich. 2003. *Daybreak: Thoughts on the Prejudices of Morality*. Edited by Maudemarie Clark and Brian Leiter, translated by R.J. Hollingdale. Cambridge: Cambridge University Press.

Nietzsche, Friedrich. 1997. *Twilight of the Idols: Or, How to Philosophize with the Hammer*, translated by Richard Polt. Indianapolis/Cambridge: Hackett Publishing Company.

Nietzsche, Friedrich. 1989. *On the Genealogy of Morals*, translated by Walter Kaufmann. New York: Vintage Books.

Nietzsche, Friedrich. 1979 [1873]. "On the Truth and Lies in a Nonmoral Sense." In *Philosophy and Truth*, edited by Daniel Breazeale. New Jersey: Humanities Press.

Nietzsche, Friedrich. 1974. *The Gay Science*, translated by Walter Kaufmann. New York: Vintage Books.

Nietzsche, Friedrich. 1969. *Thus Spake Zarathustra*, translated by R. J. Hollingdale. New York, NY: Penguin.

Nietzsche, Friedrich. 1968. *The Will to Power*, translated by Walter Kaufmann and R. J. Hollingdale. New York: Vintage Books.

Nietzsche, Friedrich. 1967. *The Birth of Tragedy*, translated by Walter Kaufmann. New York: Vintage.

Nietzsche, Friedrich. 1966 [1886]. *Beyond Good and Evil*, translated by Walter Kaufmann. New York: Vintage.

Parsons, Talcott. 1971. "Value-Freedom and Objectivity." In *Max Weber and Sociology Today*, edited by Otto Stammer, translated by Kathleen Morris. New York: Harper & Row.

Parsons, Talcott. 1951. *The Social System*. New York: The Free Press.

Payne, Christine A. 2018. *Critique Without Foundation: Friedrich Nietzsche and the Social Studies of Science*. Ph.D. Dissertation, University of California, San Diego.

Rabelais, Francois. 2006 [1564]. *Gargantua and Pantagruel*. London: Penguin.

Rehmann, Jan. 2007. "Towards a Deconstruction of Postmodernist Neo-Nietzscheanism." *Situations* 2(1): 7–16.

Reuters. 2016. "Karoshi Cases on Rise in Japan: Overworked to Death." *TaipeiTimes*, April 4. http://www.reuters.com/article/us-japan-economy-overwork-idUSKCN0X000F. Accessed June 2, 2016.

Riis, Søren. 2008. "The Symmetry Between Bruno Latour and Martin Heidegger." *Social Studies of Science* 38(2): 285–301.

Riley, Alexander T. 2005. "'Renegade Durkheimianism' and the Transgressive Left Sacred." In *Cambridge Companion to Durkheim*, edited by Jeffrey C. Alexander and Philip Smith, 274–302. Cambridge: Cambridge University Press.

Roberts, Michael J. 2019. "In Search of the Wanderer and Free Spirits: The Ascetic Absence of Nietzsche from American Sociology." *Critical Sociology* 45(2).

Roediger, David R., and Philip S. Foner. 1989. *Our Own Time: A History of American Labor and the Working Day*. London and New York: Verso.

Rose, Gillian. 2014 [1978]. *The Melancholy Science: An Introduction to the Thought of Theodor W. Adorno*. London and New York: Verso.

Rosenthal, Bernice G., ed. 1986. *Nietzsche in Russia*. Princeton, NJ: Princeton University Press.

Ryan, Michael. 1982. *Marxism and Deconstruction: A Critical Articulation*. Baltimore: Johns Hopkins University Press.

Sartre, Jean-Paul. 2004 [1960]. *Critique of Dialectical Reason*. London and New York: Verso.

Sartre, Jean-Paul. 1992 [1943]. *Being and Nothingness: A* Phenomenological Essay on Ontology. New York: Washington Square Press.

Sartre, Jean-Paul. 1968 [1957]. *Search for a Method*. New York: Vintage.

Scheler, Max. 1994 [1914]. *Ressentiment*, translated by Lewis Coser. Milwaukee, WI: Marquette University Press.

Schotten, Heike. 2019. "Nietzsche and Emancipatory Politics: Queer Theory as Anti-Morality." *Critical Sociology* 45(2).

Stammer, Otto, ed. 1971. *Max Weber and Sociology Today*. New York: Harper & Row.

Steinberg, Mark D. 2002. *Proletarian Imagination: Self, Modernity and the Sacred in Russia, 1910–1925*. Ithaca, NY: Cornell University Press.

Strong, Tracy B. 2012. *Politics Without Vision: Thinking Without a Banister in the Twentieth Century*. Chicago and London: University of Chicago Press.

Strong, Tracey B. 1988. "Nietzsche's Politicial Aesthetics." In *Nietzsche's New Seas: Explorations in Philosophy, Aesthetics, and Politics*, edited by Michael Allen Gillespie and Tracy B. Strong, 153–174. Chicago: University of Chicago Press.

Theweleit, Klaus. 1987. *Male Fantasies: Women, Floods, Bodies, History*. Minneapolis, MN: University of Minnesota Press.

Traub, Rainer. 1978. "Lenin and Taylor: The Fate of 'Scientific Management' in the Early Soviet Union." *Telos* 37: 82–92.

Weber, Max. 2004 [1917]. "Science as a Vocation." In *The Vocation Lectures*, edited by David Owen and Tracy B. Strong, translated by Rodney Livingstone, 1–31. Indianapolis, IN: Hacket Publishing Company.

Weber, Max. 2002 [1905]. *The Protestant Ethic and the Spirit of Capitalism*, edited and translated by Peter Baehr and Gordon C. Wells. New York: Penguin Books.

Wilentz, Sean. 2004. *Chants Democratic*. Oxford: Oxford University Press.

Williams, Robert C. 1980. "Collective Immortality: The Syndicalist Origins of Proletarian Culture, 1905–1910." *Slavic Review* 39(3): 389–402.

CHAPTER 11

Resuscitating Sociological Theory: Nietzsche and Adorno on Error and Speculation

Jeremiah Morelock

1 Introduction

Today sociology suffers from a kind of theoretical anemia. It could be terminal. Big claims are pushed aside as imprecise and unrealistic, on the grounds that they archaically stray from the specifics of idiosyncratic human experience or concrete facts. A passive and non-communicative stalemate between positivist and relativist paradigms persists, ironically falling into a partnership in constraining the development of sociological theory.[1] These inhibitions against theory are not entirely unreasonable. Important lessons have been learned. Today, for example, declaring totalizing theories as universally true without checking them against empirical findings has fallen far out of fashion. Positivism and postmodern relativism bring with them demands for different kinds of justification, and these are useful demands. And yet, instead of becoming more epistemically robust, sociology is becoming more epistemically evasive.

New theoretical work in sociology is being done, and advances beyond the hegemonic-complacent gridlock of positivism and relativism are occurring. However, substantive theoretical claims beyond the middle-range face much compliant resistance in being seriously discussed in the discipline's mainstream. Resting content with the conclusion that no theory is solid, we have resolved to accept and understate them with little discrimination. A cornucopia

1 The notion that scientific relativism preserves the problems with scientific positivism, only in an inverted form, has been articulated differently but with comparable force by Babich (1994) and Laudan and Kukla (1996). Babich articulates the point in the context of her interpretation of Nietzsche's perspectivalism, and Laudan articulates it in his own refutation of post-positivism, yet both expositions are similar. The argument in common to both authors is that a dogmatic relativism which staunchly prohibits anything approaching truth claims, justifies itself on the basis of the failure of truth claims to live up to positivist standards. Knowledge that would earn the right of the title is still equated with the rigidity of positivism – stated broadly: universal, absolute, empirical, and proven. The rigidity is maintained, the focus is just flipped. What positivism and relativism have in common is the prohibition against making large theoretical claims.

of diluted theoretical flavors stampedes unobtrusively through our academic journals and department halls. This often occurs ostensibly under the growing new paradigm (and metaparadigm)[2] of "pragmatism," which tends to be adopted and expressed in similarly shallow fashion to the array of theories it permits without examination (Morgan 2014).

Awareness of the discipline's malaise is common among sociologists, as is the sense that it has something to do with theory. Opinions differ over exactly what the source of the problem is, and what might be a solution. Some amount of bushwhacking away the thickets of bad theories can be found in most proposals. Healy (2017) says today we demand individual theories to account for so much at once that we block a lot of potentially fruitful new ideas. Some theories get through, but generally speaking the survivors lack mojo and are too complex and tempered to say anything substantial. At the same time that creative new ideas are blocked, lackluster theories multiply through minute differentiations only of possible interest to the specialist. Other commentators call for "empirical grounding and analytical specificity" (Ermakoff 2017), "less theory [and] more description" (Besbris and Khan 2017), and to "foreground thick and accurate descriptions of the social world as the most significant contributions researchers could make" (Mears 2017: 144). Seidman (2017) argues for sociological theory to focus on issues of popular concern, in a voice written more for the lay public rather than just for other professional academics.

While journals may be saturated with compulsory and underwhelming "theoretical contributions," simply taking a machete to the discipline will not solve our woes. As Healy (2017) emphasizes, a lot of good new ideas never make it to publication because of how fine the mesh of our gatekeeping strainer has become, and correspondingly how small and pointed our theoretical contributions are weened to be. In turn we have a dearth of new big theoretical ideas, and a flood of positivist middle-range theories and relativist "theoretical contributions" isomorphic to middle-range theories in scope.

Sociological theory needs resuscitation above the middle-range if it is going to sustain a compelling reason for existence. This requires dedicated attention to theory that extends to the epistemic. Allowing space for multiple perspectives that speculate beyond facts is the only antidote to positivist dogma. Honoring the critical interrogation of perspectives is the only antidote to relativist paralysis. Can multiple speculative perspectives and critical interrogation survive together beyond lip service? Or is theoretical anemia the only pragmatic option? This concerns not just sociological theorists, but all sociologists, because without theory to guide our research and interpret our results, sociology

2 See Bakker (2011).

is just journalism, hardly deserving of its current (tenuous) status as a social science. Sociological theory is not a parasite. If it is treated as such and left to die, the imagined host – sociology the discipline – will die along with it.

I propose learning from Nietzsche and Adorno to find a way beyond anemia. While both are well known for being critical and iconoclastic in their diagnoses of Enlightenment rationality, they also both offer positive depictions of how a liberated and liberating alternate kind of philosophy might operate. In this Chapter argue that their epistemological visions, while famous for being negative, importantly support the affirmative yet discerning use of (a) the unknown – or as I refer to it later on "the shadow between concept and object"[3] – and (b) multiplicity. I also argue that this orientation could be brought more into sociology in order to liberate sociological theory from its current malaise. To do this, I argue that their epistemologies (a) incorporate temporal *and atemporal* dimensions of becoming stemming from the philosophy of Heraclitus, and (b) can be read as directed toward abstract objects of social scientific import. I suggest their ideas point toward a metatheoretical perspective that affirms the unknown or "shadow" and multiplicity, while maintaining an attitude of critical analysis. Imagination, creativity, and the generation of new and different theories are encouraged, yet no theory is immune from critical reflection and refinement.

The structure of the paper is as follows. First, I describe Nietzsche's epistemology in relation to Heraclitus' theory of becoming. I then argue that because Nietzsche's epistemology might be read as directed toward abstract objects of social scientific substance. I follow this with an exposition of Nietzsche's concept of "error," emphasizing the importance he lent to it in his vision of liberation. I then turn to Adorno. I emphasize that Adorno's philosophy was inseparable from his socio-political convictions; hence his epistemology can be read as pertaining to abstract objects relevant to social science. I then describe Adorno's theory of speculation, explaining it through its relation to the ideas of Hegel and Heraclitus. I describe the implicit connection in Adorno's thought between speculation and his methodology of elaborating conceptual "constellations," also in relation to Hegel and Heraclitus. In conclusion I revisit Nietzsche and Adorno's similar insights concerning error, speculation and multiplicity in reference to using them for a metatheoretical lens that might help sociology leave behind its recent anti-theoretical doldrums.

3 As in T.S. Eliot's (2010) poem "The Waste Land": "between the idea and the reality falls the shadow."

2 Nietzsche on Error and Perspectives

2.1 *Nietzsche's Heraclitus*

Throughout Nietzsche's corpus he presents errors in human understanding as inevitable, even ubiquitous and intrinsic to experience. There are multiple types of error, but as a rule their necessity stems from the fact that we inevitably and mistakenly superimpose being (and universality, solidity) on becoming (particularity, flux) in how we interpret (Green 2002; Rowe 2013). Nietzsche's theory that being is a ruse that masks becoming stems from Heraclitus, the pre-Socratic philosopher who introduced the notion of becoming into Western thought. Like other pre-Socratics, his philosophy is garnered from fragments, making interpretation more ambiguous than when looking at extended monographs. However, to understand Nietzsche's theory of becoming in light of what he took from Heraclitus, Nietzsche's own interpretation of Heraclitus seems most relevant. In what follows, I present Nietzsche's take, leaving aside the further interpretation of what Heraclitus "really" meant.

> ...Heraclitus proclaimed: "I see nothing other than becoming. Be not deceived. It is the fault of your myopia, not of the nature of things, if you believe you see land somewhere in the ocean of coming-to-be and passing away. You use names for things as though they rigidly, persistently endured; yet even the stream into which you step a second time is not the one you stepped into before."
>
> NIETZSCHE 2001: 52

In the above quote, Nietzsche expresses Heraclitus' rejection of "being" as illusion, instead proclaiming reality to be temporal becoming. Nietzsche connects this to the atemporal strife of opposites, another of Heraclitus' central ideas:

> Ordinary people fancy they see something rigid, complete and permanent; in truth, however, light and dark, bitter and sweet are attached to each other and interlocked at any given moment like wrestlers of whom sometimes the one, sometimes the other is on top. Honey, says Heraclitus, is at the same time bitter and sweet; the world itself is a mixed drink which must constantly be stirred. The strife of the opposites gives birth to all that comes-to-be; the definite qualities which look permanent to us express but the momentary ascendency of one partner. But this by no means signifies the end of the war; the contest endures in all eternity.
>
> NIETZSCHE 2001: 54–55

In the above description, becoming occurs through time, but standing behind becoming are atemporal relationships between opposing principles, or – in keeping with Nietzsche's metaphor – wrestlers. They are atemporal in the sense that they are eternal, but also – and more importantly for the present discussion – they are atemporal in the sense that both wrestlers are simultaneously present for their match, these matches being primary to the appearance in time of objects bearing various qualities. To say that "honey is at the same time bitter and sweet" is to say that the object "honey" is at any given moment properly defined by *both* sides of the opposition bitter/sweet, regardless of the object honey's momentary phenomenal status as either bitter or sweet.

The painstaking analysis of how and how much Heraclitus figures within Nietzsche's own philosophy is outside the scope of this essay, but I would hazard a suggestion by way of Deleuze's read of Nietzsche as vehemently opposed to dialectics. The wrestlers analogy may have been adopted but purged of its dialectical element. Instead of just two wrestlers, with Nietzsche we have an indeterminate plurality. Portraying Nietzsche's position on dialectics, Deleuze (2006) states:

> It is not surprising that the dialectic proceeds by opposition...It is unaware of the real element from which forces, their qualities and their relations derive...[D]ifference is the only principle of genesis or production; a principle which itself produces opposition as mere appearance. Dialectic thrives on oppositions because it is unaware of far more subtle and subterranean differential mechanisms: topological displacements, typological variations. (157)

For Nietzsche, "reality" is really *a multiplicity of forces and their appearances, or perspectives*. Yet Nietzsche's attitude toward truth is not true relativism, despite the fact he eschews positivism and the assertion of singular truth (Babich 1994; Bauer 1999). Nietzsche posits a meritocratic view of perspectives: (a) in a natural sense, perspectives that are better at proliferating and/or better at serving the propagation of those who hold them, will tend to spread and last through time and (b) in a metaphysical sense, perspectives which are more life affirming, or most thoroughly harmonious with "will to power" as "active forces," are inherently superior (Deleuze 2006). In this dual hierarchy of perspectives that Nietzsche posits, the ranking factors are human ones, not truth criteria. In other words, Nietzsche's declaration of intrinsic error is not a mark against erring perspectives; rather perspectives are better or worse depending on how people use them.

2.2 *Nietzsche's Purpose, Abstract Objects, and Sociological Theory*

The above summarizes error and perspective from the outside, in terms of their general shape or form. Nietzsche is concerned with errors and perspectives in terms of how these play out psychologically and socially. What about from the inside, in terms of their content? What are the errors about and what are the perspectives on? Theories of knowledge can variously pertain to sense perceptions or ideas. In terms of content, is Nietzsche's epistemology directed more to one or equally to both?

Nietzsche is not explicit on this. Yet the contents Nietzsche is concerned with in his wider philosophy do not tend to be sense perceptions. His main purpose in interrogating "truth" is to discuss *how we relate to the idea of truth*, not whether or not truth exists independently of us. Further, his main purpose in interrogating our *ideas* about truth is *how they inform our lives*, not whether or not they correspond to a mind-independent reality (Gemes 1992). His concerns are not raw empirical data, but rather topics such as morality, art, play, philosophy, nihilism, free spirits, and so on. When Nietzsche talks about a multiplicity of perspectives he references perspectives as they inform ways of living. He is less concerned with how they inform empirical perception. It is much more important to Nietzsche how a person understands social obligation than what colors they see in a chair, for example. In "On the Thousand and One Goals" from *Thus Spoke Zarathustra* Nietzsche (1977) writes:

> Zarathustra saw many lands and many peoples: thus he discovered the good and evil of many peoples. And Zarathustra found no greater power on earth than good and evil. No people could ever live without first esteeming; but if they want to preserve themselves, then they must not esteem as their neighbor esteems. Much that was good to one people was scorn and infamy to another; thus I found it. Much I found evil here, and decked out with purple honors there. Never did one neighbor understand the other: ever was his soul amazed at the neighbor's delusion and wickedness. (170)

It would be consistent to treat Nietzsche's theories of error and perspectives as more concerned with how people use abstract objects of social scientific import than with the metaphysics of concrete objects. This theory has strong meta-level elements. In a sense Nietzsche's epistemology is a regular theory of knowledge, but in another – and I would argue, more pertinent – sense, it is a social psychology concerned with how people use and are impacted by ideas about humanity. Transposing his terms onto the question of sociological theory, theories and their component concepts can be viewed as errors and perspectives. And overall, the lesson he promotes is that all theories are errors, yet this is not a reason not to use them, nor is it a reason to consider them inherently equal and use them arbitrarily. Instead, theories should be used selectively and in service to what purposes they benefit.

2.3 *Levels of Error and Free Philosophy*

Nietzsche's most sustained treatments of error are contained in his essay "On Truth and Lie in an Extra-Moral Sense," (1979) and in his books *The Gay Science* (2010) and *Twilight of the Idols* (1997).[4] *The Gay Science* contains a framework for a fuller treatment of error within which the applicable section of *Twilight of the Idols* can be subsumed. Because of this, I discuss *Twilight* before *The Gay Science*, despite the former book being written after the latter. By treating these texts as part of a theoretical whole, I am departing from interpretations such as those of Clark (1990) and Leiter (2007), who suggest Nietzsche abandoned the error theory in his later work, wherein he turned to a more thoroughgoing naturalism including the uncomplicated promotion of science. Instead, I side with Green (2002) and Rowe (2013) in the opinion that Nietzsche's error theory was a consistent presence throughout his work.

In *Twilight of the Idols*, Nietzsche presents his most sustained explicit discussion of error, titled "The Four Great Errors." These four errors are: (1) confusing cause and effect, (2) false causation, (3) imaginary causes, and (4) free will. Rowe (2013) suggests that Nietzsche's main purpose in calling out these errors is to point to the alternative possibility of celebrating *becoming*, which is a more faithful appraisal of existence than the insistence on *being* which the four great errors are predicated upon. In a sense then, all four of these errors are derivations of the fundamental error of mistaking *becoming* for *being*. Secondarily, Rowe insists Nietzsche's main complaint about these errors is their presence within [all] religion and morality. Despite the fact that overall Nietzsche's analysis of the errors is ontological, the target of his intervention is social and psychological. In attempting to dispel religion and morality as predicated on

---

4 In his early essay "On Truth and Lie in an Extra-moral Sense," Nietzsche (1979) uses the word "lie" in similar sense to his later use the term "error." In the early essay, Nietzsche describes all language as stemming from a will to deceive. If the social implications of this are set aside, he is saying that the original function of language is to give voice to untruth. He also articulates that all concepts are untrue. To use a concept is to erroneously treat different things as if they were the same. Concepts are created by lumping together a collection of objects under some aspect or aspects that they have in common, while ignoring their differences. An ideal version of this sameness is extracted and used to measure belonging of objects under the concept.

errors, Nietzsche appears to be supporting scientific analysis in its stead; but this is not his main purpose. Far from supporting a staunchly rational approach to investigating reality, he supports a playful one. Regardless his opinions on science and the "truths" it presents to us, Nietzsche's goal is here just as in his other writings a cultural one – moving toward a more playful orientation of embracing *becoming*.

In *The Gay Science*, Nietzsche scatters his reflections on error throughout, which is consistent with the meandering and aphoristic style of the work as a whole. When Nietzsche focuses on errors here, he is either anticipating a will to error as a mark of the free spirits of the future *or* he is specifically concerned with large errors that have substantial and powerful legacies in the history of Western thought. And as in "Truth and Lie" where he describes fallacy as the very building blocks of our social world, he attributes many positive developments to these errors. One of these developments is the will to truth. Hence, even the staunch Enlightenment advocate should recognize that all of the "truths" of today owe their existence to powerful errors of the past. In "Preludes of science" he says:

> Do you really believe that the sciences would ever have originated and grown if the way had not been prepared by magicians, alchemists, astrologers, and witches whose promises and pretensions first had to create a thirst, a hunger, a taste for *hidden* and *forbidden* powers? Indeed, infinitely more had to be *promised* than could ever be fulfilled in order that anything at all might be fulfilled in the realm of knowledge. (IV: 300)

In this vision then, Nietzsche simultaneously praises and denigrates error. Instead of errors being *bad*, they are just the media by which we operate in life. The more important question for him is whether a way of thinking is healthy for life, not whether it is "actually" wrong. Some errors are more or less beneficial for various purposes. As in the above quote, some errors that are healthy for life may take the form of the immoral when they arise in a given society. Moreover, some "poisons" that are not life affirming in themselves may end up being beneficial for us in other ways or at later times. As he says is "On the doctrine of the poisons":

> So many things have to come together for scientific thinking to originate; and all these necessary strengths had to be invented, practiced, and cultivated separately. As long as they were still separate, however, they frequently had an altogether different effect than they do now that they are integrated into scientific thinking and hold each other in check. Their

> effect was that of poisons; for example, that of the impulse to doubt, to negate, to wait, to collect, to dissolve. (III: 113)

Overall, Nietzsche uses the term "error" on two different levels. On the first level, error is simply telling ourselves a story about the world; adopting a narrative to live by. These types of errors are necessarily limited and incomplete. They are inescapable for humanity. The second type of error is at the meta level: the belief that a particular error is the truth. Nietzsche lauds errors at the first level to the extent that they are life affirming. Nietzsche's wider concern is with error at the second level.

The importance of the distinction between first and second level errors lies in the hope that Nietzsche holds out for a new, liberated kind of thinking. In the modern period, a will to truth becomes rampant and seeks to overcome errors in human understanding. Scientific explanation displaces metaphysics. Nietzsche (1996) expresses some explicit admiration for this change in his earlier writings. However, this will to truth is also part of the crushing trajectory of nihilism in Western culture (Deleuze 2001). Living under the illusion that our errors are truths is not to be admired according to Nietzsche, and yet the will to truth should be questioned. First, there is no reason to believe that we are better off without errors. Second, the belief that there is a truth which can be found may be an error as well.[5] The abandonment of the will to truth is a mark of his "free spirits" (Nietzsche 2009; Mullin 2000).

Nietzsche's simultaneous praising and denigrating the will to truth is not so paradoxical if it is understood in light of his portrayal of people who adopt his preferred relation to truth. These people are beyond illusions because they embrace the perspectival nature of human realities. They are liberated from confining illusions that pretend to have captured the final word on truth. These illusions both include the errors of the past that were treated as if they were truths, as well as the modern error of searching for truth through science and reason. The will to truth is a form of nihilism, but it is also a path of progress that in relentlessly overcoming errors will lead to the overcoming of itself as well, which will pave the way for a new type of human to proliferate, which is unencumbered by all of these things. This liberation contains the positive embrace of our inevitable ignorance; i.e. of a will to error. In this liberated thinking, people would knowingly and intentionally adopt perspectives that are life affirming. The inevitability of error would be accepted, but not passively or as an excuse to brand all perspectives as equal. The free spirit of the future will

5 He indicates this is more than a possibility in his rejection of the separation of "real" and "apparent" worlds in *Twilight of the Idols* (1997).

recognize the perspectival nature of all knowledge, and so will knowingly live by errors (in the first sense), intentionally choosing and using them in affirmation of life.

His references to the first type of error always reference – even if only implicitly – the second type of error. In his discussions of the first type of error, his thesis is that they are not intrinsically positive or negative. Whether or not a belief is in error may or may not coincide with whether that belief is advantageous for life. What really matters is at the meta level: whether a person is able to liberate their thinking from the constraints of a rampant will to truth, by (a) recognizing the inevitability of error, and (b) consciously and intentionally choosing and using their beliefs in order to bring strength and vitality to their lives; to move toward greatness and to live in connection with – and expression of – their innermost drives.

As described in the previous section, Nietzsche's theory of error can be applied to sociological theory. Doing so suggests the following. All sociological theories and their component concepts are limited and incomplete, but that is not a bad thing. Sociological concepts and theories are inevitable in sociology, and different ones serve different purposes better than others. To the extent that sociological theories serve the purposes of the sociologist who uses them well, they are laudable. The cardinal mistake is belief that a theory is *actually* "true." Taking on this meta-perspective is not only more adequate to the way sociological theory operates epistemically; it is a liberated and liberating attitude which can allow space for playfulness, risk-taking, personal values, and overall vitality to flourish unapologetically in a discipline that has been knowingly plodding along, tail between legs, to its death since the 1980s (Denzin 1987). Following Nietzsche's vision, we might move the discipline into a more vibrant, free-spirited era that embraces sociological theory while superseding both positivism and relativism as guiding rubrics.

3 Adorno on Speculation and Constellations

3.1 *Adorno's Purpose – Saving Philosophy*

Like Nietzsche, Adorno (2008; 1973) sees concepts as inherently inadequate and indispensable. A – if not the – major impetus behind *Negative Dialectics* was an attempt to salvage philosophy from its progressive implosion. He identifies the present alternative of philosophies with systems that cannot be defended, versus "arbitrary" philosophical claims that cannot be defended, as needing some kind of third option in order for philosophy to be sustainable as a legitimate enterprise. Adorno hopes to salvage system-like traits in philosophy, without actually maintaining a system within which all claims are required to fit. This is evident in his transformative adoption of Hegel's dialectic, rather than dropping the structure of the dialectic entirely.

Like Nietzsche, Adorno tends to focus on culture much more than on concrete objects. With Adorno, as with Nietzsche, I propose looking at his discussion of objects as about abstract objects more than about concrete objects. Some clear evidence to justify this is that in the latter sections of *Negative Dialectics*, the "models" Adorno presents to display his method are clearly on conceptual topics: freedom, morality, and metaphysics. Other direct – and more explicit – evidence is in lecture 19 of *An Introduction to Dialectics*. Adorno's examples of "class" and "society"[6] clearly show he is concerned with properly analyzing abstract objects more than with concrete objects.

> ...if we had to show by direct reference to the object itself, let us say, what 'class' or what 'society' is, and both are concepts which reflective investigation cannot do without, we would certainly find ourselves at a loss... pre-eminently because these concepts themselves are so complexly structured, because the categorical moments are so predominant here, that we cannot get away simply by referring or pointing to the object or state of affairs in question. And as a rule these are precisely the concepts which...effectively elude definition because they involve a historical content which cannot be reified or tied down, as it were, which cannot be straightforwardly related to other concepts without those concepts forfeiting all determinacy in the process.
>
> ADORNO 2017: 197

Adorno's concern with salvaging philosophy is not just because he values it for its own sake. Whereas Nietzsche lauds life affirming conceptual errors, Adorno values philosophy for a different social reason: its relationship to political practice. In typical Marxian fashion, Adorno insists upon the interrelatedness of theory and practice, each informing and influencing the other. In aiming his negative dialectics toward the rescuing of philosophy, he was clearly preoccupied with the theory side of the equation. More explicitly, he was outspoken in his disdain for the anti-intellectual threads in the political activism of the 1960s (Skinner 2005). He repeatedly warned of the kinship between the anti-intellectual, pro-action tendencies of 1960s radicalism and the anti-reflective and pro-aggressive mentality that underscores fascist movements. He insisted

6 Soon after the above quote he gives another example: guilt about concentration camps at Auschwitz.

that the evident failures of Marx's prophesized revolution to come to fruition demanded a concerted focus on theory in order to inform further practice that might be successful rather than either aborting or devolving into authoritarianism. Saving the prospect of philosophy thus meant saving the prospect of overcoming domination (Adorno 2008).

In the published collection of his lectures on *Negative Dialectics* (2008), he articulates clearly that he holds "speculation" – as an *element* of philosophy – as valuable and intrinsic. The freedom of thought contained within the element of *speculation* was intrinsically connected to the possibility of generating political and social freedom through informed practice. Whereas Nietzsche treated error on different levels (adopting a belief vs. believing a belief to be true), Adorno's treatment of speculation is bifurcated between his and Hegel's meanings. While he provides no clear explanation of the difference between his and Hegel's notion of speculation, he distinguishes his own use of the term from Hegel's entanglement of "speculation" with identity thinking (Adorno 2008; 1973). The relationship may be clarified by understanding it as embodying Adorno's general method of following yet departing from Hegel's dialectic: he drops the second negation.

3.2 *Dropping the Second Negation*

Hegel's second negation – the negation of the negation – is the third step in Hegel's dialectic. It follows the first negation whereby an object passes into its opposite. In the negation of the negation, the relationship between the first object and its derivative opposite are contained together at a higher level.[7] Adorno drops the second negation out of the dialectic, preserving contradiction at the level of the first negation. This has many different ramifications; some are directly social and some are more at the level of philosophical method. On the more purely methodological level, whereas in Hegel's dialectic all of reality is encapsulated in systemic dialectical pyramid that culminates in the Absolute, in complete knowledge; for Adorno there is no such pyramid. For Hegel, all apparent difference is actually just a "moment" within a larger whole within which the differences are reconciled in a larger Identity. For Adorno, all the complexities and contradictions of reality are left as non-identical, as complexities and contradictions, rather than connected together within an all-encompassing

7 For example, in Hegel's Being/Nothing/Becoming nexus, Being's negation is Nothing, and Becoming occupies the stage of second negation. Becoming unifies the opposites of Being and Becoming as participating in a higher order. Their antagonism is shown to be cooperation in the positive process of Becoming, which possesses a larger reality than Being or Becoming on their own. In fact, their reality can really only be properly understood within the higher order of Becoming.

whole. Other than this difference, however, Adorno and Hegel's dialectical methods are very similar. Adorno (2008) does not abandon Hegel; he tweaks him, with far-reaching ramifications.

On the social level, Adorno's central criticism is that Hegel's second negation privileges the social whole over individuality and difference. It is commendable in Adorno's assessment that Hegel calls out independent critical thought as an emancipated form of mind in relation to unthinkingly following the status quo. Independent critical thought is in fact that negation of herd conformity. Unfortunately, Hegel declares that the even greater, more complete, self-aware way of being is through assimilating into society as it is. Rather than unthinking conformity, we have thinking conformity. With the greatest awareness then comes a knowingly conservative attitude. And so with the political question of the individual and the community, the reconciliation of the two does not result in the community allowing the individual great personal freedom. No, it consists in the individual freely submitting to the community. This has been catastrophic in the modern era when large swaths of individuals decide to find their "true" freedom in relinquishing their individuality to the horde. Groupthink is not a reliable judge; it is a holocaust waiting to happen. And yet for Hegel, even the holocaust would have to be seen as contributing to the greater good in the long term; the real is the rational. Adorno refuses to take Hegel's position. How, in good conscience, can we claim that everything that happens is meaningful, rational, and good? We cannot.

3.3 *Speculation in Hegel and Adorno*

Broadly stated, "speculation" in philosophy is the element whereby ideas extend beyond immediate facts. Philosophical thought moves beyond the empirical and the provable or disprovable, and into questions of a more ethereal nature. When it comes to speculation, the difference described in the section above characterizes the distance between Hegel's and Adorno's dialectics. In Hegel's (1977a, 1977b) early essays on Kant, Fichte and Schelling, he distinguished his philosophy as "speculative" in contrast to other thinkers who practice "reflective" philosophy (Schelling being a notable exception). Reflective philosophy limits itself to the reflection of apparent reality, with the aid of logical proof. Speculative philosophy, on the other hand, is based upon intellectual intuition (Cerf 1977). It does not require logical and empirical evidence, and does not speak the applicable language. It is generated by the engaged and speculating human mind. These speculative aspects, that go beyond reflecting the given in tight logical architectures, are also what allows Hegel's philosophy to ascend to the supposed higher levels, and to the highest level of absolute knowledge. For Hegel, reaching beyond inevitably means reaching up within an interconnected system, and collapsing into an encapsulating Identity. Hegel's speculation allowed him to make his system totalizing and teleological.

Adorno's non-identity theory is neither totalizing nor teleological. He centers his notion of non-identity on objects and their concepts. Simply put, there is always a mismatch between concept and object. While conceptual thought aims at capturing objects, it necessarily falls short of accounting for them in their entirety. In turn, there is always a "remainder," a bit of the object that escapes the concept. Adorno similarly sees philosophies that are systems as being reductive and constraining, "hypostatizing" thought. In tandem, he criticizes speculative philosophy, which weaves complex webs of relations between concepts that do not directly refer to objects, and hence only "exist" to the extent that engraving something in philosophy makes it so. The speculative philosophy that he attacks is also philosophies that contain systems. As such his attacks on speculative philosophy are intrinsically attacks on speculative *systems* of philosophy. He attacks speculative philosophy specifically on the level of elevating webs of concepts to a place of supposed greater or more fundamental reality than objects, when in fact, being devoid of objective content, they are the most remote from reality that any concepts can be. "First philosophy" thus always begins from an ephemeral, non-objective construction of the philosopher's mind, which is shaky – if not entirely fictional – ground for such a professed foundation. Adorno is vehement, yet he is not altogether opposed to the elaborate use of concepts, nor to their speculative dimensions. The essential crime he lambasts is the attribution to systems of concepts of the access to higher truth.

Adorno emphasizes putting objects first. In other words, concepts should arise from and be responsive to encountering the object, rather than the object being encountered from within the prejudices of already assumed conceptual parameters. Adorno's "priority of the object" and "non-identity" of object and concept are easy to take as denigrating of concepts to the point of total skepticism, "concretion," or a combination of the two (O'Connor 2004). Yet Adorno is a *dialectical* thinker. He has positive as well as negative aspects to his theories, including in his take on epistemology (Sherratt 2002; 1998). He may critique concepts, but he also underscores their importance.

Despite Adorno's insistence on objects always being larger than their concepts, he also maintains, albeit in a comparatively minor narrative in his work, that concepts are larger than their objects. In other words, concepts cannot capture all that is contained in the object; and yet concepts cannot be completely filled by their objects either. The part of the object that exceeds the concept is famously dubbed the "remainder" by Adorno. The excess of the concept beyond its object – left formally nameless – is the part of the concept that extends beyond fact. In this sense, conceptual thought is inherently speculative. Hence, the issue of speculation is integral to Adorno's philosophy of non-identity.

Speculation takes place within the concept – in the shadow between concept and object – as well as surrounding the concept, as it is referenced within conceptual constellations (which are explained in the following section). This zone of speculation that goes beyond logical or empirical proof risks untruth, irrelevance, and remoteness; but it is also the zone of intellectual creativity that moves human understanding forward. And speculation is a crucial part of any decent philosophy, according to Adorno. Indeed, speculation *makes* philosophy, in contrast to the bare reporting of facts (Adorno 2008; 1973).

3.4 *Constellations and Abstract Objects*

For Adorno (2008; 1973), philosophy aims at disclosing the non-conceptual, but because it uses concepts, it necessarily fails. Adorno suggests that a conceptual multiplicity should be used, comprised of different strands and clusters of conceptual thought. Each strand or cluster indicates something of the object, but fails to capture the object in total. A collection of limited lives of the object are indicated. The truths of the object – if they can even be appropriately referenced as such, which is doubtful – are multiplicities demarcated by the conceptual constellations within which the object's concept is located. There are no outer parameters to the possibilities for such constellations, and so the truths of the object are limitless.

In *Negative Dialectics*, Adorno provides three "models" which operate differently from one another and do not "link up." He suggests that the attempt to reach integration and unity is implicit in the act of philosophizing, despite its impossibility. Hence, there is a ghost of system, or totality, haunting his methodology. A *negative* totality hovers, which highlights the fact that tensions persist – and cannot be resolved – in the antinomies, differences, and multiplicities he outlines. Yet the truths of the object are not arbitrary either. The lives of the object are never free-floating; rather they are always grounded within constellations whose shapes are (a) historically contingent, related to changing socioeconomic formations, and (b) immanent to the object's concept (Adorno 2017). Adorno brings out these historical and immanent dimensions through a dialectical *process* of critique. As in Hegel's logic, *movement* is intrinsic to Adorno's method.

3.5 *Atemporal Movement*

Hegel's dialectic possesses a shifting double-meaning with regard to movement: at times it is movement in history, at other times movement in logic.

Many times, he seems to be operating by both, in varying proportions. The reader has to infer whether and to what extent any given process in Hegel's thought is supposed to happen in time vs. in an ideal space out of time. Adorno (2017) suggests that the merging of the temporal and atemporal aspects of Hegel's logic is no accident – rather in Hegel's dialectic, everything has a complex immanent logic which unfolds and changes through time.

Hegel's dialectic integrally involves Heraclitus' theory of becoming, both in terms of the thesis of fundamental flux, and the thesis of the warring unity of opposites. In Hegel's description, Heraclitus was a speculative philosopher. Heraclitus' notion of becoming defines an object by all of its changes in time. His strife of opposites defines an object as a temporal and phenomenal expression of atemporal oppositions. In this sense, Heraclitus' philosophy extends beyond the mere reflection of apparent reality, to include unseen dimensions that extend beyond present physical states. For Hegel, this suggests totality, in the sense that Hegel uses the term. In Hegel's philosophy, a multiplicity of opposites are integrated in a massive hierarchical system that unites in an all-encompassing, timeless Identity. From the perspective of totality, *all* movement is atemporal, even time.

Hegel's treatment of Becoming occurs at the start of his *Science of Logic* (2010), and essentially runs as follows. Being – that is, pure being – is without substantive contents, and so in attempting to think of it, the concept of Being must immediately pass over into its negation, Nothingness – pure nothingness. Yet Nothingness cannot be thought except in its contrast to Being, hence it passes back over to Being. Neither one can be thought independently. Each one is itself but also not itself at the same time. The overall movement between these two is what Hegel refers to as "Becoming," and it is within this Becoming that each one can exist, even as something of an atemporal flickering between itself and its negation. This flickering occurs in thought, which occurs in time, and therefore it necessarily involves a temporal element. However, the logic to it is *immanent*. The flicking is inherent in the logics of Being, Nothing and Becoming, prior to their recognition by the pondering mind. The immanent logic is true beyond time, and it is also not directly about time. Hence it is atemporal, yet comes to human awareness through temporal consciousness.

Adorno's method of constellations can be comprehended both through the notion of immanent logic and through the unfolding of history. In both cases, the lives of the object are multiple, and "truths" are to be found within process, rather than as conclusions. The process that truths follow is at once historical and immanent. Adorno's method is open yet grounded in rigorous analysis. Truths are never final or complete, and speculation is honored. Yet truths are not relative. They are connected to changing historical conditions and webs of dialectical logic. At any moment in history, concepts are within multiple immanent logical relations.

4 Conclusion: *Amor Lutum*[8]

Despite some claims that history ends at postmodernity (Baudrillard 1994; Fukuyama 1992, 1989), the social sciences have not ended at postmodernism. Since Kuhn's (1962) pronouncement of the succession of limited and incommensurable paradigms rather than their progress toward a final, complete paradigm, the idea that intellectual trends are not sacrosanct but instead have something akin to life cycles has become commonplace. Correspondingly, scholars pondered what would come after postmodernism even back in the 1990s while the movement was at its most energetic (Woodiwiss 1990; McLennan 1995; Mouzelis 1996). Pragmatism has sometimes been invoked as a new social research paradigm (Morgan 2014; Bakker 2011), although discussions surrounding it are typically obscure both in terms of (a) what "pragmatism" signifies, and (b) if – and if so, how – pragmatism transcends positivism and relativism rather than simply collapsing back into one or the other according to the predilections of the researcher. Indeed, the pragmatist "whatever works" mantra can be used as a thin veil for positivism and also for relativism at the metatheoretical level, in both cases having a prohibitive effect on philosophical examination despite ostensible openness.

I propose a return to Nietzsche and Adorno. I say "return," because they are old thinkers; their direct presence within sociology has been minimal. This Nietzsche is not the postmodern Nietzsche, nor is it the neo-Kantian Nietzsche. It is Babich's (1994) *perspectivalist* Nietzsche who operates beyond positivism and relativism, and who is channeled by Adorno (2008; 1973) not only in his critique of the concept, but also in his celebration of daring and playfulness in philosophy (Bauer 1999). Nietzsche and Adorno both do not expound total systems of philosophy. Neither do they avoid contradiction. Of specific significance for the present exposition, both criticize the trappings of Enlightenment rationality, and yet both admire rigorous analysis. Both support the creative production of new understandings, and both support cutting through myths and illusions.[9] The lesson here is not to attempt to emulate

8 Love of Dirt.

9 This could be framed as ambivalence, or paradox, but the important thing here is that in order to understand them, both sides need to be taken in. Some commentators (Clark 1990; Green 2002) interpret Nietzsche as more pragmatic and pro-science, and others focus on his

Nietzsche or Adorno with precision. Neither one would support that anyway. Yet it is at least possible – and I would argue advisable – to take on an attitude broadly akin to their epistemological perspectives.

The intervention this paper is intended to achieve is at the level of metatheory – specifically, what Ritzer (1990) has classified as *internal-intellectual* metatheory – rather than methodology. Metatheory has fallen out of fashion in sociology for decades. Criticisms of metatheory from a largely practical – also impatient and arguably anti-intellectual – point of view (Turner 1986) gained something of a hegemonic status in the discipline, effectively severing sociology from serious interrogation of its philosophical roots. At this point sociological theory has already advanced far into an underwhelming corner. The notion that the dogma of singular empirical truth and the dogma of unaccountable relativism are both indefensible; is setting in as common sense across the discipline. Yet attempts to move beyond positivism and relativism – such as pragmatism – tend to fall somewhere on a continuum between the two that ultimately cater more to one or the other side. Unfortunately such half-hearted compromise does not overcome the dilemma. Metatheory is the only way out, aside from ignoring theoretical considerations even more. In this paper I have proposed that a metatheoretical angle which supports the selective use of multiple perspectives might be helpful.

Nietzsche's perspectivalism and Adorno's negative dialectics offer us points of departure along these lines. For both Nietzsche and Adorno, the shadow between concept and object is a key element in the relationships between people and "truth" that they support. Instead of trying to eradicate the shadow, both of them support maintaining it with awareness that it is there. The shadow does not contain truth in itself, but it does allow a relationship to knowledge which is perhaps more actualized, and in this sense, as close to "truth" as we can reasonably come (while having important ulterior benefits, such as affirming life or overturning domination).

All theory draws connections that extend beyond what can be known empirically. In Western philosophy this insight is nothing new. But this understanding does not need to result in the total rejection of theory. Instead, we might embrace that every theory involves *speculation*, and recognize that it is this and the *errors* it implicates that actually let theory empower us. Theories are useful, and they are limited. Their limitations are intrinsic to their utility,

more critical stance to Enlightenment thought. Others suggest that Nietzsche changed his mind over the course of his writing career on these issues. I suggest not trying to rectify these seemingly contradictory elements, rather their contradiction needs to be preserved, and both aspects recognized.

and influence which of our values they appear to serve. Placing them above philosophical analysis and silencing critique deprives them of potential refinement. Tossing them out entirely because they form incomplete maps disempowers us unnecessarily.

References

Adorno, Theodor W. 2017. *An introduction to dialectics*. Hoboken, NJ: John Wiley & Sons.

Adorno, Theodor W. 2008. *Lectures on Negative Dialectics: Fragments of a Lecture Course 1965/1966*. Cambridge, UK: Polity Press.

Adorno, Theodor W. 1973. *Negative Dialectics*. London, UK: A&C Black.

Babich, Babette E. 1994. *Nietzsche's Philosophy of Science: Reflecting Science on the Ground of Art and Life*. Albany, NY: SUNY Press.

Bakker, J.I. (Hans). 2011. "North Central Sociological Association Presidential Address: Pragmatic Sociology: Healing the Discipline." *Sociological Focus* 44(3): 167–183.

Baudrillard, Jean. 1994. *The Illusion of the End*. Cambridge, UK: Polity.

Bauer, Karin. 1999. *Adorno's Nietzschean Narratives: Critiques of Ideology, Readings of Wagner*. Albany, NY: SUNY Press.

Besbris, Max, and Shamus Khan. 2017. "Less Theory. More Description." *Sociological Theory* 35(2): 147–153.

Cerf, Walter. 1977. "Speculative Philosophy and Intellectual Intuition: An Introduction to Hegel's Essays." In *The Difference Between Fichte's and Schelling's System of Philosophy*, by Georg Wilhelm Friedrich Hegel, edited by H.S. Harris and Walter Cerf, xi–xxxvi. Albany, NY: State University of New York Press.

Clark, Maudemarie. 1990. *Nietzsche on Truth and Philosophy*. Cambridge, UK: Cambridge University Press.

Deleuze, Gilles. 2006. *Nietzsche and Philosophy*. New York, NY: Columbia University Press.

Deleuze, Gilles. 2001. *Pure Immanence*. New York, NY: Zone.

Denzin, Norman K. 1987. "The Death of Sociology in the 1980s: Comment on Collins." *American Journal of Sociology* 93(1): 175–180.

Eliot, Thomas Stearns. 2010. *The Waste Land and Other Poems*. Peterborough, Canada: Broadview Press.

Ermakoff, Ivan. 2017. "Shadow Plays: Theory's Perennial Challenges." *Sociological Theory* 35(2): 128–137.

Fukuyama, Francis. 1992. *The End of History and the Last Man*. New York, NY: Simon and Schuster.

Fukuyama, Francis. 1989. "The End of History?" *The National Interest* 16: 3–18.

Gemes, Ken. 1992. "Nietzsche's Critique of Truth." *Philosophy and Phenomenological Research* 52(1): 47–65.

Green, Michael Steven. 2002. *Nietzsche and the Transcendental Tradition*. Champaign, IL: University of Illinois Press.

Healy, Kieran. 2017. "Fuck Nuance." *Sociological Theory* 35(2): 118–127.

Hegel, Georg Wilhelm Fredrich. 2010. *The Science of Logic*. Cambridge, UK: University Press.

Hegel, Georg Wilhelm Fredrich. 1998. *Phenomenology of Spirit*. Delhi India: Motilal Banarsidass.

Hegel, Georg Wilhelm Fredrich. 1977a. *The Difference Between Fichte's and Schelling's System of Philosophy*. Albany, NY: State University of New York Press.

Hegel, Georg Wilhelm Fredrich. 1977b. *Faith and Knowledge*. Albany, NY: State University of New York Press.

Kuhn, Thomas. 1962. *The Structure of Scientific Revolutions*. Chicago, IL: University of Chicago Press.

Laudan, Larry, and Andre Kukla. 1996. *Beyond Positivism and Relativism: Theory, Method, and Evidence*. Boulder, CO: Westview Press.

Leiter, Brian. 2007. "Nietzsche's Theory of the Will." *Philosopher's Imprint* 7: 1–15.

McLennan, Gregor. 1995. "After Postmodernism – Back to Sociological Theory?" *Sociology* 29(1): 117–132.

Mears, Ashley. 2017. "Puzzling in Sociology: On Doing and Undoing Theoretical Puzzles." *Sociological Theory* 35(2): 138–146.

Morgan, David L. 2014. "Pragmatism as a paradigm for social research." *Qualitative Inquiry* 20(8): 1045–1053.

Mouzelis, Nicos. 1996. "After Postmodernism: a Reply to Gregor McLennan." *Sociology* 30(1): 131–135.

Mullin, Amy. 2000. "Nietzsche's Free Sprit." *Journal of the History of Philosophy* 38(3): 383–405.

Nietzsche, Friedrich. 2010. *The Gay Science: With a Prelude in Rhymes and an Appendix of Songs*, translated by Walter Kaufmann. New York, NY: Vintage Books.

Nietzsche, Friedrich. 2009. *Ecce Homo: How to Become What You Are*, translated by Duncan Large. Oxford, UK: Oxford University Press.

Nietzsche, Friedrich. 2001. *Philosophy in the Tragic Age of the Greeks*, translated by Marianne Cowan. Washington DC: Regnery Publishing.

Nietzsche, Friedrich. 1997. *Twilight of the Idols: Or, How to Philosophize with the Hammer*, translated by Richard Polt. Indianapolis/Cambridge: Hackett Publishing Company.

Nietzsche, Friedrich. 1996. *Human, All Too Human: A Book for Free Spirits*, translated by R.J. Hollingdale. Cambridge UK: Cambridge University Press.

Nietzsche, Friedrich. 1979. "On Truth and Lies in a Nonmoral Sense." In *Philosophy and Truth: Selections from Nietzsche's Notebooks of the Early 1870's*, translated and edited by Daniel Breazeale. Amherst, NY: Humanity Books.

Nietzsche, Friedrich. 1977. *The Portable Nietzsche*, translated by Walter Kaufmann. New York, NY: Penguin Books.

O'Connor, Brian. 2004. *Adorno's Negative Dialectic: Philosophy and the Possibility of Critical Rationality.* Cambridge, MA: MIT University Press.

Ritzer, George. 1990. "The Current Status of Sociological Theory: The New Syntheses." In *Frontiers of Social Theory: The New Syntheses*, edited by George Ritzer, 1–30. New York: Columbia University Press.

Rowe, David Emmanuel. 2013. "Nietzsche's 'Anti-Naturalism' in 'The Four Great Errors.'" *The International Journal of Philosophical Studies* 21(2): 256–276.

Seidman, Steven. 2017. *Contested Knowledge: Social Theory Today*. Hoboken, NJ: John Wiley & Sons.

Sherratt, Yvonne. 2002. *Adorno's Positive Dialectic*. Cambridge, UK: Cambridge University Press.

Sherratt, Yvonne. 1998. "Negative Dialectics: A Positive Interpretation." *International Philosophical Quarterly* 38(1): 55–66.

Skinner, Jacob. 2005. "Critical Theory at a Crossroad: Adorno, Marcuse, and the Radical Sixties." *Inquiry Journal* 11.

Turner, Jonathan. 1986. *The Structure of Sociological Theory*, 4th ed. Chicago, IL: Dorsey Press.

Woodiwiss, Anthony. 1990. *Social Theory After Postmodernism: Rethinking Production, Law and Class.* London, UK: Pluto Press.

CHAPTER 12

The Science of the Last Man: Nietzsche and the Early Frankfurt School

Daniel Sullivan

In their late dialogues while composing a new *Communist Manifesto* for the 20th Century, Theodor Adorno and Max Horkheimer struggled to find a language to describe life in the contemporary "atomistic stage of civilization." At one point Adorno spontaneously found the right words when he quoted Nietzsche: "'No herdsman and one herd.' A kind of false classless society" (Adorno and Horkheimer 1956/2011: 33). He was invoking, of course, the figure of the "Last Man," a specter throughout Nietzsche's writings. I intend to show that this was not a coincidence. Rather, in their late empirical studies, the Frankfurt School scholars arrived at a diagnosis of how "average" individuals under modern capitalism were able to participate in atrocities such as the Holocaust. This diagnosis resonates strongly with Nietzsche's archetype. My aim is to demonstrate how the social scientific methodologies of both Nietzsche and the early Frankfurt School gave them a unique vantage on this predominant personality type in contemporary culture.

A standard story is that Nietzsche was hostile to empiricist epistemology (for reviews, see Antonio 1995; Sadler 1993). For its part, the empirical methodology of the early Frankfurt School is neglected and even maligned (e.g. Martin 2001). Attempting to counteract such misconceptions, I examine three primary questions: What was Nietzsche's vision for methods at the intersection of philosophy and science? How does this vision relate to the metatheoretical foundations of the Frankfurt School's empirical methodology? And what relevance do this vision and methodology have for the empirical social sciences today? I believe it is essential to ask these questions because the vast majority of writing on Nietzsche and empirical science centers on broad topics of epistemology, such as the possibility of transcendent rationalism (Babich 2004). Furthermore, largely in response to Habermas's (1987) *Philosophical Discourse of Modernity*, the secondary literature tends to contrast the "second generation" Frankfurt School with the apparent anti-normativism of Nietzsche and followers like Foucault (Ashenden and Owen 1999). Instead, I compare and synthesize the writings on social scientific methodology of Friedrich Nietzsche and the early Institute for Social Research (ISR).[1]

The ISR's methodology was characterized by two major assumptions that fulfill Nietzsche's vision for science as a *paradoxical* endeavor. They are: (1) sociological theory and empirical research, qualitative and quantitative methods, and individual and societal levels of analysis *must* always be employed in concert with one another; and (2) this is the case *despite* the fact that none of these binaries is ultimately reconcilable in any straightforward way. I will examine how these assumptions are exemplified in the last major empirical project of the ISR: the *Gruppenexperiment*. I will argue that this neglected vision of empiricism provides a welcome counterpoint to recent developments in the social sciences, and that it granted the ISR empirical insight into a personality type that Nietzsche would have recognized as the Last Man.

1 Nietzsche's Vision for Science

I agree with Berkowitz (1995), Clark (1990), Jaspers (1936/1997), Richardson (1996), and Stack (2005) that Nietzsche had a "passionate longing" for the truth. I further agree that Nietzsche's perspectivism led him to believe that the truth was constantly in flux and could only be approximated through a method that sought maximal knowledge of diverse perspectives. Beyond its perspectival *content*, Jaspers further highlighted the unique *form* of Nietzsche's "methodical attitude" (Jaspers 1936/1997: 172–174), a form that can be characterized as "paradoxical." Its significance lies in the effort to utilize science for the pursuit of truth in the service of important anthropocentric ends, while nevertheless maintaining a critical distance from empirical methods as conventionally understood. The goal of his science is "Not 'to know' but to schematize – to impose upon chaos as much regularity and form as our practical needs require" (Nietzsche 1968: 278). On one hand, he claimed, "The most valuable insights are arrived at last; but the most valuable insights are *methods*" (Nietzsche 1968: 261) and that "everyone now should have acquired a thorough knowledge of at

1 I recognize the complex history of the "Frankfurt School" (Institut für Sozialforschung) and the fact that it exists to this day as an active scholarly Institute affiliated with Johann Wolfgang Goethe University (for a concise German-language overview, see the Institute website: http://www.ifs.uni-frankfurt.de/institut/geschichte/). However, for purposes of simplicity in this essay, when I employ the acronym ISR – Institute for Social Research – I am specifically demarcating the "first generation" incarnation which was exemplified by Adorno, Fromm, Horkheimer, Marcuse, and Pollock, and which carried out empirical projects between 1929 and 1955.

least *one* science: then he would know what is meant by method and procedure and how vital it is to exercise the greatest circumspection" (Nietzsche 1878/1996: 202). Yet he also notoriously claimed, "It is not the victory of science that distinguishes our nineteenth century, but the victory of scientific method over science" (Nietzsche 1968: 261). Clearly, Nietzsche believed that the majority of contemporary empirical efforts did not live up to a "true" standard for scientific method. Indeed, Nietzsche outlined his vision of science largely in critical contrast to contemporary science and philosophy – an expository strategy that also figured prominently in the methodological writings of the ISR.[2]

2 Critique of Naïve Empiricism

Nietzsche continually contrasts his perspectivist method against what he refers to as "positivist" science and philosophy, "which halts at phenomena" (Nietzsche 1968: 267) in its "prostration before 'facts,' a kind of cult" (Nietzsche 1968: 226–227). He was especially critical of nineteenth century scientists who felt emboldened to reject the aims of philosophy in the embrace of what they perceived to be "claims to objectivity, to cold impersonality" (Nietzsche 1968: 229). Nietzsche already recognizes in these pilgrims to positivism certain dangerous tendencies that would be attacked approximately one century later in the ISR's critique of positivist social science.

2.1 *Fetishism or Idolatry of Method*

Nietzsche's first angle of attack on "scientific-positivistic" thought (Nietzsche 1887/1974: 288) is his argument that the worship of "objective" scientific method and simultaneous rejection of philosophical aims concealed hidden motivations. Anticipating Devereux's (1967) groundbreaking analysis, Nietzsche asserted that scientific methods are for many a means of coping with fundamental anxieties and fulfilling a metaphysical need for certainty in the void left by declining religion. This is why he often referred to scholars as "frogs and weaklings" (Nietzsche, 1887/1974: 287–290). The ISR would later take up this line of argument in nearly identical terms: "[T]his intellectual uncertainty...is so great that [people] make a fetish of certainty as such...People prefer to cling

2 In reconstructing Nietzsche's vision for social science methodology I will rely heavily on *The Will to Power* with full awareness of its controversial status in Nietzsche scholarship (Magnus 1988; Stack 2005). Specifically, the present study is partly the fruit of a focused examination of the section "The Will to Power as Knowledge" which opens "Book Three: Principles of a New Evaluation."

to pure tautology...rather than importing into the realm of knowledge the risks...imposed by an existence liable to be annihilated at any moment" (Adorno 1968/2000: 76).

Nietzsche also anticipated the ISR's critique of technical-administrative science by pointing to the role of commercial-political interests in sustaining method worship. A coterie of specialists docilely quantifying extant reality is a vision of academia perfectly suited to the unfettered growth of capitalism. Preoccupation with the form rather than the content of thought allows scholars to insert whatever themes happen to be politically popular into their well-oiled calculating machines. The essay "Schopenhauer as Educator" contains a prophetic critique of the growing culture industry and commercialization of education in Germany at the hands of "the greed of the money-makers" (Nietzsche 1874/1997: 164), a process in which scientists are seen to be complicit.

> The man of learning is to a great extent also motivated to the discovery of *certain* 'truths' ... Truth is served when it is in a position...to win the favor of those who have bread and honors to distribute...[This] 'Truth', however, of which our professors speak so much, seems to be...a self-contented and happy creature which is constantly assuring all the powers that be that no one needs to be the least concerned on its account; for it is, after all, only 'pure science.'
>
> NIETZSCHE 1874/1997: 137, 170–172

2.2 *The Reduction of Qualitative Differences to Quantitative Equilibria*

The second front of Nietzsche's war on naïve empiricism centers not on researchers' motivations for fetishizing their method, but rather the way in which that method systematically distorts the nature of reality. *The Will to Power* contains several notes in which he draws into serious question the apparent scientific advances made by "the mechanistic interpretation of the world" (Nietzsche 1968: 332) that seeks "the calculability of the world, the expressibility of all events in formulas" (Nietzsche 1968: 334). Nietzsche (1886/1989) charged that the obsession of "scientific-positivistic" thought with quantification represents a modern incarnation of asceticism that inhibits the "free spirit" of philosophy and scholarship just as theology once did. This charge is taken up again in nearly identical terms by the ISR: "Positivism is the puritanism of knowledge...Knowledge resigns itself to being a mere repetitive reconstruction. It becomes impoverished just as life is impoverished under work discipline" (Adorno 1976: 55).

The critique of fetishistic quantification is by no means a wholesale attack on quantitative methods and empiricism *as such*. It is just as much an error to adopt Nietzsche as an unabashed champion of *Verstehen* methodology as it is to position Adorno and Horkheimer as committed enemies of empirical enlightenment (see Dallmayr and McCarthy 1977; Morrow and Brown 1994).

Rather, Nietzsche is highlighting an insidious hazard of quantitative social science that reflects its underlying political nature (despite the frequent protests of scientists that their work is somehow a-political). The problem is not at all the employ of quantification in coming to grips with reality; indeed, Nietzsche insists much can be gained from this approach. The problem, rather, is the way in which quantification of all forces and phenomena encourages a tendency to *equilibrate*, rather than differentiate, entities, by viewing them either as opposite ends of a homeostatic tension-system or as somehow comparable in terms of dimension or magnitude. Deleuze describes how, in formulating laws such as that of the conservation of energy, "we pass from a principle of finitude (the constancy of a sum) to a 'nihilistic' principle (the cancelling out of differences in quantities, the sum of which is constant)" (Deleuze 1983: 46). Given his commitment to genealogical methods, Nietzsche naturally sees this tendency to level qualitative differences more as a reflection of the modern cultural environment and less as "progress" in our tools for understanding reality (Richardson 1996).

3 The Characteristics of Nietzsche's Scholarly Method

Granted that Nietzsche went to great lengths to disparage the naïve empiricism of his day; what, then, were the characteristics of his own envisioned method? Synthesizing the secondary literature with Nietzsche's own writings, I discern three fundamental aspects. The first is an unyielding commitment to truth; in short, a deeply developed "intellectual conscience" (Berkowitz 1995; Jaspers 1936/1997; Nietzsche 1886/1989). This translates into a sharp suspicion of all scholarly dogmas and a relentless reflexivity concerning questions of method, including above all one's own (Grimm 1977). Nietzsche's vision for all forms of scholarship, including both science and philosophy, is an experimental one – truth is an elusive goal that must be relentlessly pursued with the willingness to adopt and discard a variety of hypotheses, perspectives, methods, and "regulative fictions" (Schacht 2016; Stack 2005). This paradoxical approach to truth does not undermine the latter, but rather is the only legitimate way to approach it, as the ISR later realized (e.g. Horkheimer 1935/2014: 63–70).

But how should this experimental approach to truth be practiced, and what are its primary targets? In answering these questions Nietzsche was keenly aware of the contribution of the history of ideas to the condition of modern science and philosophy. Far from embracing a narrative of progressive freedom from ideological tyranny, Nietzsche focused on what had been *lost* in the historical transition from religion and classical philosophy to modern secular rationalism (along lines directly parallel to Horkheimer's later argument about the triumph of subjective over objective reason). What these cultural circumstances meant was that we had arrived at the "*age of comparison*" (Nietzsche 1878/1996: 24), during which a globalized and fluid society would be inundated with competing ideas, norms, and morals of varied cultural origin and potential for service to humankind. He insisted we "confront the task which the age sets us as boldly as we can" (Nietzsche 1878/1996: 24) by determining which ends were worth pursuing during the *Götzen-Dämmerung*. The importance of scientific method lay in the fact that we could now gather *data* to be employed in service of this central aim:

> Since the belief has ceased that a God broadly directs the destinies of the world…man has to set himself ecumenical goals embracing the whole earth…if mankind is not to destroy itself through such conscious universal rule, it must first of all attain to a hitherto altogether unprecedented *knowledge of the preconditions of culture* as a scientific standard for ecumenical goals.
>
> NIETZSCHE 1878/1996: 25

Thus, I would argue that a second distinguishing feature of Nietzsche's method, beyond its experimental commitment to radical truth, was that it was both *perspectival-psychological* (Richardson 1996; Stack 2005) and *genealogical-cultural* (Foucault 1977; Schacht 2016). He emphasized the importance of psychology for his method, while also arguing that chronic inattention to history was the "family failing" of philosophers (Nietzsche 1878/1996). Both psychology and genealogy were essential, he argued, because knowledge of an object or "law" is never valid across time and space: "Coming to know means 'to place oneself in a conditional relation to something'; to feel oneself conditioned by something and oneself to condition it – it is therefore under all circumstances establishing, denoting, and making-conscious of conditions (not forthcoming entities, things, what is 'in-itself')" (Nietzsche 1968: 301). To achieve this "conditional relationship" with his objects of study, Nietzsche gathered as much data as possible regarding the affective phenomenology of individuals located in particular cultural-historical circumstances. His aim was always to *contextualize* knowledge of morally relevant phenomena in order to make qualitative *comparisons* between them, in the hope of discovering new "ecumenical goals" for humanity.

Nietzsche critiqued contemporary scientists and philosophers for approaching the subjects of humanity and society as if knowledge of their nineteenth century incarnations was somehow valid for all time and reflective of some underlying essence (cf. Schacht 2016). He condemned a disinterested form of academic history for its own sake that would be isolated from the aims of philosophy and government. His cultural-psychological method would meet the challenge of the trans-valuation of values in the "age of comparison" by synthesizing empirical data relevant to the choice between possible human ends (Nietzsche 1886/1989: 97–98).

A final defining characteristic of Nietzsche's method must be mentioned: his vision for social science was essentially *tragic* (Olick and Simko under review; Stack 2005). Nietzsche's unyielding commitment to truth meant that he seemed prepared to accept the possibility that humanity would be unable to engage in the kind of collective self-determination that the ISR sought to promote. Perhaps, however, the tragedy of Nietzsche's vision is only apparent to those of us accustomed to straightforward solutions and the naïve views of empiricism – both celebratory and critical – that predominate late capitalist thought. One point of commonality between Nietzsche and the ISR is that they are frequently misunderstood as adopting a stance of resignation when confronted by the limits of human knowledge. What if the "tragic" element in their twin corpora stems from a shared methodological commitment to contradiction and paradox, a commitment that leads not to a door but a bridge?

4 The ISR Vision of Science as a Paradoxical Endeavor

Regardless of how one views the fruits of the labor, I contend that the ISR never abandoned its commitment – first outlined by Horkheimer in his inaugural address as Institute Director in 1929 – to the development and employ of a method that would transcend facile boundaries between philosophy and science, theory and research. Like Nietzsche before them, the charter members of the ISR were relentlessly inventive, polemic, holistic, and skeptical in their quest for truths that could improve the human condition. It is not my primary aim here to establish a link of historical influence. But by reading the methodological texts and scientific endeavors of the ISR back through Nietzsche, we may gain a fresh appreciation of the insight and promise they contain. The ISR constructed an outline of social science as a *paradoxical* endeavor. Their embrace of the role of dialectical tension in the unmasking of truth reveals their greatest methodological affinity to Nietzsche.

4.1 *The Antinomy of Empirical Research: Tension between Interpretive Philosophy and the Data of Science*

Nietzsche consistently attacked philosophy from the Socratic-Platonic tradition to his day for its defensive resistance to the findings and formulations of science (while praising the "scientific types of the old philosophy" such as Democritus and Heraclitus; Nietzsche 1968). In a similar vein, the ISR were as skeptical of relativistic philosophy as they were of positivism's smug self-confidence. Just as they opposed the strict demarcation of theoretical and empirical endeavors, the ISR simultaneously denied the notion that these two forms of understanding could be easily reconciled (Adorno 1976; Horkheimer 1993).

Like Nietzsche, the ISR believed a skeptical confrontation between science and philosophy to be crucial because they were troubled by the "antinomy of empirical research" – the tendency for scientific methods and the "disinterested" pursuit of truth to become a fetish, a means-in-itself (Frankfurt ISR 1956/1972; Pollock, Adorno et al. 2011). These concerns form the logical core of the ISR's argument against "technocratic" research of "total administration" (Adorno 1976; Marcuse 1966; Pollock, Adorno et al. 2011). They proposed that the alleged "objectivity" of value-free, method-fetishizing research simply reproduces or reifies, in symbolic-textual form, the objectivity of a totally socialized society in which individuals are themselves reduced to objects. This form of research is paralyzed and incapable of achieving the original goals of Enlightenment reason, namely some form of human liberation and betterment – Nietzsche's "ecumenical goals."

The alternative to such technocratic research was, of course, dialectical methods fused with critical theory (Adorno 1976; Horkheimer 1972/2014). From this perspective, the phenomena unearthed by empirical research are not to be merely taken at face value, chronicled and catalogued. Rather, they serve alternately as ending and starting points for the act of theoretical *interpretation*. "In sociology, *interpretation* acquires its force both from the fact that without reference to totality – to the real total system, untranslatable into any solid immediacy – nothing societal can be conceptualized, and from the fact that it can, however, only be recognized in the extent to which it is apprehended in the factual and the individual" (Adorno 1976: 32). The ISR's method involves dialectical movement between the focused investigation of concrete empirical phenomena, and acts of theoretical interpretation that illuminate those phenomena in light of a critical-historical understanding of the society in which they take place. Put differently, this method centers around the exchange between perspectival and genealogical forms of knowledge as advocated by Nietzsche.

4.2 *The Aporia of Sociology: Tension between Quantitative and Qualitative Methods*

In the notes on method in *The Will to Power*, Nietzsche proposed that both quantitative and qualitative forms of knowledge were essential for understanding uniquely human behavior.

> Everything for which the word 'knowledge' makes any sense refers to the domain of reckoning, weighing, measuring, to the domain of quantity; while, on the other hand, all our sensations of value (i.e., simply our sensations) adhere precisely to qualities, i.e., to our perspective 'truths' which belong to us alone and can by no means be 'known'!... Qualities are an idiosyncrasy peculiar to man; to demand that our human interpretations and values should be universal and perhaps constitutive values is one of the hereditary madnesses of human pride.
>
> NIETZSCHE 1968: 304–305

The problem Nietzsche alighted on is one that Adorno referred to as the "aporia of sociology": the fact that quantitative methods, for the sake of obtaining potentially "universal" reliability and generalizability, sacrifice the in-depth validity regarding human experience offered by qualitative methods. The ISR researchers clearly saw, with Nietzsche, the central role of quantification in furthering knowledge. Yet consistent with their aim of employing theoretical interpretation to illuminate the social totality made manifest in individual objects of study, ISR researchers found qualitative data to be an essential complement to their quantitative analyses.

In particular, the researchers attacked the prevailing methods of opinion research and other forms of quantitative attitude surveys as simply providing a "subjective reflection" of the total society. In other words, when individuals are demanded to have an opinion about subjects which they may only understand through socially filtered preconceptions, and presented with a preselected "cafeteria" array of responses, the results often simply confirm dominant ideologies, since the latter were built into the method from the outset. Qualitative data provide a way out for the researcher working with standardized empirical methods, granting the study an element of critical reflexivity that is typically foreclosed by quantitative research. By coaxing "webs of meaning" (Adorno 2010: 56) out from careful interpretation of qualitative data, the ISR researchers probed and problematized the reified picture presented by their statistics, refracting the patterns through a broader social and philosophical frame.

Most significantly, this foothold in qualitative methodology allowed the researchers to avoid the reduction of qualitative differences to quantitative equilibria that Nietzsche lamented. The ISR viewed inflexible procedures of standardization and replication in quantitative research as inevitably leading to such a reified condition of knowledge: "The demand for interchangeability in sociology tacitly assumes an identity of minds, and this dooms knowledge to sterility" (Adorno 2010: 49). This constant wariness is echoed in the fact that, as in the case of theory and empiricism, ISR researchers were concerned that an artificial demarcation of quantitative and qualitative study as separate domains of inquiry would subsequently sanction an artificial "harmonizing" of these two domains. If interviews are interpreted as simply reinforcing the findings of a survey, then qualitative data have not served their purpose in illuminating how "the social manifests itself through the individual" (Adorno 1968/2000: 74).

4.3 *The Dialectical Concept of Society: Tension between Individual and Societal Levels*

A possibly telling note from *Will to Power* reads: "Science: its two sides: in regard to the individual; in regard to the cultural complex (level); – valuations from one side or the other are mutually antagonistic" (Nietzsche 1968: 328). Nietzsche likely considered both of these "sides" or "levels" significant for social science because, as is well known, he was deeply suspicious of the conventional notion of the "subject." He rather saw the individual as the site of competing forces: largely non-conscious drives, as well as internalized cultural categories of morality, perception, and language (Richardson 2015). Given that these forces often manifest conflicting desires, Nietzsche considered the individual a cauldron of tension that could lash out with violence if directed by a powerful leader. The ISR scholars similarly emphasized the violent nature of the individual-social exchange, taking pains to distinguish their position from either methodological individualism or the sociological holism associated with Durkheim (Adorno 1968/2000: 27–45). The ISR vision of society is instead more Nietzschean: as a conglomerate of conflicting forces that threatens to rend apart at any moment.

What is essential for the ISR, as for Nietzsche, is the psychoanalytic insight that life under modern capitalism renders the individual a site of internalized tension and *ambivalence*. Horkheimer, Adorno, and their colleagues stressed two aspects of individual-social mediation in modernity that generated this internal ambivalence. First, they contended that any form of "solidarity" under capitalism – political, nationalistic, etc. – was ultimately a screen, constructed by the culture industry and easily shredded, stretched over an underlying social arrangement that was competitive and antagonistic to the core. Second, they emphasized the schizophrenic experience of self-awareness in a culture that trumpets the values of individualism and self-sufficiency, but locks individuals into an increasingly standardized and predetermined set of movements through a system of invisible social controls. These elements combine to produce a large number of individuals who, though superficially satisfied, rational, and content with the small pleasures of consumerism, nevertheless harbor profound self-doubts and the potential for hostility against the external forces on which they feel dependent. This ambivalent personality type – reminiscent of Nietzsche's "Last Man" – was documented in the ISR studies, and especially in their late *Gruppenexperiment*.

The ISR's vision of science as a paradoxical endeavor, balancing and recognizing the tension between epistemologies, methods, and levels of social reality, bore fruit in the large Berkeley project on authoritarianism, but also in a series of other lesser-known yet critical studies. I will conclude with a detailed reconstruction of the methods and findings of one of these, in order to demonstrate the potential and ongoing relevance of the "paradoxical" social science heralded by Nietzsche and undertaken by the ISR.

5 Paradoxical Social Science: ISR Methodology in *Gruppenexperiment*

The *Gruppenexperiment* was conducted in 1950 upon the Institute's return to Germany during the time of Allied occupation. The "experimental" aspect was the development of a new method that sought to observe the development of "public opinion" as it arises in situ in realistic social situations. Working out of three research centers in Hesse, Bavaria, and Northern Germany, the ISR organized semi-formal discussion groups of 8–16 participants who met in public places (e.g. clubs, cafeterias) accompanied by a research assistant and a tape recorder. Participants were given pseudonyms and assigned to groups based on demographic categories (e.g. college graduates, older adults, farmers, clerks, housewives). Data were collected from roughly 1,800 participants, resulting in 121 discussion transcripts (over 6,000 pages). The overwhelming bulk of rich data was processed through a form of content analysis that resulted (over iterative coding rounds) in close statistical consideration of seven key themes or "attitudes," identified as significant and prominent in close readings of the transcripts.

The group discussions were organized around a carefully constructed stimulus, the "Colburn letter," which was read at the beginning of every session. Ostensibly written by a U.S. soldier stationed in occupied post-war Germany, the letter contained many critiques of German society and broached the raw topics of collective guilt for the Holocaust and the passive German national character. This stimulus was specifically designed to elicit latent attitudes and a preformed ideology – lingering after the ostensible eradication of National Socialism – that participants normally repressed but would enact to defend their "collective narcissism" (Pollock, Adorno et al. 2011: 149).

Researchers assigned individual statements in the group discussions labels, e.g. "approving, ambivalent, or disapproving attitude" (with reference to democratic, as opposed to fascist, ideals). The content analysis involved coding statements based on their relevance for the identified focal themes. The final dependent variables are percentage counts of statement labels, stratified according to the independent variable of sociological grouping (gender, age, occupation, and levels of education and military service). These percentages are derived from counts of the labels assigned to qualitative data interpretively by individual researchers. Thus, "the use of interpretive categories already introduced a qualitative component into the quantitative analysis. This is based on our conviction that the distinction between quantitative and qualitative social research...[must] not be hypostatized by the method" (Pollock, Adorno et al. 2011: 49).

The combination of a controlled social setting with detailed transcription of individual statements allowed the researchers to document the social construction of ideology as it occurred, and to observe how the pressures of anomic social interaction in an administrative-consumerist society give rise to individual acts of conformity. The ISR summarily reported that "only about one-sixth of the speakers have a positive attitude (16%) [towards topics such as democracy, remilitarization, and German guilt], but almost three times as many have a negative one (44%) and more than twice as many an ambivalent one" (Pollock, Adorno et al. 2011: 106). The researchers interpreted the overall pattern as evidence of a consistent, reified "public opinion" that was spontaneously invoked across the discussions. This public opinion contained lingering remnants of fascism, including anti-Semitism and denial of complicity for wartime atrocities. The researchers observed that only a disconcerting minority of the participants in the discussions displayed an unambiguously positive attitude toward Western democratic ideals. Many were openly apologetic for

National Socialism, and refused to acknowledge collective guilt or to absolve Jewish citizens of any responsibility for war crimes. Of course, these disturbing attitudes were to a large extent evoked by the threat of the stimulus letter read at the beginning of the discussions. Yet notable beyond the number of clearly anti-democratic remarks was the ambivalence displayed by many participants, chronicled extensively in Adorno's separate qualitative analysis (Adorno 2010: 158–168). Individuals sometimes oscillated between condemnation of Nazi crimes and anti-Semitic remarks without conscious awareness of their self-contradicting statements.

Perhaps most interesting is the ISR's analysis of the typical group dynamics that gave rise to this post-fascist "public opinion" in the discussions (Pollock, Adorno et al. 2011: 109–147). Groups often displayed a dynamic of artificial solidarity: over the course of the discussion the members gradually moved toward conformity and a climactic point during which they would compete with each other to echo stock phrases. A spontaneous process occurred repeatedly through which individual statements gave rise to collectively endorsed opinions which in turn exerted dominion over the remaining participants. Artificial solidarity arose in the groups as participants became more familiar with each other and converged on certain standard ideological tropes. It would then quickly fade away as each individual retreated from conversation into near silence. In sum, participants drew on culturally standardized, pseudo-intellectually formulated defenses to address accusations of guilt in the stimulus letter: "How speakers submit to existing language becomes fully clear when the lost subjectivity escalates into a self-satisfied gesture, when people endear themselves to popular jargon" (Pollock, Adorno et al. 2011: 166). With few exceptions, the participants failed to achieve either critical self-consciousness or a genuine sense of interdependence with their fellow discussants.

6 Documenting the Last Man: A Nietzschean Archetype in the ISR Data

The *Gruppenexperiment* revealed that very few German citizens had strong positive attitudes toward liberal democracy, and several evidenced remnants of a fascist ideology. These historical data make a simple but important point: Accepting hindsight bias, it is unsurprising that National Socialism rose to prominence and the Holocaust occurred. The German people were simply ill-equipped to oppose fascism in any serious way, an observation reinforced by the finding that their capacity for self-criticism was not significantly improved by the experience of fascism's rise and defeat. The basic documentation of this historical reality is not as significant as the vantage point achieved via the ISR's methods on the underlying social psychological processes behind this massive failure of democracy.

The ambivalence displayed by the ISR's participants is remarkably presaged by the allegoric figure of the "Last Man," Nietzsche's herald of barbarism in modernity. Although Nietzsche did not describe this archetype extensively under this label, I interpret the Last Man as an incarnation of the bourgeois-consumerist, "passively nihilist" mentality encouraged by capitalist democracy in the modern era, a type attacked repeatedly throughout his oeuvre (see Diken 2009; Evans 1993; Owen 1995; Shaw 2014). This is the type whom Antonio (1995) called a "social simulator"; the individual who displays "the remarkable antithesis between an interior which fails to correspond to any exterior and an exterior which fails to correspond to any interior" (Nietzsche 1874/1997: 78). It has been argued that Nietzsche anticipated the "passive nihilism" of postmodernity when he described the Last Man as no longer compelled by goals for meaning or self-improvement, but rather as preoccupied by "petty pleasure" and "Mechanical activity and all that goes with it – such as absolute regularity, punctilious and unthinking obedience, a mode of life fixed once and for all, fully occupied time" (Nietzsche 1887/1967, 134–135; cf. Evans 1993; Kroker 2004). Individuals living in modern urban society are socialized to be moving bundles of reactive forces (Deleuze 1983), responding uncritically to the increasingly complex, technological stimuli with which they are confronted. Yet this passive life of reactivity comes with a price; the problematic "internalization" of hostility and festering *ressentiment*. Despite the superficially oppressive and mechanical nature of contemporary life, the modern city nevertheless threatens to become the site of a "turning point in history" which will witness "a kind of *tropical* tempo in the competition to grow, and a tremendous ruin and self-ruination, as the savage egoisms…wrestle 'for sun and light' and can no longer derive any limit" (Nietzsche 1886/1989: 211). Nietzsche's descriptions of the Last Man in capitalist modernity are of an individual compelled to maintain an aura of self-sufficient rationality, responsiveness and complacency, from which he derives an opinion on all matters; yet beneath the aura churns self-doubt, bad conscience, and the repression of forceful passions.

Conforming to Nietzsche's description of "social simulators," the *Gruppenexperiment* participants drew on culturally standardized, pseudo-intellectually formulated defenses to address the accusations of German guilt in the stimulus letter, frequently speaking in "slogans." The comportment and language through which they automatically react to the accusation of guilt resonates with Horkheimer's description of the "utilitarian cast of thought" brought on by "the mechanization of life." As a result of the individual's need for precise adaptation to an increasingly complex existence, the individual becomes psychologically passive:

> Men need directives, and their need increases the more they obey these directives; consequently they disaccustom themselves to spontaneous reactions…Society acts upon the masses in their fragmented state…*Every man becomes lonelier, for machines can calculate and work but they cannot get inspirations or identify themselves with other machines.*
>
> HORKHEIMER 1974: 26–27

As the individual's daily patterns of activity and social interaction are increasingly predetermined along paths set by expert social planners, Horkheimer believes that the last remnants of subjectivity are shifted to a group-based consciousness formed primarily on the basis of the division of labor. He explicates this psychological inculcation of the collective in a manner that recalls the formulaic *GE* discussions.

> Self-awareness in contemporary society is directly connected with belonging to some collectivity: to an age or vocational group, and ultimately to the nation…Everyone thinks and speaks in the way proper to his group or profession…The decay of individual expressiveness, which is effected in home and school through the *schematization of language*, is carried further in professional life…*causing language itself to lose its expressive quality and to take on more and more exclusively the character of a set of signs.*
>
> HORKHEIMER 1974: 133–143

This is the outcome of middle class standardization and specialization that Nietzsche foretold when he spoke of the modern individual as having a "weakened personality," as becoming like an "actor" with nothing but "rags and tatters" beneath the "mask," prompting the question, "Are there still human beings, one then asks oneself, or perhaps only thinking-, writing-, and speaking-machines?" (Nietzsche 1874/1997: 85). Anticipating Horkheimer's pessimism, Nietzsche was suspicious of language as a tool for reducing individuals to a common stratum, to psychological domination by the cultural "herd" (Richardson 2015). As the ISR found in *Gruppenexperiment* decades later, Nietzsche feared that the rise of modern media and passive nihilism would create ambivalent persons who, burdened by internal resentment, would turn to group-speak and ideology as compensation for a lack of self-awareness.

For the ISR, as for Nietzsche, the supreme danger represented by this rise in purely mimetic cognition is that totalitarian figures may utilize it to channel disillusioned resentment into violent acts. "Dominated masses readily identify themselves with the repressive agency" because it offers "free rein to indulge their imperious mimetic impulses," as previously docile individuals "seize the opportunity to identify themselves with the official social ego" and "carry out with fury what the personal ego has been unable to achieve…The superego, impotent in its own house, becomes the hangman in society" (Horkheimer 1947: 116–121). The discussion groups in the ISR study were observed to become more integrated when participants rallied in litanies of aggression against the occupying Allied forces, represented by the soldier of the stimulus letter (Pollock, Adorno et al. 2011: 139). Even amidst the wreckage of the Third Reich, a new "predestined savior" might have "altered the direction" of "the most dangerous of all explosives, *ressentiment*" (Nietzsche 1887/1967: 126–127).

7 The Lessons of Paradoxical Social Science

The ISR data have, I believe, clear significance for understanding the role of cultural and economic factors in the barbarism and subsequent amnesia of Germany in the first half of the last century. But beyond this, what is the significance of the scholarly method I have re-constructed here from their writings and those of Nietzsche?

One theme is the threatening force of ambivalence or lack of commitment. From a methodological standpoint, Nietzsche and the ISR aggressively opposed a positivist commitment to quantification and specialization that obscured important qualitative differences in social phenomena and ultimately paralyzed researchers. It is telling that among the first of many methodological critiques of *The Authoritarian Personality* was a chapter "Authoritarianism: Right and left" by Edwards Shils that functionally leveled politically significant personality differences through the neutralizing claim that extremism exists at both ends of the spectrum. Similar conclusions are being reached today among a growing group of psychologists who insist that conservatism has been vilified in social psychology, and that experiments can be designed to show bias and irrationality among people of all political stripes (see Duarte, Crawford, Stern, Haidt, Jussim, and Tetlock 2015). Such tendencies to target extremism on both sides of the political divide not only perpetuate the leveling of qualitative difference, but deflect attention from those "moderate" participants who emerged as an important problem in *Gruppenexperiment*. In the scientistic zeal to promote the virtue of compromise, contemporary social psychologists may blind themselves to the Last Man, the perhaps dominant personality type under modern capitalism that adheres to the status quo and the shield of mediocrity to cover latent hostility.

The "classics" of social psychology invoked in connection with Nazi Germany – the Asch conformity studies, the Milgram obedience studies, Tajfel's "minimal groups" paradigm – stress either high rates of clearly conformist behavior or explanations for rare nonconformity. These studies implicitly assume that atomized individuals are oriented to social groups through automatic processes of deindividuation, which are typically functional but which under the wrong circumstances can bring about disastrous consequences. These analyses are typically rooted in evolutionary-functionalist accounts, suggesting that all individuals at all times and places are subject to similar processes of social learning and obedience. Adopting a Nietzschean genealogical approach, the ISR scholars instead saw contemporary individuals as sites of inner tension oscillating in their attitudes toward the objective force of a society that confronts them as simultaneously alienating and all-powerful. The attention to detail in *Gruppenexperiment* illustrates this phenomenon through the high numbers of participants who fall in-between "extreme" positive or negative response options. These are exactly the type of participants who accounted for the majority of variance in most of the classic social psychological experiments on conformity, but whose data were overshadowed by a narrow focus on isolated causal factors. Supplementing the standard banality-of-evil narrative, the ISR's unique methods offered a glimpse of the inner tensions that permitted "average" individuals to be swayed by the presence of an authority demanding radical violence. Focusing on the majority of silent and ambivalent participants who fall through the analytic cracks of standard social psychology, the ISR made a chilling case for the role of non-commitment and self-ignorance in atrocity.

Finally, I contend that there is much to be said for the value placed on the *unfinished* and the *experimental* in the visions of social science provided by both Nietzsche and the ISR. "The Frankfurt School's intellectual legacy...should be understood in terms of the growing interest in the philosophy of Nietzsche during the course of the scholars' work in America...the fragment as a mode of considering an otherwise-totalizing society takes an increasing role" (Perrin and Olick 2011: xxxviii). This paradoxical mode of social science advises that our understanding of the individual-social mediations in which we are immersed will never be tidy or complete. In its commitment to the power of the unfinished and open, we can discern perhaps the most important lesson for our work today. The ultimate conflict in social science is not between reason and empiricism, relativism and rationalism, or hermeneutic and causal methodology. It is the conflict between *unidimensional* forms of thought that cannot tolerate contradiction, and the *multidimensional* form sought by Nietzsche and the Frankfurt School.

References

Adorno, Theodor W. 2010. *Guilt and Defense*, edited and translated by Jeffrey K. Olick and Andrew J. Perrin. Cambridge, MA: Harvard University Press.

Adorno, Theodor W. 2000 [1968]. *Introduction to Sociology*, edited by Christoph Gödde, translated by Edmund Jephcott. Cambridge, UK: Polity Press.

Adorno, Theodor W. 1976. "Introduction" and "Sociology and Empirical Research." In *The Positivist Dispute in German Sociology*, edited by David Frisby, translated by Glyn Adey, 1–86. London: Heinemann.

Adorno, Theodor W., and Max Horkheimer. 2011 [1956]. *Towards a New Manifesto*, translated by Rodney Livingstone. London and New York: Verso.

Antonio, Robert. 1995. "Nietzsche's Antisociology: Subjectified Culture and the End of History." *The American Journal of Sociology* 101(1): 1–43.

Ashenden, Samantha, and David Owen. 1999. *Foucault Contra Habermas: Recasting the Dialogue Between Genealogy and Critical Theory.* Thousand Oaks, CA: Sage.

Babich, Babette E. 2004. *Habermas, Nietzsche, and Critical Theory.* Amherst, NY: Humanity Books.

Berkowitz, Peter. 1995. *Nietzsche: The Ethics of an Immoralist.* Cambridge, MA: Harvard University Press.

Clark, Maudemarie. 1990. *Nietzsche on Truth and Philosophy.* Cambridge: Cambridge University Press.

Dallmayr, Fred R., and Thomas A. McCarthy, eds. 1977. *Understanding and Social Inquiry.* Notre Dame, IN: University of Notre Dame Press.

Deleuze, Giles. 1983. *Nietzsche and Philosophy*, translated by Hugh Tomlinson. New York: Columbia University Press.

Devereux, Georges. 1967. *From Anxiety to Method in the Behavioral Sciences.* The Hague: Mouton & Co.

Diken, Bulent. 2009. *Nihilism.* New York: Routledge.

Duarte, Jose L., Jarret T. Crawford, Charlotta Stern, Jonathan Haidt, Lee Jussim, and Philip E. Tetlock. 2015. "Political Diversity Will Improve Psychological Science." *Behavioral and Brain Sciences* 38: 1–58.

Evans, Fred. 1993. *Psychology and Nihilism.* Albany, NY: State University of New York Press.

Foucault, Michel. 1977. "Nietzsche, Genealogy, History." In *Language, Counter-memory, Practice*, edited by D.F. Bouchard, 139–164. Ithaca, NY: Cornell University Press.

The Frankfurt Institute for Social Research. 1972 [1956]. *Aspects of Sociology*, translated by J. Viertel. Boston: Beacon Press.

Grimm, Ruediger H. 1977. *Nietzsche's Theory of Knowledge*. Berlin: de Gruyter.

Habermas, Juergen. 1987. *The Philosophical Discourse of Modernity*, translated by F. Lawrence. New York: Polity Press.

Horkheimer, Max. 2014 [1972]. "Traditional and Critical Theory." In *Subject and Object: Frankfurt School Writings on Epistemology, Ontology, and Method*, edited by Ruth Groff, 185–232. New York: Bloomsbury Academic.

Horkheimer, Max. 2014 [1935]. "On the Problem of Truth." In *Subject and Object: Frankfurt School Writings on Epistemology, Ontology, and Method*, edited by Ruth Groff, 55–90. New York: Bloomsbury Academic.

Horkheimer, Max. 1993. *Between Philosophy and Social Science: Selected Early Writings*, translated by G. Frederick Hunter, Matthew S. Kramer, and John Torpey. Cambridge, MA: MIT Press.

Horkheimer, Max. 1974. *Critique of Instrumental Reason: Lectures and Essays since the End of World War II*, translated by Michael J. O'Connell et al. New York: Seabury Press.

Horkheimer, Max. 1947. *Eclipse of Reason*. New York: Oxford University Press.

Jaspers, Karl. 1997 [1936]. *Nietzsche: An Introduction to the Understanding of his Philosophical Activity*, translated by Charles F. Wallraff and Frederick J. Schmitz. Baltimore: Johns Hopkins University Press.

Kroker, Andrew. 2004. *The Will to Technology and the Culture of Nihilism: Heidegger, Nietzsche, and Marx*. Toronto: University of Toronto Press.

Magnus, Bernd. 1988. "The Use and Abuse of *The Will to Power*." In *Reading Nietzsche*, edited by Robert C. Solomon and Kathleen Marie Higgins, 218–235. Oxford: Oxford University Press.

Marcuse, Herbert. 1966. *One-Dimensional Man: Studies in the Ideology of Advanced Industrial Society*. Boston: Beacon Press.

Martin, John Levi. 2001. "*The Authoritarian Personality*, 50 years later: What questions are there for political psychology?" *Political Psychology* 22(1): 1–26.

Morrow, Raymond. A., and David D. Brown. 1994. *Critical Theory and Methodology*. Thousand Oaks, CA: Sage.

Nietzsche, Friedrich. 1997 [1874]. "The Uses and Disadvantages of History for Life" and "Schopenhauer as Educator." In *Untimely Meditations*, edited by Daniel Breazeale and translated by R.J. Hollingdale, 57–194. New York: Cambridge University Press.

Nietzsche, Friedrich. 1996 [1878]. *Human, All Too Human: A Book for Free Spirits*, translated by R.J. Hollingdale. Cambridge UK: Cambridge University Press.

Nietzsche, Friedrich. 1989 [1886]. *Beyond Good and Evil*, translated by Walter Kaufmann. New York: Vintage Books.

Nietzsche, Friedrich. 1974 [1887]. *The Gay Science*, translated by Walter Kaufmann. New York: Vintage Books.

Nietzsche, Friedrich. 1968. *The Will to Power*, translated by Walter Kaufmann and R.J. Hollingdale. New York: Vintage Books.

Nietzsche, Friedrich. 1967 [1887]. *On the Genealogy of Morals*, translated by Walter Kaufmann. New York: Vintage Books.

Olick, Jeffrey K., and Christina Simko. Manuscript under review. "Tragic Sociology." Charlottesville: University of Virginia.

Owen, David. 1995. *Nietzsche, Politics, and Modernity*. London: Sage.

Perrin, Andrew J. and Jeffrey K. Olick. 2011. "Translators' Introduction: Before the Public Sphere." In *Group Experiment and Other Writings: The Frankfurt School on Public Opinion in Postwar Germany*, edited and translated by Andrew J. Perrin and Jeffrey K. Olick, xv–lxi. Cambridge, MA: Harvard University Press

Pollock, Friedrich, and Theodor W. Adorno, et al. 2011. *Group Experiment and Other Writings: The Frankfurt School on Public Opinion in Postwar Germany*, edited and translated by Andrew J. Perrin and Jeffrey K. Olick. Cambridge, MA: Harvard University Press.

Richardson, John. 2015. "Nietzsche, Language, Community." In *Individual and Community in Nietzsche's Philosophy*, edited by Julian Young, 214–243. Cambridge: Cambridge University Press.

Richardson, John. 1996. *Nietzsche's System*. New York: Oxford University Press.

Sadler, Ted. 1993. "The Postmodernist Politicization of Nietzsche." In *Nietzsche, Feminism, and Political Theory*, edited by Paul Patton, 225–243. New York: Routledge.

Schacht, Richard. 2016. "Gehlen, Nietzsche, and the Project of a Philosophical Anthropology." In *Naturalism and Philosophical Anthropology*, edited by Phillip Honenberger, 49–65. New York: Palgrave Macmillan.

Shaw, Tamsin. 2014. "The 'Last Man' Problem: Nietzsche and Weber on Political Attitudes to Suffering." In *Nietzsche as Political Philosopher*, edited by Manuel Knoll and Barry Stocker, 345–380. Berlin: de Gruyter.

Stack, George J. 2005. *Nietzsche's Anthropic Circle: Man, Science, and Myth.* Rochester, NY: University of Rochester Press.

CHAPTER 13

The Death of Truth – Guilt, Anxiety, Dread, and Hope: Nietzschean Confessions

Christine Payne

> Have you not heard of that madman who lit a lantern in the bright morning hours, ran to the market place, and cried incessantly: "I seek God! I seek God!" – As many of those who did not believe in God were standing around just then, he provoked much laughter. Has he got lost? asked one. Did he lose his way like a child? asked another. Or is he hiding? Is he afraid of us? Has he gone on a voyage? emigrated? – Thus they yelled and laughed. The madman jumped into their midst and pierced them with his eyes. "Whither is God?" he cried; "I'll tell you. *We killed him* – you and I. All of us are his murderers. But how did we do this? How could we drink up the sea? Who gave us the sponge to wipe away the entire horizon? What were we doing when we unchained this earth from its sun? Whither is it moving now? Whither are we moving? Away from all suns? Are we not plunging continually? Backward, sideward, forward, in all directions? Is there still any way up or down? Are we not straying as through an infinite nothing? Do we not feel the breath of empty space? Has it not become colder? Is not night continually closing in on us? Do we not need to light lanterns in the morning? Do we hear nothing as yet of the noise of the gravediggers who are burying God? Do we smell nothing as yet of the divine decomposition? Gods, too, decompose. God is dead. God remains dead. And we have killed him.
>
> NIETZSCHE, *The Gay Science*

∵

1 Introduction

Thus speaks Nietzsche (1974) in aphorism 125 of *The Gay Science*. What follows is a set of reflections on Nietzsche's perspectivalist approach to questions of truth and politics in light of his anti-annunciation. What is at stake is the possibility of valid and justifiable critique absent singular and secure epistemic truth. I suggest that attending to Nietzsche's reflections on questions of truth and knowledge can provide us with a compelling framework as we continue to navigate the thorny questions of realism and relativism, of science, philosophy, and politics. Moving beyond the realm of attention to that of action, I also suggest that it is possible and justifiable to appropriate those aspects of Nietzsche's approach to truth without worrying about whether such appropriations map on to his own beliefs and values. Simply put, I consider the character and the consequences of taking Nietzsche's perspectivalist approach seriously as one way of reflecting upon the kinds of questions that sociologists of knowledge and scholars in science and technology studies ask and the kinds of 'answers' that we look and hope for.

When the larger project of which this essay is a part was first being hatched, the political landscape looked different. In light of the U.S. election in November 2016 and the seemingly endless rhetoric surrounding 'fake news,' and 'post-truth,' what was an already significant set of puzzles concerning the status of scientific facts and claims to truth have been thrown into heightened register. I offer this explicitly normative assessment upfront: critique has not and – cannot afford to – run out of steam.[1] Critique and common sense need not be

1 In a now iconic essay, "Why Has Critique Run Out of Steam? From Matters of Fact to Matters of Concern," science and technology studies scholar Bruno Latour (2004) reflects upon the worrisome appropriation of central science studies concepts and approaches (including the reluctance to allow controversies to culminate in relative certainty, consensus, and closure, a penchant for the underdetermination of theories by facts, and symmetrical approaches to truths and falsehoods) by actors involved in such projects as climate change denial and 9/11 conspiracies. In the ceaseless deployment of critique and deconstruction in the realm of epistemology, mainstream science studies has provided conceptual fodder for reactionary political agendas at the same time that it has neglected the very real political and ethical dimensions of the actors, cultures, and agendas otherwise given such critical attention in science and technology studies' accounts. Latour regrets that his prior work and the work it subsequently inspired have been marshalled to such unintended projects, and he suggests that the discipline of science and technology studies as a whole is far past due for a reckoning of how and why it is that STS has (allegedly) come to hold a curious series of intellectual alliances. As one step towards dissolving the possibility for such appropriations and seeming alliances, Latour suggests we consider a turn toward a version of realism – but a realism of 'matters of concern' as opposed to 'matters of fact.' Relative to his previous approaches, this reevaluation of the place of politics and ethics in the domain of science and technology studies is a welcome development on Latour's part. Still, it gives pause to note that Latour's understanding of what it means to attend to matters of concern involves a self-conscious step *away from* critique rather than a reiteration and reinforcement of it. As he says, "...the danger [is] no longer...coming from an excessive confidence in ideological arguments posturing as matters of fact...but from an excessive *distrust* of good matters of fact disguised as ideological

conceptualized in a zero-sum fashion. While this essay does not posture anything like an 'answer'; it does proffer a unique Nietzschean approach that can contribute to the considerations regarding the significance and scope of critiques of knowledge.

2 Perspectivalism by Way of Conceptualization

Nietzsche (1979) contends that knowledge is, and can only ever be, particularly-situated. Knowledge emerges from, and is conditioned by, historical social relations. Insofar as knowledge is perspectival it remains partial – which is to say not general, not static, not universal. There is no stable foundation outside of the relations of social actors to provide epistemic warrant or meaningful certainty for claims made 'in general.' While no fixed foundation outside of historical social relations exists to provide epistemic security or certainty, Nietzsche nevertheless understands the creation of abstract and relatively static

---

biases! While we spent years trying to detect the real prejudices hidden behind the appearance of objective statements, do we now have to reveal the real objective and incontrovertible facts hidden behind the *illusion* of prejudices" (227)? For Latour, the problem is that questions of social epistemology have been so successful in demonstrating the ideological, discriminatory, and exploitative components and goals of seemingly objective concepts and facts of science and technology that we must now turn our attention to making sure that real facts and the political and ethical matters of concern tangled up with them are taken seriously. Leaving aside the question to what extent scholars in science and technology studies have, in fact, been successful at demonstrating the work of ideology, Latour's point is fair enough – we cannot afford to deconstruct ad infinitum in the face of serious political and ethical consequences. What is worth noting is that, outside of mainstream philosophy and sociology of science, these concerns are always already assumed. Drawing explicit attention to political and ethical matters of concern – whether conceptualized in a realist or some other fashion – explicitly structures the assumptions and approaches of scholars working within Marxist, feminist, critical race and sexuality, and postcolonial paradigms in both science and technology studies proper and in its variously contributing disciplines. It seems to me that to lean away from critique for the sake of 'realist' political and ethical concerns is to give far too much away to those same unsavory political peoples and projects that Latour is so rightly anxious about. To impose my own metaphor into his meditation, if scholars of social knowledge and epistemology do not wish to have certain people in our beds, we should muster the intellectual and political organization to kick them out rather than abandon our hard fought and ongoing critical work. Rather than yield to an apparently pragmatic realism or anxiously contribute to unfair caricatures of the critical sensibilities of studies of social epistemology, I contend that Nietzsche's perspectivalism is better poised to toggle between the crucial work of providing clear and unflinching demonstrations and explanations of existing natural and social processes *and* providing equally unflinching critiques of ideology in the service of accuracy and of liberation.

concepts about empirical reality to be a necessary activity of human experience. Individuals deploy concepts in order to fix and so manipulate the material world they navigate. The process of conceptualization draws together the particular instances of experience and converts these into seemingly similar kinds of entities, in the process making possible the transformation and identification of unlike into like. In the practical interest of social communication and action, concepts function as a means for 'arbitrarily discarding individual differences and forgetting the distinguishing aspects' of what are actually distinct moments of lived experience. As Nietzsche (1979) explains:

> Every word instantly becomes a concept precisely insofar as it is not supposed to serve as a reminder of the unique and entirely individual original experience to which it owes its origin; but rather, a word becomes a concept insofar as it simultaneously has to fit countless more or less similar cases – which means, purely and simply, cases which are never equal and thus altogether unequal. Every concept arises from the equation of unequal things. (83)

Conceptualization, then, is the collapsing together in consciousness of *particular* experiences in the service of representing them as *general* for the *practical* sake of shared meaning and collective activity. What is significant is that Nietzsche's account of abstraction at this stage is normatively neutral. There is nothing inherently problematic with the process of abstraction, because abstraction is just how social actors navigate and engage with the world. The practical function of concepts is obvious enough. Identifying an object as a 'seashell' or 'pillow,' or as being 'cerulean' or 'curved,' works to designate particular empirical experiences of the world that can be meaningfully understood among groups of people. In order to make sense of shared existence and to communicate meaningfully with each other in the world, humans must make use of abstract and general concepts. There will never not be conceptualization and hence, there will never not be abstractions from the particular to the general. However, abstractions can be said to really and truly reflect a general perspective, fact, or interest only in the sense that particular experience has always already been schematized into concepts – concepts which reflect attempts to invest particular moments with general significance for practical purposes. What is significant here is that the processes for identifying general true knowledge – and distinguishing it from ideology and illusion – remain, in the last instance, socially and historically unstable and so epistemically uncertain.

There is a double maneuver at play in Nietzsche's analysis. Abstraction functions to provide a sense of stability and security as people come to feel relatively efficacious and satisfied with their self-forming and shared practices. In another sense, practical abstraction cannot actually provide sufficient epistemological grounds – and so cannot adequately justify epistemically – this stability and security. Read together, these two claims lead to the provocative conclusion that what is epistemologically unjustifiable – generalized abstraction – is socially meaningful and practically necessary. Within a given context, abstract general concepts are perfectly useful for describing and so helping to adjudicate truth in an epistemically weak sense. An individual may, for example, be able to determine usefully and meaningfully whether there is food in the cat's bowl or if current weather conditions invite the wearing of a sweater. A less pedestrian example: we may determine usefully and meaningfully whether or not there is evidence that climate change is a real phenomenon worthy of sustained attention and action. Nevertheless, outside of a particular context or perspective, general conceptual abstraction is incapable of providing adjudication in the sense of epistemic certainty. 'Particular context' is also a concept and so may also shift in meaning. Climate change provides a good illustration. The *particular* context in which the reality of climate change exists and matters is, literally, a *global* – which is not to say universal – context, and so the way in which humans approach the set of facts and meanings around this particular context will – at least potentially – be more or less global in character.

The choice of climate change as an example to be read in relation to Nietzschean perspectivalism is purposeful. As scholars and as human beings we are right to be uneasy or hostile in the face of approaches like perspectivalism that threat to result in or legitimize the inability to make and justify claims to knowledge and truth. Nietzsche's worries arise from a different but equally significant line of reasoning. As noted above, Nietzsche demonstrates that the transformation of unlike (particular) into like (general) is a normatively neutral process. However, while not *constitutive* of the process of conceptualization as such, the transformation of the particular into the general does provide the conditions of possibility for the emergence of unjustifiably stable and solid truths. Much to what would be his horrified chagrin, Nietzsche's consideration of the relationship between the particular and the general, of empirical experience and reasoned abstraction, reads like a textbook Marxist (2010) concern with ideology. Nietzsche (1979) contends:

> For something is possible in the realm of these schemata which could never be achieved with the vivid first impressions: the construction of a

> pyramidal order according to castes and degrees, the creation of a new world of laws, privileges, subordinations, and clearly marked boundaries – a new world, one which now confronts that other vivid world of first impressions as more solid, more universal, better known, and more human than the immediately perceived world, and thus as the regulative and imperative world…*in this conceptual crap game 'truth' means using every die in the designated manner, counting its spots accurately, fashioning the right categories, and never violating the order of caste and class rank.*
>
> 84–85, emphasis mine

Dynamic partial perspectives and experiences come to appear less real and true than abstract generalizations. In addition, what is designated real and true acquires a sense of being higher in value ('more human') and of carrying legitimate authority ('regulative and imperative'). Particular perspectives (unlike) are transformed into general (like) perspectives (concepts) which are imagined to be reality and truth as such – and by extension to embody goodness, and command authority.

Whether in the more mundane pragmatic interest of shared communication or the more explicitly political interest of groups exercising power and authority, the conflation of the particular into the general renders some aspects and understandings of the world real, true, and good at the expense of contingency, dynamism, and particularity. In other words, social actors work to fix relations, perspectives, and concepts in ways advantageous to their particular positions and interests. For Nietzsche, a central worry is that individuals will become attached to, and invested in, concepts – including the concept of truth – when they ought to be cultivating a healthy amount of epistemological skepticism. Crucially, however, what I loosely refer to as Nietzsche's critique of 'ideology' is not based on the presumption that there are secure and stable truths out there waiting to have the cloak of illusion lifted from them. Nietzsche's point is rather that concepts as condensers and conveyers of fluid and particular sense and meaning are necessarily abstract and so never immediate, never stable, and so always evasive of epistemological certainty and justification in the philosophically strong sense.

3 Perspectivalism: A Warning *against* Agnostic Relativism

Were this the punchline of Nietzsche's understanding of knowledge, it would appear that his analysis fits rather comfortably in the philosophical tradition of relativism. Nietzsche's contention that claims to knowledge are by turns simply pragmatic, linguistically-based, perspectival and so socially-constructed, and also prone to unwarranted conflation into The Truth of a matter – therefore meriting cautious skepticism – seems to leave little wiggle room to come to another classificatory conclusion. A well-worn series of concerns come in the wake of discussions of relativism. The specters of plurality, symmetry, social construction, under-determination, expertise and authority – in brief, epistemic uncertainty – must be considered; these epistemological concerns then extend into questions of political and ethical relativism. Everyone has their particular truths and ways of being in the world and, to borrow a phrase of Haraway's (1988), no real or abstracted 'God's eye view' exists from which some claims and practices deemed more accurate or more just than others. To borrow a turn of phrase political theorist and Nietzsche scholar Tracy Strong (2012) who borrows it from Hannah Arendt (2018), is it possible to critique and affirm knowledge claims (including political and ethical claims) in the presumed absence of a universal epistemological 'banister?'

Considering his account of perspectivalism as outlined above, it is understandable to read Nietzsche as a banner-bearing member of House Relativism. I wish to pause and consider the possibility that Nietzsche's perspectivalism leads, ultimately, beyond the distinction between truth and relativism. And yet:

> Have you not heard of that madman who lit a lantern in the bright morning hours, ran to the market place, and cried incessantly: "I seek God! I seek God!" (III: 125)

So we begin again with aphorism 125 of *The Gay Science*, wherein Nietzsche (1974) relates a parable concerning the death of God. It is understandably tempting to read Nietzsche in exactly the same fashion as those who laugh in the marketplace – as cruel and taunting skeptics, ever mocking the herd-like masses for their stupidity, banality, and their generally pathetic servitude to slavish values and standards, as well as one who cherishes and seeks out those few individuals willing and capable of radical self-overcoming towards a healthier and more creative life. This understanding of Nietzsche has much to recommend it – but in a fashion and to a set of purposes often radically misunderstood by both those who condemn and those who celebrate such an ethos.

If we pause to consider the first few lines of the death of God parable, we see that the masses are those mocking the singular madman. Here, the multitude comprises the apparently sophisticated group of atheists who knowingly taunt and laugh at the supposedly contemptible individual creature still frantically searching for his god. Given his ceaseless critique of morality, his contempt with the modern masses, and his desire to foster heroic feats of self-overcoming, what are we to make of the opening scene in this iconic 'God is dead' parable? The parable begins, as do so many of Nietzsche's writings, by tempting the reader to identify with a particular character, statement, or point of view.[2] We all-too-knowing modern readers immediately feel a sense of smug pity for the character of the madman as he wails across the town square in search of God. While perhaps less actively cruel than the townsfolk, our response as readers is similar: we modern knowers are no longer so simple-minded or naïve as to believe in a God any longer. As sophisticated and skeptical intellectuals, we modern readers cannot help but scoff at or pity someone flailing madly about in search of a God that does not exist. My suspicion is that this identification with sophisticated skepticism is in fact Nietzsche's target of critique. The parable continues:

> The madman jumped into their midst and pierced them with his eyes. "Whither is God?" he cried; "I'll tell you. *We killed him* – you and I. All of us are his murderers. But how did we do this? How could we drink up the sea? Who gave us the sponge to wipe away the entire horizon? What were we doing when we unchained this earth from its sun? Whither is it moving now? Whither are we moving? Away from all suns? Are we not plunging continually? Backward, sideward, forward, in all directions? Is there still any way up or down? Are we not straying as through an infinite nothing? Do we not feel the breath of empty space? Has it not become colder? Is not night continually closing in on us? Do we not need to light lanterns in the morning? Do we hear nothing as yet of the noise of the gravediggers who are burying God? Do we smell nothing as yet of the divine decomposition? Gods, too, decompose. God is dead. God remains dead. And we have killed him. (III: 125)

What began as an identification with the taunts of the knowing masses about the loss of God has suddenly and dramatically shifted to an identification with the madman and his terrified questions and accusations concerning the

2 As David Allison (2001: vii) notes, there is a strong sense in which Nietzsche is always speaking directly to 'you' as the individual reader, and this apparent intimacy works to draw us towards whatever series of ideas Nietzsche appears to be working up. But as Ken Gemes (2006: 191ff) suggests, Nietzsche, "employs uncanny displacements and subterfuges in order to disguise his real target." I contend that such a maneuver is particularly evident in Nietzsche's analysis of the death of God.

character and consequences regarding this loss. We suddenly share the madman's anxieties and guilt. The news that, moments ago, inspired a knowing wink and laugh now inspires chill and dread. Nietzsche's abrupt bait-and-switch works as an unexpected aid to reflection. Just as quickly as we share in the seemingly obvious guffaws encircling the seeker of God, we shift our shared concern towards the disquieting consequences of God's death. Upon reflection, the death of God presents modern individuals with a series of *problems* concerning values, morality, justification, and meaning; very much not a series of self-important *answers*.

Rather than relax in our supposed knowledge that the world has been shorn from all metaphysical and religious foundations, we modern readers and thinkers ought to take this recognition much more seriously. If the modern world really has lost its god, then under the patina of intellectual progress via a skeptical atheism, there lies the reality of a creeping cultural, political, and ethical nihilism. Nietzsche seems to be suggesting that, without a belief in a god, modern humans must confront the ultimate groundlessness of their existence – including any meanings attached to their existence. Atheism may or may not offer an intellectually – sophisticated position relative to the question of the existence of God, but it cannot by itself suggest or provide other foundations or meanings upon which humanity might secure its ideas and ground its practices. The task left us after the death of God is a sober assessment of the meaning of existence absent universal values and standards, absent some or another telos. Where are meaning and morality now? This leaves us with the question: what does this series of proto-existentialist concerns have to do with epistemological perspectivalism? I contend that Nietzsche gives us an 'answer' when he suggests that readers of his *Genealogy of Morality* (1998: III: 24) return to aphorism 344 of his *Gay Science* where he argues that:

> ...it is still a metaphysical faith upon which our faith in science rests – that even we seekers after knowledge today, we godless anti-metaphysicians still take our fire, too, from the flame lit by a faith that is thousands of years old, that Christian faith which was also the faith of Plato, that God is the truth, that truth is divine. (V: 344)

In our quest for ever greater degrees of precision and accuracy, in our desire for a ceaseless accumulation of facts and data, and in our insistence on attaining an increasing amount of scientific and technological mastery over our natural and social worlds, we transfer many of the qualities and ideals embedded in the concept of God into the concept of Truth. Nietzsche contends that in many respects, scientific truth serves as a substitute deity. This apparently paradoxical contention is teased apart in the third treatise of Nietzsche's (1998) *Genealogy of Morality*.

In this work Nietzsche seeks, among other things, to trace the emergence and development of slave morality and the triumph of ascetic ideals. Ascetic ideals can be understood as those values that cultivate and glorify restriction and constraint, deference and meekness; i.e. severe and subservient self-discipline in the face of material and psychological temptations towards excess. These values are resignifications of the physical realm that has historically been characterized by material scarcity and socio-political exploitation. In the face of such threats to our being, we develop various measures of defense by which we seek to preserve ourselves. Over time, the real and understandable reactions taken to avoid physical and psychological threats as much as possible have come to be internalized and reconfigured as cultural and moral approaches to oneself and others. Unable to conquer others and the external world, the physically and politically less powerful have resignified such powerlessness to indicate a culturally and morally superior position vis-à-vis the powerful (I: 1ff). At the same time, those made nominally more powerful in this fashion cultivate the presumption that humans are sovereign individuals who operate by means of their own free will. The presumption of free will carries with it the assumption of individual calculability and responsibility, which in turn promotes feelings of guilt and practices of punishment when actions are taken that fail to be socially predictable or acceptable (II: 1ff). Finally, ascetic ideals serve as a means by which humans are able to partially stop up the anxiety the human condition produces, by providing a table of values by which some sense of supposedly static meaning can be gleaned out of an otherwise unanchored existence (I: 1–7; III: 1ff). Ascetic ideals, in other words, function – often unconsciously – as defense mechanisms against the brute force of the material and political world as well as the existential uncertainty posed by the often harsh and seemingly meaningless world into which we are thrown.

Historically, ascetic ideals and practices have been chiefly directed by and towards the concept of theological deities – deities who provide a sense of security and meaning at the same time that they command a level of submission and self-discipline.[3] What is important about ascetic ideals in relation to the current analysis is that Nietzsche demonstrates that the gradual shift from theological to scientific beliefs, values, and practices has in fact *refined* ascetic ideals rather than *replaced* them. The presumption that scientific approaches to the world supersede and overcome religious approaches and their ascetic ideals is misguided. In their otherwise consistent skepticism, questioning, and

3 See also Nietzsche's *Gay Science* (1974: I: 1ff) and *Beyond Good and Evil* (1989: I: 1ff).

disbelief in things unproven, individuals working in the modern Western scientific tradition maintain a seemingly unproblematic allegiance to – which is to say faith in – the reality of, and value in the pursuit of, truth. Nietzsche (1998) is clear:

> These negating and aloof ones of today, these who are unconditional on one point – the claim to intellectual cleanliness – these hard, strict, abstinent, heroic spirits who constitute the honor of our age, all these pale atheists, anti-Christians, immoralists, nihilists, these skeptics, ephectics, *hectics* of the spirit (all of them are the latter in some sense or other), these last idealists of knowledge in whom alone the intellectual consciousness today dwells and has become flesh – in fact they believe themselves to be as detached as possible from the ascetic ideal, these "free, *very* free spirits" and yet, to divulge to them what they themselves cannot see – for they stand too close to themselves – this ideal is precisely *their* ideal as well, they themselves represent it today, and perhaps they alone; they themselves are its most spiritualized outgrowth, the troop of warriors and scouts it deploys on the front line, its most entrapping, most tender, most incomprehensible form of seduction: – if I am a guesser of riddles in anything then let it be with *this* proposition!...These are by no means *free* spirits: *for they still believe in truth*. (III: 24)

In other words, while the profession is predicated in part upon endlessly calling into question every concept and claim previously accepted – both in the sphere of religion and previous science – modern science stops short of calling into question the reality and desirability of truth as such. Nietzsche (1998) even suggests that not only does science and its quest for truth not negate the ascetic ideal, in fact, "science...is rather its *most recent and noblest form*" (III: 23). Because scientific truth is assumed to work at a critical remove from religious concepts and claims, it misunderstands itself as being free from theologically-inflected presuppositions and valuations. It is this invisibility of its actual character that makes science the "...*best* confederate of the ascetic ideal...it is the most unconscious, the most involuntary, the most secret and subterranean one" (III: 25). Being the most unconscious, involuntary, and secret confederate arguably renders truth the most intractable 'God' humans have.

To return to the iconic parable, perhaps the madman was mistaken and the laughing crowd premature in their merry mocking. Perhaps God is alive and well in the form of truth. In this sense, it can be argued that the death of a theological god works to open up more space for those committed to the practice of secular scientific truths [with Truth as God]. To the extent that there is anything like a zero-sum game operating between belief in a religious deity and belief in secular science, the death of God as deity would seem to offer an expanded realm in which secular science could, as it were, 'take over' for God as the ultimate source of epistemological validation and so existential justification. And this would be in keeping with one aspect of the *Genealogy* just discussed. Understood in this manner, God, in a secular sense, is not dead but unconsciously thriving, unseen in broad daylight. Perhaps what is necessary is not the *rejection* of this new ascetic ideal but an honest and self-conscious *recognition* that this is in fact what scientific truth is: 'All my reverence to the ascetic ideal, *as long as it is honest*' (III: 26). And while Nietzsche does, as always, demand we cultivate and maintain an intellectual conscience, such honest recognition proves to be only a first step, insufficient by itself. The recognition that 'we knowers' have inherited and even advanced the ascetic ideal begs a much larger and far more unsettling question. Recall again the madman's cries of anxiety to the knowing masses:

> *We killed him* – you and I. All of us are his murderers. But how did we do this? How could we drink up the sea? Who gave us the sponge to wipe away the entire horizon? *What were we doing when we unchained this earth from its sun? Whither is it moving now? Whither are we moving? Away from all suns? Are we not plunging continually? Backward, sideward, forward, in all directions? Is there still any way up or down? Are we not straying as through an infinite nothing?* Do we not feel the breath of empty space?
>
> 1974: III: 125, emphasis mine

Nietzsche may be read as suggesting that modern science and our desire for increasing stores of Truth – being transubstantiations of our prior belief in, and desire for, an omnipotent, omniscient, eternally real and true, and salvific deity – are at risk of suffering a fate similar to that of God: death. If Nietzsche's contention that scientific truth partially continues in another guise those desires and beliefs embodied in conceptions of God, then the death of God must be re-read in a heightened register. Considered retroactively, the death of God serves as an alarm, warning of the possibility of the death of stable and generally-agreed upon truths. As the presumed conviction in the validity of singular perspectives and static truths is challenged, and as challenges to traditional standards, classifications, and expertise increase, it could be that we run the risk of encountering the death of truth by way of infinite epistemic skepticism and instability.

Given his perspectivalist epistemic assumptions, and given his relentless critique of all things moral, it would not be unreasonable to read Nietzsche as reveling in our having become 'unchained,' our 'plunging continually...backward, sideward, forward, in all directions...straying as through an infinite nothing.' Insofar as such 'plunging' and 'straying' provides the potential for an increase in our ability to maintain a critical distance on claims to truth, as well as our ability to imagine and construct new 'truths' about ourselves and the world, it seems fair to conclude that Nietzsche remains open to some of the consequences stemming from the death of God, and, by extension, the death of truth. Having 'unchained this earth from its sun,' we find ourselves at relative liberty to explore, experiment, and evaluate on our own terms. This loosening of moral restrictions is tied to and echoed in a relative loosening of epistemological constraints. Indeed, Nietzsche (1974) himself reflects in a later section of *The Gay Science* on the thrilling sensations afforded by the death of God:[4]

> ...we philosophers and 'free spirits' feel, when we hear the news that 'the old god is dead,' as if a new dawn shown on us; our heart overflows with gratitude, amazement, premonitions, expectation. At long last the horizon appears free to us again, even if it should not be bright; at long last our ships may venture out again, venture out to face any danger; all the daring of the lover of knowledge is permitted again; the sea, *our* sea, lies open again; perhaps there has never yet been such an 'open sea.' (V: 343)

This is indeed a potentially emancipatory occasion considering the significance of frequently marginalized or silenced positions and perspectives working to assert themselves against the presumably universal epistemic and political status quo.

Without wading into the thorny issue of Nietzsche's anti-democratic sensibilities, it is clear enough that celebrating the release from stable and secure foundations – whether in the realm of morality or in the realm of epistemology – must remain tempered by the recognition of how potentially risky this untethering may prove for projects aimed at increasing knowledge in the service of collective philosophical, pragmatic, and political projects. If scholars provide a plausible explanation for why some groups of social actors take witches to be real and true entities, what is the consequence of adducing such an explanation,

4 It cannot be inconsequential that this exhilaration is tempered in the immediately succeeding aphorism (V: 344). This is the same aphorism that Nietzsche enjoins us to reconsider in the *Genealogy* and which relates the search for truth to a search for God; here the death of God signals the possible death of truth, and by extension a path towards nihilistic relativism rather than life-affirming liberation.

however thoughtfully-grounded in socio-cultural and historical contexts and conditions? Is the explanation meant to serve as an end-in-itself, a description of a natural or social fact meant to be stored away as a potential piece of data in yet another investigation of a new fact? What of the *conditions* that inform the otherwise well-explained claims to the truth of witches? And what of the *consequences* of the belief in the truth of witches? Likewise, if the truth and reality of some idea or fact can only be adduced in the light of those social actors who are themselves working to adduce said truth or reality, then what, if any, outside standard – epistemic or moral – can be used to *critique, challenge, or affirm* such internal accounts? In the light of relativism, we are presented with a choice between admitting the impossibility of attaining any stable and secure outside authority or admitting that, given this first premise, the only authority we can collectively turn to is the authority of authorities, i.e. we are left with relativism or relativism tempered by pragmatism.

Now that we are in the process of 'wipe[ing] away the entire horizon,' well-intentioned celebrations of social construction, symmetry, and skepticism as significant tools of scholarship may be premature and misguided. The more appropriate response to the recognition that we are 'straying as through an infinite nothing' without aid of either a compass or an anchor may be fear and frustration in the face of apparently perpetual moral and epistemological insecurity. In the face of climate change denial, in the face of creationism, in the face of anti-vaccination campaigns – in the face of brazenly moneyed interests involved and invested in every level of knowledge production – there is much to despair and struggle over. If there is any truth to the contention that the characteristics of relativism helped us arrive here, do we not indeed 'feel the breath of empty space?' Has it not indeed 'become colder?'

In assessing the consequences of the Copernican Revolution, Nietzsche's (1998) own ambivalence is apparent: '…man seems to have stumbled onto an inclined plane – he is now rolling faster and faster away from the center – whither? into nothingness? into the "*penetrating* feeling of his nothingness?"… So be it! exactly this would be the straight path – into the *old* ideal? …' (III: 25).[5] To the extent that humans are losing their importance vis-à-vis the cosmos, we are both liberated and falling fast towards potential nihilism. To the extent that we seek to level this inclined plane by way of science and the search for truth, we nevertheless remain invested in an ascetic ideal. Paradoxically, it is the

5 Compare with section 47 of *The Anti-Christ* (1977b) where the concept and character presumed of God is conceived of "not merely as an error, but as a *crime against life*."

ascetic ideal itself that has so far kept humanity from plunging into nihilism – the ascetic ideal makes sense, however painful, of the meaninglessness of existence (III: 28). Truth is meant to subvert the recognition of the meaninglessness of existence. It is possible that one day even this – truth – may, by its own self-annihilating logic, give way to nothingness, leaving us to grapple with the dialectic of liberation and nihilism – both epistemological and by extension political and ethical – yet again.

> What meaning would our entire being have if not this, that in us this will to truth has come to a consciousness of itself as a problem?...It is from the will to truth's becoming conscious of itself that from now on – there is no doubt about it – morality [now truth] will gradually perish: that great spectacle in a hundred acts that is reserved for Europe's next two centuries, the most terrible, most questionable, and perhaps also most hopeful of all spectacles.
>
> 1998: III: 27

But, whether and to what extent we find Nietzsche's cryptic warning-qua-tentative hope of epistemic and moral relativism apt, it would seem to beg the question: is this Nietzsche's critique – his confession – of himself? If Nietzsche warns us against the potential and actual threats of relativism, we may still wonder if his own perspectivalism nevertheless remains in the potential service of such a philosophical enterprise. Recall Nietzsche's perspectival characterization and understanding of knowledge claims: pragmatic, linguistic, socially and culturally-embedded, and situated in particular perspectives, and therefore fundamentally partial. In one important sense, Nietzsche must necessarily remain implicated in the drive toward potentially nihilistic relativism insofar as his meditations question the plausibility of understanding truth in a straightforward universal or realistic fashion. In another sense however, the answer to whether Nietzsche is or is not implicated in the rise of relativism has to be negative. In addition to his concerns over the death of God, Nietzsche also explicitly contends that some perspectives are indisputably *better* than others.

To the extent that perspectives are grounded in particular subject positions that remain differentially-situated in terms of class, race, gender, sexuality, and other social relations and locations, then perspectives are unequal; socio-political and cultural hierarchies are baked in to Nietzsche's understanding of perspectivalism. In a theoretical move largely comparable to that made by Sandra Harding's (2004; 1986) standpoint and Donna Haraway's (1988) situated epistemologies, Nietzsche insists on the particular and partial character of knowledge while simultaneously maintaining that some of these particular perspectives are better situated than others with regard to questions of understanding and evaluation.

Unlike standpoint and situated epistemologies, by 'better' Nietzsche does not mean to connote 'more accurate' in an epistemic sense. For Nietzsche, 'better' must be understood in a social or cultural sense. To the extent that Nietzsche has anything like an answer to questions of epistemic accuracy in the light of perspectivalism, it seems to be the supposition that the more perspectives brought to bear upon a question of objective fact the better:

> There is *only* perspectival seeing, *only* a perspectival 'knowing', and the *more* affects we allow to speak about a matter, *the more* eyes, different eyes, we know how to bring to bear on one and the same matter, that much more complete will our 'concept' of this matter, our 'objectivity' be.
> 1998: III: 12[6]

The key point to make here is that for Nietzsche, the central concern motivating his perspectivalist approach is not a question of epistemology – of accuracy, of certainty, of objectivity – at all. However important and necessary such concerns are, they are neither sufficient nor the most significant for Nietzsche. Far from privileging those perspectives that are historically marginalized, Nietzsche, at least at first glance, privileges the perspectives of history's 'winners.' In its critiques of Truth, perspectivalism aims to avoid relativism not so much by gesturing to the *epistemic* privilege of certain standpoints, but by gesturing to better and worse approaches to, and kinds of, *life*.

For Nietzsche, better perspectives are those perspectives that come from positions of relative freedom, power, health and strength; those who are in positions to act rather than merely react. He is particularly wary of ways of knowing, ways of valuing, and ways of acting that are characterized by 'ressentiment'; i.e. the reactionary mix of desire, envy, hatred, and fear harbored against the powerful, and the concomitant wish to receive recognition and admiration

6 This consideration of increasing perspectives as a means toward objectivity should be read in light of the role of measured restraint that Nietzsche (1997) discusses in *Twilight of the Idols*: "A useful application of having learned to see: one will have become, as a *learner* in general, slow, suspicious, and resistant…Leaving all one's doors open, submissively flopping belly-down before every little fact, a constant readiness to jump in and interfere, to *plunge into* other people and other things, in short, the celebrated 'objectivity' of modern times is bad taste, is *ignoble* par excellence" ('What the Germans are Missing': 6). In other words, a stress on multiplicity indicates neither a relativistic 'anything goes' nor a positivistic 'repeated verification of the evidence is tantamount to truth' approach to questions of knowledge.

for being relatively powerless. While I argue against such a reading, one can be forgiven for reading in Nietzsche a privileging of masters over slaves, the heroic individual over the dumbly blinking masses, the Dionysian Anti-Christian will-to-power over the mendaciously pitiful herds. It is not possible to travel across Nietzsche's works without encountering these distinctions. And there is some truth in reading Nietzsche as championing the first over second moment in each such pair. While it can be at turns comical and horrifying to engage in Nietzschean critique, attending only to this aspect of his thought risks creating representations of Nietzsche as an unserious trickster, proto-fascist, or self-important superman. I contend that it is worth wading through the thorny question of Nietzsche's politics in order to salvage the potentially liberatory character of his perspectivalist project. The key to appropriating the potential in Nietzsche's perspectivalism lies in reconsidering what the overarching themes motivating his analyses across the subjects of metaphysics, epistemology, ethics, and aesthetics is.

If I am reading him correctly, the central themes are the ideal of overcoming, i.e. of going *beyond* both past and present presumptions and practices, and the question of life itself. What appears on the surface to be a deeply problematic attack of slavish social actors and an equally problematic admiration for barbaric master elites turns out to be a more subtle recognition that social relations and positions – forms of life – that are now historical remain to inform the present but can in no way be recovered and repurposed. He compares and contrasts 'higher' and 'lower' forms of life not simply to praise or disparage each in turn, but in order to understand how and why present reality has the shape and substance that it does. Of course, for Nietzsche, present relations and values leave much to be desired. What is necessary, then, is a way forward – out and *over*. No admirer of Hegel, Nietzsche nevertheless deploys a version of dialectics within his texts; one that Theodor Adorno (2007), reflecting on similar subjects from a similar philosophical and cultural (if not a similar political) angle, would later describe as *negative* dialectics. Negative, because this understanding of the world remains theoretically doubtful towards, and politically averse to, teleological and all-too-tidy syntheses of conflicts and contradictions. Dialectical, because in spite of such suspicions, the approach remains committed to the possibility, however tentative, of radical change that aims beyond the present by attention to the past.

In a post-script as preface to his first book *The Birth of Tragedy*, Nietzsche (1967) reflects upon what, ultimately, he has been trying to elaborate and emphasize across his intellectual career. His realization encapsulates what it is that could and should be the response to the questions he has been considering across his works: 'To look at science in the perspective of the artistic, but at art in the light of *life*' (Attempt at a Self-Criticism: 2).

Writing one year later, also retrospectively, Nietzsche (1974) prefaces a new edition of his *Gay Science* by contending that:

> I am still waiting for a philosophical physician…to muster the courage to push my suspicion to its limits and to risk the proposition: what was at stake in all philosophizing hitherto was not at all "truth" but something else – let us say, health, future, growth, power, life.
>
> Preface for the Second Edition: 2

The basis or 'foundation' against which Nietzsche determines the relative value of a perspective is that of material lived existence. Both obvious and vague, 'life' provides us with what is at stake for Nietzsche. What perspectives, what standpoints, what facts, truths, and understandings of reality contribute to better life? What social conditions work in the service of affirming rather than negating life? What are the conditions that might yet allow us to say 'yes' to life – is it possible and, if so, how? We need not agree with Nietzsche's answers to these questions to take his philosophical point.

4 Perspectivalism: Beyond Truth and Relativism

By way of conclusion and as a way of bringing in to stark relief the through-point of this series of reflections, I briefly outline the thinking process that served as the initial motivator of my larger project on Nietzsche and the question of truth. I came to Nietzsche after Marx via the Frankfurt School; the question that drove the turn to Nietzsche was the question of ideology and the question of what Marx (1991: 959) refers to as the 'realm of freedom': the question of knowledge (consciousness) and its relation to the possibility of a better *life*. My thinking went as follows: Like Marx, Nietzsche understands the consciousness of social actors relative to their social relations, which are expressions of particular interests. Also like Marx, Nietzsche demonstrates how particular perspectives, ideas, and interests are transformed into relatively ossified, apparently general facts of the matter. Finally, like Marx, Nietzsche illustrates that the force for disrupting old ways of knowing and being and of creating new ways of knowing and being is to be located in power and desire – politics and ethics. Change occurs through active transformations in social relations. However, unlike Marx, Nietzsche's analysis of consciousness and its transformations throws into question the possibility of a general social interest by which political or ethical practices could be judged, in any ultimate sense, as more or less real, true, good, or authoritative. Whatever interests take pride of place as general social interests would not for that matter be any less perspectival, historical, and particularly-situated in definition, meaning, and substance nor any less open to contestation and transformation.

For Nietzsche, a transformation in consciousness constitutes a series of sidereal expressions rather than an uncovering or an arrival. The recognition that relations of power lie behind processes of conceptualization does not lend itself self-evidently to a political project that seeks to overturn exploitative power relations *if* such an overturning is intended as a strategy for securing transparency between thought and experience. This recognition can serve to motivate action towards *particular* political projects of overcoming. However, liberation cannot stem from, nor arrive at, a general social transparency and interest if a general social transparency and interest is illusory. From this perspective, liberatory practices, like conscious thought, can only ever be the transformation of particular social relations towards particular interests informed by particular perspectives – which as perspectives of social relations must remain in historical flux.

The question then becomes: what is to be gained by the Nietzschean deflation of general social interests into particular interests? What is at stake? The move away from designating a set of interests as universally real and true creates spaces for particular truths to exist without the risk of their being shelved under the label of ideology in favor of those claiming possession of a more real or correct consciousness or political practice. Drawing sharp distinctions between real and true general social interests and merely partial interests risks designating a particular – however radical – set of interests, values, and desires as *the* real and true general social interests, values, and desires. Simply put, it risks resurrecting the ideology meant to be extinguished.

The crucial work that Nietzsche's thought provides is the provocation to read out of perspectival epistemology and the concern over the death of God a broader series of political projects and ethical questions. Political imaginations, desires, and projects emerge historically, from multiple particularly-situated positions and perspectives. They are not and do not remain static or univocal. In the short-term, the assumption of a more correct political imagination and practice has the potential to overshadow or exclude critical ideas and actions that may overlap with, challenge, or compete with interests and projects assuming pride of place. One need only consider the debates revolving around the tactics, strategies, and goals of the contemporary American Left. The questions of whether one comprehensive social movement can or should be marshaled for the sake of its strength in numbers, whether distinct groups should focus their demands on particular issues while working in solidarity with different but related groups, or whether different groups require some degree of distance for the sake of concerted focus and against threats of cooptation all demand sustained reflection.

In the long-term, political ideas and actions shift in character, scope, and aim. The search for a general social consciousness and political practice denies the necessarily multiple lived positions and perspectives from which ideas, interests, and goals emerge. Paradoxically, it may be in the overall interest of a society to remain open to particularly-positioned, historically-shifting ways of moving forward, however fraught with contention such untidy politics must be. If we return to Marx, for example, in arguing that human flourishing in the realm of freedom is an interest that weaves together and thereby transcends the distinction between the particular individual and the general social totality, we can still pause to ask what exactly is meant by the concept of 'human flourishing.' Of what does this consist, and does it consist of the same attributes across individuals, groups, or societies? Is the meaning of human flourishing open to challenge and change? What are better and worse ways of living?

These are questions of politics and of ethics. They are contested, contestable, and often enough contradictory. The limitations of Nietzsche's agonist perspectivalism are clear. They are the limitations and frustrations and risks of politics itself. So we find ourselves in some sense back where we began, namely, back to the issue of the death of God and its Nietzschean corollary, the death of Truth. Are critique and practice – whether epistemic, political, ethical or otherwise in flavor – possible, absent the certainty of a foundational Truth? Outside the non-answer of apathetic nihilism, they are and must be. Critique (and the scholars and disciplines of knowledge, science, and technology studies) cannot now afford to run out of steam.

References

Adorno, Theodor W. 2007. *Negative Dialectics*, translated by E.B. Ashton. New York, NY: Continuum.

Allison, David B. 2001. *Reading the New Nietzsche: The Birth of Tragedy, The Gay Science, Thus Spoke Zarathustra, and On the Genealogy of Morals*. Lanham, MD: Rowman & Littlefield Publishers.

Arendt, Hannah. 2018. 'Hannah Arendt on Hannah Arendt.' In *Thinking Without a Banister: Essays in Understanding: 1953–1975*, edited by Jerome Kohn, 443–475. New York, NY: Schocken.

Gemes, Ken. 2006. '"We Remain of Necessity Strangers to Ourselves": The Key Message of Nietzsche's Genealogy.' In *Nietzsche's On the Genealogy of Morals: Critical Essays*, edited by Christina Davis Acampora, 191–208. Lanham, MD: Rowman & Littlefield Publishers.

Haraway, Donna. 1988. 'Situated Knowledges: The Science Question in Feminism and the Privilege of Partial Perspective.' *Feminist Studies* 14(3): 575–599.

Harding, Sandra. 2004. 'A Socially Relevant Philosophy of Science? Resources from Standpoint Theory's Controversiality.' *Hypatia* 19(1): 25–47.

Harding, Sandra. 1986. *The Science Question in Feminism*. Ithaca, NY: Cornell University Press.

Latour, Bruno. 2004. 'Why Has Critique Run Out of Steam? From Matters of Fact to Matters of Concern.' *Critical Inquiry* 30(2): 225–248.

Marx, Karl. 1991. *Capital: Volume 3*, translated by David Fernbach. New York, NY: Penguin Classics.

Marx, Karl, and Fredrich Engels. 2010. *The German Ideology*, edited by C.J. Arthur. New York, NY: International Publishers.

Nietzsche, Friedrich. 1998. *Genealogy of Morality*, translated by Maudemarie Clark and Alan Swensen. Indianapolis and Cambridge: Hackett Publishing Company.

Nietzsche, Friedrich. 1997. *Twilight of the Idols: Or, How to Philosophize with the Hammer*, translated by Richard Polt, introduction by Tracy Strong. Indianapolis/Cambridge: Hackett Publishing Company.

Nietzsche, Friedrich. 1989. *Beyond Good and Evil: Prelude to a Philosophy of the Future*, translated by Walter Kaufmann. New York, NY: Vintage Books.

Nietzsche, Friedrich. 1979. 'On Truth and Lies in a Nonmoral Sense.' In *Philosophy and Truth: Selections from Nietzsche's Notebooks of the Early 1870's*, translated and edited by Daniel Breazeale. Amherst, NY: Humanity Books.

Nietzsche, Friedrich. 1977a. *Thus Spoke Zarathustra*, translated by Walter Kaufmann. New York, NY Penguin Books.

Nietzsche, Friedrich. 1977b. *The Anti-Christ*, translated by Walter Kaufmann. New York, NY: Penguin Books.

Nietzsche, Friedrich. 1974. *The Gay Science*, translated by Walter Kaufmann. New York: Vintage Books.

Nietzsche, Friedrich. 1967. *The Birth of Tragedy*, translated by Walter Kaufmann. New York: Vintage Books.

Strong, Tracy B. 2012. *Politics without Vision: Thinking Without a Bannister in the Twentieth Century*. Chicago, IL: University of Chicago Press.

PART 4

All-Too-Human: The Question of the Human Condition in Light of Nietzsche

∵

CHAPTER 14

Nietzsche's Genealogy as a Critique of Racial Narratives and the Loss of Solidarity

Jung Min Choi and John W. Murphy

1 Introduction

In the past two decades, multiple discussions have been raging over Nietzsche's influence on the writings of race and racism. And similar to the way in which his philosophy has been used by both the Right and the Left to buttress their arguments, Nietzsche's perspective on race is no different. From Jacqueline Scott's (2003) piece, "On the Use and Abuse of Race in Philosophy: Nietzsche, Jews, and Race," where she points to Nietzsche's ambivalence on race to Robert Holub's (2001) account of Nietzsche's colonial mentality to William Preston's (1997: 169) charge that "Nietzsche is a cruel racist," it is clear that Nietzsche's writings have garnered extreme interest among race scholars in general and postcolonial writers in particular. Obviously, Nietzsche's influence goes beyond race, as his ideas, especially his use of geneology, have been utilized heavily by postmodernists, feminists, and queer theorists just to name several. While each camp utilizes Nietzsche in different ways, they all seem to generally agree that geneology provides a unique methodological tool (Foucault 2002) to combat the traditional binary logic that has resulted in oppression and marginalization of groups and peoples around the world. Indeed, the arguments presented in this paper owe a great deal to Nietzsche's geneology in critiquing the popular narratives on race and at the same time rescuing solidarity without the aid of essentialism.

In many circles essentialism is considered to be a remnant of the past. Since Nietzsche's negation of the ***origin*** (emphasis mine) in *On the Geneology of Morals* (2012) and *Beyond Good and Evil* (1989), along with the rise of constructionism in the social sciences, persons are no longer trapped in an identity but free to invent themselves in a variety of ways. In the field of racial and ethnic studies, this change is considered to be very important. After all, essentialism has been used traditionally to justify racial hierarchies and other modes of exclusion. With the metaphysics of domination undermined – a universal or foundational principle – roles can be challenged and new prospects proposed

(Murphy and Choi 1997). Many social critics, along with everyday persons, have found this new openness to be quite exciting and liberating.

At first this change was invigorating. A trend toward multiculturalism emerged, for example, that many persons embraced (Glazer 1997). The stigma attached to earlier identities could be confronted, with a radical pluralism able to flourish. Particularly noteworthy is that society could survive, and even benefit, from the resulting diversity. The belief that everyone had to assimilate to a particular cultural ideal, in order to avert chaos, was treated as passé.

Critics on the Right and the Left, for very different reasons, were unhappy with the rise of multiculturalism (Kimball 1990). In general, however, both argued that social order would be jeopardized by this outcome. Their basic critique was that relativism is encouraged that undermines ethical principles and thus social solidarity. Without a universal foundation, no society can be effectively or justly regulated.

Although these critics try to resurrect an outmoded thesis, at least in terms of contemporary philosophy, a real problem has arisen related to the social construction of identity. Specifically, persons are creating their narratives alone, in the absence of others. And while they revel in their uniqueness, social conflict seems to be unavoidable. Societal cohesion appears to be impossible, with everyone enthralled with their personal stories.

But constructionism does not have to end in this way. What critics and proponents of this philosophy have overlooked is that neither individual nor group narratives are created alone. While at first this statement may sound esoteric, and hardly a solution to the current lack of solidarity, a principle is involved that can unite diversity and order. Diversity and social cohesion, in other words, do not have to be treated as antagonistic. To borrow from Nietzsche, this binary way of understanding society is to act "mythologically."

But in order to appreciate this shift in thinking, the philosophy behind the demand for assimilation must be understood. Why diversity is presumed to be a threat to order, accordingly, will become clear. Perhaps more important, however, is that a new way of thinking about order is revealed, whereby diverse narratives do not necessarily have to clash and preclude dialogue. Individuals and groups can create their narratives together, without sacrificing their unique histories or experiences (Boff 2001). A base of social solidarity is thus available that does not demand the usual integration, with the traditional racial hierarchy, and obscure selective identities.

2 Realism and Assimilation

At the heart of American racial policy has been a key principle, that is, assimilation.[1] This idea has taken several forms, ranging from the melting pot to segmented assimilation. In general, however, the point is that everyone should, and eventually will, internalize a set of specific norms. And if this integration does not occur, the fear is that society will become balkanized and lose any cultural uniformity.

What is often overlooked is that this policy is an outgrowth of a theme basic to classical sociological theory. Specifically, these writers such as August Comte and Emile Durkheim were obsessed with the breakdown of society and sought social imagery that would prevent this collapse. They offered a particular metaphysics, therefore, that they thought would reinforce order. In the nomenclature of Werner Stark (1963), they became committed to social realism.

Realists believe that only society is real. In this sense, society is greater than, and superior to, the individual and all individuals combined. In the words of Talcott Parsons, a classic realist, society constitutes an "Ultimate Reality" (Parsons 1971: 4–8). Society, in other words, provides the universal referent necessary to prevent the onset of chaos; the realm of the social exists *sui generis*. Without this abstract foundation, the unity required for society to survive is difficult to secure.

Among those who write about race relations, this realism is referred to as foundationalism or essentialism.[2] The basic policy, accordingly, is that everyone should assimilate to this special normative base. Those who do not comply face social marginalization, and perhaps may even be viewed as a threat. Samuel Huntington's description of Mexicans in the American Southwest provides a prime example (Huntington 2004). He contends that their resistance to assimilation, and reluctance to downplay their cultural heritage, has transformed these persons into a social time bomb.

But assimilation is not usually characterized as a politicized process. Common sense dictates, for example, that a society with competing cultures will be unstable. On the other hand, social mobility depends on successful assimilation. How can new immigrants expect to achieve success without learning the dominant norms and language? Assimilation is thus only logical.

---

1 See Robert E. Park (1950), Milton Gordon (1964), and Nathan Glazer and Patrick Moynihan (1963).

2 See Stanley Fish (1989), bell hooks (1992).

But this process is hardly neutral. Early on immigrants were expected to adjust to the so-called Anglo-ideal. Nowadays European standards should be adopted. In either case newcomers are expected to abandon their original backgrounds and don a new identity. This new outlook, in general, is considered to be superior to the old, and specifically better suited for contemporary society. Their cultural lineage, in short, is a serious liability.

No wonder that so many critics spurn multi-culturalism. Multi-culturalists, after all, reject assimilation and champion cultural diversity. But this trend is rejected not only by conservatives. Arthur Schlesinger (1998), a classic liberal, argues that multiculturalism poses a real threat to American society. In this sense, realists tend to agree, even across party lines, that without a universal foundation a society is doomed.

Given this theoretical framework, and the accompanying assumptions, assimilation represents a sound policy. But even assimilationists recognize that diversity cannot be totally eliminated. These diverse elements, nonetheless, must be guided into their proper place in society, thereby providing some regularity and security. A method of aligning persons to their respective positions, social and economic, must be available. At this juncture is where essentialism comes into play.

3 Social Alignment and Essentialism

Even with the pressure to assimilate and become fully integrated into society, differences are present. In fact, racial hierarchies are obvious, in addition to other disparities. A central concern, accordingly, is how to prevent this diversity from erupting into widespread conflict. Essentialism is invaluable in addressing this issue.

Essentialism, or the search for truth as Nietzsche (1989) expounds in *Beyond Good and Evil*, is basically a part of Western philosophy. As early as the dialogues of Plato, persons were differentiated from others on the basis of fundamental traits. Elites, for example, have characteristics that separate them categorically from the poor. Likewise, slaves deserve to be distinguished from free persons. And more recently, minorities have a status inferior to the dominant groups. All of these distinctions rely on essential traits that are difficult, if not impossible, to change. Nietzsche, at times, falls for this trap as well in his discussion of Blacks and Jews (2012).

As a result of essentialism, there is nothing political about the social placement of persons. Those who champion a racial hierarchy, for example, can claim that prejudice has nothing to do with their outlook or desires. After all, such an arrangement is merely natural, with persons gravitating to their correct social positions. There is nothing sinister about this outcome. An essence merely clarifies what a group or person has to be.

Throughout the history of race relations, biology has been invoked to justify social placement. Certain persons or classes have been identified as unfit based on inferior intelligence or ethical character. The work related to the Bell Curve represents a recent attempt to continue this trend (Herrnstein and Murray 1994). The point is to avoid what some writers call mismatch, whereby persons, but mostly minorities, are given access to schools, jobs, or other opportunities for which they are not qualified. The message is that no-one should tamper with the natural alignment that will occur without the intervention of activists (D'Souza 1991).

What essentialism does is provide a sound rationale for an orderly integration, even in the face of obvious disparities. For example, if blacks are underrepresented in executive jobs, discrimination is not necessarily to blame. Those with low intelligence or a lack of motivation should not expect such advancement. The resulting hierarchy is simply the product of the laws of nature. In the end, persons find their proper niche in a society (Herrnstein and Murray 1994).

Many critics, however, have questioned the legitimacy of essentialism. Marxists, for example, contend that this thesis represents an ideology designed to reinforce a particular power structure.[3] Others challenge the biology that has been used to formulate this principle (Lewontin 1985). While some constructionists argue that racial and gender identities are the culmination of a performance, with no objective basis (Butler 1990). As a result of these critiques, many persons who have been marginalized feel liberated. They are no longer trapped by tainted identities that limit their possibilities but can invent themselves in any number of ways. Formerly restrictive societies can now be more open.

4 Racial Biographies

Essentialism is supported by a particular philosophy known as dualism. In the modern form proposed by Descartes, knowledge is divided into two distinct realities, that is, the objective and the subjective. In this scheme, the former is treated as real, while the latter is degraded as opinion (Bernstein 1983). Objectivity is thus available to those who have the proper training, such as scientists.

3 See Gunnar Myrdal (1944); Robert Blauner (1972); and Stephen Steinberg (1995).

With respect to essentialism, this distinction allows certain biological or character traits to be viewed as natural properties. As a result, these characteristics can be invoked, without indicating political bias, to determine the fate of persons. Disparities in health status between blacks and whites, for example, are simply the result of poor character, rather than access to care (Vega and Gonzalez del Valle 1993). Some persons have more insight, and are able to control their behavior, better than others.

But a variety of philosophies, such as those mentioned in the previous section, challenge dualism. The argument is that human action, often language, interferes with everything that is known, and thus access to objectivity is compromised (Lyotard 1984). The objectivity that sustains essentialism, in other words, cannot be achieved, due to the absence of neutrality. At best, all that is ever available is one perspective or another. Indeed, the tracing of geneology obliterates the fantasy put forth by objectivity (Nietzsche 1989).

Without a core that defies interpretation, the justification for essentialism is lost. All that is left, in fact, are claims and counter claims made about the identity of a group or person (Fish 1989). Following this revelation, some scholars began to argue that identities are merely narratives (Omi and Winant 1994). An identity is a story that contains, for example, historical and cultural elements. An identity is thus thoroughly socially manufactured and biographical.

Many persons and groups embraced this narrative rendition of identity. This novel outlook permitted them to give unique meaning and purpose to their lives. As a result, they began to take pride in their narratives, both past and present. Furthermore, each story should be treated with dignity, and never smeared by another's claims. All persons and groups should be able to tell their stories as they please – their voices should never be perverted. The result of this scenario would be a truly pluralist society, devoid of the restrictions imposed by essentialism.

As should be noted, constructionism is very alluring. The problem, however, is that persons began to tell their stories in isolation from others, thereby courting relativism that threatens any sense of community. Many theoretical and social trends have contributed to this inward turn. For example, the atomism that pervades Western philosophy, the individualism associated with modern societies, and the recent resurrection of Social Darwinism in neo-liberal economies have played a significant role in this process. Nonetheless, this shift toward narrative identities has begun to fragment society.

This charge is different from the complaint made by conservatives a few years ago about the relativism they believe was spawned by postmodernism. They worried that without a universal base of values any society would collapse into a myriad of perspectives. The usual social and cultural arrangements, likewise, would be threatened.

The problem in this discussion is significantly different. In the absence of dualism, there is no attempt to erect a universal frame of reference. Indeed, as will be discussed, such a base is not required to preserve order. Nonetheless, the ability to establish an alternative community, one that is inclusive, is jeopardized by this narrative turn. For example, the vision supplied by of Martin Luther King Jr.'s "Blessed Community" is out of reach without any prospect for solidarity.

A lot of promise was associated with the critique of essentialism proposed by constructionists.[4] The hope was that a plethora of narratives would emerge along with the tolerance necessary for all of these stories to flourish. But without any rationale for solidarity this outcome is doubtful. Individuals and groups will likely continue to revel in their own stories, with others ignored and unappreciated.

5 Narratives Together

Those who advocate for narrative identities often overlook a seminal point in contemporary philosophy. That is, narratives are never created alone, despite the claims advanced by atomists or Social Darwinists. Persons always act in the presence of others, and their respective stories crisscross many lives. These narratives, furthermore, are dealt with in various ways, including support and resistance.

This idea is not based simply on a technical matter, such as the generalizability of stories, agreement, and consensus. Rather, and much more important, the point is that social existence is fundamentally intersubjective.[5] In traditional sociology this theme is overlooked. What is usually presented is that basically persons exist apart from one another and must be joined by formal agreements, such as laws, contracts, or powerful institutions. In each case, the assumption is that persons must be forced together, because any other mode of connection is missing.

In contemporary philosophy, however, persons are viewed to exist together prior to any of these formal arrangements, that is, they are open to others (Levinas 1969). In fact, this association is necessary to formulate any agreements or representative institutions. In other words, they exist in a state of solidarity that can be transformed into legal or institutional relations (Boff 2001). And prior to being imposed by control mechanisms, order emerges

4 See bell hooks (1992), Cornel West (1994), and Manning Marable (2002).

5 See Martin Buber (2010), Emmanuel Levinas (1969).

through everyday discourse that brings persons together. Through this sort of interpersonal meeting order arises in the absence of a universal base or general reality.

Even conflict between individuals and groups signals a connection. However, the ethical implications of this realization are rarely discussed (Marx 1987). That persons and groups can peacefully co-exists, based on the recognition of their differences, is not given serious consideration, especially in the realm of race relations. In this sense, the intersubjective domain is not devoid of ethics, simply because access to absolute standards is denied. But within a realm where persons co-exist without any legitimate claims to dominance, a new discussion of inclusion must be inaugurated.

Especially important is that constructionism, understood through the method of geneology, does not result automatically in relativism. Basing identities on narratives does not mandate an inward turn. But rather, persons have to be convinced that others are absent through long-term socialization or coercion. Through political or economic influences, for example, individuals and groups can be convinced that they act alone. Any sort of real and sustained cooperation is thus a fantasy that violates human nature.

In view of contemporary philosophy, the new message is that narratives support both uniqueness and access to others. In order to convey this idea, argues Paul Gilroy, new social imagery is needed. He contends that "jazz" is an appropriate metaphor to describe how order is generated and maintained, without demanding assimilation and restricting diversity (Gilroy 1995: 79).

As opposed to the universals that have been introduced to legitimize assimilation, order is depicted by jazz to be spontaneous and the result of loose cooperation. The members of a jazz ensemble are inventive, while taking various lines of music progression into account. In the end, various streams of play are united without total integration.

Individuals or groups, in other words, can read one another's narratives, grasp the differences that exist, and appreciate the various sentiments that are conveyed. And given the absence of absolutes, none of these stories is obligated to become subservient to another. The ethic that is present, instead, requires that these narratives co-exist and that each one be treated with dignity. To introduce another metaphor, a montage of stories is present and has integrity that should be protected.

These loose arrangements are not a threat to interpersonal cohesion. In more racial or ethnic terms, order and diversity are not basically antagonistic. Order can thus occur without the metaphysics of assimilation and the accompanying uniformity. The idea is that those who adopt constructionism, as a way to subvert essentialism, are not condemned to relativism and disorder. Nonetheless, vigilance is needed to insure that other forces do not arise and turn persons inward and undermine solidarity.

6 Conclusion

Why is this discussion important? After all, more pressing issues, such as police shootings and other violence, need to be addressed. But at the core of this discussion is a very significant theme: the development and maintenance of community. And only with true social solidarity will these other problems be successfully resolved.

Everyone wants liberation, especially those who have been marginalized. But individual liberation will not solve the problems faced currently by societies. Individuals or groups withdrawing into their own narratives will not be helpful. A new model is needed, whereby persons see their respective fates as joined together in a public sphere.

With no escape from intersubjectivity, the stage is set for solidarity to become a guiding principle – not some plan for an abstract, collective humanity, but an understanding that persons are concretely linked. In the field of race relations, King's image of the "Blessed Community" provides a pertinent example. In this setting everyone has a dignified place, while a commodious order is created.

Community is important because full members do not cheat or discriminate against one another. Likewise, suspicions abate in a real community. Individuals and groups are able to create their own identities, and take pride in these narratives, while recognizing that they rise or fall together. No story is ever written alone!

Integration, nonetheless, is not enough to engender a sense of community. In fact, undertaken in the wrong way, such a policy may contravene solidarity – persons may be forced into hostile or unequal relationships. In conclusion, therefore, narratives must be accompanied by respect and care, in order for community to be achieved. True liberation is reached through these traits.

In the end, talking about narratives and their linkage is not esoteric or a distraction. Central to this issue is a fundamental association between persons that is not merely a platitude. The reality is that persons are joined, even in their diversity, and should begin to recognize this simple fact. Accordingly, discussions about narrative identities do not have to impede reaching this awareness of the collective or communal nature of daily existence.

References

Bernstein, Richard. 1983. *Beyond Objectivism and Relativism*. Philadelphia, PA: University of Pennsylvania Press.

Blauner, Robert. 1972. *Racial Oppression in America*. New York: Harper and Row Publishers.

Boff, Leonardo. 2001. *Etica Planataria desde el Gran Sur.* Madrid: Editorial Trotta.

Buber, Martin. 2010. *I and Thou*. Mansfield Centre, CT: Martino Publishing.

Butler, Judith. 1990. *Gender Trouble.* New York: Routledge.

D'Souza, Dinesh. 1991. *Illiberal Education*. New York: Free Press.

Fish, Stanley. 1989. *Doing What Comes Naturally*. Durham, NC: Duke University Press.

Foucault, Michel. 2002. *Archaeology of Knowledge*. New York: Routledge.

Gilroy, Paul. 1995. *The Black Atlantic*. Cambridge, MA: Harvard University Press.

Glazer, Nathan. 1997. *We Are All Multiculturalists Now.* Cambridge, MA: Harvard University Press.

Glazer, Nathan, and Patrick Moynihan. 1963. *Beyond the Melting Pot: The Negroes, Puerto Ricans, Jews, Italians and Irish of New York City*. Cambridge, MA: MIT Press.

Gordon, Milton. 1964. *Assimilation in American Life: The Role of Race, Religion, and National Origins.* New York: Oxford University Press.

Herrnstein, Richard J., and Charles Murray. 1994. *The Bell Curve: Intelligence and Class Structure in American Life.* New York: Free Press.

Holub, Robert C. 2001. "Nietzsche's Colonialist Imagination: Nueva Germania, Good Europeanism, and Great Politics." In *The Imperialist Imagination*, edited by Sara Friedrichsmeyer, Sara Lennox, and Susanne Zantop, 33–49. Ann Arbor, MI: The University of Michigan Press.

hooks, bell. 1992. *Black Looks: Race and Representation*. Boston, MA: South End Press.

Huntington, Samuel. 2004. *Who are We?: the Challenge to America's Identity*. New York: Simon & Schuster.

Kimball, Roger. 1990. *Tenured Radicals*. NY: Harper and Row.

Levinas, Emmanuel. 1969. *Totality and Infinity*. Pittsburgh, PA: Duquesne University Press.

Lewontin, Richard C. 1985. *The Dialectical Biologist*. Cambridge, MA: Harvard University Press.

Lyotard, Jean-Francois. 1984. *The Postmodern Condition: A Report on Knowledge*. Minneapolis, MN: University of Minnesota Press.

Marable, Manning. 2002. *The Great Wells of Democracy: The Meaning of Race in American Life*. New York: BasicCivitas Books.

Marx, Werner. 1987. *Is There a Measure on Earth?: Foundations for a Nonmetaphysical Ethics* Chicago: University of Chicago Press.

Murphy, John W., and Jung Min Choi. 1997. *Postmodernism, Unraveling Racism, and Democratic Institutions.* Westport, CT: Praeger.

Myrdal, Gunnar. 1944. *An American Dilemma: The Negro Problem and Modern Democracy*. New York: Harper & Bros.

Nietzsche, Friedrich. 2012. *On the Geneology of Morals.* Cranston, RI: Angelnook Publishing.

Nietzsche, Friedrich. 1989. *Beyond Good and Evil: Prelude to a Philosophy of the Future.* New York: Vintage Books.

Omi, Michael, and Howard Winant. 1994. *Racial Formation in the United States*. New York: Routledge.

Park, Robert E. 1950. *Race and Culture*. Glencoe, IL: The Free Press.

Parsons, Talcott. 1971. *The System of Modern Societies*. Englewood Cliffs, NJ: Prentice-Hall.

Preston, William A. 1997. "Nietzsche on Blacks." In *Existence in Black: An Anthology of Black Existential Philosophy*, edited by Lewis R. Gordon, 167–172. New York: Routledge.

Scott, Jacqueline. 2003. "On the Use and Abuse of Race in Philosophy: Nietzsche, Jews, and Race." In *Race and Racism in Continental Philosophy*, edited by Robert Bernasconi and Sybol Cook, 53–73. Bloomington, IN: Indiana University Press.

Schlesinger, Arthur Jr. 1998. *The Disuniting of America: Reflections on a Multicultural Society.* New York: W.W. Norton & Company.

Stark, Werner. 1963. *Fundamental Forms of Social Thought*. NY: Fordham University Press.

Steinberg, Stephen. 1995. *Turning Back: The Retreat from Racial Justice in American Thought and Policy*. Boston, MA: Beacon Press.

Vega, William, and Amalia Gonzalez Del Valle. 1993. "The Need for Community-Based Health Policy: A Challenge for Democracy." In *Open Institutions: The Hope for Democracy*, edited by John W. Murphy and Dennis L. Peck, 123–139. Westport, CT: Praeger Press.

West, Cornel. 1994. *Race Matters*. Boston: MA: Beacon Press.

CHAPTER 15

Nietzsche's "Anti-Darwinism": A Deflationary Critique

Peter Atterton

> The author of *Zarathustra* ... demolished so many idols only to replace them with others.
>
> EMIL CIORAN, *The Trouble with Being Born*

∵

So much has been written on Nietzsche's relation to Darwin that it is easy to suppose that there is nothing left to say that is of much philosophical value.[1] However, I wish to raise some questions about Nietzsche's "anti-Darwinism" that, if I am not mistaken, are important but have not yet been sufficiently addressed. My aim here is not simply to correct Nietzsche's misinterpretations, though I do that as well, but to suggest that had Nietzsche understood Darwin better, he would have avoided what I consider to be a major shortcoming of his (Nietzsche's) work. While biological processes and evolutionary theory constitute a substantial part of Nietzsche's conception of naturalism, it can be shown that *teleological* rather than purely causal explanations predominate in Nietzsche's descriptions of "will to power" and "will to life." These phenomena are not accounted for in terms of antecedent conditions or mechanisms but in terms of certain goals or goal-directed behaviors found within nature itself. This, of course, is the opposite of what Darwin taught and as a result threatens to derail the naturalistic, skeptical, and anti-metaphysical task that Nietzsche set himself (e.g. Nietzsche 1989a: 161). The clearest indication of this is chapter 5 of "Schopenhauer as Educator" (1997: 156–161) and "Zarathustra's Prologue" (1982: 121–137), where Nietzsche imputes to nature the goal of creating a superior type of human being that is represented as leaving the plain of animality

1 See e.g. Kaufmann (1974: 157–177); Stack (1983: 156–194); Dennett (1995: 181–186, 461–467); Ansell-Pearson (1997: 85–122); Hollingdale (1999: 56–87); Moore (2002); Richardson (2004); Johnson (2010); and Wilson (2013).

altogether. What I think this establishes is that Nietzsche's philosophy does *not* constitute the radical anti-humanism that postmodern scholars say it is, and therefore should be viewed with suspicion.

1 Nietzsche's Darwinian Origins

Although Nietzsche says that only "scholarly oxen" could have suspected him of Darwinism because of what he says about the overman (1989b: 261), it can hardly be denied that Darwin exerted a profound and lasting influence on his thought. Most commentators and biographers regard Darwin as a seminal figure for Nietzsche. Walter Kaufmann suggests that Nietzsche, while "not a Darwinist ... [was] aroused from his dogmatic slumber by Darwin, much as Kant was a century earlier by Hume" (1974: xxi). George Stack claims that "[a]lthough he says a great deal 'against Darwin,' there is no doubt that his thinking was stimulated by Darwinian conceptions and that he creatively adapted its principles to his own interpretation of life" (1983: 179–180). And in a book-length study dedicated to getting to the core of Nietzsche's fundamental disagreement with Darwin, entitled *Nietzsche's Anti-Darwinism,* Dirk Johnson draws attention to "the pre-eminence of Darwin for the development and articulation of Nietzsche's philosophy" (2010: 1).

What, then, did Nietzsche find in Darwin's thinking that played such a decisive role in the formation of his own? In 1874, in the second *Untimely Meditation,* "On the Uses and Disadvantages of History for Life," Nietzsche called attention to three Darwinian "doctrines" as follows:

> the doctrines of sovereign becoming, of the fluidity of all concepts, types and species, of the lack of any cardinal distinction between man and animal – doctrines which I hold true but deadly.
>
> 1997: 112

The fact that Nietzsche considered these tenets to be "true but deadly" is significant. It explains why Nietzsche should have had such an ambivalent relation to Darwin. Let us first consider what Nietzsche found in Darwin's theory that he could not gainsay before looking at his reservations about what he considered to be its perilous consequences and which his own thinking was an attempt to circumvent.

What Darwin showed incontrovertibly for Nietzsche is: (1) The notion that becoming and change permeate the whole of the animal and plant kingdom. (2) Talk of instantiating an immutable essence (Platonic Idea, type, or species) has no meaning, amounting to a falsification and rejection of Platonic-Aristotelian metaphysics. (3) There are no essential or absolute differences between humans and (nonhuman) animals.

The last tenet is the most important for Nietzsche. For it means that what philosophical and cultural anthropologists, in tandem with the whole orientation and trajectory of the dominant Judeo-Christian tradition in the West, consider to be insuperable ontological and ethical distinctions between humans and animals *simply do not exist*.[2] Darwin himself, of course, did not deny that humans are a unique species, like every species is unique. But humans are not unique in the sense of standing outside of nature. What we think of as our special characteristics that separate us from animals – our "reason" and "spirituality" – are explained by the same natural and evolutionary processes as those that govern the emergence of traits among animals with which they are continuous. According to Nietzsche, this was Darwin's "fundamental proposition": "Man ... is precisely a creature of nature and nothing else" (1997: 30–31). Nietzsche takes up this Darwinian idea in the following famous passage from *The Anti-Christ*:

> We have learned better. We have become more modest in every respect. We no longer trace the origin of man in the "spirit," in the "divinity," we have placed him back among the animals. We consider him the strongest animal because he is the most cunning: his spirituality is a consequence of this. On the other hand, we guard ourselves against a vanity which would like to find expression even here: the vanity that man is the great secret objective of animal evolution. Man is absolutely not the crown of creation: every creature stands beside him at the same stage of perfection.... And even in asserting that we assert too much: man is, relatively speaking, the most unsuccessful animal, the sickliest, the one most dangerously strayed from its instincts – with all that, to be sure, the most *interesting*!
>
> 1990: 136

I will come back to Nietzsche's claim that man is relatively speaking the most *interesting* animal later (a claim he repeats in *The Genealogy of Morals* [cf. 1989b: 33]). The claim is a dubious one not least because the term "interesting" has little, if any, philosophical meaning that I can discern (it is after all purely a matter of subjective opinion what various individuals deem interesting), but

2 In Continental philosophy, this thought of "indistinction" has been developed in various ways by Gilles Deleuze and Félix Guattari (1987) and Georgio Agamben (2004).

also because I think that in using the term in a laudatory way to draw a distinction between man and animals, we have here evidence of Nietzsche indulging in the vanity that humans are separate from the rest of nature, even as he is in the process of "placing man back among [*zurückgestellen*] the animals." This will become clear a little later when we look at Nietzsche's anthropocentric remarks in *Thus Spoke Zarathustra*.

The point, however, at which Darwinism is rejected by Nietzsche is the point at which it ceases to serve as a condition for life, power, and growth. Beyond the truth its doctrines contain, what makes Darwinism "deadly" (*tödtlich*), according to Nietzsche, is that it embodies values that are *radically nihilistic*. In the *Nachlass*, Nietzsche puts it thus: "goals are lacking and these must be *individuals*! We observe how things are everywhere: every individual is sacrificed and serves as a tool. Go into the street and you encounter lots of 'slaves.' Whither? For what?" (2011: 154). Darwinism is governed by the conviction that individual life is expendable; millions upon millions of individuals perish each day, but life continues through their offspring, which in turn die. Of what value is an *individual* if it exists merely to perpetuate the species, which must itself eventually become extinct? Nietzsche could no more embrace the ostensibly Darwinian view of the individual as a mere "accidental occurrence in the flux of becoming and passing away" (2011: 9) than he could return to the pre-Darwinian metaphysics and theology that had conferred on human beings the universal status of "ends in themselves." *The only alternative was to try to find a way beyond it.* In Kaufmann's words, "it was a question of creating a new picture of man in reply to the 'true but deadly' nihilism from beyond the Channel" (1974: 167).[3]

3 Nietzsche's attempt to leave what J.B. Haldane called "the relatively firm ground of scientific objectivity for the shifting morass of human values" (1990: 83) is not because he rejects evolution as a worldview, though, as we shall see, Nietzsche does make various misguided attempts to "correct" Darwin's theory of evolution by natural selection, *but because of the negative ramifications of holding it to be true*. Nietzsche appears to believe, seriously enough, that if the theory is widely accepted then no one should be surprised if there is a breakdown of social bonds and an outright *bellum omnium contra omnes* (as Hobbes dubbed it). The thinking here is like that of the character Ivan in *The Brothers Karamazov*: "If God does not exist then everything is permissible." If people no longer have a sense of being God's creatures under universal moral laws, then, Nietzsche believes, the most individualistic, exploitative, and rapacious egoism will naturally predominate (1997: 112–113). That the protestant theologian David Strauss should have welcomed with open arms the Darwinian gospel that amounted to a full-frontal assault on the moral-religious worldview of Christianity in particular was an irony that was not lost on Nietzsche. In "David Strauss, the Confessor and the Writer," published in 1873, he pilloried Strauss for clothing himself in the "hairy cloak of our ape-genealogists" (*zottige Gewand unserer Affengenealogenand*) and praising Darwin as "one of the greatest benefactors of mankind" (1997: 29) (*einen der grössten Wohlthäter der Menschheit*).

2 Nietzsche's "Anti-Darwin" Criticisms (1887–1888)

Before looking at how this new picture took shape, I wish to identify five criticisms that Nietzsche makes of Darwin. Most of these criticisms are already familiar and have already been debunked elsewhere.[4] However, the goal here is not to rub it in by showing just how a *poor* reader of Darwin Nietzsche was, if he ever read him directly at all, which looks doubtful,[5] but to explain the wrong "turn" in Nietzsche's thinking regarding the thinly-veiled teleology that is will to power.

The first four criticisms listed below are found in the "Anti-Darwin" material of the *Nachlass*, written March–June 1888. The fifth is found at length in two places: section 350 of *The Gay Science* (1887; second edition); and the "Anti-Darwin" section of *Twilight of the Idols* (1888).

1) *Progressivism*: Nietzsche aligns Darwin with the view that evolution is progressive. He attributes to Darwin three distinct but associated conjectures: 1) the whole animal and vegetable kingdom has evolved from the lower organisms to the higher; 2) the human species represents progress in comparison with other types of animals; and 3) that the human species is continuing to progress (2011: 363). What we find, on the contrary, says Nietzsche, is that "man as a species is not progressing" and "does not present any progress compared with any other animal" (363). He concludes: "that species represent any progress is the most unreasonable assertion in the world." "That the higher organisms have evolved from the lower has not been demonstrated in a single case" (365).

2) *Natural Selection:* Not only, according to Nietzsche, is there no evidence that evolution is progressive, we find in many cases the exact opposite has occurred: "the elimination of the lucky strokes, the uselessness of the more highly developed types, the inevitable dominion of the average, even sub-average types" (2011: 364). Natural selection, Nietzsche contends, favors the weak *over* the strong: "among men ... the higher types, the lucky strokes of evolution, perish more easily as fortunes change"

4 See especially: Moore (2002); Richardson (2004); and Johnson (2010).

5 Richardson writes: "Tellingly, he [Nietzsche] seems not to have required of himself a direct acquaintance with Darwin's own writings before addressing his attacks. He knows the movement primarily by way of English and German Social Darwinists. So, in particular, he refers more to Spencer than to Darwin; he has Spencer but not Darwin in his library" (2004: 16). A letter written to Malwida von Meysenbug, dated August 4, 1877, provides circumstantial evidence that Nietzsche may have read Darwin's perfunctory "A Bibliographical Sketch of an Infant" (1877). Incidentally, Richardson (2004: 17) and Johnson (2010: 16n17) both make the mistake of naming Paul Rée as the recipient of the letter.

(363). It is only the lowest who appear to have a survival value conferred on them and to be indestructible. This is seen in cases where weaker individuals with stronger "herd instincts" (364) and superior "cunning" (*List*) (362, 365) often prevail over the strongest and most gifted *but less gregarious and intelligent* individuals. If this is right and "the fruitfulness of the species stands in a notable relation to it chances of destruction" (362), we are back to square one. Darwin has simply failed to explain how "unconscious selection" (*unbewußten Selektion*) (362) could produce better and stronger individuals in place of the weak and ill constituted.

3) *Adaptation:* Nietzsche roundly criticizes the adaptationist program presented by Darwin. He attacks the program in both forms: forward and backward. He attacks the forward form since he finds an environmental "problem" that it is not solved by an organism's phenotypic trait. And he attacks the backward form insofar as he finds a phenotypic "solution" that is maintained in an environment that would call for a quite different adaptation. He writes: "Beings with exterior markings to protect them from danger do not lose them when they encounter conditions in which they live without danger – When they live in places in which their dress ceases to hide them they do not by any means adapt to the new milieu" (2011: 362).
4) *Theory of Inheritance*: Nietzsche rejects Darwin's proposed mechanism for evolution, namely, natural selection, in favor of the theory of "blending inheritance." This is the view that offspring are merely an average between the two different characteristics of their parents: "But one nowhere finds any example of *unconscious selection* (absolutely not). The most disparate individuals unite with one another, the extremes are submerged in the mass" (2011: 363).
5) *Struggle for Existence*: Finally, the most serious criticism that Nietzsche offers of Darwin concerns what he disparagingly refers to as "the incomprehensibly one-sided doctrine of the 'struggle of existence'" (1974: 292). Darwin's major error, according to Nietzsche, was his inordinate stress on "preservation" or "survival" rather than "power" and "growth." The superabundance that we find in nature, the profusion of differences in phenotype in nature, is not to be explained solely, or even mostly, in terms of the differential survival and reproduction of individuals, but rather is due to the organism's striving to becoming more than it is by surpassing its hereditary type.

Five criticisms of Darwin then: *progressivism, natural selection, adaptation, theory of inheritance, and the struggle for existence.* None of them are compelling; most reveal a misunderstanding and misinterpretation of Darwin's ideas.

Consider, first, the claim that evolution implies "progress." Nietzsche is right to criticize such a claim but wrong to attribute it to Darwin. Darwin had barely set foot off the Beagle before he had rejected the idea. In the year Nietzsche was born in 1844, Darwin wrote in a Letter to Hooker: "Heaven forfend me from Lamarck nonsense of a 'tendency to progression' 'adaptations from the slow willing of animals' &c, – but the conclusions I am led to are not widely different from his – though the means of change are *wholly* so – I think I have found out … the simple way by which species become exquisitely adapted to various ends" (1988: 2). Darwin knew that all organisms, even the simplest, are well suited ("exquisitely adapted") to their particular environment if natural selection is to perform an explanatory role. But he also understood that the idea of progress is culturally imbedded and that it is something of an anthropomorphism and human-chauvinism to consider large-brained mammals like ourselves to be "higher" than, say, insects. "It is absurd," he wrote in his notebook, "to talk of one animal being higher than another. – *We* consider those, where the {cerebral structure/intellectual faculties} most developed as highest. – A bee doubtless would when the instincts were" (2009: 189; B 74). True, Darwin never properly addresses, as far as I can see, the issue of whether complexity is a standard of evolutionary progress. Since organisms in a lineage necessarily begin as very simple biological entities and evolve towards increasing complexity, it seems reasonable to endorse a kind of *relative* evolutionary progress. Notably, on the last page of the *Origin of Species*, Darwin seemed to do just that when he wrote: "as natural selection works solely by and for the good of each being, all corporeal and mental endowments will tend to progress towards perfection" (1964: 489). This is not to endorse the idea of absolute progress, however, since there is no absolute standard (e.g. Platonic Idea) by which the evolution of a lineage is judged to be progressive. Nor does it suggest that a lineage must *necessarily* increase in complexity (consider the subterranean mole rat, a mammal, that has almost lost the ability to see due to its very small and structurally deficient eyes), but only that posterior members of the sequence generally exhibit an improvement of "corporeal and mental endowments" to the extent they confer a survival value. Whatever that endowment is, it is not the result of any internal mechanism within an anterior form. The Lamarckian view that organisms have an innate tendency to evolve in definite direction toward some definite *telos* ("Man") is one that Darwin decisively rejects. Life, for Darwin, is not linear or unidirectional ("lower to higher") with animals climbing up vertical rungs of a *scala natura* pinnacled by humans, but sprawling and opportunistic, occupying different niches opened by chance and adapting itself to vicissitudes of the environment. The fact that Darwin immediately after the passage just quoted cites four laws: "Growth with

Reproduction," "Inheritance," "Variability," and the "Struggle for Life" (489–490), but deliberately avoids speaking of a law of *progress*, and indeed expends much of his effort trying to disentangle evolution from the precisely the kind of progressive evolutionism that Nietzsche wrongly attributes to him, indicates that he was concerned with a much more ramified view of the development of life. It is therefore no slur on Darwin that the evolution of higher organisms from lower "has not been demonstrated in a single case" because that was never his intent. In fact, he did not believe it.[6]

Nietzsche's criticism of the theory of natural selection is also without merit. Nietzsche attempts to provide a counterargument to the theory by pointing out that nature often favors the weak over the strong. But it becomes immediately clear that Nietzsche is equivocating on the use of the words "strong" ("*stark*") and "weak" ("*schwach*"). In Darwinian terminology, "strong" means "fittest" in sense of differential reproductive success; "weak" simply means the opposite, i.e. those organisms that due to their being at a competitive disadvantage are less likely to survive and/or leave behind offspring. (Indeed, the usage is so unexceptionable that many readers of Darwin consider the term "survival of the fittest" a tautology, inasmuch "fittest" is defined as "those organisms that survive," so "survival of the fittest" can only mean "survival of the survivors"!) For Nietzsche, on the other hand, "strength" is nothing adaptative; it refers to a type of (human) psychological disposition or capacity to give oneself one's own rule of conduct. "I have found strength," he says, "where one does not seek it, in simple, gentle and helpful human beings, and conversely the inclination to rule has often seemed to me an inherent sign of weakness.... The powerful natures rule, that is a necessity, even if they do not lift a finger. And when they bury themselves their whole life in a garden house [*Gartenhaus*]!"[7] Strength, then, for Nietzsche, does not produce

---

6 Nietzsche appears to have reached the erroneous view of Darwin as a progressivist through reading the German popularizer of Darwin's ideas, Ernst Haeckel. Haeckel, in his book *The History of Creation* (1892 [1868]), had sought to synthesize the German tradition of *Naturphilosophie* as well as the progressive evolutionism of Lamarck with Darwin's theory descent, which he called *Darwinismus*. Indeed, it was Haeckel who spoke of "the law of progressive development, or the law of progress which we perceive active everywhere in the history of nations (as also in in that of animals and plants) [] explained by Darwin's Doctrine of Descent" (1892 [1868]: 27). Needless to add, there is no truth in Nietzsche's claim in *The Gay Science* that "without Hegel there would have been no Darwin" (1974: 305). There is no record of Darwin ever having read Hegel. This should not surprise us as Darwin could not read German and the first English translation of *The Phenomenology of Spirit* did not appear until nearly thirty years after Darwin's death!

7 "Aber ich habe die Kraft gefunden, wo man sie nicht sucht, in einfachen milden und gefälligen M[enschen] ohne den geringsten Hang zum Herrschen—und umgekehrt ist mir der

differential success; "the strong and domineering natures" even find themselves at a disadvantage in comparison with those who are *physically* strong and have "the desire to rule" yet who lack the inner strength to "'give style' to one's character" (1974: 232) and "become master of the chaos one is" (2011: 444). It is therefore no contradiction to say that natural selection favors the fittest (organisms) at the expense of the strong, since what Nietzsche is calling the "strong" is not defined in terms of (reproductive) fitness. Indeed, since the strong individuals, as Nietzsche presents them, are devoid of both cunning and gregarious instincts, in certain instance we should expect it. That would almost certainly make the strong types (since they are likely to be selected against) non-hereditary and thus merely adventitious – something Nietzsche readily admits when he says: "The brief spell of beauty, of genius, of Caesar, is *sui generis*: such things are not inherited. The *type* is nothing extreme, no 'lucky stroke' [*Glücksfall*]" (2011:363).

As far as the critique of adaptionist program is concerned, Nietzsche drastically underestimates the duration of most evolutionary change. Darwin insisted that evolutionary change is generally takes place only gradually ("Natural selection acts only by taking advantage of slight successive variations; she can never take a great and sudden leap, but must advance by short and sure, though slow steps" [1964: 471]), so gradually that one would not expect *to see* organisms adapt to new environments, especially in the absence of selective pressure against a trait, which is presumably what Nietzsche means when he says they live "without danger." Actually, Nietzsche is doubly wrong here, for when there is a selective pressure against a trait, then we occasionally do witness a change on the short timescale Nietzsche has in mind, as in the famous case of the peppered moth, which according to Sewall Wright "constitutes the clearest case in which a conspicuous evolutionary process has been actually observed" (1978: 186).

Nietzsche's criticism of Darwin's notion of natural selection of advantageous traits while defending the now discredited theory of "blending inheritance" is guilty of faulty logic, as much as anything. If blending inheritance were true, all members of a species would eventually converge upon a single phenotype, which is patently not the case. Darwin, who once held a similar view, soon came to see that it was incompatible with the observation that phenotypic traits, such as flower color, often re-emerge after a generation in which

Hang zum Herrschen oft als ein inneres Merkmal von Schwäche erschienen... . Die mächtigen N[aturen] herrschen, es ist eine Nothwendigkeit, sie werden keinen Finger rühren. Und wenn sie bei Lebzeiten in einem Gartenhaus sich vergraben!" (1980: 582, my translation).

they were not exhibited. While Darwin did not fully understand the mechanism of the inheritance (since he had not read Gregor Mendel's work on genetics), he knew that "propagation by true fertilisation, will turn out to be a sort of mixture & not true fusion" (1990: 484), with the result that when two varieties are crossed, ancestral forms often reappeared without having been "blended away."[8]

Nietzsche's criticism of the notion of the "struggle for existence" is easily the most serious criticism he makes of Darwin, yet one that is no less ill informed than the others. The criticism, which is made repeatedly in Nietzsche's published work, is not that organisms never struggle to preserve themselves, but rather that it is the exception and not the rule:

> The wish [*wollen*] to preserve oneself is the symptom of a condition of distress, of a limitation of the really fundamental instinct of life which aims at the expansion of power, and wishing for that frequently risks and even sacrifices self-preservation.... The struggle for existence [*Dasein*] is only an exception, a temporary restriction of the life-will [*Lebenswillens*]; the great and small struggle revolves everywhere around preponderance, around growth and expansion, around power, in accordance with the will to power which is simply [*eben*] the will of life [*Wille des Lebens*].
>
> 1974: 291–292, see also 1990: 86–87

8 Nietzsche also defends the Lamarckian theory of the inheritance of acquired characteristics. "All the virtues and efficiency of body and soul," he writes, "are acquired laboriously and little by little, through much industry, self-constraint, limitation, through much obstinate, faithful repetition of the same labors, the same renunciations" (2011: 518). These physiological changes acquired over the life of an organism may be passed on to its offspring, according to Nietzsche: "[T]here are men who are the heirs and masters of this slowly-acquired manifold treasure of virtue and efficiency-because, through fortunate and reasonable marriages, and also through fortunate accidents, the acquired and stored-up energies of many generations have not been squandered and dispersed but linked together by a firm ring and by will" (518). This is asserted several years before Nietzsche's "anti-Darwin" entries in the *Nachlass*, so it is unclear whether he is attempting to pit Lamarck *against* Darwin here. If so, he would wrong since even in the *Origin of Species* Darwin seems not to have ruled out the inheritance of acquired characteristics as a supplement to natural selection. As late as 1868, Darwin was attempting to demonstrate what he considered to be the inheritance of acquired characteristics through he called "the hypothesis of pangenesis" (2007: 327). True, Darwin was never convinced that Lamarckism was the whole story and even came to view it as obscuring the "simple" way evolution actually works. For Darwin, species become adapted not through "will" and the transmission of the acquired products of will, but though a *causal mechanism* that is natural selection itself.

It should appear obvious that this inordinate stress on *individual survival* (Nietzsche thinks) is precisely *not* what Darwin means by the term "struggle for existence." Indeed, it is just this sort of restriction and misreading that Darwin was at pains to avoid in the *Origin of Species* when he wrote:

> I should premise that I use the term Struggle for Existence in a large and metaphorical sense, including dependence of one being on another, and including (which is more important) not only the life of the individual, but success in leaving progeny. Two canine animals in a time of dearth, may be truly said to struggle with each other which shall get food and live. But a plant on the edge of a desert is said to struggle for life against the drought, though more properly it should be said to be dependent on the moisture. A plant which annually produces a thousand seeds, of which on an average only one comes to maturity, may be more truly said to struggle with the plants of the same and other kinds which already clothe the ground.
>
> 1964: 62

Two wolves may be literally at each other's throats, but the desert succulent is not literally struggling to survive – certainly it is not wishing or willing anything – any more than the oak is struggling to preserve its genes by strewing the ground with acorns. If there is an irony here, as Richardson (2004: 17) points out, it is that Nietzsche misreads Darwin's notion of "struggle" as sort of physical combat in precisely the same way that foreshadows the misreading of his own term "power." In using the term "struggle," Darwin is speaking figuratively, not literally; he is anthropomorphizing. The term indicates the coefficient of adversity that organisms face in preserving themselves through their dependency on certain conditions of existence as well as in leaving progeny. Different organisms "struggle" in different ways.[9]

Darwin's use of metaphor here is of relevance to us since it enables him to avoid literally ascribing *intentions*, i.e. ends, goals, to blind physical nature. The importance of avoiding teleological or goal-directness of insentient natural organisms (e.g. plants) cannot be overstated. To consider a species lineage as literally modified *in order to* accomplish an end would simply be to pour old

9 The ant *struggles* with other ants which it makes its slaves; birds *struggle* when they cooperate with each other (alarm calls, etc.) to protect themselves against predators, or penguins to protect themselves against the cold. That is why Darwin can say, without a shadow of inconsistency, that a non-conscious organism such as a plant is "struggling" to survive and have offspring as much as is a conscious organism, such as a wolf.

creationist wine into new bottles. Indeed, if there is one thing that makes the Darwinian "struggle for existence" different from the "mobile army of metaphors, metonyms, anthropomorphisms" masquerading as "truths" in the Western tradition it is that they are in reality "illusions about which one has forgotten that this is what they are" (Nietzsche 1982: 46–47). The notion of *entelechy* was really a metaphor that Aristotle thought of as a literal truth. By contrast, when Darwin speaks of the struggle for existence, he *knows* it is a metaphor, an illusion of sorts, though in fact it refers to a system of dependencies that is a fact.

However, this is not the end of the story. For the problem is not only that Nietzsche misrepresents what Darwin means by "struggle for existence," but that the notion with which Nietzsche replaces it – "will to power" and "will of life" – reintroduces a teleological and vitalist conception of organisms that Darwin's notion of struggle was precisely meant to leave behind. In the third part of this essay, I want to persuade you that despite Nietzsche's frequent attacks on "teleology," "purpose," etc., his rejection of the Darwinian mechanism of natural selection and his adoption instead of "will to power," which for the most part Nietzsche cashed out in terms of "drives," leaves him without the conceptual resources to maintain the very naturalism that his thinking was meant to present as an antidote to the history of religion and philosophy.

3 Apes, Goals, and the Overman

When Nietzsche speaks of "the will to power" (*der Will zur Macht*) we are not supposed to assume that he speaking of anything that is conscious or volitional. It designates the life of all organisms, whether or not they are conscious and whatever their complexity. Thus, Nietzsche even ascribes the behavior of "protoplasm" (2011: 345) to will to power. But it is not easy to abrogate all notions of intention and teleology from the idea of a will "to" or "towards" (*zu*) power. As Richardson puts it: "What can the towards be, if *not* an end-directedness?" (2004: 21).

We see this evolutionary directedness of nature most clearly in Nietzsche's discussion of the overman, characterized as "the meaning of the earth" (*Sinn der Erde*) (1982: 125). The overman does not enter Nietzsche's discourse until the late period, but we find a foreshadowing in the so-called early to middle period. In the third *Untimely Meditation*, "Schopenhauer and Educator," written in 1874, Nietzsche abandons the "true but deadly" Darwinian gospel of "the lack of any cardinal distinction between man and animal." In a move directly counter to the canon *natura non facit saltus*, that nature does not make any leaps or jumps, that all species are subject to gradual change in an unbroken evolutionary continuum between themselves and their earliest ancestors, Nietzsche says,

> They are those true men [*wahrhaften Menschen*], *those who are no longer animal* [*Nichte-mehr-Tiere*], *the philosophers, artists and saints*: nature, which never makes a leap, has made its one leap in creating them, and a leap of joy moreover, for nature then feels for the first time it has reached its *goal* [*am Ziele*].
>
> 1997: 159

These "true men" (the philosophers, artists and saints) leave the condition of being an animal by letting go of the "accursed" drive for self-preservation:

> To hang on to life madly and blindly, with no higher aim than to hang on to it; not to know that or why one is being so heavily punished but, with the stupidity of a fearful desire, to thirst after precisely this punishment as though after happiness – that is what it means to be an animal; and if all nature presses towards man, it thereby intimates that man is necessary for the redemption of nature from the curse of the life of the animal, and that in him existence at last holds up before itself a mirror in which life appears no longer senseless but in its metaphysical significance.
>
> 1997: 157

A sentence later Nietzsche writes:

> Yet let us reflect: where does the animal cease, where does man begin? – man, who is nature's sole concern! As long as anyone desires life as he desires happiness he has not yet raised his eyes above the horizon of the animal, for he only desires more consciously what the animal seeks through blind impulse. But that is what we all do for the greater part of our lives: usually we fail to emerge out of animality, we ourselves are the animals whose suffering seems to be senseless.
>
> 1997: 157–158

These are appallingly opinionated passages and ones that are totally out of keeping with the image of Nietzsche as the great anti-metaphysician, who in the *Twilight* rejects natural teleology: "We invented the concept 'purpose'; in reality purpose is lacking" (1990: 64). What does it mean to say, "all nature presses towards man"? Or that "man … is nature's sole concern"? *There is no way to answer this question because after Darwin there is no way to make sense of the imputation of a goal – let alone the only goal – to something as ambiguous as "nature,"* one of whose meanings, in J.S. Mill's words, refers to "only what takes place without the agency, or without the voluntary and intentional agency, of man" (1985: 389).

At this point it will doubtless be replied that that "Schopenhauer as Educator" is an opusculum written by Nietzsche before his thought has properly developed, and that by the time we get to Nietzsche's mature writings we find that he has moved on from speaking of man both as an end and as discontinuous with the rest of the animals. Rather than an end, Nietzsche's mature thought posits a human being as something to be upended or overcome (*überwunden*). If man has any justification at all, it is merely as a means to the *overman*, in relation to which humans are an atavism, a throwback to an earlier form of evolutionary life. Listen to what he says in *Zarathustra*:

> *I teach you the overman.* Man is something that shall be overcome. What have you done to overcome him? ... What is the ape to men? A laughing-stock or a painful embarrassment. You have made your way from worm to man, and much in you is still worm. Once you were apes, and even now too, man is more ape than any ape.
>
> 1982: 124

Nietzsche is obviously caricaturing the Darwinian idea that humans have evolved. But like all caricatures, though it contains a resemblance to the truth, it does so only in an exaggerated, distorted manner. The worm – ironically considered by Darwin to be the most influential species on the planet ("It may be doubted whether there are many other animals which have played so important a part in the history of the world, as have these lowly organized creatures" [1985: 105]) – is not *literally* an ancestor to the human; it symbolizes for Nietzsche our origins from relatively simple, "lowly" forms of life. That we have still much within us that is worm might be read that, despite our self-conceit and pretense to be made of more divine "spiritual" stuff, we remain united with the earth, though I suspect that Nietzsche is exploiting the popular conception of the worm as a servile and base creature that would befit a description of the slave moralist or a being that lacks dignity ("One who makes himself a worm cannot complain afterwards if people step on him" [Kant 2017: 2013]). But what can it mean in the same context to say, "once you were apes, and even now, too, the human being is more ape than any ape"?[10] Is there not here a

10 In his essay "Who Is Zarathustra's Ape?" Peter Groff (2004) gives a subtle reading of the "Prologue," which he insists is concerned with the phenomenon of mimesis. The German

clear indication that Nietzsche is trafficking in the humanist conceit that human beings are – *or at least ought to be* – higher than the ape, and that the ape represents a less than flattering picture or uglification of the human? Is this not the meaning of his claim that man is a "rope" and a "bridge" between an animal and the overman, a transitional species traversing an "abyss" (Nietzsche 1982: 126–127)?

If span between animal and overman is *abyssal* (*abgrund*),[11] then the implication is that overman is discontinuous with the animal in the same way that "true" men in "Schopenhauer as Educator" are said to have left the plane of animality altogether and are "no longer animal." That Nietzsche in *Zarathustra* refuses to call the overman "man" *does not mean* that the overman is *not* human. The meaning of the term "overman" is not "man," but it does not refer to anything other than man, i.e. *human*. Nietzsche hints at its being a new species, but not in the biological sense, only in the sense that its way of being is so different from that of the human in its current historical configuration that it makes sense to call it something other than man: the "overman." Since it is only the human, the "*as yet undetermined animal*" (*das noch nicht festgestellte Tier*) (1989a: 74), that has the possibility of self-overcoming, then it certainly makes sense to say that the human being is a means to the overman. To overcome the "man" within man is simply to rid oneself of the psychological condition Nietzsche calls *ressentiment* that results from human beings having strayed from their instincts more than any other animal.[12] This has to be the case, for we should recall that Nietzsche dubs the human the "sick animal," but also "the most interesting" (1989b: 33) because it "is more sick, more uncertain, changeable, indeterminate than any other animal" (1989b: 121). What it is decidedly

word for "ape" (*Affe*) is also a verb *affen*, meaning "to mimic" or "imitate," so that when Nietzsche says that the "ape" in comparison with humans is a "laughing stock or a painful embarrassment," he is not simply expressing "the vestigial anthropocentric conceit of humans as *higher* than apes" (Groff 2004: 19). He is saying that we *resemble* the overman as little as the ape resembles us. This is why Nietzsche also says, "the human being is more ape than any ape," a statement that would appear to make no sense unless we read it as saying that humans are more representative of superficial mimicry and imitation than apes themselves. It should not be forgotten that what the people called "Zarathustra's ape" in the third part ("On Passing By") is a man (presumably) who merely mimics Zarathustra.

11 Compare Heidegger's "abyss of essence" (1993: 380).

12 Not that Darwin would necessarily agree with Nietzsche here. See the following remark taken from Darwin's C *Notebook* (1838): "[It is] hard to say what is instinct in animals & what [is] reason, in precisely the same way [it is] not possible to say what [is] habitual in men and what reasonable" (2009: 301).

not, however, is a means ("rope" or "bridge") to something *other than animal*. And to the extent that Nietzsche insists that it is, as he had done thirteen years earlier, he falls back into the human/animal dichotomy and an order or rank between them that he himself was inspired to question after Darwin.

4 Conclusion

There is no consensus regarding whether the overman is a "goal" in the sense of something to which individuals can aspire, or something unheralded and unhoped for, as far from any humans on earth as they are from apes (notwithstanding that humans are apes!). At any rate, it is not clear that to me that there is much in Nietzsche's discourse concerning the overman that is worth the exegetical labor required to salvage it from *metaphysical conceptualization*. I tend to agree with the arch-nihilist Emil Cioran's verdict that the later "prophetic" discourse on the overman constitutes something of a backsliding on Nietzsche's part:

> He demolished so many idols only to replace them with others: a false iconoclast, with adolescent aspects and a certain virginity, a certain innocence inherent in his solitary's career. He observed men only from a distance. Had he come closer, he could have neither conceived nor promulgated the superman, the preposterous, laughable, if not grotesque chimera, fantasy, which could occur only to a mind without time to age, to know the long serene disgust of detachment.
>
> CIORAN 1993: 85, modified translation

What is clear from a Darwinian point of view is that just as little as man is the goal of nature, so is the overman. As much as man is animal, so is the overman. To the extent that Nietzsche denies either of these claims due to a misplaced and ill-informed anti-Darwinism, then it is possible to find in his work a latent humanism, even as he speaks of overcoming the human-all-too-human.

References

Agamben, Giorgio. 2004. *The Open: Man and Animal*, translated by Kevin Attell. Stanford: Stanford University Press.

Ansell-Pearson, Keith. 1997. *Viroid Life: Perspectives on Nietzsche and the Transhuman Condition*. New York: Routledge.

Cioran, E.M. 1993. *The Trouble with Being Born*, translated by Richard Howard. London: Quartet Books.

Darwin, Charles. 2009. *Charles Darwin's Notebooks, 1836–1844: Geology, Transmutation of Species, Metaphysical Enquiries*, edited by Paul H. Barrett et al. Cambridge: Cambridge University Press.

Darwin, Charles. 2007. *The Variation of Animals and Plants Under Domestication (Volume 1)*. Teddington, Middlesex: Echo Library.

Darwin, Charles. 1990. *The Correspondence of Charles Darwin: Volume 6; Volumes 1856–1857*. Cambridge: Cambridge University Press.

Darwin, Charles. 1988. *The Correspondence of Charles Darwin: Volume 3; Volumes 1844–1846*. Cambridge: Cambridge University Press.

Darwin, Charles. 1985. *The Formation of Vegetable Mould Through the Action of Worms: With Observations on Their Habits*. Chicago: University of Chicago Press.

Darwin, Charles. 1964. *On the Origin of Species*. Cambridge, MA: Harvard University Press.

Darwin, Charles. 1877. "A Biographical Sketch of an Infant." *Mind: A Quarterly Review of Psychology and Philosophy* 2(7) (July): 285–294.

Deleuze, Gilles, and Félix Guattari. 1987. *A Thousand Plateaus: Capitalism and Schizophrenia*, translation by Brian Massumi. Minneapolis: University of Minnesota Press.

Dennett, Daniel C. 1995. *Darwin's Dangerous Idea: Evolution and the Meanings of Life*. New York: Simon & Schuster.

Groff, Peter S. 2004. "Who is Zarathustra's Ape?" In *A Nietzschean Bestiary: Becoming Animal Beyond Docile and Brutal*, edited by Christa Davis Acampora and Ralph R. Acampora, 17–31. Lanham: Rowman & Littlefield.

Haeckel, Ernst. 1892 [1868]. *The History of Creation. Volume 1*, translated by E. Ray Lankester. New York: D. Appleton.

Haldane, J.B.S. 1990. *The Causes of Evolution*. Princeton, NJ: Princeton University Press.

Heidegger, Martin. 1993. *Basic Writings*, translated by David Farrell Krell. New York: HarperCollins Publishers.

Hollingdale, R.J. 1999. *Nietzsche: The Man and His Philosophy*. Cambridge: Cambridge University Press.

Johnson, Dirk R. 2010. *Nietzsche's Anti-Darwinism*. Cambridge: Cambridge University Press.

Kant, Immanuel. 2017. *The Metaphysics of Morals*, translated by Mary Gregor. New York: Cambridge University Press.

Kaufmann, Walter. 1974. *Nietzsche: Philosopher, Psychologist, Antichrist*. Princeton, NJ: Princeton University Press.

Mill, John Stuart. 1985. "Nature." In *Collected Works of John Stuart Mill. Volume X*, edited by John M. Robson, 373–402. London: Routledge and Kegan Paul.

Moore, Gregory. 2002. *Nietzsche, Biology and Metaphor*. Cambridge: Cambridge University Press.

Nietzsche, Friedrich. 2011. *The Will to Power*, translated by Walter Kaufmann. New York: Knopf Doubleday Publishing Group.

Nietzsche, Friedrich. 1997. *Untimely Meditations*, translated by R.J. Hollingdale. Cambridge: Cambridge University Press.

Nietzsche, Friedrich. 1990. *The Twilight of the Idols and the Anti-Christ: or How to Philosophize with a Hammer*, translated by R.J. Hollingdale. London: Penguin Books.

Nietzsche, Friedrich. 1989a. *Beyond Good and Evil: Prelude to a Philosophy of the Future*, translated by Walter Kaufmann. New York: Vintage Books.

Nietzsche, Friedrich. 1989b. *On the Genealogy of Morals and Ecce Homo*, translated by Walter Kaufmann. New York: Vintage Books.

Nietzsche, Friedrich. 1982. *Portable Nietzsche*, translated by Walter Kaufmann. New York: The Viking Press.

Nietzsche, Friedrich. 1980. *Sämtliche Werke. Band 3*, edited by Giorgio Colli and Mazzino Montinari. München: de Gruyter.

Nietzsche, Friedrich. 1974. *The Gay Science: With a Prelude in Rhymes and an Appendix of Songs*, translated by Walter Kaufmann. New York: Knopf Doubleday Publishing Group.

Richardson, John. 2004. *Nietzsche's New Darwinism*. Oxford: Oxford University Press.

Stack, George J. 1983. *Lange and Nietzsche*. New York: De Gruyter.

Wilson, Catherine. 2013. "Darwin and Nietzsche: Selection, Evolution, and Morality." *Journal of Nietzsche Studies* 44(2): 354–369.

Wright Sewall. 1978. *Evolution and the Genetics of Populations. Volume 4: Variability Within and Among Natural Populations*. Chicago: University of Chicago Press.

CHAPTER 16

Play as Watchword: Nietzsche and Foucault

Dawn Herrera

But say, my brothers, what can the child do that the lion cannot do?
NIETZSCHE, *Thus Spoke Zarathustra*

•••

I do not know any other way of handling great tasks than as play.
NIETZSCHE, *Ecce Homo*

In *Anti-Christ*, Nietzsche writes, "Zarathustra is a skeptic. The vigor of a mind, its *freedom* through strength and superior strength, is *proved* by skepticism" (Nietzsche 2003a: 54). This interpretive statement refers to the power of the "No" figured by the lion in Zarathustra's first speech (Nietzsche 1954: 27). The lion's no is "the creation of freedom for oneself for new creation," the assumption of the right to new values. But, Nietzsche writes, "[t]o create new values—that even the lion cannot do." In other words, there is a limit to the power of refusal. And, crucially, affirmation cannot take the form of a burden assumed – the *tragsamen Geiste* of the camel has been abandoned to its desert. At this pivotal juncture, play is introduced as a conceptual keystone, the image-metaphor of activity through which the metamorphosis of the spirit is to be understood.

Questions of refusal, its limits and what lies beyond, are consistent themes in the reception of Michel Foucault's relentlessly critical philosophy.[1] Often reticent regarding his philosophical influences, Foucault was forthcoming regarding his debt to Nietzsche. In this essay, I propose that Nietzsche's

1 For paradigmatic articulations of this concern framed in terms of Foucault's putative nihilism, see Fraser (1981, 1996), Taylor (1991), and Habermas (1994); for critiques that read his ethics as aesthetic decisionism, see McNay (1992), Walzer (1991), Wolin (1986), and Rorty (1991).

importance for Foucault is clarified through the lens of play, and that play can be considered a watchword for the interpretation of the works of both authors.[2] Three themes – the play of force, stylistic play and the play of value creation – will assist in foregrounding the importance of play in Nietzsche's work, and in tracing how Foucault adopts and develops this figure and its variations, revealing an overlooked through-line in his trajectory of thought.

•••

Play is among the most obvious conceptual hallmarks of French post-structuralist appropriations of Nietzsche, salient in the work of Gilles Deleuze (2006) and Jacques Derrida (1979; 2001 [1970]) and clearly legible in that of Sarah Kofman (1993). However, despite its interpretive prominence, the idea of play itself – as image, as concept, as phenomenon – is taken somewhat for granted. This is a general tendency in deployments of play for philosophical purposes. For example, neither Kant's crucial reliance on the idea of play in the *Critique of Judgment* nor Schiller's ebullient appropriation of that idea in *The Aesthetic Education of Man* includes much by way of consideration of what it might mean to play: It is as if the notion is self-evident.[3] On the other end of the spectrum, Derrida's explications of play, for example in the landmark "Structure, Sign and Play" (2001 [1970]) capture little of the richness or amplitude attendant to phenomenal experience or semantic variability.[4]

It may be that this tendency to endorse what "play" does or renders possible without an engaged attempt to explore the contours of its meaning is an effect of the elusive quality which makes play so fit to bridge seemingly hopeless impasses in thought. In other words, that play resists the stasis of definition

2 The proposal of play as watchword is among the closing thoughts of Georges Bataille's *On Nietzsche* (1994: 151–152).

3 For a recent work which makes the idea of play central, also thinking with Nietzsche, see Christoph Menke's *Force* (2013). Menke's original and generative application of the concept to ethics by way of aesthetic philosophy gathers neglected threads of the German idealist tradition; it also is continuous with that tradition in that the question of what the word "play" is meant to capture is not expressly considered.

4 In this essay, "*jeu*" names the substitution of contents, elements, or terms within a structure, based on and limited by a fixed center which remains itself out of play. With a view to the prospects of social science after the death of God, Derrida considers "the possibility of infinite substitutions in the closure of a finite ensemble," or play, which is delimited not by a transcendental center but by the supplementary act of signification. Cf. the more general discussion of play in terms of subject-object relations in *The Ear of the Other*, where Derrida (1985: 69) conversationally alludes to Fink's reading of Nietzsche. On Derrida, Nietzsche and play see Anderson (2003).

should come as no surprise. Nevertheless, a social scientific sub-discipline has arisen around the topic in recent decades as scholars have tried and re-tried to define it. These studies almost inevitably take their departure from the path-breaking work of Johan Huizinga (2014).[5]

Rather than review this literature here, I'll just note a general feature of such "definitions" of play, relevant due to its consonance with many philosophical applications of the concept. Consistently, attempts to think play necessitate a confrontation with its unique capacity to bear paradox. Social scientific definitions of play almost always include apparently contradictory elements: e.g. boundedness and openness; skill and chance; regulation and improvisation; regard for self and regard for others; absorption and carelessness; meaning and meaninglessness; necessity and freedom; unselfconsciousness and the consolidation of the self.

In addition to this general quality, a few key hypotheses of Huizinga's original study bear mentioning. The first posits that play tends to take two particular, paradoxical forms: Play is realized as contestation or *agon*, a pursuit of individual distinction and superiority which nevertheless fosters fellowship; and/or, it is realized in a play of representation, as an act of dissimulation or mimicry which is also somehow revelatory (Huizinga 2014: 13–18). Moreover, Huizinga and most of his antecedents tend to emphasize some version of the *autotelicity* of play, its being an end in itself – but also its immense generative capacity. In short, "play" attempts to capture in language that paradoxical movement which binds through division or reveals through deception, whose creative power is immanent to the intrinsic quality of its motive.[6] Finally, *pace* theorists who find in play a quasi-utopian normative potential, play also tends also to the risky, antinomian and "dark" (Sutton-Smith and Kelly-Byrne 1984). This, too, is among its paradoxical features: Play-activity tends to the testing of given limits and the breaking of norms. However, because its continuity depends in part on boundedness, it also tends toward the establishment and maintenance of new ones.

•••

5 Recent and notable forays into the definition of play which include accounts of its paradoxical quality, include Henricks (2006: 42–67), Sicart (2014: 1–18), Brown (2009: 17–18), Sutton-Smith (1997: 1–17), and Bateson (2000 [1972]).

6 A brief but sensitive treatment of autotelicity in play activity is given in Robert Bellah's *Religion in Human Evolution* (2011), especially pp. 76–77, 92 fn. 133, 112.

Bearing this brief sketch of the phenomenon in mind reveals its relevance to multiple and seemingly contradictory or even vexing facets of Nietzsche's philosophy.[7] His references to play are infrequent but always propositional, and play appears and reappears throughout his body of work, interwoven with his most potent and persistent metaphors – laughter, the dance, the mask, the dice-throw. Play itself is addressed in an aphorism from *Human, All Too Human*, which provides an opening onto its potential significance. In this transitional work, Nietzsche posits that play, understood in the quotidian sense of leisure-activity, is comparable to work; work is activity driven by need, and play is something that men do relieve boredom borne of the habitual urge to work when needs have been met. But there is another state, a "third condition" which stands in relation to everyday play as "floating does to dancing and dancing does to walking," a "state of serene agitation" that is "the artist's and philosopher's vision of happiness" (Nietzsche 1996: 193–194). This description gestures toward the sense in which the word play is used in *The Gay Science* and beyond, the sense with which I am concerned here.

It is telling that a classic philosophical treatment of play, Eugen Fink's *The Ontology of Play* (1960), takes its primary cues from Nietzsche's first publication: *The Birth of Tragedy* describes the artistic play of the Apollonian and the Dionysian – of the dream of harmonic order and of the intoxication of entropic chaos, in nature and art. Fink understands play itself to be the dynamic conjunction of these archetypical tendencies in the paradox of their unity. For the young Nietzsche, the play of the Apollonian and Dionysian is generative of tragedy, which serves humanity through a kind of aesthetic redemption. He writes, "It is precisely the tragic myth that has to convince us that even the ugly and the disharmonic are part of an artistic game (*Spiel*) that the will in the eternal amplitude of its pleasure plays with itself (Nietzsche 1967: 141)."[8] While he would repudiate the *Birth of Tragedy* on account of its Wagnerian influence and the "offensive smell" of Hegel and Schopenhauer, this basic insight is

7 The thesis that play is fundamental to Nietzsche's philosophy is advanced by Lawrence Hinman (1974). While his arguments are framed in terms that oversimplify certain ontological claims and are problematically voluntaristic, Hinman convincingly enumerates Nietzsche's repeated reliance on the theme; he points in a promising direction in his conclusion that play orients attempts to think with Nietzsche beyond nihilism, towards "a quite definite thinking through of existence as activity" (122).

8 The German *Spiel* (like the French *jeu*) is identical in its noun and verb forms – there is no semantic distinction between "play" and "game." The conceptual distinctions between play and game which are posited in English are not relevant here.

retained in the later Nietzsche's account of eternal recurrence, which emphasizes the redemptive power embodied in courageous and joyful affirmation of the contingent play of force (Nietzsche 1989: 270–275).

The play of force is a red thread visible throughout Nietzsche's work: The "Yea-saying" spirit of *Zarathustra* is an attempt at its acknowledgment and affirmation, while the "No-saying" aspect of his thought finds it where others have sought ground (Nietzsche 1989: 310). As part of this latter task, his analysis of social psychology in *The Genealogy of Morals* is dedicated to the exposure not just of contingency but of spirited *agon* at the inception of the most seemingly stable values. Genealogy teaches that the highest ideals of the human are grounded in the sediment of the play of force. When this play ceases to take the form of outright contestation, it takes the form of dissimulation and disguise, as the drive to self-affirmation wears the masks of altruism and asceticism.

A similar insight animates Nietzsche's discussions of the history of philosophy in *Beyond Good and Evil*'s "On the Prejudices of Philosophers." Putatively objective in its search for knowledge of the absolute, the truth claims of philosophy are motivated by the instinct of the philosopher, specifically the (im)*moral* instinct to foster valuations which will "promote the preservation of a particular type of life" (Nietzsche 2002: 7).

> But anyone who looks at people's basic drives, to see how far they may have played their little game right here as *inspiring* geniuses (or daemons or sprites—) will find that they all practiced philosophy at some point,— and that every single one of them would be only too pleased to present *itself* as the ultimate purpose of existence and the rightful *master* of all the other drives.
>
> NIETZSCHE 2002: 9

Contrary to its own self-understanding, the will to truth is an outgrowth of the internal play of force which spurs an intervention into the struggle for worldly prominence. Philosophy is distinguished in this pursuit by its particularly "spiritual" and "tyrannical" mode (Nietzsche 2002: 10–11).

For philosophers and non-philosophers alike, Nietzsche posits that the vital play of force constitutes the medium of individual subjectivity, as the contestation of affects gives rise to thought and will: "*L'effet c'est moi*" (2002: 19; cf. 17, 49). This ontology of the subject is continuous with that of the reality it encounters (Nietzsche 2002: 35–36). In *Beyond Good and Evil* and in the notebooks, "the world" is for Nietzsche "a play of force and force-waves simultaneously one and 'many.'" In the ebb and flood of its forms, it flows

> ...from abundance to simplicity, from the play of contradiction back to the pleasure of harmony, affirming itself even in the sameness of its courses and years, blessing itself as what must eternally return, as a becoming that knows no satiety, no surfeit, no fatigue—
>
> NIETZSCHE 2003: 38

In the final assessment, his name for the world – and the subject that encounters it – is "will to power." Crucially, though, "will to power" does not describe a lust to achieve some extrinsically determined status of dominion, but motive force beheld in the light of its apparently inexorable continuity; "a something that wants to grow"; not the will to a holding, but to the play of this force itself (Nietzsche 2003b: 90, 256–257).[9]

Another key entry point to the play of force can be found in *Philosophy in the Tragic Age of the Greeks,* a posthumously published early work whose central figure is Heraclitus. Nietzsche remained consistent in his admiration for the pre-Socratic until the end of his life, maintaining in *Ecce Homo* that in proximity to Heraclitus he felt "altogether warmer and better than anywhere else" (1989: 273). *Philosophy in the Tragic Age of the Greeks* introduces an ensemble of themes that would be developed through the remainder of Nietzsche's life.[10] Salient among them is play, Heraclitus' "sublime metaphor," which he summarizes as follows:

> And as children and artists play, so plays the ever-living fire. It constructs and destroys, all in innocence. Such is the game that the *aeon* plays with itself. Transforming itself into water and earth, it builds towers of sand like a child at the seashore, piles them up and tramples them down. From time to time it starts the game anew. An instant of satiety and again it is seized by its need, as the artist is seized by his need to create. Not *hybris* but the ever self-renewing impulse to play calls new worlds into being.
>
> NIETZSCHE 1962: 62

---

9 Cf. *Zarathustra*, "On Self-Overcoming" (113–116). For two discussions of this crucial distinction from perspectives that are otherwise radically divergent see Deleuze (2006: 49–52, 78–82, 85) and Pippin (2009: 84–86).

10 According to Christoph Cox, "instead of revealing a juvenile Nietzsche, this text shows him advancing positions and views that are central to his later work: naturalism and anti-dualism; a repudiation of "being" in favor of an "innocent becoming"; the characterization of becoming as a perpetual "artist's *agon*" or dice game; the promotion of an aesthetic versus a moral interpretation of the world; praise of an aphoristic and esoteric philosophical style; an empiricist and nominalist critique of the notions of substance and essence, and so on" (Cox 1999). For an extended discussion of play themes in this work, see Dursun (2007).

Aeon, or time in its eternal aspect, is figured as play – its unfolding is akin to how child's play unfolds, innocent in its absorption and its absence of extrinsic motive. By opposing this impulse to *hybris*, Nietzsche dispels the self-consciousness of the agent of creation as such and the object-consciousness that must accompany it: the desire for metaphysical certainty is held in abeyance as questions of *archê* and *telos* are displaced from the creative force and from creation, and rendered immanent to the activity itself. In this way Nietzsche's appropriation of this Heraclitean formulation draws a contrast with "the constant of presence" (Derrida 2001 [1970]) as a philosophical object. Contingency loses its status as a problem to be solved as it become integral to the basic process of (en/un)folding.

Heraclitus' metaphor of play, Nietzsche claims, is intelligible to the artist or "aesthetic" personage, insofar as they are capable of grasping the paradox it expresses:

> ...how the struggle of the many can yet carry rules and laws inherent in itself, how the artist stands contemplatively above and at the same time actively within his work, how necessity and random play, oppositional tension and harmony, must pair to create a work of art.
>
> NIETZSCHE 1962: 62

Despite the enumeration of these binaries, we should not read into this figure the appearance of a dialectic. What is productive is precisely the fact of opposing terms being held together in the "serene agitation" of play.[11]

•••

Acknowledgment of the play of force is a current which animates Nietzsche's genealogy, psychology and ontology: it is only fitting that their implicit *logoi* be understood in accordance with this theme. His approach must be thought in terms of his *gaya scienza*, the poetic alliance of wisdom with laughter, of singer, knight and free spirit (Nietzsche 2001: 28, 183); (Nietzsche 1989: 294). *Gaya scienza* positions itself against a certain kind of seriousness, personified by the spirit of gravity, Zarathustra's "old devil and arch-enemy," creator of "constraint, statute, necessity and consequence and purpose and will and good and evil" (Nietzsche 1954: 197). Accordingly, finding play of force everywhere in Nietzsche should not be taken as requisite evidence for its coronation as *prima causa* and installment at the foundation of a Nietzschean doctrine, a new

11 Fredrich Ulfers (2013) has termed this notion "chiasmic unity."

order of truth. Striving to do philosophy differently, Nietzsche endeavored to bring about through language a different way of seeing and interpreting, and consequently, modes of reception and activity, thought and communication, that would accord with and affirm the elemental motility of the given.

Accordingly, Nietzsche presents his ideal mode of thought and manner of comportment through the dynamic metaphors of play, dance and sport.[12] While many figures in his work have an ambiguous aspect, the notion of "thought on light feet" is proffered with unfailing approbation and unstinting praise (Nietzsche 2003c: 77). Knowledge itself is posited as a field of play, "a world of dangers and victories in which heroic feelings have their dance and playgrounds" (Nietzsche 2001: 324). The failure of thought is characterized as a failure to adequately play this field, an incapacity marked by an "ardent seriousness" (Nietzsche 2001: 88–89). Conversely, Nietzsche holds that the ability to dance is the measure of value, and that the dance-ground, the play-ground, is to be where the new table of values is determined (2001: 366, 368). He writes, "and I wouldn't know what the spirit of a philosopher might more want than to be a good dancer. For the dance is his ideal, also his art, and finally also his only piety, his 'service of God'" (2001: 246).[13]

Nietzsche's attempt to abide by this ethos is most apparent in the play of his style, especially his variable and poetic use of form. Writing out of a wish to be understood and to *not* be understood (2001: 381), Nietzsche affirmed his laudatory statements regarding laughter, the mask and the dance through formal variation (including verse), the use of aphorism, the subtle play of contradiction, and the teasing and mocking tenor of the prose. In doing so, he subtly affirms the instability of conceptual knowledge and the centrality of the interpretive act.[14] The absence of a solid and absolute ground does not imply that there is nothing to stand on, only that one's standing cannot take the form of

12 While *The Gay Science* emphasizes dance, *Beyond Good and Evil* describes the intellectual task at hand through metaphors of sport, of archery and the hunt: The concluding image of the preface is of the free spirit who has need of tension in the bow and of its mark (4); Nietzsche describes his investigation as a great and dangerous hunt for which he desires companions (43); the "Aftersong" is a celebrant's song which recounts the state of a "wicked huntsman" as he awaits fit friends in a realm which belongs to hunters.

13 Huizinga calls dance "always at all periods the purest and most perfect form of play that exists." "The connections between playing and dancing are so close that they hardly need illustrating. It is not that dance has something of play about it, rather that it is an integral part of play: the relationship is one of direct participation, almost of essential identity. Dancing is a particular and particularly perfect form of playing" (2014: 164–165).

14 This is the thematic which French post-structuralism has (in)famously taken up with the most zeal. Foucault (1990) foregrounds the abyssal structure and interminable task of interpretation as a hallmark of Nietzsche's legacy in "Nietzsche, Freud, Marx."

rest, but rather requires a certain kind of intellectual movement – dynamic, flexible, light, and courageous at the precipice, undaunted by the abyss. In keeping with this approach, Nietzsche at once demands the active participation of his reader and preserves their freedom as a partner in the evaluative enterprise. If the spirit of the philosopher wishes to be a good dancer, it must desire companions; As we all know (or ought to), partners heighten the dance, and one grows weary of playing alone.

•••

Nietzsche characterizes his philosophical *agon* and appearance on the field of knowledge as the prelude to a future in which a new field of play might be opened to a new kind of player, at once more innocent and more masterful. The play he anticipates is the play of value creation, in the fullness of its paradox:

> Another ideal runs before us, a peculiar, seductive, dangerous ideal to which we wouldn't want to persuade anyone, since we don't readily concede the *right* to it to anyone: the ideal of a spirit that plays naively, i.e. not deliberately but with an overflowing abundance and power, with everything that was hitherto called holy, good, untouchable, divine... it is perhaps only with it that *the great seriousness* really emerges...
>
> NIETZSCHE 2001: 247

His caveat mockingly intimates that the terrain of this aspiration lies beyond the juridical structure of moral convention, a realm that anyone who would require a pass to enter is not fitted to occupy. Its particulars remain obscure: It is possible that to understand fully what is entailed in the concept of play as Nietzsche uses it would be to grasp the sense of his project in its entirety. But it is also likely that his meaning is not, in the final analysis, meant to be grasped conceptually. As he writes in *The Birth of Tragedy,* "For a genuine poet, metaphor is not a rhetorical figure but a vicarious image that he actually beholds in place of a concept" (Nietzsche 1967: 63).

With this in mind, I return to the most salient image of play in the most poetic of Nietzsche's works: the conclusion of Zarathustra's speech on the Three Metamorphoses. "But say, my brothers," he asks, "what can the child do that even the lion cannot do?"

> Why must the preying lion still become a child? The child is innocence and forgetting, a new beginning, a game, a self-turning wheel, a first

> movement, a sacred "Yes". For the *Spiel* of creation, my brothers, a sacred "Yes" is needed: the spirit now wills its own will, and he who had been lost to the world now conquers his own world.
>
> NIETZSCHE 1954: 27

After the dutiful bearing of burdens, after the "prankish" courage of refusal, comes creation. It is figured as play, rendered possible by the third transformation of the spirit into a child.[15] This is a sign that, in the first instance, creation is suffused with a spirit of lightness, a quality linked to its being autotelic. For Nietzsche, value-creation is not undertaken out of the need for values or despair at their instability. Play figures the possibility that creation might entail a detachment from value itself as motivation for or product of the task. This is not to say that new value will not come into being as a result, only that its production does not motivate the activity, as a child learns by playing, but does not play in order to learn.

Autotelicity is further suggested by the figure of the self-turning wheel. While it may involve striving for a goal, play is autotelic: Innocent of motive, it stumbles and falls over the player's concern for an extrinsic purpose which, should it be present, must be forgotten, as the athlete or actor must forget her audience if she is incapable of playing with it, too.[16] By the same token, Nietzsche's play of creation is self-contained. The spirit wills its own will in that it wills the very movement of creation – not the solidity of the value that would result or the specious comfort of its possession. Willing its own will in the game of creation, the spirit who had been lost to the world conquers its own world. "Play," for Nietzsche, describes the mode of action by which spirit might stake itself, might win itself and its world.

This conviction is reaffirmed in aphorism 94 of *Beyond Good and Evil:* "Human maturity: this means rediscovering the seriousness we had towards play

15 Gilles Deleuze (2006) argues that the lion is the sign of Zarathustra himself, in his transmutation of negation into a creative and affirmative act (the "holy no"). Zarathustra is the man who wants to be overcome; as figured by the lion's destruction of all known values, he is the final term in the series of conditions of affirmation. But affirmation finds its *un*conditioned principle in the persona of Dionysus and the figure of the child-player.

16 Recalling the influence of Heraclitus we might also bear in mind that a self-turning wheel is on fire. On the subordinate status of the extrinsic end, see *The Gay Science* aphorism 360 ("one is used to seeing the *driving* force essentially in the goals ... but it is only the *directing* force—one has mistaken the helmsman for the stream") and in *Human All Too Human,* aphorism 240 of "The Wanderer and His Shadow" ("*End and goal.*—Not every end is a goal. The end of a melody is not its goal; but nonetheless, if the melody had no reached its end it would not have reached its goal either. A parable.")

when we were children" (Nietzsche 2002: 62). In contrast with the heavy seriousness of the spirit of gravity, the light seriousness of a child at play – unburdened by *hybris*. The paradox of seriousness and play becomes intelligible when the metaphor is beheld as a vicarious image. Coming in Part 4 of the work, which circles themes of self-transformation and resistance to it, this statement emphasizes that the knowledge Nietzsche seeks to impart will ultimately not be conceptual, but enacted, and enacted in this particular spirit.

•••

Foucault foregrounds play in the introductory remarks of his inaugural lecture course at the *Collège de France*, characterizing his own *jeu* as one of seeing the will to truth. Here, "will to truth" refers to the motive force of philosophical and scientific discourses, which function as systems of exclusion with material and practical effects and traceable histories. Foucault endeavors to bring them to light: "in short, it is a matter of seeing what real struggles and relations of domination are involved in the will to truth" (Foucault 2014: 2). But in framing his own inquiry as a game, he deemphasizes the claim to an absolute knowledge or "total history."[17]

Foucault's scholarly game of recovering subjugated knowledges is a self-conscious intervention in another level of play – the "play of force" or struggle among opposing forms of knowledge and truth.[18] Claims to scientific knowledge and truth tend to disavow the play of force. In bringing out its buried particulars, genealogy

> is a way of playing local, discontinuous, disqualified or nonlegitimized knowledges off against the unitary theoretical instance that claims to be able to … organize them in the name of a true body of knowledge, in the name of the rights of a science that is in the hands of the few.
>
> FOUCAULT 2003: 9

17 See Foucault (1972: 9–10). Daniel Defert's course summary for *Lectures on the Will to Know* posits this Nietzchean game in opposition to what Deleuze has described as Plato's ontological-theological game, the foundation of metaphysics (Foucault 2014: 272–274).

18 This thematic is legible in Foucault's emerging analytic of power, for example in his analysis of strategic relations in the lecture courses of 1975–1976 (2003), where, he challenges the juridical model of sovereignty by positing the origins of state power relations in situations of strategic play between or among adversaries, which are only later stabilized through discourses of truth.

Thus, the notion of strategic play between adversaries on the field of knowledge is redoubled in the genealogical project's relation to hegemonic discourses and their associated sociopolitical forces. As is clear in his essay "Nietzsche, Genealogy, History," the analytic of power/knowledge which emerges from Foucault's genealogical analyses represents the development and application of Nietzsche's understanding that the play of force – historically, politically, psychologically – is discernable at the basis of supposed universals, including the unified subject of reason, its "chimera of a substantial unity" (Foucault 1998: 369–391).

This doubled thematic of play/struggle as movement of recovered knowledge and mode of political engagement remained significant throughout Foucault's career, especially in moments of self-interpretation, when he frequently described domains of knowledge, their associated power-relations and discursive ensembles as "games" of truth and power.[19] This characterization draws attention to the historical contingency of regimes of knowledge and authority, and to their constitution through the assemblage of norms, hedges, restrictions and rules that qualify or disqualify a statement as true, or a power relation as legitimate.

We see Nietzsche's influence on Foucault in how, through the denaturalization of critique, he aimed to expose games of truth and power as such, and so to open new possibilities for thought and action. Critical recognition of a game for what it is carries with it the possibility of playing differently. Bringing subjugated knowledges "into play" opens liminal space that disrupts social relations naturalized in scientific discipline (Foucault 2003: 179–185). For this reason, thought is emphasized as a site of play: "Thought is freedom in relation to what one does" (Foucault 1997: 114–115).[20] Through critique and the critical attitude, which will include the self-critique of reflection, thought gives a distance from practices that allows for their problematization, clearing ground for diverse enacted responses.

Regarding the play of style, Nietzsche's influence is less overt. This is not to say that Foucault's writing is without literary moments, or that cleverness and humor do not at times lend it a piquant quality – in its expository register, his

19 "From their mutual development and their interconnection [of modes of objectivation and subjectivation], what could be called "games" of truth and power come into being—that is not a discovery of true things but the rules according to which what a subject can say about certain things depends on a question of true and false" (Foucault 1998). This self-interpretive text is from "Foucault," an entry to *Dictionnaire des Philosophes* pseudonymously written by Foucault himself.

20 Cf. pp. 117–118. This 1984 interview, "Polemics, Politics, Problematizations," was conducted just before Foucault's death.

prose exhibits considerable verve, intrepidness, even "prankish" audacity. But especially in the major published works, these qualities ornament a method that Foucault himself describes as "gray, meticulous and patiently documentary" (Foucault 1998: 369). This is the primary means by which Foucault carries through Nietzsche's efforts at refusal.

> The search for descent is not the erecting of foundations: on the contrary, it disturbs what was previously considered immobile; it fragments what was thought unified; it shows the heterogeneity of what was thought consistent with itself. What convictions and, far more decisively, what knowledge can refuse it?
>
> FOUCAULT 1998: 369

In short, genealogy seeks to reestablish "not the anticipatory power of meaning, but the hazardous play of dominations" (Foucault 1998: 376).

If this method is akin to Nietzsche's primarily in its ends, a clearer stylistic legacy is implicit in the "dance" with his reader that is enacted through Foucault's avoidance of prescriptive analyses. On face, this might appear as divergent tendency between the two authors – Nietzsche's overt polemics against any- and everyone in his line of sight can be exhausting, and his exhortations to the reader, while often gestural or metaphorical, are explicit. Foucault, on the other hand, emphasized his dislike of polemics, in which the rhetorical goal is to "abolish" the other view at any cost, preferring an exchange by which the participants test each other and in so doing push each other beyond the prior bounds of their thought. He describes this as "a game that is at once pleasant and difficult" – a clear description of intellectual *agon* (Foucault 1997: 111–112).

The discomfort Foucault expressed with philosophical authority by repute is in keeping with this commitment.[21] Perhaps most importantly, his method attempts to constitute for the reader an experience by which their framework of thought regarding some domain of knowledge might be opened to change. However, having posed the problematic, he offers no positive solution. The form of his critical refusal is key – it endeavors to not replicate the tendencies of thought that it critiques. This is the crucial legacy of Nietzsche's style.

---

21 The sources in which this position is clearly elaborated include, among others, an interview with Deleuze published as "Intellectuals and Power" (Foucault 1996: 74–82); an anonymous interview with *Le Monde* published as "The Masked Philosopher" (Foucault 1997: 321–328); and the interview with Paul Rabinow published as "Polemics, Politics, Problematizations" (Foucault 1997: 109–119).

However, whereas Nietzsche endeavored to goad the interpretive play of his reader-interlocutor by means of a self-conscious esotericism and an enigmatic authorial presence, Foucault performed this refusal by attempting to disappear into his thought – in this, their play of masks differs significantly.

Moreover, Foucault gives this Nietzschean inheritance a different, explicitly ethico-political valence by emphasizing the agonism and self-staking that are implicit in play. His assertion in "Nietzsche, Genealogy, History" that "knowledge is not made for understanding; knowledge is made for cutting" (1998) is indicative of an unapologetic understanding of his own scholarly work as an intervention in a network of material practices, with implications for action on the field of power relations. In an interview on the publication of *Discipline and Punish,* Foucault expressed the desire that his work function as a "toolkit" for practitioners (Foucault 2001: 523–524). As his archive shifted to foreground modes of self-formation, his problematizations retained their simultaneous situation in actual material practices, refusal of prescriptive universals, and underlying encouragement to act.[22]

The lively critical attitude that characterizes Foucault's method even in its most relentless erudition can be read as an assumption of the lion's position – the proving of the freedom of mind through skepticism toward established orders of knowledge, realized through rigorous archaeological and genealogical inquiry. There remains, however, the question of what lies beyond. Foucault concludes both *The Order of Things* and *Introduction to Kant's Anthropology* with explicitly Nietzschean gestures beyond the positive limitations which determine that "invention of recent date," man. The concluding gestures of these works hold out vicarious images of masks and of laughter – the face of man exploding in laughter.

A similar gesture also concludes the penultimate chapter of *The Order of Things,* but it unfolds in a significantly different way. Having traced how language was constituted as an object of positive knowledge, "burying itself within its own density as an object and allowing itself to be traversed by knowledge," Foucault posits that at the beginning of the 19th century it reconstituted itself elsewhere, as literature, "folded back upon the enigma of its own origin and existing wholly in reference to the pure act of writing" (Foucault 1994: 300). He reads his exemplars of 19th century literature in relation to the modern object-mode of being of language, as leading language back to "the naked power of speech" and the "untamed, imperious being of words." The scientization of language must thus be considered as one part of a dual movement.

22 On how Foucault's work on politics opens onto his ethical commitments, see Koopman (2013), especially Ch. 5–6.

The countermovement of literature effects a "ludic denial" (Foucault 1994: 300) of Classical values and manifests a language which has no law except the affirmation of its own precipitous existence, "so there is nothing to do but to curve back in a perpetual return upon itself, as if discourse could have no other content but the expression of its own form." It seeks to re-apprehend the essence of all literature in the movement that brought it into being; its threads converge upon the *act* of writing – "singular, instantaneous and yet absolutely universal" which "has nothing to say but itself, nothing to do but shine in the brightness of its being" (Foucault 1994: 300). Here, Foucault plays the limit of his method to sketch a paradigm of the creative act. His characterization of literary language reveals how closely related Foucault's sense of the potentiality of thought is to play in the Nietzschean register.

Early in his career, Foucault regularly explored his interest in the capacity of literary language to open onto and hold space outside the order of signification.[23] Nietzsche's name appears alongside those of Roussel, Bataille, Blanchot, Artaud, and Kosslowski. In their wake, Foucault attempts to capture in the language of philosophy the experience of play with and over the limit, experience whose very name – transgression – enunciates its refusal to be contained. The texts that result tend, properly, to obscurity and paradox; they represent an important foray in Foucault's endeavor to articulate a mode of "non-positive affirmation" (Foucault 1998: 74).[24]

In later publications, as the systematic emphasis of archaeology gives way to a genealogical focus on the relation of knowledge to power, Foucault's overt gestures to Nietzschean play at the limits of anthropological man recede from view. Then, in the concluding years of his life and work, this opening takes shape in a new archive: The analytic of ethics and subjectivity that occupies Foucault's late lectures and publications can be read through the lens of Zarathustra's third metamorphosis – the spirit that wills its own will in the play of creation.

Schematizing his work on ethics, Foucault situates self-formative activity within a game of truth – a set of rules or qualifications for the production of a statement that can qualify as true. (Foucault 1997: 281–282). This kind of "game" articulates a hinge-point between *subjectivation* (the formation of a certain kind of subject through regimes of power-knowledge, the kinds of regimes

23 James Faubion collects several exemplars of this period in *Essential Works Vol. 2* (Foucault 1998), including "The Thought of the Outside" (147–170); "A Preface to Transgression" (69–80); and "Speaking and Seeing in Raymond Roussel" (5–20).

24 For a helpful critical exposition of Foucault's notion of transgression which connects it with his late work on ethics see McNay (1994).

genealogy uncovers) and on the other hand, (self-)*subjectification* by way of ethical practice. He posits ethics as a formal self-relation which necessarily entails a game of truth, a "way in which people are invited or inclined to recognize their obligations."[25] In this kind of truth-game, play is *pratique de soi,* the practice of the self, the self-formative activity.[26]

The crucial link between Foucault's ethics and Nietzshean play is consequent to the form of this practice *as such.* The crux of ethical self-relation is not the achievement of a certain end, but rather to keep a particular game of truth alive in one's world through a concern with one's actions, habits and values. The play itself, the "self-representation of movement," is of primary importance.[27] Foucault claimed to have understood "aestheticism" to mean "self-transformation" (Foucault 1997: 130–131), recalling Nietzsche's one needful thing (Nietzsche 2001: 163). However, perhaps even more than Nietzsche's ethics, Foucault's "aesthetics of existence" must be understood in terms of its process-orientation, its insistence on the autotelic quality of the individual's self-relation in pursuit of a certain mode of being, "which happily one never attains"; it is this quality of action on the self that might permit the invention of "a manner of being that is still improbable" (Foucault 1997: 136–137).

The play-element also comes to the fore in Foucault's development of *parrhesia* or frank-speech, a mode of truth-telling whose truth inheres in the speaker's *staking of* herself rather than a claim to objective certainty (Foucault 2010).[28] Parrhesia entails both *agon* and representation. At the heart of the "parrhesiatic game" lies an intersubjective bond, a pact that promises the courage to speak the truth on one side and the courage to hear it on the other. (Foucault 2008: 12–13) Here, to play a game of truth privately or publicly is to risk oneself, to stake oneself and the bond of one's relationship[s] or even one's life on truthful speech; play risks *and* strengthens both player and relation, in their truth (Foucault 2008: 312–313). In ethical play, then, there is a juxtaposition of care and *risk,* which amounts to care of the self and other, facilitating

25 This "mode of subjectification" is basically equivalent to the rules of the game, and always takes its departure from a socially extant game of truth within which the subject has been constituted. (Foucault 1997: 263, 291).

26 The other two components of the ethical self-relation are the ethical substance, i.e. that which is recognized as the substrate for self-transformation, and the *telos,* the model or ideal of being that the ascetic practitioner seeks to achieve (Foucault 1997: 263).

27 This description of play is taken from Gadamer (1986: 23).

28 Foucault's final lecture courses tracked the movement of this form of locution in antiquity from the political realm to the relationship of friendship and ethical development. For an exposition of this thematic, see Nancy Luxon (2013).

dynamism and mutual advance in the space of meaning.[29] Foucault's interest in the "real creation of new possibilities" opened by S&M play is of a piece with this line of thought (Foucault 1997: 165).

In a late interview on the topic of the politics and relational possibilities of same-sex relationships, Foucault concludes with this statement:

> We have to dig deeply to show how things have been historically contingent, for such and such reason intelligible but not necessary. We must make the intelligible appear against a background of emptiness and deny its necessity. We must think that what exists is far from filling all possible spaces. To make a truly unavoidable challenge of the question: What can be played?
>
> FOUCAULT 1997: 139–140

This question, "what can be played?" links Foucault's account with Nietzsche's vision of human maturity, and of the third metamorphosis, from lion to child. For Nietzsche, play figures the paradoxical possibility of self-overcoming in the act of value creation, absent the fixity of transcendental principles or the ground of a stable self. "In play," the acting subject remains on the scene, but is not reified outside the context of its action – and the content of this action is not specified in a narrow sense. Indeed, the possibility of openness, innovation and the new are in the foreground. This thematic of play clarifies the claims of ethics and truth in Foucault. Ultimately, one stakes oneself on one's claim – ethically, politically, spiritually. The crucial question is whether and how it will be possible to do so in innocence, without the consolation of a guarantee, with the paradoxical light-seriousness of a dancer, an athlete, a child. This truth and this ethics remain in perpetual flight from the constraints of doctrine, vanishing in the moment they would be installed at the foundation of an order.

•••

Zarathustra concludes with a "vicarious image," which according to one's disposition may be read as poignant or pathetic, hopeful or hopelessly naïve.

29 [The polemicist] … proceeds encased in privileges that he possesses in advance and will never agree to question. On principle, he possesses rights authorizing him to wage war and making that struggle a just undertaking … the game consists not in recognizing [the interlocutor] as a subject having the right to speak but abolishing him[.] (Foucault 1997: 111–112).

As the higher men sleep, Zarathustra wakes and greets the dawn alone – they are not the companions he awaits. A flock of loving birds descends, and in their midst, a lion comes to Zarathustra, who weeps, and puts his hand in its mane. The higher men emerge from the cave. During the ass-festival, they played at veneration of a beast, who, saying "Yea," would assume their burdens. Their play was a sign of their convalescence, but it was the play of old men with the old god – it had nothing of innocence and forgetting, nothing of the new beginning. It softened but did not undo the final temptation the higher men offer to Zarathustra, the temptation to pity. The lion roars powerfully and scares them away – a resounding "no," by which Zarathustra is finally free for the new. Together, they await the imminent arrival of Zarathustra's children. His anticipation encompasses the hope of generation, of persons who will inherit his overcoming of shame and pity as a legacy, and also the hope in persons who will embody the capacity for a sacred "Yes" in the play of creation.

The challenge attendant to play as an ethos is implicit in the horizonal quality of this scene. In his early and his late work, Foucault offers multiple ethico-political lenses through which we might view this Nietzschean imperative – the play of limit-testing and transgression at the edge of subjectivity; the strategic play of opposition on the field of knowledge; the public play of ethico-political counter-conduct and frank-speech; and reflective play among the forces of one's own will in self-transformative action. The call to courageously negotiate the boundaries and tensions among these states of play without *hybris,* resentment or consolation is what Foucault, drawing from Nietzsche, confers upon his reader-interlocutors – a legacy in the form of a task.

References

Anderson, Nicole. 2003. "The Ethical Possibilities of the Subject as Play: In Nietzsche and Derrida." *The Journal of Nietzsche Studies* 26: 79–90.

Bataille, Georges. 1994. *On Nietzsche.* Translated by Bruce Boone. New York: Paragon House.

Bateson, Gregory. 2000 [1972]. "A Theory of Play in Fantasy." In *Steps to an Ecology of Mind,* 177–193. Chicago: University of Chicago Press.

Bellah, Robert. 2011. *Religion in Human Evolution: From the Paleolithic to the Axial Age.* Cambridge, MA: Harvard University Press.

Brown, Stuart. 2009. *Play: How it Shapes the Brain, Opens the Imagination and Invigorates the Soul.* New York: Penguin.

Cox, Christoph. 1999. *Nietzsche: Naturalism and Interpretation.* Berkeley, CA: University of California Press.

Deleuze, Gilles. 2006. *Nietzsche and Philosophy*, translated by Hugh Tomlinson. New York, NY: Columbia University Press.

Derrida, Jacques. 2001. "Structure, Sign, and Play in the Discourse of the Human Sciences." In *Writing and Difference*, translated by Alan Bass, 351–370. New York: Routledge.

Derrida, Jacques. 1985. *The Ear of the Other: Otobiography, Transference, Translation.* New York: Schocken.

Derrida, Jacques. 1979. *Spurs: Nietzsche's Styles*, translated by Barbara Harlow. Chicago: University of Chicago Press.

Dursun, Yücel. 2007. "The Onto-Theological Origin of Play: Heraclitus and Plato." *Lingua ac Communitas* 17: 69–78.

Fink, Eugen. 1960. "The Ontology of Play." *Philosophy Today* 4(2): 95–109.

Foucault, Michel. 2014. *Lectures on the Will to Know*, translated by Graham Burchell. New York: Picador.

Foucault, Michel. 2010. *The Government of the Self and Others*, translated by Graham Burchell. New York: Picador.

Foucault, Michel. 2008. *The Courage of Truth: Lectures at the College de France, 1983–1984*. New York: Picador.

Foucault, Michel. 2003. *"Society Must Be Defended": Lectures at the College de France, 1975–1976*, edited by Mauro Bertani and Alessandro Fontana, translated by David Macey. New York: Picador.

Foucault, Michel. 2001. "Prisons et asiles dans le mécanisme du pouvoir." In *Dits et Ecrits Vol. I. 1954–1975*, 1389–1392. Paris: Gallimard.

Foucault, Michel. 1998. *Essential Works, Volume 2: Aesthetics, Method, Epistemology*, edited by James D. Faubion. New York: New Press.

Foucault, Michel. 1997. *Essential Works, Volume 1: Ethics, Subjectivity and Truth*, edited by Paul Rabinow. New York: New Press.

Foucault, Michel. 1996. *Foucault Live: Collected Interviews, 1961–1984*. New York: Semiotext(e).

Foucault, Michel. 1994. *The Order of Things*. New York: Random House.

Foucault, Michel. 1990. "Nietzsche, Freud, Marx." In *Transforming the Hermeneutic Context*, edited by Gayle L. Ormiston and Alan D. Schrift, 59–67. Albany, NY: State University of New York Press.

Foucault, Michel. 1972. *The Archaeology of Knowledge*, translated by A.M. Sheridan-Smith. London: Tavistock.

Fraser, Nancy. 1996. "Michel Foucault: A Young Conservative?" In *Feminist Interpretations of Michel Foucault*, edited by Susan J. Hekman, 15–38. University Park, PA: Pennsylvania State University Press.

Fraser, Nancy. 1981. "Foucault on Modern Power: Empirical Insights and Normative Confusions." *Praxis International* 1(3): 272–287.

Gadamer, Hans-Georg. 1986. *Relevance of the Beautiful*, edited by Robert Bernasconi, translated by Michael Walker. Cambridge: University of Cambridge.

Habermas, Jurgen. 1994. "Some Questions Concerning the Theory of Power: Foucault Again." In *Critique and Power: Recasting the Foucault/Habermas Debate*, edited by Michael Kelley, 79–107. Cambridge, MA: MIT Press.

Henricks, Thomas. 2006. *Play and the Human Condition.* Urbana, IL: University of Illinois Press.

Hinman, Lawrence. 1974. "Nietzsche's Philosophy of Play." *Philosophy Today* 18(2): 106–124.

Huizinga, Johan. 2014. *Homo Ludens: A Study of the Play-Element in Culture.* New York: Roy.

Kofman, Sarah. 1993. *Nietzsche and Metaphor*, translated by Duncan Large. Stanford, CA: Stanford University Press.

Koopman, Colin. 2013. *Genealogy as Critique.* Bloomington, IN: Indiana University Press.

Luxon, Nancy. 2013. *Crisis of Authority.* Cambridge: University of Cambridge Press.

McNay, Lois. 1994. *Foucault: A Critical Introduction.* New York: Continuum.

McNay, Lois. 1992. *Foucault and Feminism: Power, Gender and the Self.* Cambridge: Polity Press.

Menke, Christoph. 2013. *Force: A Fundamental Concept of Aesthetic Anthropology*, translated by Gerrit Jackson. New York: Fordham University Press.

Nietzsche, Friedrich. 2003a. "The Anti-Christ." In *Twilight of the Idols and The Anti-Christ*, 123–199. London: Penguin.

Nietzsche, Friedrich. 2003b. *Writings from the Late Notebooks*, edited by Rüdiger Bittner, translated by Kate Sturge. Cambridge: Cambridge University Press.

Nietzsche, Friedrich. 2003c. *The Twilight of the Idols and The Anti-Christ*, translated by R.J. Hollingdale. London: Penguin.

Nietzsche, Friedrich. 2002. *Beyond Good and Evil*, edited by Rolf-Peter Horstmann and Judith Norman, translated by Judith Norman. Cambridge: Cambridge University Press.

Nietzsche, Friedrich. 2001. *The Gay Science.* Cambridge: Cambridge University Press.

Nietzsche, Friedrich. 1996. *Human, All Too Human.* Cambridge: Cambridge University Press.

Nietzsche, Friedrich. 1989. "Ecce Homo." In *The Genealogy of Morals and Ecce Homo*, edited and translated by Walter Kaufman, 201–338. New York: Vintage Books.

Nietzsche, Friedrich. 1967. *The Birth of Tragedy and The Case of Wagner*, translated by Walter Kaufmann. New York: Random House.

Nietzsche, Friedrich. 1962. *Philosophy in the Age of the Tragic Greeks*, translated by Marianne Cowan. Washington, DC: Regenery.

Nietzsche, Friedrich. 1954. *Thus Spoke Zarathustra*, translated by Walter Kaufmann. New York, Viking Press.

Pippin, Robert. 2009. "How to Overcome Oneself: Nietzsche on Freedom." In *Nietzsche on Freedom and Autonomy*, edited by Ken Gemes and Simon May, 69–89. Oxford: Oxford University Press.

Rorty, Richard. 1991. *Essays on Heidegger and Others.* Cambridge: Cambridge University Press.

Sicart, Miguel. 2014. *Play Matters.* Cambridge, MA: MIT Press.

Sutton-Smith, Brian. 1997. *The Ambiguity of Play.* Cambridge, MA: Harvard University Press.

Sutton-Smith, Brian, and Diana Kelly-Byrne. 1984. "The Idealization of Play." In *Play in Animals and Humans*, edited by Peter K. Smith, 305–321. Oxford: Basil Blackwell.

Taylor, Charles. 1991. "Foucault on Freedom and Truth." In *Foucault: A Critical Reader*, edited by David Couzens Hoy, 95–97. Oxford: Blackwell.

Ulfers, Friedrich. 2013. "Introduction." In *The Dionysian Vision of the World*, by Friedrich Nietzsche, translated by Ira Allen. Minneapolis, MN: Univocal.

Walzer, Michael. 1991. "The Politics of Michel Foucault." In *Foucault: A Critical Reader*, edited by David Couzens Hoy, 51–68. Oxford: Blackwell.

Wolin, Richard. 1986. "Foucault's Aesthetic Decisionism." *Telos* 67: 71–86.

CHAPTER 17

Critique of Subjectivity and Affirmation of Pleasure in Adorno and Nietzsche

Stefano Giacchetti Ludovisi

The crisis of bourgeois subjectivity is one of the crucial points of the philosophical reflection of Adorno. I will here focus my analysis on the relationship, on this subject, between the thought of Adorno and that of Nietzsche. Adorno has, in fact, followed Nietzsche's critique of the artificial character of subjectivity, but at the same time he wanted to rescue the role of the subject as the ground of criticism. As Adorno (1973) states in the prologue to his *Negative Dialectics*, his task was "to break through the delusion of constitutive subjectivity by means of the power of the subject" (xii).

What we will try to see is to what extent Adorno was able to solve this "aporetic" task;[1] saving the concept and the subject while rejecting the principle of identity which forms them. In order to do so, we should analyze the similar path followed by Nietzsche and Adorno. The line followed by Nietzsche can be summarized in 3 main phases: (1) the ascertainment of the tension between Dionysus and Apollo; (2) the genealogical critique of Socratic-scientific rationality and subjectivity, and; (3) the development of an aesthetic/poetic reason. An analogous line was followed by Adorno, and it can be summarized in the following manner: (1) the tension between "non-identity" and "identity"; (2) the genealogical critique of the general concept of idealism and of the bourgeois subject, and; (3) the model of negative dialectics as the model for rationality. The purpose of this analysis is to show both the fundamental importance of Nietzsche's critical thought in Adorno's theory and how Adorno modified Nietzsche's conclusions.

One of the core aspects of Nietzsche's philosophy addresses the tension between the two impulses embodied in the two gods of Dionysus and Apollo. In Adorno this theme is proposed in a similar form, but terminologically changed into the tension between "non-identity" (of nature) and "identity" (of "second

1 Acording to J. Habermas (1997) these aporias of Adorno's thought, as they especially emerge in the work he coauthored with Horkheimer, *Dialectic of Enlightenment*, "fail to provide a way out of the embarrassment of a critique that attacks the presuppositions of its own validity" (127, my translation).

nature"), that is, between the characteristic of nature considered *outside* the process of human interpretation and the perception that we have of nature *inside* the process of conceptual understanding.[2]

The analysis of Nietzsche's evaluation of the category of the non-identical, his reception of the Heraclitean doctrine of becoming, is here necessary. Heraclitus is for Nietzsche the highest exponent of "a Dionysian philosophy,"[3] and as such he represents only one side of what philosophy consists of. Without the moment of Apollo in philosophy, without the element of conceptual constructions, Dionysus becomes just another false ontological principle. It is only through the tension between the Dionysian moment of nature's non-identity and the Apollonian way in which we represent non-identity (therefore identifying it) that we can achieve a genuine form of understanding. The greatest problem of rational understanding for Nietzsche remains that reason has by now been completely distorted by its Socratic-scientific version. In Adorno the scheme is very similar: non-identity represents what we might call "first nature," and as such we cannot properly say anything about it, since at this level nature is pure becoming which can never be conceptually fixed. For this reason, Adorno is rejecting all those philosophies that, in one way or another (subjectively or objectively) have achieved an improper identification of this Dionysian moment. Our understanding of non-identity can only occur through the artificial creation of a "second nature," that is, through concepts. The recognition of the Nietzschean tension between Dionysus and Apollo in Adorno becomes the ultimate task of dialectics. The problem for Adorno, just like for Nietzsche, is that in history only a technical, identifying reason has been affirmed as valid. Adorno has therefore to prove its arbitrariness in order to reestablish a form of rationality that, based on his negative dialectics, can finally relate to the non-identity of nature. In other words, the problem is not with reason in general, with the fact that it necessarily has to deal with concepts and identifications; the problem, as for Nietzsche, starts when we consider identities as "true," and reason becomes "tautological." Tautological is in fact for Adorno that reason that becomes a mere instrument for calculating abstract identities, since in this way reason loses its fundamental critical capacity, which is active only when it recognizes the artificiality of identities.

Adorno's work is to show how he maintained an "extremist" defense of the concept of non-identity, while at the same time he never gave up on the idea

2 The concept of "second nature" originally comes from Hegel and it is later developed by Lukács. In Adorno it takes the meaning of the alienated world of commodities.

3 This definition is repeatedly affirmed in *Ecce Homo*, but probably is best explained in his early works on pre-Socratic philosophy.

that reason alone can take us out of the impasse it created; "Every cognition requires rationality, or otherwise [the non-identical] recoils in a timeless, metaphysical principle" (Adorno 1973: 8). Adorno rejects a merely Dionysian view since it only affirms the non-identity of nature, and such a view has always to be counterbalanced by an historical consideration of how nature is modified by Apollonian creativity. At the same time, the Apollonian, historical moment of artificial creations can never be affirmed without constantly "remembering"[4] nature's non-identity beyond it. This same tension can be observed in the polar relation between subject and object. The subject has always to consider its being part of nature's non-identity (and this, as in Nietzsche, basically means to consider the impulsive side of human life), but at the same time the object's non-identity has always to be considered as mediated by human understanding through reason.

But if so far as we have described how close Adorno's dialectical method is, as the result of his strenuous defense of both nature's non-identity and reason's necessary identifications, to Nietzsche's conception of the Dionysian and Apollonian, there is a radical difference between the two philosophers that needs to be clearly remarked. This difference is indicated by Adorno (1973) himself, when he criticizes Nietzsche for *not* having maintained any notion of essence beyond the apparent world created by human intellect.

> Nietzsche, the irreconcilable opponent of the theological heritage in metaphysics, ridiculed the distinction between essence and appearance and delivered the background world [*Hinterwelt*] over to the backwoodsmen [*Hinterwäldlern*], [...] Essence is, what is itself concealed according to the law of the bad state of affairs; to dispute that an essence would exist, means taking the side of appearance [Schein], of total ideology, to which the existent has meanwhile become. (151)

This accusation might seem, at first sight, at the very least paradoxical. How can Adorno criticize Nietzsche for avoiding a notion of essence if avoiding any ontology is exactly the point that Adorno is sustaining? What type of essence can Adorno be sustaining, if it cannot be characterized by any identification? The paradoxical situation in which Adorno finds himself is described by Susan Buck-Morss (1977): Adorno is looking "for nothing less than non-metaphysical

4 The respective notion of "nemesis" in Adorno has particular importance as the memory of the identification imposed by the subject on objects.

metaphysics" (93).[5] Adorno felt that, in order not to reduce his negative dialectics to relativism, he had to find a "Hinterwelt," some type of truth from which he could justify his critical perspective. But at this point, we should not even expect to find the affirmation of some "positive" truth in Adorno, which would contradict the spirit of his negative dialectics. And in fact, the truth that Adorno (1979) is referring to is negatively defined in one aphorism in *Minima Moralia*: "the whole is the false"; which, as he reports, is the "inversion of Hegel's famous dictum: *Das Wahre ist das Ganze* [the whole is the true]" (50). The "essence" beyond appearance in Adorno is the principle of identification that distorts reason, the cause of the falsity of "totality." For Adorno, Hegel's conclusions regarding the rationality of the real have to be completely inverted; the real is actually irrational, and not because of some metaphysical principle that condemns it to irrationality (as it was in Schopenhauer). The real is irrational because its principle of rationality is actually irrational.

Here Adorno is adopting Marx's analysis of exchange in capitalism as the key to interpret social "totality" as false. Marx's analysis of capitalism points out its irrationality by indicating how surplus value distorts the value given to a commodity. Exchange value is presented by capitalism as the result of a fair exchange of equivalents, but the attribution of value to these equivalents is biased by profit. In this way use value, the only genuine attribution of value to any goods (based on the actual needs of a person), is replaced by exchange value (based on profit). For Adorno (1973), the principle of exchange of false equivalents is the reflection of the principle of identity that he considers as the basic bias in conceptual understanding, that is, in rationality.

> [The concept of totality] is true so much as untrue: true, because it forms that 'ether,' which Hegel called the Spirit; untrue, because its reason is nothing of the sort, its generality the product of particular interests. That is why the philosophical critique of identity steps beyond philosophy. That it requires, nonetheless, what is not subsumed under identity – in Marxian terminology, use-value – so that life can continue to exist even under the ruling relations of production, is what is ineffable in utopia. It reaches deep into that which secretly forswears its realization. In view of the concrete possibility of utopia, dialectics is the ontology of the false condition. (178)

5 Buck-Morss remarks that, in so doing, Adorno was trying to pursue the same goal of Walter Benjamin.

The crucial concept in Adorno for understanding this process of identification imposed by exchange value is the one of "reification." This concept, first developed by Marx (2000) to indicate the process of attribution of value in capitalism as "a personification of the thing and a reification of the person" (87, my translation), with Lukács (1971a) becomes the originating factor of a specific form of rationality: "We are concerned above all with the *principle* at work here: the principle of rationalization based on what is and *can be calculated*" (114, my translation).[6] Adorno subscribes to Marx's analysis of capitalistic exchange, of reification, and like Lukács, he considers reification as responsible for a specific form of rationality. Unlike Marx and Lukács, though, Adorno raises the economic and historical analysis of reification to the level of a principle that regulates the whole structure of rationality.[7] This different evaluation of the principle of exchange in Adorno brings him to revise Marx's historical analysis of capitalism as a specifically modern phenomenon into a principle of general alienation of the whole society. The laws of exchange are not just the specific laws of capitalism, but they are the laws of an identifying rationality. On this point, Adorno seems to follow more the analysis of Nietzsche (1989), as it was clearly developed in *On the Genealogy of Morals*: "Setting prices, determining values, contriving equivalences, exchanging – these preoccupied the earliest thinking of man to so great an extent that in a certain sense they constitute thinking *as such*" (II: 8). According to Adorno, then, the phenomenon of capitalism is not "original" as it was for Marx; Adorno does not consider reification as depending upon specific relations of production. Adorno deliberately neglects the peculiarities of capitalism indicated by Marx (2000); namely, that only in capitalism the exchange has specific features of alienation, since it affirms not only the exchange of commodities (an exchange that occurred well before capitalism), but also the exchange of work for salary, which for Marx is "an essentially different form of exchange" (24, my translation). By neglecting this part of Marx's analysis of capitalism, Adorno neglects the crucial role of class struggle in Marx's theory. The "totality" established by "identifying reason," and not just a class society, is affected by alienation. Therefore, according to Adorno we should not expect that one class, which experiences the specific alienation of labor, would be able to bring forth a revolution, since their alienation is rooted in the only form of rationality that has prevailed in the west since antiquity. Alienation in Adorno maintains the negative connotation that Marx

6 Lukács' analysis is influenced, besides by Marx, also by Weber. Lukács, though, specifies (in a footnote, n. 8) that Weber does not relate this specific rationalization to reification.

7 For Adorno, then, there are no different forms of rationalization (as Weber sustained) that represent different forms of values. Reification is the "curse" of all rationality.

gave it in relation to Hegel's definition, but it loses the specific historical connotation that Marx gave it in capitalism. Alienation in this way still represents for Adorno the fetish character of "the world of commodities," but this world is seen as a generic "second nature";[8] the world is ruled by the principle of exchange ever since reason became "identifying."

By shifting the analysis of exchange from a specific historical phase to the general functioning of "identifying reason," Adorno (1976) not only excludes from its analysis the role of class struggle, but he also envisions society as proceeding toward a fully "administered world." Once reason is reduced to the calculation of abstract identities, the margins of critical thinking are increasingly reduced.

> To think in terms of equivalence naturally produces a kind of rationality which is, in principle, analogous to the administrative rationality, since it determines the commensurability of all the objects, the possibility of subsuming them under abstract rules. The qualitative differences between the spheres and among each single sphere are reduced, and therefore they diminish their resistance against the administration. (119, my translation)

This description of how identifying reason leads to an uncritical thought fully resembles Nietzsche's analysis of the "herd" mentality as a result of the affirmation of Socratic rationality. Yet, at this point, the basic difference between Adorno and Nietzsche is clearer. This difference can be summarized through Gillian Rose's (1978) observation that Adorno "is perhaps the only neo-Marxist to make Nietzsche's criticism of logic (identity) into social criticism" (22). While for Nietzsche society is ultimately responsible for the "identity thinking" of Socratic rationality, on the contrary, for Adorno identity thinking is responsible for our unjust social organization. So, in Adorno the critique of a rationality based on identifications (which involves the possibility of changing this form of rationality) is always accompanied by a radical social critique (a change in rationality corresponds to a change in society); a type of analysis which is neglected by Nietzsche.

8 This term, of Hegelian origins and frequently used by Nietzsche, is borrowed from Lukács in *The Theory of the Novel*, where it assumes the sense of an alienated world, defined by Adorno as the world of commodities. As Buck-Morss (1977: 228) observes, Horkheimer (1972) goes back to find the origins of the expression "Second Nature" in Democritus, who affirmed the affinity between nature and education in transforming man, originating then a second, artificial nature (216).

Adorno's affirmation of an "essence" beyond appearance, rather than a positive connotation, has only the critical function of showing the falsity of totality; a falsity that is caused by "identifying reason." For Adorno then, the only definition of essence that we can achieve is actually the one of *Unwesen* ("bad substance"). If instead we try to define what would be the "good essence," we would be immediately reproducing the same defect that flaws reason; we would be creating another identity. The idea of a positive essence must remain only as a hope that one day reason will be able to use concepts (identifications) according to the model of negative dialectics, that is, by never taking them for "true" (in any fixed, absolute sense). Only in this way, in fact, the non-identity of nature (or we could use the expression "first nature," in order to contrast it to the artificial "second nature") would be "rescued" from identification. This is the main reason for Adorno's (1973) refusal to give any positive image of the utopian moment: "The mere thought of hope is a transgression against it, an act of working against it" (402). But in Adorno the utopian moment does not have a religious connotation of a metaphysical essence beyond this world. For Adorno beyond the abstract principle of identity there is still the non-identity of nature, the "residuum" that can never be fully conceptually identified, and which is present in us in our impulses.

The "background world" is for Adorno (1973) the world seen from the perspective of reconciliation, that is, the world seen from negative dialectics: "Reconciliation would be the meditation on the no-longer-hostile multiplicity, something which is subjective anathema to reason. Dialectics serves reconciliation" (6). Negative dialectics can then give us a perspective of reconciliation only insofar as it is able to dispel the "subjective anathema" imposed upon reason. So far, we have mainly seen how for Adorno his model of negative dialectics works. In other words, we have only seen in line of principle how, according to Adorno, it is possible to solve the first "aporetic" task of his theory; saving the concept while rejecting the principle of identity. In front of the increasingly stronger tendencies of society to configure itself as a fully administered world, the chances that negative dialectics will prevail as a model for rationality are increasingly smaller. This is what brought Adorno to define his philosophy as a *melancholy science*.[9] After the experiences of fascism and the affirmation of capitalism on a global scale, Nietzsche's *gay science* has lost its joyful aspect; autonomous thought is disappearing, engulfed by "culture industry."

Before we see how Adorno describes the contemporary enslavement of consciousness to the most passive acceptance of ideology, we should first see

9 Or "sad science," as Adorno describes his *Minima Moralia*, which immediately recalls the inversion of Nietzsche's *The Gay Science*.

Adorno's analysis of subjectivity. This means that we need to address the second "aporetic" task of Adorno; how is it possible to rescue the role of the subject while rejecting the principle of identity?

As we have seen, Adorno's dialectical approach is based on the acknowledgement of the falsity of the whole, but this acknowledgement still requires some form of consciousness that can discern this "falsity." The affirmation of a critical consciousness in Adorno is precluded by the ascertainment that the idea of a subjective consciousness is already the outcome of an improper identification. If in fact Adorno's main objection to his very broad conception of idealism is that it grounds artificial identities on a "constitutive subjectivity," he still needs some type of "non-constitutive" subjectivity that can sustain critical thinking. The first step for seeing how Adorno conceives this "non-constitutive subjectivity" is to follow his "genealogical" reconstruction of how subjectivity has taken shape in history.

Adorno, following Nietzsche's model, tries in fact to write his own genealogy of subjectivity, in the first *Excursus* of the work he coauthored with Horkheimer (1972), *Dialectic of Enlightenment*: "Odysseus or Myth and Enlightenment." In this Excursus Odysseus, the protagonist of the Homeric poem, is seen as the prototype of the bourgeois individual. All the vicissitudes that Odysseus has to go through in order to come back home, all the myths that Homer narrates, are considered by Horkheimer and Adorno (1972) as the process through which the subject forms its own identity. Odysseus can go through all his adventures because he uses his reason as a tool to deceive the mythical gods, through sacrifices that allow him to trick the gods and therefore to survive. In so doing, though, Odysseus affirms the principle of cunning as the principle of rationality; the ritual sacrifice is already the archetype of barter.

> If barter is the secular form of sacrifice, the latter already appears as the magical pattern of rational exchange, a device of men by which the gods may be mastered: the gods are overthrown by the very system by which they are honored.
>
> HORKHEIMER AND ADORNO 1972: 49

Through this "cunning" rationality Odysseus can survive; he gains mastery over nature. But once Odysseus uses reason for dominating nature, he is "cursed" into dominating his own nature as well. Odysseus becomes a subject because he affirms his own "I" against a nature that is reduced to a mere "object." This is the core of Adorno's genealogy of "identifying reason," which immediately recalls Nietzsche's. Reason saved humans, in prehistory, because they were able to quickly identify a danger in nature. Identifications such as ideas and concepts were indispensable for surviving. But soon identification became a universal principle and, as such, it was applied also to the subject who, in this way, created a notion of the permanently identical "I." From the moment of its birth, from the moment that it perceived itself as "identity," the "I" starts a process of self-repression. Repression is in fact a direct consequence of the process of identification. Once nature is reduced to a calculable abstract quantity, once it is reified, it loses its qualitative aspect. So when the subject reduces itself to identity, it also detaches itself from the qualitative aspect of its own life: passions. The identity of the "I" that was affirmed in order to survive soon turns into the element that prevents the "I" from enjoying life.

> Man's domination over himself, which grounds his selfhood, is almost always the destruction of the subject in whose service it is undertaken: for the substance which is dominated, suppressed, and dissolved by virtue of self-preservation is none other than that very life as functions of which the achievements of self-preservation find their sole definition and determination: it is, in fact, what is to be preserved.
>
> HORKHEIMER AND ADORNO 1972: 54–55

The best example of this sacrifice the subject is inflicting upon itself is found by Adorno and Horkheimer in the episode of the Odyssey where Odysseus has to pass through the Sirens' sea. Odysseus knows that if he hears the Sirens he will die; their song is Dionysus' song, the call of passions, which will bring him back to the dissolution into nature's non-identity. Yet Odysseus knows that that is the only true pleasure he can experience and wants to hear them. So he uses his calculating reason; he covers the ears of his subordinates with wax and commands them to keep rowing while they are passing through the Sirens' sea. He ties himself to the mast so that he will not give up to the Siren's call; so that he will not die. This for Adorno is the situation in which the bourgeois subject still lives: "The story of the Sirens illustrates the intertwinement of myth and rational labor" (Horkheimer and Adorno 1972: 35). Odysseus, as the bourgeois, can hear the call of passions since workers are "rowing" for him, but he tied himself to the mast; he is unable to free himself from the ties of civilization that he imposed on himself. Identifying reason has allowed him to dominate nature and his subordinates, but condemns him to never actually experience pleasure. Once the principle of identity regulates completely social organization, the bourgeois can only chase a fake idea of happiness, its commoditized version, and he increasingly loses the sense of what true pleasure might be. From then on, for him there will be "no happiness without fetishism" (Adorno 1979: 121).

The "genealogy" of the subject shows what Adorno and Horkheimer mean by "dialectic of Enlightenment": reason, that as the functioning of thought is supposed to enlighten us, is actually the source of our repression. Reason had its original purpose in self-preservation, but it then soon turned against life itself. By creating a "second nature" reason allowed us to survive through its calculative moment, but then it was not able to perceive non-identity anymore. From the moment of its affirmation, the structure of identifying reason remains the same throughout history, so when the Enlightenment proposed to free us from myth, from all dogmatic beliefs, it actually regressed to a new myth of "scientific" exactness. The redeeming potential of scientific, technical reason was frustrated by the fact that reason maintained the basic, original scheme of false equivalences. While Adorno rejects the moment of "idealism" that is present in the Enlightenment, the fact that it still grounds reason on the identity imposed by the subject, he nonetheless still wants to rescue the project of the Enlightenment of affirming autonomous thought. Reason has to be changed so that it finally acknowledges that the static, "identified" notion of subjectivity affirmed a principle of individual self-preservation. The "bourgeois" subject can only chase personal profit, but in so doing he is "forgetting" that he is part of non-identity, therefore forgetting that he shares this feature with other humans. Reason created identifications (and in particular concepts) so as to establish human cooperation (here, Nietzsche's analysis of the origin of concepts is basically shared by Adorno), but then when the principle of identity became the principle of an individual "I,"[10] it turned self-preservation into an obtuse egoism. The "I" at that point was concerned only with individual self-preservation, and in that way it forgot that self-preservation can only be achieved with the help of others. Through the process of identification the others, as anything outside the "I," as the whole nature, were already reduced to mere objects of exploitation. Adorno's analysis of the origin of "identifying reason" aims at the recognition of the distortion of self-preservation; the transformation of a principle of cooperation into domination. Technical reason becomes a means to dominate nature only when nature is perceived as something external, "alien"; something that does not (yet) belong to the "I." If instead reason acknowledges the role of social cooperation as the means to achieve self-preservation, then its technical aspect, its calculative moment, can be turned

10 Although Adorno does not address this topic directly in the *Dialectic of Enlightenment*, it seems that what he addresses simply as "I" basically shares the same features described by Freud as the narcissistic phase in the process of structuring of the Ego, "the primitively narcissistic aspect of identification as an act of *devouring*, of making the beloved object part of oneself." (Adorno 1992: 89).

into an instrument of emancipation. Once nature is reified, self-preservation is maintained only through domination. On the contrary, non-dominative cooperation can be affirmed only by recognizing the artificial, "identified" character of the "I," which is the principle that reduces others to "things." The equation of reason and domination holds true only insofar as reason cannot see beyond identities; insofar as it cannot "stare the negative in the face, tarrying on it." (Adorno 1973: 106) Once reason is freed from the principle of identity that constitutes social relations, once the principle of exchange has been recognized in its arbitrariness and as the element that fosters domination, the technical moment in reason (the undistorted Apollo) will become a means to authentic solidarity:

> In schema borrowed from sexual morality, technique is said to have ravished nature, yet under transformed relations of production it would just as easily be able to assist nature and on this sad earth help it to attain what perhaps it wants.
>
> ADORNO 1975: 68

Technique was developed in service of self-preservation, but once self-preservation was reduced to the preservation of an always identical "I," technique turned against us. But even if we were able to invert technique's destructiveness and actually "assist nature," what is that nature "wants"? In order to find an answer, we should examine Adorno's notion of "primacy of the object."

Adorno's insistence on the primacy of the object should be considered as his defense of the irreducibility of non-identity into concepts. For Adorno all philosophies that affirm a principle of identity are ultimately variants of idealism. Since the principle of idealism is to reduce the non-identity of the object to the "constitutive subjectivity," in its main function of identification, primacy of the object means the priority of nature in respect to any form of subjectivist reduction. This explains Adorno's (1973) choice of materialism as a cognitive tool for reaffirming the role of the object in knowledge: "Through the transition to the primacy of the object dialectics becomes materialistic" (172). But if we follow Adorno's criticism as we exposed it, Adorno's primacy of the object cannot be the affirmation of the immediacy of the object, nor can Adorno's materialism offer a type of knowledge (as a *Weltanschauung*) that can present itself in absolute terms. His conception of materialism represents a call for a genuine dialectical relationship between subject and object. If this relation is now completely unbalanced toward the "constitutive subjectivity," our primary task should be to rebalance the dialectical tension by shifting all our attention to the object. Yet, the acknowledgment of the primacy of the object does not imply in any way a diminished role of the subject in rationality, but it is mainly the remedy against its solidification (identification) in a self-referential system of identities.

We can express the value that Adorno attributes to materialism by representing the actual situation of reason in this image: rationality is like a boat that is about to capsize,[11] overwhelmingly pushed by the identification of constitutive subjectivity. For Adorno the situation is so unbalanced, that it is now necessary to push as hard as we can in the opposite direction; that of the object's non-identity. The ideal situation would be to maintain the balanced tension between subject and object, but we are in the moment where subjective identification is about to erase even the last chances of recognizing non-identity. What Adorno in fact wants to achieve is not the complete dissolution of subjectivity (as Nietzsche wanted), but the dissolution of the ideological form through which the subject perceives itself (as an "I"). But what would be a "non-constitutive" subjectivity? What would be a subject without an "I"? Adorno here is mainly indicating that there is no such thing as a "pure" cognitive subject; every subject is mediated by the object, just as much as every object is mediated by the subject. But would not then the primacy of the object run the risk of transforming itself into the same arbitrary call to passions done by Nietzsche? Adorno rejects the notion of an objective reality antecedent to the dialectical relationship, something he would condemn as "naïve" (in the sense of pre-critical) realism. At the same time, since he refuses any ontology, he cannot even sustain any naturalistic or dogmatic materialism. Adorno rejects the idea that sensations are "spontaneously" or immediately generated, but they depend on a non-identical pattern of physical impulses. Here Adorno is reproducing Nietzsche's argument regarding the non-identity of the impulses. But if Nietzsche then, against his own conception of the non-identity of passions, affirmed some of these impulses (knowing that their affirmation was an arbitrary act of his absolutely personal will), Adorno (1973) never gave up on that temptation and reaffirmed the ban on images of non-identity:

> The materialistic longing, to comprehend the thing, wishes the opposite; the full object could only be thought devoid of images. Such imagelessness converges with the theological ban on the graven image. (126)

Adorno not only did not follow Nietzsche in positively representing impulses, but he condemned Nietzsche's choice of so doing because it transformed the

11 Nietzsche, in a letter to F. Overbeck of 1881 (1998: 134) uses this image for indicating life's situation.

critical aspects of his thought into ideology. Nietzsche, in fact, identified some passions and affirmed them as the justification for a certain form of behavior. In this way, while he criticized all values as arbitrary, nonetheless he ended up affirming some values as better than others. Adorno (2000) was fully aware of the risks in Nietzsche's perspective, and while he recognized that "a positive morality – he would not have called it morality – cannot possibly exist in Nietzsche because of the absence of a substantive, objective spirit" (172), then Adorno also realized that "having proceeded in a summary fashion, [Nietzsche] came up with a positive morality that is really nothing more than the negative mirror-image of the morality he repudiated" (Adorno 2000: 172).

> Whereas in reality this very attempt on the part of a lone individual to set up in new norms and new commandments based simply on his own subjective whim implies their impotence, their arbitrary and adventitious nature from the very outset. The ideals [Nietzsche] has in mind – nobility [*Vornehmheit*], real freedom, the virtue of generosity, distance – all these are wonderful values in themselves, but in an unfree society they are not capable of fulfillment, or at best can only be realized on Sunday afternoons, that is, in private life. [...] For what Nietzsche means by man, and what he celebrates as Superman – and it's not for nothing that the latter is based on the model of the appalling and barbaric condottiere Cesare Borgia – would be the go-getter or captain of industry today.
>
> ADORNO 2000: 172

Adorno's critique of Nietzsche is here conducted on two lines: Nietzsche should not have broken the "taboo" on images, imposed by nature's non-identity, by affirming some impulses over others and, most importantly, he should have considered the socially repressive aspects of his affirmations. Once again, this is the consequence of the fact that for Nietzsche society is responsible for alienation, and for this reason he summarily decided to violently get rid of this "decadent" society. According to Adorno (2000), Nietzsche's negligence of the social character of alienation ultimately leads his ideal of Übermensch to the affirmation of a principle of domination, since he acts as an isolated individual. The reason why "captains of industry today" cannot become Nietzsche's Übermenschen is recognized by Adorno (2000):

> because they control the labor of others, even those who rule are too implicated in the general catastrophe to be able to afford this nobility. If a prominent businessman were seriously to attempt to be as noble as Nietzsche postulates – and not merely as an aesthetic gesture – he would undoubtedly go bankrupt. (173)

As a partial defence of Nietzsche's thought, we could reply to Adorno's criticism that for Nietzsche the Übermensch cannot be the man of the past, the bourgeois individual, nor live in a society where self-preservation is reduced to blind domination. Domination would in fact imply a state of repression towards some "inferior" being, whether it be another human or nature in general, which would unavoidably turn into self-repression. In Nietzsche the Übermensch seems rather a utopian perspective than a concrete, existing figure. Yet, Adorno is signaling all the problems of the destructive phase of "lions" in Nietzsche. If "lions" can in fact affirm any value they want, if they are truly free to express any of their impulses, then we have no guarantees that they will not be acting according to a principle of domination.

Adorno's critique of Nietzsche's "morality" is further developed in the second *Excursus* of *Dialectic of Enlightenment*, "Juliette or Enlightenment and Morality," where Adorno and Horkheimer develop their general critique of a morality based on formalized reason. The principle of identification implied in rationality can "logically" justify sadism. Once the Enlightenment has abolished any "objective" way of establishing goals for reason, once reason is "formalized," then the violent affirmation of domination is just as justifiable as any other moral standard. The same critique of "rational" morality is extended by Horkheimer and Adorno (1972) to Nietzsche. Nietzsche's "push of the scientific principle to annihilating extremes" (74) hides the same defect of the Enlightenment. Notwithstanding Nietzsche's refusal of any formalism in morality, he transformed pleasure into a formal principle of life.[12] Like the thinkers of the Enlightenment, Nietzsche refused an objective reason based on myth, but once reason had no objective way of establishing the feasibility of actions, he fell back on a subjective form of attribution of values; an arbitrary affirmation of its destructiveness.

But if Adorno's critique of Nietzsche is based on the ascertainment of the impossibility of grounding morality on the arbitrary affirmation of the impulses, on what can we ground morality? The Kantian alternative of grounding it on the aprioristic and transcendental character of an ethical will is rejected by Adorno (2000). Adorno's critique of Kantian ethics is based on Adorno's refusal of any conception of freedom which is not dialectically related to the social totality:

> In second nature, in our universal state of dependency, there is no freedom. And for this reason there is no ethics either in the administered

12 Although no reference is made to Freud in this *Excursus*, Adorno is referring to a principle very close to Freud's "principle of pleasure."

> world. It follows that the premise of ethics is the critique of the administered world. [...] Freedom necessarily presupposes the freedom of all, and cannot even be conceived as an isolate thing, that is, in the absence of social freedom.
>
> ADORNO 2000: 176

The starting point of Adorno's reflection on the concept of freedom originates from the paradoxical doctrine of Kant regarding a causality born of freedom. In agreement with Schopenhauer's and Nietzsche's critique of rationality, Adorno's rejection of Kant's doctrine is centered on Kant's equation of morality with reason. The distinction proposed by Kant (1928) between the empirical and intelligible character of action shows the difficulties implicit in this conception:

> We should, therefore, in a subject belonging to the sensible world have, first, an *empirical character*, whereby its actions, as appearances, stand in thoroughgoing connection with other appearances in accordance with the unvarying laws of nature. And since these actions can be derived from the other appearances, they constitute together with them a single series in the order of nature. Secondly, we should also have to allow the subject an *intelligible character*, by which it is indeed the cause of those same actions [in their quality] as appearances, but which does not itself stand under any conditions of sensibility, and it is not itself appearance. We can entitle the former the character of the thing in the [field of] appearance, and the latter its character as thing in itself. (468)

According to Adorno, in Kant moral conduct assumes a formal purity apart from any external conditions that might affect reason; practical actions arise only from reason and are purely in accordance with the laws of reason. For Adorno,[13] the problem of the causality of nature is avoided by Kant through a substantially animistic conception[14] which has placed causality outside things in themselves, eliminating the constructive aspects of the dialectical tension between subject and object. What Schopenhauer has achieved through a critique of this Kantian conception, and then developed by Nietzsche and Adorno, is the affirmation of another form of causality that is internal and that

13 This critique of Kant is clearly developed in a series of lectures held in 1963 (see, in particular, "Lecture Five" in Adorno 2000: 44–54).

14 "[Kant] is still operating with a basically animistic conception according to which things have an inner soul and an inward determinacy" (Adorno 2000: 50).

determines a different conception of what we might call “motivation.” Schopenhauer (1989) reduced this transformation to an explicit affirmation of the total supremacy of nature’s causality over any instance of freedom, since reason passes from a status of incontestable purity to an identical status of incontestable determination. Nietzsche then tried to avoid the absolute determinism of the will by negating its metaphysical essence, but then he ended up sustaining an arbitrary affirmation of impulses, therefore affirming an individualistic form of freedom (once again neglecting the social dimension). For Adorno (1998), instead, only a dialectical consideration of freedom and determinism, of individual and society, can be sustained:

> The problem of freedom of the will probably cannot be resolved abstractly at all, that is, by using idealized constructions of the individual and its character as something existing purely for itself, but only with the consciousness of the dialectic of individual and society. Freedom, even that of the will, must first be realized and should not be assumed as positively given. On the other hand, the general thesis of determinism is just as abstract as the thesis of *liberum arbitrium*: the totality of the conditions upon which, according to determinism, acts of the will depend is not known and itself constitutes an idea and should not be treated as an available sum. At its height philosophy did not teach one or the other alternative, but rather expressed the antinomy of the situation itself. […] Whether one adheres to determinism or the doctrine of free will depends for the time being on the alternative one chooses, for God knows what reasons. (84)

To sustain an idea of a form of behavior devoid of causality and therefore purely free means to implicitly give over the principle of reason to a chaotic rule of nature, while at the same time the affirmation of the universality of nature’s laws would maintain the rule of a reason which can only act according to the principle of domination. In order to resist the blind force of nature, reason requires both “something like a universal conformity to law” (Adorno 2000: 54) and freedom from the amorphousness of nature: moral and ethical actions cannot take place either in absolute adherence to law or in absolute freedom.

The scheme of Adorno’s idea of morality mirrors his model of negative dialectics; only a permanent tension between freedom and determinism can present us a correct form of behavior. Yet Adorno, as he did for the cognitive model of reason, still believes that in our world based on the principle of identification, where the notion of freedom has become mere ideology of an unfree society, it is better to affirm again the “primacy of the object,” that is, to affirm the impulsive side of existence which is increasingly forgotten by the identity of the subject. Using a Freudian terminology,[15] we can say that for Adorno the subject is too entangled in domination to sustain the role of "moral Superego." Adorno's view of morality seems to see only the repressive aspects of Kantian ethics, and it ends up privileging a Freudian "principle of pleasure" as the main drive for our actions. Here, though, Adorno (1973) unavoidably returns to a Nietzschean view of passions as the only parameter through which we can justify our actions.

> The individual meanwhile is left with nothing more of what is moral, than what Kant's moral theory, which conceded inclination to animals, but not respect, has only contempt for: to attempt to live so, that one may believe to have been a good animal. (274)

Pleasure represents the only utopia that Adorno (1979) is willing to describe, even by breaking for an instant the "taboo" he affirmed on its positive images: "He alone who could situate utopia in blind somatic pleasure, which, satisfying the ultimate intention, is intentionless, has a stable and valid idea of truth" (61). The utopian moment where freedom is actually universal, in the end coincides with Nietzsche's stage of the Übermensch; a stage with no repression and no morality. Contrary to Freud, any form of "sublimation" of impulses is for Adorno always a form of oppressive self-repression.[16]

Here Adorno is presenting us another type of problem. If we can find an answer to our previous question concerning what constitutes a "non-constitutive" subjectivity in passions, we are now facing another problem: what could possibly be "non-constituted" passions? For Adorno the principle of pleasure could be applied only in a universally free society, or otherwise we would fall into the same mistake of Nietzsche of affirming values that "can only be realized on Sunday afternoons" (Horkheimer and Adorno 1972: 132). What today is presented as pleasure for Adorno is mainly its reified version. With the development of a "culture industry," today culture is reduced to a "system" that manipulates people's consciousness into the most passive acceptance of an ideology that defends "the power of those whose economic position in society is strongest"

15 Adorno tries in general not to adopt Freudian terminology. We can see an analogy with the early works of Freud (before his *Beyond the Principle of Pleasure*). But Adorno will reject completely Freud's later theorization and, in particular, Freud's idea that the Ego must control the Id.

16 "Sublimation [...] as all mechanisms of defense, have a narcissistic character of defense of an ever-identical 'I'" (Adorno 1976: 65, my translation).

(Horkheimer and Adorno 1972: 95). Needs are distorted by economic demands; critical capacities are increasingly weakened.

> Everyone is supposed to behave according to a "level" determined by indices and to select the category of mass product manufactured for their type. On the charts of research organization, indistinguishable from those of political propaganda, consumers are divided up as statistical material into red, green, and blue areas according to income group.
>
> HORKHEIMER AND ADORNO 1972: 97

Once people are reduced to uncritical "customers," their ability to discern their own tastes and preferences is regulated by the dictates of the market. The identification of pleasure and fetishism is basically complete; the principle of "no happiness without fetishism" (Adorno 1979: 121) is now the ruling principle. How are we then supposed to experience "blind somatic pleasure" without the risk of actually experiencing its reified version?

The whole philosophical part of Adorno's work at this point cannot do anything but to refer to his aesthetic theory in order to find a way to "de-sublimate" pleasure. If sublimation for Adorno has the meaning of reducing pleasure to a passive acceptance of the rules of identity of a commoditized society, "de-sublimation" has the meaning of gaining a sense of pleasure devoid of reification, and not of mere regression into an egoistic Id. The civilization grounded on identity thinking represents the sublimation of pleasure, so we need to de-sublimate pleasure in order to change our civilization. When we discover that even the experience of pleasure is jeopardized by the standardization of taste in the administered world, we might find ourselves in a vicious circle that has no escapes.[17] Yet, our last hope for breaking this circle is to find an alternative model for "de-sublimating" pleasure and for achieving a critical consciousness in the "administered world"; this model, for Adorno, is still given to us by art. Adorno's negative dialectics must refer to his aesthetic theory in order to leave some opening to critical thought. At the same time, aesthetic theory needs to refer back to negative dialectics in order to apply critical consciousness to

17 Jürgen Habermas (1997) developed his criticism of Adorno on the ascertainment of a similar circularity of Adorno's argument. For Habermas, in fact, Adorno's thought shows a "performatory contradiction," namely, that it starts from the observation that no critical thought is possible under the domination of instrumental rationality and yet it wants to sustain a critique of ideology. Habermas then attempted to solve this contradiction in Adorno's theory by developing a theory of communication which would reestablish Adorno's project. Adorno instead tried to come out of this contradiction by establishing an interdependency between philosophy and aesthetics.

rationality. Philosophy and aesthetics in Adorno become completely interdependent; philosophy as the Apollonian moment of rational understanding, aesthetics as the Dionysian experience of estrangement from identity thinking. The irony of this situation of precariousness is described by Bataille (1992), when he affirms that "like [Nietzsche] I'm having fun laughing at people on the shore from a disabled ship" (xiv). Once we recognize the apparent character of the intellect's constructions, we will not have the comfort of *terra firma* that is offered by the solidification of our representations, but we also recognize that on that land we are condemned to be unfree, to not discover anything anymore. We leave this land on a ship that is disabled, "weak," because we can only build it on the error, or otherwise it would be so "solid" that it will never be able to leave. We do not seek any more certainties and the security offered by reason and science, or even less do we rely on a heavenly eternal continuation of our individuality, but we finally face the ocean of our passions even if that means that we will drown in them. The bourgeois subject is terrorized by this ocean because it is too "heavy," and it will therefore necessarily drown. We should not be paralyzed by the terror of the non-identical and free ourselves from the heavy armor of self-consciousness.

> We have left the land and have embarked. We have burned our bridges behind us – indeed, we have gone farther and destroyed the land behind us. Now little ship, look out! Beside you is the ocean: to be sure, it does not always roar, and at times it lays spread out like silk and gold and reveries of graciousness. But hours will come when you realize that it is infinite and that there is nothing more awesome than infinity. Oh, the poor bird that felt free and now strikes the walls of this cage! Woe, when you feel homesick for the land as if it had offered more *freedom* – and there is no longer any 'land.'
>
> NIETZSCHE 1974: III: 124

Poetic/artistic reason has the advantage of acknowledging the non-identity of nature and therefore of our passions, as well as of rejecting the false identities of scientific reason. In its reception of the aesthetic model of Apollonian construction of identities, poetic reason shows the importance of human autonomy in constructing ever new representations of reality, none of which can claim the status of truth. But there is a basic flaw in this aesthetic model of rationality as it is affirmed by Nietzsche. The problem is that not much of "reasonable" is left for it. If in fact poetic reason is characterized by its "virtuous stupidity," its principle is actually calling for the acknowledgment that beyond the irrationality of reality there is always another irrationality. Even if we find the causes for our contemporary irrationality, that is, even if we recognize the principle of identification which regulates scientific reason, the overcoming of "identity thinking" for Nietzsche substantially coincides with the affirmation of another irrationality, this time based on the "ocean" of passions, which is properly an "abyss." The unsolved problem for poetic reason is then, as Habermas (1997) observed, the attribution of value to any claim of this aesthetic reason. The problem of an aesthetic reason is that claims of validity fall into the category of aesthetic judgments. "The responses to questions about the 'value' of truth and justice are judgments of taste" (124, my translation). Following Habermas' critique, Nietzsche is unable to avoid the deficiencies of skepticism, that is, of reducing the criterion of validity to an arbitrary parameter; the affirmation of the will to power.[18] Nietzsche's notion of a "strong" skepticism, as a result of his rejection of the traditional conception of subjectivity, does not solve this problem. "Strong" skepticism points out that Nietzsche is not concerned about the "value" of truth and yet, when Nietzsche affirms some values as "personally" better than others, he relies on some type of aesthetic judgments, at least on those linked to "interest" (pleasing). These judgments are not concerned at all about universality; there is no universality, neither objective nor subjective. What parameter is then left for Nietzsche's "personal" attribution of value? Only "virtuous stupidity," which in the end is directed by an unidentifiable (non-identical) principle of pleasure. Yet, this virtuous stupidity *might* be better (in terms of autonomous thought and freedom) than our scientific "correctness," but it might just be as destructive. The "error" of Nietzsche, as Adorno pointed out, was to affirm some passions as the basis for new values, and at that point he could not escape the criticism of not being able to justify his choice other than as the affirmation of *his* will. But the real problem is that this "error" in Nietzsche's thought is the "normalcy"; poetic reason is the affirmation of these "errors." The price that we have to pay for "Nietzschean" autonomy and freedom is the permanent risk of falling back into barbarism.

Adorno, as Nietzsche, has left for the ocean of non-identity; but he does not "laugh" like Bataille. Adorno is homesick, not for the "land" of reification, but for a critical consciousness. The type of nostalgia that Adorno has is very peculiar, since it is directed towards something which never existed. On one hand, Adorno condemns every philosophy – which he generically addresses as idealistic – that maintains a founding role for the subject. Like Nietzsche, Adorno (1973) refuses the traditional notion of metaphysical essence, and

18 "Once the defenses of subject-centered reason are razed, the logos […] hollow within and aggressive without, will collapse into itself. It has to be delivered over to its other, whatever that may be" (Habermas 1997: 311, my translation).

therefore he cannot consider either the subject or its element, pure knowledge, in ontological terms, as "in itself."

> The ideological untruth in the conception of transcendence is the separation of body and soul, a reflex of the division of labor. It leads to idolization of the *res cogitans* as the nature-controlling principle, and to the material denials that would founder on the concept of transcendence beyond the context of guilt. (400)

On the other hand, Adorno's main concern is that the dissolution of any notion of subjectivity would lead to the creation of impersonal "masses" which takes place both in "real" socialism and fascism. The assimilation into the totality of the *Unwesen* represented by our society is made possible through the creation of a standardized consciousness which represses any form of personality. Adorno, like Nietzsche, knows that in order to affirm our creativity we cannot rely on the traditional, bourgeois concept of self-consciousness, because that is the foundation of a merely instrumental reason and of "total" identification which ends up destroying both our internal nature – through psychological repression – and external nature – through the destructive model of exploitation of workers and environment affirmed by capitalism.

Adorno's critique of what he generically addresses as idealism is centered on his refusal of "constitutive subjectivity," which is responsible for the principle of identity and reification. Whenever Adorno uses the term self-consciousness he does not imply by any means an ontological self: "the self should not be spoken of as the ontological ground" (Adorno 1979: 99). The self is, in fact, determined by the impulses, but at the same time it "overcomes and preserves" the impulses through the unavoidable objectification made by thought. The price that the bourgeois subject has to pay for the certainties it constructed through perennial identities is the loss of imagination, dumbness. Adorno's *Aesthetic Theory* is fully based on the ascertainment of art's ability to provide reason with a critical insight into reality; aesthetics is the model for a critical consciousness beyond the spell of identity thinking.

Adorno then follows Nietzsche's affirmation of the moment of "interestedness" in art, but not as an indiscriminate affirmation of any passions. What is lacking in Nietzsche's thought is the consideration of how pleasure has been reduced to commoditized fetishism by economic interests. Nietzsche did not consider that "in the false world all ἡδονή [pleasure] is false" (Adorno 1979: 13).

But how can art then maintain a moment of "interestedness" if pleasure is today reduced to fetishism? For Adorno it is only negatively that we can experience what should be pleasure in art; through the painful experience of "dissonance." Dissonance in modern art represents the contradictions of contemporary society (caused by the principle of identification and reification) which are responsible for fetishism. This is the core of Adorno's (1975) evaluation of modern art, and especially modern music: "Dissonance, the seal of everything that is modern, gives access to the alluringly sensuous by transfiguring it into its antithesis, pain: an aesthetic archetype of ambivalence" (15).

The artistic model that according to Adorno (2007) best exemplifies this function is modern music, and in particular the dissonance of atonal music. By dissolving the standards of musical composition, atonality shows in its form the falsity of our social order.

> Atonality is the fulfilled purification of music from all conventions. [...] The dissonant chord, by comparison with consonance, is not only the more differentiated and progressive; but furthermore, it sounds as if it had not been completely subdued by the ordering principle of civilization. (166)

For Adorno music in general has the advantage over other artistic forms of expression of transmitting its meaning only through its compositional form, without the ulterior mediation of representations (figurative arts) or concepts (poetry and literature). Music has then the potential of showing the inadequacy of conceptual understanding, its derivation from identity thinking. Music transforms concepts into pure sound, but not immediately; the meaning that is expressed by a concept is expressed by music in the unfolding of its movements. In this way music is a critical tool for philosophy. It shows philosophy how concepts should be considered; communication of an object that does not reduce the object to a fixed identity.

> Sphinx-like, music fools the listener by constantly promising meanings, and even providing them intermittently – meanings that for music, however, are in the truest sense means to the death of meaning.
>
> ADORNO 2002: 140

Here Adorno is showing not just a strict form of nominalism – "the name is no communication of an object" (Adorno 2002: 140) – but he is rather showing that we should consider conceptual understanding as a process of interpretation that does not lead to the affirmation of permanent identities. The meaning that the concept wants to express can never be fixed, and it should be interpreted as we do when we follow a musical movement, as "becoming." Adorno follows an interpretative model for the form of artistic compositions that explicitly recalls "psychological dream case studies" (28).

The artwork should be interpreted as Freud proposed to interpret dreams; not in terms of their content (whether immediate or latent), but through their form. But the subject of the case studies represented by artworks is not the individual artist. The analysis of a work will not lead to the disclosure of a specific artist's sublimation. Artworks represent instead the case study of subjectivity as it has imposed itself in history; they trace the "neurosis" of constitutive subjectivity. The "childhood trauma" of subjectivity, described by Adorno as the origin of the dialectic of Enlightenment – the "introversion of sacrifice," the domination of nature that turns against passions – now shows its symptoms in the obsession towards identity thinking. The form of an artwork shows the basic conflict between non-identity and identity, between passions and constitutive subjectivity. The analysis of artworks' form does not lead then to a sublimation of non-identity (passions) into the principle of identity, but it should lead to the desublimation of pleasure from the principle of identity, that is, from reification. This process of desublimation should not occur "positively," as an affirmation of the impulses, but negatively, as the acknowledgment of their fetish character. Art does not affirm a principle of pleasure (which by now has been distorted into fetishism); it affirms, as Cutrofello (2005) suggests, the imperative of "resisting commodity fetishism" (265).[19] The enigmatic character of music, its riddle concerning "meaning" that can never be fully solved, becomes the most powerful tool for demystifying identity thinking.

The subject that is able to relate mimetically with nature's non-identity, in other words, the aesthetic subject,[20] is the one who can sustain Adorno's negative dialectics. This subject can also be addressed as the "over-bourgeois";[21] the subject that does not "constitutively" posit identities. The definition of "over-bourgeois" has the ability of showing the similar path followed by Nietzsche and Adorno, their common refusal of accepting the principle of identity as constitutive of subjectivity. But it also has the function of showing the difference between Adorno's conception of a new subject as substantially social, and Nietzsche's conception of the Übermensch as the affirmation of an individualistic principle. If it is true that in Adorno the characteristics of the bourgeois subject are already present ever since the affirmation of identifying reason, the term bourgeois remarks the crucial category of exchange-value as the cause of social inequalities. The term over-bourgeois then

19 Cutrofello indicates in this "maxim" the equivalent of Adorno's "categorical imperative."

20 The reference to Kierkegaard's "aesthetic man" is made explicit by Adorno's (1993) criticism of Kierkegaard in his dissertation *Kierkegaard: Construction of the Aesthetic*.

21 I gave a more detailed definition of this concept of "over-bourgeois," as it can developed from Adorno's thought, in Giacchetti (2008).

indicates that the overcoming of this subjectivity represents the end of bourgeois individualism.

The model of Adorno's aesthetics points to the affirmation of a critical social consciousness in an "aesthetic" subject, but not to the affirmation of a corresponding aesthetic rationality alternative to "identifying" reason. The task of the aesthetic model is to correct the principle of identity which structures technical/identifying reason, and which reduces reason to mere domination. Adorno affirms the equation of reason and domination only as the acknowledgment of what reason is reduced to; not as a necessary equation. The margins left to the development of a critical consciousness are increasingly reduced by the affirmation of the culture industry, but they are still present in art. Adorno's aesthetic theory shows the feasibility of developing a critical consciousness of non-identity, which then must always refer back to negative dialectics as its tool for rational understanding. This rational understanding would not simply eliminate the calculative moment of its procedure. Reason for Adorno remains a means to self-preservation. Once the over-bourgeois has rejected the constitutive principle of identity, it recognizes that the goal of rationality is not individual self-preservation, but preservation of humanity. "The subject of *ratio* pursuing its self-preservation is itself an actual universal, society – in its full logic, humanity" (Adorno 1998: 272).[22]

References

Adorno, Theodor W. 2007. *Philosophy of Modern Music*, translated by Anne G. Mitchell and Wesley V. Blomster. London: Continuum.

Adorno, Theodor W. 2002. *Essays on Music*, edited by Richard Leppert, translated by Susan H. Gillespie. Berkeley, CA: University of California Press.

Adorno, Theodor W. 2000. *Problems of Moral Philosophy*, edited by Thomas Schröder, translated by Rodney Livingstone. Palo Alto, CA: Stanford University Press.

Adorno, Theodor W. 1998. *Critical Models: Interventions and Catchwords*, translated by Henry W. Pickford. New York: Columbia University Press.

Adorno, Theodor W. 1993. *Kierkegaard. La Costruzione dell'Estetico*, translated by Alba Burger Cori. Parma: Guanda.

22 The goal that reason should establish immediately recalls Kant's categorical imperative. What Adorno rejects in Kant's formulation is the fact that in Kant this imperative is still based on an individualistic conception of the subject. "In Kant the individual is the substrate of correct action. All his examples in fact come from the private and business spheres" (Adorno 1998: 264).

Adorno, Theodor W. 1992. "Freudian Theory and the Pattern of Fascist Propaganda." In *Critical Theory: The Essential Readings*, edited by David Ingram and Julia Simon-Ingram. St. Paul: Paragon House.

Adorno, Theodor W. 1979. *Minima Moralia*, translated by E.F.N. Jephcott. Surrey: Gresham Press.

Adorno, Theodor W. 1976. *Scritti Sociologici*, translated by Anna Marietti Solmi. Torino: Einaudi.

Adorno, Theodor W. 1975. *Aesthetic Theory*, translated by C. Lenhardt. Minneapolis: University of Minnesota Press.

Adorno, Theodor W. 1973. *Negative Dialectics*, translated by E.B. Ashton. New York: Seabury Press.

Bataille, Georges. 1992. *On Nietzsche*, translated by Bruce Boone. New York: Paragon House.

Buck-Morss, Susan. 1977. *The Origins of Negative Dialectics.* New York: The Free Press.

Cutrofello, Andrew. 2005. *Continental Philosophy. A Contemporary Introduction.* New York: Routledge.

Giacchetti Ludovisi, Stefano. 2008. "The *Over-Bourgeois* and the Dissolution of Subjectivity: Adorno as Nietzsche's Scholar." In *Nostalgia for a Redeemed Future: Critical Theory*, edited by Stefano Giacchetti Ludovisi, 17–32. Newark, DE: University of Delaware Press.

Habermas, Jürgen. 1997. *Il Discorso Filosofico della Modernità*, translated by E. Agazzi. Bari: Laterza.

Horkheimer, Max. 1972. *Critical Theory: Selected Essays*, Translated by M. O'Connell. New York: Herder and Herder.

Horkheimer, Max, and Theodor W. Adorno. 1972. *Dialectic of Enlightenment*, translated by John Cumming. New York: Herder and Herder.

Kant, Immanuel. 1928. *Critique of Pure Reason*, translated by N. Kemp Smith. London: Macmillan.

Lukács, György. 1971a. *Storia e Coscienza di Classe*, translated by Giovanni Piana. Milano: Sugar.

Lukács, György. 1971. *The Theory of the Novel: A Historico-Philosophical Essay on the Forms of Great Epic Literature*, translated by Anna Bostock. Cambridge: MIT Press.

Marx, Karl. 2000. "Per la Critica dell'Economia Politica." In *Lineamenti Fondamentali della Critica dell'Economia Politica*, translated by F. Codino. Roma: Editori Riuniti.

Nietzsche, Friedrich. 1998. *Opere Complete*, edited by Giorgio Colli and Mazzino Montinari. 8 Vols. Milano: Adelphi.

Nietzsche, Friedrich. 1989. *On the Genealogy of Morals*, translated by Walter Kaufman. New York, NY: Vintage Books.

Nietzsche, Friedrich. 1974. *The Gay Science*, translated by Walter Kaufman. New York, NY: Vintage Books.

Rose, Gillian. 1978. *The Melancholy Science. An Introduction to the Thought of Theodor W. Adorno*. New York: Columbia University Press.

Schopenhauer, Arthur. 1989. *Il Mondo come Volontà e Rappresentazione*, translated by A. Vigliani. Milano: Mondadori.

CHAPTER 18

Nietzsche and Happiness

Bryan S. Turner

1 Introduction[1]

Happiness is not an idea normally associated with Nietzsche. His biographers unsurprisingly concentrate on the unhappiness that defined much of his adult life (Chamberlain 1997). A powerful sense of isolation and loneliness pervades the notes he put together in 1873 on Oedipus and the soliloquies of 'the last philosopher' (Nietzsche 1987). In the *Wanderer and his Shadow* from 1880 that eventually appeared in *Human, All Too Human,* he laments 'One is filled with autumnal melancholy to think of the greatness as well as the transitoriness of human happiness' (Nietzsche 1996: §271). The theme of happiness rarely appears in the secondary literature on Nietzsche. There are however three important exceptions: Walter Kaufmann (1974 [1950]), McMahon (2006) and Richard Schacht (1983).

While he may have been unhappy as a person, the theme of happiness was a persistent topic in his thinking. His view of happiness was drawn to a large extent from Aristotle and to a lesser extent from Socrates. They shaped his ideas about power, greatness of soul, happiness and the re-valuation of values. Great souls are not dependent on a higher power and thus the death of the 'old god' fills Nietzsche in 1887 in *The Gay Science* Book Five ('We fearless ones'). Nietzsche's distinction between joy, pleasure and happiness remains relevant as a critique of modern notions of happiness which are often connected to consumerism. Nietzsche objected to the superficial treatment of happiness that was emerging in the Europe of his day and predicted the standardization of happiness through quantitative measures that are associated with utilitarianism. Nietzsche's critique of modernity has often been mistakenly seen as individualistic and hence the political character of his thought has been overlooked or neglected (Siemans and Roodt 2008).

1 Throughout this chapter I refer to 'man' and 'men,' because to modernize this vocabulary with 'her/his' or collective references to 'people' would be to introduce a vocabulary that was alien to Nietzsche's world. Aspects of this argument regarding contemporary research on happiness appeared in Turner (2018).

To establish the idea that heroic men struggle against the pleasure-seeking herd, Nietzsche had to confront Charles Darwin's evolutionary view of mankind. For Nietzsche happiness is not a conglomeration of pleasures but a way of life in which strong-souls can flourish. He associated genuine happiness with Homer claiming that suffering and happiness go hand in hand. This aspect of happiness appears frequently in *The Gay Science* which in many aspects is the most personal of Nietzsche's works. In a criticism of Christian notions of compassion which he dismissed as 'snug cosiness,' he argues that such people will never experience true happiness – 'For happiness and misfortune (*Gluck und UnGluck*) are two siblings and twins' (Nietzsche 1974: 4: 338).

Nietzsche was mainly critical on the emphasis on feelings in modern society; he treated feelings as mere epiphenomenon of deeper forces in the composition of great souls. In his understanding of hedonism as weakness, Nietzsche provides an alternative to modern approaches to happiness as pleasure. For example, most but not all economists treat happiness as simply individual preferences in consumer society. So-called Happiness Studies present an optimistic picture of increasing life-satisfaction but such results are contradicted by an epidemic of drug dependency in the middle class in the United States. Nietzsche (1974: 4: 338) was scornful of modern happiness in liberal democracies, saying 'we do not need to plug our ears against the sirens who in the market place sing of the future: their song about "equal rights," "a free society," "no more mates and no servants" has no allure for us.'

Happiness as a way of life rather than as pleasure or comfort can thus be developed as a critique of 'modern man.' In this respect, Nietzsche was also opposed to what he called 'English Happiness' as propounded in the utilitarianism of Jeremy Bentham and James Mill. In *The Gay Science,* he also rejected 'that pedantic Englishman Herbert Spencer' and his simplistic attempt at the reconciliation of egoism and altruism (1974: 5: 373). However as I show towards the conclusion, J.S. Mill, in rejecting the quantitative approach to happiness in early utilitarianism and in criticizing the extension of the franchise to an uneducated working class, developed a theory of culture that was ironically consistent with Nietzsche's view of 'great souls.' Mill's personal encounter with unhappiness was echoed in the lives of both Nietzsche and Max Weber.

2 Nietzsche on Happiness in Greek Thought and Christianity

Happiness is often associated with good health. Nietzsche however suffered endlessly from migraine and stomach complaints. In *Ecce Homo* (1980: 39) in Chapter 1 (*Why I am So Wise*) he complained of 'the tortures that go with an uninterrupted three-day migraine and agonizing phlegm-retching.' His mother sent homemade sausages to him in Italy to avoid the digestive dangers of the local product. The quest for health is never too far below the surface of his writing and indeed he used medical metaphors frequently to describe both individuals and the societies in which they lived. Nietzsche's thought offered a diagnostic of the maladies of modernity. Partly in response to illness, he abandoned his professorship and lived for the rest of his life as a private scholar. After the mental breakdown in Turin in 1889, he was during the following twelve years incapable of coherent thought.

In Darrin M. McMahon's *Happiness: A History* there is a lengthy discussion of Nietzsche. He comments that 'The subject (happiness) is central to his work, accompanying him at every stage of his intellectual evolution,' but he qualifies that by adding 'that his passion for happiness exits in tension with a profound and enduring sadness' (McMahon 2006: 425). He recalls that Nietzsche sought refuge from unhappiness in art but eventually abandoned that project following his alienation from Richard Wagner. In addition Nietzsche strenuously rejected the idea that there was any consolation in religion and he had equally rejected the idea (associated with the Enlightenment) that reason could lift men out of unhappiness. McMahon concludes that Nietzsche, while walking in the Upper Engadine mountains in Switzerland on August 6, 1881, finally found happiness (indeed joy) in the revelation he found in the idea of 'eternal recurrence.' In *The Gay Science* (337) he spoke about a happiness that 'humanity has not known so far: the happiness of a god full of power and love, full of tears and laughter, a happiness that, like the sun in the evening, continually bestows its inexhaustible riches, pouring them into the sea...' In Nietzsche's own terms, this experience is far better described as joy rather than happiness.

Nietzsche, as a professor of ancient Greek philology, was steeped in the literature, philosophy and history of the ancient world. We know for example that Nietzsche was profoundly influenced by his reading of Socrates. He was, as it were, naturally sympathetic to Socrates who did not develop a system of philosophy and who questioned his own society by identifying problems that were intractable to easy solutions. In his use of aphorisms, Nietzsche, like Socrates, was an experimental not a systematic thinker. Aristotle was also deeply influenced by Socrates' understanding of greatness and virtue in men.

Nietzsche was indebted to Aristotle's *Nicomachean Ethics* and translated Aristotle's *megalopsychia* as 'greatness of soul.' For Nietzsche such greatness of soul requires greatness of men, their independence and autonomy, and a conviction about their own worth. We can assume justifiably that Nietzsche was very familiar with Aristotle's discussion of happiness which plays a central role in the *Nicomachean Ethics.* For Aristotle, all creatures aspire to reach their full potential and this is the real meaning of *eudaimonia* as flourishing although it is typically translated as happiness. For him, flourishing was a condition of human development in which a human being achieved his self-excellence (or *aretai, virtues* in Latin) that endow him with personal control and self-sufficiency (autarchy). Consequently women and slaves were excluded from consideration. The values behind *eudaimonia* were defined in contrast to what was the most deplorable condition of man: slavery. A living tool, a slave is not a human being, because the slave lacks self-control and independence. In this fashion, the ideal of happiness is a state in which a human being is capable of self-determination. This state of happiness was not an experience of pleasure, but involved a going beyond both pleasure and pain. Nietzsche was occasionally critical of *Eudaimonia* which he lumped together with hedonism, pessimism, and utilitarianism in *Beyond Good and Evil* (Part Seven: Our Virtues; Section 225) because he argued they had a simple and misleading quantitative notion of pleasure and pain. The mistake was to treat 'attendant and secondary phenomena' rather than examining their foundation.

This discussion of Aristotle and Greek philosophy more generally provides some further insight into Nietzsche's hostility towards Christianity. It is important to understand that for Nietzsche happiness or as he says 'Greek cheerfulness' can never be separated from suffering and tragedy. It is only by passing through suffering that great souls experience real happiness. Thus in Nietzsche's *The Birth of Tragedy* Sophocles in writing about 'the sorrowful figure of Oedipus' – a man 'destined to error and misery' – recognizes that Oedipus 'eventually, through his tremendous suffering, spreads a magical power of blessing that remains effective beyond his decease' (Nietzsche 1967: 67). This characteristic of 'cheerfulness' or happiness out of the 'birth of tragedy' was not properly understood in the early Christian reception of the Greek world and the mistaken association of comfort with cheerfulness is 'encountered everywhere today.'

In Roman Christianity Saint Augustine's discussion of the ideals of human existence had an enduring impact on the whole development of the Christian Church in the West. I concentrate therefore on Augustinian theology in order to indicate the form of Christianity that Nietzsche specifically rejects. Whereas Aristotle, in accepting the biological foundations of human existence as a given, believed that sexual fulfilment was part of self-fulfillment, Augustine, like Paul, confined sexual activity to marriage and family life as necessary for reproduction. Augustine conceived of human life as a continuum in which death marks a passage, dramatic and traumatic, but only a stage in the transition into the afterlife. His thinking about immortality in this manner required an assumption about the dual nature of human life – body/soul, flesh/ spirit, forgetfulness/memory. Augustine embraced the notion that human will is an autonomous but weak and unreliable faculty. It is incapable of directing human beings to realize their own good and thus only divine grace can intervene to save a sinful creature. In his account of happiness, Augustine adopted a term from Cicero to describe divine happiness as *beatitudo*. Thus *eudaimonia* in Christianity became a *beatitude* which we can understand as the ascetic search for divine forgiveness and salvation in the afterlife rather than fulfilment in this life (Turner and Contreras-Vejar 2018). Nietzsche was specifically hostile to this development in Christianity. More specifically he regarded Pauline Christianity as a great betrayal of the message of Jesus and argued that the early Church was driven by resentment and revenge against those who persecuted them. Official as opposed to popular Christianity suppressed the three elements that Nietzsche in *The Will to Power* (802) thought were essential to vitality namely sexuality, intoxication and cruelty. It was the 'excitation of the animal functions' that 'intensified life.'

3 Of Apes and Great Souls

We cannot underestimate the significance of Charles Darwin for the development of Nietzsche's thinking about great souls. In fact Darwinism was a challenge to a generation of thinkers towards the end of the nineteenth century (Hughes 1959). He was characteristically hostile to Darwinism as an English ideology which in *The Gay Science* he also connected to Malthusian population theory – 'The whole of English Darwinism breathes something like the musty air of English overpopulation, like the smell of distress and overcrowding of small people' (Nietzsche 1974: 292). He dismissed Darwinism with its incomprehensibly one-sided doctrine of the 'struggle for existence' (Nietzsche 1974: 292). At least in his early work, Nietzsche was wholly critical of Darwinism as a modern optimistic ideology promising the evolutionary success of dominant societies. As a positivist, scientific system, Darwinism was obviously anathema to Nietzsche as a critical thinker. Nevertheless Darwin, as opposed to Darwinism, posed an important question for Nietzsche: How can men rise above their primitive ape-like origins to evolve as higher being and hence achieve genuine happiness? Darwin's theory presented the possibility that the pleasures of human beings – food, sex, and offspring – are no different from other mammals. A confrontation with Darwin became part of that 'central' task. In his later work, it was Darwin rather than Darwinism that attracted Nietzsche and forced Nietzsche to re-think his early opposition to Darwin's ideas. Indeed with a reflection on Kant, Kaufmann (1974 [1950]: 167) says 'Nietzsche was aroused from his dogmatic slumber by Darwin.'

Nietzsche believed that in a mass society modern 'man' cannot be genuinely happy. They are merely a herd incapable of lifting themselves above the law of animal evolution. It requires superhuman effort to live a satisfying and creative life in a modern industrial society. On the other hand, the *ubermensch* must free themselves from dependency on religion. It is through struggle and the will to power that the *ubermensch* lift themselves out of animal evolution and live a life of self-creation.

One important outcome of this confrontation with Darwin was that happiness in modern society had become confused with pleasure which was a confusion typically associated with the mass of people (or 'the herd'). The great souls who take happiness seriously will always aim higher. While happiness remained a major theme of western thinking in the late nineteenth century, key intellectuals (from Weber to Freud) were inclined to argue that unhappiness (at least for the masses) rather than happiness was the constant feature of human existence.

Nietzsche's basic disagreement with Darwin rests on his insistence that the value of a man – his worth, his creations – is not something he shares with any other creature. It lies in his capacity to rise above nature and rests ultimately on his special or unique position in creation – his *Sonderstellung.* Nietzsche was convinced that this capacity to rise above the animal world was not shared by all. The mass of men – the herd – would be mired in a world of physical pleasures which they mistakenly interpret as happiness. To rise above the herd, great souls will require a strenuous remaking of their natures, and to achieve that goal the virtuous soul cannot be dependent upon the state or on the Church.

4 Nietzsche and the Critique of Happiness

True existence is achieved when people stop treating their own lives as yet another accident. In the famous aphorism in *The Gay Science* (3: 270): 'What does your conscience say? – "You shall become the person you are."' Happiness involves a heroic struggle against convention and habit to become eventually a self-constructed person. Conventional morality is thus a product of the weak through the process of resentment. Again Weber shared a similar view of the role of resentment among the socially disprivileged in his sociology of religion. Controversially Nietzsche thought that religious values were the product of the resentment of the disprivileged against those in power – the rich man on his camel and overwhelmed by goods cannot pass through the eye of a needle. A new set of values had to rise above mere resentment. At one stage Nietzsche saw artistic creativity as the essential route out of the swamp of Darwinian evolutionary optimism – hence the early infatuation with Wagner and the total work of art. However, as we know, Nietzsche eventually became disillusioned by the bourgeois character of Bayreuth in which Wagnerian culture was just another substitute for the Christian religion whose days were numbered (Newman 1946).

Great souls are not dependent on a higher power and thus the death of the 'old god' fills Nietzsche with 'happiness, relief, exhilaration, encouragement, dawn' with 'happiness, relief, exhilaration, encouragement, dawn' (Nietzsche 1974: 280). He contemptuously claimed that modern society is based on an impoverished notion of happiness – the greatest happiness of the greatest number would eventually convert men into fattened pigs. 'If happiness is defined as the state of being man desires; if joy is defined as the conscious aspect of this state; and if pleasure is defined as a sensation marked by the absence of pain and discomfort; then Nietzsche's position can be summarized briefly: *happiness is the fusion of power and joy* – and joy contains not only ingredients of pleasure but also a component of pain' (Kaufmann 1974 [1950]: 278). For many who seek to interpret Nietzsche the man, the joy he experienced around the discovery of the idea of the eternal return was truly transformative at the end of his life.

In conclusion if we can agree that happiness was a recurrent theme in Nietzsche's philosophy, then what were its over-riding characteristics? Firstly it was radically secular. Nietzsche realized that Darwin's account of selection and survival made any presuppositions about divine intervention in shaping the world completely redundant. The evolution of nature was not according to any divine plan or design. It was largely the outcome of contingency and evolutionary accidents. All evolutionary outcomes were the accidental effects of habitat, resources and the struggle for mere survival. The death of God was the inevitable conclusion and consequently Nietzsche remained endlessly frustrated by the failure of his contemporaries to grasp his earth-shattering insight. His fundamental argument was that men had to shape their own lives and take responsibility for their own fate without the intervention of the gods or the comforting support of the Church.

Secondly Nietzsche was profoundly critical of modern society (and especially of the growing influence of Prussian militarism over Germany), and feared the negative consequences of capitalist industrialization. There could never be any comfortable relationship between modernity and individual happiness. Indeed he anticipated much of the criticism of capitalism that characterized the work of Weber, whose analysis of resentment and disenchantment in modernity had a distinct dependence on Nietzsche (Stauth and Turner 1988). Weber's famous thesis about Protestantism and capitalism described the connections between Calvinistic notions about hard work, discipline, accumulation and capitalism (Weber 1930). The Calvinist believer could not be confident about personal salvation and therefore the believer could not find happiness in this world. The modern world was a disenchanted garden where uncertainty was sublimated in hard work. Success in the form of wealth became an indirect but uncertain sign of salvation. Nietzsche writing in 1888 was equally clear about the problems of modernity. He condemned modernity for its nihilism – its lack of meaning. Contemporary interpretations of Nietzsche have attempted to show the relevance of his thinking to political theory (Ansell-Pearson 1994) by concentrating on the key idea of nihilism. He was affronted by the shallow optimism of economic measures of human endeavour:

> What I attack is that economic optimism which behaves as though, with the increasing expenditure of all, the welfare of all would also necessarily increase. To me the opposite seems to be the case; the sum total of the expenditure of all amounts to a total loss; man is diminished – indeed one no longer knows what purpose this immense process has served in the first place. A purpose? A new purpose – that is what mankind needs.
>
> NIETZSCHE 1968: section 886

As we have seen, Aristotle applied *eudaimonia* to both the state and the individual. It is only within a flourishing *polis* that men flourish. Nietzsche was of course critical of an all-powerful state that would rob men of their autonomy. Kaufmann (1974 [1950]: 164) claims that Nietzsche objects to the modern state because it is the power that subordinates men into conformity by intimidation. New Testament Christianity was originally a call not to conform, but to leave father and mother, and to perfect the self. In a corrupt and declining world, great souls must refashion values including their idea of happiness. The quest for genuine happiness was an individual quest that could not rest on either the Church or the state.

5 English Happiness: Nietzsche and J.S. Mill

For Nietzsche the experience of pain and suffering is connected to the ultimate experience of happiness, but it is only accidental to the pursuit of happiness in the sense that great souls must live through and beyond suffering. In the quest to become who they are, great souls will not be deterred by the accidents of pleasure or pain. Their goal is higher namely their self-fulfillment through the test of contingent suffering. While Nietzsche railed against Christianity, he was equally critical of the optimism of utilitarianism. He humorously noted that generally men do not strive for pleasure; only the English utilitarian philosophers do. He complained in *Beyond Good and Evil* about the 'indefatigable, inevitable English utilitarians... who want English morality to prevail... they would like with all their might to prove to themselves that to strive after English happiness... is at the same time the true path of virtue' (228).

He had three objections to utilitarianism. First it was a doctrine only suitable to the masses and not to great souls, who will rise above the vulgar needs of the herd. Second, it entailed a persistent confusion between pleasure and happiness. Third, he rejected the implicit optimism of the utilitarian doctrine that implied that all societies could improve and increase happiness with the correct social policies.

Kaufmann identifies a possible fourth objection by claiming that utilitarianism is an example of consequentialism. Regardless of intention, actions are good or valuable if they have good consequences such as increasing the happiness of the greatest number. Kaufmann claims that neither Christianity nor Kant nor Nietzsche's philosophy rests on consequentialism. Thus Kant crystallized 'the Western religious tradition, which commanded man to do good because God willed it, regardless of the consequences' and 'Nietzsche's generic conception of morality is best understood in terms of a brief contrast with the rival utilitarian definition' (Kaufmann 1974 [1950]: 212). He thus rejected Mill's argument that all a priori moral reasoning (such as Kant) would find utilitarian arguments 'indispensable.'

While Kaufmann may be correct in this claim, I suggest that he fails to see the interesting convergence between Mill and Nietzsche by overlooking the fact that Mill had rejected the simple hedonistic doctrines of both Jeremy Bentham and James Mill. Furthermore there is a remarkable convergence between Nietzsche and Mill with respect for example to art.

Mill is often referred to as a founding father in the establishment social science, but he was not a system founder. He was also one of the most important critics of early utilitarian doctrines. Mill abandoned the quantitative measurement of happiness that was associated with the early principles of utilitarianism. With his secular and quantitative notion of happiness in the form of a 'felicific calculus,' Bentham's ideas about happiness appeared in 1822 in 'The Influence of Natural Religion upon the Temporal Happiness of Mankind.' The arguments of the book were contentious and he published under the pseudonym of Philip Beauchamp. Bentham had elaborated the secular principle of the greatest happiness of the greatest number as the basis of the good society and in his critique of religion he argued that the promise of pleasure or pain in an after-life was not an efficient way of contributing to this-worldly happiness. Religious sanctions for good behaviour through pleasure were 'impotent' and gave rise to 'needless and unprofitable misery' (Bentham 2003: 93). He had to assume a minimal notion of happiness which could be measured in terms of its duration and intensity. He rejected the idea that different ends or forms of happiness were significant and famously announced in 1830 that 'the game of pushpin is of equal value with the arts and sciences of music and poetry' which was later misquoted by Mill as 'pushpin is as good as poetry.' Thus pleasures are calculable and all pleasures are quantitatively the equivalent.

Mill is famous for his defence of women's rights in *The Subjection of Women*. Nietzsche's father died young and he was raised in a household of five women. He resented his mother and his relationship to women was fraught with problems. Women played little or no overt role in his philosophy. In 1876 he proposed marriage unsuccessfully to Mathilde Trampedach. His romantic attachment to Cosima Wagner did not endure, but at the very end of his life in a letter to Jakob Burckhardt, he wrote simply 'The *rest* is for Frau Cosima' (Magee 2001: 296).

Mill went through a personal crisis in 1826–1827 and he came to realize that he was not happy. He concluded that the simple assumptions of Bentham's calculus were inadequate. Later he came recognize the importance of culture which could not be measured by any simple scheme. 'I, for the first time, gave its proper place, among the necessities of human well-being, to the internal culture of the individual… The cultivation of feelings became one of the cardinal points in my ethical and philosophical creed' (Mill 1971: 86). In 1851, he discovered personal happiness in his eventual marriage to Harriet Taylor. In *On Liberty* in 1859 he rejected any simple quantitative notion of happiness, but he recognized in the essay in 'Utilitarianism' that 'Questions about ends are, in other words, questions about what things are desirable. The utilitarian doctrine is, that happiness is desirable, and the only thing desirable, as an end; all other things being only desirable as means to that end' (Mill 1910: 32).

However the definition of happiness and its measurement remained obscure. In fact 'the sole evidence it is possible to produce that anything is desirable, is that people do actually desire it' (Mill 1910: 32). Despite the problems relating to its measurement, Mill concluded that liberty was a necessary condition for its enjoyment and this basic idea framed his discussion of 'The Subjection of Women' in 1869. He realized that 'while every restraint on the freedom of conduct of any of their human fellow creatures… dries up *pro tanto* the principal fountain of human happiness, and leaves the species less rich, to an inappreciable degree, in all that makes life valuable to the individual human being' (Mill 1989: 217).

Mill took the liberty of women seriously because their subjection was incompatible with the basic ideal of human liberty, and it was personal autonomy that he saw as crucial to happiness. People had to be free to pursue their own life course without unnecessary external constraints. Thus in *The Subjection of Women,* he concluded 'If there is anything vitally important to the happiness of individuals, it is that they should relish their habitual pursuits' (Mill 2006: 216). Whereas Nietzsche thought the quest for self-realization and autonomy could only be achieved by an elite, Mill generalized this view to people in general and women in particular.

Was Mill an optimistic with respect to the happiness-seeking potential of the masses in a democratic framework? When Mill read the second volume of Tocqueville's *Democracy in America* which was published in 1840 he came to fear the spread of democratic institutions and in particular the negative impact of any extension of the enfranchise to the masses on individual freedom of conscience and belief. Any premature or hasty extension of the franchise to an uneducated working class could only threaten the integrity of individual belief. Mass democracy without the reform of mass education would stifle social change. He continued to believe in the possibility of progress but in *Chapters on Socialism* he noted that socialism cannot be considered as 'the sole means of preventing the general degradation of the mass of mankind through the peculiar tendency of poverty to produce over-population. Society as at present constituted is not descending into that abyss, but gradually, though slowly, rising out of it, and this improvement is likely to be progressive if bad laws do not interfere with it' (Mill 2006: 251). The happiness of individuals relied on careful policies to balance the welfare of the mass and the interior life of the individual. In short Mill could reasonably be said to share with Nietzsche the view that enhancing the pleasure of the masses was a threat to the autonomy of the educated individual.

6 The Herd and Happiness Studies

Despite the unresolved debate about the definition of happiness, Happiness Studies, which began to develop in the 1970s, is a flourishing aspect of social science. Well-being, satisfaction and happiness are now key issues in economic theory (Bok 2010; Frey and Stutzer 2002). In addition happiness has become a growth industry in the academy. The *Journal of Happiness Studies* appeared in

2000 and *Psychology of Well Being* in 2011. Recognition of the economic study of happiness has been conferred by a Noble prize to Angus Deaton. However the original inspiration for looking at happiness as a measure of successful social policies came, not from prestigious economics departments, but from the remote Buddhist kingdom of Bhutan when in 1972 its new king Jigme Singye Wanchuk declared that Gross National Happiness would replace Gross National Product as the true measure of national progress. His index had four major dimensions – good governance and democratization; stable and equitable socioeconomic development, environmental protection, and preservation of culture. This has been a successful policy as measured for example by life expectancy which has risen from 43 years in 1982 to 66 years in this century (Bok 2010: 2). Various countries now have happiness measures including government ministers responsible for happiness.

In general terms societies with functional welfare states and democratic traditions such as Denmark, Finland, Switzerland, the Netherlands, and Sweden have citizens who express high levels of life-satisfaction. Those countries with a stable history of Westminster style democracy and steady economic growth, namely Australia ('The Lucky Country'), Canada and New Zealand are also highly ranked in terms of individual well-being (Veenhoven 1984). In world happiness surveys such as the United Nations *World Happiness Survey* (Helliwel, Layard, and Sachs 2015), 'optimal societies' have social stability over time, high productivity of goods and services, realization of national ideals and demonstrable levels of 'liveability' as measured by health and life satisfaction. Societies that have been ravaged by war, civil conflict, and natural disasters (Ethiopia, Iraq, Myanmar, and Tanzania) have generally low scores of happiness and life satisfaction.

What would Nietzsche make of these results? At one level they represent a challenge to Nietzsche's view that the herd can know only pleasure and not happiness. Both Nietzsche and Mill would object to the idea that something as complex as happiness could be measured by simple quantitative surveys. Nietzsche was above all a truth-seeker even when truth proved to be dangerous. Thus in *Beyond Good and Evil* (39) Nietzsche argued that 'Happiness and virtue are no arguments… Something might be true although at the same time harmful and dangerous in the highest degree.'

Modern notions of happiness have departed significantly from both the perspective of the ancient Greeks and from the biblical view that ultimately neither pleasure nor pain are relevant to a discussion of happiness as the ultimate goal of human endeavor. There is however an important difference between our understanding of happiness and the idea of self-development and autonomy in both the Greek and Christian worlds. If we focus on young people rather than on general populations, then there is a close association between consumption and happiness. Thus Christian Smith's survey of young American adults in *Lost in Transition* found that they characteristically associate personal happiness with consumption and their principal aim in life 'is to have the financial means to possess and consume material goods, enjoyable services and fulfilling experiences' (Smith 2011: 107). In the new environment of economic liberalism, consumption has become a measure of self-worth. What happens when this comfortable life style is challenged by economic down-turn, familial break-up or poor health?

Recent research has indicated an erosion of happiness as well-being and self-flourishing in the United States. In particular two publications by Anne Case and Angus Deaton (2017; 2015) have shown that there has been a consistent rise in mortality and morbidity rates in the United States over the last seventeen years among white non-Hispanic men especially in the age group 25–29. Income levels are not a critical factor and in previous work it was sown that after a certain level (around $75,000 per annum) increases in income do not produce significant increases in life-satisfaction (Deaton and Kahneman 2010). It is widely recognized that education is a key factor in explaining differences between social groups, but Case and Deaton argue that this particular group suffers from 'cumulative disadvantage over life' in the labour market, in marriage, and in society generally. This social group – often associated with populism and resentment against the prevailing political system – are typically referred to as the 'left behind' in a globalized economy.

Although these economic issues may explain some aspects of the sense of anomie in contemporary American society, a much more troublesome issue is the opioid epidemic which is described as America's worst drug dependency crisis. Opioids were originally prescribed to manage pain often associated with work-related injuries or sporting activities. The U.S. Department of Health and Human Services Fact Sheet reports that 33,000 people died from an opioid-related overdose in 2015. On any average day, 650,000 people start on opioid prescriptions and 580 people initiate heroin use. In the current market, heroin is often cheaper than prescription opioids and hence when users can no longer afford or have access to opioids, they change to heroin.

From Nietzsche's perspective, Happiness Studies, as a version of utilitarianism, offer an optimistic picture of an affluent and democratic society, but one in which there is considerable unhappiness associated with widespread drug dependency. This dependency is not confined to the economically marginalized and it is widespread in the U.S. from California to New Hampshire. Because in Nietzsche's scheme happiness cannot be separated from personal autonomy and self-creation, drug dependency is a form of personal slavery.

7 Conclusion: Fate and Virtu

Let me in conclusion return to Aristotle for whom happiness was conjoined with virtue, but if so how is it obtained? If happiness is a matter of chance – we are born into a wealthy household to loving parents – then how is happiness the product of the striving of a great soul? Misfortune can nevertheless strike at a wealthy as much as a poor citizen. If happiness were to be achieved merely by chance, then it could not carry the ethical weight he wants to attach to it. We should pay close attention therefore to the literal meaning of *eu-daimonia*. Happiness is indeed the result of the good chance (*eu*) or intervention of a spirit or demon. Aristotle struggled to give a satisfactory account of happiness that is not based on status or wealth, but based on virtue. Aristotle defined happiness as 'a certain activity of the soul in accord with complete virtue' (1.13.5).

Virtue (*virtu*) is important in a world where fortune (*Fortuna*) is so fickle. The contrast was originally based on gender. *Fortuna* is female and fickle, while *virtu* is derived from *vir* or the root of virility. Much of western thought has been framed within this contrast between *virtu* and *Fortuna*. The virtuous man was one, who drawing upon his virility, could nevertheless survive misfortune and find happiness (self-fulfilment) despite the tribulations arising from life's contingencies. With the ever-present threat of misfortune, a great soul can flourish, whereas the herd, mired in feeling pleasure, cannot survive.

It is here that I can introduce the idea of *amor fati* or love of fate and its connection to the eternal return that filled Nietzsche with joy. The idea was first introduced in Book IV of *The Gay Science* where Nietzsche (1974: 223) made a new resolution – 'some day I wish only to be a Yes-sayer.' By living in such a manner, human beings can construct their lives as a work of art even against the mundane vicissitudes of ageing and physical decay.

We also need to stress that the mature Nietzsche saw life as an unpredictable flow of events in a universe that is chaotic rather than law-like. This vision signals his definitive departure from any Judeo-Christian notion of a created natural world that is orderly. However, Nietzsche's *amor fati* is not fatalism but rather an active engagement with whatever befalls one or at least it is the mark of the *ubermensch* that they are not dismayed by the apparent wilfulness of unanticipated events. Furthermore, as we have seen, pain and suffering are both the inevitable bed-fellows of fortune. Looking back to *The Birth of Tragedy*, this active reconciliation with fate gives rise to joy or what we might describe as Dionysian rapture. In *Ecce Homo* he celebrated how a great soul 'wants nothing different, not forward, not backward, not in all eternity. Not merely bear what is necessary, still less conceal it – all idealism is mendaciousness in the face of what is necessary- but *love* it.' This end state is clearly outside the realm of quantitative measures of pain and pleasure in Bentham's attempt to quantify happiness. Furthermore happiness is not about comfort or pleasure. For Nietzsche is connected with power, namely the strength necessary to embrace one's fate.

Let me conclude this discussion with some consideration of Martha Nussbaum's discussion of Aristotle in *The Fragility of Goodness* (1986). She notes that for the Greeks ethics involved 'the aspiration to rational self-sufficiency' (Nussbaum 1986: 3) and as a consequence contingency in life or the intervention of bad luck were a critical challenge to this quest for self-sufficiency. Happiness is thus an activity directed towards the good life in the face of contingency and bad luck. On this basis (and following both Aristotle and Nietzsche) she is critical of the translation of *eudaimonia* in terms of pleasure. With the heritage of both Kantian ethics and utilitarianism, happiness is 'the name of a feeling of contentment or pleasure, and a view that gives supreme value to psychological states rather than to activities... To the Greeks *eudaimonia* means something like "living a good life for a human being"' (Nussbaum 1986: 6).

It is virtue that produces happiness rather than wealth and consumption. However in his 'revaluation of values' in *Twilight of the Idols* (2003) Nietzsche reverses this relationship of cause and effect to proclaim that 'virtue is the consequence of happiness' (2: 4). What can we make of this formula that on the surface looks like an arbitrary reversal? Kaufmann interprets this reversal as meaning those who adhere unthinkingly to conventional moral guidelines are weak and in fact will not obtain true happiness. Only those who have already attained a state of happiness through pain and suffering will behave virtuously.

References

Ansell-Pearson, Keith. 1994. *An Introduction to Nietzsche as Thinker: The Perfect Nihilist.* Cambridge: Cambridge University Press.

Aristotle. 1926. *Nicomachean Ethics.* Cambridge, MA: Harvard University Press.

Augustine. 1912. *Confessions.* Cambridge, MA: Harvard University Press.

Bentham, Jeremy. 2003. *The Influence of Natural Religion on the Temporal Happiness of Mankind.* New York: Prometheus Books.

Bok, Derek. 2010. *The Politics of Happiness.* Princeton, NJ: Princeton University Press.

Case, Anne, and Angus Deaton. 2017. 'Mortality and Morbidity in the 21st Century.' *Brookings Papers* (conference version).

Case, Anne, and Angus Deaton. 2015. 'Rising Morbidity and Mortality in Mid-Lie among White Non-Hispanics in the 21 Century.' *Proceedings of the Academy of Science* 112(49): 15078–15083.

Chamberlain, Lesley. 1997. *Nietzsche in Turin.* New York: Picador.

Deaton, Angus, and Daniel Kahneman. 2010. 'High Income Improves Evaluation of Life but not Emotional Well Being.' *Proceedings of the Academy of Science* 107(38): 16489–16493.

Frey, Bruno S., and Alois Stutzer. 2002. *Happiness & Economics.* Princeton, NJ: Princeton University Press.

Helliwell, John, Richard Layard, and Jeffrey Sachs, eds. 2015. *World Happiness Report.* United Nations, OECD.

Hughes, H. Stuart. 1959. *Consciousness and Society: The Reorientation of European Social Thought 1890–1930.* London: MacGibbon & Kee.

Kaufmann, Walter. 1974 [1950]. *Nietzsche: Philosopher, Psychologist, AntiChrist.* Princeton, NJ: Princeton University Press.

Magee, Bryan. 2001. *Wagner and Philosophy.* London: Penguin Books.

McMahon, Darrin M. 2006. *Happiness: A History.* New York: Grove Press.

Mill, John Stuart. 2006.*On Liberty and the Subjection of Women*, edited by Alan Ryan. London: Penguin Classics.

Mill, John Stuart. 1989. *J.S. Mill: On Liberty and Other Writings*, edited by Stefan Collini. Cambridge: Cambridge University Press.

Mill, John Stuart. 1971. *Autobiography*, edited by Jack Stillinger. New York: Oxford University Press.

Mill, John Stuart. 1910. 'Utilitarianism.' In *Utilitarianism, Liberty and Representative Government.* London: J.M. Dent & Sons.

Newman, Ernst. 1946. *The Life of Richard Wagner.* New York: Knopf.

Nietzsche, Friedrich. 2003. *Twilight of the Idols.* New York: Penguin Books.

Nietzsche, Friedrich. 1996. *Human, All too Human: A Book for Free Spirits*, translated by R.J. Hollingdale. Cambridge: Cambridge University Press.

Nietzsche, Friedrich. 1987. *Philosophy in the Tragic Age of the Greeks*, translated by Marianne Cowan. Washington, DC: Regnery Publishing.

Nietzsche, Friedrich. 1980. *Ecce Homo: How One Becomes What One Is.* Harmondsworth: Penguin Books.

Nietzsche, Friedrich. 1974. *The Gay Science*, translated by Walter Kaufmann. New York: Vintage Books.

Nietzsche, Friedrich. 1973. *Beyond Good and Evil.* Harmondsworth: Penguin.

Nietzsche, Friedrich. 1968. *The Will to Power*, translated by Walter Kaufman and R.J. Hollingdale. New York: Vintage Books.

Nietzsche, Friedrich. 1967. *The Birth of Tragedy.* New York: Vintage Books.

Nussbaum, Martha C. 1986. *The Fragility of Goodness: Luck and Ethics in Greek Tragedy and Philosophy.* Cambridge: Cambridge University Press.

Schacht, Richard. 1983. *Nietzsche.* London: Routledge.

Siemans, Herman W., and Vasti Roodt, eds. 2008. *Nietzsche, Power and Politics: Rethinking the Legacy of Nietzsche's Political Thought.* Berlin: de Gruyter.

Smith, Christian. 2011. *Lost in Transition: The Dark Side of Emerging Adulthood.* Oxford: Oxford University Press.

Stauth, Georg, and Bryan S. Turner. 1988. *Nietzsche's Dance. Resentment, Reciprocity and Resistance in Social Life.* Oxford: Basil Blackwell.

Tocqueville, Alexis de. 2000 *Democracy in America.* Chicago: Univcersity of Chicago Press.

Turner, Bryan S. 2018. '(I Can't Get No) Satisfaction: Happiness and Successful Societies.' *Journal of Sociology* 54(3): 279–293.

Turner, Bryan S. 1981. *For Weber. Essays on the Sociology of Fate.* Boston, London and Henley: Routledge & Kegan Paul.

Turner, Bryan S., and Yuri Contreras-Vejar. 2018. 'Happiness.' In *The Wiley Blackwell Encyclopedia of Social Theory*, Volume III, edited by Bryan. S. Turner, 1030–1037. Chichester: Wiley.

Veenhoven, Ruut. 1984. *Conditions of Happiness.* Dordrecht: Springer.

Weber, Max. 1930. *The Protestant Ethic and the Spirit of Capitalism.* London: Allen & Unwin.

CHAPTER 19

Beyond Good and Evil: Nietzschean Pedagogy in the History Classroom

Eve Kornfeld

1 Introduction

The last paper in the last session on the last day of an intense, interdisciplinary, international conference on Nietzsche and Critical Social Theory seemed to be the perfect moment for a Nietzschean inversion. To match the spirit of this invigorating conference, as well as to demonstrate the pedagogy I wished to discuss, I began my talk in a most unorthodox fashion: rather than reading a paper and then inviting questions or comments from the audience, I began by asking the leading Nietzsche scholars and students gathered before me to share their own first experiences reading and teaching Nietzsche. Startled though some may have been by this inversion of the traditional conference paper format, they rose to the occasion and warmed to our subject. Scholars and students (including several veterans of my classes) spoke about their personal encounters and struggle with Nietzsche, some reaching back many decades, some only a year or two. They listened and responded to each other; eminent scholars, graduate students and undergraduates found common ground in their initial confusions and continuing fascination with Nietzsche. I then shared my own first encounter with Nietzsche, the evolution and elements of my Nietzschean pedagogy, and my longitudinal research on my students' reactions. Our lively conversation continued in the question period and beyond, again with some striking inversions, as the scholars asked questions of my students, who eagerly testified as experts in Nietzschean pedagogy. Mirroring this unorthodox session, this article eschews a smooth, objective, omniscient narrative; I will use the first person to describe a session and pedagogical approach that inverted traditional structures of authority to create new relationships between teacher-scholars, students, and texts.

2 Beginnings

The room was surprisingly full, for the last session of the last day of a packed conference. Among those attending were the distinguished scholars Douglas

Kellner of the University of California, Los Angeles (the conference's keynote speaker), Babette Babich of Fordham University (a plenary session speaker), and Martin Schwab of the University of California, Irvine (who led off our session with a learned lecture on Walter Benjamin's view of history), as well as numerous graduate students in sociology, political science, history, and philosophy. I had personally invited two SDSU colleagues: Emily Hicks, a conference presenter and professor of Chicana/o Studies, with whom I had worked on an interdisciplinary Humanities project sponsored by the American Council of Learned Societies many years before, and Patricia Cué-Couttolenc, professor of Graphic Design, with whom I was preparing to teach an Arts Alive SDSU Collaborative Course on images of childhood. Moderating the session was my graduate student, Derek Bell. Scattered around the room were Christian Alvarado, Megan Bacik, Jana Peale, Jasmine Tocki, and Linnea Zeiner, all of whom had studied Nietzsche with me at some point over the last five years in my upper-division, undergraduate/ graduate History course, "Intellectuals in Twentieth-century Europe." They had participated in the longitudinal research on student reactions to Nietzsche that I had conducted for this conference, and they were quite curious to see what I planned to do with it. As I rose to conclude the session and the conference, I knew about one-third of the audience to be free spirits, and I had high hopes that the rest would also be open to an intellectual adventure.

Although some raised eyebrows greeted my initial announcement that my portion of the session would invert the traditional conference structure, starting with discussion among the audience before I presented the results of my research, there was also marked interest in my initial questions. I asked those assembled to reflect and share whatever they could remember about their first encounter with Nietzsche, and specifically what they recalled about their experience reading and discussing his work for the first time. After a brief pause to plumb their memories, the rich, personal narratives began to pour out. Douglas Kellner led the way, recalling in considerable detail how he struggled to understand Nietzsche many years before in high school, and how his reading made him "an existentialist." Martin Schwab had also first read Nietzsche many years before as a young student in Germany; he confided that he had wrestled with small bits of the text to extract their meaning, reading and rereading only parts of Nietzsche's book, but returning again and again to it. An undergraduate underscored Professor Kellner's existential narrative, explaining that she had first read pieces of Nietzsche after suffering a debilitating injury and found his dark tone strangely curative. Several other undergraduates and graduate students noted that they had had to read tiny portions of text over and over again to try to understand it; Nietzsche was the most difficult reading they had ever done, and they had entered their first discussion of his work convinced that they had not comprehended anything. Many heads nodded in agreement. Eminent scholars and students alike had first encountered Nietzsche as a fascinating but frustrating puzzle, and had struggled hard to find meaning in fragments of text. Reading Nietzsche had been one of the greatest intellectual challenges of their lives.

My next question invited the participants to reflect upon how they taught Nietzsche to their students, and specifically whether their pedagogy mirrored their first encounter with Nietzsche or differed from it in some way. A substantial subset of the first speakers responded to these questions, basing their answers on years of teaching in the case of Professors Kellner and Schwab or on just one or two recent attempts in the case of the graduate students. Kellner and Schwab both contextualized and provided guidelines for their students in lectures that preceded their students' first encounter with Nietzsche. Using their knowledge of the full range and development of Nietzsche's work, they smoothed out the difficulties in the particular text their students would read to help them see the larger picture. Their students read more easily than they had done, perhaps skimming over the more difficult passages, and accepting their professorial guides' word for their meaning. Some of the graduate students complained that it was all but impossible to induce their students to read and discuss Nietzsche. To fill the stony silence that greeted their attempts to engage their students in discussion, they turned to lectures.

I then shared my own first encounter with Nietzsche, as an undergraduate in Carl Schorske's class in European Intellectual History at Princeton. Professor Schorske also prefaced his students' reading with lectures – and not just any lectures, but beautifully crafted, intellectually compelling interpretations that placed Nietzsche's thought in the context of the crisis of European liberalism that he had studied for more than thirty years. Like his (1980) masterpiece, *Fin-de-Siècle Vienna: Politics and Culture*, Schorske's lectures drew upon an astonishing range of disciplines and thinkers to offer a sophisticated, nuanced, interconnected portrait of European intellectuals' withdrawal from politics as a fragile liberalism collapsed around them.[1] They drew reverent awe from his undergraduate students, including me. But I was one of those students who could not wait to open any book that came into my hands, so I had starting reading Nietzsche alone (slowly, painfully, angrily, but also with a growing sense of delight and liberation) as soon as I had purchased the course books.

1 My appreciation for Carl Schorske's unsurpassed understanding of European cultural history, and his commitment to his students' intellectual development, deepened as I served as his research assistant while a graduate student. His enduring influence on everyone who studied with him was profound.

I was full of questions, problems, and objections, only some of which were addressed by Schorske's masterful lectures or in my preceptorial (Princeton's small discussion sections) led by a junior faculty member who specialized in Russian economic history. I wrestled with some of them in my final essay, but left the course vaguely uneasy and dissatisfied, wishing to read the rest of Nietzsche's work for myself. Fortunately, graduate school afforded the opportunity to do just that. I developed my own interpretation to add to that of Schorske and my other mentors, and I was ready and eager to share it.

When offered the opportunity to teach a course of my own design as an advanced graduate student at Harvard and then in my first teaching appointment at Princeton, I adopted my mentors' pedagogical structure. I gave my students contextual lectures as a preface to their reading of the challenging texts I had selected. Despite my urging to encounter the difficult texts directly, even confrontationally, my students were quite relieved to depend upon my guidance; indeed, they requested discussion questions in advance, to accompany my lectures, to smooth out the rough edges and direct them to the "most important parts." The situation did not improve when I moved to San Diego State University. My new students had read only pre-digested snippets (the academic equivalent of thirty-second political sound bites) in the anthologies and textbooks that had filled their careers before they entered my course. When I handed them Nietzsche's *Beyond Good and Evil* as the first reading assignment in my upper-division course on "Intellectuals in Twentieth-century Europe," the resistance was overt. Many of them claimed to appreciate my lectures that were designed to set the stage for their reading, but they saw no point in grappling with the difficult text themselves. Their competing obligations (working far too many hours, caring for families, rushing through 18 units or more per semester to graduate before tuition rose again) seemed much more important than struggling through a dense, apparently contradictory reading. They were quite comfortable to simply receive my interpretation – all too comfortable.[2]

Even more disturbing, those obedient students who did attempt to read Nietzsche after my introductory lectures became frustrated and resentful. I had carefully selected the first six parts of *Beyond Good and Evil* to introduce the ideas that would shape and transform intellectual life in the twentieth century, and I considered the reading assignment reasonable for an upper-division course. My students did not. Rather than carefully weighing and playing with Nietzsche's language, contradictions, and challenges, they rushed to finish the

2 Babette Babich's insightful question during our conference session about the roots of my pedagogical crisis sparked this series of reflections.

reading in a couple of hours before class. They found the difficulty of the text "useless" and tedious, the contradictions a sign of "bad" thinking and writing, and the length excessive. Most problematic, they reacted to Nietzsche's genealogy of morals and transvaluation of values with precisely the traditional morals and values he was critiquing; reading quickly and superficially, they objected to his sexist, anti-Christian, and anti-Semitic passages as immoral and reprehensible. Purposefully misinterpreting/ distorting my lectures that situated *Beyond Good and Evil* within Nietzsche's intellectual development and life, they reduced his work to incoherent ranting, a symptom of insanity. Their initial encounter with Nietzsche did set the tone for their subsequent reading, but certainly not in the liberating manner I had envisioned: with a similar moralistic gesture, they would next dismiss Sigmund Freud's *Interpretation of Dreams* as the delusions of a cocaine addict. Encountering Nietzsche failed to move my students beyond good and evil.

These realizations had brought me to a crisis of liberalism of my own. As a first-generation college graduate, I hoped that my students' college educations would be as transformative as mine had been. I wanted my classrooms to be liminal spaces in which my students could explore ideas that would challenge the social and intellectual boundaries that delimited their lives. I sought to empower them to think critically and act creatively; probing the historical construction of supposedly eternal verities and immutable categories such as good and evil seemed an essential step along this path. I resisted narrow, commercial definitions of utility and productivity. Especially this course, which traced my own intellectual journey from physics to psychology to art and music to literature to history, and included so many intellectuals whose work had enriched my life, had to be liberating for my students. It was my dessert when I could be spared from my bread-and-butter assignments teaching General Education U.S. History surveys. I could not allow my students to consume it on the run between their mind-numbing, repetitive jobs. And the liberating process all seemed to begin with Nietzsche.

I knew from my own experience that the transformational power of lectures was severely limited. Even those of us with well-developed auditory skills, listening to the most exquisitely crafted lectures, rarely felt the full impact of the complex concepts embedded in them. Our minds would wander, triggered by external stimuli or an errant thought of our own. My students, who had little experience following complicated lectures, too little sleep, far more distractions, and perhaps linguistic or learning challenges, were still less likely to engage personally with the disturbing ideas in a lecture. They rarely even tried to take notes, to augment their underdeveloped auditory skills with another learning style. However disruptive the content of my lectures might be to the received wisdom they brought to the class, it was unlikely to shake their resistance to thinking critically about the carefully-constructed structures and categories (especially the invisible category of social class) that filled American political and popular culture. They had been well trained in schools, churches, and media of all sorts to equate freedom with material consumption. Remembering my own initial resistance to Nietzsche (were his "herd" or "slaves" thinly-veiled allusions to the working class?) and Freud, I understood my students' reluctance to peel away powerful cultural values to discover latent meanings and alternative visions of freedom. If they were truly to encounter these dangerous thinkers and ideas, they would have to do so through experiential learning rather than lectures. But I had no idea how to create such an experience.

3 Time Passes[3]

Years passed before I was able to teach my "Intellectuals in Twentieth-century Europe" again. California's horrendous, recurring budget crises and the pressure on fewer and fewer faculty to meet more and more students' demand for graduation requirements (including the American Institutions General Education requirement that my U.S. History surveys satisfied) forced me into a twelve-year stint teaching 500-student courses. I taught thousands of students what I could about America's polyphonic past – and Nietzsche was all but forgotten.

The only silver lining in these cloudy years came in my weekly seminar discussions of pedagogy with my 8 graduate Teaching Assistants. As I guided their attempts to overcome our students' anomie and engage them in discussion sections, I read about, reflected upon, experimented with, and reformulated various strategies for active learning. By the end of this stormy period, when I was finally able to return to "small" (150-student) U.S. History surveys and an occasional elective course of my choosing, many of SDSU's programs were impacted and admission was more selective. My students – more diverse, more ambitious, and ever more directed by economic woes and worried parents to vocational majors and clear career paths – had changed. And so had my pedagogy.

3 Admirers of Virginia Woolf's *To the Lighthouse* will recognize this evocation of a crucial interlude in which external events alter everything. See Woolf (1927: Part II "Time Passes").

4 Inversions/Subversions

Inversions of all sorts marked my new Nietzschean pedagogy. Structurally, I inverted my previous (conventional) approach: I no longer provided context or guidance for my students' reading in preliminary lectures or discussion questions; in fact, I no longer lectured at all, simply adding my comments to the mix in the course of our seminar discussion. Nor did I allow other scholars to introduce Nietzsche and mediate my students' initial encounter with the text. Our first reading was Nietzsche's *Beyond Good and Evil*, admittedly one of the most challenging of the semester. Embracing the difficulty with Nietzschean zest – and without mediation – would create a true seminar, for my students would have to work together to divine its meaning(s).

I still considered the first six parts of the book essential reading. But now, following Nietzsche's lead, I divided these six parts into shorter, more manageable reading assignments, asking each student to read just one part deeply, slowly, and perhaps repeatedly before our seminar discussion. As in any "flipped" class without lectures, students were responsible for researching whatever they did not understand (words in several languages, references to other philosophers, historical allusions, religious traditions, etc.) before coming to seminar. Much more than in flipped science classes that provide predetermined recorded video lectures, however, my students were set free to query anything and to follow their own individual paths to understanding the part they had read. I encouraged them to come to seminar with questions, reactions, and interpretations as diverse as their personal cultural and academic experiences; they would be the experts who would guide the rest of us in understanding their parts. The inverted structure, then, also subverted traditional expectations of authority in the classroom.

At the start of the seminar, the students who had read the same part gathered in a small circle to share their questions, confusions, reactions, and interpretations. This allowed those with less experience or confidence to test their reading before explaining their part to the whole class. Again, I resisted the temptation to guide the small groups too much, or to lead them to my interpretation. I asked each group to consider and discuss among themselves Nietzsche's central question, argument, language, logic, structure, and surprises, as well as their reactions to the part they had read. Fragments, failures and reversals could be productive, I noted, invoking Nietzsche's example. I reminded them that we sought a diversity of interpretations, and warned that premature consensus would limit our imaginations and understanding, as well as being coercive and inimical to a free seminar discussion.

As I circled the room, I encouraged the quieter members of each group to speak and the more active members to listen, and gently urged those who experienced difficulty in listening to other students to consider whether this might be another, subtle manifestation of Nietzsche's will to power. When the seminar was large (35 students in one semester), I also asked each group to write their most important thoughts – including their disagreements or problems – on the whiteboard; this request afforded shy or diffident students, who often served as group scribes, another opportunity to articulate their group's interpretation, either in writing or by coaching other writers. Often this assumption of responsibility and control enabled the quieter students to find their voices in the subsequent discussion. Examining and upsetting relationships of power among more and less dominant students before they could become established in our seminar, then, our Nietzschean pedagogy – supplemented by experiential learning for both active and passive students – stretched everyone's comfort zone and emphasized the group's collective responsibility to engage directly and creatively with the text.

Finally, when most of the small groups appeared ready, we formed a large circle to listen to each group present its interpretation(s) of its part, answer other students' and my questions about it, and add to our seminar's developing understanding of the complexity of Nietzsche's thought. Majority and minority views, appreciation and dissent, were aired in an environment of free but respectful contention with each other and with Nietzsche. I offered my interpretation, laced with irony and potential contradictions/alternative readings, as one of many within the seminar discussion. I felt and expressed delight in hearing interpretations at variance with my own, asking only that my students support their arguments with references to the text and/or context. Our emphasis was on uncovering contradictions, opening up students' questions, and revealing puzzles and ambiguities in the text. In the most important inversion of a traditional lecture course, we reached no resolution of our divergent readings and reactions at the end of our seminar discussion. We left Nietzsche, as he might have wished, with unanswered questions and interpretative problems that would demand a return engagement.

And return to Nietzsche we did, predictably as we read and discussed Freud, Joyce, Sartre, and Foucault over the coming weeks, but also unexpectedly in relation to our reading of Brecht, Orwell, Heisenberg, Stravinsky, and even Woolf. At first, my probing questions invited my students to connect Nietzsche to the intellectuals who followed. With accelerating frequency and intensity, however, their own intertextual references punctuated our discussions, leading to insights I had not anticipated. The inverted pedagogy with which we had approached Nietzsche enriched every seminar discussion of the semester. By the end of the semester, when my students presented their semester-long individual research on intellectuals of the Cold War and post-colonial world in two separate group presentations, they were completely comfortable in taking center stage and sharing their divergent interpretations and metacognitive reflections with the class. Without prompting or hesitation, they also traced Nietzsche's intellectual legacy around the post-war/post-colonial world. They had taken control of their own learning and of the seminar, in large part because they had struggled together to understand Nietzsche – and become empowered in the process.

These were my observations of students' responses to my new Nietzschean pedagogy in five classes (three upper-division undergraduate and graduate History courses, and two exclusively undergraduate Honors courses) on "Intellectuals in Twentieth-century Europe" between 2012 and 2016. But would the students who had taken those classes with me agree with my view of the process and outcome? In preparation for this conference paper, I undertook a longitudinal research project to find out. Using sdsu's Blackboard system in fall 2016, I emailed a questionnaire to all of the students who had studied Nietzsche with me in these five classes, explaining that I craved their answers to four sets of questions about their initial reading, first seminar discussion, and subsequent thoughts about Nietzsche. I pledged that I would present their answers without identifying information at a conference on Nietzsche in January and perhaps subsequently in publication. Nearly half of my former students responded to my request, a phenomenal response rate for such a survey, especially since some of the old email addresses on Blackboard were no longer active. Clearly, their immersion in Nietzschean pedagogy had had an impact on my students; a few even responded while at home with their families for the holidays after finishing final papers and examinations. Although some had not heard from me in years, they still wanted to share their experiences and reflections about Nietzsche.

My first set of questions asked what my students recalled about reading Nietzsche for the first time: "What was your initial reaction to reading Nietzsche's *Beyond Good and Evil* before our first seminar discussion? What did you think of his style, argument, language, structure, ideas, etc.? Did you struggle with or against them in any way?" I was struck by the intensity of the responses, even those that were retrieved from memories of five years before. My students remembered wrestling, often self-consciously and painfully, with Nietzsche's language, fragmentary style, and arguments. They had looked things up, read and re-read difficult passages, and struggled with the arguments. Their initial reactions were frequently personal and decidedly polarized: while a few jumped for joy and registered self-recognition and affirmation as they read, others resisted his gendered images and/or his genealogy of morals and view of religion. Their resistance was much deeper and more thoughtful than the superficial rejection of Nietzsche's supposed immorality I had come to expect from years before; most recognized that Nietzsche was urging them to question the categories that structured their lives, and they feared the possible consequences.

I next asked a series of questions about our first seminar discussion of the semester: "What was your reaction to our first seminar discussion of Nietzsche's *Beyond Good and Evil*? Were you intrigued, frustrated, confused, convinced, satisfied, dissatisfied, or something else? Did you resist or embrace his ideas, style, and inconclusive/contradictory endings? Did you wish to argue with him?" Once again, my students registered intense reactions that had not faded over time. The free-wheeling conversation in their small groups had been a revelation to many, who had never participated in an open-ended seminar discussion before. Many remarked upon their great surprise at hearing the widely varying interpretations and reactions of their fellow students; how people who had read the same part of the book could have arrived at such different conclusions about its central questions, arguments and surprises had filled them with wonder. They had felt great interest in their own small group's preliminary discussion, as well as the other groups' presentations of their parts. Tracing the (convoluted) development of Nietzsche's arguments between the parts had seemed like an intriguing puzzle, and they marveled at how much more they understood in the seminar than when reading alone. Some were frustrated by the lack of resolution and definitiveness at the end of the reading and the seminar, while others appreciated Nietzsche's inconclusive conclusions – and a seminar that refused to tie up all the loose ends and resolve all the disturbing contradictions, problems and ambiguities before putting Nietzsche back on the shelf.

Recalling their rich intertextual references, my third set of questions probed my students' developing understanding of Nietzsche through the rest of the semester: "Did your reactions to Nietzsche change at all as the course considered other intellectuals' responses, resistance, or debts to Nietzsche? Did you understand Nietzsche better after reading Freud, Joyce, Sartre, or other 20c intellectuals? Did you like him more or less over the course of the semester?" In accordance with their many intertextual connections at the time, many of my former students reported developing a deeper appreciation of Nietzsche as the course turned to Freud, Joyce, Sartre, and Foucault, among other thinkers. Some had reversed their initial evaluation of Nietzsche as hopelessly obscure, as they traced echoes of his toppling of traditional categories in subsequent thinkers. A few noted that they did not really appreciate Nietzsche until they saw traces of his thought in apparently unconnected, distant intellectuals like Virginia Woolf or George Orwell. Two found Nietzsche's thought resonating surprisingly in their research on post-colonial writers and artist/musicians, and deepened their understanding of Nietzsche through their research group's performance. Most regarded Nietzsche more favorably as they returned to him with new questions shaped by their subsequent seminar reading and individual research; hence their intertextual references over the course of the semester and their enhanced memory of him several years later.

Finally, I asked my former students whether Nietzsche was a part of their lives after our seminar ended: "Looking back on your encounter with Nietzsche one or two or several years later, what do you remember most vividly about reading and discussing his work? Have you ever returned to him or discussed him with anyone outside the course? Do you think reading and discussing Nietzsche changed the way you read or think in any way?" A surprisingly large number of my students had discussed Nietzsche with friends or relatives outside our seminar. Some had read Nietzsche again (a few repeatedly) after the course ended, and two reported that Nietzsche had shaped their Masters theses in fundamental ways. One included Nietzsche in the undergraduate courses that she had just started teaching, attempting to carry her own appreciation of Nietzsche to her own students. While many vividly recalled their struggle with Nietzsche's language(s) and subversive ideas on first reading and discussion, some noted that the experience transformed the way they read (more slowly, deeply, and critically) and thought (more freely and intertextually) forever. They found his call for "free spirits" unique and liberating, and aspired to live dangerously.

Overall, my former students' recollections and reflections confirmed what I had observed in the five seminars I had oriented around a Nietzschean pedagogy between 2012 and 2016. Their reactions and resistances upon reading Nietzsche for the first time were informed, self-conscious, and personal; their experiences in their first seminar discussions were free and intense; and they returned to Nietzsche with greater understanding and appreciation both during our subsequent seminar discussions and while conducting their (apparently unconnected) individual research on post-war, post-colonial intellectuals around the world. Most significantly, many continued to read Nietzsche, and even to discuss his thought and writing with friends and family, after the course ended; some registered surprise, but also pleasure, at my invitation to continue the conversation years after their initial encounter with Nietzsche. Their struggle with and against Nietzsche enhanced the possibilities for serious engagement in my students' reading and thinking; some expressed a desire to become "free spirits" after discussing Nietzsche. A Nietzschean pedagogy led my students to a difficult and sometimes uncomfortable encounter, but one with tremendous transformative possibilities.

5 Endings

It seems appropriate to end a paper on Nietzschean pedagogy and inversions with my former students' own voices – just as those of my students who attended our unorthodox conference session brought it to a close by describing to the eminent scholars and quizzical graduate students present how our Nietzschean pedagogy had empowered them. Here, then, are sample quotations from the survey I conducted in December 2016 of my former students' recollections of their initial encounters and later reflections on Nietzsche. They were selected for their richness or insight, organized roughly by the category of question addressed (although not all of my students' responses maintained strict divisions), and edited lightly to remove personally identifying information and to avoid repetition. Undergraduate and graduate, History and Honors students' reactions are jumbled together as randomly as possible. Perhaps inevitably in a paper on Nietzschean pedagogy and inversions/subversions, this selection of my former students' responses to Nietzsche closes (rather than concludes) with a haunting, heartfelt, unanswerable, existential question.

6 On Reading

"When I first read *Beyond Good and Evil*, I expected a continuation of the ideas of 18th century philosophers and others that I was familiar with. What I encountered was an intellectual who was taking the work of his precursors and not only turning on its head but throwing it out all together. At the end of the reading I had more questions than answers. Why was he so dead-set against religion? Why did he believe himself a free spirit?"

"I was very confused by Nietzsche's message before our discussion about the text. I found myself rereading passages multiple times and doing research online in order to find meaning in some of his statements. When we began to discuss the book, it became much more clear. Upon first reading the book, I struggled with how cynical and dark Nietzsche's tone and messages were. Some of his condemnations about religion, morality, and groups of people in general made me uncomfortable. I did enjoy how each chapter of his book was connected to the other chapters, but did not contain a traditional chronological order like many other books. … The main argument I have with Nietzsche would be his treatment of women and his apparent prejudice toward them. If those with strong morals are able to find their own prejudices and assumptions, I feel that Nietzsche should be able to examine his own prejudices against women."

"My initial reaction to *Beyond Good and Evil* was one of disagreement. While it was well written, and I agreed that man may not be good in and of himself, evidenced to me by the actions of my uncle, I rejected the idea that there are some people, or groups of people, who are superior to their fellow man. I tended to disagree with Nietzsche even after the discussions, but wanted to be able to do it in person. It would be interesting should time travel ever become possible."

"I remember seeing myself a lot in his writing. His ideas (to an extent) mirror much of what I believe, but that's mostly along the whole "god is dead" line. I remember my initial reaction was overwhelmingly positive. I may be rather the cynic, but Nietzsche's ideas really spoke to me."

"Nietzsche was really an introduction to the HIST582 course for me, being situated early on in the syllabus. His word selection and phrasing was something completely different than I had ever encountered before and I remember feeling very enthralled, inspired, and energized even from the pace of his thoughts. I perceived his argument at the time to be attacking the systems around him and that he perhaps had previously "bought into" in his own studies. He projected vehemence and extremely sharp witted attacks as only someone can who has stepped outside of their comfort zone and alienated themselves for survival. I still love this about Nietzsche. In fact, he's rather like taking a shot of espresso laced with gunpowder-he wakes you up by shaking (or threatening) your constitution. There was no struggle for me in his unique language nor his brazenly brilliant ideas. In fact, I rather felt like running around campus clutching my kindle and screaming in vindication, amen."

7 On Discussion

"I actually thought that email may have been in error - who would want my opinion on Nietzsche years after the fact? I guess you do! … I did wish to argue with Nietzsche, and with my classmates. That was the best part of the class - the encouragement to voice our opinions. I think I may have embraced the contradictions and skepticism in his thoughts more than some of my classmates, and that may have been in part due to my age and experience. One does tend to understand these things more as the world beats us down over the decades."

"Our first discussion in the class was certainly eye opening. My peers had ideas and interpretations that hardly crossed my mind, but made me rethink Nietzsche. ... initially I resisted his ideas strongly. ... My views on Nietzsche absolutely changed over the course of the semester. I think that it's natural to read him without any preface and feel a lot of skepticism. His work requires deep analysis, and upon beginning this class, I at least had never had exposure to anything like this. ... Nietzsche was far different from any of the others that we read. He had a more dynamic and abstract view on the world. His erratic and somewhat confusing style reflected his view of the world as one that lacks linearity, though it took a lot more exposure to philosophy to recognize that."

"After the seminar, much more was revealed of Nietzsche's philosophy. I was intrigued and, in some cases, offended by his thoughts. I found a degree of truth in his assertion that people use their ideologies to validate their senses of morality. However, unlike Nietzsche, I believe that truth and morality are universal. Because of this, I agree that societies do try to legitimize their beliefs and ways of life by claiming they are correct; however, I think that there is an answer to the question of what is good and what is evil, whereas he found it arbitrary. I understand the inherent contradiction in saying that he is wrong because I believe my world views are right (which is precisely what he claims people do), but if there is universal truth, even if the truth that I submit myself to is not the correct one, then Nietzsche's argument that good and evil are arbitrary is wrong."

"After the discussion in class ... I came to really like the book. I found myself relating to Nietzsche's idea of no one absolute viewpoint; coming from a multicultural household I often found different aspects of my life in opposition because both cultures believed different things. Neither were inherently right or wrong and I would identify more with one viewpoint based on the situation. It was reassuring to [find a] philosopher arguing for a viewpoint that I had to realize through much trial and heartache."

"My overall reaction after our discussion was one of relief, intrigue, and satisfaction. I was happy that I understood so much more of the text after hearing my classmates' opinions and being able to voice some of my own. The seminar environment always helped me to make my own assertions and interpretations of the readings based on a synthesis of ideas and thoughts. While I did enjoy more of Nietzsche's opinions when the class discussed them, I was still somewhat frustrated with the inconclusive ending to the book. At the time, I found it too vague and brief to end his book. With more thought however, I believe Nietzsche may have ended his book this way to allow his readers to make their own truths and meanings of his work, away from the "herd" and all alone like the true nobles he speaks of."

8 On Reflection

"Reflecting on Nietzsche several years later I remember not feeling alone in seeing the world in shades of grey; I was always taught there was a right and a wrong but in studying history I noticed that people never thought they were wrong when they chose an action. I find myself musing over the concept more lately because my boyfriend sees good and evil as black and white so I channel my inner Nietzsche and urge him to see things from a different viewpoint."

"I think that the greatest lesson I learned from exposure to Nietzsche's work was the malleability of concepts such as *morality*. Nietzsche was really the first time in which it was absolutely clear to me that such basic concepts as 'right' and 'wrong' were constructs open to contestation at a fundamental level. This wasn't squabbling over the intricacies of what exactly constitutes 'good and evil,' but rather debating the idea that 'good and evil' exists at all."

"I have found myself using Nietzsche for two purposes, firstly when someone says History is easy and you just read books and memorize facts ha ha. It is definitely a text that changes people's perspectives. I vividly remember his argument about morality as a means to hold back the strongest in society, but I connected this also to his writing style. Specifically, there is no proper way to write, there is not only one form of structure. Hence the liberating feeling, that we can go 'beyond' traditional methods and be original. Exposure to him definitely propelled and reinforced me to make bold arguments."

"I return to Nietzsche regularly since my first encounter. He was present in my thesis work and I've also introduced him (in condensed versions) into the undergraduate courses that I have taught. Nietzsche definitely changed the way I think, by allowing me to question everything. [In my previous courses] there was this understood agreement that what you read, you were supposed to read because it was beneficial. This author is famous, this intellectual is brilliant, this philosopher is "right"...etc. I read these people with high regard and believed every word because I was "supposed to." Nietzsche was the first intellectual that gave me permission to be divergent, and for that I will always be indebted to the class."

"Nietzsche was an incredible way to start the year as it provided the groundwork and the feel for the rest of the semester. I was not sure what to expect initially, but I found *Nietzsche's Beyond Good and Evil* to push my intellect to its limits and oftentimes I had to look up parts I did not understand. I found the language and the structure disorienting, they weren't anything like the previous philosophers works I have read. ... Before when I read Locke and Rousseau I let their words became fact, thinking that we have two kinds of people who are inherently good and evil.... However Nietzsche's points about how they are simply two expressions of the same basic human impulses rather than polar opposites really made me put everything into perspective, not only philosophically but with everything that I have blindly accepted as truth."

"Overall, I would have to say that all intellectuals that we study did share some basic principles in ... describing the human world, but I would say that Nietzsche was different only because I struggle more with him than the others. Which as a matter of fact was one of the reasons why I remember his work the most. It was difficult and I could have had a wrong understanding of what he was saying, but I felt that was somewhat of the point. His work leaves so much to the individual's perspective and that also allows for a better discussion."

"I think that Nietzsche helped me think about the journey of life. We all face internal and external struggles, but do we retreat to attempt to answer all of life's questions or do we try to end our days with friends?"

References

Schorske, Carl E. 1980. *Fin-de-Siècle Vienna: Politics and Culture.* New York: Knopf.
Woolf, Virginia. 1927. *To the Lighthouse.* London: Harcourt Brace.

Index